The SEA and
the STATES

The SEA and the STATES

A Maritime History of the American People

by SAMUEL W. BRYANT

THE GROWTH
OF AMERICA
SERIES

Thomas Y. Crowell Company · *New York*

For E. A. B.

CONTENTS

PART I
NEW WORLD A-COMIN'

CHAPTER

1	The Sword and the Cross	3
2	Call to Life	13
3	The Also-Rans	21
4	The Rivals	31

PART II
GROWING PAINS

5	First Steps	43
6	Bad Examples	53
7	Trouble with Parents	62

PART III
REBELLION

8	The Burning Decks	73
9	Rough Winds	106
10	Gropings	143
11	Fight to a Draw	160

PART IV
COMING OF AGE

12	Harvest of the Sea	197
13	Far Places	231
14	Neighborhood Brawl	252
15	The Golden Age	263

· v ·

11671

PART V
THE ANNEALING

| 16 | A Highly Emotional War | 291 |
| 17 | Interlude | 329 |

PART VI
SELF-INTEREST

| 18 | "A Splendid Little War" | 363 |
| 19 | "Sleeping: Do Not Disturb" | 378 |

PART VII
UNFINISHED DRAMA

20	First Act	405
21	First Intermission	419
22	Second Act	461
23	Second Intermission	544
	Bibliography	565
	Statistical Appendix	569
	Index	579

LIST OF ILLUSTRATIONS

FACING PAGE

INDIANS BURNING OUT THE CENTER OF A LOG FOR A CANOE   88

AN INCIDENT IN THE DEFEAT OF THE ARMADA   88

U.S. FRIGATE *President* ENTERING MARSEILLES HARBOR   89

BRIG *New Hazard* OF SALEM   120

SHIPYARD IN PHILADELPHIA, 1800   120

"PROTECTION" ISSUED TO SAFEGUARD U.S. SEAMAN AGAINST
IMPRESSMENT, 1810   121

A BRISK GALE IN NEW YORK BAY, 1838   152

JOHN PAUL JONES   153

OLIVER H. PERRY   153

TWELVE-POUNDER CARRONADE ON A BRIG OF WAR   184

CUTTING IN A WHALE   184

MAP OF A SECTION OF THE WEST COAST OF THE UNITED STATES,
1839   185

POSTER ANNOUNCING SAILING OF A SHIP FOR THE CALIFORNIA
GOLD REGIONS, 1850   280

VIEW OF SAN FRANCISCO HARBOR, 1850   281

ENGAGEMENT BETWEEN *Monitor* AND *Merrimac*   312

U.S.S. *Missouri*, IMMEDIATELY FOLLOWING EXPLOSION IN THE
AFTER TURRET IN 1904   313

BIRD'S-EYE VIEW OF DECK OF U.S.S. *Massachusetts*, AT BROOK-
LYN NAVY YARD (1905)   376

Target Practice on U.S.S. *Massachusetts* 377

U.S.S. *Kentucky* (1905) 408

Naval Message Announcing Outbreak of World War II 409

Navigating Bridge of U.S.S. *North Carolina* 409

Part I
NEW WORLD A-COMIN'

[1] *The Sword and the Cross*

The water receded and the land emerged. Gradually the land masses solidified and the world continents were formed. Immense and trackless areas of salt water covered three-quarters of the planet. For countless ages, compared to which the span of a man's life is less than the tick of a clock, the North American continent lay undiscovered.

Then, as a fortress is stormed, but over great lapses of time between the assaults, the continent began to undergo a process which tested its impregnability. In the pre-dawn of history men and women crossed to the New World from Asia, by way of the northern land bridge; others came from Europe, as winds drove seafarers to the westward. First of the moderns were the Norsemen, who left no imprint on the land: their voyages and explorations were vagrant affairs, more useful in proving the great heart of their leaders than in' opening up the walls of the new continent.

After a few centuries had passed the Spaniards began their attack, and the breach they made in the wall was deep and permanent, for Spain in the early sixteenth century was at the pinnacle of her wealth and power. For eight centuries they had fought the Moors, driving them at last out of the Iberian peninsula: the end product of this war was a race of men quick with their swords and their tempers, avaricious and devout, amorous and fearless.

But by the start of the sixteenth century there was no work at home for their swords, and it was beneath the dignity of any proper Spanish don to sully his hands with trade. Happily, there was a solution to this technological unemployment, a solution first indicated by Columbus in 1492. Along the path to the New World lay much heavy fighting, the promise of sudden wealth, and women of unknown virtue. An even more potent motive existed: somewhere to the westward was the supposed short cut to Cathay—the Northwest Passage—and the search for this route was an aberration in the mind of every right-thinking sea dog of the day.

The conquistadors moved with speed and purpose: within twenty years after Columbus made his discovery there were seventeen settlements on Haiti alone, wherein the Spaniards had no need to work, but profited mightily. The enslaved Indians of the West Indies, augmented by blacks imported from Africa, toiled in the mines and fields, producing wealth for their masters in untold amounts, and producing also a sensation of spiritual benignity on the part of their owners. For, reasoned the Spaniards, it was by their efforts that the godless natives were exposed to the ministrations of the priests who brought the true faith to their attention, and this fact alone was enough to secure for the conquerors a claim for preferential treatment in heaven.

Such a solution of economic and spiritual matters left the Spanish dons time to engage in a madcap existence, living riotously in an atmosphere of heavy drinking and gambling—lords of their own domain. But it also left them time to dream.

To the north and west there were unknown lands; and, although the hurricanes, capable of making matchwood of the unwieldy galleons, spun like giant tops across the surface of the Caribbean, the urge to conquer and kill and win sudden wealth reduced the hazards of the sea to a routine risk of life. Their dreams were nourished, too, by captive Indians who, in an effort to please, told them what they wanted to hear, spinning tales of nonexistent cities full of gold and jewels. There were even reports of a fountain of youth.

Thus, on March 3, 1513, Juan Ponce de Leon (John of the Lion's Paunch) set forth with three small vessels from Puerto Rico and sailed to the westward. One month later he dropped anchor close to the St. John's River and, beguiled by the flowered beauty of the land, called it "La Florida." After having performed the rituals then thought proper, he claimed the land for his king, Charles V, and sailed on, exploring both the east and west coasts of Florida, putting in to shore occasionally to skirmish inconclusively with the Indians. But en route to Haiti, on the voyage home, he made one discovery of major importance: he found the Bahamas Channel, which soon became the established route for the treasure ships sailing to Spain from Mexico.

The West Indies had by 1525 become a powerhouse of Spanish activity. Haiti, Cuba, Puerto Rico, and Jamaica had been explored, conquered, settled, and made into springboards for further expeditions. Through their ports moved tons of gold and silver from the Aztec empire conquered by Cortez; their harbors were crowded with the richly laden galleons which made Spain the envy of all Europe. And from the West Indian ports smaller craft set out to the west and north, probing and testing the unknown continent.

Foremost among the early trail blazers were Ayllon in 1526, Narvaez in 1528, de Soto in 1538, de Moscoso in 1542—each a potential conquistador, eager to duplicate the successes of Cortez in Mexico, of Pizarro in Peru.

In 1521 Lucas Vasquez de Ayllon, a judge in the Haitian court, becoming unhappy at the sight of so much wealth in others' hands, employed Francisco Gordillo to do some unofficial exploring. Gordillo joined forces with Quexos, a slave hunter by trade, and together they sailed up to the Carolina coast, reaching the Cape Fear River where they induced some 150 of the natives to board their vessel, and sailed off with them to sell them as slaves in Santo Domingo. There the governor ordered the release and return to their native land of these captives, but Ayllon kept one, who was speedily indoctrinated in the mysteries of Christianity and baptized Francisco Chicorana. Francisco told alluring stories of his homeland, and in 1526 Ayllon set out to take it over, having received a patent to one million acres from Charles V. The expedition sailed from Haiti in six vessels, with five hundred men and women, eighty-nine horses and some black slaves. At the king's expense three Dominican friars went along to convert the natives, for it had by now become clear that burning and looting villages was not the best way to spread the Gospel. Ayllon dropped anchor in the lower reaches of the Cape Fear River, but in entering port he lost one of his ships. Forthwith, he built an open boat with a mast, but did not neglect to provide it with oars. Scouts were sent out, by land and sea, who returned with news of a better site for a colony to the southward, on the Pedee River,

· 5 ·

and there Ayllon began his settlement. Soon provisions ran out, and Ayllon died, a victim of malnutrition, on October 18, scarcely three months after he had started his expedition. The battered remnants of his colony decided they had had enough and 150 men and women—all who remained alive of the 500—started for Santo Domingo in their five small ships, towing the body of Ayllon in the boat he had built. Winter storms hit the survivors, and the craft with Ayllon's body in it foundered.

In June 1527 Panfilo de Narvaez, a tall, proud man with a red beard and only one eye (he had lost the other in a fight with Cortez), set out from Spain with six hundred colonists and five Franciscan friars. His mission was to start a settlement in Florida, and from the beginning he had trouble. Stopping at Santo Domingo he lost 150 colonists by desertion, and two ships in a hurricane. But in the spring of 1528 he landed at Tampa Bay with 350 men and women. Narvaez hung out the royal standard and read the royal proclamation; the friars intoned appropriate prayers. Then Narvaez made a fatal error: he sent his ships, with the women, northward to find a better harbor, and he set out by land to join them. Soon he discovered that the great and rich cities he had heard of were only mud-huts; and when the ships which, wives and all, had sailed for Cuba, did not appear, escape by sea became the only hope. Wherefore in a paroxysm of ingenuity they built five boats, each twenty-two cubits long. Stirrups and spurs became nails and axes; from the pines pitch was made, and the frameworks of the boats were covered with horsehide. Running rigging they devised from horsehair and fibers, shirts became sails, and young saplings oars. Rowing along the coast, 242 men set out in these five fragile craft. All five were wrecked by storms; the one Narvaez was in was swept out to sea at night, and he joined Ayllon in a watery death.

Undaunted by the pattern of tragedies set by his fellow explorers, Hernando de Soto started out from Spain in April of 1538, with six hundred men in nine vessels. He was thirty-six years old, and he had been appointed Governor of Florida by the King, for he was the ideal Spaniard of the age: he had seen service in Nicaragua, he had fought brilliantly with Pizarro in Peru, and he had an exquisite wife—the Doña Isabel.

The expedition left Havana in May of 1539 and after a twelve day voyage he landed at Tampa Bay. As usual, the natives were unfriendly. Then, in August, de Soto set out across the land with a part of his colony, consisting of 550 fighting men, 200 horses, some Dominican friars, a physician, and in case ships had to be built to reach Cathay, he took along a ship's carpenter, calkers, and a cooper. After much hard fighting and long marching in the interior, de Soto, mortally wounded in a brush with the Indians, died on May 21, 1542. In the night his body was wrapped in a shroud, weighted with sand, and consigned to the muddy waters of the Mississippi.

Luis de Moscoso assumed command of the expedition, and in the winter of 1542-43 he ordered a fleet of brigantines built. Forges were set up on the banks of the Arkansas river, collars of iron for the slaves were beaten into spikes, and on July 3rd, 1543 the expedition—320 Spaniards and 100 Indian slaves—sailed down the river. Seventeen days later they reached the sea, and on September 10, 1543 they entered the Panuco river in Mexico, 150 miles north of Vera Cruz. At last they were among friends. Unwilling to admit permanent defeat, the survivors of the expedition added their tales of wonders just over the horizon to the growing body of legendary cities and tribes.

The Indians told of a city whose towers were studded with precious stones; there were strange reports of a race of men who lived under water, of others who lived on smells, and of an island inhabited only by women. There was, too, a chance that exploration on the western coast of the continent might uncover the western end of the fabled Northwest Passage.

In 1542 Mendoza, Viceroy of Mexico, sent out two expeditions: one to the Philippines and the other northward along the coast of California. The expedition to the west—toward China and the Spice Islands—sailed from Navidad on the west coast of Mexico, took possession of the Philippine Islands and attached them to Mexico, in the name of the King. The northward expedition left Mexico in June, under the command of Juan Rodriguez Cabrillo, hopeful of finding the Northwest Passage. Cabrillo was by birth Portuguese, and he was a crack seaman. Setting out in two small vessels he made his way up the coast of Lower California, touching at San Quentin Bay, and thence he went northwards until on September 28, 1542 he discovered the bay of San Diego. In this well-sheltered spot he weathered a three-day storm, safely anchored under the lee of Point Loma. From San Diego Cabrillo kept on to the north, touching at Catalina Island and San Clemente Island and Santa Monica Bay. On January 3, 1543, he died, and was buried on San Miguel Island. His last orders to his pilot Ferrelo instructed him to carry on to the north. Ferrelo assumed command and sailed as far north as the Rogue River in Oregon, and then turned homeward, reaching his home port—Navidad—on April 14, 1543 after a voyage of almost a year's duration. Only a fraction of the original crews were still alive for the ship's provisions of the time were not calculated to stave off scurvy. The ships themselves were at best cranky, ill-constructed vessels, hard to handle, and all but helpless in a storm. Navigational instruments in common use were the astrolabe, compasses, hour-glasses, and a primitive type of quadrant called a cross-staff, which served to give a rough idea of the altitude of the sun.

By the meridian of the sixteenth century, although the English and French and Dutch were an eternal nuisance, Spain had only one great rival for the world's trade and that was Portugal. The Portugese had a monopoly of the route by way of the Cape of Good Hope to the Far East, and Philip II of Spain began to envy them the wealth they were getting out of the trade in spices. So, in 1559, he decreed that the Philippines should be explored and exploited, and that a route for the return voyages between the Philippines and Mexico be found. In 1564 Legazpi sailed from Navidad in Mexico to take formal possession of the Philippines, and from the islands he sent one ship, with his best navigator—Fray Andres de Urdaneta—to find the best route back to Mexico.

Sailing to the north, Urdaneta came within the grasp of the Japan current and was borne to the northern coast of California whence he made his way southward to Mexico. In this fashion, by a combination of luck and great skill, a return route was found which the Manila galleons could follow, with a reasonable chance of reaching home, despite scurvy, and winds and fog.

While all this activity along the west coast was going on, there was trouble brewing in Florida and the Carolinas. Philip II had acquired a healthy respect for the French explorers to the north, where the godless

Lutherans competed with the Catholics in the fisheries, and he was afraid that the French would move southwards, perhaps as far south as Florida. And any foreign power established there would be a direct menace to the treasure ships sailing the Bahamas Channel. The Spaniards had consistently failed to colonize Florida, chiefly because of their treatment of the Indians, of whom they had enslaved hundreds and whose homes they had burned and plundered. They tried, too late, to correct this treatment with crucifixes, and they were slow to understand that the northern Indians could not be easily enslaved, as had been the case in Mexico and Peru. And, fascinated by the tales of gold and jewels to be had for the fighting, the dull work of tilling the soil was alien to their proud hearts.

But in 1559 Philip II decided that the threat was real enough to warrant a major effort, and he decreed that colonies be established in Florida. An ornate expedition set out from Vera Cruz but was wrecked by a hurricane in Pensacola Bay. The survivors gave up in despair after wandering about in the interior for over a year.

Philip's premonition of competition came true a year later, when Jean Ribault of Dieppe led a party of French Huguenot colonists to Port Royal, on the Carolina coast. This attempt failed, but in 1564 another French expedition set out under Rene de Laudonniere and settled at Fort Caroline on the St. John's River in Florida. This colony was reinforced by three hundred more French in 1565, and became a real menace to the Spanish galleons. Philip acted with unaccustomed swiftness: he picked Pedro Menendez to erase the heretical settlement. Menendez was by profession a naval officer, and a very talented one, with several French pirate ships under his belt. His fleet of seven ships carried 2,613 men and women to the Florida coast, where on August 28, 1565, he founded St. Augustine. His base secured, he proceeded to eradicate by sword and knife and pike every Frenchman he could lay hands on. The Huguenots at Fort Caroline were decimated, with the exception of the few Catholics in the colony. Ribault himself was speared to death with pikes, and King Philip was highly pleased, for had not some of his subjects scotched the evil Lutheran sect which threatened the sanctity of the new world?

When Catherine of France heard of the massacre of her colony she was righteously indignant and to exact just reprisal she chose Domonique de Gourgues—a veteran of the continental wars, brought up in the Catholic faith himself, but first of all a Frenchman. He had been captured by the Spaniards and had served as a galley slave in their ships, so he had ample incentive for revenge. At first he set out disguised as a slaver, but after trading in slaves in the West Indies for a few months, he landed in Florida, enlisted the aid of the Indians, and fell upon the settlement of San Mateo, which Menendez had established. As many Spaniards as possible were taken alive, to be hanged from the surrounding trees. Then he sailed for home, momentarily distracted by the capture of three galleons whose crews he threw overboard, and whose treasure of gold and and silver and pearls he brought back to France with him. Thus justice was done, according to the Old Testament.

In the years that followed the Indians made incessant attacks upon the Spanish settlements and fortified posts in Florida, forcing the colonists to retreat to St. Augustine and the larger colonies. The missionaries did little better than the soldiers, for all that was needed to incur the enmity of the Indians was a white skin. In 1571 Fray Segura with six other tough and courageous Jesuits tried to found a mission on the Chesapeake Bay, but the Indians murdered them all. Menendez, eye for an eye, came up there and hanged eight Indians from the yardarms of his ship. After this unfruitful mission the Jesuits abandoned the field to work in the more peaceful Mexico, leaving the Atlantic coast Indians to the Franciscans.

As discovery was piled on discovery, and the claims of Spain to new territories grew, her responsibilities kept pace. On the West Coast, ships making their landfall at Cape Mendocino after the long trip from Manila, had frequently lost half their crews through scurvy, and were in pressing need of overhaul before continuing down the coast to Mexio. The need to establish a port where they could recover from the effects of the voyage was obvious, but so dispersed was the Spanish effort at sea that no immediate move could be made to set up such a fortified port, even with the added incentive of the rapid spread of English seafaring activity.

Besides their pillaging expeditions to the West Indies, the English had proved bothersome in the Pacific, where Francis Drake in 1579 and Cavendish in 1585 had burned and looted Spanish ships and settlements. The galleons sailing back to Spain from the West Indies, loaded with the wealth of the Incas and Aztecs had been plucked like so many hairs from the King's beard. And in 1585 the upstart English had even made a vain attempt to settle on Roanoke Island, off the Virginia coast.

By 1588 Spain had endured twenty years of insult to her claims and property, and at last her patience was exhausted. France had been taken out of the play by civil war, and King Philip seized what looked like a good opportunity to crush and annihilate England, a nation with a fast-growing navy, a Protestant religion, and a Queen who did not hesitate to use her womanly charms on the Spanish emissaries. Elizabeth bemused Philip with her wily diplomacy, backing the piratical activities of Drake and Hawkins, Cavendish and Frobisher on one hand, while protesting her good intentions on the other. But Philip, toting up the score, recalling the sack of Santo Domingo and St. Augustine, the loss of scores of galleons, decided that he had to defeat England if his far-off colonies were to continue to bring gold to him in a routine manner. So he ordered a great armada made ready, to invade England.

Thus, in July 1588, the destiny of the United States was decided, in the North Sea. The Spanish fleet was commanded by a landsman, the Duke of Medina Sidonia, and he was from the first doubtful of success. Since this was to be an invasion attempt, a great part of his fleet consisted of transports, and soldiers are notoriously useless at sea. In England there were mixed feelings: the Catholics had gone underground to escape Protestant persecution, and there was considerable unrest. The Spaniards counted on a part of the population becoming allied with them, after their landing was made. The English fleets were commanded by Elizabeth's cousin, Lord Howard of Effingham, Lord High Admiral of England.

On July 19th the armada was abreast of Plymouth, the Spanish ships looking like so many floating castles, and Lord Howard ordered his ships out of the harbor. The wind was from the south-west, and the English ships, fast-sailing and easily handled, small but heavily gunned, harried the Spaniards much as a pack of wolves bedevil a herd of buffalo. On the 27th the Spaniards anchored along the coast between Dunkirk and Calais, and during the night the English sent fire-ships among them. The Spaniards slipped their cables and drove to the northeast, still under attack by the English who maintained their position to windward. As they chased the Spaniards to the north, where they encountered winds of gale force, the Spaniards were forced to round Scotland and Ireland in order to get home. By July 30th the defeat of the Spaniards was crushingly apparent: Spain had lost ten ships on the Irish coast, and in all forty large ships had been either captured or destroyed by the English, or had foundered in the heavy seas. By the time the armada reached home, half of the men in it had been lost.

In this battle 15,000 Englishmen manned 142 ships of all types, whereas the Spaniards had 132 ships manned by 8,766 sailors, 21,855 soldiers and 2,088 galley slaves. Lord Howard, with a keen appreciation of ability, had divided his fleet and given a squadron each to Sir Francis Drake, Sir John Hawkins, and Captain Martin Frobisher, all of whom, profiting by their long experience at sea in the capacity of slavers, pirates and freebooters, performed the prodigies of valor expected of them.

The net result of the battle was to prove to Spain that she no longer held the sovereignty of the seas. From now on, the oceans belonged to anyone strong enough to hold them, and the English were quick to realize this fact. The Spaniards sent Vizcaino north along the west coast of North America in 1602, and he reached the mouth of the Columbia river. But this was the last whip-lash of Philip's ambition, and the seventeenth century was to be as surely England's as the sixteenth had been Spain's.

The years between 1585 and 1607, when the colonial ambitions of England were quiescent, were among the most bodeful in the history of mankind: the armada was routed, Ireland subjugated, Shakespeare contrived his plays, the Puritans coalesced into a minor pressure group in England, translators started their work on the King James version of the Bible, Hawkins and Drake died, and Queen Elizabeth, her nation well on the road to greatness, died in her sleep in the cold pre-dawn of March 24th, 1603.

But the distillate of those two decades remained. The impetus to force the event, to create, pervaded much of English life, and with Spain removed as a rival, the coast of North America was invitingly open. There the element of perpetual growth could be planted; there, beyond the Bermudas, the small, insular nation that was England could find partial expression of its power.

And so, in 1602, Bartholemew Gosnold set out to found a colony. He failed, but in 1603 and 1605 Pring and Weymouth prospected along the Maine and Massachusetts coasts. Interest in colonization was heightened by these three expeditions, and on April 10th, 1606, King James chartered two companies to settle and exploit the new world. The London Company was granted large rights in the south, and the Plymouth Company in the north. In 1607 the Plymouth Company sent 120 men to form a colony in the northern section of the coast, and these unfortunate people landed at Kennebec, Maine, where they sampled the rigors of a New England winter before giving up in despair. Their chief claim to the attention of posterity is that they built a small pinnace, christened the "Virginia," in which they sailed back to England.

Meanwhile the London Company, in charge of efforts to the south, dispatched 120 colonists, 104 of whom survived the trip and on April 26th, 1607, founded Jamestown, Virginia—the first permanent projection of the English Protestant spirit into the new world.

---

[2] *Call to Life*

This colony of Jamestown survived its first three years in a precarious fashion. The location of the settlement had been decided upon when the colonists found a peninsula thirty miles up the James river where six fathoms of water made it easy for them to tie up their ships to trees on the shore. Hardly had they landed before they were embroiled in petty bickerings, as cliques connived for power in the little settlement. The colonists themselves were pathetically unprepared for life in the wilderness: they were all tough men, tumultuous in their emotions, violent in action, but they had little practical knowledge of fishing and hunting, with the exception of a few leaders like John Smith, who knew how to master the environment.

Smith was both leading firebrand and chief provider in the colony; a wonderfully bewhiskered man of twenty-six years, he had always managed to find a woman to get him out of trouble. He set out on a trip upriver in a small boat, hoping to find gold and silver and perhaps China—which for all he knew might be just over the horizon. But he returned disillusioned, having been captured by the Indians and saved from death only by the intercession of Pocahontas, thirteen-year-old daughter (the aborigines matured at an early age) of a local chieftain.

Despite the wilderness guidance and practical help of such men as John Smith, the colonists died in droves from fever and hunger and Indian arrows. By 1610 over seven hundred men had been brought to the colony and only sixty remained alive, emaciated and hopeless. By June, having been reduced to eating snakes when their provisions were exhausted, they decided to abandon the colony. They were sailing off to England when they encountered a relief fleet under Lord De La Warr in Chesapeake Bay, and they returned to the palisaded collection of huts they had built on the peninsula, to try again.

From then on the colony throve. The ships bringing out colonists from England, under the flag of the Virginia Company which had taken over from the old London Company, were soon bringing back lumber and powdered fish. But the Company was unhappy about the four-month duration and consequent cost of the voyage, which followed a circuitous route from England to the Canary Islands, then west with the trade winds to the British West Indies, and north to Virginia. The fact that these trade winds blew steadily from east to west had been one of the main factors in Spain's successful colonization in the new world, for they acted as a great conveyor-belt, driving the Spanish ships to the westward. But now Captain Samuel Argall was instructed to sail to Virginia directly from the Canary Islands. He made the passage in nine weeks, two of which were spent in a dead calm, and when he reported that he had met with no untoward difficulties on the voyage it became the accepted route to Virginia.

At Jamestown, as the colonists began to know the land, the obsession of finding gold and silver and the northwest passage faded, and the colony started to prove its worth on a practical basis. Trade with England was direct, and no specie changed hands in the transactions: instead, finished goods were sent out to the settlers—and bartered for lumber, beaver and otter skins and fish. The English thought of the colony as an overseas plantation, and they expected it to save them the extra cost of buying colonial products from the Spaniards and the French.

The colonists were not long in increasing their productivity: in 1611 they started building a 12-ton shallop for river and coastal trade, and the next year John Rolfe, who had married Pocahontas, began an agricultural experiment. He planted West Indian tobacco seeds in his garden at Jamestown, hoping to grow enough for his own use and with luck to get enough of a crop to have some left over for export. John Hawkins had introduced the weed into England half a century earlier, and the Spaniards had kept the London market supplied with their West Indian leaf, then considered the best in the world. But so well was Rolfe's first crop received in London that within five years tobacco had become the main export of the colony, and it was being carried to England in ships which tied up at the shore-side trees on the peninsula at Jamestown. As a result the colonists had no need to build ships of their own, other than small craft, for they could always depend on having their crop moved to market in English ships.

The pattern of the colony soon became set along predominantly agricultural lines as the little tobacco patches spread along the river's edge. The chief obstacle to their expansion was the lack of manpower to clear more land and tend the crop. Then, in 1619, in one of those incidents fantastic in their occurrence at the precise clock-tick in time when they are most needed, a Dutch ship sailed up to Jamestown and offered to sell the colonists a new commodity: twenty black slaves, who were capable of hard work in the fields, and who were moreover docile, healthy and cheaply kept. Thus the lacking catalyst arrived, was bartered for provisions, and an essential element of future growth identified. Servitude had until then been restricted to indentured white men and women—paupers and criminals sent out from England to work in the new world.

The Dutch were as sensitive as the English to those tales of wealth in the new world that brought a dreamy look to the eyes of Europe's statesmen, all equally ambitious to line their own and their countries' coffers. In 1609 a twelve-year truce between Holland and Spain was signed, and in Holland the resultant release of national energy was turned to exploring, colonizing and trading. That year Henry Hudson, in the pay of the Dutch East India Company, set forth on a trip of exploration to find the northwest passage. He sailed, by chance, into New York harbor in his ship the *Half Moon,* and one of the crew remarked that there were many fish in the lower bay. The *Half Moon* was so brightly painted and flew so many varicolored pennants that she looked like a mysterious bird with celestial plumage to the Indians, but they came aboard to barter their tobacco for penknives and beads and bits of cloth. One valorous brave drank so much Holland gin that he became indecorous and then unconscious, but the next day he was back for more.

Hudson sailed up the river, looking for the northwest passage, but shoal water just south of Albany stopped him. On his return to Holland he was intercepted by the English and held with his ship at Dartmouth, on the grounds that being an Englishman he should be working for England, and not for their arch trade rivals the Dutch. But he got his report to Holland, where it was received with such enthusiasm that next year the Dutch East India Company sent out five ships to trade with the Indians in tobacco and furs. This trade grew rapidly, and to protect the traders from the unpredictable and often homicidal whims of the Indians, Fort Nassau and Fort Orange (later known as Albany) were built. The Dutch at that time were the carriers of the world's cargoes, and in the new world their effort was at first strictly a business proposition: they were interested in getting wealth out of the country, not in settling it. But in 1623 the ship *Nieu Nederlandt* sailed for New York with thirty families of Walloons—sturdy Protestants all. On landing the colonists scattered, some settling on Manhattan, others along the Delaware and Connecticut rivers, a few on the west shore of Long Island. In 1625, farm tools and 103 head of livestock arrived, to be followed in the next year by a few slaves, and the gin-loving settlers were soon well entrenched in the New Netherlands.

For them the Hudson River valley was a broad highway for trade with the Indians and with each other. The river lay in a fertile valley 150 miles long, and it formed a natural funnel for the furs of the back-country. To carry on their traffic in tobacco and furs the colonists developed "vlie booten," or flyboats, small shallow-draft, flat-bottomed vessels that could nose up to the riverbank at any likely-looking farm and set up business as a floating general store with the settlers. Occasionally these sea-going peddlers could pick up a few furs from the Indians, but the bulk of this business went to the established fur-trading posts.

To the north weird events were taking place: the Pilgrims had finally settled in Plymouth, Massachusetts, where they found a good harbor and good fishing, after a sixty-six day crossing in the 180-ton *May Flower*. They were complete realists about the future. They expected no sudden wealth, and were ready to work hard for a living by fishing, farming and trading. This approach to colonizing was something new in 1620, but strong motives activated the Pilgrims. They had fled from England, refugees from religious intolerance, and spent years of exile in Holland, where they could worship as they saw fit. And England, in the early years of the seventeenth century was suffering from land-hunger: her five million people felt cramped on their tiny island and they turned naturally to the sea. In Holland over a thousand ships a year were being built while the Pilgrims were there, and the Dutch were even more conscious of the sea than the English. Thus the Pilgrims were exposed to the sea-mindedness of Europe's two leading maritime and trading nations, and their absorption of this knowledge of the sea fitted them eminently well for life on the New England coast.

In that they wanted to be left alone to worship as they pleased, they were pure escapists. But they had, too, a sharp eye for profit and the practical aspects of life in the wilderness. The Indians taught them how to fish and grow corn, how to fertilize the fields with fish and shells, and, knowing the sea's value, the colonists were quick to repair the shallop they had brought over on the *May Flower,* and to use it for fishing.

But not until 1624 could they freight an English ship with cod and make enough of a profit to build two more shallops. Next year they had a bumper crop of corn and they loaded the surplus into a shallop and sailed north to trade it for seven hundred pounds of beaver skins on the Kennebec river. Thus when they had word that a trading-post run by English merchants on Monhegan Island, off the Maine coast, was about to be abandoned, they had cash on hand and they sent a boat to the island where they bought four hundred pounds worth of goods at bargain rates, and on their way back they picked up another hundred pounds worth at Kennebec. That was all the boat would hold and when she returned to Plymouth, laden to the gunwales, the Pilgrims bewailed the fact that she was not large enough to take full advantage of such heaven-sent bargains. So they cut the boat in half, and rebuilt her, lengthening her, to be ready for what the future might offer. Before long they were able to send a bark up the Connecticut river, and another to New York to open up trade with the Dutch. Ten years after its start, and after enduring many hardships, the colony was secure, nearly out of debt, and its faith in the future was boundless.

But the Pilgrims were soon overshadowed in importance by the Puritans, who were being hotly persecuted in England for their religious purism. In quick succession Salem was founded, in 1626, then Charlestown in 1628, and Medford the next year. The final Massachusetts Bay Colony charter was granted in 1629, after some slight but necessary misrepresentations, and the colony was started as a commercial fishing venture. The settlers—seven hundred Puritans—who were to found Boston, reached the banks of the Charles river in 1630 in time to hole up for the winter. In the next thirteen years, hounded by bigots in their homeland, no less than eighteen thousand Puritans came to the Bay Colony to live, and with them came a few capable, compassionate leaders, and considerable riffraff. The great migration slackened in 1643 when Cromwell's rebellion put an end to this species of persecution (substituting instead the harassing of Catholics), and many of the colonists returned to England, while others went to the British West Indies, or joined the Dutch on Long Island. But the colony had its roots down, and through the port of Boston passed most of the settlers who were to found other New England colonies. They moved inland in small groups, seeking fertile valleys for their farms, or, more often, they sailed along the coast in small vessels, searching for good harbors where they could combine farming with seafaring. Rapidly the Bay Colony became New England's commercial center, exporting fish and staves and furs, importing household goods, woolens and trade trinkets.

Inevitably the colonists began to build their own ships, for in 1629 the freight rate between England and Boston was three pounds per ton, passengers were carried for five pounds and horses for ten pounds. This was far too much money for the hard-working Puritans to let escape them, and in 1631 Governor John Winthrop launched the 30-ton, one-masted *Blessing of the Bay* on the Mystic River. The 120-ton *Desire,* built at Marblehead for the fishing trade, soon followed; and by 1636 at least six of the forty ships on the regular run from England to Boston were colony-owned.

Meanwhile there had come to Salem a rare being, a Puritan minister named Hugh Peters. Peters thought that the colonists were placing too much emphasis on the fur trade, which was bound to diminish as the animals were killed off, and that real prosperity was to be found on the sea. He saw clearly that small ships which could be easily handled by a few men were the most practical craft for colonial fishing, and he exhorted the colonists to build as many of these as they could. Any man could take a canoe and go fishing for cod, make money at it, and build a bigger craft. A 7-ton shallop could be built for twenty-five pounds, and her owner could profit mightily on the investment.

The settlers were no strangers to fishing: they had the benefit of a century of accumulated experience that their countrymen, along with Portuguese, Spaniards and Frenchmen, had handed down by word of mouth about the fishing on the Newfoundland Banks. As early as 1500 at least one hundred vessels from Europe were sailing across the North Atlantic each spring to fish the Newfoundland Banks, and to cure their catch on shore before returning in the autumn. In 1577 no less than 350 vessels sailed for the Banks, caught their cod, and dried the catch at St. John, Newfoundland. Their ships were only partially decked, unheated save for a half-hogshead full of sand on which a fire could be built, but what they learned about fishing was invaluable to the colonists who combined with the pioneers' techniques their own first-hand knowledge of the sea.

Before long Hugh Peters was showing the New Englanders how to increase their profits: he persuaded them to build their own vessels to save the freight charges to England, and when the cogency of his reasoning became apparent there was a great increase in shipbuilding along all the New England coast, with a resultant growth in both fishing and trading. The usual colony-built vessel was a small craft of less than

20-tons, partially decked to protect the cargo, and of shallow draft. In one such vessel—a sloop—John Gallup was standing down Long Island Sound in May 1936, with a crew of a man and two boys, when he was forced by a rising wind to seek cover in the lee of an island. As he neared the shore he saw a vessel about the same size as his own, which he recognized as the pinnace of a Mr. Oldham, who had sailed with a crew of two boys and two Indians. Gallup hailed the other craft but got no answer, and on running nearer discovered fourteen Indians were lying on her deck. A canoe manned by Indians and carrying goods had just started for the shore, leading Gallup to suspect that Oldham had been hijacked by the natives. When the Indians on the pinnace slipped their cable and ran off before the wind, Gallup sailed after them, and running alongside, he fired a volley of duck-shot at them. The Indians had swords, spears and some firearms, but Gallup drove them below deck, and having too few men to attempt to board he rammed the vessel. After the first crash six Indians jumped overboard and were drowned, on the second attempt there were no results, but with the third ramming five more Indians jumped overboard, and another appeared on deck, offering to surrender. Gallup ran alongside and took this Indian aboard his sloop, where he was bound hand and foot and put into the hold. Another redskin followed his example and he also was bound, but since Gallup was afraid that the two Indians together might cause him trouble, he tossed the second one into the sea. Now only two Indians were left in the pinnace; they had barricaded themselves in a small compartment below deck and they were armed. Gallup boarded the vessel and found there the body of Mr. Oldham, his head split, his hands and legs much mangled, and the flesh still warm. The corpse was thrown into the sea, and Gallup removed all the remaining goods to his own craft, stripped the sails off the pinnace, and started to tow her toward land. But the wind increased and he was forced to cut her adrift.

Such incidents were frequent in the coastal trade, and there were also informal engagements with the French in Nova Scotia, but to the colonists such matters were simply inconveniences which they had to guard against and accept as best they could.

[3] *The Also-Rans*

No matter how perilous life was on the sea, it was infinitely preferable to working the land. At sea the risks were understood and to some extent calculable, but on shore they took on the frightfulness of the unknown, as the superstitious minds of the colonists peopled the trackless wilderness at their backs with all manner of evil demons. They knew the reality at first hand, and that was bad enough: bears, wolves, wildcats, and Indians who could stalk a man on dry leaves. Many a settler went off into the woods to chop up some firewood and vanished without a trace, leaving his family and friends to explain his disappearance by their sharply imagined terrors.

The sea had its demons too, but it was a less hostile element, and one which they had sailed over and to some extent mastered. It was their sole link with the civilization they had left behind in Europe, a civilization accessible to them only on its own harsh terms, but still a last resort as a refuge should their new homes prove to be untenable. The thought was often in their minds, for they were extremely conscious of being only a fringe of humanity clinging to the coast, seldom out of sight or sound of the sea. If everything they had accomplished should suddenly be wiped out by marauding Indians or failing crops or epidemics, the sea could always be depended upon as a line of retreat.

In varying degree throughout the colonies this sea-mindedness existed: it was a predominant trait among the English in New England, the Dutch in New Netherlands, and the Swedes along the Delaware. To the south in Virginia and the Carolinas where the terrain and climate favored exploitation of the land's resources the energies of the colonists were turned inland to an extent impossible in New England.

New England was not without its own rich soil, and many settlers became prosperous farmers, but that did not prevent them from leading an amphibious life—working the sea as well as the land. The interplay of several immutable factors induced them to turn to seafaring: the farms could not be worked in the harsh New England winters; the forests were invitingly full of timber; and the sea was at hand. In many small settlements shipbuilding ways were set up along the rivers' edge and the first heavy fall of snow signaled the laying of a ship's keel. Often this was a group effort, each man donating as much of his time and money as he could, and in return receiving a share in the completed vessel. The forests were rich in stands of white oaks whose wood was heavy, tough, and so accessible that the colonists used only the choice parts of it—the gnarled branches and crotches—for the frames of their vessels. There were plenty of white pines, light and strong and straight, whose wood was ideally suited for use in decking, masts and spars. And although the Admiralty had been quick to reserve the finest trees as Crown property, marking them with a broad arrow, their surveying was irregular, and a colonist could always find what timber he needed.

Before the middle of the century seafaring had become recognized as such an important part of New England's prosperity that laws were passed to protect and encourage it: fishermen were granted the right to go ashore wherever they wanted to, to dry their catch; shipwrights and fishermen were exempted from duty in the militia; the Pilgrims laid down rigid specifications of workmanship and materials which their shipbuilders had to meet; the fishing boats enjoyed a period of freedom from taxation.

The early vessels were built as economically as possible: the colonists had no money to spend on such luxuries as the huge superstructures fore and aft which made the European merchantmen look like floating castles, nor could they always get iron for the fittings. Their shipwrights had to turn out craft stripped of all but the most essential material; often put together with wooden pegs. Most of the colonial harbors were shallow, making it imperative to broaden the hull and decrease the draft of the vessels, and this, together with simplicity of line, resulted in fast and stable ships.

In these small, easily-handled vessels the early coastwise trade began, and most of the craft were manned by Dutchmen from New Netherlands and Englishmen from New England. Pinks and sloops, shallops and snows carried merchandise along the coast, never venturing very far from land, making the short trips from harbor to harbor, and when the weather looked ominous running in to the nearest haven. A thriving trade developed between the northern and southern colonies as the New Englanders sailed down to Virginia and the Carolinas and the West Indies, exchanging their grain and lumber and fish for the products of the plantations—sugar and tobacco and cotton. Crew members had a personal interest in making their voyages safely and without damage to the ship, since they usually carried, in addition to the general cargo, some merchandise of their own which they could trade for their own profit.

Meanwhile larger ships were being built for the trans-ocean trade, which by 1646 had grown so great that the English Parliament was moved to pass an Act stipulating that only ships flying the English flag could carry colonial products to foreign markets. This Act was aimed directly at the Dutch Republic, then the chief merchant nation in the world, in an attempt to halt its growing aggressiveness at sea. Cromwell encouraged the passage of the Act, and there was nothing predatory or small-minded about the attitude which inspired Parliament to pass it, for each European nation with overseas colonies tried to monopolize the trade of its own possessions and drew up restrictions to protect its own profits. By so doing they laid the foundations of a flourishing smuggling business, wherein men of every nation tried to circumvent all the laws in an effort to turn a dishonest penny. Commerce at sea took on all the aspects of an armed trade, and no thoughtful captain would undertake a voyage without at least a few light guns aboard, which his crew had to learn how to handle.

The North American coast was ideal for the smugglers: sharply-indented, with great bays and estuaries, small rivers and inlets, it offered innumerable harbors and hiding-places into which they could dodge. There were not enough men-of-war to do more than make a futile attempt to stop this illegal traffic, and when the English colonies commissioned a few of their own ships as cruisers they were used chiefly to prevent the Dutch from moving in on their trade, and to restrain those Indians who had piratical notions.

In 1650 England tightened the noose again, this time by prohibiting all foreign vessels from trading with her colonies, unless they were licensed to do so; then, next year came another restriction—an Act which prohibited the import of any colonial goods into the realm unless they were carried in English ships, owned by Englishmen, and more than half of whose crews were English. The effect of this Act was softened only a trifle by the stipulation that European goods could be imported into England in the ships of the nation producing them. The Dutch were not appeased, for they had forged ahead at sea during the Cromwellian Rebellion in England, and war followed.

After some preliminary skirmishes brought about by the Dutch refusal to salute the English flag at sea, war was declared formally on July 8, 1652. Both nations directed their colonies in the New World to commence hostilities, but the English in the New Haven and Connecticut colonies and the Dutch in New Netherlands facing them had nothing to fight with, so they neglected to become hostile.

In European waters the English, in fighting the Dutch, had taken on men as hardy and brave as any nation had ever produced, and moreover led by skilled officers. In a series of battles the English fleet was severely mauled—once so badly (on November 29, 1652) that Von Tromp, the Dutch Admiral, after a particularly clear-cut victory hoisted a broom at the mast-head of his flagship, thereby signifying that he would sweep the seas clean of all English shipping. But in 1653, on August 7th, a four-day battle took place in the North Sea: Admiral Monk with 120 English ships, carrying about 4,000 guns and 17,000 men, engaged Admiral Von Tromp's 108 men-of-war, 8 fire-ships and 25 armed merchantmen. The first three days were spent in skirmishing, but on the 10th Von Tromp, who had kept to windward of the English, paralleled their line of battle and attacked furiously. Smoke blanketed the two fleets, flames shot towering through the smoke and great explosions were heard as ships caught fire and exploded. The English fought with such spirit that Von Tromp realized they would perish before surrendering and to force a decision he attempted to lay alongside the English flagship. A musket-ball cut him down, and, their nerve shaken by the loss of their leader, the Dutch retreated. As the smoke cleared the sea was seen to be covered with dead bodies, with the fragments and hulls of ships, still smoking and burning. Throughout the remainder of the two fleets there were dismasted vessels and ships whose sails had been perforated with cannon balls. The English pursued the Dutch as far as the Texel, and the victory was theirs beyond any doubt.

As a result of this battle the Dutch sued for peace, and the terms set by Cromwell included the provision that the English flag must be saluted by the Dutch wherever and whenever they encountered it on the sea. The war had lasted only twenty-three months, but in that time the English had taken 1,700 Dutch merchantmen as prizes, whose total value was set in Holland at close to six million pounds. From then on England's maritime supremacy, although often seriously threatened, was never lost: she had won the lead and she maintained it. Indeed, as though to test her muscles (for she did not bother to declare war), in December 1654, she sent an expedition under Admiral Penn against the Spaniards in the West Indies, and annexed the island of Jamaica.

The defeat of the Dutch and England's resultant booming, triumphant nationalism were to have profound effects on the life of the North American colonies. No one could now restrain the explosive creative spirit which, compressed in the little island off the coast of Europe, began to make itself felt throughout the world, wherever ships could sail. In the colonies the English officials, representing as they did the leading maritime nation of Europe, became puffed up with a sense of importance and power. The colonists found many of them insufferable, and delighted in bilking them in the performance of their duties, whenever those duties interfered with trade or profits.

Expansion of commerce, fishing and colonization was going on rapidly in America when Charles II came to the throne in 1660, bringing with him a diluted Catholicism and a sense of the value of the Royal Navy as a protector of the realm and of trade. His brother, James, Duke of York, became Lord High Admiral and at once set about increasing the size and power of the fleet. For although the English and Dutch governments were officially friendly, at sea their merchantmen and privateers were at swords' points, and a no-quarter war raged wherever Dutchman met Englishman. Charles II, with that appreciation of valid national policy which transcended party lines in England, promulgated more Navigation Acts to cut down the Dutch share of world trade. The Act of 1663 was a knife in the heart of the Dutch merchants, for it specified that products of the colonies could not be exported directly to other countries, but had first to be sent to England and there put ashore. Certain kinds of goods to which the Act applied were enumerated, among them sugar, tobacco and cotton. Thus tobacco for the continent had first to go to England and there be trans-shipped before it could be cleared for its destination. Again, in 1663, Parliament decreed that no product of any European country could be imported into the colonies unless it was carried in English ships sailing from English ports. To the colonists, as well as the Dutch, this was another severe blow: it meant that the goods the settlers needed, such as Spanish iron, would have to pass through English ports and would consequently be more expensive; it meant, too, that colonial exports would lose in value since they had only one market—England. The fisheries remained unaffected by the Act, for Parliament (perhaps realizing that such a ruling could never be enforced) did not include fish in the list of enumerated articles, and the colonial fishing fleets kept carrying their salted cod to Spain and Portugal, to the Azores and the Canary Islands, where the local religious customs created a large demand for this commodity.

The colonists, from Maine to Jamaica and Barbados, were thoroughly angry at the turn events had taken: they had become more and more self-reliant as the years passed, and they had become accustomed to a certain amount of self-government in that they made their own local laws and regulations. The Puritans, who were always talking about "the higher law," now invoked it and interpreted it to mean that they were justified in circumventing such restrictions on their right to make money as the Acts of Trade and Navigation. In this way they not only eased their consciences but lined their pocketbooks, and the smuggling business expanded with the deduced blessing of the Almighty.

The Dutch could only see that their livelihood was being threatened again and they were willing to fight about it. They had driven the English merchants into tears of rage by seizing their ships in the Indian ocean, off the coasts of Africa, and in the North Atlantic. Now Charles II was forced by these outraged merchants to open hostilities and the Second Dutch War began. In 1664 Charles II had given the colony of New Netherlands to his brother James, Duke of York, even though the Dutch still owned it, and before the formal declaration of war a squadron commanded by Sir Robert Carr started out to take over the

Duke's new property, pausing en route only to wipe out a few Dutch trading stations on the West African coast. The four frigates with their five hundred veteran troops under Colonel Richard Nicolls sailed up to New Amsterdam with loaded guns. The Dutch, caught without defenses, submitted peacefully to this English conquest, and New Netherland was named New York, in honor of the new owner.

In Europe the war went on, exclusively a maritime struggle, and it was highlighted in 1665 and 1666 by three great naval battles—the first and last of which the English won. But after the last large-scale battle, that of August 4, 1666, the Royal Navy was out of funds and the fleet had to be laid up for the winter. England's finances were in sorry straits: she had suffered the Great Plague in the summer of 1665; in 1666 the Great Fire burned down nearly all of London, and her financial resources were inadequate to cope with these two disasters and the Dutch as well. On the 14th of June, 1667, the Dutch fleet under De Ruyter sailed up the Thames and the Medway and burned the royal ships laid up there. For four weeks the Dutch fleet controlled the mouth of the Thames, and Charles II decided that peace was in order. The treaty was signed at Breda, Holland, on July 31, 1667, and by its terms the seizure of New York was legalized, while the Dutch got the islands of Surinam and Run, in the East Indies.

With the acquisition of New York from the Dutch (to whom the Swedes in Delaware had surrendered in 1655), the English held a continuous strip of coastal colonies from Canada to Florida, as well as their rich and productive West Indian islands. What had been a series of precarious settlements a few decades earlier was now a possession that satisfied and fed the imagination of every Englishman.

The colonists, while hostilities declared and undeclared absorbed the European nations, were building ships at an ever increasing rate, with a large percentage of them fit for the ocean trade. Ships could be built in New England for four pounds per ton burthen, while the cost in England was six pounds per ton, and the English merchants ordered enough ships in the colonies to keep the yards busy throughout the year. Often a ship was built, freighted with cod and lumber, and sailed to England where both ship and cargo were sold.

But no matter how remunerative shipbuilding and legal trade was, there were more profits in smuggling, which at first was quite open and respectable. French and Spanish ships cruised off Newfoundland, always ready to exchange cargo with colony vessels, and the Puritans were happy to do business with them. Long Island became a hotbed of smuggling activity, where goods were landed on the beaches, transferred to wagons, and sold in New York. Southward in Virginia and the Carolinas the smugglers were equally well received and the transition from legal to illegal trade was just as easily made, due to a natural sympathy on the part of the settlers for the hard-working smugglers who, often at the risk of their lives, brought them untaxed goods.

By 1672 inter-colonial smuggling in tobacco, furs and slaves had grown to such proportions that the English passed another Act which this time specified that colonial exports had to be taxed before leaving the colony, unless a bond was given to land them in the English realm. This Act served only to stimulate the ingenuity and increase the incentive of the smugglers, to make them build more and faster ships, and to engage in even more widespread and active attempts to thwart the English laws.

The Act could not be enforced by England, at that time busy in her third and last war with the Dutch. Indeed, so weakly was New York defended that a small Dutch fleet sailed up to and occupied Manhattan until they were moved out by the terms of the peace treaty in 1674.

But with peace, uneasy as it was, the English began to take a closer look at these overseas plantations of theirs that had been growing of their own accord, and appeared now to be getting out of hand. The remoteness of the colonies had made them a matter of general indifference to England while she was struggling for power in European waters, but in 1676 Edward Randolph was sent over to the Massachusetts Bay Colony, as Commissioner for the Crown.

At this time the colony was full of prosperity, rectitude and a not always mute insolence. Randolph was received with distaste, and although he was an obdurate and querulous man to begin with, the rudeness of his reception in the colony fortified these traits in his character. His complaints were innumerable, and they included everything which did not fit into his pattern of loyalty to King. Foremost was his objection to the independence of character the colonists showed, in their pretension to self-government. But he also reported that the customs officials were wormy with corruption, and that he had not the means to enforce the Acts of Trade, which were being flouted by many of the colony's 430 ocean-going ships. In 1682 he complained that the Massachusetts Colony had set up a naval office of its own, and that he was bilked in the righteous performance of his duty on every hand.

Forthwith King Charles concluded that a limit must be set to the intransigeance of the colonists on Massachusetts Bay, and that of them an example should be made, wherefore the colony's charter was revoked and the settlers lost many of the privileges they had been enjoying, while, charterless, they took on added woes.

The French were cause enough to worry any Englishman who had a knowledge of the new world: they had strung their trading posts northward along the Great Lakes, and they were moving down the Mississippi in a great encircling movement which threatened to hem in the English by restricting their settlements to the regions east of the Mississippi. In 1684 La Salle sailed from France, intent on settling the mouth of the Mississippi, down which he had sailed two years before, but he failed to find the delta and landed instead at Matagorda, on the gulf coast, where he founded a short-lived colony. In Nova Scotia the colony of Acadie—founded by French fishermen—had become as permanent a settlement as any English colony, and, with New Breton, it offered a base of operations for the French privateers who swarmed over the northern seas.

Thus, when King Charles died, early in 1685, and his brother James, Duke of York, became King James II, there was good reason for the English to take a careful look at their colonial possessions, which were now threatened by the French in much the same manner that the English had threatened the Spanish possessions a hundred years earlier.

James II was not an amiable character: he vacillated, was politically inept, and his Catholicism was violent: he infiltrated the once recusant clergy into the government departments and the universities; he, who had once been Lord High Admiral, attempted to have priests say mass on board the royal ships, and the crews were with difficulty restrained from jettisoning the holy men.

Sir Edmund Andros was the King's choice for Governor of the New

England colonies—a man, if anything, more choleric in temper than Edward Randolph, but more aware of colonial sentiment by reason of his seven years as governor of New York. Andros was an honest and loyal soldier, and he carried out with rigid will the orders of the Lords of Trade, which aimed at the unification of the northern colonies under one government, for enforcement of the Acts of Trade and for defense against the French and their Indian allies. After the revocation of the Massachusetts Bay colony's charter, this new colonial dominion was enlarged by the addition of the colonies of New York and the Jerseys, Rhode Island, Plymouth and New Hampshire—all of which Andros attempted to rule according to directives issued in London by men insulated from the colonies by three thousand miles of sea. This jerry-built dominion was not destined to live long: its collapse was brought about by events in Europe, when in 1688 England's traitorous fifth-column of Whig Lords went to work to oust James II, having found his Catholicism too heavy-handed to be borne.

In July they prevailed upon Admiral Herbert to doff his glittering regalia and don the uniform of an English sailor, so that he might carry a secret letter from them to the Protestant William of Orange, inviting him to invade England. On July 30th the Admiral left England in his disguise; within a few months William had accepted the invitation, and was on his way to England. He landed in Devon on November 5th with 16,000 mercenaries—officered for the most part by exiled French Protestants—and while James wavered, indecisive, not knowing whom to trust, betrayed even by his daughter Ann, at first fleeing, then returning to London—William of Orange with his Dutch and German and French mercenaries took possession of the throne. On December 18th James fled to France and to the protection of his staunch friend and fellow Catholic Louis XIV, who installed him in a palace at St.-Germain.

William of Orange with his consort Mary now ruled England and its six million souls. His most implacable enemy was France, and in the wars which followed the colonies could not be neutral: their very existence was threatened by the French and the Indians. Thenceforth as great wars ravaged Europe their effects were felt in America, as waves spread outward from a center of disturbance and move the pebbles on the far shore.

[4] *The Rivals*

In 1689 the mortal enmity of Protestant England and Catholic France found expression in open warfare, and in the American colonies this contest of giants for trade and power and beatitude brought about King William's War, in which the French in Canada instigated and officered a series of raids by their Indian allies on the frontier hamlets of New England, while Canadian privateers busily raided the fishing fleets on the Newfoundland Banks, and ranged American waters from Maine to the West Indies, seizing trading vessels and killing or imprisoning their crews in a frenzy of fanaticism.

The colonists of Massachusetts, Connecticut and New York, inspired to concerted action by the impact of French land and sea power, decided to send an expedition against the Canadian privateers' base of supply—Port Royal, in Nova Scotia. As leader of the joint effort they chose Sir William Phips, a home-grown hero from Woolwich, Maine, near the mouth of the Kennebec. Phips had been knighted by James II, as a reward for making an honest division of treasure which he recovered from a sunken Spanish galley in 1687, and he was reputed to be a man of great industry as well as integrity. Phips set out from Boston with eight small colonial ships and nearly eight hundred men on April 28, 1690; on May 11th the landing was made and the town seized without opposition from the French. Much booty fell to the New Englanders: the Catholic church was plundered and the altar demolished, as an expression of Protestant distaste for the symbols of Catholic ritualism. Phips himself absconded with the French Governor's personal supply of wigs, garters, nightcaps and shirts—all articles hard to come by in New England.

Vastly encouraged by this military and sartorial victory, the colonists sent a more ambitious expedition against Quebec in the fall of the same year. Phips commanded again, but this time he had thirty-four ships, ranging in size from small fishing vessels serving as transports to a

44-gun ship manned by two hundred men. In all, nearly two thousand men were in the expedition, but when the squadron had threaded the tricky channel and arrived before Quebec on October 16th, Phips was unable to make any headway against the French defenses. His landing-boats, caught by a falling tide, grounded on sand bars, and the men he was able to get ashore were easily repulsed by the French and Indians. Phips then sailed his ships close to the citadel, which he bombarded ineffectually, for at that time the emphasis in naval armament was on numerous small guns and not on the weight of metal they could throw. After Phips had bounced his round shot off the walls of Quebec until his ammunition ran low and the impending season of winter gales threatened his safe return, he withdrew his fleet and sailed for Boston.

As a result of this failure Phips' reputation was only slightly tarnished, and in 1692 he became the Royal Governor of Massachusetts, then the leading maritime colony, during a period of utter lawlessness at sea, when guns wrote the rules and every sail was suspect. Regardless of the flag a ship flew, the chances were that it had a commission from England or France or Holland or Spain to cruise as a privateer or letter-of-marque, and ships so commissioned could seize enemy or neutral vessels as legal prizes.

The colonists' ships were also vulnerable to the pirates who owed allegiance to no flag and who infested the seas: Levantine and Barbary Coast rovers cruised the waters from Spain to England in their galleys, ready to board any ship of lesser force than their own; in the West Indies renegade Europeans, after starting out with open boats at Tortuga Island, had quickly built up a formidable business as the ships they captured increased in size and they were enabled to expand the area of their operations to include all of the Caribbean, and the eastern seaboard of North America. The amiable and often devout villains who engaged in this profitable industry went under the generic term of "buccaneers," derived from their practice of "boucanning," or smoking, meat and fish in the West Indies; the Dutch knew them as "zee rovers" and the English as "freebooters"—a word the French attempted to pronounce by saying "flibustier." Few of these freebooters could compete with their archetype, Blackbeard—a magnificent old sinner who chewed up wine-glasses to prove the durability of his digestion, and who thoughtfully burned sulphur in his ship so that his crew would be sure to feel at home in the Purgatory wherein, they were convinced, they would inevitably spend eternity.

There were indigenous pirates, too, born and bred in the American colonies. Ned Low, of Boston, delighted in raiding the fishing fleets for their stores and any gear he might need, albeit he wept copious tears in his rare moments of sobriety at the thought of the shame he was bringing to his young child at home ashore. Closer to the ideal was Thomas Pounds, in pursuit of whom Boston sent Captain Samuel Pease in the sloop *Mary,* in 1689. Pounds was brought to action in Vineyard Sound, his ship flying the blood-red flag while he strutted about, shouting horrible oaths and threats at the crew of the *Mary.* After a brief, bitter engagement, in the course of which Pease was mortally wounded, the crew of the *Mary* boarded the pirate ship and brought Tom Pounds back to be hanged in Boston.

As the war went on between France and England, and as the warships of England were concentrated in English home waters to protect the small, sea-moated nation from the wrath of Louis XIV, the incidence of piratical acts rose year by year. Colonel Benjamin Fletcher, who had become Governor of New York in 1692, soon found a profitable sideline in fostering the pirate trade. Five years earlier the English had sent Sir Robert Holmes with a squadron of frigates to the West Indies to wipe out the freebooters, and his partial success there drove them to develop new fields of endeavor. Most lucrative of the new areas of activity was the Indian ocean, where the pirates based on Madagascar and there traded what jewels and gold and merchandise they had picked up at sea for the guns and rum and ammunition brought out by Yankee merchantmen, who could return to New York and sell their goods without being asked embarrassing and impertinent questions. Manhattan traders did business in many strange currencies—Spanish moidores, doubloons and pieces-of-eight, French louis-d'ors and English guineas—and dealt in strange merchandise—Far Eastern rugs, silks, sandalwood, teakwood, jewels, and gold and silver bars. On one trip to Madagascar a New York merchantman whose captain was willing to overlook the origin of the goods he bought from pirates could return home with a full cargo and smuggle it in past the bribed port officials, for a net profit of thirty thousand English pounds. Such smugglers, who often operated as pirates themselves, were known in New York as "Red Sea men," and they were not without honor in the eyes of their countrymen. Frequently they were the arbiters of style in male attire, even if a trifle flamboyant in their display of personal jewelry and gold. Their manners were often courtly and impeccable, and they were received as friends in the homes of the most reputable men in the community, who financed their adventures with the understanding that the smuggler would respect their anonymity. It was unthinkable that a pillar of the community should be proved a lawbreaker, and it was a cardinal sin for any smuggler or pirate to divulge his source of financial backing and political protection.

By 1698 the loss of revenue and trade brought about by the smugglers and pirates had reached such large proportions that the English government was moved to action. But since the Royal Navy was fully occupied in the war with Louis XIV, a private company was organized to hunt down and destroy some pirates, as an object lesson. It was clearly understood that such a company must offer some chance of profit to its stockholders, among whom were King William, Lord Bellomont (who had replaced Fletcher as Governor of New York, and who was also Governor of Massachusetts and New Hampshire), Lord Chancellor Somers, the Duke of Shrewsbury, Romney and Robert Livingston— the latter a local New York luminary. A 30-gun ship, the *Adventure-Galley,* was bought in London and partially manned there by a hundred men. A New York merchant-captain named William Kidd, who was known to be an intrepid and competent skipper, was put in command, on Bellomont's recommendation. He was supplied with a letter-of-marque, and the King gave him a special commission to cruise in pursuit of pirates. Kidd recruited a full ship's company from the waterfront of New York, and after a fruitless cruise up and down the American coast, he set out for Madagascar, which he reached in late 1697, only to find that the pirates, forewarned of his mission, had fled. As their search in the Indian ocean for pirates and booty proved futile, the crew became mutinous, demanding that the ship devote its time to a little pirating on its own account. Kidd, with a notable elasticity of ethics, accepted their demands and their luck changed. The *Adventure-Galley* seized several ships which were fair prizes, since they were flying either the colors of the Great Mogul Aurungzeb of India or of France, and Kidd could not at that time have received news that in the fall of 1697 the Treaty of Ryswick had brought about a fragile truce in the war between France and England. Then, his appetite whetted by these perfectly legal seizures, Kidd made two fatal mistakes: he captured a rich prize, an East Indiaman called the *Quedagh Merchant,* an English ship, put her crew ashore, moved his own men aboard, and burnt the old *Adventure-Galley;* he became involved with a mutinous gunner named William Moore, who, when called a "lousy dog" had the temerity to reply "If I am a lousy dog, 'tis you who have made me so!" Kidd's answer to this piece of insolence was to hit Moore such a smart blow on the head with a wooden bucket that next day the gunner died.

Kidd set sail for the West Indies and home, little knowing that he had achieved too much notoriety for safety: he had involved his backers from King William to Governor Bellomont at a politically inconvenient time, and he was doomed to be railroaded to the gallows, convicted of being guilty of the murder of William Moore and of the pirating of the *Quedagh Merchant.*

As the seventeenth century drew to a close, France and England were leading in the contest for world power. Holland, although rich in trade and shipping, was not in their class, and Spain's decline had already begun through her inability to protect her enormous empire.

France and France alone could compete with England at sea, thanks to the naval establishment built up by Colbert under Louis XIV. But gradually, as Louis came to concentrate his resources on land warfare, the French fleet suffered from lack of funds. In Brest, Le Havre, Toulon and Marseilles France's warships were decommissioned and their crews released to serve in merchantmen commissioned as letters-of-marque, or the frigates and brigs were taken over by private individuals who manned them with trained crews and sent them out as privateers. England's answer was to build more ships to protect her merchantmen and to prey on the remnants of France's merchant marine. This rivalry between England and France, keen as it was in the competition for trade in India, was even more acute in the new world and on the high seas. The English colonists along the Eastern seaboard, remembering the

French-Indian raids and massacres which had decimated many frontier settlements, and remembering too the sometimes inhuman brutality of Canadian privateers, were whole-heartedly with the English in their hatred of France.

In the lives of those colonists who had survived the fighting at sea and in the frontier settlements, as in their ancestors who had undergone periods of near-starvation and disease, there could be dimly discerned the threads of national character which were being interwoven by natural forces. Among those threads—and not the least in strength of them—were the inherited, accumulated and sharply developed traits of the men who made their living from the sea. By 1700, although the English-speaking colonists in America numbered only some 260,000 souls, the seafarers among them were already known in the world as men who were reckless, predatory, ingenious, without principle and with limitless ambition.

And, dragged as they were by their loyalties into the kingly, internecine quarrels of Europe, they were soon to be involved and their mettle tested in another war whose origins were in London and Paris and Madrid. Europe was about to undergo one of its periodic struggles; this time it was a question of Spain. The Spanish Empire was a gigantic collection of colonies which included, in the new world alone, Cuba, Puerto Rico, all of South America with the exception of Brazil, all of Central America, Mexico and Florida. This empire was in danger of partition, for it was evident that Charles II of Spain, sick in mind and body could not live much longer and the choice of an heir to his realm was undecided.

Like so many vultures the kings of Europe focused their attention on the dying man, and formed a Grand Alliance to make a profitable division of his Empire. But the Spanish people, who had been declining in numbers and wealth for over a century, and who were obviously incapable of protecting all their widespread possessions, became infuriated at the idea of pieces of their empire falling into the hands of England, Holland and France, whereupon Charles II, after checking with the Pope and being advised to stand pat against any partition of the Empire, made his will on October 12, 1700. Philip, seventeen-year old

Duke of Anjou, and grandson of Louis XIV, was the chosen heir. Three weeks later Charles died, and Louis, deserting the Grand Alliance, threw his support to the duke, who became Philip V of Spain.

Then complicating an already involved situation, the exiled James II, fellow Catholic and life-long friend of Louis XIV, died in his palace at St. Germain, and Louis, in an excess of grief and sympathy, suddenly recognized the dead king's son as James III of England. This arbitrary recognition of a king for the English throne already occupied by William of Orange fanned English hatred of France to a flaming rage, which the House of Commons promptly reflected by voting large increases in the army and navy.

While the English and French were engaged in diplomatic maneuvering aimed at lining up their allies for the coming war, William of Orange died, in March 1702, and Queen Anne became ruler of England. In May, England and Holland declared war against France and Spain, and the War of the Spanish Succession began.

In Europe, while Marlborough was demonstrating his brilliant generalship in the battles of Blenheim, Ramillies and Malplaquet, and while a combined English-Dutch fleet was seizing Gibraltar, there were modest repercussions in the new world as the French and English and Spanish colonists sided with their respective monarchs.

The colonists knew the war as "Queen Anne's War," and the usual terrifying night raids and massacres by French and Indians on the frontier settlements were followed by more intricate naval actions. The Spaniards, who had never abandoned their claim that Florida included South Carolina, sent a squadron of five ships against Charleston in 1706, and the citizens of that doughty port, whose partiality for smugglers had made it known as "Rogues' Harbor," promptly commissioned a popular local blade named Colonel William Rhett as a Vice-Admiral Rhett assembled several ships which happened to be in port, armed them in haste, and manned them with whatever seamen he could find. The French, in the midst of these frantic preparations, had surrounded the town, but as soon as Rhett got his flotilla under way the French squadron beat a hasty retreat, having lost nearly half the men in the expedition. A few days later, Rhett, eager to prove further his ability as a Vice-

Admiral, upon receiving news that a large Spanish ship was off the coast, set out in two small vessels and captured the ship, bringing ninety of the crew in to Charleston as prisoners.

But South Carolina did not stop her nautical adventures with these victories: next year a fleet sailed down to Pensacola, and after chasing many outraged Spaniards into the brush, the Carolinians burnt the town, although they could not force the fort to surrender.

The war at sea had become increasingly a war of privateers as the French Navy declined in power. Often half a dozen or more French privateers sailed as a squadron, cruising about and seizing the ships of her chief maritime enemies, Holland and England. In the years between 1702 and 1707 England alone lost 846 merchantmen, but in that same period France lost 1,346, and France's merchant marine was thoroughly vitiated.

The English-speaking colonies suffered their share of the depredations of the French privateers: in 1708 privateers based on Port Royal captured thirty-five English merchantmen, among them many of Boston registry, and imprisoned 470 seamen. And losses to the French were not noticeably less after England sent a squadron of three 60-gun ships, HMS *Rochester, Severn* and *Portland,* to clean up the north coast of Newfoundland, where the English captured in the harbor of La Couche two vessels mounting together thirty guns, with 145 men; in Carouse three more vessels, mounting sixty-four guns in all, with 210 men; and in Great St. Julian one 30-gun vessel with 120 men. As the French privateers continued their work, damaging both the colonists' pocketbooks and their pride, the traditional objective, the capture of Port Royal, became a primary war aim, not only because of the privateers which sailed out of that port, but also because Port Royal occupied a key position in the Newfoundland fisheries, being a handy place to fit out ships and dry the catch.

Two expeditions had come to nothing, in 1707 and 1709, and the third attempt took place in 1710, when four frigates and some thirty transports, commanded by a professional English soldier, Colonel Nicholson, left Boston on September 18th. Six days later they sailed into the harbor of Port Royal and landed fourteen hundred men, having lost only one ship on the rocks at the harbor mouth. Subercase, the French governor, had no more than three hundred men to defend his domain against the invaders, but he resisted as best he could and did not surrender until October 1st, when the English began to bombard the town. Forthwith the English re-named Port Royal, in honor of their Queen, Annapolis Royal.

This victory stimulated the English, whose fleets had won control of the seas from the dispersed French naval forces, to undertake an expedition against Quebec, in a co-operative effort with the colonists. Boston was all a-twitter when the leader of this new offensive—Vice-Admiral Sir Hoveden Walker, R.N.—arrived there on June 24, 1711. The Admiral was a very patronizing man, who deigned to talk to but a chosen few of the colony's leaders. Nine warships and some sixty transports and supply ships set out for Quebec on July 30th, with nearly twelve thousand men aboard, among them five regiments of Marlborough's veterans and two regiments of New Englanders. On August 22nd the expedition was in the Gulf of St. Lawrence and a thick fog settled down, followed by a strong easterly wind which rose in force as the night wore on.

The pilots were hopelessly confused, and shortly after 10:30 that night an Army officer on Admiral Walker's flagship, the 70-gun *Edgar,* awoke the Admiral to tell him that the ships were being driven on a lee shore. Walker, outraged at this interruption of his dreams, dismissed the officer and tried to go to sleep again, but soon the presumptuous man was back again: the fleet was in peril, no doubt about it. Walker rose at last from his bunk, coming out on deck in his slippered feet, with his dressing gown flapping in the wind. The fog had lifted, and in the moonlight breakers could be seen close at hand. Walker ordered the ships to beat away from the shore, but eight transports and two supply ships went on the rocks, and nine hundred men were lost.

The fleet then rendezvoused off Cape Breton, but the expedition's nerve was so badly shaken that the attack on Quebec was abandoned. The colony vessels, small transports and supply ships, returned to Boston while Walker led his fleet back to England, where his flagship exploded at Spithead, killing four hundred of the men aboard. But Walker was ashore at the time and all he lost was his official papers, a loss which helped to prevent an investigation of his failure to take Quebec by the Privy Council. Long and loud were the recriminations over this affair, as the colonists blamed the unapproachable Admiral for the failure, and the Admiral accused the colonists of supplying him with incompetent pilots.

The war ended, as far as England was concerned, when the Treaty of Utrecht was signed on April 11, 1713. Louis XIV had won his main point: a Bourbon was on the Spanish throne and the Spanish Empire was still intact. But England received from France in the new world, Nova Scotia, Newfoundland and Hudson Bay, and also won specific rights from Spain to share in Spanish trade along with a practical monopoly of the business of supplying slaves to the Spanish colonies. France kept Cape Breton Island, with its port of Louisbourg which controlled the approaches to the Gulf of St. Lawrence, and France retained, too, definite rights in the Newfoundland fisheries.

Next year Queen Anne died and George I, a coarse and stupid man who was so unfeeling that he broiled his wife's lover in an oven, became King of England and Scotland. Unable to speak a word of English, this German princeling was the best Protestant ruler available, and he took over a nation in good condition, whose eight million people had prospered during the eleven years of war and grown even more imperialistic in nature.

France, on the other hand, was in sore need of a period of recuperation, and when Louis XIV died, in 1715, the Duke of Orleans who ruled as Regent for five-year old Louis XV was as anxious as the English Prime Minister Walpole to avoid war. Thus a providential hiatus in the fighting occurred, and a period of peace which was to last until 1739 left the English colonists along the American seaboard free to develop their assets, with only such minor obstacles to progress as an occasional pirate and the natural perils of the sea to overcome.

Part II
GROWING PAINS

[5] *First Steps*

The American colonies, by 1715, had clearly indicated the extent to which the sea would influence their future growth. The colonies south of Maryland, with their large plantations devoted to tobacco, cotton, rice and indigo, were not greatly concerned with nautical matters, save when an occasional pirate ship loitered along the coast and gave them a chance to display their ability as seamen. One nest of pirates, driven from the Caribbean by the English, set up a base of operations on the Carolina coast near the mouth of the Cape Fear river and battened on the coastal shipping for a brief period in 1718. The Governor of North Carolina quickly sent out his most talented naval officer, William Rhett, against the freebooters. Rhett captured their sloop, and along with it their leader, Steed Bonnet, and a crew of thirty men. Soon afterwards the Governor, not willing to be outdone by the deeds of any man, duplicated Rhett's feat in a no-quarter action against another pirate sloop in which only a few of the pirates escaped death. Those who survived the engagement at sea were, with one exception, hanged after a trial on shore. But rarely were the southern colonists called upon to fight at sea, and their energies were directed inland at the exploitation of the great coastal plains.

It was in New England that the traits essential to successful seafaring were being constantly tempered and tested and sharpened, in the fisheries, in the whalers and slavers, and in the routine business of carrying goods to Europe and southward along the coast to the West Indies.

The shipyards had expanded enormously during the years of intermittent warfare: between 1674 and 1714 New Englanders had built no less than 1,332 ocean-going vessels, and of these 239 had been sold abroad. In 1715 there was not an idle shipyard along the whole New England coast, for the demand for ships was constantly growing both in the colonies and in England. War had caused the destruction of thousands of ships which now had to be replaced, and even in a period of peace the loss of ships to the elements was high, for there were few buoys in the channels, charts were crudely drawn, and such aids as lighthouses were almost non-existent along the American coast.

In the eight years from 1712 to 1720, seven hundred ships were built in New England, and the English shipbuilders along the Thames saw in this activity the beginning of a trend which might end with England buying all her merchantmen in the colonies. In 1724 they protested to the king that colonial shipyards were attracting their best craftsmen, and asked that a stop be put to the encouragement of colonial ship-building, with whose prices they could not compete. English-built ships not only cost more; a question of policy was involved. England was running short of oak trees, for the royal forests had been decimated by naval requirements during the wars with Holland, France and Spain. The oak groves were replanted, but not until the eve of the American revolution would the trees be large enough for use in men-of-war and merchantmen. Meanwhile it was plainly in the public's interest to safeguard what oaks remained in England by encouraging the use of colonial timber. The colonists drew on what seemed to be a never-ending source of oak and pine and spruce; furthermore, they encouraged skilled shipwrights to leave England and to come to work in the new world at higher wages, with more personal freedom, and with an unlimited opportunity to advance their own fortunes.

The ships the colonists built in the eighteenth century were rigged and modeled along European lines, and in the gradual evolution of types, the schooner, with fore-and-aft rig was developed toward the end of the century. The rigging of the schooner was a definite improvement on accepted types: with fore-and-aft sails on two masts, in place of the usual square-rigged sails, a large schooner could be handled by a few men, could be worked up and down the rivers more easily, and was less at the mercy of the constantly shifting winds of the northeastern coast than a square-rigged vessel. Schooners that carried a square-topsail as well as fore-and-aft sails were among the fastest vessels afloat, and they were much in demand for both fishing and privateering.

As trade boomed, shipbuilding kept pace, and new products were added to the fish, timber, furs and tobacco which had marked seventeenth-century colonial exports. Rice and indigo began to appear on the southern plantations, and on New England bills of lading whale oil and whale bone began to be entered with increasing frequency.

The English settlers along the south shore of Long Island had begun as far back as 1644 to post lookouts for whales which drifted ashore. Tall spars lined the beaches, and when a lookout spotted whales close offshore the townsmen would set out in pursuit in their open boats. Slowly the market for whale oil grew and by 1711 the Long Islanders were making enough money from whales which drifted ashore, and from those they killed not far from land, to inspire the Governor of New York, Robert Hunter, to demand one-twentieth of the catch. This decree the colonists ignored. For over half a century they had been fishing without paying any share of their catch to the government, and their original patents to the land they lived on included the right to keep all the fish they caught. The Long Islanders knew, better than the Governor of New York, how speculative whaling was: in 1707 they had taken four thousand barrels of whale oil, but the year before their catch had amounted to only six hundred barrels.

The whales moved in along the south shore of Long Island from November to April, when this area became their natural feeding ground, and in those months the weather was seldom fit for any but the boldest seamen to set out after a whale in an open boat manned by only six men, in an effort to make a killing with the crude harpoons then in use.

But Governor Hunter was adamant about his 5 per cent cut and he sent a sheriff to seize all the whales the colonists caught. In opposition to this shakedown the citizens of Easthampton produced a local whaler of Irish extraction, Samuel Mulford, who was blessed with an unusual amount of Hibernian obstinacy. Mulford was elected to the New York General Assembly where he attempted to win his case in vain, being constantly outvoted by the non-whaling majority. But he stood on his right to speak his mind and in open assembly he stated his case, attacking the governor's personal financial ambitions without regard for tact or consequences. The courts were in the control of the governor and before long Sam Mulford found himself fined fifty pounds, as well as being harried by a succession of court orders which made it necessary for him to spend most of his time traveling to and from New York. He determined to settle once and for all the question of whether the colonists were legally subject to rule by the decree of the governor, or whether they enjoyed the constitutional rights of English subjects. To get a decision in this matter Mulford sailed secretly from Easthampton to Newport, R.I., walked to Boston, and sailed thence for London. In London Sam Mulford's appearance was so obviously colonial that he was the object of much curiosity to the good people of the town. The pickpockets found the contents of his pockets so alluring that Mulford resorted to a fisherman's natural defense: he sewed fish-hooks in his pockets, to the grief of London's petty thieves. He was equally successful in his defense of the colonists' claims: to Governor Hunter went word that he should encourage rather than harass the whalers, and the governor remitted his 5 per cent cut on whales.

Meanwhile another center of whaling activity—Nantucket Island, off the south shore of Cape Cod—had been busy learning the technique of successful whaling. In 1690 they had hired a Cape Cod expert named Ichabod Paddock, and a few years later they felt sufficiently optimistic about whaling to invest in a sloop of their own. In the winter of 1712, while Mulford was establishing the rights of whalers, as well as of all colonists, in London, a Nantucketer named Captain Christopher Hussey was making apochryphal whaling history in an open boat off Nantucket. That winter, according to the folk tales, a sudden gale drove Hussey's boat out of sight of land, and just at the moment when his crew had become exhausted by their attempts to reach land they encountered, in the storm, a school of such whales as they had seen only once before. These whales were sperm whales, and to the Nantucket whaler the capture of one of them meant as much as the capture of a Spanish galleon meant to the English privateers, for the sperm oil taken from the head of these whales was worth eight shillings an ounce and it was in great demand by the apothecaries of Boston and London for unguents and lotions.

In these circumstances, when the odds were very good that Hussey and his crew would never reach shore again, and when it was clear that they had nothing to lose but their lives already imperiled by the gales and therefore well worth the risk involved in whale-killing, Hussey made a natural decision: he went in chase of the school. One whale was killed, and (so the ancient yarn goes), as the oil from it spread a slick over the water, quieting the waves in a mystical fashion, the boat was able to weather the storm by keeping in this smooth spot. Next day they towed the whale to Nantucket, and the story of Hussey's providential escape spread from pulpit to pulpit.

At this time the islanders owned only five sloops, but they were promptly fitted out as whalers after their owners learned that it was possible to kill sperm whales, even although they had to be sought in deep water. Three years later Nantucket had six sloops devoting their entire time to deep-water whaling, and the oil and bone of their catch was sold for eleven hundred pounds. Soon the business of whaling became so lucrative that the original system by which a boat's crew shared equally in the profits of a chase, as well as in the toil and danger, gave way to a new method of dividing the catch: as some men showed greater skill with the harpoon and the lance than others, they demanded and got a greater share of the results of the common effort.

In 1720 a small amount of Nantucket whale oil was sold in London, where the price was higher than in Boston, and where ship's gear such as canvas, cordage and iron fittings were less expensive than in the colonies. Before long the Nantucketers had established a direct and substantial trade with England, as the whalers brought in more and more oil, and took in exchange an increasing amount of cordage and canvas for their growing fleet.

The Nantucketers were not entirely dependent on the sea for a living: they had their tiny farms and their livestock to take care of their basic requirements. But their one chance of making a great deal of money in a very short time was to risk their lives as whalers. In two months aboard a whaler a man might make as much as he could in a year ashore. After a few cruises he might have enough money to buy shares in another whaler, and so increase his chances of eventually owning his own ship. Promotion on the whalers was faster than on any other vessel: a man with an unusual sense of timing, balance, keen eyes and granitic nerves, could expect to fill the post of harpooner after his first voyage, and by quick succession, as others lost their lives, he might rise to fill a first mate's berth before he had reached the age of twenty.

In Nantucket there was an additional motive, besides the all-pervading quest for wealth, which had its effect on the whaling business. The girls on the island had a reputation for being luscious as ripe plums and they banded together in a secret sorority whose members swore to marry no man until he had killed his whale. Indeed, it is doubtful if any self-respecting girl of the island would even consider bundling with a youth who did not wear around his neck the small wooden peg which on a whaler's boat locked the harpoon's line into its groove, but which on shore was worn only by the harpooners.

While the islanders in open boats and sloops were hard at work at sea during the winter months when the whales moved within range of their craft, and while a few larger vessels ventured as far away as Greenland in their search of sperm whales, to the north of Cape Cod the colonists of Maine, New Hampshire and Massachusetts were specializing in an equally profitable type of fishing.

Cape Cod, stretching out into the Atlantic like a half-bent arm, made a natural barrier which divided the early maritime efforts of the colonists by turning the energies of those who lived south of it on Nantucket to whaling, and those who lived north of it to cod and halibut fishing. By following the line of least resistance, by taking advantage of what was close at hand, the Nantucketers led the colonies in whaling; the colonists who lived along the coast north of Cape Cod found their sea-harvest on the Newfoundland Banks.

There had been thriving English, French and Portuguese fishing fleets on the Banks as early as 1615, when England alone had 170 fishing craft off Newfoundland, and France and Portugal had close to three hundred vessels together. This industry, initiated when John Cabot reported he had found good cod-fishing on the coast in 1497, was first developed by French fishermen from Normandy, and by Portuguese from the Azores who were fishing the Banks in 1504. By degrees, in order to supply the fish which were essential to the sanctity of faithful Catholics, the English moved in on this type of fishing, and with them the colonists of New England, who sent their first vessels to the Banks in 1645. By 1701 there were 121 colonial fishing vessels, manned by 2,700 men, dragging cod from the squally northern waters.

The first craft used in the fisheries of the New England coast were shallops, small, one-masted boats, broad in the beam and decked over amidships to give the crew some protection from the weather. As the need for bigger vessels grew, larger shallops were built, with two masts, since two small sails were more easily handled than one large one. These shallops were in turn supplanted by the ketches, or "catches," which the Dutch settlers knew as "pinkies," and whose distinguishing features were a pointed or rounded stern and a large square sail. The early ketch was easy to build and to handle; because of its large beam it was reasonably safe and fast, and it had a large cargo-carrying capacity, the hold being nine or ten feet deep, which made it useful for both the coasting trade and the fisheries. Their hulls were of white oak, their masts of spruce or pine, and they were decked with white pine. Generally there was a small cabin aft where the crew ate and slept. In 1700 the whole Massachusetts fishing fleet was composed of ketches built in the towns along the bay. Most of them were of less than 30-tons burden, or 10-tons register, and they could be built for about three and a half pounds per ton.

While these craft were working the Banks and in so doing training thousands of seamen in the rigors of northern fogs and gales, from the shallop a new type of vessel was being derived—the sloop, with fore-and-aft rig, broad decked and square in the stern. For boats of 30-tons the sloop was a handy craft, easily handled by a few men in any sort of weather, and after 1700 it became the most popular type of fishing and trading vessel. Many of the fishing fleet off the Banks, and nearly all the mackerel boats, were sloops, and as they grew in size square topsails were added. Soon the sloops had supplanted the ketches in the offshore fisheries and in the coastal trade, and the shipyards at Salem, Boston, Charlestown, Newburyport and Gloucester were busy turning out these fast and easy-sailing vessels.

Generations after the sloop had won favor as an economical and safe type of vessel, the schooner appeared, an even better product. The schooner was not the invention of any one man: its lines were the product of the trials and errors of many men, all seeking to build craft that could carry more goods at greater speed. A good schooner could make two trips to the Banks while a sloop was making one. With square topsails, even more speed was achieved, and during the wars it became the custom to suspect any topsail schooner of being a privateer.

While the colonial shiprights were sharpening their wits, trying to evolve safer and faster vessels, and as the lines of their craft grew cleaner, another industry—slaving—had been developing with great rapidity.

By Article 16 of the Treaty of Utrecht, signed April 11, 1713, Spain agreed to take 4,800 Negro slaves each year for thirty years and this large order was to be filled exclusively by the ships of England and her colonies. The Spanish and English kings were each to be paid 25 per cent of the profits from this business, and in England the prospects of exploiting this monopoly were so highly regarded that Article 16 was hailed far and wide as one of the main rewards of the war.

The demand for slave labor in the new world had been growing spasmodically ever since the Spaniards began their conquest and colonization of the Caribbean area in the early sixteenth century; as each colony expanded and it became evident that profitable operation of the mines, and of the sugar and tobacco plantations, depended on a constant supply of cheap labor, slaves were brought over from Africa in Spanish ships exclusively until John Hawkins of England raided the Guinea coast in 1562, captured three hundred slaves from the Portuguese and sold them in the Spanish West Indies. In the following years his exploit was imitated by other adventurers in a series of forays along the slave coast, but it was not until the English colonies in the West Indies had shown how profitable sugar plantations could be, with slave labor, that the English regularized this dingy business.

Toward the end of the seventeenth century the supply of English criminals and paupers who could be indentured was exhausted, and the blacks were an acceptable substitute. Charles II chartered a company to handle the demand for Negro slaves in 1662, but this organization, which had contracted to bring three thousand slaves a year to the English West Indies, went out of business soon after the Dutch fleet under De Ruyter wiped out its shore establishment and captured many of its ships in 1664. Not until 1672, when the Royal African Company was given its charter did the English slavers get down to serious work. By its charter the Company had a monopoly of this most lucrative trade, and so great were the profits that private merchants in London and New England demanded that they be permitted to share in the business. Parliament supported their request and in 1698 the free-lance slavers, who had been bootlegging blacks in spite of the guns of the Royal African Company, were admitted to the trade, on condition that they pay 10 per cent duty on all the goods they brought to Africa.

To the acquisitive New Englanders the slave trade was irresistibly attractive, and none among them showed more enterprise in it than the Rhode Islanders. In the ten-year period after colonial ships were permitted to share the slave trade, 103 vessels were built in Rhode Island, and a majority of these indulged in an excursion for slaves after they had sold their New England cargos in the West Indies. From Trinidad or Antigua they ran over to the slave coast, picked up a few unfortunate blacks, and traded them in the West Indies for molasses on the way home. In the Rhode Island distilleries the molasses soon became rum, which was always useful in any kind of trade.

The New England merchants quickly improved on this pattern of trade: their ships began to follow a triangular trading route which started when they loaded rum in New England, sailed for the Guinea Coast, and there exchanged rum for slaves. Then, on what came to be known as "The Middle Passage," they brought the slaves to the West Indies and there traded them for molasses which was brought home to be made into more rum.

Newport, Rhode Island, rapidly became the leading port in America in the slave trade, with Bristol and Providence not far behind. There was then no moral stigma attached to selling or owning slaves, and the few futile attempts at suppression of the trade in the early eighteenth century came from citizens of the northern colonies, where slave-owning was not a paying proposition. In the southern colonies an occasional voice was raised in objection to slaving, but there a short winter and a long growing season made it possible to keep slaves at work in the fields throughout most of the year and without them the plantations could not have existed. In the north slaves could work in the fields only during a short growing season, and they had to be fed and clothed and housed throughout the unproductive winter months. No matter how well they were cared for, they died in droves in the harsh northern climate. For these reasons the New England colonies bought comparatively few slaves, and in 1715, when there were 435,000 English colonists and 59,000 slaves in America, the vast majority of the slaves were owned in colonies south of New England. In New York they made up one-seventh of the population, in Maryland close to half, and in South Carolina the whites were outnumbered three to one by the blacks.

When Article 16 of the Treaty of Utrecht came into effect, and competition was unrestrained, the Rhode Islanders went into the business with all the ingenuity at their command, and with no loss of respect in their communities. Pious merchants and blasphemous sea-captains alike saw no discrepancy in trafficking both in human flesh and Christianity, and if some down-at-heel Quaker raised objections and pointed out that the slave trade was a tragic triangle based on greed, thriving on drunkenness and ending with agony, the answer was that slaving was as good a way as any to win converts to Christianity.

Assiduous as the colonial slavers were in pursuit of their profits, they were far surpassed by the activities of Englishmen sailing out of London and Bristol and Liverpool. Once the Spaniards had admitted them to the trade the Englishmen made the most of it, and in their greed they ran afoul of the Spanish authorities. By agreement with the Spaniards the English were entitled to send one slave ship a year to Porto Bello on the Panamanian Isthmus, and interpreting this concession as a sign of weakness, they soon were sending whole fleets of merchantmen to Porto Bello. The colonists on Panama welcomed this sudden inrush of merchandise, but the Spanish authorities were outraged. They retaliated by outfitting numerous small vessels as colonial cruisers, whose sole duty was to see that England did not exceed her contracted quota.

George I had died on June 12th, 1727 in the course of a trip he was making in Germany with his mistress. His son, George II, succeeded him, and he was a moderate improvement on his father, having a better grasp of English, and a sensitivity of character which he owed to his mother, whose lover had been cooked in the oven by his father. There is little reason to doubt, in spite of the adulterous proclivities of his mother, that George II's father was George I. Both kings had the same meaty complexions and dumb animal courage. The troubles with Spain that George II inherited were routine matters: they could be settled with guns, which then bore the motto "Ultima Ratio Regum"—"the last argument of kings": war.

A long series of blood-curdling boardings and engagements culminated in the "War of Jenkins' Ear"—a war which was forced on Walpole's government, against his wishes, in 1739, when Captain Robert Jenkins related to a Committee of the House of Commons the story of the insults he had suffered at the hands of the Spaniards. Jenkins, the Committee learned, was peacefully sailing home from the West Indies in the brig *Rebecca* when he was forced to submit to boarding by a Spanish cruiser whose captain insisted on his right to search the vessel. When Jenkins objected, he was seized and one of his ears torn off, and he was informed that he should take the ear to his king and tell him that if he had been there he would have received the same treatment. And Jenkins showed the Committee his detached ear, which he had carefully preserved by wrapping it up in cotton. As news of this humiliation spread over London the populace reacted as Walpole's enemies expected them to: they suffered a wave of hysterical nationalism, and the United Kingdom declared war on Spain on October 19th, 1739.

[6] *Bad Examples*

This war, which was not one of England's better efforts, was destined to taper off into sporadic encounters at sea after the English had suffered two extremely expensive defeats in the Caribbean. Vice-Admiral Edward Vernon, with a fleet of 124 vessels, 29 of them ships of the line and the rest transports and frigates, set out from Antigua in 1741 to take Cartagena, a major Spanish base on the Northeast coast of South America. With him went twelve thousand soldiers (four battalions of them raised by levies in the colonies north of Carolina), and sixteen thousand seamen. To oppose him the Spaniards had a garrison of only four thousand men, but they were enough. From March 9th to April 16th the fleet milled about off the coast, while the land forces besieged the fortifications. Between the land and naval forces there was an utter lack of co-operation, heightened by acrimonious exchanges between the commanding general and Admiral Vernon. Finally, when only three thousand troops remained alive, the remainder having died of disease or in battle, the expedition withdrew.

In October of the same year an expedition against Santiago, Cuba, failed as dismally, and for all their efforts to drive Spain from the Caribbean area the English had only one reward: Commodore George Anson, operating along the Pacific coast in his 50-gun ship, the *Centurion,* captured a galleon on its way from Mexico to Manila with £313,000 worth of gold and silver aboard.

The colonists soon lost interest in the war: hundreds of their men had met death in the futile attempts to take Cartagena, and the press gangs were roaming the streets of their towns, chasing likely-looking seamen to impress them into the service of the King. Not every sailor was as resourceful as the one pursued by Lt. Tume, of the sloop *Province,* who led the Lieutenant an obstacle race through the streets of Boston which ended only when he dashed up the roof of a house and halted at the top, while the Lieutenant kept going and fell to his death on the flagstones in the yard.

Even the privateers had trouble manning their ships, no matter how colorful their promises to volunteers, and no matter how fine their reputations as fighting ships. One of the best of them, the 100-ton *Young Eagle* of Boston, after a successful cruise in and around the Canary Islands during which she took ships flying the flags of Sweden, Spain, Ireland and the Pope, could not raise a full crew in her home port. Only after she had sent her drummer, with drum beating, and her first lieutenant through the streets of Newport, R.I., shouting the advantages of service in the *Young Eagle,* could she fill her complement of 135 men.

As the war with Spain degenerated into guerrilla fighting at sea, another and far greater war was in the making. Old Charles VI, Holy Roman Emperor, had died in sanctity in 1740, and there were no males to take over the throne. He had taken pains to win support for Maria Theresa as his successor but among all the power-thirsty nations around his realm he neglected to make a binding agreement with the one inevitable enemy, France.

Instinctively France allied herself with the enemies of Maria Theresa; the decision was in the nature of a reflex action, backed by the experience and tradition of two centuries of opposition to all things Austrian. England, too, reacted according to habit: she opposed France automatically, and in 1744 the War of the Austrian Succession was on.

The colonists knew this as "King George's War," and once again they suffered the frenzied attacks of the French and Indians on land, and the perpetual sniping of the privateers at sea.

While in Europe the English were losing so many battles on land that an abortive attempt was made to place a Catholic Stuart on the throne of England, in the new world the colonies were assembling shallops and sloops and schooners to make an attempt to take the French fortress of Louisbourg, on Cape Breton. Louis XV had spent some six million dollars over a period of twenty-five years on the fortification of this keystone of French power at the mouth of the St. Lawrence. The people of Massachusetts knew how formidable these defenses were, but when there was doubt about whether the expedition was a wise move, they petitioned their Governor, William Shirley, to carry out the attack as planned, regardless of whether they had English support or not. Connecticut, Rhode Island and New Hampshire joined them in the expedition, which sailed from Boston on March 25, 1745. The land forces, all of whom were New Englanders, were commanded by Colonel William Pepperell of Kittery, Maine, and the fleet itself, numbering close to a hundred sail, by Captain Edward Tyng of Massachusetts. Besides the transports, which carried 4,070 soldiers, there were twelve colonial cruisers acting as convoy. By Governor Shirley's instructions all the vessels were equipped with fishing-lines, so that the expedition could replenish its supplies with cod whenever the need arose.

Before the expedition reached Cape Breton it was reinforced by the arrival of Commodore Warren of the Royal Navy with four ships of the line, and he immediately set up a blockade of Louisbourg to protect the colonists in their siege of the fortress. The colonists landed before Louisbourg on April 30th, and after forty-seven days of siege the French surrendered. To many of the colonists this Catholic stronghold was a den of Satanic iniquity, and one venerable old chaplain, Parson Moody of Boston, went promptly and righteously to work chopping up the altar and images in the Louisbourg church.

Throughout the remaining three years of the war, while the Royal Navy defended them against threatened invasions by the French and Spanish, the colonists restricted their sea-fighting to the work of their privateers and letters-of-marque, which engaged the enemy with as much lethal violence as any pirate ships. When one small privateer, with seventy captured Spaniards in her hold, and only four colonists aboard, was faced with an attempt by the prisoners to seize the vessel, the captain wielded his ax with such skill that he cut off the Spanish leader's jaw with one blow, and when the Spaniard slipped on the blood-spattered deck, cut off his right foot with another blow. At this point the Spaniard cried for quarter, which was given him for a few hours so that he could prepare to meet his God. Then he was shot. The ferocity and cruelty which marked nearly all encounters between Englishman and Spaniard or Frenchman were a product of their rival religions: to the Catholic, as to the Protestant, there was considerable satisfaction to be gained from killing an enemy who worshiped God in such an obviously unreasonable, and sometimes blasphemous, manner.

The war ended when the Treaty of Aix-la-Chapelle was signed in October 1748, and by its terms the French regained Louisbourg, in exchange for Madras, India. Those Frenchmen who had fought for and won Madras in the miasmic heat of India were no less outraged at the disposition of their prize than were the colonists who had taken Louisbourg. But to the colonists, as to so many disappointed children, Parliament awarded enough money to cover the cost of their expedition, and the grumbling subsided. England at least had won Acadie from the French, and she kept that, calling it Nova Scotia, and began turning Halifax into a major naval base.

During the nine years of war, from the time Admiral Vernon set out to attack Cartagena up to the signing of the peace, the English lost 3,238 vessels to the French and Spanish, and took from them 3,424, most of which were of far greater value than the English ships lost. The English estimated that they had made two million pounds sterling by the fighting. Clearly, war could be made to pay, and the Treaty of Aix-la-Chapelle was at best a makeshift peace: it settled no basic rivalry between the nations. But it did mark the beginning of an eight-year period of peace, in which the American colonies made enormous strides forward in their maritime affairs.

Within two years after the peace there was a thriving trade in all the colonies: Boston, Portsmouth, Newport, New York, Philadelphia and Charleston cleared hundreds of vessels each year. The settlements still clung to the coast—nowhere did they penetrate far inland. There were, by 1750, a trifle more than one million English-speaking colonists in the American colonies, and they began to repay Walpole's far-sighted policy of encouragement by becoming one of England's best customers. The main stream of English commerce with her colonies had shifted from the West Indian sugar islands to the colonies north of Spanish Florida.

The colonists, once they were free to resume their interrupted pursuit of the maritime life, intensified their efforts: colonial fishing smacks were soon more numerous than ever off the Newfoundland coast, where they dominated the fisheries by their numbers and energy. The offshore whalers of Massachusetts began to extend the range of their cruises: in 1743 they had learned how to build furnaces and carry try-pots on the decks of their ships, and this meant that larger vessels were needed to take advantage of the innovation. Before long they were chasing sperm whales past the Gulf Stream, and north to Baffin's Bay, "trying out" the oil from the blubber of their whales and storing it in casks in their capacious holds.

The slavers, too, were entering boom times: up to 1750 slaving had been as genteel as any other form of trade. It required fine seamanship, plenty of courage and a strong stomach. In return it offered sudden wealth, or, quite often, an even more sudden death. The chief source of supply for the slavers was that fifteen hundred miles of West African coast called the Guinea Coast. In all that coastline there were but two large rivers draining the hinterland: there were no good harbors, and when the winds built up a sea from the west even the beaches were unattainable. Sand-bars lined the shore, and just outside the breakers the sharks waited patiently for the capsized native canoe or ship's boat which tried to reach the shore. The climate was murderous for the white men: sudden mists chilled them, and the heat of the sun drained them of energy and often drove them to madness. This whole shore was dotted with slave factories owned and managed by the Spanish and Portuguese, Dutch and English and French. Each factory was a stockaded fort, usually built near a good source of fresh water, and often located on one of the numerous islands which lie just off the coast. They were well fortified, with an eye to defense against native tribes and white rivals. Alongside each factory was a barracoon, a walled-in space, with a shed-like shelter, where the slaves could be kept alive until they were sold. The forts were garrisoned by soldiers from Europe who decayed morally even faster than their weapons rusted in the moist jungle heat of this fever coast, whose place-names were household words in every American seaport—Ambriz, and Anamboe, Calabar, Bonny, Piccaninny Sestus, Goree, St. Paul de Loango, the Bight of Benin and the Bight of Biafra.

In the first half of the eighteenth century slaves were comparatively easy to come by in Africa: the native chieftains were eager to help, and they frequently had a few slaves of their own to spare, for they held that the possession of a few slaves was a sign of magnanimity on their part—proof that they did not kill off all their enemies. They were beset with tribal wars, and medicine men who studied the entrails of sacrificial livestock and then pontificated to the chieftains, advising them when the time was propitious to wage war. These chieftains loved battle: a tribal raid, in which men, women and children were tortured and slaughtered with ingenious brutality, was their conception of the full life. But, being human, the natives loved to trade, which to them meant exchanging their gold and wax and ivory for rum and bits of colored cloth. As soon as they learned that slaves were worth rum, the massacres of near-by tribes slackened and the object of war became the enslavement of the neighbors, as the innate blood-lust proved less potent than the profit motive.

By the native laws debtors had to work out their debts as slaves of their creditors; thieves were enslaved by those whom they had robbed; lovers trapped with errant wives were brought into the outraged husbands' households as slaves, where the master could keep an eye on them; if a man's god was defiled by another man, the penalty was slavery. Polygamy was the law, and if a man acquired a surplus of wives and children they could be disposed of by selling them as slaves. Thus the source was apparently limitless.

When the American colonists moved in on this trade in large numbers, after 1750, they usually followed a set routine: they could expect to reach the slave coast in eight weeks' time, and once there the captain of the slaver gave a party for the local chieftains who got as drunk as possible on rum, and accepted gifts of silk and cotton fabrics from the slaver. Next day the slaver sent an officer ashore to look over the slaves in the compound, and to make his deals with the native chieftains. One good slave would be worth a hundred gallons of rum, worth eleven pounds, and the slaver had to make his bargain quickly. If he took too long in filling his ship with slaves, sickness might start and spread throughout the whole load. If he could not find enough slaves on one part of the coast he had to move on to another and there repeat the time-consuming rituals the natives demanded. Everywhere along the coast the competition was fierce: the native compounds and the European factories alike were never short of customers. Generally a ship 80 per cent slaved was considered full enough to shove off on the Middle Passage, since during the wait for the final 20 per cent of the load there was a good chance that sickness might kill off not only the slaves but captain and crew as well.

By 1753 the price of a prime slave set down hale and hearty in Barbados was thirty-five pounds, and the demand was rising as the southern colonists in America began to increase the size of their plantations of rice, indigo, cotton and tobacco. It was cheaper to work a slave to death and then to buy a new one than it was to support one in his old age. In Virgina there were slave stud-farms where the colonists played at improving the breed by crossing slaves of various tribes in an effort to arrive at a standard breed which would be both tractable and durable, and strong. But as the new world absorbed the Africans by the thousands, what few had foreseen happened: there was a shortage of slaves in Africa.

The whites had a solution for the dilemma: they began to foment tribal wars along the slave coast and far into the interior of Africa by playing one chieftain off against another, by bribing the witch-doctors to incite raids, and by asking no questions about the slaves they bought. To insure that there be no lack of captives agents were established on the coast who supplied the warring tribes with arms and ammunition. Soon the natives were using their most luscious wives for bait, so that, by playing the outraged husband they could enslave the black Casanovas, hard as they were to find in the darkness. Before long even this concession to tribal usage was abandoned and it became perilous for a native to accept an invitation to a neighbor's hut, where he stood a good chance of being trussed up in ropes and carried off to the waiting slaver in the dark of night. Native blacks from the hinterland, their curiosity whetted by the sight of the great ships with their white sails, were frequently guided aboard by more sophisticated natives, only to discover that they had been sold by their guides.

When the slaver had been filled to the satisfaction of her captain she set out on the Middle Passage, a run which was usually made close to the equator. Habitually the captain took into his cabin the most shapely native girl he could find, to help him while away the hours of the voyage to the West Indies, and by his dalliance he often remained in a stupor of extreme debilitation, for few white men could stand the pace set by the lewd nymphs of the African tribes.

The New England slavers were built for speed: the *Fame,* of Newport, had a 79-foot keel and a beam of 26½ feet—racing sloop lines. They were smaller than the English ships, but equally uncomfortable for the blacks. Usually they had two decks, and the space between was designed to hold the slaves. This space was always less than four feet high and in it the slaves lived while the cargo was being completed and during the Middle Passage. Women and children were segregated in one section of the slave deck and since they were considered harmless they were not ironed. The males were shackled in line, with various types of irons which could be bought in any New England seaport; they were stretched out like drying codfish on the slave deck, their feet outboard and their heads inboard. A full ship would be carpeted with prostrate slaves. Once a day during the Middle Passage they were brought up into the sunlight and fresh air and encouraged— by whips if necessary—to sing and dance as a means of getting exercise. While they were being aired the slave deck was washed down with salt water, but even so, no smart captain passed a slaver to leeward, where the smell could be detected three miles away. Always there was danger of an endemic disease, such as ophthalmia, infecting the whole ship, and even in the best-run slavers many died during the Middle Passage and were thrown to the sharks which trailed the evil-smelling vessels. Food and water were stored in the lower hold, and the food consisted almost entirely of yams bought along the slave coast.

Hence the need for speed: the New Englanders favored small slavers of 40- or 50-tons, which could make a fast passage and thus keep the slaves aboard as short a time as possible, cutting down the cost of feeding them and lessening the loss by sickness and death.

In the West Indies and in the southern colonies the best slaves were sold, at a profit of at least 200 per cent, and those who remained—the sickly and the weak—were brought to New England with the molasses from the sugar islands and sold at bargain rates in the seaports. The slaves became house-servants, and the molasses went into the distilleries of Boston and Providence and Newport. At the latter port the stills were operated with such finesse that one gallon of molasses could be made into one gallon of rum—an accomplishment envied throughout all New England.

[7] *Trouble with Parents*

While the colonists were pursuing their peaceful, if often unsavory, business afloat England and France were driving each other to distraction. French ships had infringed on the terms of the Treaty of Aix-la-Chapelle so frequently that England felt impelled to retaliate, and her fleets were made ready. One squadron, under Vice-Admiral Boscawen, sailed for North America to protect the colonies from a French fleet under Admiral De la Motte which was making threatening gestures in those waters. Boscawen was directed to protect all British possessions and to attack the French fleet wherever he found it; his orders were made public and the French Ambassador in London advised Louis XV of their clear meaning. Louis, thus informed, declared that the first gun fired at sea in a hostile manner would be held equivalent to a declaration of war.

Boscawen carried out his orders with dispatch: on June 6, 1755, he fell in with four French ships of the line near the entrance to the Gulf of St. Lawrence. After a 48-hour chase, at noon on June 8th the 60-gun ship *Dunkirk,* commanded by Captain the Hon. Richard Howe, caught up with the 64-gun French *Alcide,* and after some preliminary hailing, opened a cannonade so intense that the French ship struck her colors. Thus the Seven Years' War started, although it was not formally declared until 1756, after the usual diplomatic alignments had been arranged.

In the American colonies there had been small and well-ordered border disputes in 1754, but in the next year these matters developed into a small-scale inland war when neither the French nor the English would give up their claims to disputed territory. The problem to be settled was this: could France, by throwing a string of trading-posts south from the Great Lakes along the rivers to New Orleans, keep the English from expanding to the westward? The English had never fixed any limit to the westward in their colonial land grants, and now here were the French, hemming them in to the east of the Alleghenies, spreading their pernicious (to the English) religion among the native Indians, and fortifying their trading-posts. Could any bumptious colonial or any haughty Englishman be expected to watch this process unmoved?

The matter was not destined to be settled by the colonies, but as a side issue in the war brewing in Europe. In the coming war, the action between the *Dunkirk* and the *Alcide* was the last bit of yeast added before the ferment started.

England, with her delicately tuned intelligence sources, knew that war was inevitable. But her population was but a third of France's and she needed a strong ally on the continent—some nation to hold and fight and drain French blood on land while English ships were beating down the French at sea. With gentle compulsion Prussia was urged to ally herself with England and Frederick the Great, sensing the opportunities of such an alliance, yielded to the persuasive plan: England would help with funds and supplies and even some British regulars, but the brunt of the land-fighting was to be borne by Prussia. The agreement was signed in January 1756, and in May France allied herself with Austria. Thus the two Catholic empires faced the Protestant kingdoms.

Before France and Austria could act, Frederick attacked and engulfed Saxony, absorbing her army into his own. Not until November 1757, in the battle of Rossbach, was the tide definitively turned to the Protestant side: in this battle Frederick's twenty-eight thousand men crushed the fifty-five thousand forces of the Catholic allies in detail when they tried to outflank him. By this defeat France was severely crippled on land, and England was free to pour her resources into the war at sea.

In the new world the objective was to drive the French out of Canada as a prelude to breaking their power on the North American continent, and the first step in this campaign was the capture of Louisbourg. An English expedition under Admiral Holbourn had sailed bravely up to the fortress in 1757, sighted sixteen French ships-of-the-line in the harbor, and sailed away intimidated by the sight of so many floating batteries. That same year William Pitt became England's Minister of War and the decisions he made, although not felt until the next year, were epochal in the war: he picked military leaders who were young and tough, with a limitless ambition for England's cause. Boscawen, most venerable of the lot, was forty-seven: he was in command of the fleet that sailed for Louisbourg in 1758. Amherst, forty years old, was the land commander of the expedition, and with him was Wolfe, aged thirty. The fleet rendezvoused at Halifax in May and it was assured of success by its very size: forty men-of-war manned by eight thousand sailors, and twelve thousand troops in the transports —nearly all of them British regulars, for Pitt was taking no chances on the colonial militia who had shown a preference for home and its comforts to the rigors of campaigning against the French and Indians. Without undue trouble the soldiers were landed and the fortress besieged, while the fleet blocked any hope of reinforcements, until, after a valorous defense, French honor was satisfied that nothing further could be done to defend the place. Louisbourg surrendered in July, and with it the British dominated the St. Lawrence Gulf. The way was clear for an attack on Quebec.

Wolfe went back to England that fall, the embodiment of the young kingdom of Great Britain—assured, skilled in warfare, in character a strange blend of knightly manners and utter realism—to prepare the expedition against Quebec.

In January 1759, 250 ships set out from Portsmouth on the Hampshire coast for Louisbourg, en route to Quebec. Forty-nine of this great fleet were men-of-war, manned by fourteen thousand sailors and marines; the rest were supply ships and transports. Temporarily delayed by ice in the harbor at Louisbourg, the expedition sailed up the St. Lawrence river in July, threading the tricky channel. On July 31st Wolfe attacked and his forces were thrown back; not until September 13th, under cover of darkness, did he infiltrate his men onto a small beach the French had been using to bring supplies into the city, and thence up to the Plains of Abraham. That night five thousand regulars landed and the next day they slaughtered the French and their colonials and Indians. In the approved romantic manner Wolfe died, a victim of French marksmanship, and the mortally wounded Montcalm, commander of the French, survived him by only a day. Repeatedly Montcalm had asked Paris for reinforcements, but they were refused him on the grounds that it was not possible to cross the ocean with any sizeable force without being almost certainly intercepted by the English whose men-of-war were blockading the coast of France.

By their inability to cross the ocean in force the French lost both Louisbourg and Quebec, and with those keys to Canada in English hands, Montreal fell in the next year and with it all of Canada. A final, devastating blow to French ambitions on the sea came when a huge fleet Louis XV had prepared for the invasion of England and Scotland was dispersed before the two main sections of it could assemble at Brest for the operation. From then on the French could at best offer sporadic opposition, by the activities of her privateers, to England's offshore supremacy. That this opposition was dispersed and unplanned made it none the less injurious to the English, who lost in the first four years of the war over 2,500 vessels to French privateers, although they still had, in 1760, close to eight thousand merchantmen at sea.

While this diffuse sea-fighting went on, and was even intensified after France had hardly a single ship of the line in fighting trim, George II died and his grandson George III, obese, beet-red in complexion, as virtuous as his grandfather had been sinful, on October 25, 1760 became King of Great Britain. England at last had a ruler who could speak English without trouble or accent, although this accomplishment was balanced by several handicaps: the new king really wanted to rule, and he was subject to periods of insanity; even when officially sane, his stupidity made him an obstacle to rational government. He was twenty-three years old.

Within two years Spain entered the war against England, in time to lose Havana and Manila before the Peace of Paris was signed on February 10, 1763. By this treaty it became evident that much had been decided by the years of fighting: France lost everything in the new world except a handful of islands in the Caribbean—Martinique and Guadeloupe and Sta. Lucia—and the two small islands of St. Pierre and Miquelon off the Newfoundland coast, which were put at the disposal of French fishermen who kept their rights, by the treaty, to fish on the Grand Bank and in the Gulf of St. Lawrence, much to the dismay of sage Englishmen who knew that this concession would encourage the rebirth of the French merchant marine. The Spaniards were barred from the fisheries, greatly to the annoyance of those devout fish-eaters, but Havana and Manila were restored to them in exchange for Florida. France gave Louisiana to Spain, as a sop for the loss of Minorca, which France had guaranteed to her.

For Great Britain the war had proved a fulcrum: France was tottered out of North America, Spain disgorged Florida and all territory east of the Mississippi; in the Caribbean England kept the Grenadas, Dominica, Tobago and St. Vincent. At the end of the war, after seven years of incessant fighting, the Royal Navy which had made these gains possible consisted of 286 vessels in commission, 125 of them ships of the line of 40 guns or more, and 93 vessels in reserve, 67 of them ships of the line. Seventy thousand men manned this unrivaled force, and with it a small, insular nation had not only protected its possessions but also had won a great empire.

Ahead were twelve years destined to be peaceful ones for the colonists in America, but they were years shot through with intimations of the conflict to come. No sooner had colonial trade revived, after the Peace of Paris, than Grenville brought his Stamp Act before Parliament on March 10, 1764. By it England expected to collect a small percentage of the cost of the war from the colonists whom her soldiers and sailors had protected from the French and Spaniards. But in the colonies, where peace meant profits, there were violent protests: the Virginia Assembly declared that no external authority could tax Virginians; a congress attended by representatives of nine of the thirteen colonies met at New York in the fall of 1765 to give emphasis to their opposition to any such tax. Then Edmund Burke, with Pitt's help, repealed the Act on February 22, 1766, little suspecting that such forbearance on England's part would be thought in America a confession of weakness.

The aristocrats who ruled England had misread the character of their colonists: in an age when greed and thievery, as well as courage and stamina, marked the English-speaking people, the colonists had more than their share of these characteristics. It was not uncommon for the New England fishermen to plunder weaker ships, to stage sudden raids on defenseless settlements, to steal fishing equipment from each other and the Canadians; many merchant captains, driven by their wild lust for money, undertook illegal adventures in trade which were certain to fail utterly if their vessels ran afoul of the King's ships, but which—if successful—would double or even treble the value of the cargo. To such men the Caribbean was an open book; they knew the ports of Europe and the Spanish and Portuguese Islands and West Africa as well as they knew their native harbors.

Between the colonists there was little unity: the northerners considered the southerners a contemptible type of Englishman, with loose morals, impious, barbarously cruel to their slaves, usually knavish in their relations with other men; to the southerners the yankees were cheats and deadbeats, addicted to a sharpness of dealing which bordered on stealing, inhospitable, sanctimonious hypocrites who worshiped God with sniveling words while in their minds they were calculating the possible profits of the next voyage. There were, regardless of location, two traits which marked all the English-speaking colonists: they were tough physically—their heritage from ancestors who had survived the passage from the old world to the new—a trip which often cost half the passengers their lives; they were intent on profits, to an extent difficult for even an Englishman to understand. In England among the patrician ruling class there was little comprehension of the perils involved in winning a living in the New World, whether on land or at sea, and consequently the venality of the colonists and their rage at the slightest threat to their money-making activities inevitably brought exclamations of startled contempt from the English law-makers.

Soon another attempt at taxation came out of Parliament: this time it was the work of Charles Townshend, whose cupidity matched that of any colonist. The Townshend Acts, intended to ease the English tax burden by putting a part of the load on the colonists, consisted of an import tax on English paper, glass, tea, paint and lead unloaded in the colonial ports. Opposition took the form of agreements among colonial merchants not to import taxable goods, and in New England as trade fell off violence increased. In the port of Boston, when the sloop *Liberty,* owned by John Hancock, was boarded by customs' officials in an effort to collect the duties, a mob of Bostonians chased them away and the governor called for help from Halifax, which was forth-coming in the form of two regiments of redcoats. For eighteen months the English regulars were quartered on the town, and then an incident occurred which led to the first bloodshed: on March 5, 1770, a few Bostonians could not resist the targets the redcoats offered and they began tossing snowballs and cat-calls at the soldiers of the king; soon the fun of plastering the dignified redcoats with snowballs attracted a crowd, and the crowd became a mob. In self-protection against this outrageous form of warfare, which made a mockery of their uniforms and their king, the soldiers fired on the colonists, killing four of them. Even while such firebrands as Sam Adams, and Hancock, and Joseph Warren—whose financial interests were involved—were distorting the incident in the "Boston Massacre," Parliament was repealing the Townshend Acts, with the exception of the one on tea, which was maintained as a token of the right of the government to tax the colo-nies.

That same year the colonial trade showed evidence of its recupera-tive powers: Rhode Island had 150 slavers at work, and Nantucket cleared 125 whalers; the trading vessels of the colonies were a familiar sight in all the ports of Europe. But Parliament was content to let matters rest, and with Europe and India open to English traders there was no pressure from that quarter for restrictive legislation aimed at the colonial merchants.

For the next three years Parliament showed little interest in the colonies, but if Parliament was bemused, being more occupied with domestic than colonial affairs, there were Englishmen at work along the New England coast who were very much concerned with the blithe contempt the colonists showed to His Majesty's rules and regula-tions. Soon after the Peace of Paris the colonists had revived the an-cient art of smuggling, and the customs officials had fitted out lightly-armed sloops and schooners to patrol the coast and halt the smug-gling. A series of minor demonstrations against these revenue cruisers, and against the habit the Royal Navy had of impressing colonial sea-men into the King's service whenever a vessel was short-handed, came to a climax in 1772 in Narragansett Bay.

In March of that year the 102-ton schooner *Gaspé,* carrying four

3-pounders and a crew of twenty-seven men, commanded by Lieutenant William Dudingston, arrived in the bay, and soon his diligent pursuit of the smugglers and his arrogant manner toward the colonists, had won him the hatred of the local population. On June 9th the New York to Providence packet, the *Hannah,* with Captain Benjamin Lindsay in command, set out from Newport for Providence, and soon the *Gaspé* followed, ordering the packet to heave to and be examined. Lindsay refused, and as a fresh southerly breeze sprang up and carried him out of gunshot the *Gaspé* began the chase. With both vessels carrying every stitch of canvas the *Hannah* led the *Gaspé* twenty-five miles up the bay, and lured her into shoal water seven miles south of Providence where she ran aground, while the packet, drawing less water, sailed smugly on.

The *Hannah* continued up the bay to Providence, leaving her pursuer grounded on the bar, and soon after sunset all Providence knew that the obnoxious *Gaspé* lay helpless and could not move until three hours after midnight, when the tide would float her free. Eight longboats were gathered, their oars and oarlocks muffled, and a drummer went through the streets calling for volunteers to man the boats. By ten o'clock the crews were ready, armed with staves, paving stones and a few firearms, a sea-captain at the tiller of each boat, and Captain Abraham Whipple in command of the flotilla. As they approached the unsuspecting *Gaspé,* in line abreast according to the best naval tradition, Whipple hailed and demanded to be let aboard. Dudingston, outraged at such temerity, fired his pistol at the boats, but without effect, and one of the Rhode Islanders, Joseph Bucklin by name, drew a bead on the Lieutenant and sent a ball crashing through his arm and into his groin. The Lieutenant had hardly hit the deck before the colonists boarded and seized the *Gaspé.* The bandaged Dudingston and his crew were taken off the schooner, and the colonists then set fire to her, watching her burn to the waterline and blow up as flames touched off her magazine.

Promptly, as news of this outrage reached the authorities, the English government offered a reward of a thousand pounds for the arrest of the leader of the attack, and five hundred pounds for any of his men. But there was no leak, and when Dudingston faced a court-martial in

England in the fall of the year for the loss of his ship, he was honorably acquitted and immediately promoted, as a fitting reward for his zeal. In spite of his wounds he lived to become a rear-admiral.

The burning of the *Gaspé* was soon followed by an incident which showed a similar spirit: the East India Company, being low in funds, persuaded the government in England to grant it the monopoly of supplying tea to all the English colonies, and while this tea rotted in many damp cellars along the seaboard, and was not permitted ashore in New York and Philadelphia, the Bostonians took more dramatic action. On December 16, 1773, led by men disguised as Indians, a mob of Bostonians boarded one of three East India tea-ships in port, and poured close to 350 chests of tea into the bay.

Then in quick succession the moves which were to end in open warfare followed: Lord North closed the port of Boston in the spring of 1774 and named General Gage military governor. The first Continental Congress met at Philadelphia on September 5th, 1774; seven months later, on April 19th, 1775, General Howe fought his way back from Concord and Lexington, losing over two hundred of his two thousand men to the marksmanship of the "Minute Men." Harried by events, for the spirit of rebellion was running like fire in a ship's rigging throughout the colonies, the Second Continental Congress met in May at Philadelphia; on Thursday, June 15th, the delegates chose as commander-in-chief of the armed forces the forty-four-year old Colonel George Washington. He was the only delegate in uniform. Two days later English troops fought Americans at Bunker Hill. The affair was beyond conciliation.

Part III
REBELLION

[8] *The Burning Decks*

The colonists, divided between loyalty to their king and to their pocketbooks, were in no condition to wage a successful war against England on the sea. But by a happy coincidence the British were not especially well fitted to fight the colonists, for the Admiralty was suffering from the dry rot of twelve years of peace. Appropriations had been cut down to ease the national debt, and corruption was widespread among the jobholders and political appointees who ran the Royal Navy. Admiral Hawke had retired in 1771, worn out by his efforts to combat the decay of his fleets, and he was succeeded by the phlegmatic John Montagu, Earl of Sandwich, who was to last for seven years as First Lord of the Admiralty. Sandwich had by 1775 run the Royal Navy into a condition approaching dissolution: this he achieved with the help of a coterie of cronies who handled the procurement of supplies and the issuance of commissions as a form of political graft, and by his own sluggish nature, which could only be aroused by such major calamities as the murder of one of his mistresses by a former lover. To such a man the rebellion in the colonies was a minor incident, calling for no undue alarm, in spite of the stream of dispatches coming to him from Admiral Graves in Boston, asking for more ships to patrol the eighteen hundred miles of colonial coastline.

In June 1775 Graves had twenty-nine vessels, and it is doubtful if more ships alone would have solved his problems: he was an unusually stupid man, domineering, unimaginative, and further handicapped by a lack of orders clearly defining the manner in which he should carry on hostilities against the "provincials."

But if Graves was hog-tied by Admiralty inertia and his own doltishness, there were plenty of rebellious colonists who were happy to profit by such conditions, and they began at once to collect the best means of offense at sea they had: the whaleboats. As early as April 25th orders had gone out from the Committee of Safety in Boston to send all available whaleboats to Boston, and in July they were being used to annoy the British, burning lighthouses, raiding the islands in the bay for hay and livestock, and when pursued escaping by the strenuous rowing of their crews from the heavier British longboats. Graves was sorely tried by the operations of these swift, lightly-manned craft, which seemed to him to number three hundred (although it is likely that the total was closer to a hundred), and his dignity was ruffled by the insouciance with which they annoyed his forces. But to the Whig colonists, advocates of freedom, they were a heady tonic, and concrete evidence of Britain's feet of clay.

As Graves disposed his vessels along the coast, from Portsmouth, N.H., to New York, the mere presence of these symbols of royal power encouraged the local Tories to remain true to their king, and helped to define the cleavage of the colonists into the ranks of the rebels and of the loyalists. In the twilight period between peace and belligerency, by mutual necessity the British vessels patrolling the coast made arrangements with the local inhabitants by which both lived more comfortably: the British were allowed to buy food and supplies on shore, in spite of the outraged cries of rebel patriots, and in return the colonial trading vessels continued to bring in fish from the banks and cargoes from the West Indies.

Counting on the elasticity of the patriotism of the citizens of Machias, Maine, Ichabod Jones of Boston set out for that port in May, 1775, with two small sloops loaded with foodstuffs which he hoped to exchange for lumber. He was convoyed by the *Margaretta*, a schooner commanded by Midshipman Moore, and on his arrival at Machias he had little difficulty in persuading the local loyalists to do business with him. But when he gave preferential treatment to them in selling his supplies the patriots rose in their wrath: under the leadership of the rebel Jeremiah O'Brien, on June 10th and 11th, an engagement developed which throws a shaft of illumination on the type of people the British considered both seditious and rebellious.

June 10th was a Sunday and the officers of the *Margaretta* were in church, worshiping in the Protestant fashion, when they descried an approaching, noisy band of colonists, obviously intent on capturing them while they were occupied with the niceties of the Divine Service. Quickly, by way of the windows, the British decamped, and reached their schooner, from which they fired a few blanks over the town to dampen the patriots' spirits. Then they weighed anchor and reached a spot of comparative safety some four miles below the town. The colonists, following on land, began a desultory fire on the schooner with muskets and the *Margaretta* was forced to move again, anchoring this time in the bay.

Next morning a party of the patriots seized one of the lumber sloops and brought her alongside a wharf, where they gave three stentorian cheers as a means of attracting volunteers for an attack on the *Margaretta*. Armed with axes, pitch-forks and a few muskets, thirty-five men set forth in the lumber sloop, favored by a light northwest breeze. Once under way, being mindful that all proper warships must have a captain, they chose Jeremiah O'Brien to be their leader. The *Margaretta*, sighting this crowded craft obviously bent on hostilities, weighed anchor and crowded on sail to avoid a battle, since her captain was uninformed of the events which had transpired at Concord and Lexington: to him these wild provincials must have appeared to be half-pirate, half-madmen. The schooner fled, hotly pursued by the sloop, and as the wind freshened the sloop closed in, until Moore opened fire with his four light guns and fourteen swivels (which were large muskets mounted in crotches). One man was killed on the sloop, which in turn fired on the schooner, killing her helmsman and clearing the quarterdeck. As the schooner broached to, the sloop gave her a thorough raking and ran alongside. A brisk musket fire was exchanged at close quarters, with Moore busily tossing hand grenades until the amateur warriors of the sloop boarded the *Margaretta* and shot him down.

O'Brien and his crew, thirsty for more victories, transferred the guns and swivels of the *Margaretta* to the lumber sloop and set out for further adventures. They took two small British cruisers, and carried their prisoners to Watertown, Massachusetts, where the provincial legislature was holding its sessions. As a reward for his exploits O'Brien was appointed a Captain in the colony's naval forces and sent out with his last two prizes under orders to seize all vessels bringing supplies to the British forces in Boston, where the besieging rebels were in dire need of muskets and powder and flints.

The colonists had but one source of arms and ammunition in large quantities: the store-ships which the Admiralty sent at irregular intervals to the British forces in America. Habitually such ships were unarmed and but lightly convoyed. These were the prizes which the provincial legislature considered legal, and these only, for they were reluctant to begin unlimited hostilities at sea by commissioning privateers and letters of marque while there yet remained a chance that the rebellion could be localized and carried on without undue bloodshed.

But by September 1775 the need for military supplies had become so great that General Washington, then commanding the colonial militia besieging Boston, directed Captain Nicholson Broughton of the Army on September 2nd to take a detachment of soldiers and with them proceed to Beverly, Massachusetts, where he was to take command of the schooner *Hannah,* which had been outfitted at federal expense. In the *Hannah,* with the soldiers as crew, he was to cruise in search of British ships carrying arms, ammunition, provisions and soldiers.

Broughton, being a native of Marblehead, found his army training no obstacle to success as a naval officer: he had a highly profitable cruise during which he took several prizes whose cargoes were of material aid to the colonial militia, and Washington soon commissioned more vessels to augment his exasperatingly small supply of muskets and cannon and powder.

Early in October word came to the Continental Congress that two store-ships were en route to Quebec from England, unconvoyed, and loaded with military supplies. Congress—unaware of Washington's unofficial navy—instructed him to borrow ships from Massachusetts, Rhode Island and Connecticut, all of which had a few small armed vessels of their own, and with these colonial cruisers capture the two store-ships. None of these colony vessels were available at such short notice, but Washington's unauthorized fleet had meanwhile grown to six vessels, which were a constant source of satisfaction to him, capturing as they did numerous store-ships and bringing their prizes into port. Unable to carry out his orders from Congress with colony ships, Washington detached two of his raiders (the *Lynch* and the *Franklin*) on October 16th and sent them north under Captain Broughton and Captain John Selman to cruise near the mouth of the St. Lawrence river and to seize the store-ships on sight.

But Broughton and Selman missed their quarry in the fogs and storms, and then, not wanting to return empty-handed, they turned homeward, stopping at St. John's long enough to abduct the governor and two leading loyalists, and to loot the governor's home. Washington, wrathful at such ungentlemanly behavior, ordered the kidnaped Canadians returned home, and invited Broughton and Selman to return to their regiment and resume war on land, since their lack of the finer sentiments obviously unfitted them for naval activity. Both officers refused and quit the service of their country for good.

Meanwhile Congress had been busy pondering the creation of a national continental navy. On October 3rd the Rhode Island delegates, acting on instructions given them in August by their state assembly, introduced a resolution calling for action on the matter. Two days later a Naval Committee was appointed and at the same time Congress ordered Washington to attempt the capture of the Quebec-bound store-ships; on October 13th, when their nautical helplessness was made evident by their need for, and lack of, men-of-war, the Congress ordered the brig *Lexington* and the sloop *Reprisal* bought and fitted out to seize any store-ships they could find. The emphasis was still on the use of colonial armed ships only as a means of capturing supplies.

Then Admiral Graves, having examined his conscience and, mulled over his vague orders, came to a conclusion: he must have revenge on the seaports which supported the colonial cruisers, and on October 16th Captain Henry Mowat, acting on the Admiral's orders, dropped anchor off Falmouth (now Portland) Maine. His force consisted of HMS *Canceaux* and HMS *Halifax,* carrying a total of fourteen guns, and the armed transports *Symmetry* and *Spitfire,* with a hundred troops aboard. His instructions were to burn the town to a crisp.

Mowat had suffered the indignity of having been made prisoner at Falmouth earlier in the year, and when the chance came to flee he had broken his parole, but in spite of these experiences he showed no vindictiveness in the operation he now engaged in. The townsmen were warned and given ample time to collect their valuables and to leave their homes before the bombardment commenced at 9:40 A.M. on October 17th, 1775. By sunset the town was in ruins.

Colonial reaction to this act of reprisal was immediate and far-ranging: other towns were on Admiral Graves' list of intended victims —Salem and Machias, Newburyport, Portsmouth, Marblehead, Ipswich, Gloucester—every seaport which had ever thwarted the operations of the British by acting as a base for colonial cruisers looked to its own defenses against a sudden, threatened descent on the town by Captain Mowat. The news of the burning of Falmouth seeped through the colonies, and added ballast to the arguments of the rebel leaders: here was an example of downright cruelty. The agitators made the most of it: the crevice between loyalist and patriot widened and became a ravine—soon it was to become an unbridged chasm.

The members of Congress, stimulated to action by this evidence of British barbarism, which left three hundred families without shelter in a New England winter, called for strong measures: on October 30th they ordered two vessels, the *Alfred* and the *Columbus,* bought and fitted out for the purpose of *defending* the colonies; on November 10th a Marine Corps was ordered created; and on December 13th, 1775, the construction of thirteen frigates to carry on hostilities against the British was authorized.

Contributing to this sudden consciousness of the sea was the experience Washington had enjoyed with his six small commerce-raiders: on the evening of November 29th he had received good news, which he promptly passed on to Congress, from one of the officers he had commissioned—Captain John Manly. Commanding the *Lee,* Manly had captured the brigantine *Nancy* at the entrance to Boston harbor. The *Nancy* had lost her protecting convoy and was herself unarmed, although laden with stores of a military nature, including 100,000 flints, 2,000 muskets and a 13-inch brass mortar—all items Washington had been trying desperately to locate. The inventory of the swag delighted the members of the Naval Committee: here was plain proof of what a ship with a few guns could contribute to the cause.

Early in December the Congress had appropriated $100,000 to buy four men-of-war; on December 22nd they issued a list of the officers who were to serve in the toddling navy.

Never was the creation of a corps of naval officers handled with more regard for the political weight each aspirant carried: the commissions were frankly awarded on the basis of political expediency, and with little regard for the appointees' abilities as leaders and mariners. New Englanders, being wise in affairs of the sea, dominated the Naval Committee, and when the list came out it reflected the influence of such men as the venerable and learned rum-pot, Stephen Hopkins of Rhode Island, and of John Adams, the cogent, sardonic Massachusetts rebel. Hopkins' share of the patronage amounted to three apointments, all relatives of his: Ezek Hopkins, Commander-in-Chief (at $125 per month); Abraham Whipple, Captain of the *Columbus;* and John B. Hopkins, Captain of the *Cabot*. Adams, good friend and drinking-companion of Stephen Hopkins, inserted a relative of his own in the list: Dudley Saltonstall, Captain of the flagship *Alfred*. As a sop to the Philadelphians, where the Congress was meeting, Nicholas Biddle was given command of the *Andrea Doria*. The rest of the list of eighteen names included one happy choice—Paul Jones—who was made first lieutenant of the *Alfred,* at the insistence of his patron, Joseph Hewes of North Carolina. Before long Jones was to be known as "the North Carolina Captain."

Out of the coming conflict a few of these eighteen officers were to emerge as naturally great fighting-men, but the great majority of them were doomed to be defeated—if not by superior British strength, then by their own inferior qualities as naval officers.

When the time came to find crews for the ships being brought into commission there was no undue difficulty: the privateers were not then being commissioned, and there was so little commerce that many a sailor was on the beach, or in the army damning the war and hoping for a soft berth at sea. As an inducement, seamen as well as officers were to share in the prizes, to the extent of one-half the value of all warships taken and one-third of all other vessels. Men were recruited for the duration of the cruise only, and since novel conceptions of liberty were at large it was a foregone conclusion that there would be a certain amount of trouble in enforcing discipline. John Adams, mindful of the sometimes mutinous conduct of the men in Washington's private navy, had condensed a copy of the British Naval Code, dating from 1749, and the resultant Naval Articles had been approved by Congress on November 23rd. They embodied all the harsh penal laws which the British had found useful in running a navy; and as a further insurance against seamen who thought liberty unlimited there were the marines, who could always be counted on to handle disorderly sailors. But to the recruits such impediments were acceptable: the idea of a navy without rules and regulations was inconceivable.

On January 5th, 1776, the infant navy was ordered by the Naval Committee to proceed to the southward and engage Lord Dunmore's fleet which had been burning towns and plantations in Virginia, causing much misery to the local patriots and encouraging the southern loyalists. Ezek Hopkins was in command of the eight vessels, and not until February 17th did he lead his squadron out to sea. Then, making a loose interpretation of the discretion allowed him in his orders, he prudently by-passed the enemy men-of-war and headed for the Bahamas. En route the squadron captured two small sloops and from their crews learned that the island of New Providence was rich in military stores and virtually unprotected. To Hopkins this looked like too good a chance to pass up: he could prove the worth of his command, in which his confidence was limited, and at the same time obtain badly-needed supplies for the army. Surely such an action was preferable to pitting his ships against Lord Dunmore's experienced men-of-war. After a brief stop at Abaco in the Bahamas he proceeded toward New Providence.

The squadron sailed bravely up to the town of Nassau in broad daylight, and the local governor—who knew an enemy when he saw one —forthwith loaded nearly all his powder on two ships and sent them out of the harbor to safety during the night. Then Hopkins landed his marines—220 strong—under Major Samuel Nicholas: they marched four miles to the town and fort, both of which they captured without losing a man. The booty consisted of seventy-one cannon, fifteen mortars and twenty-five casks of powder, which was loaded into the American ships in the course of the next few days. On March 17, Hopkins sailed for home, confident that he had earned his pay, and that his easily-won supplies would be of tremendous value to Washington's army in the siege of Boston.

But on that same day the British were evacuating Boston, with eleven hundred loyalists, after eleven months of siege, to seek refuge in damp and barren Halifax.

Members of the Continental Congress were delighted: here was further proof that the British were not invincible; here, too, was a good time to make a muscle at the King. The pressure to commission privateers had been growing: it was a really necessary formality, for if some stout-hearted commerce-raider from the colonies happened to be captured by the British he could be, rightly, treated as a pirate, if he had no commission. The matter needed to be regularized, and the seamen were entitled to what protection Congress could give them; on March 23rd the law was passed and it became legal to commission privateers and letters of marque and reprisal (the former being vessels whose sole aim was commerce-raiding, the latter—letters of marque and reprisal —being primarily merchantmen which went armed and wolfish about their business). The New Englanders had won one of their main arguments, and now dozens of the vessels which they had could legally be converted to this type of warfare. On April 7th Congress ordered the embargo lifted: American ships were authorized to trade with any nation but Britain and the self-imposed restrictions of the association of merchants were discarded.

Meanwhile Hopkins, plugging along to the northward, his ships deeply-laden, slow, foul-bottomed, and many of his crew sick with small pox, took two puny prizes: the 6-gun schooner *Hawk* and the 12-gun brig *Bolton*. And then, not far from New London, at 2:30 on the morning of April 6th, in pitch-blackness, Hopkins was himself attacked.

The man who thus dared the naval might of the colonies was Captain Tyringham Howe, in the 20-gun, 451-ton ship *Glasgow*. Howe had no idea how many ships he was engaging, and the brig *Cabot* came into action first, getting one broadside into the British ship before she realized she was out-classed when she took two broadsides from the *Glasgow*. Then came the turn of the *Alfred,* which had drawn near in the light and variable wind: a lucky shot carried away her wheel block and ropes and she broached to. *Alfred* took three raking broadsides before she could get under way again, and the ships mulled about in the utmost confusion, with *Andrew Doria, Columbus* and *Providence* taking little or no part in the action. When Howe of the *Glasgow* saw the size of the force he had so blithely attacked he crowded on all sail and bore away toward Newport, hoping to lead the Americans within reach of the British squadron on patrol there. At 6:30 A.M. Hopkins signaled an end to the chase; the squadron turned back to collect its prizes and proceed to New London, which it reached on April 11th.

The town went wild with joy over the news of the battle, and soon word spread to all the colonies: the colonial navy had won a noble victory, in which a few light vessels had forced a heavier opponent to flee. But on reflection, the public began to ask: why was the *Glasgow* able to escape? It was shameful—a disgrace to the American squadron. Reacting to the general bitterness, Congress ordered Hopkins and Whipple and Hazard (of the *Columbus*) court-martialed.

There was but little balm for hurt colonial pride in the single-ship action which had been fought on the day of the *Glasgow* engagement: Captain John Barry, in the *Lexington,* had won a two-hour fight with the armed sloop *Edward* off the Virginia capes, and in so doing he had maintained admirable standards of tenacity and valor. But news of this fight only made Hopkins' failure seem even more abysmal.

In New London the ships could find no recruits: all the best seamen were eager to serve in the privateers where a man could make a financial killing without being subject to naval discipline. No one was anxious—save for a few country bumpkins, sons of rebels—to serve in a navy that couldn't catch one British ship with five of their own. Hopkins borrowed two hundred soldiers from Washington—a short-term loan—to replace his sick and wounded, and the ships moved to Providence where they were by slow degrees fitted out for further duty. But they were never to sail again as a squadron: they went out on their various assignments as they became ready for service: Paul Jones, now commanding the *Providence,* returned Washington's soldiers to New York, carried out routine convoy duties and cruised in search of prizes; Biddle, in *Andrea Doria,* took two transports full of troops and many lesser prizes. It was the beginning of commerce-raiding warfare—the only type of war the handful of ships of the regular navy had the power to wage. Seldom were their cruises even moderately successful: the total effect of their operations in the winning of independence was negligible. British men-of-war blockaded the colonial ports; at will her armies were moved up and down the American coast. The colonial vessels which were to cause Britain the most trouble were the privateers, manned by the hard-bitten, greedy and vengeful seamen of the colonies.

In the summer of 1776 the privateers continued to come out of the rivers and harbors from Maine to Georgia in a nondescript manner but in respectable numbers. Many of the New England vessels were converted bank fishermen, sloops and topsail schooners, now freshly painted, with new and longer masts and spars, armed with a handful of four-pounders and a few swivels. Seldom were they of more than sixty tons burden, and on occasion they worked in packs, joining forces in easy familiarity with whatever rebel vessels were at hand.

On June 17th a brig owned by the Connecticut colony, the 14-ton *Defense,* was working her way out of Plymouth when she heard the thud of cannon-fire to the northward. *Defense* crowded on sail, anxious to join the party, hopeful that the firing signified the capture of more fat British merchantmen, which—uninformed that the British had evacuated Boston—had been plopping into the hands of the colonists like so many codfish. Near dusk *Defense* came up with the cause of all the noise: four small American schooners, which had been beaten off after attempting to take two British transports. The transports had run in to Nantasket Roads and anchored there. One of the schooners was 8-gun *Lee,* of the Massachusetts colonial marine; the other three were privateers. Captain Harding of the *Defense* and the captains of the schooners laid out a plan of operations: backed by the schooners, whose support was of more moral than practical value, *Defense* stood in to the Roads shortly before midnight and anchored within pistol shot of the transports. Challenged by the British ships, Harding ordered them to strike, and the reply came back: "Ay-ay, I'll strike!", followed by a broadside. The action lasted for more than an hour, until suddenly both British vessels struck their colors. *Defense* found the transports loaded with soldiers, and they, along with their commanding colonel, were made prisoners-of-war. Next morning, prowling the bay in company with the schooners, *Defense* took a third transport, with one hundred red-coats aboard. Five hundred British soldiers in all were taken from the three transports and as prisoners of the Americans they were useful pawns, exchangeable for colonists held by the British.

There was no dearth of prisoners, on both sides, for the colonists were now waging an active guerrilla sea war. South Carolina, Virginia, Maryland, Pennsylvania, as well as the New England colonies, had their own colonial cruisers ranging the coast from Newfoundland to the West Indies in a fine display of patriotism and profit-making. Their officers often held two or even three commissions: as state naval officers, as privateers and occasionally as officers of the United States of America, as the confederation was known after the declaration of Independence. Whatever their commissions they were quick to perceive that Britain commanded the seas only when the wind was right. There was nothing quite so mirth-provoking as a becalmed ship-of-the-line.

In increasing numbers British men-of-war came over to take up their stations on the coast: ships of the line, frigates, brigs, sloops and tenders—all intent on making the blockade effective. But on gale-swept nights, when the British were snugged down, warm and dry, an occasional privateer would come booming out of port, all canvas set, sometimes passing within pistol-shot of the anchored enemy; with a rude and usually harmless broadside by way of derisive salute to the king, and before the royal ship could beat to quarters, the privateer would be off in the storm-scud, lost to sight.

By the autumn of '76 a few privateers had shown up in European waters and had sent their prizes in to Spanish ports, much to the annoyance of the British ambassador who pointed out that the disposal of such prizes would compromise the Anglo-Spanish treaty. But the Spaniards considered that anyone who could injure the detested English was worthy of special benevolence, and the prizes were sold quietly, decorously and in utter secrecy. Such transatlantic adventurers were exceptional in the first two years of the rebellion, when most of the privateers were working in American waters.

One favorite hunting-ground was the Gulf of St. Lawrence, where the colonials were so numerous that they got in each others' way and cluttered up the seascape. Time and again a privateer in these waters would sight a strange sail, make a quick estimate of its strength, and either fight or run. When running, if the stranger began to gain, overboard went the guns and the ship's stores; in moments of extreme stress the crew were set to work at sawing away the bulwarks, a process that relieved the tension of the chase and was thought to be advantageous in increasing speed. All too often such cases ended when both vessels, cleared for action, ran up the American colors. But there was no way to recover the precious guns and supplies that had been jettisoned.

Among the privateers, as well as the continental cruisers, a fine disregard for the proprieties of international law held sway: no smart privateering captain ever sailed with his true colors flying, for the object was to surprise, out-guess, trick—by any means within the power of man's mind and arm—and capture enemy vessels. If some staid British merchantman was dull enough to think that a British flag meant that the vessel flying it was British, he was likely to be disillusioned as soon as the stranger came within range and ran up his true colors.

In the Gulf there was good hunting for the smaller privateers, which could take small fishing sloops and trading vessels without any risk, and when things got dull they could always run in to shore and plunder a helpless fishing settlement, thinking, in all sincerity, that they were to some extent paying the British back for the burning of Falmouth. The always present threat of British men-of-war based on near-by Halifax was to a great extent diminished by the abominable weather—intermittent fogs and storms—in which the privateers could often escape pursuit.

The richest hunting grounds were in the West Indies, and nearly all the privateers working out of southern ports made the Caribbean their area of operations. Even before the rebellion the British had found two means of cutting down on losses to pirates and privateers: convoys, well-guarded by men-of-war, and merchantmen armed heavily enough to risk making their runs unescorted. At Portsmouth, England, and Dublin, Ireland, the convoys for the West Indies were assembled leisurely and publicly. Their size, the strength of their escort, their destination and sailing dates were common knowledge, and since it took several months for the ships to collect there was always, during the revolution, plenty of time for the colonial agents to get the information home. Acting on such news the privateers could waylay the convoy, ready to cut out a prize if the escort wandered afield, or to pick up stragglers if storms dispersed the fleet. It was not uncommon for such convoys to number more than one hundred merchantmen, and the privateers found that by working in pairs one of them could decoy the men-of-war in a futile chase while the other, after hiding over the horizon, closed in and went to work cutting out prizes.

By the end of '76 there were at sea 136 privateers whose commissions had been recorded, and there were dozens more whose owners had dispensed with the time-consuming formality of getting permission from Congress to fight the enemy. These latter worthies simply forged their own papers and set out to make their fortunes.

But in 1777 the number of privateers at large dropped to only 73, cut to that number by captures and by losses to storms and shipwrecks. Almost plaintively the historians, searching for a bit of optimism, singled out a 12-gun privateer which cut capers in the English channel. This vessel hove in sight of one of the Jersey Island's ports, was fired on by the local fort, drew out of range, and picked up an inbound brig worth $35,000. To make matters worse the privateer landed a boat near dusk and captured two officers of the garrison who were out shooting rabbits. But in the West Indies the colonists found new and unexpected support, in the French pirates who were hi-jacking the merchantmen in those waters. Suddenly these pirates blossomed forth with commissions from the Continental Congress, and as full-blown privateers they operated out of Martinique and Guadeloupe, terrifying the merchants and seamen who plied the inter-island routes, and sniping at the big merchantmen en route to and from England. Their vessels were of good size, most of them with twenty or more guns, and manned with notoriously hispid crews of up to 125 men. One such vessel counted in its crew of 125 men only two American citizens, but its American flag was as large as that of any Continental frigate. No longer patibulary, the courage of these pirates soared, and with it their captures.

Among the Americans the main cause for the decline in privateers was pure bad judgment. It is doubtful if there were any better seamen in the world than the colonists who had learned their trade in fishermen, whalers, slavers and merchantmen, and who were moreover familiar with guns and the waters in which they cruised. But there was one trait on which many foundered, and that was the intoxicating effect that victory combined with profits had on the acquisitive facet of their natures. A six-gun sloop might start out with fifty men for crew, and with luck take six prizes. (To take more prizes than you had guns was considered unlucky.) Into each prize the sea rover would have to throw a prize crew, and eventually her own crew would number no more than fifteen men. This was an invitation to rebellion in the prizes, where a man's parole was broken as freely as it was given, and it weakened the privateer herself, making her an easy victim for any fully manned vessel that came along.

The exuberant inexperience of many colonists helped to swell the number of American seamen who fell into British hands: overly optimistic and fortified with rum a band of colonists would sometimes pile into a small unarmed sloop and with muskets and pikes garnered from attics and junk-shops attempt to take a larger British vessel. Even sober-sided patriots would set out in vessels of less than twenty tons, with ten or fifteen men and boys for crew, hoping to make their fortunes by a lucky capture. As prisoners such volatile spirits were likely to join other unfortunates in the prison ships anchored in the East River between New York and Brooklyn, where they were subjected to such harsh treatment while awaiting exchange that a fierce hatred of all things British was branded by pain and often agony in their minds. Most notorious of these prison hulks was the *Jersey*, an old 64-gun ship of the line which had been surveyed out of the service of the king.

Her calking had fallen out and the wind blew snow through the cracks in her planking; there was never enough to eat and seldom enough water to drink. Prisoners, if they had the cash, could buy an occasional mouthful of sausage and some fresh vegetables from the bumboats that came alongside in fair weather, but their habitual diet consisted of worm-eaten ship's bread, salt beef from which all the fat had been cut, and once a week a portion of bitter gruel made of musty oat-meal and water. The one meal a day was cooked in a large copper tank, five feet square and four feet deep, and the only fuel available was green chestnut. Even when the fire was started at seven in the morning it was impossible to get the mess in the tank to boil before noon. On stormy, cold days it sometimes took until three in the afternoon. The ship was verminous and there were few blankets.

Anchored in the East River nearby were several hospital ships, packed with prisoners from the *Jersey*. The attendants were male nurses, colonists who had become hardened to suffering, frequently drunk, and always anxious to rob the dead. Sick men were packed away in pairs on the bunks, and if a man's bedfellow died during the night the still-breathing prisoner had to wait until daylight before the nurses would take the corpse away. Contemporary writers estimated that eleven thousand American seamen died aboard the *Jersey* and her brood of hospital ships during the years from 1776 to 1783.

Only slightly less feared by American seamen was Old Mill prison in England, located between Portsmouth and Portsmouth dock. Here other Americans were imprisoned, after an examination which invariably ended with the words: "You are severally and individually committed to Old Mill prison, for rebellion, piracy, and high treason on his Britannic Majesty's seas, there to remain during his Majesty's pleasure, until he sees fit to pardon or otherwise dispose of you." In Old Mill conditions were more tolerable than aboard the *Jersey:* there was more and better food, and the prisoners were allowed to govern themselves within the walls, to study, and to earn money by making gimcracks and ship models. But only a handful of men ever escaped from Old Mill's granite walls, or from *Jersey's* wooden ones; and the hatred generated in both prisons stood the colonies in good stead in future years, whenever an impelling motive was needed to bring men to fight the British.

In the summer of 1777 there did not seem to be much future in being a rebel. The British men-of-war were taking American vessels right and left; the currency was nearly worthless, vitiated by lack of public confidence in the cause. To make matters worse, in July General Sir William Howe loaded nearly two-thirds of his New York garrison on ships and sailed for Philadelphia by way of Chesapeake Bay, went on to defeat Washington at Brandywine, captured Philadelphia in late September

Indians Burning Out the Center of a Log for a Canoe (from De Bry, *Travels to America*)

An Incident in the Defeat of the Armada: Diego Florez de Valdez' Galleon Springs Her Foremast and Is Taken by Sir Francis Drake in *Revenge*

U.S. Frigate *President* Entering Marseilles Harbor, 1806

and forced the ragged Americans into winter quarters at Valley Forge.

Even native ingenuity seemed doomed to failure: David Bushnell, a Connecticut farmboy who was graduated from Yale University in 1775, had invented a clam-shaped submarine called *The American Turtle* and this vessel, manned by an army sergeant named Ezra Lee, had proved a failure in an attempt on Lord Howe's flagship, 64-gun *Eagle,* in August 1776. The *Turtle* was an ingenious invention, but it was futile against the Royal Navy.

General John Burgoyne, proud co-author of a plan to cut the colonies in two by invading from Canada, by way of Lake Champlain, Lake George and the valley of the Hudson to New York, was marching down from the north, thinking that Howe would meet him half-way. But Howe's orders had been misplaced, put in the wrong pigeon-hole in London, and when he received them, Burgoyne was beyond help. Trailing his baggage-train of those comforts without which no sensible British general would ever dream of traversing the wilderness, Burgoyne blundered on to the southward, to meet final defeat at the siege of Saratoga on October 17, 1777, when he surrendered to General Horatio Gates the remnants of his army of Hessian and British mercenaries. During the last days of the siege Burgoyne distinguished himself for coolness by dandling his mistress (wife of one of his junior officers) on his knee while he imbibed deep draughts of champagne with his free hand. He was defeated not because the Americans were good, but because he was hopelessly incompetent.

But here was good news at last—a major victory at a time when it was sorely needed. Congress, which had fled from Philadelphia to Baltimore, made ready duplicate copies of the official news of the victory, and off to France with the original copy went the packet *Perch* on October 31st, sailing from Boston. Two days later Paul Jones, with the duplicate copy, left Portsmouth, N.H. in *Ranger,* flying the new flag of stars and stripes. *Perch* won the race, making Nantes on November 30th; *Ranger,* having tarried in a fruitless attempt to cut some prizes out of a British convoy, came in two days later.

The news *Perch* brought had a decisive influence on the French court, and on Louis XVI. The king was in favor of immediate intervention in the cause of that liberty and democracy whose political theory was largely a creation of French writers and romanticists. "La democratie" had been bandied about in the salons ever since Voltaire and the Swiss Rousseau had taken up their quills and with gallic wit and logic and literary excellence proved beyond any doubt that all was not perfect in the world. Demanding human equality and democratic government, Rousseau's *The Social Contract,* written in 1762, made it inevitable that the sympathies of France would be with the United States in a fight against tyranny.

On February 6, 1778, an Anglo-French treaty of commerce and alliance had been signed. But nevertheless, on June 17th the war between France and England began when Admiral Keppel ordered two French frigates and a schooner pursued. The French 40-gun *Belle Poule* fluttered away after a two-hour fight with 32-gun *Arethusa,* which had fired the first warning shot, but the other two French vessels were taken. The niceties of international law having been observed, France could now aid the colonies openly instead of clandestinely. Hereafter there would be no contentious British ambassador to protest the sale of American prizes brought into French ports; they could be sold openly, and the money derived from their sale turned over to Ben Franklin in furtherance of the rebel cause, which was now the cause of France too.

Before becoming allied with France, American privateers had been operating out of French ports and had made the channel crossing so unsafe that the French merchantmen had been able to take over a large share of the trans-channel trade, and now those same Americans could count on active help in combat from French ships, and on French sailors to help man out their vessels. On that same day when the treaty of alliance was signed in France, in London the House of Lords was being informed by Alderman Woodbridge that since the beginning of the rebellion American privateers had caused Britain to lose by capture or destruction 733 vessels, 174 of which were retaken by the British. Underlining the effect of the privateers for the enlightenment of the Lords came William Creighton's statement: he estimated that by February 6, 1778, losses to British merchants brought about by privateers had reached the value of at least two million, two hundred thousand pounds. These losses were particularly annoying to the nation which still claimed to have "a peculiar and Sovereign Authority upon the Ocean, by the Laws of God and Nature." 174 privateers with 1,838 guns and 9,236 men and boys had caused all this damage, and in addition had captured close to eleven thousand British seamen for whom replacements had to be found by the press-gangs of the Royal Navy, an activity which added immeasurably to the unpopularity of the war among the English people.

Bases for privateers in France and in the French West Indies were but a minor contribution of the French under Louis XVI. The French navy, which Choiseul had started building up after the Seven Years' War, was still growing. Choiseul had been dismissed from office in 1770, but his policy was carried on and in 1778 France had eighty ships of the line and 67,000 seamen—enough sea power to enable her to challenge Britain's claim to supremacy at sea. Forthwith the Count d'Estaing was ordered to proceed to America with the Toulon fleet, and he sailed on April 15th with twelve sail of the line, five frigates and a sloop. The Admiralty sent Vice-Admiral Byron to find and attack the French fleet but he was overtaken by a heavy gale and his ships disabled and dispersed. The British in America had been ordered to evacuate Philadelphia and to concentrate on New York, and while d'Estaing sailed leisurely westward the British arrived in New York and made ready to defend the port. D'Estaing, never in a hurry, paused to chase 28-gun *Mermaid* ashore, and to enter the Delaware; finally he turned up four miles off Sandy Hook and dropped anchor on July 11th. To oppose the French squadron Admiral Richard Howe (brother of William, who had been replaced by Sir Henry Clinton), had command of ten sail of the line, a 32-gun frigate and nine lesser vessels. He had, too, the whole-hearted support of New York's numerous tories who suspected that the French were idolators, and immoral to boot.

The French spent the next ten days at anchor, industriously replenishing their water casks and stores, while Howe disposed his inferior force in a defensive fashion, grimly determined to beat off any French attack on the port of New York. On the 22nd, when wind and tide favored the French, he thought they would surely come in and fight. D'Estaing, as expected, got his fleet under way, but to the astonishment of the Englishmen he simply hovered about the entrance until noon (he was listening to his pessimistic pilots), and then hauled off to the southward, content to have made a display of his strength.

A week later the French fleet appeared off Newport, R.I., which d'Estaing and the colonists planned to take from the British in a joint operation. D'Estaing put two ships of the line and two frigates on station in the East and West passages to Narragansett Bay, bottled up the British ships in Newport and so frightened their commanding officer that he sank or burned them. The French then took Conanicut Island, destroying the British batteries on Beavertail and in the Dumplings which commanded the entrances to the Bay. On August 8th the French cannonaded the British batteries protecting Newport, without much effect, and the next day Admiral Howe appeared in the offing with a reinforced squadron. Howe did not feel justified in attacking the French, whose twelve great sail of the line could out-gun him, and whose ships had the weather gage. But d'Estaing, pinned in the Bay by southerly winds, was uneasy, and on the 10th he got under way and stood out to sea. During that day and the next the two fleets, having made every preparation for action, circled each other like stiff-legged dogs. Before their growls could become bites a heavy gale blew up and both French and British were scattered far and wide. Neither Howe nor d'Estaing had shown any real inclination to fight, the former because he considered himself up against a superior force, the latter from sheer prudence. But d'Estaing may have been thinking of earlier troubles he had had with the British: he had been made prisoner in 1758, before Madras, and he had broken his parole. When magnificent old Boscawen heard of this he growled that if he ever caught the man he'd chain him to the deck like a monkey.

But with Howe off to refit in New York, d'Estaing returned to the entrance of Narragansett Bay, loitered there briefly, and then went on to Boston to repair his storm-damaged ships. The joint French-American plan to take Newport had turned out to be a dismal failure, and in the summer d'Estaing sailed for more lucrative cruising grounds—the West Indies, where he picked up a few unimportant and undefended British islands and fought an inconclusive battle with Admiral Byron in defense of Grenada. His chief contribution to the rebel cause was one of which he was unaware: by shifting his operations to the Caribbean, where he could use his fleet with direct benefit to France, he drew south from the American coast all but a few of the British ships which had been stationed there. The number of American privateers in service rebounded as soon as the coast was clear.

In the summer of '78 the Continental navy was in a parlous state. Biddle in 32-gun *Randolph* had fallen in with 64-gun *Yarmouth* on March 7th, and to give his five squadron-mates time to flee, had attacked the ship of the line. After a running fight of half an hour *Randolph* exploded. Five days later *Yarmouth* picked up four men clinging to a piece of wreckage and they were all who were saved from *Randolph*. It was a glorious gesture, worthy of comparison with the working habits of the privateersmen. As the frigates of the Continental navy were captured, wrecked or sunk, their officers became unemployed and many of them, men like Joshua Barney, John Barry, Alexander Murray, went into either the cruisers maintained by the states or into privateers.

Native tories, observing how successful the rebels were as privateers, took it up with the aid of the British. Several New York tories sent out their merchantmen, armed and commissioned by the British but manned by colonists, to take prizes in the coastwise trade. As a result commerce was driven away from New York, Connecticut and Rhode Island. Newport had its tory privateersmen, most obnoxious of whom was Captain Hazard, who sailed in 14-gun *King George* with eighty men and boys. In the summer of '79 Silas Talbot, in the sloop *Argo*, with 12 guns and sixty men, was cruising south of Long Island, hoping to run in with one of the tory privateers, whom Talbot had been ordered to eradicate. He was specially intent on taking Hazard, for they were both from Rhode Island and Talbot felt that Hazard was giving the colony a bad name by his cannibalistic activities as a privateer. At midday a sail was sighted, and she turned out to be Hazard in *King George*: *Argo* ran alongside, gave the brig a broadside, boarded and drove the Newporters below deck. Not a life was lost on either side, and Talbot sent his prize in to New London where the tories from Newport were exposed to the insults of the patriots who had been looking forward to the capture of Hazard and his crew for months. Talbot in *Argo* resumed his cruise and in rapid succession he freed an American privateer taken by the British, seized an armed merchant brig, took the British privateer *Dragon* in a four and a half hour duel, and then another one, the privateer brig *Hannah*. When *Argo* reached port with her rigging in tatters, her timbers shivered by shot and shell, the good citizens of New Bedford regarded her with joy mixed with awe. This diminutive vessel had taken ten times her weight in prizes and in guns and made a fortune for her crew. After refitting, *Argo* went on to run her total of prizes taken to twelve vessels and three hundred prisoners. The southern New England coast was cleared of tory privateers and, his assignment finished, Talbot was ordered to turn his command back to her owner.

As news of victories like Talbot's spread through the colonies there was a great renaissance in the privateering field. Syndicates were formed, stock issued, ships fitted out and built expressly as privateers. The business rapidly became regularized, and among the "Articles of Agreement" the crews signed were fine details: the reward for sighting a sail which became a prize was set at five hundred dollars; the first man to board an enemy vessel got one thousand dollars. There were bonuses which established the worth of a lost limb at four thousand dollars, of an eye, two thousand, of a joint, one thousand. Officers and men shared with the owners all prize money resulting from the sale of captured goods and ships.

In the north the British were also active. Sir Henry Clinton, thinking it would be useful to have a post on the Penobscot whence he could snipe at the Boston sea traffic, ordered General McLean to lead an expedition down from Halifax to establish the base. On June 16th the troops landed, 650 in all, and began to clear the land. When news of this reached Boston the Massachusetts General Court decided to oust the British and an expedition was assembled. Dudley Saltonstall was placed in command, a tragic choice, for he was a psychopathic case, incapable of leadership or decision, and the fleet of thirty-seven vessels—eighteen armed (eleven of them privateers) and nineteen transports sailed up to the Penobscot on July 25th. A landing was attempted and failed, but by August 12th the Americans had taken possession of several islands on the south side of the harbor and had made a landing on the peninsula, where they set up their batteries. On the night of the 12th an informer told General McLean the rebels would make an attempt to storm his half-completed fort. While he was making ready to receive the assault, suddenly the Americans abandoned their camp and works, embarked their troops, baggage and artillery. Coming over the horizon was Commodore Sir George Collier, in 64-gun *Raisonnable,* with six light ships in support. The American look-out vessel had spotted the squadron, and now the American vessels formed a cresent across the mouth of the river, as though they intended to fight. But when three of the British men-of-war drew near—*Blonde* and *Virginia,* of thirty-two guns each, and 20-gun *Galatea*—the Americans broke and ran up the river, led by Saltonstall in 32-gun *Warren,* and Holmes in 22-gun *Sally,* followed helter-skelter by the rest of the Americans—six 20-gun frigates, and three of 16-guns, 7 brigs, together with nineteen sail of transports. Collier threw out the signal for a general chase, and as the ships fled up the river and were trapped, they surrendered or were burned by their own crews. Both banks of the river were lined with burning hulks and when Collier totted up the score he found that there were thirteen prizes. Twenty-four sail had been completely destroyed. Thoroughly gratified, he returned to New York with his prizes. After that defeat the Continental Navy as an even mildly offensive force was finished, and never again in the war of the rebellion was its strength regained.

D'Estaing was the only hope: he had the only force in American waters capable of meeting the British, and after being goaded to action by Congress he was willing to try again. On August 20th he sailed north with twenty sail of the line and eleven frigates, carrying 5,500 troops, intending to free Savannah of the British and their tory allies, who included free blacks and the inevitable mulattoes. The French, leisurely as ever under d'Estaing, landed their guns and bombarded the town on October 3rd, and then tried to storm the British lines. They were repulsed and driven into the swamp, losing nearly twelve hundred officers and men. With difficulty they re-embarked and sailed back to France, save for a few fragments of the expedition which returned to the West Indies. The Americans were now without any effective French help along the coast of the United States, and they had to depend on their privateers to do what damage they could to the British.

Spain had declared war on Great Britain on June 16, 1779, but she was of limited help, her main interest in America being the recapture of Florida, and to that extent she was a modest drain on British resources in the colonies. Her major effort was in European waters, and the chief American beneficiaries of her entrance in the war were the American privateers who could now operate out of New Orleans, a handy base for the Caribbean area.

As far as the Continental Navy was concerned it was up to Paul Jones to keep some semblance of spirit in the organization. This short, heavily-muscled, blue-eyed Scot had been born in 1747, the son of a gardener who had married a farmer's daughter. By 1779 he had demonstrated time and again that he could take care of himself under any conditions. As a boy he learned about life in the Royal Navy, then went into the slavers, becoming third mate of the *King George* and chief mate of the *Two Friends,* worked in the merchantmen, and in 1768, while on the beach in Jamaica, did a turn as a ham actor in John Moody's troupe, playing the part of young Bevil in "The Conscious Lovers." At sea again, his volcanic temper got him into trouble with the Law when he killed the ringleader of a mutinous crew, and he vanished from sight and record. There is evidence that he was making a living as a pirate part of the time. In need of an alias, he changed his name from John Paul to Paul Jones, turned up in North Carolina in time to catch the virus of the pre-revolutionary days, found a patron in Joseph Hewes, influential ship-owner, and when war started wangled a commission as a First Lieutenant in the Continental Navy. Among the officers of that navy Jones was far and away the best qualified: he had learned the polished and skilled seamanship of the slavers and pirates, he was used to the cut-throat engagement both trades entailed, and he now had a chance to turn his anti-social instincts against the nation which had, unjustly, he thought, made him an outcast. In addition he had two other rare qualities: the habit of command, and a sense of the dramatic, which soothed his voracious vanity.

As a naval officer he toadied to the Naval Committee, knifed his rivals skillfully in letters to his patron, and by sheer lack of competition —for he was unrivaled as a single-ship commander—obtained command of the *Ranger,* put her in commission in spite of a shortage of stores and only one suit of sails. There was only one barrel of rum for the crew aboard when *Ranger* sailed for France in November 1777.

In European waters Jones worked *Ranger* to the limit, taking prizes, pausing only to make an attempt to burn the shipping at Whitehaven. There were only a few ships protecting the British coast, and Silas Deane, one of the American commissioners in France, had been looking for someone to burn such ports as Liverpool and Bristol. In England Deane was thought responsible for the incendiary activities of Jack the Painter, a well-known fire-bug, and he may indeed have been Jack's abettor, but proof is lacking. But here was Jones, who knew the coast of England well, and in April of '78 he tried to burn the shipping at Whitehaven, but failed. Only one ship burned satisfactorily, and Jones moved up the coast to his birth-place, St. Mary's Isle, where he demonstrated to his boyhood acquaintances how far up he had come in the world, and then he returned to France.

His next command was the best he could obtain: an ancient East Indiaman called *Duc de Durac,* worm-eaten, crank, her old timbers exuding a heady aroma of arrack, cloves and tea—reminders of former cargoes from the East Indies. In this floating antique with castellated poop, rearmed with forty-two guns, rechristened *Bon Homme Richard,* and accompanied by a squadron of mongrel consorts, Jones sailed out of L'Orient on August 15th and on September 23rd, 1779, off Flamborough Head on the Yorkshire coast fell in with 44-gun *Serapis,* a new frigate which was escorting the Baltic convoy home to England. What followed was essentially a single-ship action, since the rest of Jones squadron, by now reduced to *Alliance, Pallas* and *Vengeance,* took little part in the battle.

The action opened at about 7:20 in the evening, in swirling mists, and lasted until Pearson in *Serapis* hauled down his flag at 10:30. During those brief hours Jones magnetized his men by his spirit: he was like a flame, touching with fire, transmuting the gross material of his crew into inspired action. A harvest moon came up and threw a baleful light on the men-of-war, exposing them to the full view of hundreds of spectators on the Yorkshire cliffs. They had never seen anything like it, nor had Pearson of *Serapis.* Here he was up against something beyond reason, beyond all human experience. After beating *Richard* into a wreck, Pearson, a humane man, called out: "Do you strike?" Back came the reply, half-cry, half-howl: "I have not yet begun to fight!" Soon thereafter Pearson struck his colors. *Richard,* hardly a hulk, was kept afloat all day during the 24th while her wounded were taken off, and next morning at 9:00, with *Pallas* standing by, she was abandoned. An hour later she dove, bows first, beneath the waves, to the inexpressible grief of Paul Jones, who wanted to get her into port as proof of the impossible.

Of all the actions fought by the Continental Navy, won, lost or drawn, *Richard* vs. *Serapis* was the one that most inflamed men's minds with pride of country: it marked the immaculate absolute in obstinacy, courage and savage leadership. On it the minds of future American sea-fighters mused, and even dullards who never left dry land were jolted out of their complacency by the sheer ferocity of the battle.

Back in the colonies Clinton had little to fear at sea. It was true, the Spaniards had brought the weight of their navy to bear, but it was only a potential threat. Even with Spain's sixty sail of the line added to France's eighty, Britain still outnumbered them both with 150 line-of-battle ships. With d'Estaing's fleet back in France, the coast was clear, and Clinton sent an expedition south from New York in December 1779 to take Charleston, South Carolina. Next May the city capitulated, and the British captured four of America's remaining eight frigates. Then the rebellion in the south degenerated into a series of bloody, internecine raids and battles in which whig fought tory with the backing of their respective governments. The Carolinas could be counted out of the war.

Meanwhile the privateers had been growing in size and destructiveness. One man, Elias Hasket Derby of Salem, seeing that many of the early privateers were lost because they were unfit for the business, had the wit to put the matter on a research basis. A wealthy shipowner before the rebellion, he had seen his business ruined by the war, and to recoup his fortunes he turned his talents as a capitalist to the privateers. In his shipyards he made a study of design and rigging and armament, and soon he was building topsail schooner privateers big enough to fight off British sloops-of-war, fast enough to run away from heavily gunned ships, and capable of being converted to cargo-carrying letters-of-marque. Other shipowners, too, were developing the new breed of privateer: big vessels mounting twenty or more guns and manned by at least 150 men and boys. There were so many of them that it was difficult to get crews, and an enticing ritual was developed to attract the necessary men and boys. With fifer, drummer and color-bearer, an officer would swagger through the streets of a seaport, shouting the benefits of service in his ship, and telling all true patriots to repair to the tavern, there to eat and booze and sign the articles. The tavern rendezvous bill for one month could easily reach a total of nearly fifteen pounds, for a hundred and thirteen bowls of punch and grog and cherry toddy. The owners paid, and the men were brought aboard drunk or sober, along with an occasional country bumpkin who had clomped in to town and wanted to try to rival the fame of Paul Jones. In 1780, 228 privateers with over three thousand guns were at sea, and their sails dotted the English and Irish channels, making misanthropes of many a gouty English merchant.

The best operator of the lot, Jonathan Haraden of Gloucester and Salem, came up from service in the colony cruisers to take command at the age of thirty-five of the Salem letter-of-marque *General Pickering*, 180 tons burden, fourteen six-pounders, forty-five in the crew, men and boys. Haraden was one of those rare beings who do not come fully alive until they are in battle, and by the end of the war he was being credited with having taken some sixty vessels, whose guns totaled over one thousand.

Haraden sailed for Spain in *Pickering* in May of 1780, loaded with sugar for Bilboa, carrying a commission as a letter of marque, and en route he fell in with a British cutter of 22 guns which he beat off after a two-hour fight. In the Bay of Biscay, during the night, he ran alongside the British privateer *Golden Eagle*, twenty-two guns, and yelled to her that he was an American frigate, ready to blow her to hell if she did not strike her colors. *Eagle*, in consternation and perhaps remembering what had happened to *Serapis*, struck at once. Haraden took up his interrupted course for Bilboa, his prize with him, and soon after dawn on June 3rd as he was nearing port the lookout spotted a large sail coming out of the harbor. From his prisoners Haraden learned that she was *Achilles*, a 42-gun privateer out of London, with a crew of 140 men. During the day light winds prevented the two vessels from engaging, but *Achilles* took Haraden's prize. That night Haraden chose his position with skill and a knowledge of the lay of the land, putting *Pickering* behind some shoals so that when *Achilles* attacked she would not have any advantage of position. Early next morning *Achilles* moved in. Thousands of Spaniards lined the shore, attracted by news of the impending battle, eager to see their allies the Americans kill a few British. It was better than a bull-fight.

As *Achilles* came within range, *Pickering* began to rake her with broadsides. Then the wind failed. For three hours the Britisher tried to bring his ship in, to close with *Pickering,* but always he was out-maneuvered by Haraden, who knew it would be fatal to let himself be laid alongside by the heavily-manned enemy. Finally *Achilles* turned and ran, breaking out a sail as large as a ship of the line's, and although Haraden chased her, she out-footed him. Haraden re-took *Golden Eagle,* and came into port escorted by a regatta of delirious Spaniards who carried him through the streets of the city on their shoulders. They had seen him, in a vessel that looked like a ship's boat compared to *Achilles,* rout the larger ship in the best bull-fighting tradition, and they gave him the kind of a welcome usually reserved for a famous matador who had dispatched with grace and precision an enraged bull: banquets, parades, speeches and fiestas.

On his way home Haraden fell in with three merchantmen off Sandy Hook, two of fourteen guns and one of twelve. In spite of some natural timidity on the part of his crew he attacked the three ships, taking them one by one, in a series of lightning-like single-ship actions.

In a later cruise, still in *Pickering,* he came up against a king's packet, a brig heavily-armed and manned, bound for England from the Carib-bean. After a four-hour duel Haraden hauled away to take stock of his damages, and he discovered that he had but one round of ammuni-tion left. This last round he rammed home, and, running alongside the packet, told her captain that he had precisely five minutes to strike his colors. Then Haraden took out his watch and read off the vanishing minutes to the Englishman, while his crew stood by with lighted matches ready to touch off the shotted guns. The Englishman broke, hauled down his colors, and when *Pickering's* crew went aboard the packet they saw a deck covered with wounded and dead. Blood made the deck slippery underfoot and dripped from the scuppers.

While the Americans specialized in their privateering activities the French and British were pouring power into the Caribbean, making that area of lush and profitable sugar islands the cockpit of the war in the Western Hemisphere. Remnants of d'Estaing's fleet which had retreated to the West Indies after the siege of Charleston were reinforced on March 22, 1780, by a squadron under Comte de Guichen, increasing the strength of the French fleet in the Caribbean to twenty-three sail of the line. On March 27th de Guichen's opposite number, Admiral Rodney, arrived in the role of commander-in-chief of the West India station. In his command were twenty sail of the line. The French and British fleets met in battle on April 17th, and after a four-hour engagement the French sailed away. The British were left so disunited and crippled that Rodney found it inexpedient to pursue the French, who considered themselves the victors. Then Spain sent in twelve sail of the line to help swing the balance of sea power in favor of the Allies. Rodney tried but failed to intercept the Spaniards, whose arrival raised the odds against him to such an extent that he dared not risk battle with the combined fleets of his enemies. To make matters worse for the British, Rochambeau turned up in Newport, R.I., in July with seven sail of the line and fifty-five hundred troops. The British in Newport had evacuated the city in advance, warned of the impending arrival of the French, and Rochambeau occupied the city without firing a shot. To Rodney this was an added distraction, and when de Guichen sailed from Martinique in August with fifteen sail of the line Rodney suspected he might be going north to join forces with Rochambeau. De Guichen was, in fact, going back to France, but Rodney had no way of knowing this and to help protect the British in New York against a possible joint attack by de Guichen and Rochambeau he sent half of his fleet to New York, leaving the rest in Jamaica. He arrived in New York on September 12th, to find that Rochambeau had disposed his seven sail of the line in such a strong defensive position in Newport harbor that an attack on them appeared foolhardy. Behind his anchored ships and land batteries Rochambeau and his men enjoyed the amenities of life in Newport (whose uncouth natives were wide-eyed at the amount of cosmetics the French officers used), while a few British ships stood patrol off the entrance to Narragansett Bay.

When Rodney was certain of the disposition of the French naval forces he returned to the Caribbean where he learned that Britain had declared war on Holland on December 20th. Immediately he made a descent on the Dutch islands of St. Eustatius and St. Martin, where the Americans had been accustomed to buying large quantities of contraband goods for their army. Rodney found and seized in the harbor of St. Eustatius two hundred merchantmen, six men-of-war, and three million pounds worth of supplies.

During that winter of 1780–81 the British forces at sea were spread very thin: they were everywhere on the defensive, in the Baltic, the North and South Atlantic, in the Indian ocean, in the Mediterranean and Caribbean seas. British ships had to be ready to fight off any French, Spanish, American or Dutch vessel that came within range. To make matters worse, each convoy of merchantmen had to be heavily escorted to protect it from the attacks of the privateers of all nations. There simply were not enough ships in the Royal Navy to handle all the business, for the oceans were like a web whose center was the Admiralty, sensitive to the faintest pressures—which represented enemy fleet or convoy or land movements—on strands leading to the remote ports of the world. Each enemy move demanded a countering move, in terms of the shifting of fleets or of fleet units.

Word came to the Admiralty in March 1781 that de Grasse was setting out from Brest for the West Indies with twenty-six sail of the line and a large convoy of merchantmen, and Rodney was so advised. De Grasse sailed by way of the Azores, where he detached five of his sail of the line and sent them to the Indian Ocean under the command of Suffren, while he went on westward to the Caribbean with his twenty-one ships and his convoy. He reached Martinique on April 28th, where he was joined by four sail of the line. The odds were now overwhelming in favor of the French: they had twenty-five sail of the line in the Caribbean, as against eighteen British ships. Qualitatively the French men-of-war were better than the British with the sole exception that the hulls of the British ships were sheathed with copper and they were as a result faster than the French. De Grasse chased the British into Antigua, moved on to take Tobago on June 2nd, and came to anchor off Haiti on July 26th, 1781. There he was given dispatches from Rochambeau and Washington, brought by the French frigate *La Concorde,* urging him to bring the weight of his fleet against the British either off New York or in the Chesapeake. Rochambeau recommended action in the Chesapeake and de Grasse agreed with him, sending him word by *La Concorde* that he would sail for the Chesapeake with his fleet and as many soldiers as he could pick up in the French garrisons in the West Indies.

De Grasse had carried out the first part of his orders: he had established a local supremacy at sea in the West Indies. Now he was free to help the Americans and he moved with un-Gallic speed, gathering men and supplies, borrowing gold from the Spaniards so the Americans could meet their debts and pay their soldiers, arranging for the Spanish fleet to guard the interests of France while he was gone. Two hundred French merchantmen he ordered to remain in port: he had some business to attend to in the north—he would be back later on to see that they were escorted safely to France. For a few weeks de Grasse functioned with the enthusiasm of a young blade, in spite of his sixty summers, bringing to bear on this operation everything he had learned since he had gone to sea at the age of twelve in the service of the Knights of Malta in their galleys, everything he had learned in forty-two years of service in the French Navy.

Rodney was ill: on August 1st he sailed for home with four sail of the line, a proper minimum squadron for an Admiral of his rank; six other sail of the line had been detached to escort the Jamaica convoy back to England, and the rest of the fleet sailed north under Admiral Sir Samuel Hood to reinforce Admiral Thomas Graves in New York.

Meanwhile the Allied plan began to develop with the precision of a jig-saw puzzle: Rochambeau left Newport with his troops, marching to join Washington's ragged forces along the Hudson; de Barras sailed from Newport on August 27th with eight sail of the line and the siege artillery and supplies in eighteen transports: the various forces were converging on their common destination—Yorktown, where Cornwallis had holed up, blocked in by Lafayette and the joint French-American forces.

The six thousand troops of Rochambeau and Washington crossed the Hudson on August 24th and marched southward. De Grasse with twenty-four sail of the line anchored in Chesapeake Bay on August 30th, and on September 5th Admiral Thomas Graves appeared with nineteen sail of the line, a 50-gun ship, and six frigates. The French were first sighted at 9:30 A.M., anchored inside the Virginia Capes, and action commenced at 4:15 P.M., with the wind moderate from the northeast and the weather fine. After a two-hour running fight, with the action bearing to the southward, the British hauled to the wind and ceased action. De Grasse kept them in sight for five days, playing with them, drawing them off, so that de Barras could slip unmolested into the Chesapeake with his siege train and eight sail of the line. When de Barras arrived, the British, hopelessly outnumbered, burned their damaged 74-gun *Terrible* and sailed back to New York to refit. The Rochambeau-Washington force was ferried down the bay to join Lafayette's command, and the siege of Yorktown began on September 30th under the supervision of French engineers who were expert in the use of siege guns. Fifteen thousand French and American soldiers faced seven thousand British, and when Cornwallis capitulated on October 19th, 1781, two thousand of his men were in hospital. Nine days later the expected British reinforcements arrived off Yorktown—twenty-two sail of the line under Admiral Hood—but they were too late, and they turned back for New York, which, with Charleston and Savannah, were the only strongholds remaining in British hands in all the thirteen colonies.

Yorktown marked the end of Great Britain's major efforts in the war against the colonies: it had been six years and six months since Lexington. When the news of the defeat was brought to Prime Minister Lord North in his home in Downing Street, he gestured wildly and began pacing the floor, saying over and over again: "O God! it is all over!" The tory government of King George was discredited, the results of the interference of the king in government made all too clear. The realm was heavily in debt, taxes were ruinous and the whigs had all the political ammunition they could use.

Still the merchants were losing ships to the privateers, 449 of which, from America alone, were at sea in 1781. The Royal Navy was still in action at opposite ends of the earth, fighting fleet actions in the Indian Ocean, where Admiral Sir Edward Hughes and the Frenchman Suffren tore each other's fleets to pieces; in the Caribbean, where in April of 1782 Rodney finally defeated and captured de Grasse. The last action of the war was fought off Pondicherry in the Indian ocean on June 20,

1783, when Hughes met Suffren for the fifth time, and then had news of the peace a few days later.

Peace had been a long time in coming. On November 30th, 1782, articles between the United States and Great Britain had been signed, but they were not to go into effect until France and Britain made peace. And that did not finally come about until September 3rd, 1783, when the definitive articles were sealed. By the treaty, called the Peace of Paris, the independence of the United States was acknowledged, and because of the insistence of John Adams the Americans retained their fishing rights off Newfoundland and in the Gulf of St. Lawrence. Spain regained Florida and everything west of the Mississippi, France kept a few West Indian islands, and Britain, Gibraltar. American loyalists who chose to leave the new-born nation gathered in New York and Charleston and were evacuated in British ships. On November 25th, 1783, the last British men-of-war sailed out of New York harbor, and the thirteen colonies were left to work out their own destiny.

When the war ended there were only two vessels of the Continental Navy afloat—*Alliance* and *Hague*—and they were promptly sold by order of Congress. The nation was happy to forget about a navy that had cost so much and accomplished so little; only the names of Paul Jones and Nicholas Biddle were worth saving, and they entered into and became a part of the folklore of the colonies. Some three hundred privateers were still afloat, and they were promptly converted to the ways of peace. During the war the privateers had cost Great Britain eighteen million pounds worth of damage, had captured some twelve thousand British seamen, and had trained thirty thousand Americans in the use of guns and ships. They had forced insurance rates to new highs for British merchantmen, had raised the cost of living in England, and had taken in all nearly two thousand British vessels. From the day *Reprisal* reached France with Ben Franklin and a cargo of indigo, and two prizes taken en route, until the last prize was brought in, the people of France and Spain and Holland had been given telling proof of the vulnerability of the British to even a small seafaring nation of three million people. In the most despondent days of the rebellion their exploits, often greatly magnified in the press, had given new life to the rebels. Their prizes supplied guns and powder and trade goods, along with much hard money for the colonial cause. In their names is the evidence of the spirit of the men who sailed and fought them: *Bloodhound, Black Snake, Disdain, Panther, Revenge, Retaliation, Viper, Wild Cat*—and *Liberty*.

---

[9] *Rough Winds*

The thirteen colonies stretched south from the Great Lakes and Canada to Florida, inland from the sea to the Mississippi. In the Gulf of Mexico Spanish interests were dominant, and her settlements at Pensacola, Biloxi, Mobile and New Orleans carried on a decorous trade, troubled only by smugglers. On the West Coast Spanish influence had been extended north during the years of the revolution. With the help of the inevitable Franciscans the Presidio at San Francisco was founded in 1776, Los Angeles in 1780, Santa Barbara in 1782. These, with San Diego, made California a Spanish preserve, and the indolence of the dons was but mildly disturbed by the Russians to the north.

The Muscovites, following the current fashion, had been expanding southward along the coast of Alaska ever since Vitus Bering, a Dane in the service of the Czar, had discovered the Aleutians and the Bering Strait in 1741. Siberian fur-traders soon found that Alaska was fabulously productive of furs, and by 1771 they were bringing sea otter and seal skins into China, where such peltries were in great demand by the merchants and mandarins.

Spain kept an eye on the Russians, mindful that they might impinge on Spanish interests, and expeditions were sent to the north to find out exactly what the Russians were doing, and to set a limit to their operations. By 1776, motivated by anxiety about Russia, the Spaniards had explored the West Coast as far north as Sitka, and for the moment the Russians were restrained from moving into California.

The British knew that the Russians were carrying on some sort of bizarre trading activity north of California and along the Alaskan coast, but not until Captain James Cook voyaged to the Northwest coast in 1778 did they realize the extent of the profits the Russians were making. Cook's findings were soon public property in the American States, for in 1783 John Ledyard of Connecticut, who had sailed with Cook, published in Hartford a journal and chart of the voyage, reporting that the Indians bartered sea otter skins to the Russians for a few beads, and that the Russians then sold the skins in China for as much as a hundred dollars apiece. Confirming Ledyard's narrative, and banishing all doubts, came Cook's own account of his third voyage, published in 1784.

News of the existence of this El Dorado and awareness of the value of the China trade, provided strong stimuli to the American merchants and shipowners, who had suffered painful financial losses during the revolution. But now they found that it was not easy to pick up and mend the threads of trade broken by the war, for the independence they had won also entailed dependence on their own efforts and capital to build and man ships and to find markets for their goods. There was a brief flash of prosperity, but only the fisheries quickly regained and held their prewar place in the economy of the states. In every other field of seafaring there were innumerable obstacles to be overcome before the profits could be counted.

In 1784 the merchantmen of all nations were moving again on their lawful tasks, still armed, but not quite so heavily. The explosive quality of the times made for general distrust, and there were always the pirates in the Caribbean and the Mediterranean to contend with; Holland and France and Spain moved cautiously, licking their wounds; Britain was not so utterly sure she ruled the waves, for the French Navy was a worthy rival. At Brienne, in France, in that summer of 1784, the young Napoleon told his father he wanted to be a naval officer—so great was the prestige of the service after the part it had played in the American revolution, so sure were the French that future battles would make promotion and pay in that service swift and sure. The giants of the world were uneasy in their roles of peaceful neighbors, with each nation alert to detect and turn to its own advantage any weakness in the policy and power of another. In that atmosphere the young American nation was disturbed in mind, but anxious to learn, inspired by the profit motive.

At first American coastal trade was active and prosperous, but soon the various states, each functioning as an independent republic, began to compete with each other, trying to lure trade away from neighboring states by levying port dues and taxes on the ships and goods of their rivals. James Madison was moved to point out that New Jersey, caught between Philadelphia and New York was like a keg tapped at both ends, and that North Carolina, between Virginia and South Carolina, was like a patient bleeding at both arms.

The West Indian trade, by custom and usage a projection of the coastal trade, had been a mainstay of colonial commerce in pre-war years, when colonial fish, corn, lumber, cattle and horses were traded in the islands for sugar, rum and indigo. But trade with the British islands had been closed by an Order in Council in July 1783, and before the smugglers could evade the Order in adequate numbers thousands of slaves had starved to death, and with them hundreds of impoverished whites.

Hardly had the peace been declared before the British made clear the line their policy would follow in dealing with American trade: *Bedford* of Nantucket arrived in England on February 3rd, 1784, with 487 barrels of whale oil, followed soon by *Industry* with a similar cargo. The oil was sold at a profit, and the British merchants, who had nurtured their own whalers during the revolution, manned them with captured American seamen, and established a whale fishery off the coast of Brazil, protested vehemently against this competition. Without delay a duty of eighteen pounds per barrel was levied on all oil imported in foreign ships.

American shipyards had built hundreds of vessels for British merchants before the war, and had built them at half the cost of English ships. And as the specter of American shipyards building more and more vessels for England arose, the British government ruled that the king's subjects could not buy any more American-built ships.

In what they hoped would be a final blow to the revival of American commerce, the British ruled that the only American products which could be brought to England in American ships were naval stores the kingdom lacked—masts, spars, pitch, tar and turpentine—and indigo. To make matters even more difficult, ships from America could carry to England only the products of the state from which they sailed.

British frigates which were short-handed made a practice of cruising off the American coast and filling out their crews by impressing seamen from any American vessel that came within reach of the frigates' guns. There were thousands of deserters from English ships, and it was hard to tell, said the British, whether a man was an American, or an English deserter. Passports and proofs of colonial birth were not acceptable: if a man had the physique and appearance of a useful hand, it was decided arbitrarily that he was British and he was taken aboard the man-of-war to serve the King.

In the face of such difficulties, and by a process of elimination, there were only two major and lucrative trade areas open to those merchants and shipowners of the thirteen states who wanted to make a lot of money in a hurry: the Far East and the Northwest coast.

China, India, Sumatra and Java offered the best immediate chances for large profits, for from those regions came the spices and teas and silks which had been the lifeblood of the Honorable East India Company ever since its founding in Queen Elizabeth's reign. Americans knew the Company well, for it held, by sanction of Acts of Parliament, a monopoly of all British trade in the Far East. But now that the American States were no longer a part of the British Empire this trade was open to their ships.

The voyages the Americans undertook fell into a pattern: they started out for the Canaries, then followed the route of the East Indiamen, south to Table Bay at Cape Town, and thence by way of the Sunda Straits (between Sumatra and Java) to Canton. The elementary hazards of the trip were increased by the lack of navigational instruments and accurate charts, by pirates from the Barbary States who roved about the Canary Islands, by the natives of the islands in the Java Sea who had found the white men to be highly undesirable customers because of their habit of descending on native villages to plunder their homes and violate their wives. Then, too, China's coast had its own indigenous pirates, well-organized and often equipped with war-junks they had captured from their government.

But if the risks were great, so were the profits, and the Americans had a native product much in demand in China: the ginseng root, sweet-tasting, esteemed by Chinese as an aid to the virility on which their concubines made such exhausting demands. But before American-Chinese trade could find its full growth there was another deterrent to be overcome—the British ships at Cape Town. These East Indiamen, en route home from China or India, loaded with teas and silks and spices, invariably stopped at Table Bay to take on provisions. Company goods could not be bartered, but the captain of every Indiaman had the use of fifty-six and one-half tons of his ship's cargo space for his personal trade ventures. Such men, seeing the provincial Americans at anchor in the bay, could make a nice profit by trading their tea for the Americans' ginseng. It posed a nice problem for the Yankees: should they take the cash, avoid the risk of the trip on to China, and let the uncertain profits they might make at Canton go? Some, whose environment had made them practical men, took the cash.

Thus 40-ton *Harriet* of Hingham, Massachusetts, sailed loaded with ginseng from Boston in December 1783, under the command of Captain Hallet. She felt her way southward along the African coast and made Cape Town, where the English captains offered Hallet two pounds of fine tea for one of ginseng. Hallet could not resist the immediate profit, and the deal was made.

Then came *Empress of China,* 360 tons, and she sailed from New York on February 22, 1784, equipped with a "sea letter" from Congress which humbly requested of every official the ship might encounter that she be received with goodness and permitted to transact business wherever she might anchor. *Empress* had been financed to the tune of $120,000, chiefly by New York merchants, and ginseng formed the major part of her cargo. The ship rounded the Cape of Good Hope, crossed the Indian ocean, got safely through the Sunda Straits, and was sailing past Java when she fell in with two French merchantmen which had been converted from men-of-war for the China trade. As recent allies, the French were cordial, and together the ships sailed for Canton, reaching the anchorage on August 23rd. *Empress* traded her cargo after abiding by the intricate rituals the Chinese had devised to regulate their dealings with the white barbarians, and reached New York on May 11, 1785.

She had made a profit of thirty thousand dollars—a net gain of 25 per cent on the capital invested—but her various shareholders did not consider this a sufficient return on their money, in view of the risks involved, and the voyage was not considered a successful one.

The New Englanders looked down their wine-red noses at such petty pickings, a trifle annoyed because they had not reached China first. They had not been idle, but cautious. Salem's E. H. Derby had been feeling out the ground: in June 1784 he sent the bark *"Light Horse"* with a cargo of sugar to St. Petersburg, and opened the Baltic trade; in November he sent his *Grand Turk* to Cape Town with instructions to gather information on the China trade, and to exchange her cargo for anything profitable except slaves. 300-ton *Grand Turk* had been built in 1781 as a privateer, and for this voyage she carried twenty-two guns, and a mixed cargo valued at $27,000. At Cape Town her captain, Jonathan Ingersoll, consorted with the English captains, picking up news of the market in China, and trading ginseng for tea. One captain offered a princely sum for the rum aboard *Grand Turk,* and aroused Ingersoll's suspicions to such an extent that Ingersoll found out that the reason for this munificence was that St. Helena was bone-dry and in grave need of any sort of rum. Off he sailed to the island, which he loaded with rum, and then he made for the West Indies where he exchanged the rest of his cargo for island produce. When *Grand Turk* returned to Salem in the fall of 1785 she had made a profit of 100 per cent on the voyage. Since this represented a normal and reasonable gain Derby sent her out again after a brief refit, but this time under a new captain, Ebenezer West, an ex-privateersman who had spent four years in a British prison. She was off for the Indian ocean on December 5th, but finding no market for her cargo at Mauritius she went on to Canton, where she found *Empress of China* in port on her second trip. *Grand Turk* was indoctrinated in the formalities of the trade by the resident American agent, Major Shaw, and she sold her cargo, then loaded with tea and silks and chinaware and sailed for home. She reached Salem on May 22, 1787, and disposed of her cargo with a profit of 100 per cent.

Other ships from America had been testing the trade newly opened to them in the Far East: *United States* left Philadelphia in March 1784 and traded in Pondicherry, French India; *Chesapeake* and *Betsy* were in Calcutta taking on goods, and *Hope* showed up in Canton. *Experiment,* the smallest of the lot to reach the Far East, sailed December 18, 1785, from New York's East River. She was a Hudson river sloop of eighty tons built for the Albany–New York river trade, but now she was commanded by Captain Stewart Deane, ex-privateersman, alumnus of four years in England's Old Mill prison. Deane had eleven men, one officer and two boys for crew; for self-defense his vessel carried six guns, two swivels, pikes, muskets, pistols and cutlasses. Deane took his single-stick merchantman to Canton without incident, traded his ginseng for tea and silks, and returned with profit to the plaudits of all New York. The trip home from Canton had taken only four months and twelve days, and with such an example of success before them the merchants of the States began to send more and larger ships to the Far East. In 1789, so profitable had the trade with China proved, there were fifteen American ships in Canton Roads at the same time.

In the meantime action had been taken to garner the profits of the fur trade in the Northwest. A syndicate was formed for that purpose in 1787, and six men financed the venture, subscribing a total of fifty thousand dollars. The syndicate bought *Columbia,* a two-decked, 213-ton three-master, square-rigged, armed with ten guns. She had been built by James Briggs of Scituate in 1773 and she was thought an old vessel, for ships' lives were short in that age of violence. Both Ledyard and Cook had pointed out the difficulties of navigation on the Northwest coast, and it was evident that *Columbia* would need a tender—a small craft to cruise among the islands and inshore, to carry on trade with the Indians and stock *Columbia* with furs. Such a craft was located: *Lady Washington,* a 90-ton sloop, with the square topsail favored by all New England single-stickers. John Kendrick of Wareham, Massachusetts, an ex-privateersman, was selected as leader of the expedition and captain of *Columbia;* his friend Robert Gray, ex-privateersman of Boston, was given command of *Lady Washington.* Great pains were taken in fitting out the vessels: they were completely overhauled, refitted and provisioned for what everyone knew would be a long and arduous voyage. And on September 30, 1787, they set out from Boston with their cargoes of knives, iron, tools, toys and beads. The commanders had precise orders: they were to proceed to the Northwest by way of Cape Horn, deal fairly with the natives, be wary of the Catholic Spaniards, gather furs and trade them in Canton for tea which they were to bring home to Boston. The two vessels sailed by way of the Cape Verde Islands, a lotusland where two of their key men jumped ship—the surgeon, and Woodruff, their guide, who had been with Cook. These were heavy losses, but Kendrick and Gray sailed on through the South Atlantic, leaving the Falkland Islands on February 28th, 1788, to round Cape Horn. The sea was not kind to them there: the season was late and gales drove the waters against the currents, building up huge seas; waves swept their decks, and the winds threw *Columbia* on her beam ends, nearly capsized her. Then, in one dark, roaring storm the vessels became separated. For a month their crews fought the cold and the gales, fisting the frozen canvas in, driving the vessels on to the westward. It was mid-April before *Lady Washington* took the long Pacific rollers, her crew hardly daring to believe that they had left the furious Cape behind them. Sailing north, in June she caught the northeast trades, and from then on it was fair sailing for the little sloop. Early in August she dropped anchor near Cape Mendocino, and at Cape Lookout became involved in a fight with the Indians, who knifed the cabin-boy to death. She sailed on to the rendezvous—Friendly Cove, in Nootka Sound, Vancouver—and made port on August 16th, 1788. Seven days later *Columbia* staggered in under short canvas: two of her crew had died at sea, and the rest of them were weak as kittens from scurvy.

Nootka in 1788 was British territory, having been purchased from the Indians a few years earlier by Captain John Meares, a one-time Royal Naval officer, for a brace of pistols and some copper. He had begun to settle the land with Chinese he transported from Canton, and he cultivated their natural domesticity by supplying them with wives brought from Hawaii. He had built a fort and a little vessel named *Northwest America* which was used to collect furs along the coast and in the inlets. The Americans began at once to make themselves at home in Friendly Cove, building a large house and in their spare time turning the iron they had brought with them into chisels and knives. One chisel, in the spring trading in 1789 was worth one otter skin, but later that year the Indians became more sophisticated, and demanded as many as eight chisels for one skin. *Lady Washington* cruised along the shore, her shallow draft permitting her to visit the Indian villages she sighted, and as she exhausted her trade goods for furs she turned the harvest over to *Columbia* and set out to barter for more. It was while this innocent business was going on that a most ferocious Spaniard named Don Estevan Martinez sailed into Nootka in a heavily-gunned Spanish man-of-war, the *Princessa*. He took possession of the colony in the name of his king, captured three British ships which came unwittingly into the harbor, but left the Americans untouched. All his zeal came to naught, for England demanded and received reparations from Spain for the damages he had caused English traders, and England won, too, recognition of her right to sail and trade in the Pacific, which up to that time had been claimed by Spain as a purely Spanish ocean. During Martinez' visit the Americans Kendrick and Gray were demurely preparing to sail. The captains exchanged vessels, and *Columbia,* now commanded by Gray, sailed late in July 1789 for Canton. She called at Hawaii to take on water and firewood and provisions, and to let the crew have a frolic ashore, then went on to Canton where she sold her furs and loaded with tea. Kendrick in *Lady Washington* followed only as far as Macao where heavy weather kept him from sighting *Columbia* as she sailed for Boston by way of the Cape of Good Hope in February 1790. Six months later *Columbia* stood in past Boston Light and received a tumultuous welcome from the city, with artillery banging out salutes and the crowds cheering. She had been gone nearly three years, and had circumnavigated the planet. But her profits were not up to the 100 per cent mark, and two of her backers withdrew from the syndicate.

It was a changed country *Columbia* returned to: the Federal Constitution had been drawn up a few weeks before the expedition had sailed in 1787, it had gone into effect in March 1789, and George Washington had been inaugurated on the sun-drenched morning of April 30, 1789. The first creaking machinery of government had begun to get into motion. Congress was conscious of the need to protect the youthful merchant marine from the ravenous competition of the European nations and it had passed a customs act giving American vessels a 10 per cent discount on tariff rates on imports, and in addition had ruled that tea brought into the States in foreign vessels should be taxed at more than double the rate American ships paid. Since the tea came from India and China this ruling secured American trade with the Far East for American ships. Then, in July 1789, Congress passed an act permitting vessels built and owned in the United States to enter home ports on payment of tonnage duties of six cents a ton, whereas foreign-built and owned ships had to pay fifty cents a ton. By the same act it was ruled that foreign vessels in the coastal trade had to pay duties at every port of entry, while the Americans had to pay only once a year. The young nation was learning fast, and given such encouraging treatment by Congress the merchants and shipowners reacted by building and fitting out more merchantmen: there was even an abortive attempt to form an American East India Company, and for this purpose the 600-ton *Massachusetts* was designed along East Indiaman lines and launched at Quincy, Massachusetts in the fall of 1789. But her trip to Canton was not a success and the project was abandoned, being beyond the means of private capital.

In December 1789 there were only 123,893 tons of American shipping registered for foreign commerce; a year later the total had risen to 346,254 tons. The benevolence of Congress included not only the ship-owners and merchants but also the seamen. In 1790 an act was passed which specified that all seamen were to have the benefit of a written contract defining their rate of pay and the duration of the voyage; the responsibilities of masters of vessels were defined, and they were constrained to consider the welfare of their crews as well as the profits of the owners. Heavy penalties awaited any captain who abandoned members of his crew in foreign ports, and the ship itself could be held as security for the payment of fines.

In this atmosphere of privileged discrimination for American ships and seamen the remaining members of the syndicate which had backed *Columbia* and *Lady Washington* determined to try again. *Columbia* was given a thorough refit, including new masts and spars, and in late September, 1790, with Captain Gray in command, she set out again for the northwest coast, under orders not to trade with Spaniards and to insult no one unless first insulted. *Columbia* arrived in June, 1791, at

Clayoquot on Vancouver Island, a port much favored by the fur-traders, and she began trading along the coast in company with *Lady Washington,* which Kendrick had brought back from Macao, by way of Japan (where he had been ordered off), earlier in the year. It was a hair-trigger business, with the natives displaying much cunning, attempting even to seize the *Lady Washington,* and killing four members of the expedition. That fall Kendrick in *Lady Washington* sailed again for Macao with a full cargo, and Captain Gray of *Columbia* went into winter quarters at Clayoquot. He built there a small fort and a new tender for *Columbia*—the 44-ton *Adventure,* and having heard of a great river in the region he set out in the spring of 1792 in *Columbia* to find it. Sailing to the southeast he fell in with Commodore Vancouver's squadron of three ships, which was sailing north to explore the coast. The two commanders exchanged civilities, and Gray was warned that he was wasting his time looking for the legendary great river. But Gray kept doggedly on down the coast, discovering and exploring Gray's Harbor, beating off an attack by Indians in war-canoes; and at dawn on May 11th, he found a passage leading into an unknown river. With a favoring wind, *Columbia* set all sails, crossed the bar and sailed into the river on the tide. Gray went on, ten miles upstream, noting several Indian villages, and for several days he traded with the natives, then went fifteen miles further up-river. At that point he hazarded the guess that the river might be navigable for a hundred miles, reversed his course and made for the river's mouth. On May 19, 1792, he landed with his crew and named the river Columbia, in honor of his ship, and claimed the region it dominated for his country. Thus, to the pretensions of Spain and Britain and Russia in the mysterious northwest area was added a most valid claim by the United States. Gray resumed his trading, and when he had a full cargo for *Columbia* he sold *Adventure* to the Spaniards for seventy-five otter skins and sailed for China. He repaired leaking old *Columbia* at Macao, sold his furs and loaded a cargo of tea and chinaware, santeens and nankeens. When he reached Boston in July 1793, the news of his discoveries impressed no one, and the syndicate was not made sufficiently happy by the profits of the voyage to underwrite another trip.

For every unsuccessful voyage there were a dozen profitable ones and the upsurge of American shipping continued as the citizens of the seaport towns were given proof of the profits to be made in trade. The gambling spirit prevailed, inspiring adults, as well as children not yet in their teens, to engage in financial adventures of their own. These they undertook by scraping together a few dollars and turning either the money or its equivalent in goods over to the friendly captain of a merchantman bound for foreign ports, who handled the investment as wisely as he could and often returned with a profit of over 100 per cent on the speculation. Thus, John Tucker of Salem gave one hundred Spanish dollars to the captain of *Messenger,* bound for the Far East; in Batavia, Java, the captain spent $90.19 for ten bags of coffee which he sold in Antwerp on his way home for $183.75, making a neat profit for his optimistic investor, who undoubtedly sped the vessel on her voyage with nightly prayers for her safety and for the health of the captain.

In the seaport towns boys had usually left school, with some knowledge of reading, writing and arithmetic by the time they were thirteen or fourteen years old. Then, if they could, they went to work in the counting-house of a prosperous merchant, where the talk was always of ships and cargoes and remote harbors. There they learned the rudiments of trade, the lingo of the sea, and their young eyes bugged out with amazement at the sight of the profits their employers made. As soon as the opportunity offered, or was created by influential relatives, they went to sea in search of their fortunes. As a result of exposure to this system there was never any shortage of alert young blood in the fabulous business, and the merchant marine kept expanding steadily, with only a temporary recession in 1793 caused by trouble in Europe.

France, bankrupt and leaderless, had drifted into revolution; the Bastille had been stormed on July 14, 1789, and Louis XVI's head, detached from his body by the guillotine, had thudded into a basket in January of 1793. Britain was aghast at such excesses and not a little worried about the potential effect of the revolutionary virus on her own empire. Clearly, there was a chance that this crazy idea of human equality might become pandemic, and the disturbing concept of democratic government was one alien to the formal thinking of the aristocrats who ruled Britain. To them the reign of terror by mobs drunk on wine and liberty was an indecent spectacle, and in addition the British people felt their hereditary distaste for all things French. France, anticipating trouble with Britain as an inevitable by-product of her new form of government, declared war on February 1, 1793. The British were not unhappy.

The French were fighting for an ideal that inflamed men's minds and they were already at war with Austria, Sardinia and Prussia, while Russia and the Pope looked at the new republic askance: there was but one possible maritime ally for the Revolution—the United States, whose treaty of alliance of 1778 with France was still in effect. By that treaty the Americans guaranteed French island possessions in the West Indies, and if the United States abided by its treaty obligations, as France expected it to, then war between Britain and the United States would follow, for it was unthinkable that the British would not attempt to seize some of the lush French islands in the Caribbean. But President Washington, mindful of the naval and military impotence of his country, trimmed his sails to meet the wind: neutrality became the American policy, and France was disillusioned.

As a neutral nation the United States soon found seafaring a path beset with pitfalls. Britain was in no mood to observe the niceties of international law which the small maritime nations had been trying to establish for their own benefit, nor was she in a position to let her archenemy France grow stronger with the help of neutral shipping. The United States, as the leading neutral maritime nation, was caught in the cross-fire: both France and England seized her vessels. It was preferable to be taken by the British—they paid for the condemned cargoes at a fair price, including even freight charges. But the Americans objected to this on two counts: first, they could get higher prices in France for their foodstuffs, and second, such seizures were an infringement of neutral rights. The French were not as meticulous as the British in paying for the cargoes and ships they seized: the atmosphere of the revolution was not conducive to judicial impartiality, but to chaos, and the local Committees in the French ports made their own rules, much to the bewilderment of the Yankee merchantmen.

While the Americans were suffering severe losses in European waters, they were also carrying on a teeming trade with the French West Indian islands which had been opened to their vessels as a matter of expediency, and scores of small sloops and schooners were busily trading in that area, bringing in foodstuffs and lumber in exchange for sugar and tobacco. In November, 1793, the British throttled this trade with an Order in Council which ruled that no neutral could trade with France or with any French colony. This was, they said, an order based on the "Rule of 1756"—a relic of the Seven Years' War calculated to keep neutral merchantmen from moving in on colonial trade in time of war and thus nullifying British control of the seas. The principle was debatable, but the guns that enforced it undeniable.

Before the Americans trading in the Caribbean had any intimation that the Order in Council had been issued their ships were being seized by the hundreds. Not only were vessels suspected of trafficking with the French seized but also those sailing for British West Indian ports loaded with foodstuffs—a trade permitted by local proclamations so that the islanders could avoid famine. The Americans, regardless of their destinations, could not win: there were too many British men-of-war, too many penurious British naval officers and officials, all anxious to line their pockets with prize money.

Congress, unable to take offensive action, passed an embargo act intended to prevent American vessels from leaving port, and this act had not been long in effect before the British revoked their Order in Council of November 1793 and issued a new one—an action taken not because of the embargo but because it had suddenly become clear to them that there was no substitute for American vessels as cargo-carriers for the West Indies. Under the new Order in Council only those vessels carrying merchandise directly from the French colonies to Europe could be condemned. With restrictions lifted on trade between the United States and the French West Indies, the Americans took up once more the flourishing business of importing great quantities of coffee and sugar to their home ports, trans-shipping it, and setting out for Europe with it. The British admitted, in principle, that the transshipment in American ports broke the voyage and took the curse of hostile origin off the merchandise, making it truly of neutral origin.

Word of the new Order in Council reached Congress early in April 1794, and that same month Chief Justice John Jay was empowered to negotiate a treaty with the British. Off to London he went, where the British examined him with the care a group of scientists would give to an insect of undetermined species. With clinical precision they put their fingers on his weakness—vanity. Jay was outrageously vain, and being easily flattered he was charmed to hear that while the British did not agree with him, they nonetheless admired graciously and extravagantly his personal acumen and the wisdom and cogency of his arguments.

The negotiations were completed in November 1794, and the new treaty, in its commercial clauses, represented the limit of the concessions Britain could make without impeding her military and naval operations. By its terms mixed commissions were to rule on the legality of seizures of American vessels; there was to be "a reciprocal and perfect liberty of commerce and navigation" between the United States and the British Empire, in theory. For it did not work out in practice. When the treaty's terms were made public in the United States there were cries of pain and rage from the public, and charges that Jay had been diddled by the nefarious British diplomatists. In the American Senate, after much debate, the treaty was ratified with the sole exception of Article Twelve. This Article granted the Americans the right to direct trade with the British West Indies provided the trade was carried on in vessels of no more than seventy tons burden, and provided, too, that American vessels should not export from the United States any molasses, coffee, sugar, cocoa or cotton—the produce of the West Indian islands. Strictly interpreted this condition would have prevented the tremendously profitable re-export of Caribbean island produce from American ports and for this reason it was rejected by the Senate. The rejection was a matter of indifference to the British, who opened their trade with the West Indies to the Americans (in vessels of less than seventy tons), by executive order because it was both profitable and necessary to the welfare of the islands and the kingdom. The war with France had made it necessary for the Royal Navy to draw heavily on the British merchant marine for seamen, and by taking advantage of the eagerness of the Americans to carry the trade between the West Indies and American ports, while the British retained the direct trade between their colonies and Europe, there was obtained a substantial relief in the need for seamen and ships, and at no great financial loss.

Brig *New Hazard* of Salem (from Reynolds, *The Voyage of the New Hazard*)

Shipyard in Philadelphia, 1800: Building of the Frigate *Philadelphia*

No. 380

United States of America.

I, ISAIAH WESTON, Collector of the District of NEW-BEDFORD, DO HEREBY CERTIFY, That *Alden White*

an AMERICAN SEAMAN, aged *Eighteen* years, or thereabouts, of the height of *Five* feet *8 1/2* inches *Light Complexion largescar outside of the left thigh an anscar on the inside of the left Ankle Born in New Bedford County of Bristol and state of Massachusetts*

Isah. Weston Collr

has this day produced to me proof in the manner directed in the Act, intitled, " An Act for the relief and protection of American Seamen ;" and, Pursuant to the said Act, I DO HEREBY CERTIFY, that he is a CITIZEN of the UNITED STATES of AMERICA.

IN WITNESS WHEREOF, I have hereunto set my Hand and Seal of Office, this *twenty ninth* day of *July 1810.*

"Protection" Issued to Safeguard U.S. Seaman Against Impressment, 1810

Moreover, the British Caribbean possessions were assured of a constant supply of food and lumber and livestock, and of the continuance of the American market for their sugar and coffee. The Americans, for their part, continued to re-export island produce to Europe; and now for the first time they were assured by Jay's treaty of definite contracted rights which, once established, enabled them to make their plans and to carry them out without fear of sudden British attacks, legal or illegal, on their shipping. From 1797 to 1807 relations between Great Britain and the United States, because of this treaty, were kept on an even keel.

The French, already suspicious of American intentions to evade their responsibilities under the 1778 treaty of Alliance, had now further cause to effervesce in a wrathy manner: this Anglo-American treaty clearly favored the maritime supremacy of Britain, at the expense of the French Republic. It placed the United States in the position of being so friendly to Britain that it amounted, in French eyes, to being unneutral. The Americans were, in fact, not disposed to flout the power of Britain, although they had tried to discharge some of their treaty obligations to France: French privateers were fitted out in American ports, and French prizes were brought into American ports; the embargo was lifted and a convoy of 130 merchantmen loaded with provisions had sailed for France from Chesapeake Bay in the spring of 1794, escorted by five French men-of-war, in an effort to ease the famine which threatened France.

The convoy arrived safely in France, but there its value was soon forgotten in the naval disaster which befell the Republic on June 1st, 1784, when the British Channel fleet, under Lord Howe, met and defeated the French fleet under Villaret. From that day on the French navy, vitiated by the lack of discipline and the loss of experienced officers by murder or flight, was worthless as a weapon. By the end of the next year the French Committee of Public Safety was convinced that the fleet could not win a battle, and what remained of it was kept in port, while the crews wandered off to fight on land or to man privateers. And thus in late 1795, despite the contumely they had heaped on the United States because of Jay's treaty, it became more important than ever to France that American ports be kept open to French privateers and their prizes. But why, reasoned the Americans, should the French be favored over the English, at the risk of war, and especially when the British paid for the goods their armed vessels seized, while the French did not?

To the French, confirming their suspicions of Jay's treaty, there soon came incontrovertible proof that the Americans were unfriendly; any remaining doubts vanished when French privateers were warned away from American ports, and it was made clear that France could expect no practical aid from the United States. The French Minister was recalled in November 1796, and President Washington, then nearing the end of his second term, called James Monroe back from Paris, where he had been representing the United States as Minister. Charles Pinckney replaced him, but the French refused to recognize the new Minister, letting him cool his heels in Paris for a month and then summarily ordering him to leave the country. This insult to the United States, coupled with the continued seizures of American vessels by French privateers, created a diplomatic impasse in 1797. There was only one solution—armed force.

Fortunately John Adams, a man with a firm grasp of maritime affairs, took office as President in March 1797, backed by a Federalist majority in both houses of Congress. His plans for a navy moved rapidly forward, with the help of French depredations on American commerce. Relations with France grew progressively worse: France decrees had followed one another with bewildering rapidity, but, in sum, they meant only one thing: ruin for neutrals trading with Britain. Early in March the French Directory passed a decree ruling that Americans serving in British ships would be treated as pirates if captured; that all American vessels had to carry a list of crew members, the "rôle d'équipage" specified in fine print in the 1778 Treaty of Alliance, and that vessels without such lists could be confiscated and their crews jailed. The Americans got the point, after losing scores of vessels, and furnished themselves with "rôles d'équipage." Meanwhile Congress made a muscle, empowering the President to complete and put in commission the frigates *United States, Constitution* and *Constellation,* three of six which had been authorized three years earlier when war with Algiers threatened briefly to make them necessary. But the Algerines had been pacified, and the frigates had become in subsequent years a political football, kicked here and there by the inland anti-Federalists led by Jefferson. Now at last the ships were coming into being, and none too soon, for an American peace commission, consisting of Elbridge Gerry, John Marshall and Pinckney, was undergoing peculiar experiences in Paris.

They had arrived in October, and Talleyrand, the French Foreign Minister, had sent around three ward-heelers who operated under the labels of "X" and "Y" and "Z." They intimated that a bit of bribery was in order; $250,000, say, for Talleyrand, and a loan to France of ten million dollars. That would be enough to call off the privateers and to adjust all matters of disagreement. The Americans, startled and shocked by such callous, realistic diplomacy, rejected the suggestions.

In January 1798, the French government, lacking a legal right to justify the seizure of American vessels now that they carried "rôles d'équipage," decreed that any neutral vessels found at sea with goods produced in Britain or in any British colony were subject to confiscation. In April the American Congress published the detailed record of the peace commission's negotiations with "X," "Y" and "Z," and the public reacted to this exposé with violent demonstrations against France, with profuse professions of loyalty to the federal government, and with yards of bad, although patriotically-inspired, verse. The slogan was "millions for defense, but not one cent for tribute!", and the public's sentiments were quickly transmuted into acts of Congress.

The defense of the nation was at that time entrusted to one department, that of war, and the secretary of war drafted a letter to the appropriate congressional committee recommending, in April, that Congress adopt a plan of armament and defense, including the building of twenty small vessels, and in the event that war was declared, urged Congress to authorize the construction of six ships of the line. Congress was sufficiently impressed to empower President Adams to acquire, by building, purchase or hire, twelve vessels of not more than twenty-two guns each, and to get them to sea. For this purpose an appropriation of $950,-000 was voted. On April 30th a navy department was created; in May Adams was authorized to instruct the commanders of public vessels to capture and send into port any French cruisers, public or private, which might be found along the American coast, and to free whatever American vessels might have been captured by them.

Congress, now in the proper mood, passed law after law to bridle the French privateers with an American naval force: arrangements were made for the condemnation of captured French vessels and for the imprisonment of their crews; the President was authorized to accept twelve more armed vessels which the various states were in course of donating to the cause, and since gifts of that nature were frowned upon, public stock was issued in payment for such vessels. In June the President's good friend Benjamin Stoddert of Maryland, a wealthy merchant, took office as Secretary of the Navy, thoroughly aware of how little he knew about the job, but anxious to learn.

On July 7th, Congress abrogated the 1778 treaty of Alliance with France, and all other conventions with that nation which were still in force; on July 9th American men-of-war were authorized by a crucial order to capture French vessels wherever they might be found, and President Adams was empowered to commission American vessels as privateers and letters-of-marque. The Marine Corps, which had been dissolved with the navy of the revolution, was re-established, and the construction of three more frigates was authorized. The two republics were now thoroughly enmeshed in an undeclared war in the best monarchist manner.

Stoddert was faced with a problem of no mean proportions: he had to improvise a navy after hostilities had begun. Happily he had a wealth of men and ships and material to draw upon. But the only frigates actually at hand were *United States, Constitution* and *Constellation,* all launched the year before, and just now getting ready for sea. Of more immediate value were the state revenue vessels, built from the keel up as armed vessels. Generally these were brigs, of between 150- and 200-tons measurement, carrying ten to fourteen guns and crews of from fifty to seventy men. By the time the big frigates were at sea enough of the revenue vessels had been taken into the federal service to give the organization a patina of professional polish. The nondescript nature of the nation's sea forces was further enhanced by the inclusion of merchantmen; it was comparatively easy to transform them into men-of-war; it simply meant adding more guns, at a sacrifice in speed and sailing qualities, and turning them over to naval commanders. *Ganges,* under Richard Dale, had returned from a voyage to China in the spring of '98; promptly she had been bought and fitted out as a public armed vessel and sent to sea on May 22nd under Dale's command. In June she was followed by *Constellation,* Captain Truxton commanding, and by *Delaware,* Captain Decatur. A few days out of port *Delaware* fell in with the privateer schooner *Le Croyable;* Decatur took her and sent her in for condemnation. *United States* and *Constitution* finally got to sea in July, and others followed until by the end of the year there were twenty-three naval vessels at sea—eight of them ex-merchantmen, eight others former revenue vessels, one the captured *Le Croyable,* now named *Retaliation,* and six bona fide men-of-war built for the business. In addition, some two hundred letters-of-marque had been commissioned, and were at large, carrying their cargoes and enough guns to protect themselves from small privateers.

But John Adams, remembering how the effectiveness of the revolutionary navy had suffered from the competition of the letters-of-marque and privateers for prime seamen, had a phobia about privateers. He took steps to make the new federal navy so attractive that no sober sailor would prefer private service to service in the public armed ships of the nation; sailors in the navy were to be paid fifteen dollars to seventeen dollars a month—seven dollars more than their corresponding ratings could get in the merchantmen; aspirants were ushered around the ships, given a glimpse of the crew's quarters, permitted to feast their eyes on the ration list and lick their chops at the prospect of such fine fare. As an added attraction, they were told, sailors in the federal service shared in all prize money awarded the ships in which they served. With such incentives there was no lack of volunteers, from whom only the best-qualified men were chosen, and ships were fully manned in a matter of hours. Nor was there any lack of officers, many of them with experience in the revolution; others, the young blades, had service in the merchant marine behind them; and dozens of young hopefuls of proud parentage went off to sea as midshipmen. True, a certain amount of political patronage had to be handled, for the good will of Congress was as necessary as guns to the growing fleet. Good, if not the best, men got the best commands: Barry and Truxton and Nicholson skippered the three big frigates; Decatur, Bainbridge, and Preble had to be content with less responsible billets.

The fighting was all to the southward, for the American coast was soon cleansed of enemy privateers and they moved to the West Indies, attracted to the business there like sharks to the slave ships. The Americans set up a system of convoys to protect their merchantmen, and early in August Captain Truxton in *Constellation,* 38, with *Baltimore,* 20, Captain Phillips, went to Havana and escorted a convoy of sixty sail back to their home ports, bilking the French cruisers which had been lying in the harbor at Havana, waiting to pounce on the merchantmen as soon as they left port. *Baltimore* then started off with a convoy bound from Charleston to Havana and en route she fell in with a heavily gunned British squadron which cut out three of her wards, impressed five of her seamen into the King's service (for *Baltimore* had left in such a hurry that she had no commission aboard to prove that she was a United States warship), and made off with the prizes. Throughout the transaction Phillips of *Baltimore* made no fight in defense of his ship and men, and on his return to the United States he went post-haste to Philadelphia to report the whole affair to his government. Forthwith he was dismissed from the service without trial, a sacrifice to the burgeoning nationalism of the young Republic.

Meanwhile a squadron under Commodore John Barry had gone to take up its station in the Caribbean, patrolling the area, protecting American vessels, snapping up privateers wherever they could find them, and in general performing in a highly effective manner. A second squadron, under Commodore Truxton in *Constellation,* 38, gathered at its rendezvous off St. Kitts, and dispersed to patrol its prescribed area. *Constellation,* under Truxton's command, had developed a spirit of its own, a pride of ship unique at that time, and she was a taut ship, hankering for a fight when she met the French frigate *L'Insurgente* five leagues off Nevis on February 9, 1799. After an hour of hard, close fighting, *Constellation* shot out of the smoke, wore round, and hauling athwart the enemy's stern, was in position to rake her with every gun when the Frenchman struck his colors. *L'Insurgente* had lost seventy men—twenty-nine dead, forty-one wounded—while *Con-*

stellation's casualties were only three wounded. News of this victory was most pleasing to the national pride, a fillip was given to the popularity of the service; in the taverns and coffee shops the elders waggled their beards, saying the action was proof that Americans had an aptitude for naval activity.

The tone was set, and the standards defined for the navy by the early incidents: Phillips was the horrible example of what not to do; Truxton the paragon of naval virtue and victorious results. When the squadrons returned in the summer of '99 to discharge their crews, many of whom had shipped for a one-year term only, they had no trouble replacing them. John Adams' fear of losing men to the privateers had been proved groundless: the British had left so few French merchantmen afloat that it did not pay to fit out privateers to look for them. Prize money, the high wages in the navy, and the pride men took in serving in men-of-war, were enough to offset the attractions of the merchant marine, whose men were engaged in adventurous, if not patriotic, doings.

Most fantastic of the pioneer merchant voyages were those of Captain Jonathan Carnes of Salem. While at Bencoolen, on Sumatra, he had learned by chance that pepper grew wild on the island's northwest coast, and on his return home he shared his secret with Jonathan Peele, who built the schooner *Rajah* for him. Carnes armed his new command with four guns, signed on a crew of ten, loaded with iron, dried fish, tobacco and brandy. All this activity was carried on while the ship's destination was kept secret, much to the annoyed curiosity of all Salem. Sailing in late '95, Carnes did not return until the spring of '97, but when he did his schooner was loaded to the hatches with pepper, and the profit on the voyage was 700 per cent. In the same unobtrusive and secretive manner *Rajah* was fitted out for a second trip, and when she set out she was trailed by several hopeful merchantmen who intended to find out where the pepper originated. Carnes gave them the slip, and returned home with another tremendously profitable cargo of pepper. But on the third voyage his source of pepper was discovered and thenceforth he had to be content with a mere 100 per cent profit, and the knowledge that he had initiated a trade that made Salem the center of the world pepper trade, a position the town held for generations.

Rivaling the exploits of Carnes was another Salem product, Richard Cleveland, who at the age of twenty-three, with five years of seafaring behind him, turned up in Le Havre in 1797, determined to make his fortune. Cleveland had a touch of the Mad Hatter in him, and a sublime self-confidence that sustained him in the performance of his wildest notions. At Le Havre he managed to purchase, on credit, a 38-ton cutter, which had been a Calais-Dover packet; coppering her and fitting her out cost him a thousand dollars, half of his capital, and he raised two thousand more from friends to buy a cargo suitable for trading at the Isle of France in the Indian ocean. Hardly had he left port before his vessel encountered a gale and he had to beach her on the French coast. Repaired, and with three new crew members to replace those whom the storm and the beaching had frightened away, Cleveland set out again for Cape Town and the Indian Ocean. The cutter, *Caroline* by name, was manned by a bizarre group of men: first mate was Reuben Barnes of Nantucket, a nineteen-year-old who had been in the whale fisheries and who therefore knew ships from the keel up—a steady, watchful and intelligent man; first of the fore-mast hands was a surly, towering Prussian who had spent eighteen months in a British merchantman, after deserting the Duke of Brunswick's army wherein he had seen enough land fighting; then came the cook, George, a six-foot three-inch tall Negro, black as ebony, who had been a slave in Savannah but who had been given his freedom when he saved his master's life in an attack by an enraged Indian. George was so tall and thin that he was in constant fear of listing so far to port or starboard that he would fall overboard, and to protect himself he never made his way fore or aft without holding on to some support with both hands. The third hand was a seventeen-year-old English boy who had so recently recovered from the small-pox that he was very feeble, as well as being almost blind. Smallest and youngest of the lot was a fourteen-year-old French boy, a faithful replica of a baboon in appearance; he had served in French privateers and learned some horrible oaths in an English prison. With this crew Cleveland reached Cape Town, where he sold the *Caroline* and her cargo, and made his way to Canton. There he bought a cutter not much larger than *Caroline,* picked up a crew of nineteen renegade water-front bums, deserters from men-of-war, deserters from Indiamen, and even two escaped convicts from a Botany Bay prison ship. Cleveland and faithful George, the cook, were the only Americans aboard when the cutter set out for the Northwest coast of America to find a cargo of furs. There was a mutiny and Cleveland put it down; attacks by Indians were fought off; the furs were loaded, and brought back to be sold in Canton. Cleveland was away from Salem for seven and a half years, and on his return, at the age of thirty, he had been around the world twice, and had increased his two thousand dollars to seventy thousand.

In European waters the American merchantmen found adequate profits and excitement during the closing years of the eighteenth century, as Napoleon's lightning-like campaigns shifted from nation to nation. The Americans, nibbling at the periphery of the European trade, could never be sure of any condition other than one of constant hostilities, and a typical voyage was one made by Elias Hasket Derby, Jr., in 1799. Commanding the twenty-gun ship *Mount Vernon* out of Salem, bound for Gibraltar, he made the passage in seventeen and a half days. The first two weeks at sea were uneventful, but as the *Mount Vernon* neared Spain French privateers were constantly in sight. Luckily Derby had a fast ship, for he fell in with a fleet of fifty sail—so many of them that he thought they must be British. They turned out to be French, and after exchanging broadsides with one of them, he came to the conclusion that the odds against him were too great, and he scampered off, chased by the French whom he easily outdistanced. By midnight the rocket signals of the pursuers were almost out of sight. Next day he was chased by two frigates which he lost after nightfall, and then a French lateen-rigged vessel tried to take him, off Cape St. Vincent, chasing him nearly to Cadiz. There being no British fleet at Cadiz, Derby came to the conclusion that the city must be in French hands, so he proceeded toward Gibraltar. Off Algeçiras Point he was attacked by a large lateener of piratical aspect, loaded with over a hundred men. Shotting his guns with six-pound grape, Derby gave them a broadside, then bearing away, poured in fire from his stern guns. The pirate struck his ensign, but Derby had no room for so many captives, and he continued to Gibraltar.

Mount Vernon and her cargo of sugar and coffee had cost the Derbys $43,000, but on this one voyage she made a profit of $100,000 on the original investment.

While the merchantmen were fighting their way to and from foreign ports, to St. Petersburg, the Red Sea, Smyrna, Batavia, India, China, the Northwest coast of America, in the Caribbean the United States Navy had extinguished nearly all the large French privateers. Truxton, still in *Constellation,* was cruising off Guadaloupe on the 1st of February, 1800, when he sighted a heavy French frigate, and set out in chase. Next day he caught up with her, for she was heavily laden, and in a five-hour engagement, running into the dark of the Caribbean night, the Frenchman was thoroughly beaten. She turned out to be the *Vengeance,* 54 guns to *Constellation's* 38, and she was so shot up, having taken 188 round shot in her hull, and suffered the loss of 50 men killed and 110 wounded, that she barely made port in Curaçao. *Constellation* lost twenty-five dead and fourteen wounded, had her mainmast shot out of her, and Truxton got her into Jamaica for repairs. News of the fight clinched his reputation as the nation's leading naval officer, and the Congress presented him with a special gold medal in token of the national esteem and trust.

The French were gradually coming to realize that they were suffering more from the loss of the trade which the Americans had formerly carried for them than they were gaining by fighting the American warships in the Caribbean; and Talleyrand began to offer tentative explanations of the peculiar behavior of the Messieurs "X," "Y" and "Z," whose dealings with the American peace commission had precipitated the fighting. The naval engagements had gone almost unnoticed in a France fully occupied by Napoleon's thundering campaigns, and with most of the big French privateers taken, the business was left to small ones, called picaroons, little better than pirates, not really worthy of representing France.

Stoddert had been worried about these picaroons: they were an infernal nuisance, many of them little more than rowboats, but when an American trading schooner lazed in a sun-hammered Caribbean calm, she was easy picking for a picaroon. The big American frigates, the smaller corvettes, and the converted merchantmen were no use in work against them: they were too slow, drew too much water to work inshore, and there were not enough of them. The frigates were fast for their class —none faster afloat than *Constitution*—but they could not chase every lateen-rigged lugger into its cove. Something new was needed, and Stoddert ordered two light, fast vessels built—*Enterprise* and *Experiment*—and sent them down to the islands in late '99, to convoy American ships and to try their metal against the picaroons. Both vessels were schooner-rigged, built on the eastern shore of Maryland along the lines of the Baltimore craft which, in turn, had been modeled after those French privateer-luggers common in American waters during the American Revolution. It is doubtful if there were any faster vessels afloat than *Enterprise* and *Experiment,* and yet they were light enough to be moved by sweeps, for all that they carried twelve long sixes, a species of gun that preceded the use of the light carronade.

Experiment made her first cruise under the command of Lieutenant-Commander Maley, and began convoying shipping through the narrow passages of the West Indies, where vessels were exposed to attacks by large barges manned from the shore. Near the start of 1800 she was becalmed in the Bight of Leogane, with several sail of merchantmen in convoy. Out from shore came ten barges, filled with Negroes and mulattoes, thirty to fifty of them to each boat, all armed with muskets, cutlasses and pikes, and in some of the boats light guns and swivels. Thinking *Experiment* a merchantman, they attacked her and were beaten off with grape-shot, but went on to take two of the convoy which were too far off for *Experiment* to protect. Twice the barges went to the shore, landed their killed and wounded, took on replacements, and twice *Experiment* routed them. After seven hours of intermittent fighting the picaroons, having lost two of their barges and suffered many casualties, retreated. *Experiment* attempted to follow, using her sweeps in the dead calm, but she was obliged to give up the chase in order to continue watch over her convoy.

Enterprise, twelve guns and seventy-six men, had fallen in with battered *Constellation,* as that frigate was making her way into Jamaica after her fight with *Vengeance,* and Truxton sent the schooner to Philadelphia with dispatches. Not until March was she back in the Caribbean, and while working her way toward St. Kitts, rendezvous of the

Windward Squadron, she met a large brig off the Mona Passage. Setting out in chase, with her American ensign flying, *Enterprise* caught up with the stranger, who unfurled Spanish colors, and opened fire on the schooner. This was most impolite, for Spain and the United States were at peace: so *Enterprise* poured a broadside into the brig, counted her guns—eighteen of them—and after exchanging fire for twenty minutes the vessels separated, as though by reason of mutual respect. The captain of *Enterprise,* who could not endure being fired on without returning the fire, no matter what flag the aggressor flew, was Lieutenant-Commander John Shaw, twenty-seven years old, an American by preference. He was born in Ireland, of English parentage, and since his father had sired more progeny than he could with his pay as a British cavalry officer conveniently maintain, a family council of war was held, and John, with an older brother, sailed for New York in 1790 to make their fortunes in the new world. John Shaw went on to Philadelphia, then the political capital and largest town in the infant republic, delivered various letters of introduction, decided he would make the sea his calling for he had acquired a taste for the life on the trip to America. He had no trouble obtaining a berth on an Indiaman and in the next six years he made four trips to China, during the second of which, in *Sampson,* the ship was attacked by Malay proas in the Straits of Banca, after night had fallen. Six four-pounders chased the proa-men off, but the action was spirited and bloody. Studying hard, Shaw made third officer on his third trip to Canton, and on the fourth he went out as first officer. With four voyages to China to his credit, Shaw was well qualified for a command of his own, and early in '98 he was in the West Indies, master of a Baltimore brig. Returning to Baltimore that spring, after undergoing some insolent treatment by the French in the Caribbean, he found the country on the verge of war with France. Dale was out in *Ganges,* and there was no time to lose; influential friends in Baltimore applied to the Navy Department in his behalf and he was commissioned a Lieutenant, at the age of twenty-five, ordered to *Montezuma,* in which he served until late in '99, chasing and being chased by privateers, convoying and cruising in the Caribbean. He had been at sea nine years, and the year of active service in a man-of-war, added to his experience in merchantmen, had made him a master of his profession when he took command of *Enterprise* that fall, as a Lieutenant-Commander.

After the brush with the Spaniard, *Enterprise* kept on patrolling, looking for a worthwhile opponent. In quick succession she took *La Citoyenne,* six guns; *La Seine,* six; *L'Aigle,* ten; *La Pauline,* six; *La Guadaloupéenne,* seven: all smaller, lighter vessels, some of which hardly fought back long enough to warm up *Enterprise's* guns. *L'Aigle* fought well at first but her crew's nerve failed when the Americans boarded: it was difficult to understand—all the crew of *L'Aigle* had suddenly gone down the scuttle and were below deck—until Shaw found out that one of his round shot had glanced off the top of the French captain's head, half-scalping him and knocking him out; another shot had gone directly through the center of the French lieutenant's chest; and a third had grazed the side of the third lieutenant's head, taking off part of one ear and much of the skin, spinning him senseless to the deck. This, her man said, was the luck of the *Enterprise:* no one was brash enough to claim that they had aimed individual cannon balls at *L'Aigle's* officers.

Not until near the end of her cruise did the schooner meet an enemy worthy of her 165 tons and twelve guns: the unlucky ship was the privateer *Flambeau,* a brig mounting twelve guns and throwing heavier metal than *Enterprise,* and manned by a crew of one hundred and ten, compared to eighty-three in the American schooner. In a running, close-range battle that lasted only forty minutes, *Enterprise* forced the Frenchman to strike, and found aboard her forty men killed or wounded. *Enterprise* herself had ten casualties, but this was one of the hottest actions of the war, and it crowned the reputation of the ship and her commander. *Flambeau* was taken into St. Kitts as prize and because *Enterprise* had taken a vessel of superior force, the whole amount, instead of the usual half, of the prize money went to her officers and men. Thus far, in eight months, *Enterprise* had captured six enemy vessels, recaptured eleven American merchantmen, and now Shaw was ordered home, suffering from dysentery. He reached Washington early in January, 1801, to find peace with France was at hand.

Secretary Stoddert could look back on his work with pride; besides setting up the sea-going navy, he had begun a shore establishment, stretching the meaning of Acts of Congress to the breaking point in spite of the screams of the Jeffersonians. In 1799 Congress had appropriated one million dollars toward the construction of six great 74-gun ships-of-the-line: $200,000 more for a reserve of timber and forest lands for future naval use; and $20,000 for the construction of two dry-docks. Broadly interpreting the Congressional intent, Stoddert, with Adams' backing, bought land for navy yards at Norfolk, Washington, Philadelphia, New York, Boston and Portsmouth, N.H. Work on the six seventy-fours was started, and in late 1800 Stoddert began making the navy taut, drawing up a new Naval Code which included scourging, cutting out the dead wood in the naval establishment, recommending a peacetime organization which he hoped would survive the hostility of the incoming Jeffersonians. There was still a slim Federalist majority in both Houses of Congress, but the bill that came out of Congress made it permissible to cut the navy to the bone when peace came and if the Jeffersonians so desired.

The President was empowered to discharge all but nine of thirty captains and commanders, all but thirty-six lieutenants (a reduction of 75 per cent); only 150 midshipmen were to be kept in service. Those discharged were to be given four months pay, and those retained were to get full pay only when on active duty. In other words, they would have to work for their money. And the President was authorized to sell all but thirteen of the nation's men-of-war; if he chose to do so, he could decommission seven of those thirteen.

Peace with France was ratified on February 3rd, 1801, ending the war that had never been declared, and the adjustment of the navy to peace was left for the incoming administration to handle. Thomas Jefferson took office in March; Stoddert was replaced by Robert Smith of Maryland, as Navy Secretary. The new Secretary, of a paunchy shipping family, turned out to be indolent, of little use or influence in naval matters. Jefferson was inclined to think that navies were a necessary evil: how necessary he could not quite decide. But Gallatin, his Swiss-born Secretary of the Treasury, had a more positive approach to the matter; he wanted to balance the budget, and this couldn't be done with a large naval establishment to support. Therefore, reduce the navy, cut it to fit the budget, and everything would be solved. All that had to be done was to act along the lines so thoughtfully indicated by the out-going administration: all but fourteen of the nation's thirty-four men-of-war were sold, and seven of those retained were decommissioned; *Enterprise* was saved—she was a national pet: work on the six ships-of-the-line was discontinued; navy yard activity was restricted to the accumulation of materials for use in case of emergency; officers and men were discarded by the hundreds. Jefferson even proposed a novel plan: why not build a huge shed in Washington and haul the navy up under it, safe from salt water? Damned nuisance, navies, thought the Jeffersonians—cost a lot of money and went around fighting at the drop of a hat.

The shed plan was never carried out, even though it did look like a good time to economize: the Napoleonic wars were winding down, articles preliminary to the Peace of Amiens having been signed in the fall of 1801. Clearly, Britain and France were intent on peace and no one could foretell that the peace would last only eighteen months. The world in late 1801 was in a relatively quiet mood, and for the United States there were only a few small dark clouds on the seaward horizon. In the spring of the year, news had filtered across the ocean to America that Spain had ceded Louisiana to France by secret treaty, having already given her half of Santo Domingo. But what about Florida? Was that included in the transfer? No one could be sure.

A tremor of apprehension shook the government when Napoleon, assured by the preliminary peace treaty with Britain of some freedom of action at sea, sent a great expedition of twenty thousand men and over twenty ships-of-the-line to re-establish French authority in Haiti in December 1801. The island had been in the hands of rebellious slaves ruled by Toussaint L'Ouverture, who had even negotiated a treaty with the British, and now it was time to bring the island back into the fold. Twenty thousand men were hardly enough: they died like flies from yellow fever and were killed by hundreds in the jungle fighting. By 1803 they held at most a few ports, and their nearest sure base of supply was Louisiana. But in war or peace, the Americans were uneasy at the presence of such a force in the new world, on their doorstep, under the power of the highly volatile and unpredictable Napoleon. Jefferson sent word to his resident minister in Paris, Robert Livingston, to open negotiations with France for the purchase of Louisiana, and dispatched James Monroe to help him. In April 1803, the French position in Haiti was hopeless: renewal of war with Britain impended, and in that event the French forces in Haiti would be caught between the black rebels and the British warships. Louisiana, useful to Napoleon only as a means of support of his forces in Haiti, would become worthless, cut off by British sea power. With Haiti all but lost, Louisiana was a liability to Napoleon: there was even a good chance that Britain would take it over, for it was poorly defended and the London papers talked of an expedition of fifty thousand men. At this point Napoleon decided to sell, Monroe arrived in Paris, and the details of the deal were settled by April 30th: the whole of Louisiana as Spain had possessed it was sold to the United States for sixty million francs—twelve million dollars. Sixteen days later France and Britain were again at war, for Britain could not bring herself to give up Malta to the Knights of St. John as she had agreed to do; but Louisiana was no longer fair prey, and the province's forty thousand inhabitants came under the protection of the American Constitution.

Jefferson faced a second problem involving sea power at the start of his administration. This one was in the Mediterranean, where the Pasha of Tripoli, having become dissatisfied with the tribute paid him by the United States, declared war on May 14, 1801 in the accepted Turkish fashion—by cutting down the flagstaff at the American consulate—and loosing his corsairs on the American merchantmen in the Mediterranean. For years, ever since shortly after the close of the Revolutionary war, the United States had paid tribute to the Barbary States—Algiers, Tunis, Morocco and Tripoli—in order to enable American ships to trade peacefully and unmolested in the Mediterranean. Every maritime nation in Europe likewise paid tribute, and if in addition the nations had powerful navies, the corsairs left their ships alone. But small nations, weak in sea power, suffered: for if the corsairs had no merchantmen to capture, what could they be expected to do for a living? American ships were in the same class as Danish ships, as far as they were concerned, treaties and tribute notwithstanding. In this view the corsairs had the enthusiastic support of Britain, which operated on the theory that any damage done to the trade of other nations would be to the benefit of British trade.

Jefferson added up the score, pro and con: peace was nice to have; but in ten years the United States had paid close to two million dollars in tribute to the Barbary States; it might be cheaper in the long run to fight them now; the navy, small as it was, was eating its head off, doing nothing; why not send it to the Mediterranean? It would not cost much more, and it might accomplish something. So, when war seemed certain early in May, Jefferson sent out Commodore Richard Dale in 44-gun *President*, with *Philadelphia*, 38; *Essex*, 32; and little *Enterprise*, 12.

The squadron's wings were clipped by their instructions: since Congress had not declared war, activity was restricted to "spirited defense"; when *Enterprise* took a Tripolitanian poleacre the pirate's guns were thrown overboard and she was told to move along. About all the squadron could do was to give protection to American merchantmen bound for Leghorn or Malta, and this service they performed in a routine manner. Dale was ordered home late in 1801, and Richard Morris became commodore, flying his broad command pennant in *Constellation*, with five other vessels in his squadron. An Act was passed by Congress, authorizing the seizure and destruction of the ships and property of the Barbary States, but still not declaring war. Even with that authority, Morris could accomplish nothing; he was recalled, his inept performance examined by a board of inquiry, and he was dismissed from the service.

Two years of failure were beginning to tell on Jefferson; he was politically embarrassed, and it was decided to carry on the war more energetically; to this end, Edward Preble was ordered to hoist his broad command pennant in *Constitution*, and he sailed from Boston, August 13th, 1803, for Gibraltar, where he was to pick up the rest of his squadron:

> *Philadelphia*, 38—Captain Bainbridge
> *Argus*, 16—Lieutenant Hull
> *Siren*, 16—Lieutenant Stewart
> *Vixen*, 12—Lieutenant Smith

Nautilus, 12—Lieutenant Somers
Enterprise, 12—Lieutenant Decatur.

Argus and *Siren* were new, fast brigs; *Vixen* and *Nautilus* new schooners, built in the spring of '03, about 160 tons each, with crews of from 75 to 95 men. By chance, all the vessels were wonderfully well commanded: Stewart, Smith, Somers and Decatur were all under twenty-five years old; with the exception of Preble all the ship captains were unmarried, and most of them were intimate friends, having grown up in the service together. The navy was all their present life and all the future.

They didn't like the cut of Preble's jib at first: too much discipline, no warmth, a man subject to black rages, and where had he come from, anyhow? True, he had commanded *Pickering* in the West Indies in '98 and '99, had not accomplished much with her; then he had taken *Essex* out to the China seas, convoying merchantmen without notable incident during the last part of the trouble with France. His reputation dated from an age they could scarcely imagine—the American Revolution, when Preble was known as a wild, impetuous fighting man, and men spoke of his cold nerve and his consuming hatred of the British in reverent tones in the taverns. Now here he was in command of a crack squadron, pacing up and down the quarterdeck, silent, tough, sour, exacting—a product of the New England soil, his character a distillate of the age, molded as inevitably as a gun in its casting. The old-timers knew about him.

Edward Preble was born in 1761, in Falmouth, Maine—that same town the British under Captain Mowat had burned in 1775. As a boy he showed considerable spirit; the neighbors said he had "a bit of the brigadier" in him—that is, he took after his father, an irascible old general of the militia. There was much poverty in Maine in '77 and '78, and the old brigadier was forced one summer to muster his five sons and set them to work digging potatoes in the family fields: Edward suddenly threw down his hoe, declared he would do no more such work, and ran away to sea, shipping out on a letter of marque bound for Europe. On his return, in spite of a severe trip, he decided to follow the sea as a career, and his father obtained a commission for him as a midshipman in the Massachusetts State naval forces, in early 1779. Preble was ordered to *Protector,* Captain Williams commanding, and he was aboard when she fought *Admiral Duff* in a close and sharp encounter that ended when *Duff* exploded. It was while he was on *Protector* that he saw the sea serpent: the ship was lying in one of the bays of the eastern coast, waiting for the rest of a squadron, on a clear and calm day, when a large serpent was discovered lying quite motionless on the water. Captain Williams studied it for some time with the glasses, then ordered Preble to take a boat and to destroy the creature. Midshipman Preble armed twelve men as boarders, and with them manned a large boat that had a swivel in its bows; they shoved off and pulled directly toward the monster, which was about one hundred and fifty feet long and thick as a barrel. As the boat neared it, the serpent raised its head about ten feet above the water, looking about it. Then it began to move slowly away from the boat. Preble pushed on, his men pulling with all their force, and the serpent being not far away, the swivel was loaded with bullets and discharged: the serpent simply increased his speed and soon ran out of sight of the boat. Preble, not a loquacious man, was reluctant to talk about the incident in later years, for the scientists had even then proved to their own satisfaction that such things could not be.

Protector took part in the fatal expedition Saltonstall led to the Penobscot, and there Preble was captured by the British, taken to New York and thrown into the prison-hulk *Jersey*. He was placed on parole, allowed to go ashore, and finally exchanged for a British officer. Returning to Boston he found a berth as first lieutenant in another state cruiser, the *Winthrop,* Captain Little commanding. In her Preble made his reputation: word came to Captain Little of a large armed brig lying in the bay at Penobscot, and he resolved to take her while she lay at anchor; Preble as first lieutenant was to lead the boarding party of forty men, but *Winthrop* came alongside the brig at such a clip that only fourteen men managed to make the brig's deck, Preble with them. Little called out to ask if he should send more men, and Preble replied, "No— I have too many already!"—a remark that broke the spirit of the British. By this time the gunners of the British shore batteries were awake, and Preble had to work his prize out to sea under a brisk fire. He fought out the rest of that war in *Winthrop,* and when the navy of the revolution was discarded in 1783, he was discharged, at the age of twenty-two, and went into the merchant marine. It was when the French war began in 1798 that he applied for a commission and was given command of *Pickering.* That was about all the squadron knew about him at Gibraltar in the fall of 1803, and the reputation was difficult to square with the man; they had to see him in action to believe it all.

Preble did not keep them waiting long: shortly after he arrived at Gibraltar in *Constitution,* and was cruising nearby at night, a strange man-of-war was sighted close at hand. *Constitution* beat to quarters and closed, both vessels hailing each other. Preble ordered the name and nationality of his vessel to be given to the stranger, and in return to demand the identity of the stranger, under penalty of getting a shot if the demand were refused. The stranger answered that he would answer a shot with a broadside, and this insolence was too much for Preble: he sprang up into the mizzen rigging himself, seized a trumpet and roared, "This is the United States ship *Constitution,* 44, Commodore Edward Preble. I am about to hail you for the last time; if you do not answer I will give you a broadside. What ship is that? Blow your matches, boys!"

Back across the black water came the answer: "This is His Britannic Majesty's ship *Donnegal,* 60 guns!" Preble shouted he didn't believe it, that he would stick by him until morning to see for himself. A boat soon came from the stranger, explaining everything: she was the frigate *Maidstone* and had given a false name to allow her people time to get to their guns in case of trouble.

Word ran through Preble's squadron: "If the old man's temper is wrong, his heart is right!"; he had been ready to take on a British ship of the line with 44-gun *Constitution,* and that meant he lacked nothing, for he was obviously a masterly ship captain. Now he was getting the good will of the squadron. They knocked about in the Mediterranean; renewed the treaty with Morocco, visited Cadiz, notified Tripoli that they had started a blockade of the coast, put a consul ashore at Algiers, went to Malta. In Malta Preble received heart-breaking news: *Philadelphia* had run on a reef in a chase off Tripoli, had lowered her colors to the barbarians, and—worse yet—the Tripolitanians had re-floated her and brought her into port where she was anchored under the guns of the forts. Bainbridge, and all her crew were prisoners. The loss rankled and was hard to bear; Preble sailed down to reconnoiter the harbor at Tripoli, and to make a show of his force. Bainbridge suggested, in a smuggled letter, that *Philadelphia* could be burned at anchor in the harbor, and Preble agreed. A captured ketch, named *Intrepid,* was turned over to Stephen Decatur, loaded with men, and with *Siren* as escort the ketch set out for Tripoli to take and burn the captured *Philadelphia*. Preble waited fifteen days for them in Syracuse, Sicily, and when *Siren* came in sight she was flying the signal of success. Decatur in *Intrepid* with his eighty-four men had boarded the *Philadelphia* at night as she lay under the guns of the forts in Tripoli, with two hundred men aboard, and they had routed the natives, laid their demolition charges and were running out of the harbor when *Philadelphia* exploded in sheets of flame.

Preble worked *Constitution* hard, in and out of various ports, convoying, official visits, chasing corsairs. No one could blockade Tripoli effectively in the winter—it was always a lee shore that time of year, but in July, 1804, Preble was ready to attack.

On July 25th he was before Tripoli with fifteen sail—everything he could get together: one frigate, three brigs, three schooners, along with two bomb ketches and six gunboats borrowed from the King of Sicily, who was also at war with the Pasha of Tripoli. 1060 Americans manned the ships, and they faced a well-defended city, 118 guns in fixed fortifications, 19 gunboats, a brig, 2 schooners and 2 galleys. The Pasha's fighting men numbered between twenty and thirty thousand and they were not to be taken lightly: although indifferent gunners, they were well-built, bold in battle and with fearful reputations in hand-to-hand combat; no officer was anxious to let those blood-thirsty, death-seeking pagans get over his plank sheer with their scimitars.

Preble was getting ready to bombard when a gale blew up and dispersed the fleet; August 3rd he was back again and the battle opened. The enemy gunboats came out, were met in a hammer-and-tongs engagement and driven into port. Four times in the next thirty days the Americans came back to bombard the town, maintaining a close blockade when they were not actually fighting. By September 4th the Pasha was morose and jumpy, making a nuisance of himself in the harem, and he offered terms. His people were hungry and no one know what the mad Americans would do next. Preble rejected the terms; he had another ace to play.

The night, the ketch *Intrepid,* which had been loaded with fifteen thousand pounds of powder and some two hundred shells, moved toward the port, manned by thirteen volunteers, commanded by twenty-five-year-old Richard Somers. A powder-train had been laid to set off the explosion in the inner harbor, while the crew was to make its escape in two accompanying boats. Soon the ketch came under the fire of the Pasha's batteries, and two galleys closed to investigate her. At this moment a light was seen on *Intrepid's* deck, as though someone were carrying a lantern along hurriedly. Half a minute later a tremendous flash illuminated the harbor, a burning mast, with its sails, was seen in the air, and the roar of the explosion swept out to sea. Later the thirteen bodies of the volunteers were found, those of the officers identified by the lack of callouses on their hands, and Preble reported that Somers had blown up his ship rather than submit to capture. There is no doubt that Somers had a premonition of death, and that he was capable of such an extreme act of heroism, but, more likely the lantern bobbing along the deck was being carried below to investigate damage from the shore batteries, and the powder-train was set off by accident, before anyone could attempt to escape in the boats.

Preble was making ready for another attack when the northers set in; keeping three men-of-war off Tripoli to maintain the blockade, he sent the rest of the squadron to Sicily. On the 10th his relief, Commodore James Barron, hove in sight and Preble left to settle his accounts at Malta, Syracuse, Palermo and Messina before sailing for home. He left behind him in Tripoli an abashed Pasha, willing to give up all claims to tribute, and to scale down the ransom for the American prisoners. The Bey of Tunis, impressed by Preble's campaign and the growing strength of the American squadron, was willing to follow suit; Algiers became less voracious.

Barron had brought out with him an agent empowered to negotiate a treaty, Colonel Tobias Lear by name, and the colonel was as eager to pacify Tripoli with his diplomacy as the naval officers were with their guns. Barron, in desperately poor health, relinquished his command to John Rodgers on May 22nd, 1805, and the negotiations continued, with Lear holding out the olive branch. Finally he accepted the Pasha's terms: no more tribute and three hundred dollars ransom for each American prisoner. It was rank appeasement, but the squadron had to accept Lear's decision, and peace was finally signed in June, when the Pasha assembled his eight-man council and put the question: "War, or peace?" The vote was four for peace, four for war: the Pasha broke the tie, hauling his signet out of his clothes and sealing the treaty as he said, with resigned dignity, "It is peace."

Even the Pope was jubilant: his coasts were particularly exposed to the ravages of the African corsairs; he had lined them with towers to repel their raids, and now his temporal realm could have a respite from their inroads. Publicly he proclaimed that the Americans had done more to suppress the barbarians than all the rest of Christendom combined. The victory and the glory were all Preble's: he was wined and dined by everyone; Congress gave him a gold medal and a sword; Jefferson asked his advice and offered to make him Navy Secretary, but ill health prevented him from accepting further public service. He had won a difficult campaign, at a cost of only thirty men killed and twenty-four wounded, and more important, he had given the navy a new and high pride in itself, and had taught the young bucks, Decatur and Hull, Stewart and Chauncey and Trippe, a lesson in sound planning coupled with infinite courage. And he had taught them selflessness: none of them ever forgot it.

[10] *Gropings*

In the spring of 1805 the Americans had cause to beat their chests and make the proud noises symptomatic of a no longer incipient nationalism: their navy had earned its salt; their merchant marine was in a period of forced growth that had the shipowners and traders giddy with joy. Jefferson was re-elected by a great majority, carried into office on the wave of prosperity and optimism.

The nation had even produced a man of undoubted mathematical genius—Nathaniel Bowditch of Salem, Massachusetts—whose work in the field of navigation was bringing him increasing renown both at home and in Europe. Bowditch, born in 1773, had been exposed to formal schooling for only a brief period. He was of an impoverished family and at the age of twelve had gone to work for a ship chandler in Salem. In the shop he encountered algebra and at first glance he became fascinated; within a few years he had achieved a local notoriety in matters mathematical. Meanwhile there had come to Salem treasure in the form of the library of Dr. Richard Kirwan, of Cloughballymore, Ireland, albeit through no fault of the learned doctor. He had sent his library on its way to London in the fall of 1780, on board a merchant vessel, and an American privateer at large in those waters had seized the ship as a prize and absconded with the books. The privateer got safely home to Beverly, Massachusetts, and among the selected parts of cargoes she had taken from prizes was the library of Dr. Kirwan. News of the forthcoming sale of the books spread to Salem, where a group of literate merchants joined forces, bought the books, and with them founded the Salem Atheneum's library. Bowditch was given the run of the library, and he absorbed knowledge from Kirwan's books like a parched seaman guzzles rum of high proof; he was in his element at last, with access to such works as Hamilton's Conics, Emerson's Mechanics, and numerous enchanting Mathematical Papers of the Royal Society, of which Kirwan had been a member. The student copied book after book by hand so that he might carry their contents to sea with him, and to sea he had to go for there was no other way for him to make a living. He was twenty-two years old when he first shipped as a captain's clerk on the Salem merchantman *Henry,* bound for Mauritius, and this voyage marked the beginning of nine years at sea on various vessels. During that time he worked on his mathematics and applied his knowledge of figures to the practical problems of navigating a ship. He came to know the constellations of the Pacific and the North Atlantic oceans intimately and since the duties of a captain's clerk were neither exacting nor exhausting he had enough idle time to teach the crews celestial navigation, and, as a form of mental relaxation, to pick up several foreign languages. In 1801 he finished the work that was to be the cause of his celebrity, a work called "The New American Practical Navigator." It was not, strictly speaking, an original effort: an Englishman, John Hamilton Morse, had written a navigation handbook and Bowditch had taken this handbook and corrected over eight thousand errors in it, many of them of a nature perilous to the mariners who used it. The revision was so thorough that the American product was in effect a different book, although still faintly resembling the original. Bowditch published his "Practical Navigator" in 1802, under his own name, and since it was an unrivaled aid to navigators few vessels, British or American, went to sea without a copy. Soon "The Practical Navigator" was being used by the Russians and the Swedes and the French as word of the book's value spread among the maritime nations of Europe, where a genius in another field of human endeavor was hard at work.

In Europe Napoleon's Grand Army moved lightning-like to Ulm, defeated the Austrian general, Mack, and six weeks later routed the Russian and Austrian main forces at Austerlitz; in the interval between the land battles, Vice-Admiral Lord Nelson defeated the combined fleets of France and Spain off Cape Trafalgar and then expired on HMS *Victory* with gratifying heroism, at 4:30 P.M. by *Victory's* time, October 21st, 1805. Of this battle a sailor wrote to his father, saying "I bid Fear kiss my bottom, and set to in good earnest . . ." and "We have taken a rare parsel of ships, but the wind is so rough we cannot bring them home, else I should roll in money, so we are busy smashing 'em, and blowing 'em up wholesale. . . ." From Trafalgar on, in the rigid declension of the years, Britain's faith in her navy was adamant and the age-old rivals poured their energies into fighting on the elements on which they had won their greatest victories—the French on land and the British on the sea. Napoleon's armies drove on in their endless fight for the revolutionary ideal, opposing all the ancient forms of government—the Prussian monarchy, the Papacy, the House of Hapsburg, Russia, aristocratic Britain—while the British, weather permitting, ruled the seas. The

French sent out their cruisers and privateers, splendidly-built, swift vessels, to prowl for British merchantmen; the British reacted by barring French merchantmen from the oceans.

Into this chaotic war of giants sailed the American merchantmen, willing to do business with either side, their hatches open to the highest bidder. By 1805 the bulk of the Atlantic trade was in American hands, and even Spanish gold and silver from the mines in Mexico and Peru was being brought to Spain in American ships; fleets of Yankee merchantmen carried the products of the French and Dutch and Spanish islands in the Caribbean, and of Batavia and the Philippines, to the United States. There the cargoes were landed to make them neutral in conformity with British rules, and re-shipped to Hamburg, Copenhagen, Lisbon, Emden, Cadiz and Antwerp, where they were exchanged for manufactured goods. There seemed to be no end to the transfers of the vessels of European nations to the safety of American flag and registry; in no other way save by this escape to the protection of neutral ownership could they hope to avoid capture by the British. American tonnage in foreign trade rose to a total of 744,224 tons in 1805—an increase in two years of 158,312 tons—and 91 per cent of all American trade was carried in American vessels.

The British took a jaundiced view of the whole situation: not only were they losing a market for their manufactured goods as the Americans imported goods made on the continent of Europe, they were also permitting a rival merchant marine to grow with unnatural rapidity. And there was a legal question involved: were these importations of French and Dutch and Spanish colonial produce into American ports, and then their subsequent export, really carried out in good faith? Too often, it was suspected, the voyages between such colonies and their mother countries were broken by a stop in American ports simply to take the curse of hostile origin off the cargoes. By coming home, unloading the cargo, putting up bond for the customs duties, making a few trifling repairs, and re-loading the cargo, an American could claim that his cargo originated in the United States and was therefore—as neutral property—not legally susceptible of seizure. The British admitted the neutral character of such cargoes, but they also suspected the Americans of widespread abuse of the principle, for it was common knowledge that the Yankees were sharp customers, tricky dealers, ready to sell their grandmothers for a Spanish dollar.

A decision in the High Admiralty Court came in May 1805, fired like a warning shot across the bows of a ship. *Essex,* a merchantman of Salem registry, had sailed out of Barcelona to Salem, landed her cargo there, paid duties on the goods, undergone minor repairs, loaded the same cargo and sailed for Havana. Off Morro Castle she was seized by the British and the case brought before the Admiralty Court for adjudication. According to the precedent established in previous cases it was reasonable to suppose that *Essex* would be freed, and great was the surprise and consternation along the American seaboard when she was condemned, on the grounds that the cargo was never intended for the American market, that the stop at Salem was only a pretence since the duties paid had been almost wholly returned.

Confronted with this decision, many American merchants simply abandoned such a risky business and put their ships to work in trade with Britain. Others of more valiant spirit, calculating that the higher prices they could get for their cargoes in European ports made such voyages worth hazarding, ignored the ruling and kept clearing their vessels for the continent, trusting to their speed and guns to evade search and seizure.

To make sure that the Americans were obeying the rules, British men-of-war hovered off American ports, making a close examination of every vessel in a zealous effort to find some irregularity in the ships' papers which would justify sending her into Halifax for condemnation. On a clear spring evening in April 1806 the sloop *Richard,* an unarmed coaster, was sailing blithely along off Sandy Hook when she was hailed and a warning shot fired over her bows by HMS *Leander,* a frigate. A second shot followed, and as *Richard* was heaving to, a third shot decapitated the helmsman, John Pierce, a popular man in Manhattan. Next morning *Richard* made New York and as news of the incident spread from the waterfront throughout the town, the rage of the burghers knew no limits. Boats from the British men-of-war were chased out of the harbor; British naval officers fled from the mobs; a grand jury decided that Captain Whitby, of *Leander,* was guilty of murder, and early in May President Jefferson ordered his arrest should he ever be found inside the United States.

Regardless of anti-British sentiment in the public mind, the resurgence of American shipping remained contingent on continued obedience to British rules and regulations, and soon the British were impelled, by Napoleon's successes, to extend their blockade of the continent to include all ports between the Elbe and Brest. No neutral ships could enter any port between Ostend and the Seine; only if they carried neutral or British cargoes could they trade in ports included in the extended blockade. In October 1806, Napoleon broke the Prussian army at Jena; next month he was in Berlin, where he issued a decree proclaiming a blockade of the British Isles. There was no French navy to put such a blockade into effect, but the decree gave an aura of legality to the seizure of any ship sailing to British ports, and the French privateers took many prizes under its authority.

Caught thus between two fires—the British Orders in Council and Napoleon's Berlin Decree—the American politicians raged and debated, pro-French Jeffersonians versus pro-British Federalists. In April, Congress had passed an act (but did not put it into effect immediately), called Nicholson's Non-Importation Bill, which forbade the buying of goods in Britain that could be bought elsewhere. Still the British and the French persisted in treating the United States as a punching bag, to be attended to in idle moments, not really worth bothering about in the midst of a major war. In January 1807 another Order in Council was issued, ruling that no trade with any ports under French control would be permitted. By a process of elimination, the only nations in Europe that Americans could trade with were Britain and Sweden.

Thus matters stood in June 1807, when USS *Chesapeake,* a new frigate of thirty-eight guns, was fitting out for sea at Hampton Roads, taking on guns and stores. Two French frigates were at Annapolis, and a British squadron had gathered in Chesapeake Bay to keep the Frenchmen from getting to sea. While the British were engaged in this duty several of their seamen deserted, and it was suspected that they had signed on as crew members of *Chesapeake.* One of them, from HMS *Halifax,* was reported to have run across a British naval officer on shore and to have insulted him in a verbal exchange that left the officer seething with impotent rage. Vice-Admiral Berkeley, in command of the Halifax station, ordered all his captains, in case of meeting *Chesapeake* at sea, outside her territorial waters, to search her for deserters, and at the same time to offer to have their own vessels searched by the Americans. On June 22nd *Chesapeake,* flying the broad command pennant of Commodore Barron, stood out to sea and HMS *Leopard* of the British squadron, a 50-gun ship, weighed anchor, passing the Capes ahead of *Chesapeake.* About ten miles offshore *Leopard* closed and hailed, saying she had dispatches from the British commander-in-chief, and both ships hove to. *Leopard* sent a boat over with a letter from her captain, attached to Admiral Berkeley's order; after a half an hour's rumination the boat was recalled, and it brought back word that Barron would not submit to a search of his ship, that his crew had been recruited in Boston, that he knew of no deserters from the British squadron on his ship, that his instructions were not to permit his ship's company to be mustered by any but their own officers, and that he hoped the matter could be settled harmoniously. *Leopard* then edged down toward the American frigate, hailed her twice, and received no satisfactory reply, fired a shot across her bows, followed by a second. Repeated hails brought no answer from the American: the *Leopard* fired her broadside. *Chesapeake* was totally unprepared for battle, and after taking three broadsides from *Leopard,* without being able to return the fire, Barron ordered the flag hauled down, and just as it was coming down the Americans managed to get off one harmless symbolic shot. Three British officers, with a party of men, then came aboard *Chesapeake,* mustered her crew, and picked out four men as deserters. Among them was the man from HMS *Halifax,* who had cocked a snoot and enraged a British naval officer, and three American sailors. On *Chesapeake,* as she sailed back to Hampton Roads, there were eighteen wounded and three dead. The affair brought the question of impressment of seamen to a crisis, and fomented a transient broth of energetic nationalism in the United States that transcended all party lines.

As soon as the news of the incident reached Washington, Jefferson issued a proclamation requesting all British warships in American harbors to leave at once, and barring their further entry into American waters, with the exception of vessels bearing dispatches. Instructions were sent to the American Minister in London, James Monroe, to demand reparations and the abandonment of the British practice of impressing seamen: Canning, the British Foreign Secretary, was regretful about the incident but firm in defending the practice of impressment. Discussions between Monroe and Canning were unsatisfactory—the Briton, witty and sardonic, issued squid-like clouds of ink, obscuring the issue in lengthy communications. Monroe was baffled. There was much to be said on either side: thousands of British seamen had deserted their ships, merchantmen and men-of-war, to take advantage of the high American wages and the relative safety of service in neutral vessels. Thirteen years of almost constant war with the French had made severe demands on the manpower of Britain, and press-gangs roamed the streets of British towns, quick to seize any man, drunk or sober, who might be made into a sailor. No matter if you were married and the sole means of support of your family: the King's ships had to be manned, and once aboard a British man-of-war you might as well be in prison, so closely were you watched and guarded while in port. Landsmen and seamen alike hated and feared the press-gangs even more than they did the jail, and at the slightest opportunity, particularly when in American ports, crew members of British men-of-war and merchantmen deserted, swimming ashore at night if necessary, escaping the harsh service of the King. Once ashore in the United States it was not difficult to get protection: there were always Americans who could buy birth certificates for one dollar from a notary, and who would sell them to you for fifteen. By mid-1807 there were unnumbered thousands of British-born seamen aboard American merchantmen and men-of-war; between six and seven thousand others, with some proof of American citizenship, had been taken by force from American ships and were serving in British vessels. It was difficult to tell them apart. They looked alike and spoke the same language, although with different accents. Monroe and Canning argued the matter endlessly and to no avail. The British disavowed the work of *Leopard,* but in October an order went out to all British ships directing them to impress British subjects on neutral vessels. It was an order based on military necessity: Britain was imperiled by Napoleon's defeat of the Russians at Friedland and the Muscovites subsequent inclusion in the Continental system. It was no time for Britain to worry about sea-men's accents, when her very survival was threatened.

Jefferson could not help but recognize the chasm that separated British and American and French interests in late 1807: new Orders in Council restricted American trade even more drastically than before; Napoleon issued his Milan Decree, equally disruptive to neutral commerce, in reply to the Orders in Council. It was time to look to the long-neglected defense of the United States, and Congress passed an appropriation bill of $852,500 for the construction of 188 gunboats, called "Jeffs," because they represented a cherished and derided part of the President's theory of naval defense. Jefferson signed the bill on December 18th.

Gunboats were de rigueur in all European navies, where they were used for inshore work. The United States had imported in 1803 models of those used by the Kingdoms of Spain and of Naples; nine of the craft had been ordered in 1804 and eight of them reached the Mediterranean in time to take part in the final demonstration of strength against the Barbary States in 1805. The ninth was lost at sea without a trace, en route to Gibraltar. These vessels were long, narrow and low, sloop-rigged, armed with one heavy 32-pounder in the bow and another in the stern. Only fifty feet in length, they were manned by a crew of twenty officers and men. With their guns stowed below deck, and provisions for a trans-Atlantic voyage aboard, their gunwales were hardly two feet above the water. Lieutenant James Lawrence, commanding Gunboat #6, en route to the Mediterranean in 1805, had been sighted by a British frigate whose captain thought his craft was a raft manned by survivors of a shipwreck, there being a cloud of canvas and no visible hull.

To Jefferson the gunboats appeared to offer a solution to many problems: they were cheap to build, and that made Gallatin happy; they could be hauled out of the water and stored under sheds when not needed; and they would restrict any offensive warfare that the hot-heads might feel impelled to start, since they were worthless when opposed by any larger man-of-war. They fitted into his plans for a passive coastal defense, along with forts, land batteries and floating batteries. The idea was derivative, could be traced back to Washington's 1775 whaleboat navy at Boston, and it was in harmony with Jefferson's romantic idea of democracy: the seamen for his gunboats were to spring aboard at the first threat of peril to the nation, forming a sort of Minute Men of the sea, and for a man who took his Rousseau seriously, there was a good deal to be said for the whole idea. In 1805 the construction of 25 gunboats had been authorized, in 1806 50 more were ordered; and now, with 188 being built, there would be enough to string along the whole coast, in all the major ports. In case of war he would keep the frigates in port, safe from harm, and use them as receiving ships for crews for the gunboats.

Behind this Chinese Wall, thought Jefferson, the American nation could withdraw, refusing to trade with Britain or the nations in Napoleon's continental system, living in an idyllic and bucolic fashion, the farmers tilling their fields while their wives made the spinning-wheels whir and the cows mooed gently in lush pastures. All that was needed to put the theory into practice was a law. Nicholson's Non-Importation Bill had gone into effect on December 14, 1807; that took care of keeping British goods out. To keep American goods in, Jefferson sent a message to Congress recommending "an inhibition of the departure of our vessels from the ports of the United States"—an embargo, in short— and Congress passed the recommended legislation on December 22nd 1807, prohibiting all exports from the United States by sea or land.

By means of these two laws Jefferson expected the British, deprived of American foodstuffs and raw materials, to be coerced into revoking their Orders in Council. It was not that he loved Napoleon—he detested Britain, and the best fate he could hopefully visualize for the British Isles was a successful invasion by the French and the consequent establishment in Britain of a republican form of government. But, being a realistic politician, not anxious for war, he informed the British government that the embargo was a precautionary measure, designed only to prevent the impressment of American seamen and the seizure of American ships. This sly, subjunctive interpretation of the intent of the act deceived no one in the British government, and the test of Jefferson's theory began with both sides awaiting results, the British sceptically, the Jeffersonians hopefully.

Soon it became apparent that Jefferson had utterly misjudged the resilient character of the Americans who made their living by foreign trade; he expected them to eschew all dealings with the British, but,

A Brisk Gale, New York Bay, 1838

Oliver H. Perry (from Cooper, History of the Navy of the United States of America)

John Paul Jones (from Cooper, History of the Navy of the United States of America)

their means of livelihood and their profits denied them by act of Congress, they at once began to find ways of evading the law.

Fortunate were those ships that could get out of port before the embargo went into effect; they were welcome in Britain, and as they made themselves available for carrying British cargoes without touching at American ports, they found protection from the French privateers and cruisers by sailing in British convoys, guarded by the guns of British men-of-war. Other ships whose owners foresaw the embargo in time cleared for lengthy voyages in the Pacific, where there were great opportunities in "forced trade," a popular expression used to denote smuggling backed by the force of armed ships.

The ship *Dromo,* 600-tons burden, twenty-six guns, with a complement of one hundred men and boys, cleared from Boston a fortnight before the Embargo Act was passed, bound (according to the articles) for the northwest coast of America, thence to China and back to the United States. In her signal locker were the flags of all the maritime nations, ready to be used to disguise her true nationality whenever the occasion demanded. Two and a half months after leaving Boston *Dromo* sighted land for the first time—Tierra del Fuego—and began working her way around Cape Horn, with the green hands learning the first rule of work aloft—"Use one hand for the owners and one for yourself." Ten days later she was clear of the Cape, and sailing north, when her captain mustered his crew and explained the real object of the voyage: forced trade with the Spaniards along the Pacific coast, who were known to be eager to buy all sorts of manufactured goods, having been but scantily supplied because of the war in Europe. Moreover, Spain's authority in her colonies had been weakening and it was unlikely that any powerful Spanish men-of-war would be met along the coast. *Dromo* first called at Conception Bay, Chile, where she sold twenty thousand dollars worth of goods; sailing north she gave well-fortified Valparaiso a wide berth, touched at Coquimbo where she traded more of her cargo and took on fresh provisions, moved on to Huasco, to the Galápagos Islands (for turtle and terrapin), and thence to Arica in Peru, where in two weeks heavy sales were made. South of Callao she had a brush with a Spanish lugger, a guarda-costa, fought her way free, with three dead and two wounded, and made the Cocos Islands to take on fuel and stores. Sailing northward along the Mexican coast the ship traded at several small ports, steered clear of Acapulco, where the well-escorted Spanish galleons rendezvoused, was chased by a Spanish frigate, and, in order to give the frigate time to cool off, made for Shelvack's Island, seven days to the west-north-west, to spend a month taking seals.

At Shelvack 3,200 seals were clubbed to death, skinned and staked out to dry—a lucrative day's slaughter, for in the Canton market the pelts would bring from seventy-five to a hundred dollars each. It was now time to risk entering the Gulf of California, and *Dromo* sailed for Guaymas, which she reached in six days. The town was guarded by a small fort mounting ten guns, garrisoned by fifty men and a colonel of gracious demeanor, who was prevailed upon to send to Mexico City for permission to let the ship open trade with the town. In the intervening three weeks the officers and crew of *Dromo* were received as honored guests in the town, where the blond northerners wreaked havoc with the affections of the señoritas. By the time permission to trade (with 15 per cent duty to be given to the government) arrived, word of the ship's cargo had spread up and down the coast, and the inhabitants had gathered their money and valuables, set up tents along the beach, and were ready to transact business: for years they had not been able to buy cloth of any sort, and now the Americans sold them coarse Irish linen for one hundred dollars per piece, silk stockings at eighty-four dollars a dozen, calicoes at seven dollars a yard; and the private "ventures," or personal cargoes, of crew members were traded for pearls and gold and silver. So fond did the natives become of the Americans that they urged them to stay and settle at Guaymas, and one young sailor who had managed his affair with the only daughter of a rich don very adroitly, had some difficulty in disengaging himself from her affections when the time came to leave. $140,000 worth of cargo had been sold at Guaymas when *Dromo* weighed anchor and sailed, late in December, 1808, for the Hawaiian Islands. There they took on provisions, finding the females gentle and docile, finely proportioned and with pleasing countenances. The ship's rigging was stripped and overhauled by the crew; every yard and mast being sent down (except the lower masts), examined for weaknesses, then re-rigged before the ship cleared for Canton. At Canton the sealskins and Spanish dollars were landed, a cargo of tea, chinaware and silks loaded, and on October 1st, 1809, *Dromo* sailed for home. It was March 5th, 1810, before she made fast alongside Boston's India Wharf, much to the delighted relief and profit of her owners, after a voyage of over two years.

Such luck was exceptional: the majority of American ships which were caught in port by the embargo stayed there, their masts foresting the harbors of New York, Boston, Philadelphia, and a host of minor towns. By mid-February 1808, 369 American vessels lay idle in New York, their owners biting their finger-nails and their crews looking for work. Those who suffered most directly and immediately were the seamen, by nature improvident, who found themselves on the beach with their earnings vanished in the grog-shops and bordellos, and no ships sailing. By slow stages they worked their way north to the Canadian ports, and signed on British merchantmen at a fourth of the wages they had been paid in American ships. More men were thus forced into British service than had ever been impressed.

Coastal trade was permitted, and the small vessels engaged in this type of commerce soon devised methods of reaching West Indian and Canadian ports with their cargoes. Who could object if the captain of a coaster turned up with a story of being forced far off his course by gales, and having to put in at the nearest friendly port to refit his vessel? The British were quick to encourage such voyages: orders went out to all British warships to leave such vessels strictly alone, regardless of whether they had papers or not. They were the first signs that the embargo had sprung a leak, and with careful nurturing, the leakage grew. Quebec and Halifax became busy centers of commerce as the New Englanders brought their cargoes north and exchanged them for British goods; Amelia Island, off St. Mary's river, in Spanish Florida, became a depot for the exchange of smuggled goods, and the British West Indian islands carried on a thriving contraband trade. On land, by sledge and wagon, a steady stream of goods flowed back and forth across the Canadian border.

In April, 1808, Napoleon issued his Bayonne decree, proclaiming the confiscation of all American vessels that entered ports under his control, explaining (tongue in cheek) that if they did enter his ports they must have done so illegally, since they were not allowed by law to leave the United States. Trapped thus without warning scores of American vessels were seized in European ports.

The embargo became increasingly embarrassing to maintain: Jefferson wrote plaintively to Gallatin in August, saying, "I did not expect a crop of so sudden and rank growth of fraud . . ."; the navy was called on to support the act, and proud Decatur in the frigate *Chesapeake,* his long nose wrinkled in disgust, captured two American merchantmen off Block Island and sent them in for examination. Congress authorized the President to permit vessels to sail in ballast to bring home goods belonging to American citizens, and 590 merchantmen thus licensed cleared for foreign ports; only a few returned, the rest accepting the Orders in Council and going to work for the British.

Nor was the embargo having its expected effect on Britain; a good harvest had prevented hunger, and the liberation of Spain and Portugal from Napoleon's power provided a market for exports. The cotton mills had suffered, and there had been a rise in unemployment, but as a coercive measure the embargo was inadequate.

But Jefferson was determined to make his theory work, and as the iniquity of Americans deprived of their profits was made clear to him, he became stubborn. New England town meetings passed petitions and resolutions for the repeal of the embargo; there were even outright threats of secession in some sections; it made no difference to Jefferson— they were his political opponents for the most part, British-loving Federalists—and he represented the will of the majority. The act was an abject failure—no one could fail to see that—by January 1809. The gunboats were too slow to catch the agile smugglers; there were too few larger warships to cover more than a fraction of the coast. But there was one final turn of the screw to be made: Gallatin, who as Secretary of the Treasury was charged with the enforcement of the embargo, suggested in a letter to a Congressional Committee a way to cut off the now torrential leaks in the embargo—stop them at the source. Congress passed an Act for the Enforcement of the Embargo on January 9th, ordering rigid inspections of all vessels before they could clear port; even fishing smacks could be stopped and searched; no American vessel could load without a permit and without putting up bond worth six times the value of the cargo, to guarantee that the merchandise would be delivered to an American port; goods could be seized even if only suspected of foreign destination.

The rage of the Federalists rose to a frantic roar; members of Jefferson's own party became mutinous; there was a real threat to the unity of the nation. Then, Jefferson and Congress lost their nerve: the embargo act was repealed March 1st, 1809; three days later James Madison took office as President, and Jefferson retreated to Monticello and the ruminative vegetal life of a cultured farmer, far from the sea.

Under Madison the United States remained a side issue in the European war; relations with France and England improved only intermittently: a Non-Intercourse Act which had replaced the embargo went into effect; the British issued new Orders in Council, less drastic than the old ones of 1807; the Non-Intercourse Act was suspended (it only invited smuggling), negotiations with Britain broke down; the Non-Intercourse Act was resumed; Napoleon issued his Rambouillet Decree, by which he confiscated over a hundred American vessels in his ports. In 1810 Congress passed a bill extending the benefits of American trade to France and Britain, with the understanding that whichever nation accepted the offer first would have the sole benefit of the trade. The British jumped at the offer, and that year American tonnage in foreign trade reached 981,019 tons, most of it sailing with the permission of the British. Then Napoleon saw his chance to break up the party: he offered to revoke the decrees of Berlin and Milan if the British would do the same with their Orders in Council. In November 1810, Madison proclaimed that if Britain did not revoke the Orders in Council within three months a Non-Intercourse Act would be put into effect against her. On March 2nd, 1811, diplomacy having failed, the new Non-Intercourse Act aimed only at Britain was passed; on May 16, 1811, the American frigate *President,* Commodore John Rodgers commanding, sighted the British sloop-of-war *Little Belt* fifty miles off Cape Henry. Rodgers was on the prowl for a British frigate which had impressed an American seaman, and he mistook *Little Belt* for a frigate: in the resulting engagement *Little Belt*—outgunned and outweighed by the American—was terribly cut up, suffering nine killed and twenty-three wounded.

When Congress met that fall war was on everyone's mind, and in anticipation of it Congress voted to increase the army to a total of 35,000 regulars and 50,000 volunteers. All the navy got was an appropriation of $600,000, to be spent over a three-year period in buying timber. Next spring, in secret session, Congress met to pass an Embargo Act which was to remain in effect ninety days: learning of the proposed bill four or five days before its passage, Federalists sent word to the seaports of the coming restrictions. With four days warning, the merchants and shipowners went to work loading their vessels feverishly; drays rumbled through the streets day and night, and by the time the new embargo act was passed, every ship that could find a cargo was out of port, carrying goods worth a total of fifteen million dollars, most of them destined for the British armies in Spain.

The winter of 1811-12 had been a severe one in the British Isles; Napoleon's continental system included nearly all of Europe; the United States was closed to British trade by the Non-Intercourse Act, and there was widespread unemployment. A crop failure made malnutrition endemic among the poor, and the government came under great pressure to revoke the Orders in Council, so that American foodstuffs could be brought in and exchanged for the manufactured goods crammed in every warehouse. By June 16th the pressure had risen beyond the safety mark, and the Orders in Council were revoked. Two days later, not knowing that an embargo had at last proved effective and forced the revocation of the Orders, the American Congress declared war on Britain. The motto this time was "Free Trade and Sailors' Rights!", meaning, respectively, the right of the United States to carry on trade without having to submit to foreign laws imposed by force, and the right of seamen of any nationality to the protection of the American flag when they were serving under it. Thus the fight for the principle of freedom of the seas began.

The war was destined to be an unpopular one in the United States where the hirsute frontiersmen and farmers of the inland states had no conception of the resources Britain could bring to bear in the land fighting and they blandly assumed, with a vanity produced by the isolated introspective lives they led, that a few thousand untrained militiamen, lords of the birds in the trees and the rabbits in the fields, could conquer thinly-populated Canada in a trice. Their Congressmen—the flamboyant "War Hawks"—were the ones most incensed when Madison sent proof to Congress that British agents were boring from within in an attempt to bring about the secession of New England and Louisiana. This information, coming as it did with the request for a vote on war or peace, compelled the Hawks to scream "Yea!", and their votes in the declaration of war were decisive.

In the states whose welfare depended upon seafaring most citizens thought the war a nuisance: they wanted to be left alone to carry on their trade as neutrals, if necessary and when convenient under British license. Many of the New England Federalists, beneath the skin, were not far removed from the Loyalist colonials of the Rebellion, and their sympathies were with Britain by reason of close association through years of mutually beneficial commerce. The last thing these Yankee merchants and shipowners wanted was a war that would undoubtedly ruin their shipping business. Their Congressmen voted against it, but they were too few.

The British accepted the declaration with appropriate aplomb: hatred of the Americans was broadspread in Britain, where the defeat of thirty years earlier still festered in their memories—it was not easy to forget that their King had been humbled and their army defeated by the uncouth colonials. Meanwhile there was no rush about the matter; Napoleon had invaded Russia a week after the Americans declared war and he was worthy of their absorbed attention. The war with the United States would keep; when they got around to it with their hundreds of warships and their thousands of seasoned troops it was inconceivable that they would not win with dignified facility.

[11] *Fight to a Draw*

As word of the war with Britain rippled across Europe, making the United States, if not an ally, then at least an amicable co-belligerent with Napoleon, hundreds of the merchantmen in continental harbors sped for home, keeping a sharp lookout for British privateers and men-of-war. Hopeful of intercepting scores of them was Vice-Admiral Herbert Sawyer, in command of the Halifax-Bermuda station, whose ship commanders salivated freely at the prospect of so many rich prizes. Only by luck was the anticipated catch denied them.

Madison, that June, was not quite sure what to do with the American Navy: it was so small—only fifteen ships in commission, not counting the gunboats squatting at anchor in the harbors—that it seemed a shame to risk it against the British; perhaps it would be wiser to dismast the warships and use them as anchored floating batteries, in accordance with Jefferson's plan. That way they could keep out of the fights they would surely lose, and offer some protection to the ports. Doubts as nagging as his advisers assailed him; even the opinion of naval officers varied on how to use the ships, although they were unanimous in opining that they should be used offensively. That was to be expected, for every naval officer's heart was burning with rage at *Leopard's* un-revenged attack on *Chesapeake,* and they were sickened with disgust at the treatment they had received at the hands of Congress. Still, how could anyone know what was the right thing to do?

Commodore John Rodgers, in New York with five ships, lost no time: his orders permitting, he took his squadron out to sea three days after war was declared, in search of a rumored Jamaica convoy. Customarily the West Indian convoys sailed to the north-northeast, along a route roughly parallel to the American coast, until they picked up the westerly winds several hundred miles off the New England coast and bore away to the east and the British Isles. Two days out the American squadron sighted HMS *Belvidera,* 32 guns, and USS *President,* 44, led the chase, bringing *Belvidera* under fire, inflicting and taking minor damage. But *Belvidera* got away and brought the news to Sawyer in Halifax that an American squadron was at large, and that she had been fired on—had someone declared war? A few days later word reached Admiral Sawyer that war had been declared, and—sacrificing the prizes his ships could have made had they been cruising singly—he sent them out in a squadron, to look for the American warships. It was a futile search, for Rodgers was hundreds of miles to the eastward, and on July 29th the British squadron rendezvoused with a homeward bound Jamaica convoy, and escorted them to within a few days sail of the British Isles. With the British drawn far away from American waters the coast was clear and American merchantmen from Europe reached their ports, only seventy of them being captured in the first three months of war. Meanwhile the American squadron had missed both Jamaica convoys, and the British squadron had missed the Americans.

In the late summer and fall of the year the seaport towns were the scene of frenzied activity: flags flew on the street corners to indicate rendezvous points for those who might want to sign on the privateers; the taverns resounded with patriotic songs, blasphemous oaths and uninhibited boasts of what would happen to the proud British.

As though to still the doubts of those who took Britain's tradition of naval supremacy too seriously, a providential single-ship action took place on August 19th. That day, HMS *Guerrière,* a 38-gun frigate, was several hundred miles off the Nova Scotian coast, in latitude 40° 20′ North, longitude 55 west, loafing along under easy sail on her way in to Halifax, when she sighted USS *Constitution,* 44 guns. *Guerrière's* captain was James Richard Dacres, a veteran of much fighting with the French and the Turks, proud as Lucifer and sublimely over-confident, weaned on the Royal Navy's seemingly endless record of victories. On *Constitution's* quarterdeck was Isaac Hull, trained under Preble and Truxton, a masterly mariner addicted to good gunnery, by turns frenetic and phlegmatic.

At 4:50 P.M. *Guerrière* opened fire with her starboard broadside, wore around and let go with her port broadside, but most of the shot fell short. Fifteen minutes later *Constitution* opened fire with such precision that *Guerrière,* to avoid being raked, wore around and drew slightly ahead of *Constitution*. Hull ordered the main-topgallant-sail set, to close the gap, and at 6:00 P.M. both frigates were in position for close action. *Constitution* poured in her broadsides: *Guerrière's* mizzenmast shuddered, collapsed, and went by the board, acting as a drag in the water, and Hull backed his sails, ported his helm and began to pour more broadsides into the British frigate at such close quarters that her timbers shivered. As *Constitution* forged ahead and crossed *Guerrière's* bows, the latter's bowsprit caught in *Constitution's* rigging, and both captains prepared to defend their ships against boarding attempts. An exchange of musketry between the boarding parties caused some severe losses, and the marines in *Constitution's* tops picked off *Guerrière's* officers and men, wounding Captain Dacres who nevertheless kept on exhorting his men to die for King and country. This phase of the action did not last long; in a few minutes the ships dropped clear of each other, and *Guerrière's* starboard guns were brought to bear on the American frigate: so close was the range that wads from the guns started a fire on *Constitution's* deck. But *Constitution's* guns had been doing their work, and at 6:30 P.M. *Guerrière's* foremast and mainmast fell over the starboard side and she became a helpless hulk, her gun muzzles dipping into the waves as she rolled in the trough of the sea. *Constitution*, with all sticks standing, stood off to repair her damaged rigging, while Dacres tried to regain control of his ship by rigging a spritsail, in the best bulldog tradition, never willing to admit defeat. But when *Constitution* returned at 6:45, intending to renew the action if necessary, *Guerrière* fired a lee gun as a sign of defeat, and hauled down the union-jack from the stump of the mizzenmast.

Dacres was a sorely puzzled as well as a painfully wounded man when he stepped on board the *Constitution* to offer his sword to Hull: he could not quite understand how he had been beaten, and he decided that it must have been pure bad luck; then, as if to emphasize the irrational tone of the whole affair, Hull refused his sword, but took his fore-and-aft hat! During the night the crew was taken off *Guerrière*, and next morning it was found that she was not worth taking into port as a prize: thirty shot had taken effect below her waterline, and with masts and rigging gone there was nothing to do but set her afire. This was done at 3:00 P.M. on the 20th of August, and shortly thereafter, as flames reached her magazine, she exploded. With her exploded the popular myth that British ships could not be beaten, and therein lay the morale value of the engagement: over the young republic swept a new disrespect for British sea power and a buoyant optimism.

Contributing to the victory were certain factual elements which it would have been indiscreet at that time to mention: *Guerrière's* crew numbered 244 men, whereas *Constitution* had 456 men; *Constitution's* weight of broadside was 736 pounds to *Guerrière's* 570 pounds; *Constitution* was almost a third larger than *Guerrière*—1,533 tons to 1,092 (British measurements). The two ships, both technically "frigates," were therefore far from evenly matched, as the casualties show: *Guerrière* lost twenty-one killed and fifty-seven wounded, and *Constitution* seven killed and seven wounded. British naval historians, seeking to explain the unprecedented defeat of a British frigate in a single-ship action, were quick to seize upon the discrepancy in size of the two ships, and to find something not quite honest in the way Americans had built such a powerful ship as *Constitution* and called her a "frigate."

On the score that they built bigger and better frigates than the British the Americans were guilty, and specifically one Joshua Humphreys, Quaker son of a Pennsylvania farmer, was to blame. Humphreys, born in 1751, was apprenticed in his youth to a ship carpenter, and he came to know the innards of ship-construction as well as any man in America. He had been appointed naval constructor in 1794, and he brought to his duties a mind unhindered by tradition. His approach to the construction of warships was fundamentally logical: the United States could not compete in numbers with the Royal Navy—there were not enough funds for that—so Humphreys decided that what the United States needed in its warships was quality rather than quantity. He thought the ideal warship would be one with enough speed to run away from a ship of the line and with enough offensive power to fight anything less than a ship of the line. The results were the "Humphreys' frigates," for which he prepared models in 1794; *Constitution, United States, President, Constellation, Congress* and *Chesapeake*. All of them were basically like *Constitution,* longer (204 feet) and broader of beam (44 feet, 8 inches) than the usual frigate, capable of providing steady gun-platforms, and very fast. Their broadside guns appeared to be all on one deck, not ranged in tiers as on the standard ship of the line, and they were really a new class of ship, although dubbed "44-gun frigates." *United States* was launched in 1798, and that same year *Constitution* inched reluctantly down the ways,* but for years the real strength of these ships remained a mystery to British officers.

When the facts at last came out, the English historian William James, in his massive *Naval History of Great Britain* (vol. 6, page 6), argued with a mixture of admiration and defensive patriotism that "If we consider that it is only to add about four feet to the extreme breadth of the *President* to make her a larger ship than the generality of British seventy-fours (i.e. ships of the line), and that her yards were as square, and her masts as stout as theirs, some idea may be formed of the size and formidable appearance of the American 44-gun frigate. Having had ocular proof of the manner in which the *President* was fitted, we shall take her for our guide. This beautiful ship had fifteen ports and a bridle of a side on the main deck, eight of a side on the quarterdeck, and four of a side on the forecastle. This gave the ship fifty-four ports for broadside guns; but she had the means of mounting sixty-two broadside guns. For instance, instead of her gangway being of the usual width of four or five feet, it was ten feet. This deviation from the common plan was to allow room for the carriage and slide of a 42-pounder carronade; and a novel and ingenious method was adopted to obviate the necessity of uniting the quarterdeck and forecastle bulwarks, and consequently of destroying that single-decked appearance which, for the purpose of deception, it was necessary to maintain. Between the quarterdeck and the forecastle bulwarks was the same open or untimbered space (known as the waist-hammock netting) as in any other frigate, but the stanchions for supporting the hammock-cloths were of extraordinary stoutness, and so arranged along the gangway as to form ports for four guns, which could be as effectively mounted as any in the ship."

Actually the American frigates never mounted sixty-two broadside guns, but fifty-six were not unusual, distributed as follows: thirty long 24-pounders on the main deck, and on the quarterdeck and forecastle twenty-four 42-pounder carronades and two long 18-pounders—a com-

* Her launch is described with muted hilarity in A. B. Tourtellot's *The Charles.*

bination of power that earned them the British designation of "line-of-battle ships in disguise." Naturally, no one wanted to bother about such details when victorious *Constitution* (carrying 55 guns as against *Guerrière's* 38) came into Boston at the end of August, 1812: she was proof that an American frigate had whipped a British frigate—and a frigate was a frigate. Men and boys of adventurous and patriotic spirit surged forward to enlist in the fighting ships. The privateers were manned in a burst of optimism; in New York the highbinders, butcher boys, cookey boys and indomitables from the slums of Five Points and Pawley's Hook rushed to sign on the privateers, whose decks were soon littered with bums in various stages of drunkenness. The city of Baltimore took the lead in getting private armed ships to sea: as early as July 12th the *Rossie* cleared, with Captain Joshua Barney in command. *Rossie* was schooner-rigged, with the clear delicate lines and lofty spars that were to make her home port famous as the birthplace of the clipper-schooners—so named because they clipped down the wind like hawks. She was armed with ten short 12-pounders and three long guns, and had a crew of 120 men, but it was her captain who made her the despair of the British. Barney was in his fifty-third year, a veteran of the American Revolutionary privateers and naval vessels, an alumnus of British prison-ships and Old Mill Prison where he learned to hate the British, an ex-frontiersman, ex-naval officer in the service of France, crack shot and unsurpassed commander. *Rossie* was of a type familiar to him: he had gone to sea at the age of eleven in a Baltimore pilot-schooner, a miniature clipper, and in his hands *Rossie* found a man who understood her. Such privateers were built for speed —not battle; they had to be swift enough to escape enemy frigates, yet strong enough to carry guns and take weakly-armed, slow-sailing merchantmen. There was no profit to be made in fighting men-of-war. Lightly built and heavily sparred to carry a cloud of canvas, fragile, sensitive to the helm, they were perilous ships to sail and fight in— and their captains had to have judgment and daring to match their ships' speed and fragility. Barney was at sea ninety days in *Rossie,* cruising off Nova Scotia and then in the West Indies, and in that time he captured eighteen vessels, seven of which were burned at sea after the most valuable and least bulky parts of their cargoes had been transferred to *Rossie*. The rest were sent in as prizes, to run the total prize money of the cruise up to one and a half million dollars—most of which went to the government in taxes and to the schooner's owners.

Rossie was exceptionally lucky: most of the privateers which got to sea in the first few months of hostilities were small and hastily manned craft, provisioned for only a short cruise, their chief purpose being to take their prizes before word of the war got about. They headed for near-by Canadian waters—for the area around Nova Scotia in particular, where the trade routes from the West Indies and the British Isles converged. Between July 1st and August 25th, twenty-five of them had been taken by the British—an indication of the speed and indiscretion with which many craft unfitted for the business had been sent to sea. But over a hundred others had taken close to two hundred prizes by the time Admiral Sir John Warren arrived at Halifax in late September to take command of the combined transatlantic stations of Newfoundland, Halifax, Jamaica and Barbados. With him came his wife, a fearsome creature who was commonly expected to take his place should he ever be recalled. Warren could at first do little about the privateers: he had not enough cruisers to contend with them, his frigates were either cruising in squadrons, or helping to guard the British convoys in which all British merchantmen had been ordered to sail. He had come to Halifax with instructions to propose an armistice, and as soon as he arrived he opened negotiations by sending word to Washington that it might be wise to try to find a peaceable settlement of the issues. Word came back that impressment must be stopped—and that was a point which Warren had no authority to discuss, so the trial balloon of peace collapsed. The next policy he followed was one nicely calculated to do Britain the most good and the United States the most harm: the British and Spanish armies in Spain and Portugal needed all the foodstuffs they could get from America—therefore, let the Americans carry this trade, and license them to prevent their being intercepted by British privateers and men-of-war, and make them pay for the licenses. Canada and Bermuda and the West Indian islands were also dependent on the United States for grains and meat, and that trade was to be licensed, too. Warren had an acute estimate of the American character; he knew that if a New England Federalist were offered the choice between no trade at all and trade under British license, he would take the license and go about his business, damning the government in Washington and its pro-French, anti-British sentiments. Hundreds of American vessels took up licenses, paid heavily for them, and began carrying supplies for the British: that fall in a two-week period twenty thousand barrels of flour arrived at Halifax in ships from Boston, many of them flying Spanish or Swedish flags. Conveniently, from Warren's point of view, the licensed trade helped to foster the spirit of disunity in New England: given time, he hoped to foment actual secession of the Yankee states from the rest of the nation, and to a British officer it looked as though the rift, made clear in the partisan papers, and by the eagerness with which licenses were sought, could be made a permanent cleavage. Meanwhile the orders were: play with them, cater to their love of money, connive with them, do nothing to disrupt their licensed trade.

As the winter weather became uncomfortably severe, Warren moved from Halifax to Bermuda, and on the voyage his ship of the line sighted so many privateers that he became much agitated, and, protection of commerce being his primary duty, he wrote to the Admiralty requesting more warships to contend with the swarms of Americans cruising for British merchantmen. Britain had at sea, as of September 1st, 1812, 686 men-of-war—120 of them sail of the line, 145 frigates, and the rest cruisers of various sizes. Of these Warren had been assigned seventy-nine—three ships of the line, fifteen frigates and sixty-one smaller craft, sloops-of-war fit for cruising against the American privateers. They were vastly outnumbered by the privateers, which numbered (with the letters of marque) six hundred in December 1812. And the Americans were growing bolder every day: they landed at the little towns along the Canadian coast and sacked and plundered the colonists; they had even taken vessels at anchor in such ports, manned them and sailed away with them.

The British frigates under his command were really not safe alone: he could never tell when they might run into one of the big American frigates that outclassed them, and then there were all sorts of explanations, excuses, apologies to be made to the Lords of the Admiralty. *Macedonian,* 38 guns, met *United States,* 44 Commodore Stephen Decatur in command, on October 25th in a strong south-south-east breeze and was forced to haul down her colors after a two-hour fight; then *Java*, 38 guns, in late December fell in with *Constitution*, 44 Commodore William Bainbridge, and after a four-hour battle surrendered, so much cut up that she was not worth saving and had to be burned at sea. This was little short of outrageous: first *Guerrière*, then *Macedonian*, and now *Java*, and the London papers squealing like stuck pigs at the insult to the flag. No matter if the British ships were manned by such human dregs as the press-gangs could catch, no matter if they did not have full crews, no matter if the American frigates were so heavily gunned that the British called them "ships of the line in disguise"—defeats of any nature at sea were insufferable and inexcusable. The Americans, unused to naval victories, began to change their attitude toward the British men-of-war: few men outside the naval service had expected an American frigate to force a British frigate to strike her colors, but now it was clear that they could be beaten, and national vanity battened on the fact, helped by the newspapers' natural inclination to report the battles as having been fought between ships of equal strength. Congress, highly impressed, authorized the construction of six 44-gun frigates and four 74-gun sail of the line, but it was too late and none of them got into action.

By January 1813 Admiral Warren had received reinforcements; he had eleven ships of the line, thirty-four frigates, thirty-eight sloops-of-war, and fourteen miscellaneous craft: total—ninety-seven. The Admiralty thought it was enough, and with pained dignity informed him that in addition to his own command fifteen other warships, including five sail of the line, were based on the Azores and St. Helena, all busy chasing Americans. At any rate, Warren had enough ships to carry out his orders, and in February 1813 the commercial blockade of the Chesapeake and Delaware bays were complete, and off such unblockaded ports as New York and Boston squadrons strong enough to keep the American frigates and private armed ships in harbor maintained a close patrol, while permitting the neutral and licensed merchantmen to come and go. In March, the commercial blockade, which included neutral shipping and coastwise trade, was extended to cover New York, Charleston, Port Royal, Savannah, and the Mississippi River; the only trade remaining was forced to the ports north of New York, in accordance with the policy of fomenting disunity in New England.

Holed up in Boston in the spring of 1813 were the American frigates *President, Congress, Constitution* and *Chesapeake,* in various stages of seaworthiness. In April, taking advantage of foggy weather, *President* and *Congress* eluded the British squadron on patrol off Boston and got to sea. *Constitution* was undergoing alterations and in late May only *Chesapeake* was fit for immediate sevice. The British patrolling squadron consisted of the 38-gun frigates *Shannon* and *Tenedos,* and when the proud and energetic commander of *Shannon,* Captain Philip Broke, discovered that his only possible rival was 38-gun *Chesapeake,* Captain James Lawrence, he ordered *Tenedos* to go away and stay away until June 14th so that he could tempt *Chesapeake* out for a fight. On May 29th he was informed that *Chesapeake* was ready for sea, and at last it looked to him as though the honor of the Royal Navy could be refurbished in an equal battle with an American frigate. This would not be one of those tough 44-gun Americans against a more lightly armed British ship, but a well-matched, even duel. And, having been in command of *Shannon* with the same crew for five years, Broke had confidence in his ship. It remained to insult the American sufficiently to bring him to battle, and Broke quilled a masterpiece of insolent politeness to Lawrence, saying:

"As the *Chesapeake* appears now ready for sea, I request you will do me the favor to meet the *Shannon* with her, ship to ship, to try the fortune of our respective flags. The *Shannon* mounts twenty-four guns upon her broadside and one light boat-gun; 18-pounders upon her main deck, and 32-pounder carronades upon her quarter-deck and forecastle; and is manned with a complement of three hundred men and boys, besides thirty seamen, boys, and passengers, who were taken out of captured vessels lately. I entreat you, Sir, not to imagine that I am urged by mere personal vanity to the wish of meeting the *Chesapeake,* or that I depend only upon your personal ambition for your acceding to this invitation. We both have noble motives. You will feel it as a compliment, if I say that the result of our meeting may be the most grateful service I can render to my country; and I doubt not that you, equally confident of success, will feel convinced that it is only by repeated triumphs in *even combats* (and here he underlined the words) that your little navy can now hope to console your country for the loss of that trade it can no longer protect. Favor me with a speedy reply. We are short of provisions and water, and cannot stay long here."

The letter was sent in by a discharged prisoner, but by the time he got ashore *Chesapeake* was under way, and he delivered the challenge to Bainbridge at the navy yard. *Chesapeake* rounded Boston lighthouse under all sail, with flags flying at the fore- and mizzen-mast heads and in the main rigging, one of them a motto-flag with the words "SAILORS' RIGHTS AND FREE TRADE," and another, a motto-flag with the words "DON'T GIVE UP THE SHIP." Shortly before six P.M. the battle began, and within twelve minutes Broke led a boarding party aboard *Chesapeake*. Shortly thereafter the *Chesapeake* was in British hands, her captain mortally wounded and the marine sharpshooters cleared out of her main and mizzen tops. At the height of the battle Captain Lawrence managed to gasp, "Never strike the flag of my ship!", or (for the reports varied), "Don't give up the ship—fight her 'til she sinks!" Six days later he died aboard *Chesapeake* as she was being taken to Halifax by a prize crew. His death was in violent, almost protesting contrast with the activities of other Americans in the regions of the Delaware and Chesapeake bays.

In those waters, where the main weight of the British naval effort in American waters was concentrated in the spring of 1813, the venality of the inhabitants amazed even the British naval officers, inured as they were to corruption and avarice. Both bays had been blockaded in February, and in April Admiral Warren, with Rear-Admiral George Cockburn as his second in command, brought a strong force including three ships of the line into Chesapeake Bay. The British enjoyed themselves enormously, turning away all neutral merchantmen, sailing up the bay past Baltimore, capturing cattle, frightening the farmers out of their wits, destroying military stores wherever they could find them, and capturing any American vessels they ran across. Their only opposition on land consisted of an occasional patriot who banged away at them with a musket; on water there were a few scuffles with the Americans in which the fighting was severe enough to show that the country was not entirely spiritless. The American gunboats—the "Jeffs"—proved their worthlessness, much to the distress of the local citizenry who had thought highly of them; and the frigate *Constellation,* 36 guns, holed up at Norfolk, while *Adams,* 24 guns, found safety in the Potomac. By May the blockade was so effective that Baltimore and Philadelphia were cut off from sea-borne trade, the coastal trade in small vessels was extinct, and the only ships that could pass the British patrol were those with licenses permitting them to do so.

Of these there were scores, for the region was the source of much of the wheat and flour production of the United States, and there was always a demand for such foodstuffs to supply the armies in Spain and Canada, and the civilians in the West Indies and the British Isles. At the same time the British warships could count on buying all the fresh meat, fruits and vegetables they needed from the farmers along the shore, and could get information of military value from paid informers among the natives. Collaboration with the enemy had reached such extremes by July that Madison asked Congress to prohibit all exports, and when the Senate refused to pass the requested legislation he took matters into his own hands and ordered the navy and the army to arrest all vessels in the blockaded area which showed any indication of carrying food or supplies to the British. If such vessels flew Swedish or Portuguese or Spanish flags it made no difference; they were nearly always Americans sailing under false colors, and they were to be seized regardless of the flags they flew. Madison, confronted with incontrovertible evidence of the materialistic nature of his countrymen, was highly incensed, and he used strong language in his order to all naval officers, speaking of collusion with the British as "palpable and criminal intercourse . . . carried on with great subtlety and treachery by profligate citizens. . . ." Here, at last, was something for the gunboats to do, and they were very busy that summer trying to keep the "profligate citizens" from giving aid and comfort to the enemy. Such citizens continued the business as best they could, reasoning with quaint logic that it was highly unfair for the unblockaded New Englanders to be making all the profits, and doing their best to right the wrong done them by circumstances.

The invasion of Canada by land, which the War Hawks had expected to be a pleasant excursion, had bogged down because of incompetent commanding officers and raw, flighty militiamen: along the northern border there was only one precipitate of the war worthy of being hailed in the press as a great and flawless victoy, and that was an engagement between Oliver Hazard Perry and Acting Commander Robert Heriot Barclay on Lake Erie. Both had an odd assortment of lake-built vessels manned by crazy-quilt crews of soldiers, woodsmen, farmers, with a smattering of sailors. Barclay's flotilla consisted of six warcraft throwing a total broadside of 459 pounds, while Perry had nine vessels whose total broadside force was 880 pounds: the two met on September 10th, 1813, shortly before noon, in light and variable winds. Perry distinguished himself by closing with the enemy in the approved fearless style, and when his flagship, the *Lawrence,* was so shot up that she could no longer fire a gun, he hauled down the ship's motto-flag which bore the words "DON'T GIVE UP THE SHIP," and moved to *Niagara* to fight on. Out-gunned and out-fought, the British surrendered after three hours of battle and Perry scribbled a message to the local army commander, General W. H. Harrison, saying, "We have met the enemy and they are ours"; to Navy Secretary Jones he sent a report in the Nelsonian manner: "It has pleased the Almighty to give to the arms of the United States a signal victory over their enemies on this lake." The victory did indeed contribute greatly to American land operations in the area by preventing British control of the lake, and by enabling General Harrison to re-affirm American interests in the west; nevertheless, when the year ended all American troops had been driven out of Canada and the British there were in a position to take advantage of any favorable decisions they might win in Europe.

Many things had gone wrong with Napoleon: forced to retreat from burning Moscow in the winter of 1812, he had started again with levies of green conscripts and older troops gone stale on garrison duty; but his magnificent cavalry—his sword-arm—was gone, the horses eaten during the rout from Russia and the replacements not of the same quality; he suffered periods of languor and mental lassitude (for he was forty years old), and the disaster came in October 1813 at Leipsic when three enemy armies totaling 150,000 men converged on him. He had but half that number of troops, and the attempt to beat the enemy in detail failed; his army broken, he retreated into France, pursued by the enemy. In the opening months of 1814 he fought with his old brilliance, but by April the last levies had been made and his Marshals were sure that nothing could save him from defeat; Marshal Ney, well called "The Bravest," had to tell him: "The Army will not march." On April 6th the Emperor abdicated, soon thereafter to be taken to the tiny island of Elba, which, with his title and a guard of veterans of the Grand Army, was all that remained to him of his Empire. For the British, after twenty years of almost constant warfare, a new and splendid vista opened, marred only by the minor trouble of the war with the United States.

Plans were quickly formulated to end that dispute: the entire coast of the United States was to be blockaded, and there were to be three invasions—at Niagara, down Lake Champlain, and at New Orleans. Simultaneously the coast was to be raided whenever possible. In the Pacific conditions had been stabilized: the Americans had been driven out of the northwest fur trade, and the Spaniards to the south in California were peaceful, as were the Russians who had moved southward and built a trading post at Bodega, California, in 1812, with the permission of the Spanish. True, the Russians had fortified the post and refused to leave, but that was a Spanish problem. For the British in the Pacific there was only one fly in the font: Captain David Porter in *Essex*.

Essex had left the Delaware in October 1812 with 319 men aboard, and provisions for a six-month cruise; she sailed from one rendezvous to another, trying to join Bainbridge's squadron, first at Port Praya in the Cape Verdes, then at Fernando de Noronha, then at Cape Frio, sixty miles from Rio; but Bainbridge was always one jump ahead of her, and her cruise thus far most unsatisfactory—no prizes except for a little 10-gun King's packet, the *Nocton,* which disgorged £11,000 in hard money. From Cape Frio the trail led to St. Catherine's Island, off the Brazilian coast, and while there Captain Porter heard of *Constitution's* victory over HMS *Java,* a thousand miles away; he left St. Catherine's on January 26, 1813, toying with the idea of going to the next indicated rendezvous—St. Helena; but his provisions were running low and the Spanish South American ports were still sufficiently Spanish—and therefore pro-British—to be closed to him as a source of supplies. Meditating, Porter estimated his chances in four given circumstances: he could continue cruising about in the Atlantic, facing capture by the British; he could attempt to run the patrol of British warships off American ports and presumably fall in with a ship of the line that would blow *Essex* out of the water; he could keep chasing Bainbridge all over the South Atlantic and be likely to starve before he found him; or—(and this was a stroke of imagination, a brain throb) he could round Cape Horn, get all the provisions on the Pacific coast he needed, capture enough enemy whalers to keep his ship properly outfitted, and in general carry on with all the freedom of a privateer. The latter course had the added attraction of taking him far out of reach of the Navy Department and the crochets of land-bound politicians. So, off to the Pacific it was, and after a tempestuous passage around Cape Horn, with the crew on reduced rations, *Essex* carried the flag into the Pacific. She had only one small and imperfect chart of the ocean.

Porter decided to put in at Valparaiso, and *Essex* sailed to the northward, through foggy weather; on March 13th she suddenly rounded the Point of Angels, shot into the roadstead of Valparaiso and was becalmed under the guns of a fort. *Essex* was flying British colors, a precautionary measure, and Porter kept them flying while he looked over the shipping in port—mostly Spaniards, and one lone American with her boarding nettings triced up as a means of preventing sudden attack. That was a bad sign: no one rigged boarding nets in a friendly port—they were intended to help ward off boarding parties. Porter took *Essex* out to sea to think the matter over and to try to pick up some information without letting everyone know that an American frigate was in Pacific waters. He raised no ships he could get information from, and two days later he was back in Valparaiso, where he learned, much to his amazement, that Chili had declared herself independent of Spain and that he was a welcome visitor. At the same time he had word that the Viceroy of Peru had sent out cruisers against American shipping and that the British whalers had been equipped with letters of marque and were chasing any Americans they could sight. There were known to be twenty-three American whalers in the Pacific: they had set out before war was declared and they were so many innocents, friendly as pups, and as easily picked up. His presence in those waters was a God-send to them.

For a week *Essex* took on provisions and while she was so engaged an American whaler came into port with news that a New Bedford whaler had been taken by a British letter of marque, and Porter put out to sea at once, to protect his countrymen and to capture the enemy. The first enemy he fell in with was a Peruvian cruiser, one of the Viceroy's bright ideas, and she was taken without a fight, her guns and ammunition tossed over the side; thus spanked, she was sent on her way with an explanation to the Viceroy that Spain had not declared war on the United States and that therefore his actions, as a representative of Spain, were misdirected. Porter continued toward the Galapagos Islands, a favorite rendezvous for whalers, and cruised there from April until October, capturing twelve British whalers in that area—all well-found, fine vessels of close to 400-tons burden, armed with guns of various caliber, officered and manned in large part by Americans, either impressed prisoners or Nantucket Quakers. The best of the prizes was fitted out with a collection of twenty very light guns, yclept *Essex Junior,* and command of her was given to Lieutenant John Downes, who had been a midshipman with Porter during the war with Tripoli. It was even better than old times, and *Essex Junior* was sent with three of the prizes into Valparaiso, returning in late September with word that a British squadron under Captain James Hillyar had sailed for the Pacific and that his command consisted of 36-gun *Phoebe,* and the sloops-of-war *Cherub* and *Raccoon.* Porter thus far had done wonderfully well: he had taken over half of the twenty-odd British whalers in the Pacific, and driven the rest far off, but his ship was in no condition to fight a heavier frigate. He decided to refit, to get his ship ready for action with *Phoebe,* and the nearest port where he could do that without fear of interruption was at Nukahiva Island, in the Marquesas. There were so many prizes to be disposed of that it was embarrassing to know what to do with them: two were given to prisoners to take to the British Isles; three were sent to the United States (all of them captured before they could make home ports); and three others he took with *Essex* and *Essex Junior* to the Marquesas, where they anchored in late October, 1813.

At Nukahiva the frigate was overhauled, provisioned and refitted with materials from the three prizes, while the crews of the vessels lived in native huts ashore, making free with the ingenuous maidens of the island. A slight war on land broke the monotony: a troublesome rival tribe had to be chastised, and the marines and sailors carried out a successful jungle campaign on behalf of the tribe that had befriended them. In December Porter set sail, much to the dismay of many of the seamen who had found the native attractions unsurpassed, and headed for Chili and the British squadron. The Americans reached Valparaiso on February 3rd, 1814, and five days later Hillyar with *Phoebe* and *Cherub* arrived, *Raccoon* having been ordered to the northwest coast. Until late in March *Essex* and *Essex Junior* lay at anchor in the neutral harbor while Porter tried to figure out a way to escape: finally the decision was forced on him when on March 28th during a fresh south wind one of *Essex's* cables parted and the other anchor began to drag as the wind drove the ship out to sea, where *Phoebe* and *Cherub* were waiting, their motto-flags flying. Porter got on sail, and was doubling the headland when a violent squall carried away the maintopmast, so crippling the ship that all he could do was run her close to the coast and anchor, trusting that Hillyar would honor the neutrality of the anchorage. But Hillyar could not resist the sight of a partially incapacitated enemy and he closed with both his ships to polish off *Essex*. *Essex* was pounded as she lay helpless within pistol-shot of the shore, and when 154 of her 225 men had been either killed or wounded or lost overboard, Porter hauled down the flag. The British were now free to write off the Pacific as finished business and to turn their attention to the Eastern seaboard of the United States.

There, along the Atlantic coast in the spring of 1814 events began to assume an aspect most pleasing to the British. The Admiralty split up kindly, bumbling old Admiral Warren's command and allocated the various parts of it to a covey of younger men, among them Vice-Admiral Sir Alexander Cochrane and Rear-Admiral Sir James Yeo. Yeo was placed in charge of operations on inland waters, while Cochrane was in command along the Atlantic and Gulf coasts. This change in command, reflecting as it did Britain's ability to detach large naval and land forces from Europe as Napoleon gathered impetus on the road to disaster, signaled the start of the final phase of the war with the United States.

Cochrane's appointment was an unhappy choice from the American point of view: he was a man of venomous disposition, and his sense of dignity revolted at the temerity the United States had shown in daring to war with the British Empire. It amounted, in his eyes, to lèse majesté —so might the King have felt had he been given a tweak by a strange chambermaid. To his new command Cochrane brought a good deal of uninformed zeal: among his daydreams was one in which he visualized the liberation of thousands of slaves with whom he would create a Cossack-like cavalry corps, each slave thirsting, in theory, for the blood of his master. His orders were elastic enough for him to take whatever reprisals he thought necessary to chastise the presumptuous Americans, who to his way of thinking were still knavish provincials. The attitude was a peculiarly British one, derived from the insular thinking that colored British nationalism; it was not much changed from the attitude Essex had brought to the wars against Ireland over two centuries earlier. The difference in its application this time was one of distance: instead of the enemy being just across the Irish channel, he was an ocean distant and his settlements were scattered along a coastline of tremendous length.

Cochrane relieved Warren on the first of April, 1814; on the 24th the Americans revoked their Embargo Act and the dammed up trade of the eastern seaboard gushed out just in time to provide numerous small prizes for the new British naval offensive. The coastal waters came alive with swarms of sloops and schooners which surrendered on sight, and, although they seldom carried cargoes of any great value, in the aggregate they represented a tidy amount of prize money. The big merchantmen, to the great sorrow of the British naval officers, nearly always sailed under neutral flags or with British licenses, and conditions became reminiscent of the fall of 1813 when ships flying Portuguese, Spanish or Swedish flags passed in and out of Boston, and when the Portuguese consul grew rich selling registry under his flag to all comers at one thousand dollars per ship. Then blank licenses were available in Boston where they could be filled out with a minimum of forgery. The British would have preferred to fight an honest and patriotic enemy who sailed under his true colors and refused to give aid and comfort to the enemy—thus only could they have obtained the prize money they so sorely needed. To them the materialism of the American trading community was therefore doubly contemptible: it deprived them of prize money and it was odiously traitorous.

By the spring of the year it had become clear that the policy of trying to foment disunion between New England and the rest of the nation had failed. The Americans seemed to have no great love for each other, but they preferred to keep their identity as Americans to the alternative of becoming British. Doubtless the exploits of their navy and their privateers had a good deal to do with creating this pride of nationality; in any event the policy of divide and rule, which had worked so well in Ireland, had proved futile, and the thing to do now was to defeat the whole pack of scoundrels regardless of where they lived or how they voted. With Napoleon out of the way, the means were available.

Peace with France was signed on May 30th and on the next day a blockade of the entire east coast of the United States was proclaimed, confirming publicly what Cochrane had been doing on naval orders ever since he had relieved Warren. When the full force of the blockade fell on New England there were still plenty of Federalists who were willing to do business with the British. Blockading men-of-war found that they could buy anything they wanted from the shore and they were never lacking fresh vegetables, newspapers and intelligence of military value. Did *Constitution,* in Boston, have a furnace for heating shot? "Oh, my, yes! She can heat forty-five shot in fifteen minutes. . . ." The venality of the New Englanders was as undiluted as that of the citizens who lived along the shores of the Chesapeake Bay, but it was even more unrestrained and publicly displayed. Lieutenant Henry Napier, after a few weeks of cruising along the New England coast in HMS *Nymphe,* wrote in his diary: "Sunday, 29 May. All the people exceedingly discontented with the war and all join in abusing the government. Self, the great ruling principle, more powerful with Yankees than any people I ever saw. Begin with a dollar and proceed to any amount, you may always buy a Yankee in almost any rank and station!" That was a precise estimate of the type of people who came running to meet a British man-of-war's boat when it neared shore to purchase provisions under a flag of truce. There was, it is true, a certain amount of slyness on the part of such Americans as these, an anxiety to tell the British what would please them most and so perhaps create an atmosphere conducive to higher prices, but the rock-hard practicality of the New Englanders easily overcame any faint twinges of conscience they may have felt. On occasion a ship's boat would be fired on by the local militia, but such signs of belligerency were exceptional, reflecting only a highly localized sentiment, due generally to the strong-minded leadership of a few patriots in an isolated community.

A brisk traffic under British licenses continued throughout the summer, with coastal traders going about their business in their usual fashion, carrying cargoes to Halifax and bringing back manufactured goods in return. The British warships stopped them all, looked over their licenses for flaws, and if they could find the slightest excuse—if perchance the license had expired during the voyage because of adverse winds—the vessel and cargo would be seized. Few of the legitimate prizes were worth sending to Halifax: they were burned at sea and their crews put ashore at any convenient place. Fishing craft, too, were issued licenses, but as the blockading warships developed a habit of stopping them when they returned fully-loaded, and helping themselves to what fish they fancied, the Americans became quite wary of fishing licenses, and only a minute part of the peace-time fishing fleets put to sea.

The only really exasperating opposition the British ran up against in northern waters was that offered them by the privateers. Off Nova Scotia and Newfoundland, in the St. Lawrence Gulf, there were always privateers to chase and seldom could they be caught. Fog banks hid them, and sudden squalls, and when closely pursued at night they developed the trick of suddenly snugging down all their canvas and simply lying doggo, all but invisible, while the British drove on without being able to locate them in the darkness.

But Cochrane's blockade, in a commercial sense, was proving to be an undoubted success, bringing great financial distress to whole communities and cutting American trade to a tenth of its pre-war value. And while this slow process of strangulation was going on, undramatically and remorselessly, another part of British grand strategy was taking place in the Chesapeake. There the astringent Rear-Admiral George Cockburn had returned in the spring and renewed his raiding activities against sporadic resistance. In August he was joined by Major-General

Ross with several thousand troops, many among them veterans of the war in Spain. Cockburn suggested to Admiral Cochrane that it might be a good idea to attack Washington and Cochrane gave his blessing to the idea—it would be an act of reprisal for the damage the Americans had done in Canada where they had fought an unnecessarily cruel and incendiary war. With General Ross and some four thousand soldiers and marines Cockburn started to put his plan of attack into operation: he chose a novel route—by way of the Patuxent River and Bladensburg. The only obstacle in his path turned out to be Commodore Joshua Barney, in command of sixteen of the detested gunboats, the "Jeffs," and a sloop. Barney had given the British in the Chesapeake as much trouble as he could with his command, but now the odds against him had risen too greatly, and he moved his sailors and marines ashore, leaving only enough men aboard the flotilla to blow up the ships anchored in the Patuxent at the first sight of the enemy. Thus, when the British rounded Pig Point they were greeted by the sight of the sloop burning, and shortly thereafter the gunboats began to explode like so much popcorn. Only one failed to burn in a satisfactory manner and that, with the incidental merchant schooners in the river, became a British prize. Barney retreated with his sailors and marines to Washington, where he found that the government and the people placed an amazing amount of faith in the militia, and consequently expected an easy victory over the British. But as the British advanced, and the militiamen marched bravely out to meet them, Barney was extremely worried about the outcome. It turned out that he had made a correct estimate of the militiamen's worth in battle, for when they met the British they fled like barnyard fowls, terrified by the rockets the British launched at them. This was a new type of weapon, and they were hideous things, much worse than bullets: you could watch each rocket coming at you and they gave the appearance of chasing each individual man. To Barney's sailors and marines they were an old story: they had seen rockets fired at night at sea as signals, and they had met rocket-fire in their previous engagements with the British. And thus it was that Barney found himself about a mile from Blandensburg, on a hot and humid August day, with five hundred sailors, a hundred marines, and a battery of five guns. He placed the battery so that it commanded the main road to Washington and sat down to await the event. The British came marching up the road six abreast, with the easy swing of veteran troops; Barney's battery halted them with a broadside. About six hundred American soldiers, in good position on high ground on the flank, were dispersed by a volley of rockets, to Barney's great mortification. The sailors and marines were left to fight off the British alone, and the British worked around to their rear, finally encircled them after taking heavy losses, and when the Americans' powder and shot were exhausted Barney told them to escape by whatever means they could. They picked a thin segment of the British line and charged through it. Barney was out of the battle, with a musket-ball in his thigh, and he was taken prisoner, immediately paroled, and his wound cared for by the British surgeon.

Cockburn and Ross continued with their troops on the road to Washington without opposition. The President and his official family had fled, their trust in militiamen evaporated by the debacle. That evening the Capitol was set afire, and as it burned the British heard heavy explosions from the Navy Yard where the Americans were destroying everything of value. Then the local fort went up in flames, and the British turned their attention to the White House, which was undefended, and, as headquarters of the Commander-in-Chief, that too was burned. The Treasury and War Department came next, and their burning rounded out the day's work. Next morning the office of the Secretary of State was burned, along with the government's printing materials, the extensive rope-walks some distance from the city, and the great bridge over the Potomac. The Navy Yard was given a few finishing touches to render the demolition complete there, and two men-of-war nearing completion were set afire. The value of the public property so destroyed reached a total of £365,463; damage to private property was negligible. That evening the British withdrew, marched back to the Patuxent and regained their ships without molestation. The citizens of the United States were aghast at the ease with which the whole operation had been carried out, and the war became more unpopular than ever.

Fortunately the British thought they could repeat their excursion against Washington at Baltimore. But at Baltimore, although the battle was touch-and-go for several hours, the militia stood firm behind fixed defenses and the British took heavy losses. Even their rockets were of no help before Baltimore; Francis Scott Key thought they looked very pretty and wrote about "the rockets' red glare" in his poem, even as the British fell back in defeat.

To the north, in the land fighting, the British had been equally un-lucky: two offensives were aimed at the United States—at Niagara and Lake Champlain. The Niagara drive was stalled at the Battle of Lundy's Lane in late July; the Lake Champlain drive, which was the more threatening since it would have cut the nation in two had it succeeded, came to a crisis in September. General Sir George Prevost, with at least ten thousand of Wellington's veteran troops fresh from the war in Europe, had marched down from Montreal, following the same plan that had led Burgoyne to disaster in 1777. That was one of the nice things about the British—they could always be counted on to use an old plan in similar circumstances at a later date: it didn't seem to matter whether the plan had failed or not when it had first been used—the mere fact that it had been followed proved that it was a sterling idea, needing only a little polish to be as good as it ever was. And so Prevost moved southward, two-thirds of his army supplied with beef by avaricious American contractors, and in September he was in the town of Plattsburg, New York, just across the river from the fort held by fifteen hundred American regulars and a few thousand militiamen of dubious worth. As he progressed down the west shore of Lake Champlain, Prevost had enjoyed the protection of a British squadron under the command of Captain Downie, whose ships prevented the American lake squadron from causing undue trouble to the British army.

But at Plattsburg the whole forward movement ground to a halt: the fortifications were well-built—West Point engineers had seen to that—and it would be difficult and costly to storm the works. But if Downie would synchronize his attack on the American ships anchored before the fort with the land attack by Prevost, then everything would go well. The American squadron was commanded by a Captain Thomas Macdonough, an intrepid fire-eater who knew his business: he had four ships larger than a gunboat, and ten gunboats, with a total of eighty-six guns and about nine hundred men. His position, anchored about a mile and a half from the forts, within Plattsburg Bay, was defensively strong. Downie had ten gunboats too, and four larger vessels, with a total of eighty-three guns and rag-tag crews to the number of 714 men and boys, many of them without previous experience aboard ship, although the gunners were experienced men. On September 10th Prevost sent a message to Downie, requesting his immediate co-operation and casting slurs on his zeal in a manner calculated to get immediate results. Downie was not ready, but the pressure was great, Prevost was also Governor-General of Canada, orders were orders, and he agreed to go in and dig the American squadron out the very next morning. The signal was arranged: when his flagship, the *Confiance,* rounded Cumberland Head she would scale her guns—that is, fire blank cartridges without shot—and that would be the signal for the land forces to begin the assault on the fortifications. Then the Americans would be caught between the captured guns of the fort and the guns of Downie's squadron. At daybreak the British squadron got under way and stood over toward Plattsburg Bay. At about seven A.M. the American squadron was sighted at anchor and the British flagship scaled her guns. But Prevost, instead of ordering the attack at the signal agreed on, decided his men should have something to eat before battle, and he ordered them to go to their breakfast. To compound Downie's troubles the wind died and the American gunboats rowed toward him in a wavering line that reflected the varying degrees of bravery of the commanding officers. He was soon under fire from their guns, but Prevost's men continued with their breakfast, within sound of the firing. The British gunboats advanced gallantly toward the Americans, and the battle was joined. The main rivals—Downie's *Confiance* and Macdonough's *Saratoga* began to slug it out unmercifully in perfectly calm water, their guns double-shotted at point-blank range. Under such conditions no gunner could very well miss his target and the slaughter on both vessels was ghastly. After fifteen minutes of firing a shot hit a 24-pounder carronade Downie was standing behind, knocked the gun against his groin with such force that he died soon after. Macdonough was twice knocked unconscious; once when a shot cut the spanker boom in two and the spar fell on him, and again when a shot drove the head of a gun-captain against him and knocked him in the scuppers.

· 183 ·

But he came back for more; gradually the more seasoned crews of the American ships gained the upper hand—ultimately they forced the British to strike their colors, with the exception of some gunboats which fled from the carnage after all the larger British men-of-war had surrendered.

The defeat of the British was a decisive one: Prevost was unable to continue his advance while the Americans held undisputed control of the lake, and he led his magnificent army back to Canada. In London where the government had been expectantly awaiting news of a great victory, counting on it to win concessions from the Americans in the peace talks then going on at Ghent, this defeat was disastrous, and there was a sudden deflation in their demands. Macdonough's victory was one of those minor engagements which had major results, and since its importance was recognized at the time, Congress voted him the usual medal, and the New York legislature gave him a small estate on Cumberland Head from which he could overlook Plattsburg Bay—the scene of his victory—and ponder the luck that had kept him alive to enjoy his fame.

It was not until the last six months of the war that the privateers reached the crest of their effectiveness: the slow, inept ships had been swept up by the British frigates and cruisers, leaving only the swiftest and best-handled at large. Among those privateers which had survived and proved most profitable, one type of vessel gained a unique reputation: the Baltimore clipper schooner. Judged in the cold light of performance, in terms of escapes and of prizes taken, no other vessels had proved so durable and productive as private armed ships, and plans for building them were eagerly sought from Georgia to Maine. Their captains grew misty-eyed at the sight of them; Captain George Little wrote: "Once more, then, I am in command of one of the most beautiful models of a vessel that ever floated on the ocean—I mean a Baltimore clipper schooner, of one hundred and forty tons burden, with proportions as scrupulously exact as if turned out of a mould. The workmanship was in all respects as neatly executed as if intended as a beautiful specimen of cabinet excellence; her spars were in perfect symmetry of proportions with the hull, and she sat upon the water like the seabird that sleeps at ease on the mountain billow. She was well armed and manned, and, like

Twelve-Pounder Carronade on a Brig of War (by E. W. Cooke, 1828)

Cutting in a Whale (from Davis, *Nimrod of the Sea*)

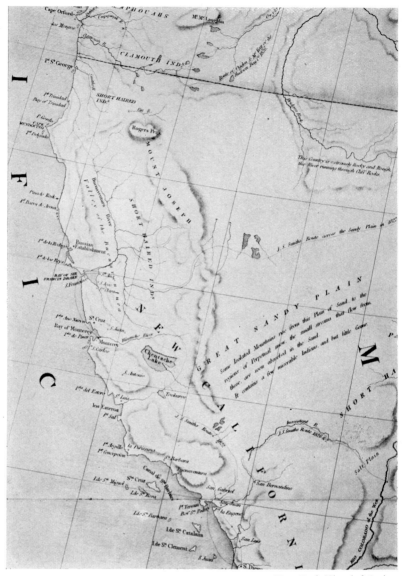

Map of a Section of the West Coast of the United States
(by David H. Burr, 1839)

some aerial being, as report had it, would at my call outstrip the wind."

Speed meant profit to the owners of the privateers, and they had an added incentive to build competent ships: there was an increasing wariness on the part of the volunteers who manned such craft. The seamen were becoming more sophisticated; even the waterfront drunks could no longer be counted on to throw themselves into a wambly merchantman equipped with a few added guns and a commission to seize enemy ships. No canny salt was eager to sign on a vessel unless she looked as though she could outrun the enemy, or unless she had already established a reputation for successful cruises. Too many men had been thrown into British prison-hulks and prisons to make the chance worth taking otherwise, and the smart seaman did his mental arithmetic, calculating his chances of survival, with a good idea of what failure would mean. Tales of the hardships awaiting prisoners were common knowledge in the seaport towns; they were founded on grim fact—on firsthand experiences related by the few who managed to escape, and on the uncensored letters the prisoners were allowed to write.

Their complaints reflected the relatively high standard of living the Americans were accustomed to, even aboard ship. The treatment they received at British hands simply reaffirmed the public's hatred of the British. There is no doubt that prisoners were cruelly treated—insulted, abused, inadequately fed and clothed and sheltered, but such treatment was normal in the British merchant marine and navy. The American prisoners in Stapleton prison, near Bristol in England, received each day an allowance of a pound and a half of black bread per man, and a half a pound of raw, fresh meat, the bones being included in the weight. Sailors in the Royal Navy would have envied such fare: the food they had to eat on His Majesty's ships was fit only for swine—weevily hardtack and meat so old it was like chunks of ebony, foul drinking water, rancid butter useful only for greasing the guns, maggoty oat-meal gruel. There were red worms in the cheese, green worms in the drinking water and beige worms in the biscuits. The British sailors had their half-pint of often diluted rum each day, and that served as an opiate; the American prisoners had plenty of fresh water and if they had money they could buy whatever they fancied. But to Americans used to the rations aboard naval vessels, on privateers and letters of marque, their basic prison diet was outrageous. To many of them it meant slow starvation and death.

The prison hulks American prisoners were usually kept in soon after their capture were condemned ships of the line with the spars and guns taken out of them, uniformly uncomfortable places to live in. They were located at the more important naval stations convenient to American waters—at Halifax, Bermuda and Jamaica, as well as in ports in the British Isles and at Gibraltar. At Jamaica they were famous for the variety of the animal and insect life that teemed in their old timbers and between decks—lizards and roaches, snakes and centipedes, gluttonous lice and fleas—an unappetizing and mostly inedible life. Rations on such hulks varied as greatly as the dishonesty of the supply officers, who as Royal Naval officers had developed to a fine art the technique of improving their personal financial position by feeding the prisoners as little as possible, and by buying that little as cheaply as possible. Typical were the rations aboard the *St. Antonia* prison ship, anchored in Portsmouth harbor: for each man, half a pound of beef and a pound and a half of bread each day, and in addition a pound of fish and a pound of potatoes twice a week. The victuals were poor in quality, often condemned for naval use but judged good enough for prisoners. Thirty of the eight hundred prisoners aboard *St. Antonia* died, unable to withstand sickness in their enfeebled condition, their will to live broken by the constant pressure of hunger and cold and inactivity.

From the prison hulks the Americans, most of them from privateers, were transported at irregular intervals to the prisons on land, where they were equally unhappy. Melville Island, near Halifax, handled the overflow from the hulk anchored close offshore. Into the island's stone prison, a two-story building forty feet wide by a hundred and thirty feet long, were packed nine hundred and fifty prisoners. It was a matter of no importance to the British agent in charge whether they survived or not; he ordered them to "die and be damned," and a good many of them carried out at least the first part of the order. In the British Isles prisoners were moved from the hulks to either Stapleton or Dartmoor prisons, where they joined the hundreds of Frenchmen who had been captured throughout the latter years of the Napoleonic wars. There were three prison buildings at Stapleton, each with a capacity of fifteen hundred men, and the yard was guarded by a wall fourteen feet in height, topped by cannon and sentinels; outside the wall was a ditch twenty feet broad; from their prison the men could gaze on the castle, deer parks and gardens and lakes of the Duke of Devonshire's estate—a lovely panorama and the only pleasing sight that was their lot. But it was also a sharp reminder of their lost freedom. The French prisoners had become adjusted to the life at Stapleton. Many of them had lived there for six or eight years, and had taken full advantage of the privileges allowed them: they traded with the country folk, exchanging lace and plaited straw, bonework of exquisite execution—ship models and musical instruments—for food and currency. The Americans, new at being imprisoned, could not bring themselves to work at such painstaking tasks; they were restless men, many of them habituated to gambling and drink, and always frantic with hunger. A few industrious ones plaited straw for ladies' bonnets, and by incessant work at this craft earned one shilling a day, enough to buy bread and coffee to augment their minute official rations. Not until the latter half of 1813 did the American government act on the numerous petitions for aid that the prisoners sent to Reuben Beasley, the American agent who was supposed to have their welfare at heart, and then the allowance finally granted them was at the rate of six shillings and eight pence per man per month. With care the sober-sided prisoners could buy enough food with their allowance to live tolerably well; the irresponsible ones, on the other hand, in obedience to life-long habits acquired along the waterfronts, found it more pleasant to spend their money gambling and wassailing in a brief, lurid escape from reality; then, out of funds and hungry, they would repair to the swill-pile, composed of potato and turnip skins and whatever scraps of food had been thrown away by their more conservative comrades, to glean the choicer morsels in an attempt to placate their hunger.

When the war with Napoleon came to an end the French prisoners were sent back to France, and many of them were reluctant to leave, for they had built up their prison crafts to a point where it was not unusual for one of them to have saved from a thousand to two thousand guineas. Removal of the French left only four hundred Americans at Stapleton and since they were not numerous enough to justify the expense of keeping the prison garrisoned, they were transferred to Dartmoor, one hundred and ten miles distant, in weekly drafts. It was a change for the worse.

Dartmoor was some fifteen miles northeast of Plymouth in Devonshire, surrounded by a dreary waste of moors, bogs and crags among which even the natives occasionally lost their way and wandered about until they starved to death. Rumor had it that witches had their habitation among the crags, and the wily wayfarer would not be caught out at night in that region. The depot, as the British called Dartmoor prison, consisted of seven stone prisons encircled by two walls, each twelve feet high, the outer one measuring a mile in circumference, and the inner one, thirty feet inside, was loaded with sentries. By forced marches the prisoners from Stapleton started for Dartmoor, under heavy guard, and expected to make twenty miles each day. But prison life had so enfeebled them that the usual draft took nine or ten days to make the trip, the weakest being transported in carts. When all had been transferred to Dartmoor the population of that place totaled over six thousand Americans, scattered throughout the seven prisons. Blacks were segregated in Prison Number Four, isolated from the other men by two stone walls fifteen feet high: their sufferings can only be imagined, for they were an illiterate lot, seldom in touch with the whites, and those white men who have left journals of their life in Dartmoor were far too concerned with their own troubles to worry about the mental and physical trials of the black men.

Dartmoor's reputation was an evil one, and justly so. Officers and men were given the same treatment, and the officer who had run his ship with a discipline thought excessive by his men was likely to be tied to the whipping-post and soundly flogged. The criminal element—the "rough-alleys"—at first far outnumbered the men of principle and they ruled the prisons with brute force, in an atmosphere of excessively bad morals. Matters improved when the Americans who had been serving in British ships and who refused to fight their countrymen were sent to Dartmoor from the prison hulks; these were men of character, and they helped the conservatives to establish order and a rough type of justice. A constitution was drawn up to regulate prison life, and a great majority of the prisoners swore allegiance to it. Judges were appointed and penalties for law-breaking enforced; several types of schools were organized—in reading and navigation and writing. But always there were the eternally damp granite walls, the poor food, the bright yellow convict uniform with "TO" (for Transport Office) stamped on them, and the hot-tempered, cruel Captain Thomas George Shortland, Royal Navy, who ruled the depot with despotic authority. Attempts to escape almost invariably failed: the guards could be bribed to sell the password, but then they could not be depended upon—they would alert the sentries to be on the look-out for the very prisoner who had bribed them, or they themselves would pick him up as he tried to walk out past them. The one bright spot in the prisoners' existence was the physician in charge of the hospital, Dr. George McGrath, a skillful and considerate man who was constantly trying to improve conditions for his charges.

With officers and men facing such a thoroughly unpleasant future in case of capture, the privateers at large in the latter half of 1814 performed prodigies. Many famous cruises had been made before them: *True Blooded Yankee,* a French-built brig fitted out at Brest, but manned by Americans and a few British sprung from French jails, took twenty-seven prizes off the British Isles and sent the best of them into French ports, before she was finally captured. *Yankee* of Bristol, R.I., scoured the West African coast and came home in the spring of '13 with $296,000 worth of loot, having captured eight vessels; by war's end she had run her score up to thirty-four prizes worth close to three million dollars. *Comet,* commanded by Captain Thomas Boyle, a Baltimore romantic, took twenty prizes in the West Indies in early 1814 and burned most of them after taking off specie, and goods of small bulk but great value. There were many other fabled privateers: three-masted *America* of Salem, converted from a merchantman and run like a man-of-war, sent twenty-seven prizes safely into port; *Governor Tompkins,* 14-gun schooner of New York, tangled with a British frigate and managed to escape, went on to take twenty prizes, three of them worth over half a million dollars apiece. Most of the successful cruises were made in European waters after the middle of 1813, for by that time the British convoy system had proved so effective in American waters that the privateers had to look for prizes far afield. In European waters there were friendly French ports—Nantes and Brest were the favorites—and prizes taken in

European waters were much more likely to reach safety in French ports than they were if sent to the United States. In the waters around the British Isles, off the coast of Spain and the Azores and Canary Islands, the traffic was heavier and the chances for prizes so much the better.

It was at Fayal in the Azores that *General Armstrong,* anchored in the harbor and trusting that the neutral Portuguese waters would be a safe refuge, was attacked by the ship's boats of a British squadron. The privateer fought them off, killing sixty-three and wounding one hundred and ten men, before her captain ordered her abandoned and scuttled. In a similar engagement, off Nantucket, when the boats of the frigate *Endymion* tried to take the becalmed *Prince de Neuchatel,* the British ran into unexpectedly strong resistance. The privateer's captain, Jean Ordronaux, seeing that his men were in danger of losing the fight, resorted to the approved action of commanding officers in extremis—he grabbed a lighted match and held it over the powder-magazine, threatening to blow up the ship if his men did not rally and drive the British off. It was a technique that seldom failed, and *Endymion's* men were thrown back in disorder.

The ideal in privateering was approached when Captain Thomas Boyle, having made his reputation in *Comet,* was given command of *Chasseur,* a Baltimore clipper, in 1814. This command was by way of reward for services rendered, and it was a happy union of the best type of privateersman and the best type of vessel. *Chasseur* was a brig, and she carried sixteen long 12-pounders, and a complement of a hundred officers and men. Boyle was something of a dandy, a gentlemanly person, soft-spoken, considerate of his prisoners and his men, incurably romantic. He seems to have been driven by an acute distaste for the British—his Irish ancestry may have had something to do with this. But he was never cruel, always insouciant. As for the war, he enjoyed it immensely. He was without peer as a ship-captain and he used *Chasseur* like a rapier. Joshua Barney of *Rossie* was of the same metal, but in comparison Barney was iron where Boyle was Toledo steel. On his first cruise in *Chasseur* Boyle took eighteen merchantmen. His favorite cruising grounds were the English and Irish channels: once he was pleased to send in a sardonic proclamation to be posted at Lloyd's in which he declared with mock solemnity that he was instituting a blockade of the

British Isles. The British, in the fall of 1814, must have thought there was a vestige of bitter truth in the proclamation: they were losing merchant-men by the dozen to the various privateers, and the Royal Navy ships never seemed to be fast enough to catch the Americans. The losses were great enough to make an impression on the British government at a time when negotiations for peace with the Americans were being carried on.

The American peace mission had been in Ghent since June of 1814, and the British, expecting good news of their offensives in the United States, were in no hurry to reach an agreement. But when news came to them of the defeat of the British squadron on Lake Champlain by Mac-donough, and of Prevost's retreat to Canada, they were willing to come to terms. The American envoys abandoned their insistence that the British cease impressments; John Quincy Adams' firm stand for the maintenance of fishing rights for the Americans in the Newfoundland and Labrador fisheries turned out to be a rear-guard action. The treaty of Ghent was finally signed on December 24th, 1914, and the undecided problems of the war—land boundaries and trade relations, damage claims, and the question of naval forces on the Great Lakes were turned over to joint commissions to settle. The British had had enough of war: the people were war-weary and there was distress in the agricultural areas; the national debt was heavy and mounting, and at the Congress of Vienna there were ominous signs. Wellington was offered the chief command in the United States and he refused, saying he saw no way to win without first establishing supremacy on the lakes—and he saw no way to establish that supremacy.

The war tapered off: two weeks after the peace was signed the British lost the Battle of New Orleans to General Andrew Jackson; the priva-teers gradually got word that the fighting was over, but not before *Chasseur* fought the British-manned American-built *St. Lawrence*—a ship of equal size—and beat her soundly. The last shots of the war were fired at Dartmoor prison on April 6, 1815 when the rioting American prisoners so goaded Captain Shortland with insulting remarks that he ordered his troops to shoot, and thus initated the "Dartmoor Massacre," which, with the burning of the federal buildings at Washington, dramatized the perfidy of the British in the minds of the Americans.

In the course of the war 526 American privateers and letters of marque, fighting for profit and often for revenge, captured 1,344 British vessels—a severe and constant drain on British resources. Of the twenty-two American warships that got to sea during the war, and took 165 prizes, only the frigate *Constitution,* the sloops-of-war *Wasp, Hornet* and *Peacock,* and the brig *Tom Bowline* were at sea when the war ended. The rest of the warships had either been captured by the British or were bottled up in port. The navy's record was clear and honorable: they had been all but chased off the sea by superior numbers, but not before they had made the point that only superiority in numbers had brought about such sad results. On the positive side there was much in their favor: they had won the crucial victory on Lake Champlain; Barney at Bladensburg had proved the worthlessness of militiamen when compared to sailors and marines; and they had two new mottoes to weave into their growing tradition of heroism—Lawrence's death-inspired, fine words "DON'T GIVE UP THE SHIP," and Perry's "We have met the enemy and they are ours . . ." The big frigates had done so well in single-ship actions that it was proved that if given the ships, the navy would supply the victories. Even Congress thought so, and voted the necessary funds to create a permanently effective fleet.

With the work of the privateers added to that of the navy, there is no doubt that the men on the sea fought Britain to a draw on behalf of the whole nation. The breed had turned out to be a tough one, and against the darksome backdrop of political ineptitude, civilian venality and army failures, the work of the privateers—motivated by self-interest though they were—shines like a shaft of light in the darkness. The navy's accomplishments were more on the order of lightning flashing against a night sky: it set a high record for all men to note, and then vanished, leaving only a few great oaks riven and splintered as evidence of its innate, infrequently-used and undeveloped power. The officers who manned the navy ships were a strange group to find in that time of self-seeking men: they could have gone into privateers and made more money but they did not. They preferred to hurt the British with as many guns as possible; they thought highly of honor, both personal and national, and they were determined to prove the worth of their beloved ships. They were conscious of being among the pioneers, and they sought fame quite frankly. A good deal of their spirit was Paul Jones' legacy to them, a legacy mellowed by the years, the ugly lines eroded and the bitter facts forgotten; more of it was Preble's. From the past came ample inspiration for Perry's stubborn courage, Macdonough's sound strategy, Lawrence's pride. They were not religious men, and perhaps therein lies a part of the explanation of their success—they made service of their country a religion.

With the end of hostilities, there yet remained the usual reverberations to still: pirates in the Caribbean, Algerine corsairs, troublesome South American countries. It was enough to keep the navy occupied, while the merchants and shipowners started to reconstruct their trade.

Part IV
COMING OF AGE

[12] *Harvest of the Sea*

There was much to be done—the coast to be marked and buoyed, lighthouses to be built, the old, work-worn ships to be refitted and new ones to be constructed, crews to be found for them, and the war-scattered shipyard craftsmen to be gathered again and put to work. In an atmosphere of peace and political tolerance the work of reconstructing the merchant marine went forward swiftly. Relations with Britain, too, were conducive to productive work: the two nations had discovered that war, at least between themselves, was not a profitable occupation; their men of government had learned their lessons and henceforth the normal bickerings and maneuverings for national advantage between the two nations were settled without resort to war, by means of the decisions of various commissions whose members evolved sundry pacts, all decorously sealed, signed and deposited in the archival files, but embodying in their terms sufficient logic and realism and justice to give them the force of acceptable law. The two war-weary nations, having exhausted their physical strength, had to resort to the use of reason to find a way of getting along together, and this was an amazing result of the war, as unexpected as though two embattled elks, antlers entangled, were to lie down in mutual respect and exhaustion, and then to rise and work themselves free of each other, and to go their respective ways in peace.

While this halcyon mood still endured, a proposal of the British Foreign Minister, George Canning, was transmitted to Washington by Richard Rush, the American Minister in London. The message arrived in Washington on October 9, 1823. James Monroe was then President, and John Quincy Adams was his Seceretary of State. Canning's proposal was that both the United States and Britain declare that Spanish America was in fact independent, that neither nation wanted any of Spain's former possessions in the New World, and that neither nation could remain indifferent to the transfer of any part of the formerly Spanish lands to any other power.

Adams was opposed to the idea: he was not ready to eschew the acquisition by the United States of further Spanish territory, for he was mindful of the possible expansion of the United States to the southwest, and, furthermore, his republican nature rebelled at the idea of becoming allied with monarchical England. Monroe and Thomas Jefferson, whose opinion was sought in matters of high policy, were in favor of accepting Canning's proposal. But Adams persuaded the Cabinet to his way of thinking, which was based on the premise that the United States might just as well proclaim the New World off bounds to England and the Continent as to the Continent alone. Wherefore, President Monroe, in his annual message to Congress, delivered on December 2, 1823, proclaimed the basic principles of what came to be known as "The Monroe Doctrine." In his message the President said that the United States government believed that the European powers could not extend their political system to any part of the Western Hemisphere "without endangering our peace and happiness." In addition the message declared that colonization in the New World was at an end. To these basic tenets other corollary principles accrued with the passage of the years, beyond the imagining of any man then living.

Thus it was in a time of dulcet, unaccustomed internal and external peace that the American mariners and merchants began to spread their sails and let their imaginations soar. There was at last a chance to explore thoroughly the potentialities of a wisp of steam.

Years before, in 1782, the Englishman James Watt had invented a steam engine, a bulky and awkward contrivance, but the best in existence at the time. He owed much to the earlier work of Thomas Newcomen, and to the few and scattered pioneers who during the Dark Ages had tried to harness steam. By refining the known inventions and adding to them his own ideas, such as double-acting engines and separate condensers, Watt devised engines that worked well enough for him to manufacture and sell.

The early American effort in this field was rich in imaginative efforts if not in permanent results. Among the American inventors was James Rumsey, who made a living as a bath-tender in a Virginia resort; in the ample spare time his work permitted he pondered the force with which water gushed from the pipes and decided that it would be practical to mount an engine on a boat, draw water in through a pipe in the bow, and expel it forcefully at the stern, and in this way force the boat ahead by water-jet propulsion. A boat powered according to his plan was tested and it turned out to have a speed of nearly four knots an hour. But there was no money for further experiments, and Rumsey went to England in search of financial backing. While there, and before he could begin to exhaust the possibilities of his ideas, he died.

John Fitch of Pennsylvania was another indigenous inventor: he acquired a monopoly of steam navigation in New Jersey waters and each boat he built showed improvement over the earlier models. In 1790 he constructed and powered one which attained a speed of eight miles an hour in still water: this craft had her paddle-wheels at the stern, and she made over thirty trips between Philadelphia and Trenton as a river packet. The idea was proved sound, but there were no dividends and the project was abandoned when a boat built for the Mississippi River traffic was wrecked and the company Fitch headed became insolvent. Fitch knew that he had a practical idea, but he also appreciated men's reluctance to risk their money on such a novel project. Hopefully he went to the Ohio to try again, but meeting with no success there he unobtrusively committed suicide.

Robert Fulton, another Pennsylvanian, knew of these experiments and of other less successful ones. They were all parts of a jigsaw puzzle and the problem was to merge the best aspects of the various inventions. Fulton was an artist by nature and early inclination, so gifted that in 1793 he went to England to learn the latest painting technique from Benjamin West. In England his imagination suddenly became fired with the innumerable uses to which steam power could be put, and he proceeded to round up and master all the known data and the principles involved while he carried on his experiments in steam. This method of approach was considered not quite cricket at the time: it bordered on the theft of others' work and thought, but to Fulton it was simply an application of the time-honored artistic habit of learning from the acknowledged masters.

When he had a firm grasp of the fundamentals he went to Paris for backing, but Paris in 1794 was in the middle of a revolution and had no time for such affairs. Even Fulton's plea that British oppression could be permanently erased by the use of steam-powered vessels brought him no help, and he returned to England. There he published a booklet on the use of steam in navigation, but the public remained apathetic. He returned to France and, converting his inventive abilities to the belligerent tone of the age, began to work on the possibilities of submarines and torpedoes. Napoleon was not interested. But the American Minister to France, Robert Livingston, who had dabbled in steam navigation experiments, saw the value of his countryman's ideas and he supplied the necessary backing for experiments in surface vessels powered with steam. Their first boat collapsed and sank as soon as it was launched on the Seine in 1803—the weight of the engine was too great for it. Fulton hauled the engine up out of the Seine and built a stronger hull for it, and this time the vessel was a success. It was terribly slow-moving, but it proved that the main problems had been solved.

Livingston had formerly been awarded the monopoly of steam navigation on the Hudson, in association with John Stevens and Nicholas Roosevelt, and although the monopoly had expired before advantage could be taken of it, this man Fulton appeared to be the missing ingredient in the matter, and possibly the monopoly could be regained. At any rate, when Fulton drew up plans for an engine to be used on the Hudson, Livingston supplied the money and Fulton went to England to get his engine manufactured. Watt built it for him for £548; the boiler was built by Cave & Son, at a cost of two shillings and two pence per pound, or a total of £476, 11s, 2d. Permission had to be obtained to export the engine and boiler, for it was against British government policy to permit the export of such useful items, which might be used in competition with British interests.

In New York Fulton ordered the hull for his engine, and to the consternation of his builder, Charles Brown, he ordered a keelless hull 140 feet long, with a beam of 13 feet and a draft of only 7 feet. These proportions were at that time anarchistic: the usual rule of thumb was to build ships whose length would be three and a half times their beam, and whose draft would be at least half their beam. Yet here was this madman Fulton ordering a vessel more than ten times as long as it was broad. They called it "Fulton's Folly."

Finally the ship was launched, christened *Clermont* in honor of Livingston's home on the Hudson, and the engine and boiler were installed: engine with a twenty-four inch cylinder and a four-foot stroke; boiler twenty feet long by seven feet deep by eight feet wide, set in masonry. Dry pine was to be the fuel. Two paddle-wheels, with a diameter of fourteen feet, were to drive the ship. The whole vessel—machinery and hull—embodied Fulton's ideas, the result of much hard thinking and the application of tested principles.

On August 17, 1807, the ship was ready for her first test, and the waterfront was crowded with mocking citizens whose vulgar remarks made Fulton's soul quiver with pain. But at one o'clock he ordered Captain Moses Rogers to cast off, and the wheels began to turn. Then they suddenly stopped. The mob was delighted: the gadget didn't work, just as they had claimed all along. Their coarse comments went unheeded by Fulton, who had noted that the paddle-wheels needed minor adjustments and who was hard at work making them. When the corrections had been made and the engine started again, the *Clermont* moved steadily across the river and began to steam surely up-river, close by the west bank to avoid the current. Twice during the night she stopped to take on fuel, and as she made her way up the Hudson in the darkness, belching sparks and smoke, the natives were terrified at the sight of her. Those who were afloat on the river often quenched their fears by diving overboard and striking out for the shore to escape the frightful vision of a ship moving contrary to the laws of God, up the river, without sails and obviously on fire. After a twenty-four hour run she was at Clermont, Livingston's home on the Hudson, one hundred and ten miles from New York City. That evening Livingston and his friends came aboard, and as a fitting climax to the trip he announced the engagement of his niece, Harriet Livingston, to the hero of the day—Robert Fulton. The engaged couple blushed becomingly. Next day the *Clermont* made the run to Albany in eight hours, at an average speed of nearly five miles per hour, and while she was at Albany she picked up some paying passengers for the return trip. From that time on Fulton was an undoubted success, and the *Clermont* went into operation as a regular New York–Albany packet, complete with time-tables and fixed rates, enjoying the monopoly of steam traffic on the river granted by the state legislature.

Three more river steamers were built for the Hudson traffic: the *Car of Neptune* in 1808, the *Paragon* in 1811, and the *Fire Fly* in 1812. Then the war intervened, and Fulton died in 1815, leaving the company in the hands of less inspired men. In 1825 the monopoly was broken; a rival line put three steamers of improved design in service on the river, and by 1832 there were four competing companies in the trade. That year they were combined and the excess boats were put to work on a night line that had such a strong appeal for the customers that it rivaled the day line in profits.

Fulton's chief rival in the race to get steam on the Hudson had been John Stevens, who had built a small propeller-driven steam boat in 1802 which attained a speed of nearly four miles an hour. Stevens had been forced to abandon the idea of using propellers in larger boats because there were no craftsmen in the United States who were skilled enough to make the engines he needed. When, in 1807, the competition for the monopoly of the Hudson river steamer traffic was keenest, Stevens built the paddle-wheel *Phoenix*. But Fulton's *Clemont* won by two weeks the honor of being the first to steam up the Hudson, and since the Hudson was closed to Stevens by the monopoly won by Fulton, Stevens sent *Phoenix* off to the Delaware in 1808, in charge of Captain Moses Rogers and his son, Robert Stevens. There she proved to be a profit-making ship.

Slowly, after the war, the idea of steam spread from the Delaware and the Hudson to the Great Lakes and to the Ohio and Mississippi rivers: by 1819 more than a hundred steamers had been built, most of them for use in sheltered inland waters. Fulton had built ships with an eye on the transoceanic trade: the *Emperor Alexander* was built for the Russians in 1812 but war prevented her getting overseas; during the war he worked on a vessel fit for fighting at sea—the *Demologos*—(also known as the "Fulton Steam Frigate"), but she did not get to sea until the war was ended.

In this new field of steam the leading mariner was Captain Moses Rogers of New York. He had commanded *Clermont* on her first run, and had taken *Phoenix* from New York to the Delaware and operated her there. But he was a deep-water sailor and running tea-kettles up and down quiet waters was not enough for him: he had a powerful urge to be first across the Atlantic in a steamer, and in 1818 he prevailed upon two Savannah, Georgia, merchants to buy a ship and to equip her with steam as well as sail for the Savannah-Liverpool trade. The ship chosen was one hundred feet overall, with a beam of twenty-eight feet and a draft of fourteen feet. She was fitted out in New York with an engine and boiler built in New Jersey, and with iron paddle-wheels that could be brought inboard when the sea and wind rose and sail alone could be used. Rogers took the ship, christened *Savannah,* from New York to Savannah, and she cleared for Liverpool on May 22, 1819 Off the Irish coast she was hailed by a British revenue cutter whose captain thought she was afire, but after his fears were calmed she proceeded to Liverpool, completing the voyage in twenty-nine days. She had used her engines for a total of eighty hours. From Liverpool she went on to St. Petersburg in a leisurely manner, stopping at ports along the way, and late in the year she returned to New York. The apparently insolvable difficulty was that she had to carry so many cords of wood for fuel that she had little space left for cargo, and her owners despaired of ever making money with her. In New York the machinery was taken out of her and sold and she reverted to the life of a routine sailing ship, content to depend on the wind for her motive power.

In the river traffic and on the lakes steamers proved profitable, but on deep water where the wear on the engines and the strain on the hulls were certain at times to become extreme, hulls were strained and engines quickly worn out, and in repairing and replacing them the profits were lost. To the cagey capitalist, putting money in steam looked like a bad risk when compared to the results that could be obtained with sailing ships, which were of proved excellence and for which there was an imperative need. For the war with Britain had left the whole merchant marine in need of reanimation.

Among the first to recover from the blight of the war years were the New England fishermen, whose vessels the British had driven from the high seas. The small boats that had fished the alongshore waters had come through the war almost unscathed: they were seldom worth the bother of chasing and burning as far as the British were concerned, and they could in any event be easily replaced. But with the bigger sloops and schooners—the vessels that had been built for work on the Banks—it was another story: those that were of no possible use as privateers lay unused in the ports, often laid up out of reach of British cutting-out parties from the blockading warships. The crews of these vessels had scattered like startled gulls at the outbreak of war: most of them went into the privateers where their knowledge of the sea was most likely to bring them profit and where the element of risk that made fishing so entrancing to them was present in an adequately high and primordial degree. During the war they fished for prizes and for men's lives, and when peace returned to the states they were off to the banks again, as tough and optimistic as ever.

They immediately ran into trouble. At Ghent the peace commissioners had been unable to arrive at any solution of the fisheries problem: the British insisted that the war had canceled the rights the Americans had won by the treaty of 1783—the rights to participate in the alongshore fisheries of Nova Scotia and Newfoundland, and to land along the coast of British North America and dry their catch. John Quincy Adams had argued in vain against this contention. In the final treaty no mention was made of the matter. This lack of commitment by the British was, for them, an exceedingly sage and farsighted move: they knew the value of the fisheries as a training school for seamen, and as a means of building up a pool of sea-wise men who could be used to man the king's ships in time of war. Obviously, if the Yankees were allowed to create a large fishing fleet, their maritime and naval power would be increased accordingly. Indeed, had not the British prison-ships and jails been well-filled with Yankee fishermen captured in privateers in the recent war? Therefore, to cripple the maritime activities of this pushing young rival nation the first important step to take was to impede the fishermen with every possible legal and diplomatic obstacle. The Collector at Halifax growled that he would chase the Yankee fishermen off the fishing grounds, and in the summer of 1815 a British sloop-of-war harried them, ordering them to stay at least sixty miles away from Nova Scotia. That ruined the summer's fishing, but it provided a good opening for John Quincy Adams, then American Minister to the Court of St. James, in his renewed, almost personal, campaign to restore to the Americans the rights they had enjoyed under the treaty of 1783.

The British ruled that the fishermen were not to be subjected to the arbitrary whims of royal naval officers; the warnings of the zealous sloop-of-war were disavowed by the government: but these were the maximum concessions they could bring themselves to give to the Americans. The right to fish inside the three-mile limit, and the right to dry their catch on any portion of the coastline they chose was denied them. To Adams, a stalwart admirer of the cod and halibut and mackerel, as well as a keen diplomatist with an understanding of the economic and naval value of a strong fishing industry, the British rulings were only the opening moves in the game. He offered vehement objections to the decisions, and finally the dispute was referred to a special commission. The commission labored and produced the Convention of 1818 and thereby solved some matters of principle involved. By the Convention the American-Canadian border was extended westward to the Rocky Mountains; the Oregon Territory, that vaguely-defined region located between Spanish California and Russian Alaska, defied permanent solution then, and it was decided to leave the territory open to joint Anglo-American occupation and exploitation for ten years, and during that decade the Spanish and Russian claims to the territory were peacefully eliminated. But the fisheries problem was such that an immediate settlement of some sort was needed, and the Convention did manage to arrive at a working agreement which was a compromise of rival claims. By the Convention the activities of the Americans were severely restricted: whereas formerly they had been permitted to land and dry their catch on any unsettled part of the Canadian provincial coast, now they could land only on the barren coast of Labrador and on the south coast of Newfoundland to cure their fish. They could no longer fish at will inside the three mile limit: now they were restricted to vaguely delimited parts of the Labrador and Newfoundland coasts. But, since the two nations involved were not without the rudiments of Christian virtue, the Americans obtained the rights to seek shelter from the tempests, to make emergency repairs, and to purchase provisions at any place along the coast. In return for all this the Americans gave up their rights to fish inside the three mile limit of the prohibited coastal areas. It was not a bad agreement, in view of the fact that the territory concerned was indisputably British. Its chief fault was that the sections of the coast where the Americans were to be permitted to engage in alongshore fishing were not precisely defined, and that lack of definition became the cause of many unhappy incidents. But the Yankee fishermen did not look at the matter in that light: distance oversimplified the dispute and made it a question of right or wrong as far as they were concerned. They thought that they had been bilked and that the best fishing grounds had been arrogantly denied them. But they were willing to try to make the best of the decision, and in this effort they were blessed with a sympathetic Congress which subsidized their work with bounties.

Experience had proved that there was no substitute for the incentive provided by governmental bounties: when the bounties of 1792 were removed in 1807 the fishing fleets dwindled rapidly and Congress tried to stem the decline in 1813 by enacting another bounty law which provided two dollars and forty cents a ton for vessels of twenty to thirty tons, and four dollars a ton for vessels of over thirty tons. But the war made this a futile gesture, a mere indication of good intentions. In 1819 the amount was raised to three dollars and fifty cents a ton for vessels of five to thirty tons if they stayed at sea for four months, and to three dollars and fifty cents a ton for vessels of over thirty tons if they stayed at sea for three and a half months and if their crews numbered ten or more men and boys. Thus encouraged the Yankees took to the sea in their fishing craft—the brigs and sloops and schooners that they had evolved by generations of experience. Even with the bounty it was a hard life: few fishermen could average more than eighteen dollars a month, and with the hordes of children their wives produced this was barely enough to live on, even with the utmost economy of management. Small wonder that the term "tight-fisted" was an apt description of the New England character: where the lives of men had to be risked to earn the barest essentials of life there could be no squandering of pennies, and the habit of Spartan living, and of the sharp thinking that could be discerned in Boston bankers a century later, became inbred in thousands of New England families.

The fishing industry, as it grew in size after the War of 1812, remained a family business: it was not unusual for a whole crew to be composed of relatives—uncles, sons, nephews, cousins and in-laws. Even a ten-year-old child, if he chanced to be related to the proper people, could make the three to five month trip to the banks and back. Such minute fishermen were called "cut-tails," a term derived from the method used to pay them: they were paid only for the fish they caught themselves and as proof of their prowess with a line they had to cut a piece of the tail of each fish they caught. Exposed to the fascination of the business at such an early age, and growing up in it, the Yankees of the fishing villages and large ports along the New England coast saw no great allure in the westward migration that attracted thousands of their land-minded countrymen. Before they realized it the cut-tails had grown up as an integral part of the pattern of the fisheries, and it was not a pattern to be easily exchanged for life in some inland valley where a man would be tied to a farm, hemmed in by hills and with the excitement gone out of his life as he became a drudge looking at the earth rather than the sky. At sea life was a constant challenge and a gamble, under conditions that changed perpetually from day to day and even hour to hour. The fishermen almost without exception refused to exchange the tiller, with the sails and sea ahead to look at, for the plough, with the less appealing view that went with it.

With this spirit, convinced that their lives would be well spent on the fishing grounds, the New Englanders began to test the British regulations. They were deprived of their habitual grounds, and so perforce they went to grounds that were further away from the power of Great Britain. One such fishing ground was George's Bank, northeast of New England, and one of the North Atlantic's most productive fishing grounds. George's Bank had won and kept an evil reputation ever since 1730, when some Marblehead fishermen had worked the Bank sporadically. By 1821 its ill-repute was well-established in the folk-lore of the fisherfolk, and when three doughty Gloucester fishing vessels sailed for the bank in the spring of that year they were conscious that they were taking their lives in their hands. The peril on George's Bank was not entirely mythical; although tradition had it that the water would rush in over a fishing vessel and sink it like a stone, the real danger came from the fact that the bank itself was covered by much less water than the surrounding ocean bottom. As the tides rose and fell a huge volume of water passed over the bank, creating a strong current and in times of storms creating shoals which became well-known, like North Shoal and Cultivator Shoal. Vessels anchored on George's Bank might break adrift in the strong current and be driven on the shoals before their crews could get them under control. The three Gloucestermen reached the bank and one schooner was selected as the guinea-pig for the experiment. Spare hands on the other two schooners were put aboard her, and thus reinforced, while the others stood uneasily by, the chosen vessel dropped anchor and began to ride the tide safely. No krakens put in an appearance, and the superstition about the bank was banished.

Within the next few years fleets of Gloucester schooners were hauling large cod and halibut out of the tidal current over George's Bank, each man handling a hand-line with a nine pound sinker, for a lighter lead was not enough to counteract the current and reach the bottom. It is doubtful if any more perilous place to fish could have been found: besides the tides there were gales and fogs to contend with, and only a well-found and well-manned vessel could enjoy a modicum of safety there. The schooners were seldom of over eighty tons register; there was no incentive to build larger craft which would have only the dubious advantage of size, for the bounty payments stopped after the payment on the first eighty tons.

Besides Gloucester, the ports of Marblehead and Newburyport, Provincetown and Portsmouth and Boston, as well as a score of lesser ports, sent their schooners to George's Bank and the Grand Bank, each ship manned by eight to twelve men and boys, three-fourths of whom had to be American citizens to qualify the ship for the bounty. The crews were for the most part Yankees, although there was a slight infusion of Canadians and Nova Scotians, who were equally at home on the banks. 530 sail, nearly all schooners, some of them with square topsails, were reported off the coast of Labrador in 1820, and aboard this vast fleet there were no less than 6,000 seamen. Thousands more were on the fishing grounds off Newfoundland. Habitually such vessels represented the co-operative and collective work of an entire village, with many citizens, as well as the crew, holding shares in a vessel. If she returned there was much rejoicing, if not, another row of tombstones with the words "Lost at Sea" on them marked an inscrutable disaster. Insidiously a few of the more competent men acquired whole schooners, or in unusual cases even fleets of five or more vessels, which were worked on shares by the crew but with the owner getting by far the largest bite of the profits. By 1831 the tonnage of vessels in the deep-sea fisheries had reached 103,450 tons: in 1814 it had been only 8,863. The groundwork was firmly laid for an enduring industry.

While the fishermen were re-establishing their way of earning a livelihood, the merchantmen were learning the new rules that governed their activities. By a notable act of Congress, on March 3, 1815, the United States offered reciprocity to any foreign nation that would do away with discriminating duties; Algiers, Sweden and Great Britain quickly saw the advantage of reciprocal trade treaties and they agreed to the offer. Britain stood to profit most by the agreement, for the reciprocity applied only to trade between the United States and the British Isles. No longer could discriminating duties be laid on the direct trade between the two nations, but the canny British retained for themselves the trade of their North American and West Indian possessions, and the only part of the realm outside the British Isles that remained open to American vessels was the East Indies. The result of this treaty was that American vessels were soon excluded from the British West Indies, and the lumber, salt fish, flour and livestock of the United States could be carried to the islands only in British ships. As soon as the regulations took effect the British began to send their ships to the United States, loaded with manufactured goods which competed with the infant, war-created industries in the American cities, and the British ships loaded with American produce which was traded in the West Indies for plantation products for which there was always a good market in England. By this triangular trade not only the merchant marine but the whole mushrooming industrial life of the United States suffered, and suffered to such an extent that Congress was inspired to retaliate by barring the entry of British ships that came from British ports where American ships were not allowed. Congress was in a nasty mood in March, 1817. On the first of the month the American Navigation Act was passed, and by this act foreign vessels were forbidden to take part in the coastal trade of the United States. Section four of the act set forfeiture of their cargoes as the penalty for those vessels which were owned wholly or partially by subjects of a foreign power and which attempted to engage in the coastal trade. And since the risk was not worth taking, the act gave the sanctity of law to the already highly-effective existing monopoly which had been achieved by placing high duties on foreign vessels in the coastal trade. By the same Navigation Act the way was cleared for more reciprocal trade treaties, which were negotiated in later years with all the maritime nations.

Still the British remained obdurate and continued their policy of excluding American ships from the British West Indies. It was a policy that endured until 1849, and while it was in effect the century-old pattern of smuggling returned, with the connivance of local British officials in the islands who wanted their compatriots to have the benefit of the lowest possible prices. Many a nameless schooner, loaded with foodstuffs from American farms and the cheaper grades of manufactured goods from American factories ran down the coast and into an island port to sell her cargo.

Equally irksome to Americans trading with the West Indian islands were the regulations the Spaniards enforced in their possessions: duties varied from island to island, depending on the avarice of the local officials and on the virulence of their anti-American sentiments, both of which geysered after the United States took over Florida in 1819. Tonnage duties were $2.50 a ton in Cuba and $1.00 a ton in near-by Puerto Rico for American vessels and invariably they were less for British vessels. The discrepancy was pointed out to the Spanish government, but without effect. Then Congress retaliated with similar high duties on Spanish vessels in American ports and Spain finally saw the error of her ways.

Thus, between the British exclusion laws and the whimsical Spanish duties, with pirates and hurricanes to brave, the Americans trading in their small vessels with the Caribbean islands led an adventurous life. The brig *Polly*, 130 tons, sailed from Boston for St. Croix one December, loaded with lumber and foodstuffs. In the Gulf Stream she ran into a gale, her hull began to leak and she capsized. Her cargo of lumber saved her from sinking and after her masts were cut away she was righted. Her crew perched on the cabin and hung there for twelve days, alternately soaked by the seas and burned by the sun, and always famished. On the twelfth day the Indian cook, perhaps in the course of recalling the scene of his youth, remembered that he knew how to make a fire by rubbing two sticks together and from then on the crew had hot meals instead of raw pork. On the eighteenth day their water supply was exhausted, but they managed to catch a little rain-water. After forty days their salt pork was gone; on the fiftieth day the mate died, and the cook and two seamen soon after. The survivors ate the barnacles on the ship's hull, and a large shark they caught loitering near the vessel. They recovered a tea-kettle and a pistol from the wreckage and with them devised a crude still to make fresh water. By the middle of April the barnacles were all gone, but they caught another shark and numerous small fish. Not until June were they finally picked up by the ship *Fame* of Hull, England, bound homeward from Rio de Janeiro. The wreck of the *Polly* had drifted close to two thousand miles in the one hundred and eighty-seven days since the storm.

Trading vessels that reached Caribbean waters had to run the gauntlet of the pirates who throve in that area in the years directly after the War of 1812. Most of these villains were of Spanish or mixed blood, and they were exceedingly ferocious. The loss of Florida gave them additional cause to plunder Americans since it enabled them to color their activities with the idea that they were avenging a wrong done to their native land. To the Latin mentality, extremely emotional at best, such an incentive was a laudable one and it intensified their natural penchant for rancorous cruelty: their victims were beaten, kicked, screamed at, and dipped in the sea until half-drowned; if a paroxysm of rage seized the captain of a piratical vessel the prisoners were sometimes murdered instantly. By 1819 their activities were so widespread that the United States sent its leading hero, Captain Oliver Hazard Perry, of "We have met the enemy and they are ours" fame, to clean out the pirate nests. But before the Captain could accomplish much he died of a fever he caught on the mosquito coast and the pirates continued their depredations. By 1823 the pirates had committed at least three thousand piratical acts in Caribbean waters since the spring of

1815, and it was not until 1825 that the navy had the situation well in hand. By that time such officers as James Biddle, David Porter, Matthew Calbraith Perry and David Glasgow Farragut had all had a crack at the pirates and had improved their professional repute in practical fighting.

In the formative post-war years, cut off from legal trade with the British West Indies and Canada, the Americans were driven far afield in their search for profits. It was soon discovered that the Baltimore clipper schooners were admirably suited for slave-running; they had speed enough to run away from the men-of-war that patrolled the slave coast, and their between-decks accommodations were not so bad that they brought about a ruinous rate of casualties among the slaves. Speed was of the utmost importance at this time, in this business, for public opinion had been gnawing away at the trade, and by 1815 it had lost the last vestiges of its erstwhile respectability.

The Pennsylvania Quakers had been the first group to agitate against the slave-trade, and this they had done to no avail, other than the absorption by themselves of righteousness, as early as 1693. From then on opposition was sporadic and impotent until 1774, when it became evident to many rational persons that the liberty so well expounded in the Declaration of Independence applied to all human beings. There seemed to be no justification in excluding people of dark pigment from the benefits expected to be derived from the revolution, and after much cerebration the United Colonies agreed not to purchase any slaves after December 1, 1774. Taking a firm moral tone, they eschewed the whole business in theory. But although the words were inspiring indeed, being indicative of the highmindedness of Americans and of their Christian charity, both amiable attributes rare in that age, it was clear to many seafaring men that there was cash to be made in no small amounts in the business of running Africans to the colonies. Whereupon they entered the trade, to the great benefit of their fortunes if not of their souls. The trade with Africa was outlawed formally in 1807, when both the United States and Great Britain abolished it by law; that year, in March, an Act was passed by Congress which superseded several earlier and ineffective ones. The new law made slaving illegal on a national basis by ruling that slaves intercepted on their way to the United States would no longer be the property of the slaver but would become subject to the regulations of the state in which they were landed. In this way the slaving ship-owners and mariners made no money, but the slaves were no better off than if they had been landed secretly. The reason for this peculiar disposition of the blacks was that the southerners were terrified at the thought of what might happen if thousands of slaves, rescued from the slavers, were given their freedom and turned loose among the docile and domesticated plantation hands. Behind this fear lay the memory of the Haitian revolt and the massacre of the whites there. But the legislation was the best that could be obtained at the time, and it undoubtedly had a deterrent effect on the wholesale importation of African slaves, who, in any case, were becoming scarce.

There were slaves to be bought in Africa, after much difficulty, and they were transported to slave depots on the periphery of United States territory: Amelia Island in Spanish Florida was a thriving center of the trade until Andrew Jackson captured it in 1818; the West Indian islands were conveniently near and too numerous to patrol effectively. The pirate Jean Lafitte brought his booty to the hide-out at Barataria, among the bayous southwest of New Orleans, until he was driven out after the War of 1812 by a joint Army-Navy expedition. Then the remnants of the Baratarian pirates moved to Galveston Island, where they formed a self-governing community, and then to Matagorda and Amelia Island in 1817. By that time Amelia was probably the largest slave depot the world had ever created: thousands of them were landed there and bought and sold in a free, highly competitive market. Slaves taken by the pirates, or smuggled in by the slavers, were routed overland in small groups to be sold on the plantations of the southern states. It was estimated at the time that between 1815 and 1818 some twenty thousand slaves per year were smuggled into the country in one way or another. Slaves landed on Amelia represented an investment to their owners of from $175 to $250 each. Once on a plantation they could be sold on the black market at from five hundred to one thousand dollars each, depending on their physique and health and the nature, war-like or placid, of the tribe of which they had been members. When Amelia was a hive of slaves, all waiting to be brought into the United States, the business became a national scandal and in 1818 Congress passed a well-intentioned but ineffective law to stem the trade. Next year there was a stronger law, enabling the President to use naval vessels to extirpate slaving by Americans, in Africa or anywhere else. Meanwhile it became increasingly difficult to distinguish between pirates and slavers and privateers, all of whom abounded in the Caribbean Sea and who often acted interchangeably as best fitted the circumstances. Not until 1820 was the definitive anti-slavery bill passed by Congress: it made death the penalty for participation in the slave trade, and in 1823 this bill was made perpetual by Congress. Even the southern states were for it: Virginia was reaping a heavy crop of infant slaves on her slave-breeding farms, some of them of a light-brown hue, and her leading citizens were anxious to cut off the foreign product which competed with the domestic production; in other southern states, wherever there was a surplus of slaves created by the breeding-farms, there was an equal anxiety about the effect the imported article would have on prices. The southerners involved in making money legally from slave-breeding were politically smart, and their influence in Congress, when added to that of the anti-slavery pressure groups, was enough to put teeth in the anti-slavery legislation.

In 1819 Congress appropriated $100,000 to enforce the anti-slavery law, and in the next year three American warships patrolled the West African coast, in conjunction with units of the Royal Navy. But appropriations soon dwindled to a point far below the need in following years and it was not until 1842 that the United States, by the Ashburton treaty with Britain, agreed to maintain an effective anti-slavery squadron off the slave coast. Just before that time there were some very able specialists operating in Africa, among them Don Pedro Blanco of Malaga, who had his establishment near the Gallinas lagoon and whose international credit rating was excellent. In 1839 he retired, a multimillionaire, to bask on the Italian riviera. Another successful operator was the Brazilian creole, Da Souza of Whydah, who mined the tribes of Dahomey. Both of these men lived in an excessively ornate manner, with harems composed of women of every color and in courts which would have been the envy of the Caesars. There was a steady market for all kinds of feminine finery at Whydah and Gallinas, for as the harem favorites changed from night to night each one had to be given new gifts by the master, gifts of fine linen, jewels, silks and wines. The masters, Da Souza and Blanco, were sybarites, and the less complex American mariners who dealt with them and visited their palaces, eyed their galaxies of houris and armed guards and slaves, came away stunned by the splendor of the court life and by the dissipation, feasting, gambling and sensuality of the two men. But the Americans invariably came away with their ships laden with slaves which they could always sell in Brazil, or smuggle, with luck, into the United States. Once landed on the Florida coast they could be hidden in the interior until there was a demand for them, and then they could be sold as escaped slaves who had been caught hiding out in the wilds.

Among the more notorious slave-ships were several former privateers, most famous of which was the *Saucy Jack*. Manned by very tough characters, these ships went armed to defend themselves against the warships, and on occasion they beat them off in the best privateering manner. Such engagements were extremely wearing on the slaves: the hatches had to be battened down lest the blacks become over-stimulated by the gunnery, and when the hatches were closed that meant that there was no ventilation below deck, and the slaves stifled in fetid air. It is problematical if they were ever more miserable than at such times, for the common practice was to rig wind-sails over the open hatches to scoop fresh air down to the slaves, and to give them the best possible treatment to keep them alive and well and worth high prices. With the trade effectively outlawed, the profits increased with the risks, and many shipowners could not resist making an attempt to cash in on the demand. In 1835 the 90-ton Baltimore clipper *Napoleon,* owned by Don Pedro of Gallinas, made several trips from Cuba to the slave coast and back, with 350 slaves aboard on each trip, among them a hundred boys and girls. The cost in Africa per head was $16, and in Cuba they were worth an average of $350 each; the net profit on each trip was $100,000.

There was no great difficulty in the years of such profits in getting men to man a slaver, and among the crews were many Americans. The more articulate of them justified their occupation by believing that the slaves were actually better off with them than as free natives in the African jungles, where they might be tortured or killed in a tribal war, or made a human sacrifice in an Ashantee rite. At Coomassie such rites

involved a hundred boys and girls, who were first tortured with dia-
bolical ingenuity by tribal warriors. Such sadistic orgies rivaled even
the work of the priests of the Inquisition, although lacking the latter's
refinements. After torture the natives marked for sacrifice were massacred in a most regrettable manner: the heads of some would be
crushed, while others, less fortunate, were disembowled and vivesected
and left for the dogs to eat. The Americans who knew of such rites
reflected that native life at best was not good, and that they were doing
the blacks a favor by taking them out of reach of such horrors and bringing them to the relatively better conditions in the United States.

In the United States the debates on slavery were endless: the most
consistently anti-slavery group was the clergy and since their bible was
inconveniently lax on the matter of slave-running, they were wont to
quote the best available text, from Timothy I, Chapter I, verses 8, 9, and
10, by which "menstealers" are ruled persona non grata by Paul the
Apostle. The slavers' standard reply to this line was that they didn't
steal the slaves—they bought them. From that point on the arguments
became both jesuitical and blasphemous, and sight was lost, in the
welter of words, of the fact that slaving was a tremendously lucrative
way to make a living. Of course, such pragmatic men as the slavers had
to be could not assess the theological and moral and ethical arguments
of the anti-slavery crusaders, and lacking a grasp of dialectics, they
became outlaws, losing all claim to righteousness and heaven, and
theirs became a much-condemned activity in which no virtuous man
would take part. And thus the trade reverted to the criminal elements
of several nations who continued to sieve blacks into the West Indies
and then, by way of little-known harbors, into the southern states.

While these unsavory doings were taking place, there was a purely
legitimate, equally competitive branch of the merchant marine in
process of growth, and this branch was the young North Atlantic packet
lines. The British had run packets—the term applied to any vessel that
sailed at regular intervals between two ports—as early as 1756, when the
king's packets brought the mails and very important personages to and
from New York and Falmouth. These ships were invariably small and
fast, seldom of more than two hundred tons, and they were usually

brigs. They went armed and disciplined as his majesty's ships. The early British packets met with so many maritime disasters that they came to be known as "coffin brigs," but they established the need for such a service and the New England merchants set up a packet line of their own in the last part of the eighteenth century. John Hancock, one of Boston's leading spirits in the maritime field, owned the *Boston Packet,* which linked Boston and England with a fair regularity, but British men-of-war and privateers drove the American packets from the sea. Sailing on a definite date was their vulnerable point: they were easy to waylay and capture if they kept to their schedule, and if they did not sail as advertised they were of no more use to shippers than any other vessel.

Not until the era of peace began in 1815 were conditions propitious to try again. In 1816 the Black Ball Line was established with four rugged ships of close to four hundred tons each—the *Amity, Courier, Pacific* and *James Monroe.* A large black ball painted on the foretopsail identified ships of this line. From the very first sailing the venture was a success: merchants and passengers had become used to regular sailing dates on the river packets, and the habit spread easily to transatlantic crossings. The requisites for the packets were speed and safety: they were among the largest and fastest ships of that day, soundly built, but carrying clouds of sail, square-rigged, commanded by men who made a habit of getting the most out of their ships by driving them unmercifully. It made no difference if there were sails lost or risks taken—the object was to get to and from Liverpool as fast as possible—and the captains had to make decisions that balanced the factors of speed and danger to a nicety. The Black Ball packets sailed on the first of every month, and in the first nine years of operation the line's packets averaged twenty-three days per trip between Sandy Hook and Liverpool, and forty days per trip for the return voyage, during which head winds were inevitable.

Competition was not slow in entering the field: the Red Star Line put its packets on schedule in 1821, sailing on the 24th of every month. To the Black Ball Line this looked as though the rival line's packets were starting a week ahead of the Black Ball packets, so the latter began an additional service with ships sailing on the 16th of every month. These schedules left a two-week period in which there was no packet service, and into the breach stepped the Swallow Tail Line, with a weekly service, and the field was full. The idea spread to other cities: Philadelphia began sending packets to Liverpool and to London; three lines made the New York–Havre run regularly. The coastwise trade began to support coastal packets between New York and Charleston and New Orleans, and thence to Vera Cruz, where a packet line kept trade with Mexico lively. The coastal lines functioned as feeders for the transatlantic packets, as well as for trade between American ports; they funneled merchandise into New York and helped to make the city grow and become a center of trade.

Of the Atlantic packets there were never more than fifty in service at the same time, but by the regularity of their departure—and they sailed in fair weather or foul—and by the speed and seamanship with which they were worked they gave the nation something to be defiantly proud about, and they were soon acknowledged, even by the British, to be the best ships in the trade. By 1824 the American packets had won the bulk of the North Atlantic freight and passenger trade, by their sheer efficiency.

The Black Ball packet *Pacific* was typical: she was fitted out in a luxurious fashion for the benefit of her passengers; the dining saloon was fourteen feet wide by forty feet long, and down the center of it ran a mahogany table flanked by mahogany chairs; there were archways over the entrance of each stateroom; the paneling was done in mahogany and satinwood. On both sides of the dining saloon there were seven cabins, complete with mirrors and furnishings worthy of cabin-class passengers. In the steerage there were other arrangements, thought adequate for the immigrants who sought work and freedom in the new world: there they were packed in like cattle, with little ventilation and poor food, not greatly better off during the passage than the slaves from Africa. One packet, the *Independence,* 734 tons, drove her way back and forth across the Western Ocean, as the Atlantic is known to seamen, for 29 years, making in all 116 round trips, and bringing 30,000 passengers to the United States. Her log recorded 1,500 births and 200 marriages.

Mostly by packet, an average of fifty thousand immigrants came to the

United States each year in the decade from 1830 to 1840. A majority of them were Irish peasants, with Germans forming the second largest nationality and English the third. In the ten years after 1840 the rate of entry rose to an average of 150,000 a year, all of whom were absorbed in the various states without undue trouble. The Irish congregated in the cities, where they formed a source of cheap if not docile labor at a time when they were needed on railroad and canal construction jobs, for which type of work they were well-fitted. Of course, they brought their religion with them, and the intolerant New Englanders and New Yorkers sneered at such Papists, forced them to keep to themselves by refusing to associate with them, and prevented, for the time being, their assimilation in the Puritan stock which was even then sadly in need of vitalizing, new blood. But the Irish, as soon as they became acclimated—and this did not take them long—began to produce numerous policemen, politicians and priests as well as hod carriers. The Germans moved westward to the rich farmlands of Wisconsin and Missouri where they flourished in a peasant-like manner and contributed much to the stability of the nation; the English seldom strayed far from the sea ports.

Gradually the size of the packets increased, although they kept a family resemblance. They were painted black, with a white or a varnished port streak, and they carried a supply of livestock and poultry in the housed-over longboat between the main- and foremasts so that their passengers could be certain of having fresh lamb and pork and turkey and chicken throughout the voyage. By 1838 a packet was a vessel of considerable size: *Roscius,* of the Dramatic Line—whose vessels were named after famous dramatists and thespians and whose mark was a huge X on their foretopsails—was of 1100-tons burden, with a main deck 170 feet long, a 36½ foot beam, and a hold 22 feet deep. The distance from her keelson to her main truck was 187 feet.

Two elements that went to make the packets successful remained constant: the type of officer who commanded them and the type of seaman who worked them. The master of a packet was a rare blend of gentleman and ruffian: he had to be at home among the cabin passengers in the dining saloon, able to admire a well-turned ankle without outraging a husband, fit to exchange politically discreet banter with the ladies and gentlemen, and of sufficiently genteel table manners to sit at table with them. He had, too, to be master of his ship beyond dispute—to know navigation and seamanship, and to be of great enough physical strength to endure the strain of long spells on deck in foul weather. Such men were hard to find, and when the packets first began their runs they were usually commanded by men with experience in privateering. Such men knew best how to drive their ships in a perpetual race against time, and were used to calculating risks. For their work they earned close to $5,000 a year, getting $30 a month pay, 5 per cent of the freight charges, 25 per cent of the cabin passenger fare (which varied from $100 to $140 per head), the money paid for the mail (2¢ for each American letter, 2 pence for each British letter), and, if a captain so desired, as a special perquisite he could take his wife along free of charge.

The crews were of another class: they were the "Liverpool Irish"—the "packet rats"—brought aboard drunk or drugged by the crimps who ran bordellos and bars in Liverpool's Booble-alley, Gibralter-place and Rottenrow. They got as much as eighty dollars for each man they brought aboard, and they thought it a clever dodge to collect for carrying a dead man aboard and dumping him in a forecastle bunk the night before sailing time, explaining all the while that the corpse was only in a drunken stupor. Trafficking as the crimps did with burkers and kidnapers, the crews were sometimes a mixture of the dead and the unfortunate living. If the mate paid good money for a corpse, thinking he was getting a drugged seaman, and then discovered his mistake when he came to sort the quick from the dead, and had the body tossed over the side, there was that much more work for the living to do. But these men were able to handle the work: they were nearly subhuman in mentality, but of great strength and utterly fearless in the wildest storms. They could be counted on to get the canvas in and to do it with speed and skill. They were the bucko mate's province: he had to be able to beat them individually and cow them collectively, or he would lose his job.

In a few instances, as soon as a packet manned by the packet-rats left Liverpool the forecastle doors were nailed fast and the crew had to remain on deck for the duration of the voyage—only in this way could their officers be sure of getting them up in the rigging and at work when they were needed. Among themselves the packet-rats abided by a rudimentary code of honor: they would not steal from one another, but woe betide the stranger in their midst. He would lose the very clothes off his back and the shoes off his feet, stolen while he slept. First discipline for a crew of such creatures consisted in breaking off the points of their sheath-knives to restrain their normally murderous inclinations and to establish the mastery of the officers. American seamen refused to sail with them, and the Western Ocean packets came to be manned exclusively by them. They lacked the intelligence to perform anything more than the most rudimentary duties aboard ship—hanging out and hauling in sail—and the packets were overhauled and tuned-up between voyages by the craftsmen in the shipyards. As soon as a packet reached New York or Liverpool her crew vanished among the waterfront dives, where nameless and ingeniously devised vices flourished and a true packet-rat could enjoy the rewards of his work to his heart's content.

Spectacular as the packets were in their swift passages, in the manner in which they were sailed, in the orgies of their crews ashore, their chief contribution to the growth of America lay in their bringing the bone and gristle of European and Irish peasant stock to infuse the thinning blood of the Anglo-Americans with a new vitality. While this process of bodily growth was going on, the sea was also serving to enlarge the mental horizons of Americans.

By 1815 the world as Americans in the seaboard towns knew it was no longer a thing to be feared: the continents, save at the poles, had been delineated and the moods of the sea were known and respected even if not understood. In the little seaport towns of New England, towns like Edgartown, Barnstable, Nantucket, Salem, Sag Harbor, New Bedford, there was an awareness of the world, of its scope and variety, which seeped into the body politic through the schools and colleges and in coffee-shop gossip. Newspapers of the day spoke of far-off ports and exotic cargoes. To this awareness of the world the whalers and sealers contributed in great measure, for where there was water they could go.

Sealing in the South Atlantic was an incidental by-product of whaling, dating from 1774 when Captain Gamaliel Collins and Captain David Smith of Cape Cod set out for the Falkland Islands to look for whales. Instead, on these South Atlantic outposts, they found thousands of seals and sea lions, all basking pleasantly on the rocks. They slaughtered a goodly number of both and found, on their return, that there was enough profit in their skins and their oil to make the trip worth the trouble. In later years, between wars, numerous vessels followed their lead, pushing always further afield in search of the seal rookeries, and by 1820 there were thirty sealers at the South Shetland Islands, on the fringe of Antarctica. As sealing was carried on then it was rather risky business: the seals in their colonies were spotted from the ships, and the boats were manned and lowered away, their crews armed with clubs. Getting ashore on the rocks, through the surf, was the hazardous part of the job: once ashore they had little to fear from seals, and they clubbed them to death by the thousands, skinned them, and then made the difficult trip back to the ship. Guns were not used to kill seals because the holes made by the shot lowered the value of the skins.

Among the thirty sealers at the South Shetlands in 1820 were five from the South Sea Company of Stonington, Connecticut, under the command of Isaac Pendleton. One of the five was tiny *Hero,* of less than fifty-tons burden, Captain N. B. Palmer commanding. Pendleton sent him to the southward to look for other seal rookeries, and to the south Palmer found a land without seals but of continental dimensions. He was on his way back to the South Shetlands when fog hemmed him in and he hove to, awaiting clear weather. That night ship's bells were heard to port and to starboard, and the crew began to think that spirits were haunting them. Next day, as the fog lifted, Palmer saw on either side of his command a Russian warship, and he made haste to have *Hero's* best American flag hoisted. The Russian commodore invited him aboard the flagship where he learned that the warships had been sent out on a voyage of discovery by the Emperor Alexander, in an attempt to bring new glory to the Muscovites. The Commodore asked Palmer if he knew what islands those were, just to the north, and Palmer told him that they were the South Shetlands, and that if he wanted to enter the harbor there for provisions he would be happy to act as pilot for the Russian ships. At this offer the Russian was much dispirited, for he had already counted the islands as a new discovery, and here in a cockle-shell was a Yankee offering to act as a pilot. Admiration for a race whose members could put so small a vessel so far from home, and yet be thoroughly at ease, struggled with disappointment in the Russian. Yet he congratulated Palmer on this evidence of American initiative, and Palmer, gratified at such condescension, told the Russian of the great land area to the south, just over the horizon, and at the news of this discovery, of a magnificence worthy of the Tsar, the Commodore said in an excess of enthusiasm that he would name the land Palmer Land, in honor of the Stonington skipper. Palmer went on about his sealing, not overly impressed with his discovery of the Antarctic land mass.

Five years later the seals in the southern seas had been slaughtered with such efficiency that they became too scarce to hunt profitably, and the sealing fleet grew steadily smaller, cruising chiefly for sea lion oil, and considering themselves lucky to take a few thousand seals. But as sealing fell off, the whalers increased their activities.

For the whalers the period between the Revolutionary War and the War of 1812 had been one of exploration and of improvement in techniques and equipment. By 1815 the whale-ships had grown considerably in size, and the duration of their voyages had been lengthened to three or even four years; usually they were square-rigged ships of about four hundred tons, with heavy, bluff bows, four or five whale-boats slung on davits along their sides, thick, sturdy spars, their sails stained by the smoke from the trypots on deck. A lookout perched in the crow's-nest, which was usually a barrel but sometimes a simple wooden ring, and scanned the sea for the spouts of whales. Such vessels could not be mistaken for any other type of craft—they were too distinctive, too purely functional. Speed was of no use to them; they were built for punishment, with heavy rigging and stout masts, tubby, with coppered bottoms, not handsome in any sense, but so durable that they lasted for years and seldom needed extensive repairs. Their crews thought that the whale oil which seeped into the planking and frame preserved the wood from decay.

The whale-boats they carried were the product of over a century of trial and error, and by the early nineteenth century they had been stand-ardized: they were twenty-eight feet long, six feet beam amidship, round-bottomed, lightly-built but immensely strong. Two men could carry one of them easily. The general practice was for each boat to carry a ship's officer, who acted as the boat-steerer, using a twenty-foot oar as a rudder. There were five oarsmen, and the bow-oarsman acted as harpooner. A small mast and sail were carried in each boat, and they could be quickly rigged for use in case the wind came from a helpful quarter. As a boat neared a whale silence was enforced—even the oars were muffled, and when the range was short enough the harpooner threw one or more of his harpoons into the whale. Then there was frenzied effort to back the boat away from the whale, whose first in-stinct when struck was to sound. A whale-line, capable of bearing a 3-ton strain, was attached to the shank of the harpoon, and linked the whale to the boat. As the whale sounded the line ran out, and if the whale fled the "Nantucket sleigh-ride" began, as the whale towed the boat across the seas at high speed. Sooner or later the whale had to come up to breathe, and in order to be ready for that moment the bow-oarsman changed places in the boat with the officer. From the bow the officer drove a lance into the whale, aiming behind the shoulder for a vital part, trying repeatedly to reach the innards of the cachelot. The lances were not over twelve feet in length—half wooden shaft and half iron, with a steel blade on the point. The wooden part was detachable, joined to the boat by a short line, and it could be used to thrust more lances into the whale. The coup de grâce was one which would have delighted the aficionados of the bull-ring: a lance, with the wooden shaft set in its socket, was driven into the whale at close quarters, into the vitals of the animal, and there twisted and turned in an attempt to make a mortal wound. Clearly, bravery and skill were needed for this business, and no better small-boat handlers existed than the whale-boat crews, whose lives depended on their ability to get away from a har-pooned whale, then to close again for the kill with the lance, finally to escape the death flurry.

When the whale turned "fin out" and was dead, it was brought alongside the whaler and the work of cutting-in began. As the blubber, sometimes five feet thick, began to unwind, like the skin of a potato peeled spirally, and as it came over the whaler's side, it was cut off in sections and lowered into the hold, while the whale's huge head—one-third of the length of the whale—was severed for the head cavity oil in it. Then the try-works were started: the fire under the great kettles on the brick works on deck amidship was started with scraps of old blubber, and the new blubber was brought up on deck, cut in sections, the oil boiled or "tried" out of it and then stowed in barrels in the hold. The whole operation was a messy, mephitic and bloody job: often the crew worked long into the night trying-out the day's catch, and to win their willing efforts in the work, the "lay" or share system served very nicely. By this system each man on a whaler received a percentage of the profits of the voyage, after, of course, the owners took their slice, which in some cases amounted to two-thirds of the value of the oil. What was left was divided among officers and men according to their special abilities: the captain might get $\frac{1}{18}$th, the first mate $\frac{1}{27}$th, the second mate $\frac{1}{37}$th, the seamen $\frac{1}{75}$th. There was no standard scale; each man, before signing the ship's articles, could argue for as big a share as he thought he could get. The owners found that among introspective seamen self-examination brought self-esteem, whereas comparison brought modesty. In such haggling a knowledge of fractions was essential: green hands, fresh from the farms, would object to a share of $\frac{1}{100}$th, but be jubilant at $\frac{1}{200}$th. If there were no profits, no one got anything, but it was a rare occasion when a whaler's captain dared to return home with an empty hold: that meant failure, and a blot on his professional reputation, verbal harpoons tossed at him in the village taverns by luckier or more able men, and an irate wife in tears at the shame of it. The thought of a dry voyage was so frightful that the captains took terrific risks to fill their barrels, and the crews were willing to follow where the captains ordered. Always there was the incentive system at work—the shares of the profits—keeping the look-out awake and keen, the cooper knocking together his barrels from the staves carried for that purpose and making sure that there were no leaky ones, for a barrel that was not oil-tight would cost him money; for the same reason the harpooners kept their blades sharp and the oarsmen kept their boats sandpapered and varnished and ready to go at a moment's notice. Crews numbered from thirty to forty men, and they were almost exclusively

New England born and bred, with a light spicing of Portuguese from the Azores and a few natives picked up on Pacific islands. A ship or bark of three hundred tons would have a captain, four mates, a cooper, carpenter, cook, steward, four boat-steerers (also good as harpooners), twenty-two men and boys: in all, thirty-five officers and men, three times the number of hands needed on a merchantman of similar size.

Two main types of whales were the quarry: the sperm whales and the right whales. The sperm whales were the largest and the most dangerous to attack—one famous one was "Mocha Dick," a whale with a nasty disposition who was immortalized as "Moby Dick" by Herman Melville—but they were the ones that brought the biggest reward. The sperm oil taken from the head cavity was pale yellow in color, smelling faintly of fish, and highly prized for use in light machinery and in lubricating spindles. With this sperm oil came a waxy substance called spermaceti, clear and liquid when taken from the whale's case, but solidifying a few minutes later, much in demand for candlemaking. In addition to the sperm oil and spermaceti, sperm whales yielded a good amount of "train oil" from their blubber, not worth as much as the sperm oil, but a valuable commodity on its own account. An unusually healthy, well-fed bull would yield as much as 145 barrels of train oil, each barrel holding thirty-one and a half gallons, although the average bull's blubber produced from eighty to a hundred barrels, and a cow's only twenty-five. The right whales, of which the arctic bowheads were a species, varied in the amount of oil they produced, from 25 to 250 barrels, and while their oil was not of the same high grade as that of the sperm whales, they were rich in whalebone, which was much esteemed in the making of corsets and bustles for stylish ladies. As a rule the right whales were found far to the north or far to the south; the sperm whales preferred temperate waters.

When the whalers set out in 1815 to carry on their livelihood, they scattered throughout the Atlantic and to the Pacific. The English had discovered the grounds close to the South American Pacific coast, and that had become a favorite haunt for whalers, with Callao, Peru, as a base of supply. But in 1818 a Captain George W. Gardener searched there without luck, and then turned westward in hope of finding whales. Some fifteen hundred miles west of South America he saw the tell-tale spouts that meant a school of whales, and he cruised most profitably there, returning with a full hold. He passed the word around among his friends and soon the "Offshore Grounds" were famous in New England whaling ports: roughly the new grounds covered the area from Latitude 5 to 10 South and Longitude 105 to 125 West—just below the equator, fifteen hundred miles from the Marquesas and the Society Islands, fifteen hundred miles from Peru. In that area schools of five or six hundred whales were not uncommon, and by 1820 there were fifty whalers on the "Offshore Grounds."

Soon the whalers were off the coast of Japan, whither a merchantman bound home from China had directed them, reporting to whalers in the Sandwich Islands that he had seen schools of whales there. By 1822 there were thirty whalers off Japan, a dangerous coast off which to work, for the storms and uncharted islands were an invitation to disaster, and the crews of whalers driven ashore on the forbidden islands of Japan met with rude treatment, being taken prisoner, kept in cages and dungeons, constantly beaten and abused. In 1835 Captain Barzillai T. Folger, in *Ganges* of Nantucket, took a right whale off Kodiak Island and opened the northwest whale fishery, whose main port later became San Francisco; bowheads were found off Kamchatka eight years later, and in 1848 Captain Royce in the bark *Superior* of Sag Harbor found them in the Arctic—tame whales which could be killed as easily as cows. The mob followed him, and in the next three years 250 ships dodged about among the ice floes and took the bowheads as fast as they came up to breathe. Other whaling grounds were found in the Indian Ocean; in fact, the whole expanse of the earth's waters was examined by the whalers, who in the course of their voyages discovered some four hundred Pacific islands, named them with good resounding Yankee names, marked them on their charts and noted them in their logs. In a typical incident, Captain Pendleton of New London sighted a peak rising sheerly out of the ocean and this whetted his curiosity. He sailed closer to it and examined the coastline, finding at last a channel in the wall of the mountain, with fourteen fathoms of water in it, leading into the interior of the mountain. Through this passage he sailed and suddenly found himself in the center of an immense bowl—the crater of an extinct volcano. It was Deception Island.

As the scope of the hunting grounds grew, the fleet of whalers increased: there were 203 ships in 1829, 552 in 1840, 652 in 1842, 736 in 1846, with a total tonnage in the latter year of 233,189 tons. Gradually the center of activity shifted away from Nantucket and toward New Bedford: Nantucket had led the way in the early days, but as the size of the whalers grew the ten feet of water over the bar across the entrance to Nantucket harbor was too little: any ship of over a hundred tons had trouble getting over that bar, in spite of everything the Nantucketers could do. Unloading on lighters helped for a little while, but if the barrels of oil were lightered out at a mainland port that meant extra cost as well as trouble, and in any event it was an uneconomical way to do business. Petitions to Congress in 1803 and again in 1806 were of no help, for the Quakers on Nantucket had not strong enough political backing to offset the seamy record they made as pacifists in the war of the Revolution. In 1806 Nantucket sent thirteen whalers to sea and New Bedford eight; twelve years later New Bedford cleared twenty-five whale ships and Nantucket only eighteen; in 1846, the golden year of whaling, New Bedford sent out sixty-nine whalers and Nantucket only sixteen.

The value of the catch rose to above six million dollars in 1835; in 1845 sperm oil reached a peak of 4,967,550 gallons, worth 88¢ a gallon. Right whale oil, in 1840, was worth 33¢ a gallon and that year 11,593,483 gallons were brought to port. There were some famous catches in that era: *Uncas* of Falmouth came home in 1831 with 3,468 barrels of sperm oil worth $88,000, after a thirty-two month voyage; *Loper* of Nantucket took 2,280 barrels in fourteen months; *Sarah* of Nantucket, in three years, brought back sperm oil worth $89,000—3,497 barrels of it; *William Hamilton* of New Bedford brought in 4,181 barrels of sperm oil worth $109,000; and *Coral* of New Bedford reached the top with a cargo worth $136,000, composed of 3,823 barrels of right whale oil, 195 barrels of sperm oil, and 31,700 pounds of whale-bone.

Men were happy to set out on the long voyages when the rewards could be so great, and the life was full of the promise of action. But they had their full share of trouble afloat: the crews sometimes mutinied, unpopular officers were "lost at sea," after being tapped deftly behind the ear with a belaying-pin by a seaman with a grievance, during the night watches. In 1842 there was a particularly nasty mutiny aboard *Sharon* of New Bedford: one of her crew sliced off the captain's head with a cutting-spade, used more properly for cutting blubber, while the boats were away chasing whales. Three men had been left aboard as ship-keepers, and they formed the party of mutinous hands: arming themselves with axes, belaying-pins and harpoons, they held the ship against the boats' crews until, during the night, the third mate got aboard and killed two of the three mutineers. When the rest of the boats' crews came aboard the third culprit was found hiding in the forehold, from which he was extricated and prepared to meet his fate.

The whales sometimes showed an intelligence disconcertingly logical: one huge sperm whale—and they reached a length of eighty-four feet— attacked the whaler *Essex* in the South Pacific in 1819, when she was cruising peacefully on the Offshore Grounds. One of her crew spotted the spermaceti dead ahead, at a time when *Essex* had three of her boats out, with her captain in one of them. This whale, instead of sounding in the way well-behaved cachelots were wont to do, took a shallow dive and came up driving at the ship full ahead, hit it like a battering ram and starting the planks. While the pumps were going the whale, which had passed under the ship and regathered its strength, suddenly attacked again: this time the bows were crushed, and as the whale swam out of sight, dazed but proud, the mate aboard *Essex* barely had time to get a spare boat in the water and to abandon ship before she capsized. The mate's boat joined forces with the other three boats, and together they salvaged a supply of bread and water from the hulk of the *Essex* before she started to break up and sink. The four whale-boats started out for the South American coast on November 22nd; they were close to the equator, and nearly fifteen hundred miles from Callao, Peru. Storms separated the four boats, and the men were tortured by thirst and hunger and exposure to the sun and the salt spray; not until late in February were the survivors rescued: in all, only eight men remained alive of the thirty who had set out in *Essex*. Other ships were attacked by whales—the *Ann Alexander* on the Offshore Grounds, and *Pocahontas* off the coast of Brazil. It is likely that such attacks were cases of mistaken identity, the whales taking the whale ships for a particularly large species of whale, and therefore worth attacking. It was a much more common occurrence for whalers to lose several of their boats in fights with the whales, especially after harpoons had infuriated them, for then their flukes and tails churned the water white and smashed any boats within reach. "A dead whale or a stove boat" was the rule, and there is even a tale of a captain who fought what appears to have been a duel with a whale—he rode the whale's hump, was shaken off, rolled upon in the water, pushed under, came up, was dunked again by a knowing fluke, and finally, half-paralyzed, was rescued by his chief mate.

The custom grew, after the War of 1812, of calling at Pacific islands—the Society Islands and the Marquesas and the Hawaiian Islands—to take on provisions of fresh vegetables and fruits and water and meat. A whaler left home loaded with salt meats, hard bread, dried beans and peas, rice, some molasses and flour, and scurvy resulted from this sort of diet if it was not augmented by fresh foodstuffs. Then, too, the crews needed what was termed a "frolic," which started as soon as a whaler entered an island port. The native girls swam out to welcome them, wearing nothing but flowers and the frangible grass skirts they favored for ease of movement. The scenes that followed, especially when the crews were provided with native liquor by the canoes that came alongside, were shocking to the more carefully reared members of the crews: they were scenes of unbridled license, of gross impropriety, for the native girls had no sense of shame; they were not aware that indiscriminate copulation was frowned upon in the best social circles, and the missionaries had not then had time to spread Christian morality in all the out-of-the-way places the whalers frequented. But the frolics seldom lasted more than three days, and then the business of taking on provisions began, giving the few incurably romantic or antisocial members of a crew a chance to jump ship and shack up with some native beauty under a breadfruit tree. Reports, in detail, of such frenzied frolics do not appear in the logs of the whalers, nor in the letters sent home by their crews, who were prudent men, but the word got around in the whaling towns of New England, in the taverns when men were in their cups and boastful, and by degrees the scandalous tales came to the ears of the wives. In extreme cases the captains' wives took drastic action: they sailed with their husbands on the long cruises, took their chances with the elements, and sometimes undertook to bring moral enlightenment to the crews. But it was an impossible task for a woman to achieve, and on the islands the whalers visited, in the years after the frolics, there were sure to be a few Anglican-looking tribal members.

[13] *Far Places*

The whalers were not the only Americans who found their way into outlandish harbors in the years following the War of 1812: equally eager for profits and willing to take risks were the men who traded among the South Pacific islands and in the China sea. Often the life they led was an extremely dangerous one; not exceptional was the cruise of the *Friendship,* a Salem ship commanded by Captain Charles M. Endicott, which dropped anchor in the roadstead off Quallah Battoo on the Sumatran west coast in September 1830, hoping to pick up a cargo of pepper. The natives, with whom Salem merchantmen had been trading for years, had somehow come to the conclusion that the logical way to get such trade goods as the muskets, axes and cotton cloth the *Friend-ship* carried would be to seize the ship. So they laid devious plans for an act of piracy: one night a canoe went out to test the vigilance of the watch kept on *Friendship,* and when they were hailed by the watch, and given no chance to draw near the ship, they offered to trade some bags of pepper they had brought along to disguise the real purpose of their nocturnal visit. The trading went on during the night, with the crew of *Friendship* ready to fight at the gleam of a kris, and about sixty bags of pepper were brought aboard. Having been thwarted in this first attempt, the natives tried another artifice: they decoyed the captain and with him the second mate, John Barry, and four men, ashore by telling them that the new pepper crop they were awaiting had begun to come in, and that they could get at least a hundred bags a day on shore. Endicott and his party landed, and for a few days the trading went smoothly, although the natives took a great deal of time bringing the bags of pepper down to the landing where the scales were. Then, Po Adam, a friendly native merchant, warned Endicott that there was trouble brewing among the natives, and Endicott sent Barry from the landing to take a look at *Friendship* from a near-by hill-top. Barry reported back almost immediately, saying that there was trouble on the ship, and that he had seen men jumping overboard. Endicott mustered his shore party and, after warning them to show no exceptional excitement, they shoved off in the boat for their ship. As they rowed down the river they saw packs of natives running along the river's banks, waving their spears and swords and screaming strange Malay oaths. In the river, dead ahead of the boat, was a native proa, manned by a dozen natives of blood-curdling aspect, intent on stopping the fleeing Americans. Endicott ordered full speed ahead, for the best solution seemed to be to ram the native craft, but when the natives saw Barry in the bow of the boat, brandishing his sword, their courage dissolved and they backed water. The natives along the banks of the river were thrown into a frenzy at this escape, and later on Endicott learned the reason for the intensity of their frustration: they had decided to reward those who killed the white men according to their idea of the value of the white men's lives—the captain's death was to be worth one thousand dollars to whichever native killed him, the murderer of the mate was to get five hundred dollars, and seamen's lives were worth a hundred dollars each. When the ship's boat had cleared the land Endicott saw *Friendship* still anchored in the roadstead, sails furled, but swarming with natives. The Americans rowed thoughtfully toward their captured ship, pondering their predicament. The nearest help was at Muckie, a port some twenty-five miles down the coast, where some American merchantmen were known to be in port, and while Endicott was estimating his chances of reaching Muckie three large proas packed with natives cleared the river's mouth and started toward them. At this opportune moment the heavens clouded over and thunder and lightning played among the mountains, promising them trouble with the elements as well as with the natives. The Americans started rowing along the coast, leaving the proa-men to help sack the ship, and stopping only at the Soosoo River to fill a keg with fresh water, they kept rowing throughout the day and on into the night, bound for

Muckie. During the night the storm hit them and the seas rose; they double-manned two of the oars, and Endicott steered by instinct toward Muckie. Then the rain and the wind abated and a star came out; they rigged a sail from some gunny sacks they found in the boat, and with a fair wind made good time toward Muckie, which they reached about one o'clock in the morning. There they found three American ships, and as soon as they explained to their countrymen what had happened to *Friendship* the three made sail in all haste and set out up the coast for Quallah Battoo. By daylight they were within sight of the *Friendship,* which the natives had moved close to shore to facilitate the looting which they had been busily carrying on all night. Word was sent ashore by a passing proa that if the natives would give up *Friendship* peacefully the native town would not be bombarded, but soon a canoe brought back the answer, inviting the Americans to try to take the ship. Then there began a spirited little gunnery duel between the ships and the batteries on shore, in which the natives' guns were silenced, and no damage done to the American ships. With all danger from the forts ended, the Americans manned three boats with well-armed men and set out, rowing, toward *Friendship,* intending to storm her simultaneously on both sides and at the bow. As soon as the natives on the captured ship saw the grim-visaged crews in the approaching boats they began to jump overboard and swim for the shore, in their haste to escape. When the Americans, unopposed, regained the deck of *Friendship* there was not a soul aboard, and her blood-stained decks attested to the bitterness of the fight her men had made. The ship had been so thoroughly looted that Endicott decided to head for home, with the remnants of his crew, four of whom he found ashore, where they had been wandering in the jungle without food after escaping from the pirates. Three of his men had been killed and one grievously wounded. *Friendship* reached Salem in July 1831, where Endicott found the population in a state of great excitement, for the news of the fighting at Quallah Battoo had been brought to the United States by a faster ship that *Friendship* had fallen in with at St. Helena.

The American government moved rapidly to avenge this piracy: less than a year later the frigate *Potomac,* John Downes commanding, anchored off Quallah Battoo and sent a landing force ashore. The sailors and marines stormed the forts and set the town afire; *Potomac* then leisurely bombarded the town at close range, and the natives, their homes in ashes, were immensely impressed by the protecting power thus displayed. When Endicott returned several months after the bombardment, looking for pepper, he found a chastened population, and for a long time afterwards any Americans doing business in that port were treated with the respect the guns of *Potomac* had won for them.

But in other parts of the South Pacific the natives were not so enlightened, and they formed an element of danger as unpredictable as the sea and wind. The Fiji Islands, where the natives were of unusually warlike and cannibalistic habits, and where the coast was not well defined on the charts, attracted the more adventurous traders: the whale-ship *Oreno* was wrecked there, and the brig *Charles Daggett* had to fight her way out of Kandora in 1833, losing six men killed and several wounded in the process. *Glide* of Salem, with a large crew of thirty men, had several brushes with the Fiji Islanders in 1830 and 1831, before she finally dragged her anchor in a storm and was driven ashore on Miambooa Island. By pure luck the natives there were friendly, not having had enough dealings with the white traders to learn the advantages of corrupt practices, and they were, moreover, notably reasonable savages, not given to sudden rages, willing to talk matters over in a rational manner. The shipwrecked men were taken to the council-house where judgment was passed upon them by the local king, and the high priest with his minor priests, and tribal warriors. The high priest was in favor of treating them as though they were pigs; that is, he wanted to have them knocked on the head, cooked and eaten, thus becoming "long pigs." His opinion was worth a good deal, for the wreck of the *Glide* was attributed to his occult powers by the faithful, and in the discussion that followed he had numerous supporters. But he also had a reputation for being an ill-natured savage, and the king and his warriors seem to have taken into account both his disposition and his chronic hunger, for they ultimately judged that the white men were not to be hurt. For several months they lived among the natives, and then they were picked up by the bark *Peru,* of Salem, along with the survivors of the wreck of the brig *Niagara.*

The cargoes that attracted traders to these dangerous waters were, besides pepper, sandalwood, tortoise shell, and bêche-de-mer, or sea-cucumbers, which were plucked from the reefs by the natives and then boiled and dried and sold in China where they were used to make a soup fit for gourmets. Between the East Indian islands and China a steady trade was carried on in American ships, and this trade was but a side-line in the regular commerce with China, whose exports had by 1835 become of major importance to the United States. In the twelve months from October 1, 1834 to September 30, 1835, imports to the United States from China reached a total value of $5,987,187, and although this was only a tenth of the value of imports from England, and was exceeded by imports from France and Cuba and Mexico, it still represented a large volume of goods being carried from a distant land. Indeed, the American government was so conscious of the value and importance of this trade that in 1835 the Navy's East India Squadron was established to protect it. Tea from India and China, to the amount of 14,410,480 pounds in 1835, valued at $4,520,719, made up the chief part of the cargoes of the China traders, but they brought back, too, silks and sateens and nankeens, porcelains and chinaware and shawls, and occasionally a log of sandalwood which on the Yuletide hearth at home provided a fitting aromatic accompaniment to the traveler's tales of China.

In China the Americans had entrenched themselves in the good graces of the government by observing the rules laid down by the Chinese to regulate trade with the foreign devils. The groundwork had been well laid, and four American commission houses had been established in China, where they were permitted to carry on trade through Chinese intermediaries. It was not a bad life for the Americans who lived at Canton and carried on this trade: servants were plentiful and obsequious, and the poorest clerk working for Russell and Company, or Olyphant, or Heard, or Wetmore—the other commission houses— could afford a servant. An acquisitive man, as most of them were, could make money rapidly; white women were not then allowed in China, but for those whose Puritan upbringing was faulty, there were always the flower-boats in the river, staffed with fragile-looking girls who were themselves flower-like.

Trade was their only reason for being there, and the American houses joined forces and presented a united front to compete with the British East India Company: they were remarkably successful in this effort, and the British lost large slices of their trade to the Americans, who moved in on this profitable commerce with energy and quick wits, and fast ships.

In the Far East the need for speedy vessels developed when it was reported that the British schooner *Jamesina,* a small, swift opium runner, had sold £330,000 worth of Indian opium in Chinese ports in 1833. And she was only one of three such vessels whose cargoes were helping to lull the inhabitants of the Celestial Empire into dreams full of amiable dragons and houris. To win part of this trade the American commission house of Russell and Company sent out to Canton fast little armed vessels like 100-ton *Ariel,* 150-ton *Zephyr,* and the brig *Antelope,* of 370 tons. Speed was essential in an opium runner, for they needed it to escape the pirates of the East Indies and the China coast, and they needed to be first in the Chinese market with each year's new crop of opium; their sailing qualities had to be good so that they could beat up the Chinese coast against the northeast winds. Soon they were being called "opium clippers." Such craft, whose speed was built into them without any sacrifice of their seaworthiness, were characteristic of American-built sailing ships in that they were the answer to a specific demand for speed.

Wherever there was need for speed, whether in a Baltimore privateer in 1812 or in an opium clipper in 1835, the lines of such vessels became sharper, their spars longer, and their hull lower. But seldom were they of more than two hundred tons, and in the case of the Baltimore privateers they were mostly schooner rigged. By a curious combination of circumstances, whose precise nature it is difficult to deduce now, one Isaac McKim had an exceptionally original idea in 1832: he wanted a square-rigged ship built that would follow the sweet lines of a Baltimore clipper schooner, but that would be more than twice as large. He was a Baltimore shipowner and merchant of great resources, and Kennard and Williamson of Baltimore built such a ship for him at their Fell's Point shipyard. The owner had a wife, Ann by name, of whom he was very fond, and so the square-rigged clipper was named the *Ann McKim.* The new ship was of 493 tons register, 143 feet in length, with a 31-foot beam, and she drew 17 feet of water. Isaac McKim did not mind spending money on an idea, and the *Ann McKim* was a pet idea: her coppered bottom, live oak frames, mahogany deck fittings and twelve brass guns made her the talk of the waterfront. She went into the China trade, winning a reputation as a ship of swift voyages, but not necessarily a ship that a hard-headed, money-minded merchant would care to duplicate; she did not carry enough cargo for that, and great speed, while handy in a privateer or in running opium, was not as important in a merchantman as large carrying capacity and moderate speed. Isaac McKim died in 1838 and the ship was sold to Howland and Aspinwall of New York, who operated her for ten years and then sold her to the Chileans at Valparaiso. During the first years of her life the *Ann McKim* was a question-mark in the discussions of ship-owners and designers: she was the only one of her kind in the world, and wherever she went she was a topic for debate. The merchants watched her, saw her prove her ability, but still they remained reluctant to put their money into building others like her. They could meet what competition there was with what they had in the way of ships, and the *Ann McKim* continued to be an isolated dream expressed in oak and canvas until 1839, when a few hardy souls attempted to combine speed and size.

That year *Akbar* was built by Samuel Hall in Boston for John M. Forbes of Russell and Company; she went into the China trade and made Canton after a voyage of 109 days from New York; *Helena*, 650 tons, built by William H. Webb, followed in 1841 and *Paul Jones*, 620 tons, slid down the ways in 1842, and in one voyage, from Hong Kong to Boston, took only 111 days; then *Houqua*, 706 tons, made the passage from Hong Kong to New York in 90 days in 1844—an average speed of 158.6 miles per day. Larger vessels went into operation between India and China at the same time: *Montauk*, 540 tons; *Panama*, 670 tons; *Coquette*, 420 tons, most of them carrying opium and all of them coining money for their owners. These ships were the forerunners of the clippers: they were all large and fast and square-rigged—like the *Ann McKim* in the sense that they duplicated her virtues, if not her lines, and thus paid homage to the bright idea old Isaac McKim had when he ordered her built.

In the era that such ships opened the word "clipper ship" came to have a special meaning, and the ship that was the prototype of future clippers was the *Rainbow,* ordered in 1843 by Howland and Aspinwall (owners of the *Ann McKim*), from Smith and Dimon of New York. John Willis Griffiths was the designer, and he lengthened the bow above water, hollowed out the water lines, thinned and sharpened the ship forward, so that her greatest beam was further aft than in former ships. *Rainbow,* 750 tons, was launched in January 1845, and she was really a new type of ship. The calamity-howlers predicted that she was too sharp in the bows, and would crack up in any kind of a sea, but she turned out to be both fast and dependable, although her decks seemed always to be wet with the seas she took. *Rainbow* went out to Canton from New York in ninety-two days, and came home in eighty-eight days; beyond dispute, she was then the world's fastest ship, and she went into commission just in time to reap the benefits of the surging China trade.

Opium-smuggling had become unfashionable, even as slave-running had, and the American government took a high moral tone in the matter: Commodore Lawrence Kearny was sent out to the Far East in 1842, as commander of the Far Eastern Squadron, to see if there was anything he could do to help legal trade and at the same time keep American vessels from bringing opium to China, a practice much frowned upon by the Chinese government. Kearny was a man with an excellent record: he had been in the War of 1812, and then he had fought the Spanish pirates off the coast of Cuba and the Greek pirates off the Cyclades with considerable success. In China he looked the situation over and came to the conclusion that his powers did not include the right to interfere with merchantmen trading peacefully in Chinese ports or on the high seas, even if they were carrying opium. The most he could do to restrict the opium-smugglers was to search for flaws in their papers which would enable him to send them home for a judicial clarification of their status. It was a weak, if ethical, way to enforce the moral policy Kearny had proclaimed on his arrival in China, when he announced that he was against opium-smuggling in American vessels. But even if the policy was ineffective in practice, it won him the good-will of the Chinese government, and when he urged that the five "treaty ports" of Canton, Shanghai, Foochow, Amoy and Ningpo, which had been opened to the British by the Treaty of Nanking in August, 1842, be opened to Americans too, his request was well-received. Ten months later, on August 1, 1843, the Chinese government opened the treaty ports to the trade of all nations, and when the American government was so informed, the Chinese gave due credit to Kearny for his part in bringing about the decision.

The concession to open the five ports to all nations was helpful, but Kearny had a congenital suspicion of British machinations (the British had already adhered to Hong Kong), and he was anxious to have American commerce with China protected by a formal treaty which would extend to Americans in China the same rights the British had. The American merchants naturally favored such a treaty, and another greatly interested group was that formed by the Protestant missionaries, who were working in China under the handicap of a late arrival on the scene. The Catholics had been there centuries before them, as early as the thirteenth century, and the ornate rituals of the Catholic church exerted a much stronger influence on the pageant-loving Chinese than did the austere and colorless Protestant form of worship. In the competition to save Chinese souls the Protestants were up against the best proselytizers the Catholics had—the Jesuits. There were no Protestants with the flexible ethics of such a man as Matteo Ricci, an Italian Jesuit who, when informed that the Chinese thought that their country was the center of the world, promptly drew a map for the Manchu Emperor proving that such indeed was the case! The American missionaries were in obvious need of all the help they could get, from God or government.

In such circumstances the American government, urged by Kearny, the merchants and the missionaries began its counterplot: Daniel Webster, President John Tyler's Secretary of State, singled out Caleb Cushing to be the American Commissioner in China. Cushing was well-fitted for the position: son of a Newburyport shipping family, he was aware of the importance of foreign trade; he had been graduated from Harvard, which at that time was considered an accomplishment, and had become a lawyer and been elected to the U.S. House of Representatives. In his new capacity, being custodian of the national honor, Cushing went out to China escorted by a sloop-of-war, a frigate and one of the new-fangled sail-and-steam boats; to make the Chinese suitably aware of his importance he wore the uniform of a Major-General, with some added gold braid to increase the effect. The resultant, resplendent apparition worked wonders as a means of impressing the Chinese, but, even so, Cushing had to resort to veiled threats of warships just over the horizon, after soft words had proved inadequate to break down Chinese opposition to his request for a commercial treaty. But the treaty, at last signed on July 3, 1844, at Wing Hiya, regularized American trade in the treaty ports, granted extraterritorial privileges for American citizens in China, and nailed the door to China open. Cushing finessed the question of opium-smuggling in American ships by disentangling the American navy from any responsibility for the enforcement of China's anti-opium regulations; at the same time the protection of American warships was withdrawn from the opium-smugglers. From the navy's point of view this was unfortunate, for the service was full of zealous officers who had never heard a gun fired in battle.

Indeed, in the years after 1825, by which time the pirates in the Caribbean had been eliminated, the navy had been having a dull time at sea, and its most spirited actions were fought on Capitol Hill, where the Senators and Representatives fulminated pro and con on the question of whether the navy should be improved. There was no cogent reason to increase the number of ships in commission, and the debate that raged in Congress over the 1827 Navy Bill represented a fumbling effort to find a naval policy that would not be at odds with the Congressmen's varying conceptions of democratic government. President John Quincy Adams of course favored a powerful navy, for he was the elder son of John Adams and he had inherited the Massachusetts maritime tradition as well. But the bill, as written, was harmless enough: by it naval expenditures for the next six years were set at $500,000 per year; navy yards were to be stocked with timber and modernized, two dry-docks built and a naval academy started. On the last item there arose a great dissension: a naval academy would breed a caste of militarists who would arrogate all the best billets in the navy, leaving little or no political patronage, clamored the opposition, adding that the merchant marine was an adequate source of naval officers, and that there were enough naval officers anyhow—if there were more of them they would be likely to spend their time agitating for more ships. The bill was finally passed without the provisions for the establishment of a naval academy, and by their votes the congressmen faithfully reflected the sectional interests of the nation. New England and New York were for anything that would aid and abet commerce; the inland, agrarian states were for the least expensive navy possible.

Their type of man, General Andrew Jackson, took office on March 4, 1829, and he promptly defined the navy's place in the scheme of things: its chief business, he said, was to protect commerce, and he at that time considered that a national militia, plus the leagues of ocean that lay between Europe and the United States, offered ample protection for the nation. At the time it was a perfectly reasonable policy, for the only potential enemies were France and Great Britain, and the conception of oceans as insulation against attack was still popular. If anyone had pointed out then that the sea was in actuality a conductor over which power could be projected, it would have made no difference: the ships themselves were so slow that the idea of the sea as protective insulation was still valid.

The navy was not greatly interested in changing the types of warships then in existence, although when in March 1836 the Board of Navy Commissioners, headed by Commodore John Rodgers, submitted to the Navy Secretary a program listing what they would like to have in the way of ships, they included in their recommendations twenty-five steamers, along with twenty-five sail of the line, thirty-five frigates, twenty-five sloops-of-war and twenty-five miscellaneous small craft. Of course they stood not a chance of getting all these ships, or even a sizeable part of them, and such funds as the navy had were not large enough to permit any expensive experiments in steam. Given the choice of spending money on sail or steam, any naval officer in a policy-making position would have backed sail. Steam was a luxury, not yet proved practical for warships, whereas the ships of the line, frigates and sloops-of-war were a known quantity, dependable, efficient, inexpensive to operate and a pleasure to command. Moreover, an officer who had command of a warship had learned his business through years of service; he had, in fact, mastered an art and that was an achievement not to be complicated by the introduction of engines and boilers about which he knew nothing.

A frigate then had a ship's company of about five hundred men and boys, and it was a self-sufficient community, carrying everything except women: poultry and livestock, water and rum and medicine and a chaplain. There were three major decks: spar and gun and berth, and every man aboard had his fixed duty in an arrangement arrived at through years of hard-won experience. The seamen were divided into starboard and larboard watches, and the watches in turn were divided according to the duties of the men in them. Thus, there were the topmen of the fore, main and mizzen masts who handled all orders affecting anything above the main yards of their particular masts. Top-men had to be young and active, and they took fierce pride in their work, even to the extent of looking at lesser sailors askance, only occasionally inviting them to visit the top, which was a large circular platform on the mast, railed around, and large enough to permit twenty or thirty men to relax in it. There were "sheet-anchor men," who worked on the forecastle, handling anchors, jibs and fore-yard, and were of necessity the most experienced of all the crew. Aft of them were the "after-guard," who concerned themselves with the mainsail and spanker, and hauled the lines on the aft part of the vessel. One deck down, on the gun-deck, were the "waisters" who had the humiliating duty of looking to the cleanliness and well-being of the pigs and chickens and who were held in contempt as sons of farmers. One more deck down, on the berth-deck, were the "holders" who worked among the water tanks and food casks and cables, and who always amazed the other men when, on rare occasions, they showed up in the sunlight, pallid and blinking, like slugs suddenly exposed when a boulder is turned. Five feet separated the berth-deck from the gun-deck, and in that space the men slung their hammocks, each man allowed eighteen inches in which to spread his swaying bed.

In a frigate there were in the neighborhood of fourteen officers: captain, first lieutenant (or executive officer), six junior lieutenants, surgeon, purser, chaplain, sailing-master, marine officers, and "passed midshipmen" who were later to be called "ensigns." It was a generally accepted fact that officers from the southern states, who during their formative years had become accustomed to handling slaves, were the most popular with the crews: the northerners, given authority, were apt to become tyrannical. After these wardroom officers came the warrant officers—the boatswain, gunner, carpenter and sailmaker—not quite wardroom quality, but high enough in rank to lord it over the petty officers. Below the warrant officers were the "reefers" or midshipmen, who had been sent to sea to learn the profession at first hand. Ranking even below the midshipmen were the petty officers, and then as a last group separating the seamen from the hierarchy of rank, came the master-at-arms, who with his ship's corporals and marines sergeants made sure that orders were promptly executed by the seamen. This complex microcosm, with its hallowed rituals, and its caste system as rigid as that of India, was not easily or quickly developed: it was the outgrowth of the slow accretion of experience, and like a barnacle it cohered tenaciously to men-of-war. Naval officers would have jumped overboard before they would have sanctioned the slightest change in the organization of ship-board life, and, moreover, to them a frigate or a ship of the line looked like about the most perfect instrument for fighting on the high seas that mankind could devise.

There were, it is true, several drawbacks in the nautical life from a seaman's point of view: they had to eat breakfast at eight A.M., dinner at noon and supper at four P.M. During the remaining eighteen hours of the day they ate nothing. Flogging was still legal, and the cat-of-nine-tails, which multiplied each stroke nine-fold, was frequently injudiciously used for minor infractions of discipline; sometimes the rum supply gave out, and when this happened it shook a man's faith in the navy; the crews always included thieves who would steal the buttons off your coat on a dark night, and who formed gangs to waylay the man who saved his money. American-born citizens were not happy as sailors aboard naval vessels; the limited advancement a seaman could expect was not worth the effort or the hardship, and they preferred service in the merchant marine, where they could win quick recognition and promotion. As a result the crews consisted of social pariahs, misfits, with an occasional British-trained sailor who had tired of serving in the royal navy. "The gallows and the sea refuse nothing" was then a very relevant saying.

But, having a navy in being, some useful way of using it had to be found, and Congress was equal to the occasion. A law was passed in May, 1836, which authorized the fitting out of an expedition to explore the seas in which the whalers and merchantmen had been sailing. Nearly two years later, after the politicians had exhausted the patronage possibilities involved in the assignment of officers and scientists to the expedition, Lieutenant-Commander Charles Wilkes was given command. His instructions were: "To explore and survey the Southern Ocean, having in view the important interest of our commerce embarked in the whale-fisheries, as well as to determine the existence of all doubtful islands and shoals; and to discover and accurately fix the position of those which lie in or near the track pursued by our merchant vessels in that quarter, and which may have hitherto escaped the observation of scientific navigators." Wilkes was further informed that: "Although the primary object of the expedition is the promotion of the great interests of commerce and navigation, yet all occasions will be taken, not incompatible with the great purpose of the undertaking, to extend the bounds of science, and to promote the acquisition of knowledge. For the more successful attainment of these objects, a corps of scientific gentlemen, for the departments of philology, zoology, conchology, geology, mineralogy, and botany, with artists and a horticulturist, will accompany the expedition, and are placed under your direction. The hydrography and geography of the various seas and countries you may visit in the route pointed out to you, will occupy your special attention; and all the researches connected with them, as well as with astronomy, terrestrial magnetism, and meteorology, are confided exclusively to the officers of the navy, on whose zeal and talents the department (of the navy) confidently relies for such results as will enable future navigators to pass over the track traversed by your vessels, without fear and without danger."

Wilkes' squadron consisted of the sloops-of-war *Vincennes* (flagship) and *Peacock*, the brig *Porpoise*, store-ship *Relief*, and tenders *Sea Gull* and *Flying Fish*. In August 1838 they put out to sea from Hampton Roads, on a cruise that was to last three years and ten months. In November they arrived at Rio de Janeiro, having sailed by way of Madeira and the Cape Verde Islands. Over those parts of the ocean wherein shoals or reefs had been vaguely reported, the vessels sailed in line abreast from three to five miles apart, in open order, blanketing an area twenty miles wide, and correcting the charts as they went. Leaving Rio in January, they doubled Cape Horn, rendezvoused at Orange Harbor and sent *Peacock* and *Flying Fish* off to the southwest to try to get beyond the most southerly point Captain Cook had reached. Ice-fields drove them back, and in May they sailed for Valparaiso. The first night out a gale overwhelmed *Sea Gull* and she vanished with her two officers and fifteen men. Next stop was at Callao, the whalers' port of call, and from that point the squadron took a course due westerly across the Pacific, through the "Offshore Grounds," and past various island groups which were surveyed. They arrived at Sidney, Australia in November 1839, and there the expedition shed its scientific men, leaving them to explore the flora and fauna in New Zealand and New Holland: the warships were off on a perilous voyage to the south. January 11, 1840, *Vincennes* and *Porpoise* sighted the solid barrier of ice in lattitude 64° 11′ S., longitude 164° 53′ E. *Peacock* reached the ice on the 15th, and *Flying Fish* on the 21st, both to the westward of the other vessels. To their great delight, as they cruised through sixty degrees of longitude along the barrier of ice, they saw in the distance mountains thousands of feet high, covered with perpetual snow. The vessels were in almost constant danger from the gales and shifting ice fields; *Flying Fish* was driven away, to the northward, and *Peacock* narrowly escaped destruction when she ran into a deep bay filled with icebergs, taller than her masts, that closed on her and so damaged her rudder that for a while it was useless. On her escape from the bay she was found to be so seriously damaged that she returned to Sidney. *Vincennes,* too, and *Porpoise,* were driven by gales along the edge of the barrier of ice, dodging between icebergs, but through skill and luck escaped unscathed.

When the brief, capricious Antarctic summer was over the vessels turned northwards and spent the summer exploring and surveying the islands of the Southern Archipelago: New Zealand, the Friendly Islands and the Fiji Islands were chartered, and in all 154 islands and 50 detached reefs were surveyed, and numerous harbors sounded. This work was not all peaceful: in the Fijis the natives were hostile, and the village at Sualib Bay was burned in reprisal for an attack by the inhabitants; on Malolo, another brush with the Fiji Islanders cost the lives of two Americans, and Sualib town was attacked to avenge their deaths. It was a sharp action for about fifteen minutes, and then, after a rocket had been fired into the village, and the native huts were set afire, the villagers fled to the hills, leaving seven dead on the field of battle.

In August the expedition left the Fiji Islands, sailing for the Sandwich (Hawaiian) Islands for supplies; on their way they went by separate routes so that each ship could explore the widest possible area, and the existence and position of several islands were determined. During the next winter they roamed from the Society Islands westward to the Kingsmill group, and the scientific gentlemen made exhaustive surveys of the Sandwich group. Throughout 1841 the expedition kept to its work, with *Peacock* the only loss: she went aground off the mouth of the Columbia river and broke up shortly after her people got safely ashore. An American brig in the river at that time was purchased to replace *Peacock*, and named *Oregon*: with *Porpoise* she surveyed the Columbia river as far as the river was navigable. *Vincennes* had meanwhile been charting the harbor at San Francisco, and had surveyed the Sacramento river. In late November the expedition set out for home by way of the Cape of Good Hope, pausing to fix the position of some reefs in the Ladrones Islands, and to chart the Sulu Sea between Borneo and the Philippine Archipelago. Here they negotiated a treaty with the Sultan of Sulu that granted the United States a most-favored-nation clause, stipulated that the Sultan would afford full protection to the merchant vessels of the United States and would aid the shipwrecked mariners of any nation. This was a minor diplomatic triumph, for the Sultan's subjects included numerous pirates, all of whom were addicted to head-hunting. In February, 1842, the squadron met at Singapore, where *Flying Fish* was sold, being judged unseaworthy for the voyage home, and late that month they headed for home, arriving at New York in June 1842. The beneficent results of this expedition's work were immediate and widespread: merchantmen, whalers, and men-of-war had for the first time accurate charts of a large part of the Pacific ocean, and especially of the waters in which they were most likely to sail. On the fringe of the Antarctic continent the United States had reason for a claim in the Victoria Quadrant, for Wilkes had made his discovery a few days before the French under Dumont D'Urville had sighted the frozen peaks. Even on English maps the name appeared: "Wilkes' Land," on the coast of the new continent, far within the limits of the drift ice and of the pack ice. That year of 1842, the year of the return of the expedition, witnessed a sudden appreciation of the peace-time utility of a navy, but the applause for the Wilkes' expedition had hardly died down before an ugly incident marred the record.

The brig-of-war *Somers,* returning in the fall of the year from the West African coast suffered an attempted mutiny: there was no justification for the attempt, her captain, Alexander Slidell Mackenzie, was a fine officer and an author as well, with a good deal of imagination. But among the midshipmen was Philip Spencer, son of the Secretary of War, and he had acquired a blemished record by previous misdeeds on other ships. He stirred up discontent, planning to seize the ship and set up in business as a pirate, with captured gold and women as the chief rewards. Warning of the intended mutiny came to the captain's ears, and he ordered Spencer to be put in irons, and the suspect was shackled to the deck. At this treatment the crew became unquiet, and they in turn made the officers' nerves jumpy. Two more men—boatswain's mate Samuel Cromwell and seaman Elisha Small—were put in irons because of suspicious conduct. Spencer's locker was broken open and searched: in it was found a list of how the brig would be manned when (and if) he took command. It may have been only a midshipman's fancy—it may have been the real thing: the officers spent a sleepless night, in the course of which a fourth man was discovered trying to rob the wine-chest. Next day he was flogged, and during the flogging the crew gave a demonstration of such mute insolence that the officers were led to believe that a mutiny might break out at any moment. The thing to do, then, was to string up the suspected leaders—Spencer and Cromwell and Small—to the yardarm, and let their grotesque aerial dance be a warning to the others. This was done—although there was no legal justification for such punishment: Article XIII of the Articles of War read: "If any person in the navy shall make, or attempt to make, any mutinous assembly, he shall, on conviction thereof by a court martial, suffer death." There was no court martial on the *Somers,* but when the brig reached New York in the autumn, a court martial was convened, to determine Captain Mackenzie's right to execute men. After a lengthy investigation he was acquitted of all blame in the affair. The verdict was to be expected:

the navy was closing ranks, heads pointed outward at the civilian world, for the navy was threatened with steam—whether they wanted it or not.

There had been a few mavericks—naval officers who had come out for steam with undisciplined enthusiasm—who had rammed their ideas through by resorting to their personal political connections when it became apparent that if the navy was to have steam warships it would be in spite of, and not because of, the navy itself. Indeed, there had been an unconscionable delay in the use of steam by the navy: the old "steam-battery" *Demologos,* unfinished during the War of 1812, was carried on the Navy List as "Fulton Steam Frigate," and she served as a receiving ship at the Brooklyn Navy Yard until a powder explosion destroyed her in 1829. She had been a marine architect's misconception: 152 feet long, with a 57 foot beam, she displaced 1,450 tons and had twin hulls with a paddle-wheel between that drove her about five knots an hour. She would have been more useful, with her thirty long 32-pounders, as a floating battery in harbor defense than as a man-of-war. The idea of a floating battery was to prove unexpectedly durable: in 1837, when the second *Fulton* was built through Navy Secretary Mahlon Dickerson's efforts, he thought of the new vessel as a valuable addition to the coastal fortifications. And in his opinion *Fulton II* had the added virtue of being incapable of crossing the ocean for offensive action. She could never become a lighted fuse in the hands of hot-tempered men, for she was built only to repel enemy attack on the American coast. To this end, *Fulton II* was armed with the new Paixhan guns that threw shells loaded with powder and exploded on contact, instead of the old solid shot. Under the command of Captain Matthew Calbraith Perry, younger brother of Oliver Hazard Perry, she banged away with her guns in target practice off the Jersey coast, proving the worth of the new guns to the navy's high command. Perry became quite proud and fond of her.

Meanwhile there were outside forces at work on Congress: the French and British navies were far ahead of the American in the use of steam, and Congress wanted to know why the Americans hadn't done something about it. There had been a threat of war with France, and the British were sniping at the Monroe Doctrine: the navy looked as though it needed a touch of modernization. There were, too, a couple of politically-smart naval officers pulling the strings quietly in the halls of

Congress: Matthew Perry, related by marriage to several politicians, and Robert Field Stockton, a power in New Jersey politics, grandson of lawyer Richard Stockton who had been among the signers of the Declaration of Independence.

Stockton had a good grasp of mechanics, and he was also the chief promoter of the Raritan and Delaware Canal, and therefore interested in anything that promised cheap towing-power for the canal-boats. He was in Europe in '38, as Senior Lieutenant on 86-gun *Ohio,* when he heard about the Swede John Ericsson, who had patented a design for a screw propeller in 1836. The same year an Englishman, Francis P. Smith, had taken out a similar patent. Ericsson had built a small boat equipped with a propeller and tried her out successfully on the Thames: the Lords of the Admiralty had even taken a ride, but were reluctant to give him financial backing when they had an Englishman in the field with the same idea. But Stockton was open-minded, and after the Swede had explained how his gadget worked, the naval officer raised one thousand pounds and ordered an iron steamer to be built and equipped with engines and a propeller designed by Ericsson. The result was a 70-foot vessel, the *Robert F. Stockton,* built in '38 and brought to the United States in the spring of the next year. Ericsson arrived a few months later. The little steamer went into service on Stockton's canal, where she won her owner's heart.

The navy bill for 1839 had been passed by this time, and it authorized, but did not appropriate the money for, the construction of three steam warships: Stockton tried desperately to get one of the three steamers equipped with a propeller. He advanced all the best arguments for the new device: it would permit a ship to carry her boiler below decks, and it would do away with the paddle-wheels that obstructed the orderly placement of guns; a vessel with engine and boiler below deck would be more seaworthy, have greater stability, and thus provide a better gun platform. But he had no luck until Harrison and Tyler won the presidential election in 1840, during which Stockton helped to swing New Jersey to the winning side. As a reward for his services in the campaign the new administration gave Stockton permission to build a screw-propelled warship, and she was built in 1841, with Ericsson's help, and christened *Princeton.* Word of the new ship's prowess spread quickly, and her influence was felt first in the coastal packet lines, where the propeller began to displace the cumbersome paddle-wheels as new coastal steam packets were built.

Matt Perry had not been idle: by heckling his politically powerful relatives he had wangled the necessary funds out of Congress to start construction on two of the three steam warships authorized by the 1839 navy bill. They were completed in 1842, and they were sister-ships—the *Missouri* and the *Mississippi*. Both vessels carried ten Paixhan guns, two 8-inchers and eight 6-inchers, and they displaced 3,220 tons each. At the same time another paddle-wheel steam warship was built, christened the *Union,* but she was a miscarriage, with only six guns, and machinery perpetually breaking down, not worth the powder to blow her to hell. But *Princeton* and *Missouri* were a huge success, and thus within a period of five years both steam and the screw propeller won a foot-hold in the American Navy. It was just in time, for there was trouble brewing with the Mexicans over Texas and California, and with the British over Oregon, and the navy showed not the slightest signs of being able to protect the country. The steam warships were, in fact, the only cause for an optimistic faith in the navy, on the part of the public.

Discipline in the service was slack, with officers drinking themselves silly and crews living in fear of the "cat." In 1845 there were only seventy-six vessels in the navy, eight of them steamers, and a young man could scarcely hope to command a frigate before he was gray-haired or bald. One of the navy's worst handicaps was the abysmal ignorance of the general run of officers, who were content to vegetate in soft billets ashore or to laze around at sea in a drunken semi-stupor induced by too much wine. There was no point in being ambitious or energetic, and a soporific lassitude pervaded limbs and minds alike. There was a crying need to educate them, but not a chance to get legislation passed to set up a naval academy that would make patricians out of plebeians who were so admirably democratic. John Adams had proposed a naval school as part of a military academy as early as 1800, but that plan had failed, as had suggestions made by Jefferson and by John Quincy Adams, and the education of midshipmen had been left to the tender mercies of the chaplain, on small vessels, and school-masters, who were political appointees, on the larger ones. In 1839 a school for midshipmen had been established in Philadelphia, where midshipmen who had already served years at sea were prepared for the examination they had to take before they could become "passed midshipmen." Until 1845 this school served as the only land-based seat of learning in the navy, and it was obviously inadequate when such complicated things as steam engines and screw propellers were being put to use on warships. That year James Polk became President, and foreseeing trouble ahead, he picked George Bancroft, philosopher, historian and diplomat, to be his Navy Secretary. Bancroft could not rest in the presence of ignorance, and so he moved with diplomatic unobtrusiveness to establish a more effective naval school: he wrote to Polk, asking if he had any objections to the navy's taking over Fort Severn at Annapolis for the purpose, and Polk approved the idea of transferring the fort from the army to the navy provided the army had no objections. So Bancroft wrote an amiable letter to the Secretary of War, W. L. Marcy, asking if he would approve the transfer, and Marcy assented to the transfer in August 1845, it being understood that his son, Passed Midshipman Samuel Marcy, would be the assistant instructor in mathematics at the new academy. At eleven o'clock on Friday morning, October 10th, 1845, between fifty and sixty midshipmen were mustered at Fort Severn, and the Superintendent, Commander Franklin Buchanan, an educated and exacting man, read to the assembled officers, instructors and midshipmen a letter from the Navy Secretary, and in a few words defined the purpose for which the school was being started: it was to turn midshipmen into officers and gentlemen of a type that would have made Paul Jones proud. An ability to navigate, drunk or sober, was not enough; now you had to be an educated man, too. It was the start of the naval officer caste—a group of men for whom there was much work to do.

[14] *Neighborhood Brawl*

The work that the navy had to do concerned Mexico, which had whirled out of the Spanish Empire in 1812 with more territory than she could protect. Texas had freed herself from Mexican rule in '36, and won recognition as a sovereign nation from the United States, Great Britain, Belgium and France. The problem that had everyone puzzled was how to fit Texas into the United States. For ten years the question of her annexation was the Gordian knot of American politics, not cut until 1845 when President Tyler signed the joint House and Senate resolution that permitted her entry into the United States as the 28th state. A day later the new President, Polk, took office. The slogan "Manifest Destiny" expressed the temper of the nation: it meant expansion to the west and south and northwest—to California, Mexico and Oregon. It was one of those periods in which the people of the United States felt yeasty and full of beans, ready to spread republican government as widely as possible, even at the cost of war. The Oregon question was to be settled peacefully in 1846, when the 49th parallel was accepted as the northwestern boundary of the United States, but in 1845 Mexico was ripe for the plucking: California lay invitingly open to attack, and the American government thought the British had designs on that province. Naval officers shared the suspicion, as they had for several years.

In 1842 Commodore Thomas Jones commanded the American Pacific Squadron, and in the summer of that year he was in Callao, Peru, with the frigate *United States,* 44 guns, the sloops-of-war *Cyane* 20 and *Dale* 16, and the schooner *Shark* 12. While in Callao he read, in a Mexican paper, a manifesto issued by the Mexican government that was so violently worded that he thought war must have at last begun over Texas. At the same time, in an American paper he found a report that Mexico had sold California to the British; and then, to add to the bodeful signs, the British frigate *Dublin,* flying the flag of Rear Admiral Thomas, dropped in at Callao, took on provisions, and mysteriously departed in the night. Jones deduced that she had gone to the northward, to take possession of California. But it was the policy of "manifest destiny" for the United States to seize California in the event of war with Mexico, and so Jones sailed suddenly from Callao with his squadron on September 7, 1842, bent on forestalling the supposedly nefarious plans of the British. *Shark*, on second thought, was sent back to Callao to keep in touch there, and *Dale* went to Panama to land a special messenger with dispatches for Washington.

On October 19th *United States* and *Cyane* anchored in the harbor of Monterey, where there was no evidence of British authority, but where Jones' suspicions of British intentions were confirmed, perhaps by some local Americans who were anxious for California to become one of the United States. At any rate, the Commodore decided to demand the surrender of the province, and next morning the governor signed the articles of capitulation, in vain protesting that he was ignorant of the existence of a state of war. The American flag replaced the Mexican, and drooped sadly over the tiny fort, whose guns had not even been fired. Next day Jones discovered that he had made a terrific mistake—there was no actual evidence that Britain had bought California, or that Mexico intended to sell; and—worst of all—there was no war between Mexico and the United States. It had all been a horrible blunder, and he rapidly returned California to its rightful owners, his alacrity matched only by his respectfulness, and retired with as much dignity as he could from the scene of his conquest. The excess of zeal the Commodore had shown caused his recall, as a peace-offering to the Mexican government, and he was replaced by Commodore John Drake Sloat. Sloat's orders were to avoid aggressive acts unless war was declared, and in that event he was to seize San Francisco and to become as aggressive as possible.

Sloat kept close to Mazatlan, on the Mexican coast, in the *Savannah* 44, sending his smaller vessels off on minor and peaceful missions. Since his orders would not permit fighting until war was declared, it was critically important for him to get accurate news quickly, and to do this he set up a line of communication across Mexico, making use of numerous trading houses, to keep himself informed of events in the United States and Texas. On June 7th 1846 word came over the grape-vine to Mazatlan that the battles of Palo Alto and Resaca de la Palma had been fought and that the Americans under Zachary Taylor had routed the Mexicans, driven them south across the Rio Grande. But there was no word of a declaration of war. Sloat made his own decision: he acted as though war had been declared (as indeed it had been, on May 12th by the United States and on May 23rd by Mexico), and he sailed northward in *Savannah,* leaving *Warren* at Mazatlán to await further news.

On July 2nd he reached Monterey, where he found *Cyane* and *Levant,* and learned that *Portsmouth* was at San Francisco. A landing-force of 250 sailors and marines went ashore without opposition and the flag was raised while the guns of the ships roared out a 21-gun salute. Marines were garrisoned in the town, and California was well on its way to becoming American territory. The next few weeks were full of conquests: a Major Frémont turned up with a small party which was augmented by volunteers, trappers and traders and hunters, until it numbered 160 men, who were sworn into the service of their country, and sent to take San Diego. On July 9, San Francisco capitulated to Commander Montgomery of *Portsmouth;* by the 11th the flag was hanging over Sutter's Fort on the Sacramento, at Bodega on the coast and at Sonoma.

Then there arrived on the scene the steam-fancier, canal-owner and politician, Captain Robert F. Stockton, in the frigate *Congress* 44, just in from the Sandwich (Hawaiian) Islands. Stockton reported for duty July 15th, and two weeks later Sloat relinquished command to him, and sailed for Panama, on his way home. He had carried out his orders, and now it was up to the new commodore to secure and extend the conquests. He was to have six months in which to do it, and the period was one of considerable naval activity. Santa Barbara, San Pedro and San Diego were taken, the latter by Major Frémont's battalion, which had been landed by *Cyane.* Los Angeles, the political center of the province, fell to the combined Stockton-Frémont forces on August 13th, and Captain Gillespie of the marines was left in charge of the garrison there.

From then on the warships were kept busy running up and down the coast, shoring up garrisons here and there, tracking down rumors of uprisings, and in general acting like so many bird-dogs in an autumnal field. Los Angeles had to be taken all over again, Gillespie having been driven out by the Mexicans, and Stockton led a force of six hundred men to recapture the place. They fought their way through the Mexicans under

General Flores in two pitched battles, during which Stockton distinguished himself by sound tactics and coolness under fire. The force entered Los Angeles early in January, 1847, and after brief negotiations the Mexican governor, Don Andres Pico, yielded possession of the province to the Americans. It was a fitting finale to Stockton's tour of duty in the Pacific, and the province of Upper California was well under control when he turned his command over to Commodore William Branford Shubrick, who arrived in *Independence* 54, toward the end of January. Stockton, always original, found a party that was about to return to the United States by crossing the Rocky Mountains, and he joined them, making his way homeward overland.

The new Commodore, Shubrick, found little left for him to do in Upper California, so he proceeded to pick up pieces of Mexico. Guaymas was taken, and then Mazatlán, the most important trade center on the west coast, a town of eleven thousand inhabitants. There was a flurry of excitement when the garrison at San Jose, commanded by Lt. Heywood of the marines, was besieged by three hundred Mexicans. Heywood had only 27 marines, 10 seamen and 20 California volunteers, but he stood off the Mexicans for over two weeks, and then, just as the water supply was failing, *Cyane* anchored off the village and sent a landing force of 102 officers and men ashore who rescued the dehydrated but still valiant garrison.

Upper California, at the time of its conquest, was inhabited by a few thousand peons and Indians, with Catholic missionaries to look after their spiritual life and some wealthy and patrician Mexican ranchers to tell them what work to do. After the invading Americans had consolidated their victory the natives resumed their sedentary existence, ennervated by the climate, dozing contentedly in the shade of the missions, importing their clothes and even their wine from the United States. Of the total population twenty per cent were American citizens, and wherever the native hovels huddled around a mission there was likely to be an American trader who dealt in hides and skins and rapidly made his fortune. The conquest of this potentially invaluable region was effected by only a handful of ships: *Independence* 54, *Congress* 44, *Savannah* 44, *Portsmouth* 20, *Warren* 20, *Cyane* 20, *Prebel* 16 and *Dale* 16, working in cooperation with Fremont's volunteers and with the few regular army dragoons who had managed to straggle across the mountains in time to join the fighting.

While these martial events were taking place on the Pacific coast, there was equally important naval activity in the Gulf of Mexico. The land fighting between the Mexicans and the Americans had not been going well: the American army had ground to a stop in the wastes south of the Rio Grande and it looked as though the soldiers might be stuck there forever, at the rate they were going. And so, in a strategy newly devised in the autumn of 1846, the navy was called upon to help. The new plan was to get to Mexico City as soon as possible by way of Vera Cruz, the port nearest to Mexico City. But first Vera Cruz had to be attacked and taken by sea, with troops transported in ships. Then the troops could drive up over the mountains to Mexico City, much as Cortez had done three centuries before.

Until this new strategy was decided upon naval operations in the Gulf of Mexico had been restricted to blockade duty along the coast. Commodore David Conner was in command of the Home Squadron thus engaged, which consisted of three 44-gun frigates, three sloops-of-war and two brigs. They were enough for blockade duty, but a special effort was called for when there was trouble with the province of Yucatán. Yucatán maintained a nominal independence of Mexico then, and claimed that it was strictly neutral in the war. But when munitions began to enter Mexico through Yucatán an expedition set out to enforce the province's claimed neutrality. The center of the trade in munitions was the town now known as Villa Hermosa (called Tabasco then, in the official reports, and San Juan Batista later). Villa Hermosa is on the Tabasco river, some seventy-five miles from its mouth, and its seaport on the Gulf is called Obregon now (then it was known as Frontera).

Commodore Matthew Calbraith Perry was given command of the expedition, and at his disposal were placed the steamers *Mississippi* and *Vixen,* the schooners *Bonita, Reefer* and *Nonata,* and the revenue service's steamer *McLane* and schooner *Forward.* The flotilla arrived at Obregon and took the port without resistance, capturing several vessels and two steamers, one of which, the *Petrita,* was taken into service. Loaded with two hundred officers, seamen and marines, *Petrita* steamed up the river towing the lighter vessels of the squadron. After two days they arrived at Villa Hermosa, and seized several merchantmen there; then the squadron formed in line-of-battle abreast of the town, within half-musket range, and an invitation to surrender the town was sent ashore. The answer came back quickly enough: Mexicans would never surrender to the Yanquis, and as for Commodore Perry—he could commence firing as soon as the spirit moved him. One can almost see the twirled moustachios and the bared teeth of the outraged Mexicans. Perry ordered *Vixen* to open fire, and at the third discharge the Mexican flag on the fort was shot away, and then Captain Forrest landed with his marines and seamen, under the protection of the ships' guns. The enemy began a distracting fire with muskets, to which the flotilla replied in kind, and this sort of thing kept up throughout the rest of the day and started again the next morning. Forrest's men were pinned down by the fire, and Perry saw that there was no future in trying to take the town again such determined opposition, so he collected his force and sailed off down the river, satisfied that he had broken up the arms trade, if only temporarily.

That autumn the navy made two attempts to take the town of Alvarado, but both failed; an attempt to take Tuxpan failed when the brig *Truxton* struck on the bar and her officers and men, with the exception of one boat's crew which managed to escape, were forced to surrender to the Mexicans. These were all actions incidental to the blockade; the main naval effort did not start until October 1846, when Commodore Conner received orders to take Tampico, which was needed as a place where troops and supplies could be concentrated for the contemplated attack on Vera Cruz, and where an assault would divert attention from the real objective. Thus the new strategy started when the naval forces converged on Tampico in early November.

It was a major effort, involving eleven warships, including the *Princeton* and the *Mississippi,* which towed the smaller craft as the squadron moved out of the anchorage at Anton Lizardo and arrived two days later off Tampico. Three hundred men were landed by the ships' boats, and they all walked into Tampico standing upright, for the city had been deserted by its garrison. Inquiries disclosed that the Mexican troops had fled with their munitions to the village of Panuco, twenty miles up the river from Tampico, and Commander Tattnall followed them with a small force, routed them and destroyed their military stores.

Active preparations to take Vera Cruz and its ancient castle of San Juan d'Ulloa began in early 1847. There was need for some kind of decisive action, for the army was still bogged down in its drive southward from Texas, not halfway to Mexico City after nearly a year of fighting. The war was in danger of becoming politically embarrassing. To speed up the offensive against Vera Cruz bomb-ketches and steamers were purchased and equipped and commissioned and sent to the Gulf of Mexico: the *Ohio* 74 was diverted from its intended Pacific duty, and, with the sloops *Germantown, Saratoga* and *Decatur* was sent to join Commodore Conner's command. When the full force was assembled between the island of Salmadina and Point Anton Lizard, ten to twelve miles eastward of Vera Cruz, it consisted of all the warships the United States could lay its hands on in the Atlantic and Caribbean; and on the transports were nearly twelve thousand soldiers under Major-General Winfield Scott. The possible landing points in the vicinity of Vera Cruz were carefully examined, and it was decided to land on the beach near the island of Sacrificios, three miles south of the city. Sixty-five large surf-boats, specially constructed for the purpose, each capable of holding a hundred men, were apportioned among the warships and were manned and officered from the fleet, the whole landing flotilla being placed under the command of Captain Forrest of the frigate *Raritan*. On the morning of March 9, 1847, the soldiers were transferred from the transports to the men-of-war; each of the frigates took between 2,500 and 2,800 men, with their arms and cumbrous accouterments; the sloops took nine hundred each, and the smaller vessels as many as they could pack in on their decks. A few minutes after ten o'clock that morning the transfer was completed, and the naval vessels got under way for Sacrificios, with General Scott and Commodore Conner on the steamer *Massachusetts,* and Commodore Perry on the *Raritan*. It was a beautiful day for an amphibious landing: clear skies, a fresh yet gentle breeze from the southeast, and a perfectly smooth sea. Within three hours all the warships were anchored in their allotted places off Sacrificios. There was no confusion, and the debarkation started at once, according to plan:

Princeton was ordered to take a position abreast of the landing beach, close to the shore, and the surf-boats were loaded with soldiers and directed to rendezvous astern of her. There they formed a double line-ahead, according to regiments and companies, with the regimental flag flying in the head boat of each regiment. While this movement was going on, the steamers *Spitfire* and *Vixen,* with five gunboats, were ordered to close and to be ready to cover the beach with their fire. They were able to get in close, since they had a draught of only five to eight feet, and they lay there with their 32-pounder shell guns swiveled shoreward to protect the army. When all was in readiness *Massachusetts* fired the landing signal, the surf-boats cast off from *Princeton* and from each other, squared away in line abreast, and pulled for the beach. The first line of boats disgorged its soldiers who charged across the sand, up the dunes, and then stopped abruptly: there was not a Mexican in sight. The surf-boats returned to the warships, picked up the second line of the army, landed them, and then, without waiting to form in line abreast, they hurried back and forth between ships and shore, pouring the troops in as fast as they could. In a few isolated instances loaded boats grounded on the bar, some twenty yards from dry land, and the soldiers had to wade through waist-deep water to get ashore. But by ten o'clock that night twelve thousand men had been landed on the beach by the navy, with stores and provisions for several days, and without the loss of a single life.

Next job facing the navy was the bombardment of Vera Cruz, and preparations went ahead for that. Meanwhile on March 21st Conner relinquished command of the Home Squadron and made ready to leave for home in *Princeton:* he had been Commodore for three years and his health had suffered severely on that tropical coast. The new Commodore was Matthew Calbraith Perry.

On March 22nd Vera Cruz was completely surrounded and the Governor was invited to surrender. When he declined, shells from the army's land batteries and from *Spitfire, Vixen* and the five small gunboats began falling into the town. But there was no chance for the men on the larger naval vessels to help, and to assuage their warlike spirit General Scott graciously permitted them to land some guns and form a battery of their own. The guns landed were three eight-inch Paixhans and three

32-pounders, all of which were mounted and then served by men of the various ships in rotation, so that everyone could get a shot at the Mexicans. This battery, during the siege, fired one thousand Paixhan shells and eight hundred round shot into the enemy's walls and forts, at a cost of seven dead and eight wounded. The bombardment of Vera Cruz lasted for four days and then, with no hope of relief, the Mexicans surrendered their wrecked city.

Articles of capitulation were signed and exchanged late in the evening of March 27th, and at 10 A.M. two days later American troops garrisoned the city and the castle. At noon General Scott sat down in the Palace of Vera Cruz and penned a dispatch to the Secretary of War:

> "Head-Quarters of the Army,
> Vera Cruz, March 29, 1847.

"Sir: The flag of the United States of America floats triumphantly over the walls of this city and the castle of San Juan d'Ulloa. . . ."

When the American troops entered the city they found that scarcely a single building had escaped the bombardment: shot and shell had destroyed many homes; fires had swept the wreckage; roofs had been blasted in and walls leveled; massive pieces of masonry lay in angular heaps from which the corpses of human beings and the carcasses of horses and mules protruded. From the city an intolerable stench arose in the clear spring air. But at last the key to Mexico City had been found.

While awaiting provisions and transportation for his army, Scott ordered a lateral expedition sent against the port of Alvarado, and in this, the third attempt against that town, three separate forces were synchronized in the operation: Perry sent Lieutenant Charles G. Hunter in the steamer *Scourge* to blockade the harbor; General John A. Quitman set out overland with his brigade of volunteer troops, and Perry went slowly along the coast, gearing his progress to that of the land forces. The main prize was to be the supplies and the horses and mules of the Mexican garrison, but it so happened that Lieutenant Hunter was an enthusiastic officer, and he proceeded to take the town of Alvarado with *Scourge,* and then he went on to capture Tlacotalpan, which surrendered without a fight. Perry arrived two days later, to find that his too zealous subordinate had cleaned up the opposition but in so doing had enabled the Mexicans to escape with all their transport and supplies before General Quitman could hem them in and capture the booty. After Alvarado came Tuxpan, and a large expedition of fifteen vessels, ranging in size from *Mississippi* to the gunboats, set out to invest that port. Perry arrived off the bar on April 17th, and the next morning the landing force of 1,900 officers, seamen and marines were ferried ashore in thirty barges, and with them went four pieces of light artillery. Perry supervised the landing from *Spitfire,* and as the Americans moved toward the town there was but feeble defense by the 650 Mexicans who garrisoned the place. The forts were taken without trouble, and the whole attack was deemed a success, except by the three American seamen killed and the five officers and six men wounded.

With this capture the policy of the United States changed, for now the whole coast was effectively controlled by the navy, its towns either garrisoned or blockaded, and the American government decided to permit a re-opening of commercial activity, but this time with the revenues from port duties and import taxes being diverted into the U.S. treasury. It was a vestigial expression of the old, hard-to-kill theory that war could be made to pay for itself, and the blockade was raised, a naval force sufficiently large to collect revenues remained on duty in the ports, and a modest amount of money flowed into the treasury.

But in Yucatán there was still trouble: Villa Hermosa was unquiet, and there were reports of arms-smuggling in the area. Perry gathered a force of thirteen warships and sailed up to Obregon on June 13th. *Etna* and *Bonita* were already there, on blockade duty, and from the various ships a landing force was formed, numbering in all 1,173 men, with seven pieces of artillery. Perry moved his broad command pennant to the steamer *Scorpion* and with the rest of the shallow-draft craft in tow started up the river for Villa Hermosa on June 14th. On the following day the flotilla was fired upon by Mexicans hidden in the chaparral, at a point about twelve miles below Villa Hermosa, but fire from the ships routed them. The flotilla went on up the river until it encountered obstructions placed in the stream. On the shore opposite the river-block was a well-built breastwork from which a strong body of Mexicans kept up a harassing fire on the vessels halted in the river. Perry decided to land at this point, and as the heavy guns of the warships raked the entrenched

Mexicans a landing force got ashore. In ten minutes the entire detachment was landed, with their seven pieces of artillery, which they dragged up a steep bank, twenty feet high. Three more pieces were landed from the bomb-vessels, and then the column moved to the attack with great enthusiasm. Enemy outposts were driven in and the Mexicans broke and ran from their breastwork. Meanwhile the steamers had worked their way past the obstructions in the river and were able to cover the landing force as it advanced against the town. A mile further upstream they came upon the chief Mexican defenses, located on a point commanding the river, and manned by three hundred regular and three hundred irregular troops. The combined fire of the ships and the landing party made this action a brief one. When the firing there ceased the Americans marched on to Villa Hermosa, which was taken after a few slight skirmishes. Thirty Mexican soldiers, of the 1,400 engaged in the defense of the city, were dead. The American losses were nine wounded. And with the fall of the city the Mexican army was cut off from its last source of arms.

During this period, when the navy was securing the coast, the army under General Scott was marching inland, and with them was a detachment of marines from the naval squadron, under the command of Lt.-Colonel S. E. Watson; his detachment joined the main army in the vicinity of Mexico City, in time to share in the final assault. Attached to General Quitman's division, the marines went into action on September 12, 1847, when they helped to storm the fortress of Chapultepec, erstwhile "Halls of Montezuma," and the fortifications that protected the city's Belen Gate. Chapultepec is located on a hill, and at the base, on the left flank, were two batteries of considerable strength and a wall fifteen feet high: General Quitman's division attacked at this point, and a storming party was formed from the different volunteer corps of the division. Thus, a part of the marine detachment, under Major Levi Twiggs, second in command of the marines, joined in the assault on the 13th of September, in a concerted attack by the different army divisions under the immediate direction of General Scott. Quitman's division advanced over difficult ground, under heavy fire from the fortress, the batteries and the breastworks. Storming parties, including some marines, led the column, and a battalion of marines was posted in a position from which it could support the storming parties. As the column advanced Major Twiggs was killed, at the head of his command; then the outworks were carried and the way to the fortress opened. Marines accompanied the division as it fought its way along the causeway toward Belen Gate, and took part in the costly and protracted battle by which this avenue into the city was opened. In these actions the marines lost Major Twiggs and six men killed, two lieutenants and two sergeants wounded. And when soon after the American flag flapped over the national palace, the Mexican government could find no element of hope with which to console themselves. Upper and Lower California were in American hands, and even the Pacific coast ports of Mazatlán and Guaymas; in the Gulf of Mexico no arms could be smuggled past the blockading American warships, and there was no hope of help from any source. Peace was signed at the little town of Guadalupe-Hidalgo on February 2nd, 1812, and by the treaty Mexico ceded to the United States a vast region including California, Nevada, Utah, parts of Arizona, New Mexico, Colorado and Wyoming. In addition there could now be no more argument about the southern boundary of Texas: it was the Rio Grande. Mexico's wounded pride was salved with $18,000,000 and thus was the destiny of the United States first made manifest.

[15] *The Golden Age*

The navy, having functioned with such brilliant success in the Mexican War, its victories only slightly dimmed by the fact that Mexico had no navy at all, resumed the placid demeanor which is its lot in the hiatus between wars, and engaged in scientific, exploratory and diplomatic cruises calculated to increase the national prestige and broaden the scope of maritime commerce. One officer, Matthew Fontaine Maury, in this period achieved international fame, and were the latter-day benefactors of mariners to be canonized he would be numbered among the saints.

Maury was born in Virginia in 1806, moved with his parents to Tennessee while still a child, and entered the navy as a midshipman in 1825. His early career was not meteoric: he cruised to France in the *Brandywine* frigate, circumnavigated the world in *Vincennes,* served as sailing-master in the *Falmouth* sloop-of-war in 1830 in the Pacific. It was while he was on the latter duty that he began to evince an avid interest in the winds and currents of the ocean, for they had a direct bearing on his duties as sailing-master. On this cruise he began to write articles for the *American Journal of Science,* and to gain therefrom a reputation as a literate naval officer. In 1834 he married, and found time to complete two years later a classic text-book for students of navigation—*A New Theoretical and Practical Treatise on Navigation.* The navy took the new book to its heart and drummed its lessons into the minds of the midshipmen.

Then there occurred, in 1839, a providential accident: Maury was traveling from Tennessee to Virginia by stage-coach, and on the trip the coach was wrecked and he was lamed for life, judged unfit for further duty on men-of-war, and in 1842 placed in charge of the navy's depot of charts and instruments in Washington. A less energetic man would have been content to let old log-books continue to gather dust in the depot, but Maury, no longer able to be active physically, of necessity focused his industrious imagination and driving curiosity on the log-books. With the help of a small clerical staff he culled facts relevant to the ocean's currents and winds from the old logs, gave meaning and system to the data, and published his findings in 1847 in a book called "Wind and Current Chart of the North Atlantic." Then he instituted the practice of equipping merchantmen and warships with specially-designed logs in which observations of winds and currents were to be entered. Completed logs were sent to him, providing more fodder for his researches. There were of course many skippers who refused to bother with the new-fangled idea, but Maury rewarded ships which kept his logs with copies of his "Sailing Directions," which explained the use of his wind and current charts, and by following his tips on the probability of the winds and the certainty of the currents they would encounter on their voyages, faithful addicts of the Maury system found that they could save days on a voyage and therefore dollars for their shipowners. When it became clear that a vessel following his directions could save from ten to fifteen days on the New York to Rio de Janeiro trip, all opposition evaporated and the logs began to be widely accepted and diligently kept.

In later years Maury made the system a universal one, enlisting the aid of foreign vessels, so that his sources of information became world-wide. By 1855 his sailing directions had cut the average time of merchantmen on the voyage between New York and San Francisco from 180 to 133 days, and that same year he published his "Physical Geography of the Seas," a study of the ocean that exploded many myths popular with mariners and landsmen, and replaced them with scientific facts. The total effect of his work on the merchant marine is literally incalculable: at least a thousand American merchantmen and whalers, as well as scores of the ships of other nations, kept "Maury Logs" and were guided by his "Sailing Directions," and the saving in time and money and human life passes all reckoning. At the very least he must be credited with helping to foster the swift growth of shipping in the years following the Mexican War.

American tonnage in foreign trade had risen from 810,000 tons in 1837 to 1,047,454 tons in 1847; in the next decade it was to reach 2,268,196 tons—an increase of over a hundred per cent in ten years. A coincidence of favorable factors created this rainbow era of seafaring: the Mexican War, which gave the United States a vast and sparsely settled empire in the west; the availability of large amounts of capital for shipbuilding; Maury's work, which made the profits greater and more certain; the repeal of the British Navigation Laws in 1849; and, most direct of all in its impact on the growth of the merchant marine, the discovery of gold in California.

On January 24th, 1848, shortly before the peace treaty with Mexico was signed, James Wilson Marshall, a 38-year-old foreman at Sutter's Fort in the Sacramento Valley found gold while he was superintending the construction of a mill-race on the American River at near-by Coloma. At first the discovery seemed incredible, and Marshall and Sutter sent the yellow metal to San Francisco to find out if it was actually gold. There the nuggets were certified to be pure gold and the news spread and the gold rush began. It was a fantastic spectacle.

There were three ways to get to California from the Eastern states: overland, a long and dangerous route with Indians to be fought and blizzards to be endured; by sea around Cape Horn, less dangerous and more comfortable, but costing two hundred dollars in passage money; and by ship to the Isthmus of Panama, then overland to the Pacific and up the west coast by sea. Men in the Eastern states tried frantically to get passage to California: preachers left their pulpits, grooms their brides, fathers their babies, and any young man on the loose turned automatically westward. There was a chance for every man to make a fortune overnight, simply by digging gold out of the California soil. But first a man had to reach the Golden West, and everyone had the same idea at the same time. There were not ships enough to transport them all.

Any vessel that could move in a wind could find passengers: even the slow and often aged whaleships went into the business of carrying the gold-hunters to the new El Dorado; small sloops and schooners began to carry men down to Colón on the Panamanian Isthmus, whence the passengers had to cross a land full of malaria and yellow fever and poisonous snakes, and then hope for passage up the west coast. Just in time to reap the benefits of the demand were two men of the shipping fraternity, George Law and C. S. Aspinwall. The American government had become aware, soon after the peace with Mexico was signed, that the new region in the far west was uncomfortably distant from the east coast, and in order to join the two sections more closely the government awarded contracts to George Law to carry the mails from New York to Colón, and to Aspinwall to carry them north from Panama to California and Oregon. The contracts specified that the mails should be carried in steamships, and the route, being between American ports, was considered part of the coastal trade and therefore closed to foreign shipping.

In this service the sail-and-steam ship *California,* a wooden-hull vessel, cleared from New York in October 1848, bound for San Francisco by way of Cape Horn, loaded to the gunwales with passengers and freight. She threshed along to take up her route in the Pacific, with her paddle-wheels going whenever possible and her sails always ready to be helpful. *California* was a big ship for the time: length 200 feet, beam 33 feet, draught 22 feet, tonnage, 1,058. Two others joined her in the Pacific, the *Panama* and the *Oregon,* and began carrying gold-hunters north from Panama to California. All three had more business than they could handle, and on the east coast the rush was even worse. Larger vessels were built—*Illinois,* of 2,123 tons and *Ohio,* 2,432 tons and *Georgia,* 2,727 tons—and they went to work hauling the hopeful from New York to Colón. By 1855 a railroad traversed the isthmus and as Law fed the passengers into Colón they were carried by train to the Pacific, whence Aspinwall's ships carried them to California. In the first decade of their operations the two steamship lines, known as the Pacific Mail Line after their merger, ordered built and put into service twenty-nine steamers. Since foreign competition was barred the line prospered mightily. At first the steamers could not begin to carry all the people who wanted to get to California, and the pressure to build faster and larger sailing ships fell on the shipyards of New York and Boston. They were ready to handle the orders that poured in on them, drawing on their knowledge of the packets, and of such ships as the *Ann McKim,* and the *Rainbow*—John Willis Griffiths' first extreme clipper— and the veteran speed-ships of the China trade—*Sea Witch,* a Griffiths-designed ship built in 1846, and *Samuel Russell* (1847), *Architect* (1847) and *Memnon* (1848). The knowledge of design was there, and the craftsmanship: the packets and the early clippers proved that.

Indeed, by 1849 the British had become uncomfortably aware that their merchantmen were fast becoming obsolescent, and when, that same year, the Navigation Laws were repealed, after bitter debate in Parliament, British ship-builders and ship-owners were exposed to such competition as they had never before encountered. Now British merchants could buy American-built ships, and trade with the British Isles was thrown open to American merchantmen.

Soon after the laws were repealed the American clipper *Oriental,* of 1,003 tons, built in 1849, carried a cargo of new tea from Hong Kong to London, arriving in December, 1850, after a voyage of ninety-seven days. There were few Britons who had ever seen anything like her, although they had heard from their mariners of these tall Yankee ships that ghosted past their pudgy Indiamen in any kind of a wind. But here was the authentic thing at last and anyone could take a look at her as she lay in the West India Docks. Her masts dwarfed every other ship in sight and her low, lean, black-painted hull made the Admiralty's collective mouth water. Such a sail-carrying machine as *Oriental* had to be seen to be believed, and the Admiralty asked and were given permission to send their designers aboard with calipers and measuring rods to take off her lines. They swarmed over her, amazed at the detailed excellence of the craftsmanship that had been built into her. She was 185 feet long, with a 36-foot beam, and a depth of 21 feet. Just to make sure they were on the right track the Admiralty soon after took off the measurements of another Yankee clipper—the *Challenge,* a 2,006 tons ship, 230½ feet in length, with a 43½ foot beam and a depth of 26½ feet. The British vainly put their best architects to work in an attempt to duplicate the big ocean runners, and some of them in later years produced creditable ships for use by British merchants—ships like *Stornoway* and *Chrysolite* for the tea trade. Their best efforts approached the average American-built clippers, but never seriously threatened Yankee supremacy in this type of vessel. When the Baltimore-built *Architect,* 570 tons, rushed from Canton to London in 107 days with another tea cargo, beating the rest of the tea ships by a week, the London merchants were much disturbed: they had nothing in her class, and when she began to get £8 per ton for carrying tea, while the usual rate was £4 per ton, they saw how far behind they had fallen in the years of protected trade, and they entered the market for American-built ships.

But before the British demand for American-built clippers could be filled there were scores of clippers to be built for American owners who wanted such ships for the California trade. The Americans could not help making money with what ships they had in 1849 and 1850, but the profits to be made from the gold rush were so enormous that they ordered built more and better ships without regard to cost, and in these ships speed and carrying capacity were equally important. For California, inundated by the influx of gold-hunters, was suddenly caught short of nearly everything a civilized community needs. San Francisco became a tent-city, with butter selling at $1.50 a pound, hens at $4.00 each, flour at $40.00 a barrel. There was an acute scarcity of lumber in the tent-city: in mid-1849 lumber selling in New York at $12.00 per thousand feet brought $500.00 per thousand feet in San Francisco. For several years after the gold rush started freight rates to the west coast fluctuated between $40.00 and $60.00 per ton, and many vessels were freighted with a cargo that paid for the cost of their building. Speed, too, meant money in the bank, for fast voyages meant more voyages, and more voyages meant more profits.

In response to this fierce demand for fast and able ships the designers' thoughts turned naturally to the types of extreme clipper ships, for they were the ships that had made the most consistently fast voyages in the tea trade, and the shipyards began to turn them out in 1850—full-rigged ships with concave, inward-curving bow waterlines and tall, raking masts. Such ships had a beauty that was breath-taking: in them great strength and gracefulness and purpose were combined, and, as among the few perfect products of men's minds and hands, they may be likened to the Gothic cathedrals of Europe, albeit different motives inspired the builders and different cargoes were in the holds.

John Griffiths had pioneered the design with *Rainbow* and *Sea Witch,* and his work was brought to perfection by a native of Nova Scotia, Donald McKay, who came to New York in 1827, at the age of 17. McKay studied design and worked in New York for ten years, and then moved to Newburyport where he began to build packet ships. These were so successful that his fame spread and he was persuaded to move to Boston in 1844. Be it noted: he loved music and was a talented amateur violinist. His first clipper was launched in December 1850, and she was the *Staghound,* of 1,534 tons. She was followed in 1851 by *Flying Cloud,* 1,783 tons, which made the New York to San Francisco run in eighty-nine days. Two more clippers came out of his Boston yards in '51, and in 1852 he built the *Sovereign of the Seas,* of 2,241 tons.

The *Sovereign* was too big and too radically-designed a ship for any merchant to order built: McKay built her with his own money, sinking everything he owned in her, and then, acting as merchant, he loaded her with goods and sent her off to San Francisco from New York in 1852 under the command of his brother, Lauchlan McKay, with 105 men and boys for crew and 2,950 tons of cargo in the holds. At the time she was the largest and sharpest ship in the world, and Brother Lauchlan was a man who knew his trade. He drove the new ship to San Francisco in 107 days—not record time, but very fast considering the fact she lost a good part of her top hamper west of Cape Horn and repaired the damage while under way at sea. *Sovereign* went on to the Hawaiian Islands in ballast, loaded sperm oil for New York, and on the way home, using Maury sailing directions, covered 3,114 nautical miles in a ten-day period, arriving in New York eighty-two days out of Honolulu.

With *Sovereign* an undoubted success, McKay followed with his major effort: the *Great Republic,* of 4,555 tons register, 325 feet long, 53 feet wide, stowage capacity 6,000 tons. McKay built her in 1853 to give the British-built clippers in the Australian trade some competition, but before she could put to sea she was gutted by fire and scuttled as she lay alongside a New York dock. Raised, and rebuilt with her sail-plan considerably modified, she was still capable of making the transatlantic run in thirteen days. McKay was somewhat chastened by the ill-luck of the *Great Republic* but he went on to build smaller, less grandiose clippers: *Lightning,* of 2,084 tons, came off the ways in 1854, and she was only one of four ships he built that year for the British, for use in the Australian trade. *Lightning* sailed in February of '54 from Boston for Liverpool, and with McKay on board on this her first voyage she lived up to her name, making a run of 426 miles in 24 hours—an average speed of 18½ knots per hour, and a record never surpassed by a working sailing vessel. *Lightning* was 244 feet long, with a beam of 44 feet and a depth of 23 feet.

There were other great builders of clippers: William Webb of New York, Samuel Hall of Boston, and Jacob Westervelt of New York, each of them nearly as talented as McKay, but his genius dimmed their ability.

The secret of the clippers' speed was only partially in their lines and in the great strength of their hulls and spars that enabled them to carry enormous areas of canvas and to stand the strain of driving like narrow, tapered wedges across the seas; more important in the record-making voyages were the men who commanded these ships. The clipper captains were, without exception, men who had been brought up close to the sea, and who had worked their way to positions of command after the usual long and hard apprenticeship. It took years of experience and an alert mind to fit a man for command of one of the big ships, each of which had her little foibles and crochets; it took, too, a tough physique, for the clipper ship master had to be handy with his fists, and like the packet skipper he had to be capable of staying on deck for lengthy periods in dirty weather. He had to know his ship from keel to truck to be able to judge to a nicety just how much sail she would carry in any sort of wind without carrying away yards and sails, and that took good judgment blended with superb seamanship. In addition to these basic requirements, the men who could master the intricacies of the clippers had to be at home in the drawing-rooms of the New York and Boston merchants whose goods freighted the ships. Above all, they had to be competitive-minded, and since there were no foreign vessels to compete with on the New York to San Francisco run, the captains of the American clippers raced each other, shaving days off rivals' records: *Sea Witch* made the run from San Francisco to New York in ninety-seven days in 1850; in the next year, *Surprise* lowered it to ninety-six days and *Flying Cloud* set the record for all time at eighty-nine days.

After the rush to California started in 1848, and the "Forty-Niners" began to pour into San Francisco, the clippers in that trade had little choice of cargo in San Francisco. There were no bulky freights to be exported from California, and the clippers could either sail in ballast back to New York, or cross the Pacific to load a cargo of tea for London or New York or Boston. If they did cross to China for tea, they would return by way of the Cape of Good Hope, and thus circumnavigate the globe as casually as a man crosses a street. Nearly every clipper captain had four or five such trips to his credit, and was as a result familiar with the winds and currents from Cape Horn to the Sunda Straits to the Narrows of New York.

One exemplary clipper captain was Robert Waterman of New York, born in 1808. He went to sea in a China-bound merchantman at the age of twelve as a cabin boy, and through the years that followed worked his way aft to become first mate on the Black Ball Line packet *Britannia*, and on into commands of his own. In 1843 he was captain of *Natchez* and until he took over she was a wholly undistinguished vessel. She had convex, outward-curving waterlines and no one ever called her a clipper. Yet Waterman took her from Canton to New York in ninety-four days in 1843, and in the next year he made the same voyage in her in seventy-eight days. Four years later, in *Sea Witch,* an extreme clipper of 890 tons, he made the run in seventy-seven days—a record. Clearly, with Waterman in command, the ship itself was not as important as the way she was handled. In 1850 he did a turn in steam, taking the Pacific Mail Company's steamer *Northerner* from New York to San Francisco. Thus it was that he knew all the answers when he took command of the clipper *Challenge* in 1851.

Challenge cleared New York for San Francisco in July, 1851, with a crew of fifty-six men and eight boys, half of whom were in no way qualified to go to sea. Such a crew was not exceptional at the time: whenever a ship dropped anchor in San Francisco Bay the seamen, and sometimes the officers, deserted and made for the hills, where there was gold, and by 1851 there was a great dearth of qualified seamen on the east coast. Even the waterfront loafers had worked their way west, leaving only the most obnoxious and incompetent seamen to man the ships. Many a landsman got to the gold fields by passing himself off as a seaman, and the Irish packet-rats had streamed across the North Atlantic, on their way to California by any means available. To the crimps who supplied the ships with crews, all men were so much raw meat, and Waterman's crew on *Challenge* was a fair example of the kind of men a clipper captain had to use to run his ship.

There was only three American-born men aboard: the rest were Irish and British, Swedish, Danish, Spanish and Norwegian. They were at once dirty, depraved and dolorous, and it is unlikely that they had ever been aboard a ship with such fine accommodations for the crew: like all the big clippers, *Challenge* had a deckhouse divided into two parts by a bulkhead, one part for the port watch and the other for the starboard watch, and in these living quarters the men could get rest uninterrupted by the tramping in and out and above which marked the old forecastle. Their food was the same as that of the officers.

But from the crew's point of view there were several drawbacks: *Challenge* had, as did all the California clippers, eight studdingsails and three skysail yards which took a great deal of work to handle, and she was fond of knifing through heavy seas, taking green water over her narrow bows, and drenching anyone on deck. There was nothing romantic about her to her crew: they were alien to the aesthetes among the passengers who found much to admire in the humming vibration of the great ships under way, in the white of canvas against the sky, in the seas myriad moods, the celestial display of stars, moon and sun with their attendant variety of optical phenomena—halos, coronae, iridescent clouds and the sun's last green ray. The seamen had a great deal too much work to do to bother with such pleasant things: they had orders to obey. Waterman did his best to get them into shape for Cape Horn: he put down a mutiny with singular forcefulness, bashing in the skulls of two men with a belaying-pin accurately wielded and instilling the fear of a like fate in the rest of the crew. But off Cape Horn three men fell from the icy yards to their death, and another five died of a venereal disease which they had presumably acquired ashore. No matter how much Waterman may have known about the sea, he could not possibly have cured these men with the medicine chests then carried on every vessel of over 150 tons on a foreign voyage. "Parson's Sailors Physician" was the standard guide to all diseases and to the use of the medicine chest, which was stuffed with calomel and jalap, balsam copavi, castor oil, salts, laudanum, Friars' balsam, sticking plaster, blue stone, blister plaster, lancets, syringes and bandages. If calomel and jalap, worked off by glauber salts, did not work, the patient was blistered and bled. If the patient survived this treatment the captain had a right to be both pleased and surprised.

Even with the remnants of his half-green crew Waterman made San Francisco in 109 days, and there it was charged that he had shot five men off the yards for not moving fast enough in their work. The character of the man was such that the charge was believed by many, and unrestrained rumor gave it the semblance of authenticity, so that "shooting a seaman off a yard" came to mean a captain who was not only exceedingly tough, but an excellent shot as well. Waterman refuted the charge, demanded and got a full investigation that cleared his name of murder, but the rumor, like a miracle, could not be dispelled.

The clippers brought thousands of gold-hunters to California, and even more came by the Isthmian route. From a sleepy lotusland of some seven thousand souls in 1847 the region suddenly grew into a populous state, with 207,000 men and women in it in 1852. Only the most spirited of women, among them many professional harlots, made the trip, and once in California they were in clover. The professionals took in gold-dust by the can and nuggets by the handful; one such lady, of French extraction, is reported to have netted fifty thousand dollars in one year; others, having demonstrated a mastery of their calling, married wealthy and amorous gold-finders who wished to live in a sanctified and leisurely manner, much envied by their less fortunate companions.

In all there were 161 California clippers launched in the six years from 1850 to 1855; after 1855 clipper-building diminished—only eight were built in '56 and four in '57—for the route across the isthmus, with the railroad coming into operation in 1855, became the preferred way to get from east to west and was quite adequate for the number of people who still wanted to get to California at that time. The clippers, always expensive ships to operate, with their large crews and the extensive repairs to rigging and spars that they always needed after their fast, straining voyages, were no longer a sound business proposition when freight rates dropped, as they did in the depression of 1857 to ten dollars per ton, and passengers were no longer anxious to pay two hundred dollars to get to California by way of Cape Horn. The clippers were created for a special type of service and by a happy combination of forces: when those forces disappeared the clippers became luxury items, remembered with etched clarity by all who sailed in them. So might a great white bird have rushed across the sky, turning men's faces and thoughts upward, and then vanished, leaving an indelible flash of exaltation in men's minds.

In the 12 years between 1843 and 1855, 2,656 merchantmen were built in American yards, and of them no more than 256 were "clipper-built"—a term that was often loosely applied to any sharp and handsome craft. These 2,400 ships not deemed worthy of the name "clipper" were the run of the mill merchantmen that reaped their best harvests with the abolition of the British Navigation Laws. Their work was not spectacular, but it was on a firm foundation, and the total value of the foreign trade carried in these hundreds of unremembered vessels reached close to $360,000,000 in 1855. They were busy carrying goods from and to every nation in the world that had a seaport, with the exception of the island nation of Japan. And the American government got around to doing something about the Mikado's Empire in 1852, sending Commodore Matthew Calbraith Perry off to blast his way in, if necessary.

Matthew Perry was an ideal choice for the job. Younger brother of the Lake Erie hero, Oliver Hazard Perry, he had a sense of his own dignity as a representative of the United States, and an awesome presence acquired on the quarterdecks of warships. The expedition which he led to Japan in 1853 was just in time: there was much competition on the part of Russia and Britain to get there first.

Japan had experienced Western civilization and found it not to its liking: in 1542 three Portuguese were shipwrecked on the coast and they were followed by the usual influx of traders and Portuguese Jesuits. St. Francis Xavier arrived in 1549, and the persecution of the Christians began in 1587. Enforcing the Anti-Christian Law of 1614, the shogun Iyeyasu rounded up all foreign priests—Jesuits, Franciscans, Dominicans and Augustinians—loaded them on seven ships and sent them to Macao whence they could reach their homelands. By 1638 Christianity in Japan had been driven underground, where it could not breed forbidden doubts about the Emperor's god-hood, and that year Japan entered a period of absolute seclusion. From that date on, until 1739, no foreign ship approached Japan's coast without permission. On May 25,* 1739, a Russian ship, painted black, about a hundred feet long and with a crew of thirty men, approached the coast and men from the ship gave Russian coins to a farmer, thereby establishing the nationality of the craft.

The Japanese maintained contact with the Western world through the Dutch traders restricted to the tiny island of Deshima, near Nagasaki, and it was because of this link with the outside world that a few American ships made voyages to Japan during the years of seclusion. In 1797 the ship *Eliza* was chartered by the Dutch East Indian Company at Batavia to take a cargo to Deshima, and the same arrangement was made in 1799 with the ship *Franklin,* in 1800 with *Massachusetts* and in 1801 with *Margaret.* Then, for years, there was no commercial contact with the Japanese by the Americans.

Those few Americans who by hazard landed on Japanese soil during

* Japanese lunar calendar date.

the years of seclusion were likely to regret it, for the Japanese government was determined to protect the nation's isolation. In 1845 Captain Budd, in *Manhattan* of Sag Harbor, brought twenty-two shipwrecked Japanese back to their homeland; it was an act of pure philanthropy on his part and great was his surprise when he was warned not to return, with shipwrecked Japanese or anything else. Next year the commander of the East India Squadron, James Biddle, who had released some American whalemen from the Nagasaki jail, returned in an effort to extract a commercial treaty with Japan, but he too was warned away, and rather than precipitate an incident he withdrew from Japanese waters.

The whalers from New England and New York continued their activities off the coast of Japan, regardless of the dangers. The crews could not help having an uncomfortable feeling about their chances if they should be driven ashore on that hostile and barbarous shore, and the phrase "a stove boat off the coast of Japan" came to be synonymous, among seamen, with particularly desperate trouble of any sort. Before long the shipowners began to bring pressure to bear on the government to end this unhappy state of affairs.

In 1853 Japan's isolation was threatened from three sides: Russia was seeping down from the north, moving into the Kuriles, and to the Japanese she was the main threat to continued seclusion, but in addition there was pressure from the British and French, originating in Hong Kong and Chinese ports, and, late in the field but anxious to learn was the new young republic of United States, now making indecent advances, backed by guns. The Japanese government was kept informed of events in the outside world through commercial intercourse with the Dutch traders at Deshima, and although this intelligence did not penetrate to the public, it was of inestimable help when the Japanese government had to make a momentous decision. The government's accumulated knowledge of Western civilization dated from the sixteenth century, from the time of Spain's enormous empire, when trade with Japan was open to the world and Japanese merchantmen traded with China, Siam, Cambodia, Annam, the Philippines and the South Sea islands. As early as 1610 Japan had sent a mission across the Pacific to Mexico to study trade conditions and mining methods; three years later a Japanese envoy voyaged across the Pacific and Mexico and the Atlantic to the court of Spain in an attempt to open up trade with Mexico, and on to Rome to see the Pope. From what they could find out about the world three centuries later there seemed to have been few moral and ethical changes made, although there were reports of new and more lethal weapons in existence.

No matter how much the Japanese knew about the rest of the world, they could not have had any idea of the kind of man Matthew Calbraith Perry was—ruthless, stiff-necked, the embodiment of "Manifest Destiny," not above making use of his political connections to oust a fellow-officer, Commodore J. H. Aulick, from command of the mission to open Japan. With Aulick euchred out of the assignment, Perry went to take command of the Far East Squadron in 1852, empowered to make a display of force in Japanese waters and to try to obtain a treaty of friendship and commerce. The mission assumed great importance in the Navy Department, for with steam rivaling sail, far-flung coaling-stations had a new importance, and the establishment of coaling stations was among the aims of the expedition. A large squadron was made available to Commodore Perry: the steam-frigates *Mississippi* 10, *Susquehanna* 9, *Powhatan* 9, the corvette *Macedonian,* razeed from a frigate of the same name, three 20-gun sloops—*Saratoga, Plymouth* and *Vandalia,* and three storeships—*Southampton, Supply* and *Lexington*. The squadron rendezvoused at Hong Kong and then moved on to Napa on Okinawa in the spring of 1853, and on July 2nd Perry sailed for Japan with the flagship *Susquehanna, Mississippi, Plymouth* and *Saratoga.*

On July 8th the four black ships anchored off the town of Uraga, at the entrance to Tokyo Bay, twenty-seven miles from Tokyo. Perry then began an exhibition of seclusion that rivaled that of Japan: he ordered away the Japanese guard-boats, refused to treat with any dignitaries of lesser rank than his, which was indeed very high, and made use of his officers in all transactions with the Japanese. The Japanese were highly impressed: in just such a fashion did their own officials act, and the more unapproachable, the more rigidly ceremonious a man was, the greater was his standing in their eyes. Perry must, ipso facto, be a man of inordinate importance, transcending in splendor the local governor and approaching in personal sublimity the court circles of the Throne. They made concessions to him and his guns out of admiration, convenience and a willow-like pliancy of mind which saw that seclusion could not last forever.

Perry moved his ships closer to Tokyo, strictly against Japanese regulations, and began to send out boats to take soundings in the Bay, when the Japanese seemed to be delaying a final decision on his request that a special commissioner be appointed to take the letter of the President of the United States to the Mikado. Finally the demand was accepted, but first, as befitted the solemnity of the occasion, there had to be a ceremony and a building had to be made ready for the reception of the Commodore so that he could deliver the letter with suitable formality. When the building was ready Perry moved his squadron in close to shore so that the ships' guns covered the landing and the ceremony, and on the morning of July 14th he landed with an escort of four hundred officers, seamen and marines, who formed ranks in the midst of some five thousand Japanese troops. The Royal Commissioners, Princes Idzu and Iwami, received the Presidential letter, then hinted that it would be nice if the squadron moved further away from the capital, as soon as it conveniently could. Perry had other ideas: he ordered the squadron to move closer to Tokyo, hoping that this "would produce a decided influence upon the pride and conceit of the government, and cause a more favorable consideration of the President's letter." That night the vessels anchored ten miles further up the bay, and next morning *Susquehanna* steamed ten miles closer to Tokyo, to a point within seven miles of the city. From that distance the Americans made a leisurely examination of the shipping in the harbor. After this display of force, which the Japanese thought most indelicate, Perry sent word to the Mikado that he would return in the spring of the next year to receive the answer to his request for a treaty of amity and commerce, and the squadron set out for Okinawa to winter there.

Less than a month after Perry had left Japan a Russian squadron under Admiral Efimii Vasilievitch Putiatin appeared at Nagasaki, with requests from the Tsar that Japan permit Russia to trade in that country. Thus to the American pressure was added that of Russia, and when consideration of Perry's demands began in the council rooms at Tokyo, a powerful political clique, the Kai-Koku party, argued forcefully that, since there was no point in fighting a war Japan was sure to lose, and "as we are not the equals of foreigners in the mechanical arts, let us have intercourse with foreign countries, learn their drill and tactics, and when we have united the nation as one family under the Emperor, we shall be able to go abroad and give lands in foreign countries to those who have distinguished themselves in battle." The logic of this point of view was unassailable and the decision was made to accept Perry's demands.

In early 1854 Perry was spurred to sudden activity by the mysterious movements of French and Russian ships in Chinese waters: he had no intention of letting them beat him in the race to open Japan, and in February he set out for Tokyo Bay with all the ships he could assemble: steamers *Susquehanna, Powhatan, Mississippi,* and sail-ships *Macedonian, Lexington, Vandalia, Southampton* and *Saratoga.* The squadron anchored ten miles above Uraga, close to the spot where the conference had been held the year before. Perry insisted that the final ceremonies be held even closer to Tokyo, although arrangements called for the meeting to take place twenty miles below Uraga. The Japanese protested, but Perry was inflexible in his demand, and he began a war of nerves, moving his ships up the bay by slow stages until they were within eight miles of Tokyo, and the Japanese—fearful of what might happen to their capital—agreed to meet him where he stipulated.

A building was constructed on the shore opposite the ships and to this conference hall Perry went on March 8th, with an escort of five hundred men, all fully armed, the marines looking especially imposing in their full-dress uniforms. Five Commissioners from the Mikado received him, broke bread with him when he explained the significance of that ritual to them, and engaged in negotiations that lasted three weeks. On March 31, 1854, the Treaty of Kanagawa was signed: by its terms two ports, Hakodate and Shimoda, were opened to American ships to serve as trading centers and coaling-stations, shipwrecked Americans were guaranteed kind treatment, American consular agents were permitted to live in one of the ports, and the United States was promised that any rights granted to other nations would be extended to the United States as well.

During the conferences the presents sent to the Mikado by the American government were landed, and mechanics from the ships put them into operation: a telegraph with a mile of wire was set up, and a circular railroad big enough to demonstrate the practical value of this means of transport for the swift conveyance of people and goods was put into operation. There were among the gifts some guns and powder which hinted that the United States was a nation at once strong and of explosive possibilities. The Japanese politely presented gifts to the United States: lacquered work and silks, of exquisite craftsmanship, the products of arts they had learned from the Chinese.

On his return to the United States Perry received the plaudits of the politicians and the public and the merchants, and in their fulsome praises he basked contentedly. Congress authorized the printing of the Commodore's report, and three large volumes were forthcoming, with wind and current charts and harbor surveys, much detailed information about Okinawa and recommendations for other coaling-stations in Far Eastern waters. As a projection of American power to the Far East, in spite of the vast distances involved, the mission gratified the believers in "Manifest Destiny": the nation had grown a few more hairs on its chest, and its voice took on a deeper timbre.

While these great events were taking place in Japan, in the Black Sea, thousands of miles away, the Crimean War was getting under way, and in the course of that war a new and fundamentally original type of warship was put to the test in a manner that was to affect the future of the American navy and of every nation in the world.

The causes of this war have an antique yet curiously modern fascination: Nicholas I, Tsar of the Muscovites, wanted Constantinople, even as Peter the Great had, and he moved his forces against Turkey in 1853. France and Britain became involved because France had plans for Syria and Britain for India which would have been disjointed by a Russian victory; moreover, Napoleon III needed to infuse a bit of "la gloire" into his despotic rule of France, and Britain could not rest easily with a major power like Russia in the Eastern Mediterranean. Thus a bizarre alliance came into being, with Turkey and Britain and France united to defeat Russia.

The naval actions began at Sinope, on November 30, 1853, when six

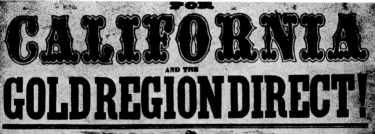

The Magnificent, Fast Sailing and favorite packet Ship,

JOSEPHINE,

BURTHEN 400 TONS, CAPT.

Built in the most superb manner of Live Oak, White Oak and Locust, for a New York and Liverpool Packet; thoroughly Copper-fastened and Coppered. She is a very fast sailer, having crossed the Atlantic from Liverpool to New-York in 14 days, the shortest passage ever made by a Sailing Ship. Has superior accommodations for Passengers, can take Gentlemen with their Ladies and families. Will probably reach SAN FRANCISCO THIRTY DAYS ahead of any Ship sailing at the same time. Will sail about the

10th November Next.

For Freight or Passage apply to the subscriber,

RODNEY FRENCH,

New Bedford, October 15th. **No. 103 North Water Street, Rodman's Wharf.**

Hudson Historical Bureau, New York

Poster Announcing Sailing of a Ship for the California
Gold Regions, 1850

View of San Francisco Harbor from Telegraph Hill (by Wm. B. McMurtrie, 1850)

Russian ships of the line armed with smooth-bore shell-guns demon-strated that shell-fire had made wooden ships obsolete by all but annihilating a Turkish fleet of eleven warships. Only one Turkish ship, a steam-powered vessel, escaped, and brought the news to Constanti-nople where there was consternation in naval circles. Word of the battle spread across the seas, and even the Americans were impressed: David G. Farragut, then a Commander, requested duty as an observer in the Crimean War, but an unsympathetic Navy Department sent him instead to San Francisco. Napoleon III was the only man who took the lessons of Sinope to heart: in October 1854 he ordered floating armored batteries built which could be used offensively, and the result was a class of five ships, the *Lave, Dévastation, Foudroyante, Congréve* and *Ton-nante*. These ships had wooden hulls protected by iron plates 4 inches thick, displaced 1,400 tons, were 164 feet long, had a beam of 42½ feet and a draught of 8 feet. They carried eight shell-guns (50-pounder smooth-bores), and a crew of 320 men. Masts were demountable; steam engines supplied auxiliary power by means of a single screw. The decks were thinly plated with iron, and the helmsman was protected by a bullet-proof conning-tower. Fans ventilated the engine-room and gun-deck. With their spoon-bows and gray war-paint the iron-clads presented a thoroughly lethal appearance, well-calculated to instill fear in the hearts of the enemy. Napoleon gave the design of his iron-clads to the British and after much debate the Admiralty ordered four of them constructed, but they were not completed in time to take part in the war.

The three French iron-clads first commissioned went out to the Crimea escorted by frigates, for they could not be trusted alone because of their unseaworthiness, and in late 1855 they joined the British and French squadrons in the Black Sea to help form a great armada of eighty warships and ten transports. The Allied fleet feinted toward Odessa on October 8th, and then a week later appeared off Kinburn, a narrow sandspit on which Russian forts protected the estuary of the Dnieper river. Troops were landed and the Russian works isolated. Then, during the night of the sixteenth the French took soundings close to the works and laid buoys to guide the iron-clads. On the seventeenth, soon after dawn, the iron-clads steamed in to within eight hundred yards of the forts and opened fire with their broadsides. Russian shot bounced off their armored hulls, and the shells from the iron-clads devastated the Russian batteries. After three hours of this unequal fighting the Russians hoisted a white flag, and reports of the damage to the iron-clads, on which the forts had concentrated their fire, began to come in to the French commander, Admiral Bruat: *Dévastation* had taken seventy-five hits, *Lave* and *Tonnante* about sixty each, and the net damage consisted of nothing more than slight dents in the iron plates. Bruat reported to Napoleon that the future of such vessels was limitless, and the French began at once to apply the lessons learned at Kinburn to all their naval construction.

There was no parallel alacrity in American naval circles, where naval policy was reverting to the principles of the War of 1812 and emphasis was placed on building fast sail-and-steam frigates and sloops, useful for commerce-raiding in war and capable of carrying the American flag with dignity in peace, but by no means suitable for fleet actions. They were a modern application of the functions Joshua Humphreys had built into his frigates half a century earlier: speed enough to flee from superior force, strength enough to defeat inferior vessels. Not until six years after Kinburn, when *Merrimac* was salvaged by the Southerners at Norfolk and iron plates were hung on her wooden hull, was the United States to have an iron-clad of its own.

By 1856, when the Crimean War ended, with Russian ambitions in Turkey temporarily checked, elements of decay were already discernible in both the naval and maritime strength of the United States. In Congress the slavery issue sharpened the edge of debate and infused men's minds with sectional rather than national interests. In this atmosphere of mutual distrust naval appropriations suffered, and during the next five years no warship bigger than a frigate was constructed, and only five of them—sail-and-steam, screw-propelled vessels—came off the ways, along with thirteen small steam-and-sail screw sloops. The merchant marine, too, entered a period of decline: with the falling off of demand for California clippers, tonnage built and operated began to diminish. There was a brief revival of demand for the services of American ships during the Crimean War, when Britain and France needed additional ships to carry troops and supplies—Donald McKay's *Great*

Republic was chartered to the French government and ferried sixteen hundred British soldiers to Marseilles from Liverpool in one trip—and there was a brisk market for American foodstuffs and goods in the British Isles and in France. But in 1857 a period of economic depression verging on panic set in and many American merchantmen lay idle . in port. This was, too, the era of the great railroad land grants, and capital was drawn inland into the country to develop its resources, rather than to the sea to export its products.

On the North Atlantic British alertness to the value of steam and the consequent subsidies granted by the British government to steam-ship lines began to show results, driving the American packets by slow degrees into second place in the North Atlantic trade. In the early 1850's it had been an exhilarating experience for packet passengers to line the rails and jeer at the pudgy steam-sail ships they passed in mid-Atlantic, with the packet captain sailing his ship close to windward to give the steamer's people the full benefit of his passengers' witticisms, but by degree the tables were turned, and dark plumes of smoke came to rise and pass on the horizon while the packet sailed along as best she could with whatever wind there was, and suffered the occasional indignity of having a steamer's skipper pass close enough to windward to blanket the spotless packet with smoke and soot.

No one in the United States had been overly worried about competition when two British steam-sail packets reached New York in 1838— the *Sirius,* after a seventeen and a half day passage, and the *Great Western,* in less than sixteen days. Racketing paddles drove their hulls along at an average speed of ten knots per hour, and the packets could do better than that. At the time the Admiralty became interested in this demonstration that British steam-sail vessels could cross the Atlantic as successfully as they could run to Hamburg, Rotterdam, Lisbon or Gibraltar, and the Sea Lords asked for proposals for a steam service to the United States which would be worthy of financial backing by the British government. Soon more British steam packets were in operation, burning coal instead of wood, basking in the favor of the Exchequer. There was little rivalry from the Americans, except for one man—E. K. Collins, who strove mightily to get Congressional backing. He finally obtained a mail contract and a small subsidy for a line of

American steam-and-sail packets, and by the fall of 1850 he had four of these vessels in operation: *Atlantic, Pacific, Baltic* and *Arctic*. The British line founded by Samuel Cunard ten years earlier met this competition with habitual aplomb. The American-built vessels were faster than the Cunarders, more luxuriously appointed, and so pleasing to the national pride that Congress raised the line's annual subsidy from $385,000 to $853,000. But trouble lay ahead for Collins: first the *Arctic* collided with a French steamer off Cape Race in a fog and in sinking carried over three hundred people to their deaths; *Pacific* sailed from Liverpool and was lost without a trace; then the sectional interests of the nation became involved in the subsidy. The southerners could see no sense in part of their taxes being used for the benefit of a small group of northern shipowners who were unsympathetic to slavery and who thus threatened the stability of southern economy. Congress, sensitive to such pressure, first reduced the subsidy, and then in 1858 abolished it altogether. Collins gave up at that point, asked Congress to free him from his contract, and let his creditors take over the steamships and sell them. He busied himself with other, more profitable enterprises, and the British steamers, with their government's backing, moved in on the trade. There was no comparable support by the American government, and without the inspiration of guaranteed profits American capital left the field to the British.

A few crack sailing packets hung on, in spite of the British steamers. As late as 1859 the packet-rats were hanging out and hauling in canvas on the Red Cross Line packet *Dreadnought,* Captain Samuel Samuels commanding. *Dreadnought* had been launched in 1853, and she registered 1,413 tons, and had made the voyage from New York to Liverpool in 13 days and 8 hours in early 1859—a distance of 3,018 miles. On occasion, Captain Samuels took his wife along with him, for she raised the tone of the whole ship, being a practising Christian even at sea. On Sundays Divine Services were executed on deck and with all flags flying. When a passenger asked Mrs. Samuels why the flags were bent on when there were no ships to see them, she replied: "God sees them. They are hoisted ashore on Sundays, why shouldn't they be hoisted at sea? We feel ourselves nearer to Him on the ocean, as only six inches of planking separate us from eternity!" But the mollifying presence of his wife did not prevent Samuels from running his ship with a heavy hand, and he had no illusions about his crew. He wrote of them: "The Liverpool packet sailors were not easily demoralized. They were the toughest class of men in all respects. They could stand the worst weather, food, and usage, and put up with less sleep, more rum, and harder knocks than any other sailors. They had not the slightest idea of morality or honesty, and gratitude was not in them. The dread of the belaying-pin or heaver kept them in subjection. I tried to humanize these brutal natures as much as possible, but the better they were treated the more trouble my officers had with them."

With such a crew Samuels set out for New York from Liverpool in July, 1859. They were, even for packet-rats, a particularly virulent group, known as the "Bloody Forties," and there were thirty of them, all habitués of a Liverpool den run by a woman of evil repute named Mrs. Riley. They had sworn to throw Samuels overboard, to give him the "deep six," and thus rid the world of a man they considered a tyrant. Off Queenstown, Ireland, there was the first sign of trouble: the helmsman replied to a command in an impertinent tone. Samuels knocked him unconscious, took his knife away from him, had him handcuffed and put in the after-house which served as a brig. This touched off the mutiny, for the men refused to work, and their leaders, Casey and Sweeney and Finnegan, kept their spirits up. As the breeze freshened, Samuels ordered in a thunderous tone, "Take in the royals!"

Back came the answer from forward: "Go to hell!"

The officers and boys furled the royals, and meanwhile the crew went without food, for Samuels had proclaimed that no work meant no food aboard his ship. After fifty-six hours of profane and intermittent negotiations, with no sleep for the Captain and no food for the crew, Samuels went into the steerage and enlisted the help of seventeen of the German emigrants. He armed them with iron bars, and awaited the attack he knew was bound to come before long. In the night two of the crew crept forward to beg forgiveness, and they threw their knives overboard as proof of their docility. But Casey and Sweeney and Finnegan were still in firm control of the rest of them.

At 3:45 A.M. the trouble broke: Casey and Sweeney attacked. Captain Samuels met them with a leveled pistol, and Casey retreated down the forecastle; the captain's dog, Wallace by name, drove at Sweeney's throat, and the rest of the mutineers plunged into the melee, knives flashing in the dim light. At this moment the Germans began wielding their iron bars, knocking the Irish dizzy, and driving them forward. Hemmed in, they were given one minute to throw their knives overboard. Said the obdurate Finnegan: "You shall be the first to go, you damned psalm-singing bastard!" The Captain kept his temper, reasoned with the men, promised them fair play, and suddenly the knives went spinning into the sea under the rising sunlight. Finnegan alone would not surrender—nor would he apologize for his harsh words—so Captain Samuels knocked him headlong into the forecastle. When the doctor had repaired him, he begged the captain's pardon, and the mutiny was over. Samuels tugged at his voluminous sideburns and moustache, and decided in a spirit of Christian charity to forget the whole affair.

Captain Samuel Samuels was a very valiant man, and it would be pleasant to record that all his confreres were of the same ilk. Unfortunately they were not: between 1826 and 1851 thirty-two vessels and their captains did not return to their home ports and have never been accounted for: they did not founder in some terrible storm at sea, or drive on uncharted reefs—their captains simply sold them abroad, and then shaved off their whiskers and changed their names.

By 1861 there was only one American-built steam-packet in the North Atlantic trade, and she was the Collins Line *Adriatic,* sold that year to the Galway Line and operating under British flag and registry. The British steamers, waxing faster and more commodious on a subsidy that reached $4,537,223 in 1860, continued to take the cream of the North Atlantic freight and passenger business. In other. fields of maritime activity the Americans held their own, and American tonnage in foreign trade rose slowly from 2,268,000 tons in 1857 to a peak of 2,496,894 tons in 1861. In addition to this tonnage there were 182,106 tons in the deep-sea fisheries and 2,657,293 tons in the protected coastal trade. Great Britain's total tonnage was slightly larger, but the Americans prided themselves on the fact that their ships were in general faster and more efficiently operated. The discovery of petroleum in 1859, when Drake's oil-well was brought in, initiated a new source of light and lubrication that was so much less expensive than whale-oil that the whale fisheries, in which the Americans excelled, were certain to come upon troubled times, even if there had been no scarcity of whales. The whalers had over-exerted themselves and killed off a great many of the great sea-beasts, without any regard for the difficulties a whale faced when he wanted to become a father: the act of impregnation involved much complicated maneuvering on the part of both parents, and a baby whale faced at best a difficult life.

In sum, the major influences in the decline of the merchant marine were: lack of American government subsidies for steam-driven ocean liners, a lack that permitted the British to pervade this field; Britain, with more advanced industrial techniques than the United States, could build steamers with iron hulls and engines and boilers more cheaply than the Americans could, and moreover the Americans could not buy foreign-built vessels for American-flag registry because the protective law of 1789 was still in effect; American capital and labor, lured inland by the profits to be made in railroads and mines and oil, willingly let the British take over the carrying trade. Then, in 1861, came the bodeful, accelerating factor—the Civil War—from which the merchant marine was not to recover for over half a century.

Part V
THE ANNEALING

[16] *A Highly Emotional War*

In broad outline, slavery, an important ingredient in the South's economy, caused secession and secession caused war. Secession was a matter of principle: should there be central rule by the government at Washington? Or should there be rule by the principle of federation? The southern states were sure that they had the right to secede and there was much legal documentation to prove their contention. But the Federal government, granting that the right to secede existed, had Federal property to protect: forts and arsenals and navy yards in Southern states, and Federal warships at sea. The South insisted that forts, arsenals and navy yards had been conveyed to the Federal government to be held in trust, with the reservation that a state could re-enter and occupy such establishments when they ceased to be used for the protection of the state which had made them available to the Federal government. On legal grounds, on the documents then blanketed by the smoke of guns, the charges of political partisanship, the miasma of vaporing hatreds, the South was clearly right. But, by a different interpretation of the documents, the North too could claim God's aid in the battle.

Abe Lincoln was elected President of the United States in November, 1860; in December the state legislature of South Carolina voted unanimously to secede from the union. For several months, while other states joined South Carolina, and Jefferson Davis was inaugurated as President of the Confederate States of America, there was a chance that the slaves states might depart in peace and form their own union, economically dependent on slave-holding, and devoted to the cultivation of a provincial type of aristocracy modeled on the British pattern.

There had been trouble at Fort Sumter, in the harbor of Charleston, South Carolina, where Major Anderson was in command of 129 Union troops: a merchant-steamer, *The Star of the West,* was chartered by the Federal government and loaded with provisions and 250 recruits for Anderson's reinforcement. She sailed from New York on January 5th, and on entering Charleston harbor on January 8th, with the stars and stripes flying, she was fired upon by Southerners who had occupied Fort Moultrie and forced to put out to sea without having landed either provisions or men. For the time being no further attempt was made to relieve the fort.

Lincoln was inaugurated on March 4, 1861; a week later the seceded states adopted a constitution of their own. Still there was hope for peace, and as late as March 31st the New York to Savannah steamers continued to leave New York, carrying the Federal flag at the peak and the Confederate flag at the fore. But always there was Sumter—a thorn in the Federal flesh—and it could not be banished by words; nor could the problem it posed for Lincoln be forever left unsolved. On April 8th the President issued an order that supplies were to be sent to the fort by sea: had he not taken the inaugural oath, swearing that he would "to the best of my ability, preserve, protect, and defend the Constitution of the United States?" Jefferson Davis was informed of this order and he instructed his General Beauregard to keep trying to get the Federal forces out of Sumter peacefully. But Beauregard's subordinates, a group of trigger-happy men, got out of hand: when Anderson said he would surrender the fort on April 15th unless ordered by Washington to defend it, they refused his offer and a Southern battery opened fire on the fort on April 12th, shortly before dawn. In the evening of the 13th Anderson capitulated: his provisions were running low, and he had no expectation of relief.

Two days later Lincoln issued a proclamation calling upon Virginia and the other states for 75,000 troops to enable the Federal government to repossess the forts, arsenals and navy yards seized by the seceded states. In effect the proclamation asked: "What side are you on?" Virginia could not be neutral, and in that state, as in the others which had not then seceded, the proclamation was regarded as a declaration of war. No longer could there be any hope of peace and the forces of the rival republics gathered in preparation for civil war—that most ferocious of all types of warfare.

There was an equal lack of readiness for war on both sides, for men's minds had been unwilling to concede that the conflict was inevitable. Less than a year before, in May, 1860, so far from the thought of war was the nation that the Federal government had transferred 114,868 rifles and muskets from Northern arsenals to arsenals in Southern states, for use in case any insurrectionists went berserker, as John Brown had at Harper's Ferry. Since there had been no formal preparations for war the South was at the outset at a great disadvantage. The Northern states with 22 million free people, had most of the industrial resources of the nation; the South, with some nine million people, three and a half million of whom were slaves, was still an agricultural region.

On the sea the discrepancy in strength was enormous: of the ten navy yards owned by the United States at the outbreak of war—at Kittery, Maine, Portsmouth, New Hampshire, Charlestown, Massachusetts, Sackett's Harbor, New York, Brooklyn, New York, Philadelphia, Pennsylvania, Washington, District of Columbia, Norfolk, Virginia, Pensacola, Florida and Mare Island, California, only the Norfolk and Pensacola yards were available to the South. As the Southern states seceded they managed to seize only a few armed vessels, mostly revenue cutters. A few other ships were purchased, so that at the start of the war the total Confederate Navy numbered ten vessels, mounting, in all, fifteen guns. The United States Naval Register for 1861 listed 90 American warships, of which only 42 were in commission—21 being unserviceable and 27 available but decommissioned. The 42 warships in commission were on their assigned stations: 12 vessels of 187 guns in the Home Squadron; 3 vessels of 42 guns in the East Indies; 22 vessels of 236 guns in the Pacific. These ships were manned by some 7,600 men. Gideon Welles, Lincoln's Navy Secretary, at once ordered all warships that were in any degree seaworthy to be put in commission, and soon there were 76 vessels, mounting 1,783 guns, that flew the stars and stripes. But this was only the beginning: Welles purchased 136 more vessels, had them altered for war service, mounted with 518 guns and put into service; construction of 52 vessels of 256 guns was begun in government and private yards. By December 1861 the United States Navy consisted of 264 vessels, carrying 2,557 guns, manned by 22,000 seamen. Its aggregate tonnage was 218,016 tons. By drawing upon the industrial resources and the mechanical skill of the Northern states, Welles was able to construct by 1865, 200 new vessels with 1,520 guns—74 of them iron-clads. And there were 1,242 officers who decided, after making their ethical calculations, to serve the Federal government; among them men like David Farragut and Samuel DuPont, who were fortunate to have the services of Benjamin Franklin Isherwood as the navy's chief engineer, and John Ericsson as ship-designer extraordinary.

The fortunes of the Confederate Navy were placed in the hands of Stephen Russell Mallory of Florida, who had been born in Trinidad in 1813, the second son of an American civil engineer, Charles Mallory of Reading, Pennsylvania, and an Irish orphan named Ellen Russell, whom Mallory met and married in Trinidad. Soon after Stephen's birth the family moved to Florida, and at the age of fourteen he was sent to the Moravian School for Boys at Nazareth, Pennsylvania, where he received three years of intensely pious schooling. That was all the education he ever had or appeared to need: he became Collector of Customs at Key West, and then a member of the United States Senate, where he was chairman of the Naval Committee. Thus when Jefferson appointed him Secretary of the Confederate Navy in the spring of 1861, Mallory knew what he was up against and what limited resources were at his disposal. He wrote to Commander Raphael Semmes, who had been sent to New York on February 21st by Jefferson Davis to purchase arms and munitions, asking Semmes to try to buy two strong steamers of light draught. But Semmes, who had been amazed at the eagerness of Northerners to sell munitions to the South in February and throughout March, and who wrote "Some of these men who would have sold body and soul to me for a sufficient consideration, occupied high social position and were men of wealth," was unable to find anyone willing to sell him two steamers. Mallory was convinced that iron-clads were the answer to the South's naval problems: if he could get enough of them, then all the wooden warships of the North would be worthless. He ordered construction of iron-clads in the Southern states, being convinced, as he said in his first report, that "Iron-clad steamships capable of resisting the crushing weight of projectiles from heavy ordnance must at an early day constitute the principal part of fighting vessels of all naval powers." There was a possibility that iron-clads could be bought in Europe, and

Lieutenant James H. North was sent abroad to see what he could find. But no one in Europe had any iron-clads for sale, and so Mallory sent Naval Agent James D. Bulloch to England to see if he could procure warships there. Other agents went to Canada to try to purchase steamers but they found that the Federal government had bought every steamer available in Canadian waters. Bulloch had better luck in England: he contracted for the *Florida* and the *Alabama*—two ships that were to cause much sorrow in the Northern states. Between June 1861 and December 1862 Mallory signed contracts for the construction in Southern seaports of forty gunboats, floating batteries and warships. The work went forward with a frenzied urgency which was matched by the Northern shipyards, for this was essentially a race against time.

When he took office Mallory was Secretary of a navy that existed only in his mind: there was timber in the South, but it was all in the forests; the iron was in the mines, for the South had never been self-sufficient in iron-making. Selma, Alabama, developed into a munitions center of considerable size as the war progressed, but in the beginning the South's only major foundry was that of the Tredegar Iron Works and Belona Foundry at Richmond. There were only two navy yards, of which the Pensacola Yard was not a construction yard but a repair base and a shelter. When the Norfolk Navy Yard fell into the hands of the Southerners it was a god-send, even if burnt and damaged, for Norfolk had a dry-dock, and some wooden hulls, and the Southerners found there 1,198 cannon, 300 of them Dahlgrens, among them 134 heavy guns. In that spring of 1861 there was not a single rope-walk in all the Southern states: everything had to be initiated—the hemp sown, the crop harvested, men taught how to run a rope-walk and make various sizes of rope—for a ropeless navy was inconceivable. Within a year a rope-walk was in working order and the Confederate Navy was spared the exquisite embarrassment of not being able to tie up its ships or to hoist their sails.

The only asset Mallory had for his projected navy was an abundance of naval officers: by June, 1861, of 1,563 United States naval officers, of whom 671 were of Southern birth, 321 had resigned from the Federal service. It was not a decision that a man could make easily: years of friendship at the naval academy, years of service afloat under the Federal flag, hardships and dangers endured, and wines imbibed in scores of foreign ports with fellow-officers made resignation a soul-searching process. Their dilemma can best be understood by supposing that in the year 2000 A.D. a world federation of nations is in being, and that a group of professional officers from each nation command the common pool of ships and instruments of war; a rebellion takes place against the central authority and officers must choose between service to the central, unsentimental government, or service to the insurgent nation of their birth—the nation in which they were born and on which emotions conjured up by such words as "home" and "family" and "friends" center. Only a man of very compelling principles could reject a direct plea to fight for his homeland on the side of his friends and family. Those 321 naval officers of Southern birth and breeding who returned to the South to accept commissions in the Confederate Navy (at the same rate of pay they were drawing in the United States Navy), were in no way guilty of treason: they were men who could weigh the legal arguments for and against their resignations and quit the service with clear consciences. Among them were some very capable officers: Franklin Buchanan, Matthew Fontaine Maury, Raphael Semmes, Catesby Ap. R. Jones, John M. Brooke. An appeal had been sent out in January 1861 to Southern officers to bring their ships to Southern ports, but of all the officers who "went South" none brought their ships with them. There were not enough warships for all of them to have sea duty, and Mallory juggled them around, sending some to open and staff navy yards, others to command river boats.

But while Mallory had an inundation of naval officers, he was very short of seamen, and recruiting was barely able to replace men lost by death, discharge or desertion. There was no supply of trained seamen to draw upon in the South, and as late as 1864 there were only 3,674 enlisted men in the Confederate Navy.

Whereas the United States Navy could begin to blockade the coastline of the Southern states in April 1861, the Confederate Navy was doomed to revert by its lack of resources to the commerce-destroying warfare which had marked the War of 1812. And, since they possessed no merchant marine of their own worth notice, the Southern states had to pick up such merchantmen as they could lay their hands on: by

May 26, 1861, they had seized thirty Northern merchant vessels in Southern ports, captured another twelve at sea, as well as fifteen steamers on the Mississippi, and fitted out the best of the lot as warships. But this was a pitifully small fleet, whether used as warships or merchantmen, and to redress the balance of power at sea the Southern states began to commission privateers and letters of marque.

Privateering was a form of warfare to which the weaker of two maritime nations had always turned in time of war, and it was moreover the one field of maritime activity in which the Southern states had a modest tradition of success. That tradition was of great appeal to the South, in spite of the blight cast upon privateering by the Federal government, which tried to prove that privateers were nothing more nor less than pirates. It was a position from which Lincoln receded later on, but in 1861 the Southern jurists and historians had to argue strenuously that privateering was an ancient and honorable way of waging war. They pointed out that the license issued by a belligerent to a private armed ship to capture enemy goods had its origin in the Middle Ages, when Princes licensed their subjects to cross their neighbors' frontiers to make reprisals for injury; that the practice was extended to the High Seas in the fourteenth century; that there was a general acceptance of privateering in the latter part of the sixteenth century; that privateers commissioned by the Prince of Orange in 1570 had helped the Netherlands in the revolt against Spain; that the French and British had used these licenses without limit in their interminable wars; and that in the American war for independence, as in the War of 1812, American privateers had made a substantial contribution to victory. Why, asked the Southerners, after centuries of acceptance, should privateering suddenly become piracy in 1861? Had not 1,500 American privateers with 15,000 guns captured 530 British vessels and their cargoes, worth $5,000,000, in the Revolutionary War? Had not Northern ports sent hundreds of such vessels to sea? And they quoted Niles' Register, a mine of nautical data, to prove their points: "A list of privateers," said Niles, "fitted out and chiefly owned in Salem and Beverly, Massachusetts, from March 1 to November 1, 1781 . . ." and the list ran on: 26 ships with 2,645 men; 16 brigs, 870 men; 8 schooners, 235 men; 2 sloops, 70 men; 7 shallops, 120 men: in all, 746 guns and

3,940 men. Were they all pirates who had fought at sea against the King of England? True, by the Treaty of Paris which ended the Crimean War in 1856, Britain, France, Russia, Prussia, Austria, Sardinia and Turkey had agreed that "Privateering is and remains abolished"—but that applied only to the signatories of the treaty—not to the United States.

Maryland, which the South considered more Southern than Northern, although the state remained neutral, was a fountain of inspiration to the privateers. Baltimore and the little ports on Chesapeake Bay had a long and worthy record of hell-raising at sea; from April 1, 1777 to March 14, 1783, 248 privateers and letters of marque sailed out of the Chesapeake, carrying 1,810 guns and 640 swivels. In 1793, when the Napoleonic Wars started, Baltimore sent to sea between forty and fifty privateers under the French flag to cruise against British merchantmen, and nearly all of these ships were built, fitted out, armed, manned and officered by citizens of Baltimore. Within five months after the War of 1812 began Baltimore had sent to sea 42 privateers and letters of marque, manned by 3,000 men and armed with 330 guns. Tom Boyle and Joshua Barney were Baltimoreans, and as such their work was considered a part of the Southern heritage of glittering work at sea. From Baltimore *Rossie* had gone out in the War of 1812 and in 45 days had taken prizes worth $1,289,000; *Rolla* in a short cruise took 7 merchantmen worth $2,500,000; *Amelia,* in 85 days, won $1,000,000 worth of prizes. In the 3 years of that war, from 1812 to 1815, 250 American privateers captured over 2,000 vessels, and Baltimore claimed that her privateers had taken a third of the total. Aside from Baltimore there was little tradition from which the Southern officers and men could draw inspiration: in the War of 1812 the other Southern ports had sent out only sixteen privateers.

Thus Jefferson Davis had both legal precedent and emotional tradition to pave the way for successful privateering by Southerners. But there were appallingly few Southern vessels fit for the business; even so, they had an effect out of all proportion to their numbers on the merchant marine. The privateer *Savannah* was the first to be commissioned, and her letter of marque was endorsed "No. 1" and dated May 18, 1861. She was a fast schooner of fifty-four tons register, a peacetime pilot-boat in Charleston harbor. Her modest armament consisted of one 18-pounder mounted on a swivel and in her waist, and she carried a crew of thirty-two officers and men. On June 3rd she went to sea under Captain T. H. Baker, and on the next day captured a Maine brig loaded with Cuban sugar. *Savannah* escorted her prize to Georgetown, South Carolina, and then turned back for deep water and more prizes. The first sail she sighted was the USS *Perry,* and *Savannah* mistook her for a merchantman, since her guns were run back and her ports closed. Full of the wine of her victory over the sugar brig, *Savannah* closed on the man-of-war, drew so close that when *Perry* triced her ports up and ran her guns out and began shooting, there was no chance of escape and Captain Baker hauled down the stars and bars. The crew of the privateer were put in irons and would possibly have been hanged as pirates had not Jefferson Davis threatened retaliation, man for man, if they were not treated as prisoners-of-war.

This was an inauspicious start for the ambitious program of privateers that Davis had in mind, but on June 28th another southern privateer got to sea: she was the brig *Jefferson Davis,* which had once been the slaver *Echo,* built in Baltimore in 1854, of 230 tons register. She was full-rigged and carried five guns, seventy-five officers and men, four prize-masters. In a lucky seven-week cruise, under the command of Captain L. M. Coxetter, she captured ten merchantmen, with a value of $225,000. The prizes were taken in waters as far apart as Nantucket Shoals and the northeastern coast of South America. There was consternation in Northern mercantile circles and the Navy Department assigned eight warships to track down and sink the elusive privateer. But Coxetter, running low on provisions and water and with half his crew manning out prizes, put in toward St. Augustine, and while trying to cross the bar, his ship struck and was lost. He and his men were the heroes of the hour, and the ladies of St. Augustine entertained them enthusiastically.

Two of *Jefferson Davis'* prizes were retaken, and what happened to one of them illustrates the depths of furious emotion and violence that the war had laid bare. The schooner *S. J. Waring,* of Brookhaven, Long Island, had been captured 150 miles off Sandy Hook on July 7th, and Coxetter had put Montague Amiel, a Charleston pilot, aboard as prize-master, with two mates and two seamen. He left aboard the prize William Tillman, a colored cook, two seamen and a passenger, Bryce Mackinnon. Under her prize crew the *Waring* headed for Southern waters, and on the evening of July 16th she was fifty miles south of Charleston, her captain and mate fast asleep in their cabins and the second mate dozing on deck near the wheel-house. Bryce Mackinnon left an account of what happened: "I was awakened," he wrote, "from a light sleep by a peculiar sound in the captain's room, which I knew instinctively could only have been produced by an axe cleaving Amiel's skull. No sooner did the 'thush' strike upon my ear than I leaped out of bed, and leaning against the door-casing in the partition, saw the steward dart through the twilight—for he had extinguished the light—noiselessly as a rat, across the cabin toward the mate's room. I saw also, at the same glance, Captain Amiel rise from his berth and attempt to follow him, but the blood blinded him, and he fell to the floor, with a horrid gurgling sound in his throat. All this was but the work of a second. The cleaving of the skull, like the flash of a gun preceding the report, was followed by a weak, faint cry, like that of a sick child, and the gurgling in the throat. I knew then his wound was mortal. Stooping sideways, the steward entered the second mate's cabin, and once more swung his axe, but not so effectively.

"The mate started up with a 'God damn you—don't strike me again,' and clutched at the steward's breast, but the steward eluded the wounded man, ran on deck to where the second mate lay near the wheel-house, and keeping his axe behind him, demanded 'What's all this noise about?' The second mate, who had been aroused by the outcries of the captain and mate, had raised himself up on his elbow, and stared at the steward in a half-stupid, half-fascinated way, not seeing the pistol which Stedding, the man at the helm, had pointed at him for use in case of necessity. As he turned his face toward the steward, the latter drove his weapon home to the base of the skull. Stedding and the steward then tumbled him overboard. He rose on the wave, with a hoarse cry, when about two lengths astern, the water having raised him; but he must have soon gone down to his long account.

"Then the steward came down to the cabin where I still stood, while Stedding stood pistol in hand, to guard the deck. The captain cried faintly twice to me by name, 'Help me—help me,' but he was past help. Another swishing blow of the axe, and he did not repeat the cry. Then the steward returned to the second mate's cabin, where, seated on a pile of starch boxes, his legs drawn up, and his head between his knees, was the half-stupefied man. Again and again the axe fell, and again and again the cry 'Don't do that' fell on my ear, each time fainter than the last. Stedding now came down, and the steward and he took the corpse of the captain by the feet, and dragging it up the companion-way, tossed it overboard. Stedding and the steward once more came down, and each taking the mate by the shoulder led him from the place where he had crouched on the starch boxes. He seemed to walk, with their assistance, as they went up the companionway, but his head lay a pulpy mass upon his shoulder, and a moment later a loud splash along-side told the fate of another of the privateers."

Left with no one aboard who knew how to navigate, the black steward took command of the schooner and followed the coast up to the pilot ground off New York, where the pilot-boat *Jane* took her in hand.

An odd assortment of makeshift vessels went into privateering under the stars and bars: converted from slavers, revenue cutters, pilot-boats and fishing schooners, they were nearly all small and lightly armed. There were probably no more than thirty of them at the most; among the few large ones were *Calhoun,* a steamer of 1,058 tons; *Judith,* of 250 tons; *Sallie,* of 140 tons. The others, like *Petrel, York, Five Brothers, Music* and *Freely* operated with indifferent success, capturing an occasional merchantman and in turn being captured. As the blockade grew in power the only Southern privateers left were small craft that darted out of the inlets along the coast and seized any passing vessel they could; the big, fast ships took up blockade-running, where there was more profit. Few as they were, by August 21, 1861, the Southern privateers had captured close to sixty Northern vessels, four of which had been re-taken, at a loss of only two privateers to the Northerners. Marine insurance premiums went up, and many New England ship-owners sold their vessels to the British, under whose flag they would be protected from harm. On August 10th the New York *Herald* raged "We are satisfied that already twenty million dollars worth of property had been lost in various ways through the operations of these highwaymen of the seas . . . English bottoms are taking all our trade . . . our shipping interest is literally ruined."

But, in reality, the Southerners had lost the Tom Boyle and Joshua Barney touch, if indeed they ever had it, and no matter how gallantly they tried they could not overcome their lack of ships, seamen, designers, mechanics, engine-shops, shipyards and craftsmen: an effective navy and merchant marine could not be improvised.

Meanwhile the blockade was tightening. Gideon Welles had set up the North and South Atlantic Blockading Squadrons; Federal warships began to converge on the eastern seaboard, and new construction in Northern yards began to come off the ways. The North's main problem was one of bases: south of Fort Monroe in Hampton Roads there were no mainland ports which its vessels could use, and there were 3,500 miles of coast to guard. Orders went out that started the re-taking of the chain of forts that stretched southward to Florida, and late in August 1861 a joint army-navy expedition sailed from Hampton Roads to take Hatteras Inlet, the key to North Carolinian waters. The Southerners had taken advantage of the indecision in Washington and by the time the expedition was under way the forts on both sides of Hatteras Inlet were well-manned. There was nasty weather on the day of the landings; nevertheless the surf-boats went ashore loaded with soldiers, much as they had in the Mexican War, but this time most of the boats were lost in the surf, although the men managed to get ashore safely. The warships closed in to help subdue the garrison in Fort Clark, and after four hours of bombardment and fighting the soldiers and marines took the fort. Three days later Fort Hatteras, on the west side of the inlet, surrendered to storming parties from the ships after a naval bombardment had softened up the fortifications. From then on the Northerners were able to prevent the Southern armies from receiving supplies from abroad by way of the ports to which access was barred by the captured forts. As possession of these forts provided, too, a base from which further operations could be sustained, within two months another joint expedition was sent out from Hampton Roads, this time with fifteen thousand soldiers under General W. T. Sherman, and the warships and transports under Captain Samuel F. DuPont, commanding the South Atlantic Blockading Squadron. The objective was Port Royal, South Carolina, and on November 7, 1861, the Northern amphibious forces attacked and won the forts. DuPont organized an advanced base there, and from it his Blockading Squadron operated against Charleston and Savannah. Slowly, as ships became available, the Northerners extended their line of bases down to Florida, occupying St. Augustine in March, 1862, and leaving only Savannah and Charleston available as major ports for the Southerners on the Atlantic coast. Then the emphasis of the Northern strategy on the seas shifted to the Gulf of Mexico, where the ports of Mobile and New Orleans were doing a thriving business, and early in 1862 the Western Gulf Blockading Squadron was organized and its command turned over to Captain David G. Farragut.

The writing was on the wall for any Southerner to see: the Northern warships were beginning a slow strangulation of Southern commerce, and in time the blockade would make it impossible to import guns and powder from Europe. Mallory realized this early in the war, and when Naval Constructor John L. Porter and Lieutenant John Brooke came forward with plans to convert the hull of the *Merrimac,* which they had raised from the mud of Norfolk Navy Yard into an ironclad, he ordered them to proceed with all haste. The work of transformation started in July 1861. *Merrimac* had been a 40-gun steam frigate of 3,500 tons, built in 1855 at Charlestown, Massachusetts, and she had created a moderate stir in British naval circles when she visited the British Isles on a cruise, being a species of warcraft new to the Admiralty. But she had been burned, scuttled and sunk on April 20, 1861, when the Northerners abandoned the Norfolk Navy Yard to the Virginians. On May 30th the Southerners had raised her and put her in drydock, where Engineer William P. Williamson began to putter with her engines, trying to undo the damage the salt water had done to them. The plan Porter and Brooke had for her was derivative in nature, based on the work that had been done by Robert Livingston Stevens in ironclads. Stevens, second son of John Stevens III, had helped operate his father's Hudson River ferry-boat, the *Little Juliana,* in 1804, and after the War of 1812 he had submitted plans to the Congress for a steampowered, shot-and-shell-proof ironclad warship. After thirty years of tergiversation Congress finally ordered this ship constructed according to plan, but as work was begun on her improvement in armament came so rapidly that the plans had to be changed from year to year and Stevens died before he could finish his ship. The progress Stevens had made in his work was generally known throughout naval circles, and, along the lines Stevens had visualized, conversion of the *Merrimac* to an iron-clad began. She was cut down to the waterline and a 170-foot shed was built on her mid-ship section, with the sides of the shed slanted at an angle of forty-five degrees on each side. These sloping sides were of pitch-pine and oak, two feet thick, extending from the waterline to a height of seven feet over the gundeck. Iron plating was laid on the wooden shed, and since the Tredegar Iron Works could handle only two-inch-thick plates, two layers were used, the under layer being placed horizontally and the outer layer vertically, and both bolted through the woodwork and clinched inside. A cast-iron ram four feet long was fastened on her bow, and her engines (which the United States Navy had condemned before the war) were patched and the defective parts replaced. In January 1862 the work was still going on. There were reports that *Monitor,* the Northern ironclad, was nearing completion in New York, and the need for speed, the sense of anxiety, so pervaded the work on *Merrimac* that the blacksmiths, strikers and finishers working on her volunteered a pledge, saying "We, the undersigned blacksmiths, strikers and finishers, agree to do any work that will expedite the completion of the *Merrimac,* free of charge, and continue on until eight o'clock every night; or any other work that will advance the interests of the Southern Confederacy." There were many delays, and chief among them was the inability of the Tredegar Iron Works to produce the iron plates, for the Tredegar Works had also to supply the requirements of the Southern army and the railroads. In February 1862 she was placed under the command of Captain Franklin Buchanan, the ranking officer in the Confederate States Navy. Buchanan had been born in Baltimore in 1800, had been appointed as a midshipman from Pennsylvania in 1815, had founded the Naval Academy, fought at Vera Cruz in the Mexican War, been with Perry in Japan, and made his emotional calculations in 1860–61, deciding to join the Southern insurgents. As captain of *Merrimac* he collected eighty seamen from a New Orleans regiment, augmented them with two hundred volunteers from the army,

picked up a score of seamen in Norfolk who were willing to try anything, and made ready to go into action in the iron-clad. Mallory wrote
to him, saying *"Merrimac* is a novelty in naval construction" and that
was putting it mildly: she was 257 feet long on the waterline, with a
beam of 57 feet, 4 inches, and a draught of 23 feet. Her battery, the
creation of Lieutenant Brooke, consisted of ten guns, two seven-
inch rifled guns fore and aft, and in each broadside four guns—three
9-inchers and one 6-incher. Her speed was, at the very best, six knots
an hour. She was christened *Virginia* by the Southerners but henceforth
she will be referred to as *Merrimac,* for the appeal of alliteration has
proved stronger than her Southern name. On the morning of February
8th, 1862 she was ready to put out into the Chesapeake Bay.

Her crew attended church services that morning, with an inde-
terminate effect, but hoping to avert a long stay in perdition in case they
should all get killed. This bit of precaution attended to, Buchanan ordered her lines cast off, and, shedding workmen as she went, she moved
into the channel. At 8:30 A.M. a quartermaster on USS *Congress* saw
smoke rising in the channel behind the woods on the Norfolk shore and
he said to an officer, "I think *that thing* is coming down at last, sir." Buchanan, sensing the historic implications of the moment, delivered himself of an oration to the mustered crew, saying, "Men, the eyes of your
country are upon you. You are fighting for your rights—your liberties—
your wives and children! You must not be content with doing only your
duty, but *do more than* your duty! Those ships (and here he gestured
toward the Federal fleet) must be taken, and you shall not complain
that I do not take you close enough. Go to your guns!" Into a circle of
guns on the Northern ships and forts the *Merrimac* steamed, trailed by
five small and excited Confederate warcraft. They counted the odds
against them: there were five large enemy ships, all wooden-hulled: 50-
gun *Congress,* with a brother of Buchanan's aboard; 50-gun *St. Lawrence;* 30-gun *Cumberland*—First Lieutenant George Morris in command, while her captain attended a Court of Inquiry on *Roanoke;* 46-
gun steamers *Minnesota* and *Roanoke* (although *Roanoke's* driveshaft
was broken); and on Fort Monroe and the Rip-Rap were batteries of
heavy guns. The day was clear and warm.

As the ironclad passed Sewell's Point the Northern ships beat to quarters and the USS *Zouave,* a gunboat, was sent to take a closer look at the monstrous Southern ship. *Zouave* fired her 32-pounder at *Merrimac,* but the shots glanced off the iron plates and the big ship did not even bother to return the fire. By one o'clock *Merrimac* was within range of the major units of the federal fleet and they loosed their broadsides at her, but the shot and shell bounced off her armored sides. The heavy guns on the federal forts had no better luck. Not until shortly after two o'clock did *Merrimac* open fire on *Congress* and *Cumberland,* getting in a broadside on *Congress* and wiping out a gun crew on *Cumberland* with one shell. Buchanan had decided to use his ram on *Cumberland* and he steamed at full speed—about five knots an hour—toward her. At 2:50 P.M. *Merrimac's* iron ram drove squarely into *Cumberland's* starboard side, and the ironclad backed away, losing her ram, but leaving a hole in *Cumberland* "big enough to drive a horse and cart through." Meanwhile *Congress* had slipped her anchor, loosed her bow topsail, and run up her jib in an effort to escape to shoal water. But as *Merrimac* backed away from *Cumberland* the iron-clad threw a broadside into *Congress.* That one broadside, wrote one of the officers on *Congress,* turned the frigate's gun-deck into a slaughter-pen, "with lopped-off arms and legs, and bleeding, blackened bodies scattered about by the shells, whilst blood and brains dripped from the beams."

Buchanan turned back to finish off *Cumberland,* having called out to the stricken ship to surrender and received the reply from Lieutenant Morris: "Never! I'll sink alongside!" *Merrimac* stood off, two hundred yards away, and for thirty-five minutes poured broadsides into the frigate, being abetted in this slaughter by the small Confederate vessels which had moved in for the kill. Deck by deck *Cumberland* settled, firing always at impervious *Merrimac,* and when she finally came to rest on the bottom of the bay, her masts were still above water and she was still flying the stars and stripes at her peak and the red "No Quarter!" flag at her fore. Smoke from the guns drifted over the scene and in the semi-obscurity the iron-clad turned away.

The refusal of *Cumberland* to strike her flag in the face of insuperable odds ranks among the world's great deeds of heroism, deserving a place in the nation's memory, where it may be of use as an inspiration, unless forgotten. At the time *Cumberland's* defiance of the ironclad made the spirits of the Northerners soar, and at the same time it showed them the completeness of the holoblastic, venomous hatred that existed in Southern minds. Captain Buchanan, an officer of the United States Navy for forty-six years, had turned his guns on his former shipmates and massacred them while he remained safe behind two feet of oak and pine and four inches of iron. Truly, thought the Northerners, these Southerners are a pack of insane bastards, and this is going to be a war to the death. The Southerners, considering themselves the aggrieved party, thought even harsher things of the Northerners.

"Having sunk the *Cumberland*," wrote Buchanan, "I turned our attention to the *Congress*. . . ." *Congress* had grounded in shoal water and *Merrimac* took a position 150 yards astern of her and began raking her fore and aft with shells. *Congress* could bring only her two stern-chasers to bear on the iron-clad, and before long they were put out of commission by *Merrimac's* raking broadsides. Fires broke out aboard the frigate, and the acrid smell of burning oak choked the wounded and the dying, while icy water from the fire-hoses added to their agony. After one hour of punishment *Congress* hauled down her colors and ran up the white surrender flags at the gaff, half-mast and main. Buchanan ordered a party to go aboard her to accept the surrender of the ship, secure her officers as prisoners, allow her crew to land, take off the wounded, and then to burn the vessel. The surrender-party was promptly fired on by the troops on shore, and withdrew. At about this time Buchanan was wounded by the fire from shore, and after ordering hot shot fired into *Congress* so that she would be totally destroyed, he transferred command of *Merrimac* to Lieutenant Catesby Ap. Rogers Jones. Soon *Congress*, with sixty wounded still aboard, was burning briskly enough to warm the hearts of the Southerners, and *Merrimac* turned to deal with *Minnesota*. But the tide had been ebbing rapidly and the ironclad could not get within range so she steamed back to her anchorage, whence her crew could see *Cumberland's* stars and stripes waving from the masts of the sunken ship, and *Congress* a fiery torch wracked by explosions that drowned the screams of the wounded. Nestled under the guns of Fort Monroe were the remnants of the Northern fleet.

In that bloody day's work two great ships had been destroyed and 257 Northerners killed or drowned; *Merrimac* had lost two men killed and eight wounded, and had suffered only superficial damages. A wave of hysteria swept Washington; Secretary Stanton told a Cabinet meeting in the White House that *Merrimac* would change the whole course of the war, would destroy every naval vessel she met, would lay all the seaboard cities under contribution, was probably on her way to Washington and "it is not unlikely we shall have a shell or a cannon ball from one of her guns in the White House before we leave the room." There was but one hope, the Cabinet thought, and that was little *Monitor,* an experimental iron-clad built by the Swede John Ericsson.

Work had begun on *Monitor* in New York in late October 1861, and she had been built in great haste—launched in a hundred days. Her underwater hull was conventional enough: length 172 feet, beam 41 feet, draught 10 feet. But on her low mailed deck Ericsson had built a revolving circular iron tower and inside the tower had mounted two heavy guns firing 11-inch, 180-pound shot. Fifty-eight volunteers, under Captain John L. Worden, made up her crew, and of them sixteen were assigned to the duty of handling her guns and the machinery that revoved the turret. On her way from New York to Hampton Roads in early March 1862 she encountered heavy weather and nearly foundered, but she arrived in Chesapeake Bay on March 8th in time to hear the distant rumble of gunfire. Late that afternoon a pilot came aboard with the news that *Merrimac* had all but wrecked the Northern fleet and at once *Monitor's* deck was cleared for action and her turret given a few trial whirls. As the details of the battle were given to them, with full emphasis on the "perfidious inhumanity" of Buchanan, the iron entered their souls. Briefly, by the light of burning *Congress,* the Southerners glimpsed the little iron-clad and knew that some strange craft had come into the harbor. But just what she was they were not sure: she might be a floating water-tender, or some new kind of ammunition ship. *Merrimac* first saw her on Sunday, March 9th, soon after dawn, and she looked like "a cheese box on a plank" or "a tin can on a shingle." Catesby Jones, commanding *Merrimac,* recognized this strange craft as his true opponent, and he steamed out to meet her. Worden, on *Monitor,* advanced to an uncertain fate: his crew was exhausted, his engineer sick, flat on his back in his bunk, his ship's steering-gear and turret machinery crank and rusty. But his ship represented the Union, and even if she was held in general contempt by the navy and called "an outlandish thing," she was the only vessel capable of facing *Merrimac* without going down to certain defeat.

Merrimac, moving to meet *Monitor,* exchanged fire with grounded *Minnesota,* and while so engaged *Monitor* closed. At 8:30 A.M. *Merrimac* opened fire on *Monitor* with her bow-chaser, but *Monitor* lay so low in the water and her turret was so small that she was difficult to hit. *Monitor* steamed up close to *Merrimac,* dwarfed by her great size, and at point-blank range fired her two guns. The 180-pound shot glanced off *Merrimac's* iron-plates, and then *Merrimac* brought her broadside to bear on *Monitor's* turret, striking it repeatedly but inflicting no damage. The duel settled down to a futile exchange of shots, with *Merrimac* firing every fifteen minutes and *Monitor* every seven minutes. Vainly the gun crews on *Merrimac* tried to get a shot into the revolving turret, but on *Monitor,* as the gun ports on the turret were opened and the guns run out and fired and then run back and the ports closed, the turret was swiftly revolved so that blank iron was the only target that she presented to *Merrimac's* guns. The Southerners found this technique exasperating, explained it as habitual Northern cowardice and a fair example of Yankees wanting to hit without being hurt. Worden became resigned to the inability of his ship to damage *Merrimac* with her guns, and he attempted to ram, aiming at *Merrimac's* propeller, but he missed by two feet. Catesby Jones, thwarted in his attempt to destroy both *Minnesota* and *Monitor* by gunfire, in turn attempted to ram *Monitor,* but the Northern ironclad, although struck by *Merrimac,* slipped out from under her like a floating board, and no damage was done to either vessel. *Monitor* then retired for fifteen minutes to replenish the powder and shot in her turret from her magazine, and returned to the battle, receiving the fire of *Merrimac* which was now aimed at her most vulnerable point —her conning-tower. One shell hit the pilothouse at 11:30 A.M., and Worden, who was at one of the peepholes, was temporarily blinded by the explosion and much cut about the face by the iron fragments. He fell back bleeding profusely, and turning to Lieutenant Greene asked if *Minnesota* was saved. When the Lieutenant said she was, Worden murmured "Then I can die happy." But this splendid closing line, delivered in the classic manner amidst swirling smoke and the boom of guns, became irrelevant when Worden's wounds were found, later on, to be superficial. *Monitor* drifted aimlessly for twenty minutes and then under Lieutenant Greene, who had taken command, she turned again toward *Merrimac*. But that vessel was withdrawing, and Greene did not follow hotly, being content to fire a couple of shots at long range.

Neither iron-clad had been seriously damaged and neither had lost any men in the battle. Each of the two rival republics therefore claimed the victory, and charged each other with cowardice, filling the columns of newspapers and magazines with their varying reports of the engagement. Nearly twelve years later, when John Ericsson was given a chance to criticize the galley proofs of an article intended for an encyclopaedia, he contradicted nearly every statement in the article, and as he wrote his rebuttal his wrath rose until he was moved to append a postscript saying "The original written under strong emotion, being nearly unintelligible, I forward the copy." It was years before the historians could point out, with reasonable personal safety, that while *Merrimac* undoubtedly won the engagement of March 8th, her fight with *Monitor* on March 9th was a draw: tactically the battle of the iron-clads was indecisive. Strategically it was a Northern victory, for *Monitor* prevented *Merrimac* from completing the destruction of the Northern fleet in Hampton Roads, ended the fear of the seaboard cities that *Merrimac* would attack the shipping in their harbors, and banished the fear that the White House would become a target for *Merrimac*. Overseas the lack of clear-cut results from the battle of the iron-clads cast further doubt on the South's future. In the Admiralty there was much debate over the relative merits of mounting guns in turrets, as *Monitor's,* and in broadsides, as *Merrimac's.* In Northern navy yards there was rejoicing at *Monitor's* performance, and the Navy Department was quick to order more of the same type.

For two months after the engagement the iron-clads by their mere existence acted as guardians of their causes: *Merrimac* refitted and came out but *Monitor* would not fight, being considered the sole defense between Washington and *Merrimac* and too valuable to hazard in a display of fireworks; *Merrimac* in turn guarded the James River and the approach to Richmond, until the Northern land forces began to descend on Norfolk, and on May 11th, 1862, she was scuttled and abandoned to the great dismay of all Southerners. *Monitor* was sent to sea soon afterwards, and in a gale off Cape Hatteras she foundered, taking sixteen men down with her in her final plunge.

By the spring of 1862 the blockade of Southern ports was beginning to show results: there were growing shortages of materials and munitions, and an increasing tendency on the part of the Southern government to issue paper money. But the blockade was a dull and uninspiring operation, with only occasional flashes of dramatic value when some fast blockade-runner managed to get clear of the warships and to show them her smoke, and its part in the slow strangulation of the South was like the constriction, slow but steady, of an anaconda.

In addition to the blockade there was another, even more arduous duty for the Northern warships to perform, involving the projection of sea power inland, up the Mississippi. Lincoln summed up the case, saying: "The Mississippi is the backbone of the Rebellion; it is the key to the whole situation." By this he gave due weight to the tremendous value the river had as a means of transportation in the Southern states: much of the South's food supply came from the slave states west of the river—from Missouri, Texas, Arkansas, and from the bulk of Louisiana, where the fertile plains were untrammeled by war. Over the river and its tributaries farm produce and supplies could be distributed to the Southern armies and the civilian population. At New Orleans the river transportation system merged with sea-borne commerce and joined the Southern states to the outside world. The North lost no time in starting to win control of the river, first by working down from the north with river craft based on Cincinnati and Cairo, and then by working north from the Gulf, where a blockading squadron had been operating with only moderate success from its base at Ship Island.

A plan was devised by Gustavus V. Fox, Assistant Secretary of the Navy, to use the navy to take, and the army to hold, New Orleans, and a squadron was assigned for this task. David Glasgow Farragut was placed in command and he arrived at Ship Island in February 1862, flying his broad command flag from USS *Hartford,* a screw-sloop. As a naval officer, Farragut approached the ideal: he combined audacity and brains, leadership and selflessness. Curiously enough, by birth and upbringing he was wholly Southern, having been born in Tennessee and raised in

New Orleans. His mother was a native of North Carolina, and his father was of Spanish ancestry: in the boy there was a mixture of chivalry and commonsense, and a heritage of illustrious deeds dating from the thirteenth century when one of his ancestors, Don Pedro Farragut, fought valiantly to drive the Moors out of Spain. The odds were that he would "go South" and take up the cause of his homeland, but he did not: when Southern relatives asked him to join them he pointed to the stars and stripes and said, "I would see every man of you damned before I would raise my hand against that flag." He had served in the navy ever since the War of 1812, in which as a midshipman he had been aboard *Essex* during her engagement with *Phoebe* and *Cherub*. By what thought processes he made his decision to fight on the Northern side we can only conjecture: perhaps he took his oath of allegiance literally, without bothering to define terms, and with a full recognition of the binding power of the deity by whom he had sworn to obey all orders. He was a very religious man, and he never expressed any doubt about the rectitude of his decision.

At any rate, here was a case of the environment of the sea and ships erasing the appeal of hearth and home, overlaying one set of emotions with another and stronger set. To Farragut, home meant first of all the deck of a warship with the United States flag flying over it. When he arrived at Ship Island he was in his sixtieth year, sage in mind and sprightly in body, still a proficient swordsman and fond of gymnastics, including somersaults. His orders read: "You will proceed up the Mississippi River and reduce the defenses which guard the approaches to New Orleans, when you will appear off that city."

The situation and the orders were such that they left him some liberty of choice: Ship Island, a hundred miles east of the forts guarding the mouth of the river, was large enough for use as a rendezvous, and from that point the Northern fleet set out in April—eight capable warships and nine gunboats. The two forts—St. Philip and Jackson—which had to be passed before New Orleans, ninety miles up the river, could be reached, were armed with 116 guns of various caliber, and the plan to attack which the Washington strategists had in mind entailed the destruction of these forts as a necessary preliminary to the capture of New Orleans. First things first, thought the strategists, but Farragut had other

Engagement Between *Monitor* and *Merrimac*

U.S.S. *Missouri*, Immediately Following Explosion in the After Turret in 1904

ideas: he calculated that if he ran past the forts and took New Orleans, the forts, cut off from provisions, would wither and die, and he issued orders to carry out his ideas.

The first step was taken when the Northern squadron sent two gun-boats to break the boom the Southerners had fixed across the river near the forts, and when a passage had been broken through the boom the fleet began to move through it, in line-ahead, on April 24th. Within twenty minutes the whole squadron passed beyond range of the forts and began to dodge the spirited attacks of Southern warcraft, cutting through the motley armada of enemy riverboats that milled about franti-cally. The Southerners afloat were brave men, but untrained in ship-handling and naval tactics, and the Northern professionals knifed through them like tempered steel through aged cheese. Meanwhile the Northern troops from the transports were being assembled at Sable Is-land (reached by way of the bayous), twelve miles from the forts, and from that point they were transported to a rendezvous five miles upriver from the forts. With the forts thus neutralized, on the 25th the joint force moved on New Orleans, and without losing a man captured the defenses five miles downstream from the city, which had been built to withstand an attack by land, but not by sea. For five days, while negotiations lead-ing to surrender went on, there was disorder in the city, and then on May 1st the Northern troops garrisoned the city, under General B. F. Butler. The general, his finer sensibilities blunted by land warfare, ruled with Draconic severity, warning the citizens on May 15th that any women who made insulting gestures toward Northern soldiers would be handled as "women of the town plying their avocation."

The fall of New Orleans was a major disaster to the Southern cause: with its fall the last hope of winning recognition from France and Britain vanished; with one of their largest exporting centers in enemy hands, the link between sea and river was broken and the free flow of grain and cattle from the west disrupted.

Meanwhile the Northern blockading squadrons, with their bases either made secure or won for them by the warships, operated without having to waste time in long voyages back to the Northern states for repairs and provisioning: at their disposal were Hatteras Inlet, Port Royal, Roanoke Island, Norfolk, Beaufort, Fernandina, St. Augustine,

Key West, Pensacola, Ship Island and New Orleans—all points at which the anaconda's pressure could be revitalized.

As major ports left to the Southerners there remained only Mobile, Alabama, Wilmington, North Carolina, Charleston, South Carolina, and Savannah, Georgia. The constriction of the blockade tightened perceptibly in the months following the surrender of New Orleans.

Farragut moved his vessels up and down the river, going as far north as Vicksburg, where his force joined temporarily that of Captain C. H. Davis, which had come down from the north: these were largely futile and useless maneuvers, ordered by Washington strategists who were guided by the looks of things on the maps and who had no conception of the difficulties of river navigation. Farragut's heart was not in this work on fresh water, but he carried out his orders dutifully and was rewarded on August 20th when he arrived at Pensacola to take over the command of the Gulf blockade and hoisted his flag as the first rear-admiral in the United States Navy. He had earned the promotion.

During 1862, 163 new warships, among them many ironclads, making a total of 427 vessels, joined the Northern fleets, and the personnel to man them was drawn from the wealth of sea-wise mariners who had been trained in the merchant marine, and in the fisheries. Even with the Northerners' natural addiction to the sea it was difficult to find enough trained seamen for all the new ships, and Gideon Welles reported plaintively that "While every sound and able-bodied man of proper age can be made into a soldier, there are comparatively few of the population who can be made into sailors. The latter may be considered experts." In the implacable school of experience, guided by the old-timers, the "green hands" from the mountains and valleys of the North learned their new trade and the behavior of guns fired in anger.

But still there were not enough ships to make the blockade totally effective, for they had to contend with not only blockade-runners but also with commerce-destroyers like *Florida, Alabama* and *Shenandoah*. Insurance rates on Northern merchantmen rose to exorbitant heights, and transfers of merchantmen from American to foreign flag and registry rose accordingly, from 126 ships of 71,673 tons in 1861, to 135 ships of 74,578 tons in 1862, to 348 ships of 252,579 tons in 1863. *Alabama* began her destructive career in the fall of 1862 and to her operations a good part of the increase in shipping transferred in 1863 can be attributed.

Captain James D. Bulloch, CSN, had indeed been a very busy man in the British Isles, negotiating for the construction of fast ships which could be used by the South as commerce-raiders, and his efforts were rewarded by the acquisition of *Florida, Alabama, Shenandoah* and *Rappahannock,* although the latter never got to sea. *Florida* was the first one out, sailing from Liverpool in March 1862, and after a difficult voyage she reached Mobile, Alabama, in September, where she was fitted out and manned for an extended cruise. Her chief prize was the clipper ship *Jacob Bell,* which was homeward bound to New York, from Foo Chow, China, with a cargo of teas and silks. *Florida* sighted her off the Windward Islands on February 12, 1863 and after a long chase captured and burned her, causing a loss to the Northerners of $1,500,000. *Florida* went on to run her string of captures up to a total of thirty-seven, with a value of over three million dollars, before she was captured while at anchor in the neutral harbor of Bahia, Brazil, on October 7th, 1864, by the USS *Wachusett,* whose captain had no regard for the amenities of international law. Brazil was outraged at this breach of her sovereignty, and the Northerners agreed to the demand of the Brazilian government that *Florida* should be returned to Bahia and turned over to the Southerners, but before that could be done the *Florida* met with an "accident" in Hampton Roads, first being in collision with an army transport and then diplomatically sinking at her moorings when a Northern naval officer settled the thorny problem by opening her watercocks and letting her fill quietly and go to the bottom of the bay.

Bulloch had nearly finished with his negotiations for the construction of *Florida,* in June 1861, when he began the business of getting Laird of Birkenhead, opposite Liverpool, to build a small steam sloop-of-war, on a model he described with considerable exactitude. She was known in the shipyard as "No. 290," and to history as the *Alabama.* Bulloch paid Laird £47,500 for her, and on July 29, 1862, she steamed out of the Mersey, just in time to escape an order sent down from the Foreign Office that she should be detained on the complaint of the American Minister that she was destined to become a Southern man-of-war. *Alabama* was 220 feet long, with a 32 foot beam, and of 1,040 tons burden. She was barkentine-rigged and her propeller could be raised from the water when she was moving under sail alone. Using her sails she could occasionally make ten knots an hour; with steam and sail she could reach 11¼ knots. She carried six 32-pounders in broadside, a 100-pounder rifle forward and a smooth-bore 8-inch shell gun abaft the mainmast. In command of the small but formidable vessel was Captain Raphael Semmes, a native of Maryland, a veteran of the Mexican War in which he served as flag-lieutenant of the Home Squadron under Commodore David Conner, and by nature much interested in law, international and maritime. His ship was formally commissioned *Alabama* on August 24th at Terceira, in the Azores, or Western Islands, with a ship's company of 149 officers and men. Three weeks later she began her career by plunging into the Yankee whaling fleet off Fayal and making prizes of several of them. Then Semmes took her north to the Newfoundland Banks, athwart the track of the grain ships bound from New England ports to Europe. In three October weeks the raider made sixteen prizes, and then she ran down the coast and into the Caribbean, putting into Port of France, Martinique, in mid-November. Here some of her crew, pining for their daily tot of grog, smuggled rum of such potency aboard that when they drank it they started a mutiny. Semmes was equal to the occasion: he ordered the reeling mutineers doused with cold water and as the rebellious seamen were thus shocked into sobriety their bellicose attitude evaporated. After coaling from a tender at Blanquilla, Venezuela, *Alabama* lay in wait between Haiti and Santo Domingo, hoping to capture one of the treasure steamers that plied between Colón and New York, loaded with gold from California, but the steamer she stopped was *Ariel,* bound for Colón from New York, with only $9,500 in her safe and 500 women and children among the passengers. Semmes released her on a ransom bond for $261,000, to be payable "after the recognition of the independence of the Confederate States." *Alabama* next moved into the Gulf of Mexico and lured one of the blockading squadron— the gunboat *Hatteras*—twenty miles out to sea, and sank her in a thirteen minute battle. Southward she sailed, down the Brazil coast, taking many prizes, and then to the marine crossroads at the Cape of Good Hope. There the raider captured twenty-four vessels and destroyed all but one of them; on she went across the Indian ocean, through the

Sunda Straits and into the China Sea, where there were slim pickings. Back to the Atlantic she sailed by way of the Bay of Bengal and down the east coast of Africa, reaching Cherbourg, France on June 11, 1864.

The Northerners had been making dogged efforts to catch her, sending several of their best ships to points at which the Navy Department deduced the raider would appear, but they had always been either too early or too late, and *Alabama* had never had to fight her way out of a trap. But in the harbor at Flushing, in the Netherlands, was the U.S. steam-corvette *Kearsage,* Captain John A. Winslow, and on June 12th a telegram arrived from the American Minister in Paris, reporting the arrival of *Alabama*. *Kearsage* made ready to put to sea at once, and she steamed down the channel, touching at Dover, arriving off Cherbourg on June 14th. Inside the breakwater the stars and bars flying from *Alabama* were visible, and Winslow ran into the harbor, identified the raider beyond any doubt, and then lay to outside the three mile limit.

Semmes was in a quandary: his ship was not supposed to fight men-of-war—her value to the Southern cause lay in her ability to destroy merchantmen and whalers. But the Northerners had accused him of cowardice, of piratical acts, and the French officers at the Cherbourg naval base expected him to fight. And, since he had the honor of the South to defend, and the rival vessel was no larger than his own, he sent Winslow of *Kearsage* a challenge, asking him not to leave until *Alabama* had been made ready for battle. In view of Semmes' background, in which magnolia blossoms and mint juleps, good horsemanship and vivacious Southern damsels combined to symbolize chivalry, his decision was inevitable: no Southern gentleman could refuse a duel, especially with a detested Northerner.

Kearsage was, like *Alabama,* a full-rigged steamer, and she displaced 1,031 tons, carried seven guns and a crew of 163 men. She was a trifle faster than the Southern ship, and the weight of her broadside was 366 pounds, compared to *Alabama's* 306 pounds. Two factors which Semmes did not give due importance to were the quality of her crew and a bit of Yankee ingenuity about which he was uninformed: the Northern ship's crew were professional seamen who had been trained together and who knew their gunnery, whereas *Alabama's* men were mostly riff-raff from British and French waterfronts, a crew of desperadoes, salted with only a few experienced British gunners, and with experience in only one naval engagement, and that against the small gunboat *Hatteras;* the Yankee trick which Semmes did not know about consisted of a belt of chains hung over the sides of *Kearsage* to protect her engines and covered with one-inch deal boards. (Farragut had used the same device when he forced passage between the forts below New Orleans.)

Shortly after ten o'clock on the morning of June 19th, a Sunday, while the crew of *Kearsage* were gathering for divine service, *Alabama* started out of the harbor. Winslow flipped his prayer-book closed, ordered his ship cleared for action, slipped his cable, and stood out further to sea to avoid any breach of neutrality. He thought *Alabama* must be the more powerful ship of the two—otherwise, Semmes would not have been willing to fight. Following *Alabama* came the French ironclad *Couronne,* intent on protecting the neutral waters of France, and the English yacht *Greyhound,* whose amiable owner wanted to satisfy the desire of his children to see the fight. The breakwater at Cherbourg and the cliffs at Dover were thronged with spectators, all happily expectant at the thought of front-row seats at a naval battle. *Couronne* returned to port when she had escorted *Alabama* outside the three mile limit.

Kearsage seemed to be in flight: she steamed out until seven miles from shore, and then came about and steamed directly at *Alabama:* at 10:57 *Alabama* opened fire, but *Kearsage* was then a mile distant and suffered only minor damage to her rigging. The two ships began to steam in spirals, broadside to broadside, as each ship tried to rake the other. *Kearsage* opened fire at nine hundred yards; gradually the range was closed to five hundred yards and at this close distance *Kearsage's* heavier guns began to demolish *Alabama. Alabama's* shells did not pierce the chain-armor on *Kearsage* and when Semmes ordered shot used instead of shell, he had no better luck. *Kearsage's* gunnery was superb—the heavy guns aimed at the enemy's water line, and the light ones at her deck. After one hour and ten minutes of battle *Alabama* was in a sinking condition, water rushing into her, and although Semmes tried to run her aground, before he could get far water reached her engine room. He hauled down her colors and flung his sword into the sea. One boat was sent to *Kearsage* to make the formal surrender, and another was loaded with wounded, then, at 12:50 *Alabama's* bows rose high in the air and she plunged beneath the waves. *Kearsage* made no immediate effort to save the men left swimming in the water—after all, they were treasonous pirates to the Northern way of thinking— and the yacht *Greyhound* picked up as many as she could, Semmes among them. *Kearsage* then lowered two boats to pick up the remaining survivors, and took them to Cherbourg. *Greyhound* took her rescued to the English coast, where Semmes was lionized and presented with a sword to replace the one he had thrown into the sea. In the fall of the year he made his way to Louisiana by way of Havana, and after living uneventfully throughout the rest of the war he descended to the practice of journalism to earn a living.

Of *Alabama's* crew of 150 officers and men, 9 were killed, 21 wounded and 10 drowned in the battle. *Kearsage's* casualties consisted of only three wounded gunners. But the sightseers along the coasts of France and England had seen enough of the battle to banish any doubts they may have cherished about the invulnerability of the fabulous Southern raider. When the news of the navy's victory reached the Northern states there was unbounded jubilation, extending from shipowners' mansions to waterfront taverns and official circles.

The last of the great Southern raiders—the *Shenandoah*—originally a British merchant steamer—sailed from London in October 1864, and under Captain James I. Waddell set out for Australia. She left Melbourne early in February, 1865, and sailed northward against the whaling fleets in the Okhotsk Sea, Bering Sea and Arctic ocean. By June 28th she had captured and burned thirty-four whalers and ransomed four, thus obliterating the American whaling industry in those waters. Not until August 2nd, when she spoke the British bark *Barracouta,* could her captain be convinced that the Southern cause was lost: but on that day he learned that Jefferson Davis had been captured and that the Southern military forces had capitulated.

For years after the war had ended the Northern claims for damages from Britain—the "Alabama claims"—were a bone of contention in international law: finally they were adjudicated by a Geneva Tribunal which directed Britain to pay the United States $15,500,000 in satisfaction for ships destroyed by raiders built in British ports. Eleven commerce-destroyers in all figured in the claims; they had captured 258 vessels whose total value was $17,900,633: all but $4,000,000 of the damages were caused by *Alabama* and *Shenandoah*—$6,547,609 being charged to the former, and $6,487,000 to the latter. On the record, Bulloch had invested the South's money well when he acquired both ships for £92,500, or less than half a million dollars. Directly to their flamboyant work can be attributed the accelerated decline of the American merchant marine and the demise of the whaling fleets, but in the effect they had on the outcome of the war they were a distraction of no great importance, for there were enough Northern warships both to hunt them and to maintain the blockade.

Lincoln had scribbled his signature on the Proclamation of Blockade on April 19th, 1861, and on May 27th another proclamation extended the blockade to include the coasts of Virginia and North Carolina, so that the whole of the Southern seaboard from the Virginia Capes to the Rio Grande became in theory an unhealthy place for neutral and Southern merchantmen. The difficulty was that by international law a blockade must be effective in order to be legal, and in the summer of 1861 the North did not have enough warships to make the blockade effective. There were 3,500 miles of coastline to patrol, and the Navy Department promptly purchased and commissioned anything that could float and carry guns—tugs, ferry-boats, steamers, sloops, schooners, ships and barks—and dispatched them to guard Southern ports. Most of these vessels were unseaworthy and their unseaworthiness made the need for bases on the Southern coast a pressing one.

The blockade was of absorbing interest to Britain and France, Holland and Spain: those nations had imported $20,000,000 worth of Southern tobacco in 1860, on which the British government had collected $21,000,000 in duties; France, $18,000,000; Holland, $20,000,000; Spain, $5,000,000. Southern cotton worth $150,000,000 was exported annually to Britain in the years before the war, and over five million people in the British Isles owed their livelihood to the manufacture of cotton goods. To a less extent Europe depended on the Southern states for sugar, rice, indigo and such naval stores as turpentine and rosin. But it was cotton that was the linch-pin of Southern finances, and the lever by means of which the South hoped to move Britain from its neutral position. The Southerners calculated that the lack of cotton in British mills would create so much unrest that the British government would be forced to recognize the Confederate States as a free nation, and perhaps come actively to the aid of the South. The Northerners looked at the other side of the coin: they thought that by blockading the South and preventing the export of cotton Britain would be made eager for an early end of the fighting, and would therefore do nothing to encourage the South and thus draw out the length of the war. As it turned out the Northerners were right, for the British government acted with restraint even when thousands in the British Isles were thrown out of work because of the lack of cotton and forced to resort to the poor-rates, or dole, for a bare subsistence.

The blockade developed in three distinct phases: the first phase lasting until the summer of 1862, the second until the fall of 1864, and the third through the winter of 1864-5. In the first period, up to the fall of New Orleans, when there were few ships in the blockading squadron, blockade-running was not at all hazardous; in the second period, as the blockading vessels increased in number, the blockade-runners began their halcyon days. The Northerners set up, in all, four squadrons: the North Atlantic Blockading Squadron operated from Chesapeake Bay to Wilmington, North Carolina; the South Atlantic Squadron from Wilmington to the Bahamas; the East Gulf Squadron from the Bahamas to Pensacola; the West Gulf Squadron from Pensacola to Matamoras. At first the only blockade runners captured were those small and slow sailing vessels which optimistic Southerners had loaded with cotton and sent out to Havana, Nassau, Bermuda, and to St. Thomas in the Danish West Indies. As the process of attrition eliminated the unfit vessels, the runners left in the business were fast steamers, and later in the war, specially-built craft from the British shipyards on the Clyde river.

As the war progressed the neutral ports closest to the Southern states entered a period of wild prosperity: Havana traded with New Orleans until the capture of that place in 1862, and with Mobile, Alabama, after that; Nassau was the center of the blockade-running traffic with St. Augustine until the Northerners took that city in 1862, and then the Nassau trade went to Savannah, Charleston and Wilmington; Bermuda specialized in trade with Wilmington, but also ran goods to Charleston and Savannah. To stop this traffic the Northern warships along the Southern coast, at the entrance to the major ports, were divided into inshore and offshore patrols, forming graceful crescents which on the maps in Washington appeared to close the harbors. In reality the blockade leaked in numerous places, and so the North began sending ships to watch the neutral ports from which the runners set out for Southern ports. Bermuda and Nassau were so closely guarded that the British residents therein ruefully claimed that they were being blockaded. But no matter how vigilant the blockading warships off neutral ports were, the runners found ways of clearing from the ports with their cargoes of luxury goods and munitions: in Nassau they could put out to sea after sunset, and, guided by the expert local pilots, steam along the shore within the three-mile limit, using the familiar shallow channels among the reefs until they reached the open sea where they could trust to their speed to escape pursuit. But by June 1863 the Northerners had captured 855 blockade-runners, and as more and faster warships went into service in the blockading squadrons, attempts to run the gauntlet became increasingly precarious. When the profits involved in running the blockade became so great that the risks were worth taking, in the British Isles blockade-running companies were formed and shares in them eagerly sought by speculators. The business demanded specially constructed steamers, and in 1863–4 these new craft came out of British shipyards and went into operation under British officers. They had to be fast, of shallow-draft, and yet able to carry a sizeable amount of cargo, and the vessels evolved were wooden-hulled, of from four hundred to five hundred tons, with extremely fine lines— often nine times as long as they were broad. Generally they were paddle-steamers, burning anthracite coal to avoid making smoke, and some of them could make seventeen knots an hour. To make it difficult for the blockading vessels to spot them their funnels were designed so that they could be telescoped, their masts were lightly rigged— mere poles without yards and only a crow's-nest on the foremast—and they lay low in the water, with no more than eight feet of freeboard, their sides painted a dull gray. In the darkness they were practically invisible at two hundred yards.

Among the English captains in this trade the most famous was "Hobart Pasha," who served under the name of "Captain Roberts," and who carried thousands of stays from Nassau, where they cost one shilling each, to Charleston where they sold for twelve shillings each, being much in demand by ladies who wished to emphasize certain points of physical attraction and disguise other less appealing protuberances. "Hobart Pasha" made several successful trips, and went on to become The Hon. August Charles Hobart, Marshal of the Turkish Empire and Vice-Admiral in the Royal Navy.

As a blockade runner, having taken her sights and fixed her position at noon, steamed toward Wilmington, North Carolina, timing her run so that she arrived after darkness had fallen, she hugged the shore, exchanged signals with watchers on the coast and in the forts, and made her final high-speed dash past the Northern warships. Quickly her cargo of munitions, invoiced as "hardware," and of such luxuries as silks, brandies, laces, fine linens, cutlery and stays was unloaded and she began to take on bales of cotton, packing them into her hold and even stacking them in two tiers on her decks, with some extra bales on top of them all for the captain's personal account. Then the ship was searched for stowaways and fumigated with sulphur to drive out any Southerners who might have sneaked aboard in an effort to desert the Southern cause. Such deserters were dealt with harshly, on occasion being set adrift in the Gulf Stream in an open boat with a few days' supply of water and a pair of oars. At sunset the blockade-runner took compass bearings on the blockading warships, knowing that they would anchor throughout the night, and then, in the darkness, it was a comparatively easy job to steam silently between them out to deep water. Even if the runner was hailed, she had the speed to show her heels to the warships, and frequently, so strictly was silence enforced—even to the extent of barring roosters in the poultry carried as provisions—the runner escaped undetected. Her chief danger then was that some fast warship might sight her at sea, by day, and catch her. But the odds were about even that she would escape: in the period from November 1861 to March 1864, eighty-four steamers were engaged in the trade, and of these thirty-seven were captured, twenty-five were lost in marine accidents, and twenty-two remained safe and actively at work, paying the cost of their construction and operation time and again to the owners.

So enormous were the profits in the business that a blockade-runner had to make only a few successful trips to repay her owners for the cost of the ship. Salt at Nassau sold for $7.50 a ton and in Richmond for $1,700; coffee worth $240 a ton in Nassau brought $5,500 in Richmond. Freight rates ranged from $300 to $1,000 per ton of 40 cubic feet—in December 1862 in Nassau it was $500 gold, payable in advance, to any Southern port. Wages for the officers and crew of the runners rose as the risks increased, so that a captain who had earned $150 a month before the war could get $5,000 a month for commanding a blockade-runner; a seaman's monthly pay reached one hundred gold dollars a month, with a fifty dollar bonus thrown in after every successful trip. The net monthly profit for the owners on a trip out of Nassau and back was in the neighborhood of ninety thousand dollars gold.

At Nassau the wharves were piled high with cotton, and the bales were stored in vacant lots and even on lawns; the warehouses were full of supplies for the Southern states, and the streets were unsafe for the solid citizens at night, for the tempting wages afloat and ashore had attracted low characters from every British and American port. In Wilmington matters were even worse: speculators from all over the South converged there to bid at the weekly auctions of imported goods; robbery and mayhem by day and murder and rape by night were common: there was great poverty among the populace, striking in contrast to the magnificence in which the agents and employees of the blockade-running companies lived. Theirs was a sybaritic and unprincipled life, complete with fine wines, clothes and foods, and the pick of slave girls. The price of food went beyond the reach of many people: a roast of lamb cost a hundred dollars, and a pound of tea five hundred dollars. The Confederate, or Southern, paper money, which in September 1861 was almost equal in value to specie, declined in value to 225 Confederate paper dollars to one gold dollar a year later, and in September 1863 a gold dollar was worth 400 paper dollars, in September 1864 a gold dollar was worth 2,000 paper dollars.

The blockade, by preventing the export of all but an estimated 15 per cent of the South's cotton, had cut the base from under the Southern states' economy. Equally disastrous were the effects of the blockade on

Southern morale: since freight rates were so high, the tendency of the blockade-running companies was to bring into Southern ports those goods which took up the least space and brought the highest profits. Luxury items, ladies' trinkets and gentlemen's liquors displaced materials badly needed by the Southern armies and warships, such as steel, iron, copper, zinc, guns and ammunition of all types, chemicals and acids, engines, boiler iron, and medicines for the wounded and the ailing. Rage entered the hearts of the Southerners who saw the blockade auction sales attended by rich and acquisitive operators who were making enormous fortunes because of the war. Public sentiment forced the Southern Congress to pass an act on March 1, 1864, prohibiting the import of luxuries, and providing that articles imported contrary to the law should be forfeited. There were many dire predictions in Nassau and Bermuda when this law was passed: it would end the blockade-running business, many thought. But in January 1865 there were as many runners in the business as ever, although by that time all the work they had done was in vain.

The Northerners, after their first fumbling efforts to make the blockade work, seem to have suddenly grasped the tremendous power of the weapon in their hands. They were, no doubt, distracted by the endless marching and counter-marching of the land armies, and they were slow in understanding that, while the blockade and the proper use of the sea could not by themselves win the war, they were the major ingredient in the victory that was cooking.

In the summer of 1864 there were still four major ports in the hands of the Southerners: Mobile, Savannah, Charleston and Wilmington; and a trickle of goods continued to come into the South by way of Matamoras on the Rio Grande, with the full approval and connivance of the French, who had set up Prince Ferdinand Maximilian, Archduke of Austria, as Emperor of Mexico in the spring of the year. The Navy Department designated its ace naval officer, David Farragut, to command the expedition against Mobile, and in early August he had enough ships assembled to make the attempt: four ironclads with their guns in turrets of the *Monitor* pattern, and fourteen wooden ships. The Southerners had an ironclad ram, the *Tennessee,* of which they were extremely proud, for she was akin to the *Merrimac* in design and armament, and three wooden-hulled river gunboats, paddle-steamers. The defenders at Mobile, while hopeful that *Tennessee* would prove her worth, did not place all their hope in her: they scattered some 180 mines, or "torpedoes" as they were then called, throughout Mobile Bay. These were ingeniously contrived weapons, one kind made of tin in a cone-shaped form with a cap and trigger and the other made out of a beer-keg or a barrel filled with powder and rigged to explode on contact.

On August 5th at 5:30 A.M. the Northern fleet got under way and about an hour later were taken under fire by the forts. Farragut climbed into the rigging of his flagship, *Hartford,* and as the smoke of battle rose in the air, he moved higher for a better view, until, fearful that their intrepid leader might fall from his perch, an officer ordered a seaman to clamber after him and lash him to the rigging. A detachment of soldiers from the Signal Corps aboard *Hartford,* who were there to handle communications with the Northern forces on land, were sent below decks for safe-keeping, until there should be need for their services. The Northern ships advanced hesitantly, and *Brooklyn,* one of the ironclads, came to a stop. Farragut signaled her to go ahead, and the answer came back: "Torpedoes." At this moment, in the roar of battle, Farragut resorted to prayer, saying: "Oh, God who created man and gave him reason, direct me what to do. Shall I go on?" An unidentified voice seemed to reply: "Go on!"—and Farragut ripped out the order, "Damn the torpedoes! Go ahead!" *Hartford* shot ahead, over the line of torpedoes, which could be heard grating harmlessly against her hull, and led the fleet onward up the bay, in spite of the loss of ironclad *Tecumseh,* which hit a torpedo and sank in short order with much loss of life. The Southern ironclad *Tennessee* fought briefly and then fled to the protection of the guns on Fort Morgan. By 8:35 A.M. Farragut's fleet had passed the fort and the torpedoes and come to anchor in the Bay. Then *Tennessee,* with the South's premier sea-dog, Franklin Buchanan, aboard, steamed out to do or die. After engaging various ships of Farragut's fleet she was rendered helpless, and Buchanan fell wounded to the deck with one leg broken below the knee by a flying piece of iron. It was around 10:00 A.M. when *Tennessee* hoisted the white flag, and Farragut sent his fleet surgeon aboard to help care for the wounded. Buchanan greeted the surgeon in a polite, though savage, tone, and was taken away to Pensacola as a prisoner-of-war. After the naval battle the forts on the bay were isolated by the Northern naval and land forces, and they capitulated one by one. On August 23rd Fort Morgan surrendered to the combined bombardment of the warships and the Northern land batteries, and Mobile was sealed up, useless as a port to the South. The total cost to the Northern fleet was 145 men killed, and 170 wounded; the South lost 12 killed, 20 wounded and 127 taken prisoner.

Savannah, closely blockaded by Admiral Dahlgren's squadron, fell to the Northerners soon after General W. T. Sherman captured Fort McAllister on December 13, 1864. With the fort, which had guarded the seaward approaches to the city, in Northern control, communications with Dahlgren's squadron were opened, and with the fleet's cooperation assured Savannah was doomed. Sherman was pleased to present Lincoln with the city as a Christmas gift.

Only the ports of Wilmington and Charleston now remained in Southern hands, and of these two ports Wilmington was the more important, for there was direct rail connection between that city and the South's capital, Richmond. So Wilmington became the objective of a huge joint army-navy expedition. A Northern fleet of seventy-five vessels under the command of Admiral David Dixon Porter descended on Fort Fisher, which guarded the approach to Wilmington. An unsuccessful attempt to take the fort had been made in late December, 1864, when troops from the transports had been landed, but after one look at the fortifications their commanders had declared them unassailable, and they had withdrawn discreetly, to the great annoyance of Admiral Porter. On the second attempt, on January 13, 1865, the warships bombarded the fort for three days, and then, with the land forces divided in two columns, one on the west side of the island composed of soldiers and one on the east side composed of sixteen hundred sailors and four hundred marines, the land advance began. The sailors, armed with cutlasses and pistols only, reached the fort's ramparts, then broke and fled in disorder; a detachment of marines was unaccountably absent at this crucial moment when they might have chased the sailors back to the fight. So great a brouhaha did these naval forces make that they drew most of the fort's defenders to the eastern side of the fort, and the soldiers coming down the west side were able to breach the walls with little opposition and to occupy the fort. With Fort Fisher in Northern hands the use of Wilmington as a port and supply base for the Southern armies was ended, and there remained only Charleston to invest to deprive the South of all access to the sea.

Charleston's fall came in February, 1865, when the joint forces of Admiral John Adolf Dahlgren and General Alexander Schimmelpfennig were concentrated against that city. Dahlgren's fleet had been co-operating with the Northern armies under General W. T. Sherman since the preceding November, and toward the end of January the admiral had collected his ships near Charleston to keep the rivers clear of mines and to neutralize the land batteries so that his supply ships and transports could safely land their military stores and keep the Northern armies adequately supplied. Sherman himself bypassed the city, leaving Schimmelpfennig to handle the land operations against it. There was a sustained bombardment by naval batteries on Cumming's Point directed against Fort Moultrie on Sullivan's Island during the night of February 17th, and when Northern scouting parties landed from the warships next morning they found the fort evacuated; Acting Master Gifford, commanding two tugs assigned to him, then entered the harbor and accepted the surrender of other fortified points, while the Northern land forces took possession of the lines of defense around the city itself, and of Fort Johnson, and—at long last—of Fort Sumter.

Thus, in the final agony of the war, in the early months of 1865, the Southern states were without useful ports, and it became a physical impossibility for blockade-runners to operate. The fall of Charleston was followed by a few minor convulsions on land, but these were death flurries: the South no longer had the will or the ability to carry on the fight.

The Northern navy had grown from 90 vessels in 1861 to 671 in 1865, from 1,563 officers and 7,600 men to 9,000 officers and 51,000 men, among whom were 7,500 volunteer officers and 42,000 seamen who had learnt their seafaring in the fisheries and the merchant marine. Throughout the war they had captured or destroyed 1,504 Southern vessels, warships and blockade-runners of all types, 295 of them steamers. In addition they had cooperated with the Northern armies in every major seaboard operation the army was able to undertake, and had to a great extent contributed to the solution of the army's supply problems by transporting munitions and provisions to the land forces. But it was by maintaining the blockade that the navy worked most effectively for a Northern victory: had it not been for the blockade, the South could have fought on forever.

---

[17] *Interlude*

Among the more endearing traits of formal historians is a habit of quoting poetry when dealing with moments of crisis. This is doubly useful, for it demonstrates that in spite of the facts and statistics with which they must cope, they are also aware of less concrete evidences of the past; moreover, in history there are moments when the human suffering involved is so great that an emotional approach is the best means of recording the character of the times. It is, then, symptomatic of the period between the Civil War and the Spanish-American War— a brief thirty-three years—that there is no marine poetry worth quoting: it is all land-verse, and had an American poet appeared whose major theme was the sea, he would perforce have written a threnody in sapphics. For the American habit of seafaring was well along the road to extinction after the Civil War, and for a variety of potent reasons.

When the fraternal blood-letting ended in the spring of 1865 close to 260,000 Southern and 350,000 Northern soldiers had been killed in the fighting, but four million blacks, mulattoes and quadroons—no longer "slaves"—enjoyed a sensation of freedom. The nation faced a herculean task of reconstruction: throughout the South transportation was at a standstill, with bridges destroyed, roads in disrepair, and only a handful of steamboats remaining on the rivers. Hundreds of thousands of the defeated Southerners were left without shelter or food. Many among them died of starvation; the living endured insults from Negroes in army uniform, and were cheated of their few remaining possessions by the carpetbaggers. In the lobby of a Savannah hotel a venerable Southern brigadier stood quietly while a drunken Northern sergeant cut the buttons off his uniform: his near-by staff officers froze into immobility, fearing reprisals, their rage turned inwards. Such incidents were not uncommon, and escape from them lay to the westward where there were millions of acres of fertile land. Westward went the more stalwart and energetic of the Southerners, to begin life again in a region where there were neither Negroes nor carpetbaggers.

There was much work to be done, not only in the West and the South but in the North, and the land absorbed the energies of the people much as waves breaking on a beach in a rising tide sink into the sand, and, constantly recurring, move farther and farther inland. Little remained at sea to attract the attention of a distraught nation: capital was happier in railroads, public utilities, mills and factories, where a 12 or 14 per cent return could be expected; labor was unwilling to suffer the hardships of seafaring for less money than could be made on land. Even had the will existed over a third of the American ships engaged in foreign trade were gone: 751,595 tons had escaped to foreign registry during the war, and they were not permitted to return to American registry; the Southern commerce raiders had destroyed nearly 110,000 tons more. The deep-sea fleet, which in 1861 totaled 2,496,894 tons, in 1866 was down to 1,387,756 tons: in those 5 desperate years the percentage of foreign trade carried in American vessels dropped from 65.2 to 32.2.

Meanwhile the British had profited mightily by their neutrality, having made such progress while the Americans were killing one another that at the close of the war they were firmly entrenched as the world's foremost carriers of ocean commerce. Not subsidies alone had brought this about: in 1857 only 121 British steamers were receiving subsidies, while 2,011 were not. But the subsidies had been so cannily granted, as in the North Atlantic packet line rivalry, that the result had been to discourage competition by the Americans. The unsubsidized British vessels, during the war, had merely tightened their grip on the heavily populated continental markets that lay at their doorstep. In addition, the British were building better ships than the Americans: they were building ships of iron.

As early as 1810 there had been a shortage of oak in the British forests, a result of the tremendous demand for ships created by the Napoleonic wars, and the shipbuilders had learned to make use of iron wherever possible as a substitute for oak. Then in 1843 Isambard K. Brunel, who had built the *Great Western,* turned out 3,500-ton, single-screw *Great Britain,* whose hull was entirely constructed of iron. *Great Britain* proved that 30 to 40 per cent of the hull's weight could be saved by building ships of iron, and that the weight saved could be used for cargo-carrying. When that saving had been made clear to the shipowners, Britain began building iron ships at an ever-increasing tempo, and by 1866 the British were building the best ships in the world. Along with the demand for ships there grew up in Britain an industrial plant of a capacity and competence much greater than America's: the best engines and boilers came from Britain, and the most experienced mechanics. No American shipyard could compete in price or quality with the British. Nor could Americans buy British-built ships, for a law, dating from 1789, was still in effect, and it forbade the purchase of foreign-built vessels.

The Americans had acquired some experience and skill in building modern ships during the war: several gunboats with iron hulls had been built, and *Wampanoag,* one of several 17-knot commerce-raiders designed to catch *Alabama, Florida* and *Shenandoah,* had been completed. These were all good ships, fast and seaworthy, but too costly for private capital to build, especially when the expanding railroads could take all the output of American boiler-works, engine-shops and mechanics, and a government up to its neck in land-problems was in power in Washington. For the moment, the sea was relegated to a position of minor importance, both in official circles and in the minds of Americans. It was land that mattered, and in February 1867 there came a chance to acquire Alaska—577,000 square miles of territory. Since the start of nineteenth century Alaska had been governed by the Russian-American Company, whose charter expired in 1861. The Russian government was not anxious to renew the privileges of the company, whose officials had dealt harshly with the natives, and whose operations were monopolistic. But if the company was withdrawn from Alaska, some type of colonial government would have to replace it, and that would be an expensive item in the Russian budget. In case of war it would be difficult to protect, for the Russians did not have a large navy. The Tsar's finances, never enough for his purposes, were in their habitual condition, and he decided to sell this white elephant to the Americans. Baron Stoeckel, Russian Minister at Washington, was instructed to offer the territory to the United States for $10,000,000. William H. Seward, Secretary of State, thought $5,000,000 a fair price, and after haggling politely for a decent period they settled on $7,200,000 as a reasonable compromise. Stoeckel sent off a dispatch to the Tsar, telling him that the Americans were willing to buy at the compromise price. Then, on the evening of March 27th, 1867, while Seward was indulging in a game of whist at home, Baron Stoeckel called to inform him that the Tsar approved the price. Stoeckel, a civilized man, suggested that the next morning would be a good time to sign the papers, but Seward, with uncouth energy, suggested that they make the treaty then and there. The appropriate State Department clerks were routed from their beds to draw up the treaty, and at 4 A.M. it was in final form, ready to go before the Senate a few hours later, much to the surprise of that august body. There was little debate, for the Americans were well-disposed toward the Russians, chiefly because Russia had been friendly toward the Federal government during the Civil War. Then the Russians had refused to intervene when invited to do so by Napoleon III, and in 1863 they had even sent a fleet on a friendly visit to the Northern states. Largely as an expression of good-will the Senate passed the treaty, with only two dissenting votes, and the House voted the necessary funds soon afterwards. A potential source of dispute between the two nations was thus removed, for the treaty was meticulously drawn, and by its terms Russia relinquished her last foothold on the North American continent.

In spite of the national obsession with land a few optimistic but ill-advised attempts to break into the North Atlantic trade were made in the years from 1866–1870. Each attempt failed, for there was no subsidy, and the lines were competing with subsidized British companies. The need for some sort of regular service to Brazil, one of America's largest markets, had induced Congress to pass, in May 1864, an act which granted a $150,000 annual subsidy, in the form of a mail contract, to a line of steamers linking closely the United States with South America; in February 1865 another mail contract act subsidized a West

Coast-China-Japan service by the Pacific Mail Company, which built four wooden-hull paddle-steamers for the trade. These were the creations of necessity, and the funds were grudgingly awarded. To make matters worse, the Suez Canal was opened for traffic in November 1869, and in the next year five hundred steamships took the short route to the Far East from Europe, making it even more difficult for the American sailships to retain their hold on Far Eastern trade. A partial solution was found to the problem of keeping some sort of American merchant marine in existence when the Pennsylvania Railroad Company formed the American Steamship Company which in 1872-3 built four iron steamers at Cramp's yard on the Delaware. With the support of the railroad, the steamship line operated between Philadelphia and Liverpool for twenty-five years. Other railroads followed suit, extending their freight-carrying ability overseas, but the obstacles against any full-scale revival of the merchant marine were too great: by 1879 only 23 per cent of American foreign trade was being carried in American ships. In the thinking of most Americans the sea became a large body of water whose chief virtue was that it separated the United States from the rest of the world. There seemed always to be trouble of some sort in Europe, and the Far East was so far away that travelers' tales of the heathen Chinese and the diminutive, flower-loving Japanese gained wide credence. The nation, mentally isolated from the world, looked in upon itself and found that it was to a great extent self-sufficient. In this atmosphere a provincial, frontier type of nationalism flourished, condemning all things of foreign origin, convinced that life in the United States was palpably superior to life anywhere else in the world. In 1880 the population reached the fifty million mark—but millions of citizens had never seen salt water.

It was difficult to find American crews for American ships: generally there were no stoves in the forecastles and no blankets for the men unless they supplied their own. Food varied from fair to bad, and pay was low: $8.00 a month for boys, $12.50 for ordinary seamen, $18.00 for able seamen. Captains were paid $100.00 per month, and first mates $50.00. Even the British wage scale was higher than that. No attempts were made on board ship to train the boys to become officers by teaching them the rules of the road and the niceties of navigation. Private ventures, by means of which seamen had formerly been able to supplement their wages, were no longer tolerated: every cubic foot of cargo space that could be filled was claimed by the shipowner, and forecastles and deck-houses became smaller and more noisome as the owners tried to squeeze the last foot of cargo space out of their ships. Under such conditions few Americans would go to sea, and crews came to be composed chiefly of foreigners—Irish, German, Dutch and Scandinavian —who, even if slow-witted, were strong and willing. Inevitably there were a few American lads who went to sea, leaving tearful parents behind them, but drawn irresistibly to the life afloat by the yarns of their elders. Such youths were of the incurably adventurous and romantic minority who found splendor in the trembling vibration of a ship at sea, in the kick of a ship's wheel in a stiff breeze, and in the brief visits to exotic ports where the liquor was heady and the native women's principles were as fragile as gossamer. But when such escapists came to weigh the pleasures against the discomforts and the perils, they were unlikely to sign on for a second trip.

One cheering aspect of the condition of the merchant marine in the years after the war was the gradual increase in costal shipping tonnage. By the Navigation Act of 1817 the Americans had made this trade a native monopoly, and under the benign protection of the Act coastal tonnage rose steadily, and ten years later, with 732,938 tons, exceeded the tonnage of ships in foreign trade. In 1838 coastal tonnage passed the million-ton mark, and in 1868 it was over two and a half million tons, while foreign trade tonnage had dwindled to less than a million and a half tons. From 1869 on, the coastal trade increased steadily, for in it profits were assured by the lack of foreign competition, and shipowners who could not compete in the foreign trade began to operate their vessels in the coastwise trade.

The coastal steamers, running on regular schedules, carried passengers and the more valuable freight items, but the sailing schooner by its innate efficiency managed to hold its position in competition with steam until the closing years of the century. A distinctive American type of craft was evolved for the trade: the three-masted schooner, of about three hundred tons. They were inexpensive to build, for there was still plenty of native timber, and to operate, for they needed only nine or ten men to handle the simple fore-and-aft rig. As the schooners increased in size to six hundred or seven hundred tons, it was discovered that the cost of operating them remained low, and they were kept busy carrying lumber and coal and ice up and down the coasts, and in fair weather or foul. As the schooners grew in size it became customary to install small steam engines on their decks to hoist the sails and trim the sheets —a labor-saving device that added greatly to their economical operation. Soon schooners of four, five and six masts were being built, and iron and steel hulls began to supplant the wooden ones. The coastal ships were not all "harbor-jumpers," sailing in short jumps from one port to another: many of them sailed direct from Maine to Texas, a distance of 2,600 miles, or from Boston to Seattle, a 15,000 mile trip around Cape Horn. Many small Pacific coast schooners, their decks as well as their holds loaded with lumber, made the long voyage to the eastern seaboard. By 1901, when tonnage in foreign trade totaled but 879,595 tons, in the coastal trade there were 2,462,084 tons in steam and 2,070,411 tons in sail. Together, the schooners and steamers of the coastal trade formed a hard core of shipping on which the nation could rely in time of war, and from which the vessels in foreign trade could obtain an occasional American mariner. In the easy comradeship of the waterfront it was a simple matter for a seaman who had a longing for new sights to leave his coaster and take his chances on a merchantman bound for alien and unfamiliar ports.

Closely related to the coasting vessels were the New England fishing schooners, which up to the heyday of the clipper ships were clean-bowed, round-bottomed craft, built of oak for strength and durability. These were the craft designed for work on the Grand Banks, and they called them "bankers." From March to November they could make three trips to the Banks, and then, during the off-season, go into the coasting trade. On these working "bankers" the grace and strength of the clippers had a direct influence: in the 1850s, at Essex, Massachusetts, they began to build "bankers" with longer and leaner lines and taller spars. They called the new vessels "clipper schooners," and when the Gloucester fishermen took the new type to their hearts, the rest of New England followed their example, for ships that were good enough to satisfy the exacting demands of Gloucester were clearly the best ships in the business. The new and faster schooners brought in more and greater profits, and helped the fishermen weather such deterrents as a panic in 1853, a Reciprocity Treaty which permitted the duty-free entry of Canadian fish in 1854, and the cancellation of the federal fishing bounties in 1858. Still the fleet continued to grow, until it reached a peak of 193,459 tons in 1862. Then the war's effect began to be felt, as the Northern navy grew in number of ships. The New Englanders were not easily attracted to naval service, but the fishermen could not resist the high government bounties offered for enlistments in the navy, and as the schooners came back to their home ports many of their crews fell prey to the blandishments of the naval recruiting officers, quit their schooners and went off to help win the war. By 1866 the deep-sea fisheries tonnage was down to 89,386 tons, and the Canadians were giving the Americans some severe competition. The Reciprocity Treaty of 1854 was annulled in 1866 and that was a help, but in 1871, by the Washington Treaty the Canadian ships were again allowed to sell their fish duty-free in American ports. Meanwhile the Canadians had moved in on the European markets and were helping to satisfy the insatiable demand of their devout customers, and in the Southern States, where dried fish had been the customary food for slaves, there were now no longer any slaves, and as free men the Negroes were unable to buy fish for themselves. Not until 1885 were the Canadians excluded from the duty-free selling of their fish in American ports, and by that time the damage had been done. Competition had brought about improved techniques: the pre-war method of carrying dories and hand-line fishing from the dories, a practice that had come into great favor in the 1850s, was advanced by the simple expedient of carrying more dories on the schooners. A cod, faced with a hook dancing merrily on the end of a line hanging from a dory, found the lure more attractive than one hanging limply from a schooner and rising and falling with gentle decorum. Trawls—long lines anchored and buoyed, with shorter lines studded with hooks hanging from them—replaced the handline in fishing for halibut; and purse-seines—large nets with which a crew in a long-boat could trap whole schools of mackerel—made the handline method obsolescent in the mackerel fisheries. But no matter how efficient the fishermen and their schooners became, men still left the sea for the higher wages and greater comforts of mill and factory work. At the same time the public was becoming more addicted to, and better able to afford, meat from the western prairies. By 1899 there were only 42,901 tons registered in the deep-sea fisheries, and that was enough to supply the market with all the fish it could absorb.

The whalers, too, reflected the widespread decline of seafaring, dropping from a total tonnage of 105,170 in 1866 to 11,017 in 1899. The impetus for the decline, of course, had been given by the Southern commerce raiders when they had decimated the Atlantic and Arctic whaling fleets. The New England ports made a brave attempt to revive the ancient tradition, and in the summer of 1871 there were forty-one whaleships back at work north of the Arctic Circle. They had followed the retreating ice north through the Bering Strait and into the Arctic Ocean in June and July, and in August they were almost at Point Belcher, hunting the bowheads and right whales. Close to the coast there was a lane of open water, varying in width from three to ten miles, and dotted with floating ice. Whaleboats scouted in this lane, or "lead," of open water, looking for the frosty spouts of whales, and often following smaller leads as they appeared in the pack ice. At night the ships anchored, and there was much fog, with always variable winds. On August 11th, while the boats were away, the wind shifted suddenly and began to force the ice toward the coast, trapping the ships and their whaleboats. The ship-keepers made sail in haste to keep ahead of the approaching ice field, and when the field grounded in shoal water the ships lay huddled in a lane of open water now no wider than a few hundred yards. For two weeks the whalesmen hunted their quarry, meeting with great success, and on August 25th a gale from the northeast drove the ice field back and enlarged the lane of open water to a breadth of four to eight miles. The Eskimos came aboard and, with inherited wisdom, warned the captains that there would not be another chance to escape the ice—that a southwest wind was coming. But the whales were being taken in large numbers, and there were still empty barrels in the holds: the captains decided to hang on for a few more days.

Then, on September 2nd the gale came, from the southwest. By the 12th all but seven of the whalers lay trapped in the ice, and those seven which had escaped to open water were eighty miles away. There was nothing to do but abandon the trapped ships and attempt to reach the seven free ones in the whaleboats. On the 14th, at noon, a strange flotilla got under way: close to two hundred boats, loaded with twelve hundred men and a handful of women and children, began to thread their way through the floating ice toward the open water and safety eighty miles away. After spending the night on the ice, they reached the seven lucky ships and in them were transported to the Hawaiian Islands. Next year a fleet of twenty-eight American and four foreign whalers returned to the Arctic hunting-grounds, for sperm oil that year brought $1.45 a gallon and whalebone $1.28 a pound. These ships found that of the thirty-four whalers trapped in the ice the year before, only one—by some whim of the ice floes—remained afloat: the rest had been ground to flotsam and jetsam. Four years later the ice trapped twelve more ships, but still others came back, as undaunted and optimistic as ever.

At the end of 1883 there were only 125 American whalers left in the business, which was becoming more hazardous both financially and physically every year. Petroleum, gushing at that time in ever·increasing volume from the Pennsylvania oil fields, was competing on a widening scale with whale oil as a lubricant and as a source of light; the whales had been almost exterminated; the work of killing them led the ships year by year to the more perilous grounds off the north Alaskan coast. Even in those remote waters the whales had become man-fearing and far from plentiful. Forty-two of these remaining 125 whaleships were in the Arctic ocean and the Bering Sea in '83; of them, eighteen were from New Bedford and the rest from San Francisco Bay. That season five vessels fell victims to the ice and many of the others were damaged, yet the New Bedford fleet took 122 bowhead and 23 right whales, and the San Francisco contingent 100 bowhead and 12 right whales.

In the summer of 1884 the U.S. Revenue Marine Cutter *Corwin*, a steam-and-sail vessel, was on duty in Alaskan waters, operating for the protection of the seal fisheries and the sea-otter grounds, sending out exploring parties to map the wilderness, making notes on birds, fish and Eskimos. On August 10th *Corwin* was at anchor off Point Marsh and in the neighborhood were some thirty whalers. That morning the weather was bright and clear, with a light-to-gentle breeze blowing from the east. About eleven o'clock in the morning the weather turned squally, and the wind, increasing in force by the minute, hauled gradually to the southward. By two o'clock a strong south-southwest gale had developed, and most of the whalers were under way, working under shortened sail. At three o'clock the bark *George and Susan,* which was still anchored, parted one of her cables and began to drag. Sail was put on her and she tried to work away from the shore, but in the effort she dragged afoul of the bark *Mabel,* anchored nearby, breaking *Mabel's* mainyard and carrying away her own head gear and jibboom. The gale, mounting in force, drove *George and Susan* ashore, where she struck hard on the beach and in a few hours had seven feet of water in her hold. As she struck some of her seamen, working with habitual speed, cleared away two boats, manned them and headed for the beach. The surf was by now tumultuous and both boats were swamped. Three men were drowned in the gelid water, and the rest reached land in a condition bordering on exhaustion.

Corwin had seen all this happen and she made haste to go to the help of *Mabel,* which was inside the breakers and in danger of driving on the shore. *Corwin* entered the breakers and anchored near *Mabel* in four and a quarter fathoms of water, with ninety fathoms of chain. She made ready a surfboat and then, steaming ahead to windward, lowered the boat, which ran a small line to *Mabel.* To the running line a large hawser was bent, but as *Mabel* was hauling it on board her cable parted and she began drifting shoreward. Sails could not save her, and as she felt the full force of the wind and waves she struck hard on the bar and then drove ashore, broadside on, about a quarter of a mile north of *George and Susan.* Within half an hour, as seas broke over her, her masts had gone by the board, and she bilged, filled with water, and became a total wreck. *Corwin,* aided by her steam engines, moved offshore to a less perilous position, and in the evening, as the gale abated, she sent a doctor ashore to care for the survivors, and then moved on to shepherd the rest of the fleet to safe anchorages.

Such incidents were routine in the Arctic whaling fishery, in spite of the skill of the captains and officers of the whaleships, who were among the most competent mariners in the world. Their crews were not of the same breed: they were filthy, unused to soap and water, reeking of stale blood and blubber, covered with vermin. Among the foremast hands insanity was more frequent than in any other class of seamen; that they shipped on these voyages at all is evidence of a tendency toward irrationality, and the grueling work in the Arctic wastes often drove the mildly unbalanced to utter insanity.

Each year fewer and fewer American whaleships put to sea, until in 1901 there were only forty of them left, with a total tonnage of 9,534.

There was one last flourish of the windships in the 1880s, when the Pacific coast grain trade reached its height. The least expensive way to get the grain to European markets was to load it on the big three-masted, square-riggers that were still at work in the world's merchant marines. San Francisco and Portland were the centers of the trade and to these ports came British, American, Norwegian and German ships, to load for the long haul around Cape Horn and to Europe. The British wind-jammers in the trade were iron-hulled, but nearly all the American vessels were wooden-hulled, Maine-built, fast and strong, but not with so much speed that they sacrificed carrying capacity. In them there was a good deal of the clipper, modified by the need for an ability to carry bulk cargo. The American grain-ships averaged about sixteen hundred tons each, a trifle larger than the British ships, and at the same time faster. For a few years there was rejoicing along the water-fronts of west coast ports and in the Maine shipyards—perhaps sail was not a thing of the past, after all. So they hoped, but the British, with the assistance of public-spirited shippers and insurance brokers, took the grain-carrying trade away from the Americans. In 1889 there were only thirty Yankee ships in the trade, whereas there had been close to a hundred ships four years before. In those four years, while the ousted American ships entered the coasting trade, the number of British ships carrying grain to British and continental ports rose to 167. The American public remained apathetic: what difference does it make, said the farmers, who carries the grain to market?

That what happened to the grain-ships and the other merchantmen in foreign trade made a difference to all the United States became apparent to the American Congress in 1890. That year measures were initiated to halt the decline of the merchant marine, after a quarter of a century of neglect. The lack of interest the Congress had shown in the years after the Civil War was a normal outgrowth of the public's apathy toward maritime matters. Congress reflected the public's desires with felicity, for the Congressmen were careful to vote in a way that would harm them least in their constituencies. And the people, in those years of indecision, were preoccupied with the material development of the nation's internal resources. Industrial development had been tremendous, as had settlement of the West. By 1890 people were saying that there was no longer a frontier—although there was still plenty of land to be developed. But the nation was showing signs of being less introspective, and there was discernible a tendency to be aware of the outside world—a hint that the nation's mental horizon was broadening.

Wars in Europe had not impinged on the American consciousness to any great extent. But when disconcerting incidents involving the national dignity occurred, the American reaction had been brief and violent. Thus, on October 31st, 1873, when the *Virginius,* a vessel with a shady reputation in the Caribbean, but with an American flag and captain, was captured by a Spanish guarda-costa, the *Tornado,* on the high seas after a chase that started in Cuban territorial waters, there was a great and clamorous anger in the United States. The Spaniards, triggerhappy because of Cuban insurrectionist activity, suspected that the passengers on *Virginius* were a junta en route to help the revolutionists overthrow the Spanish government of Cuba. At any rate, the Spanish authorities at Santiago summarily shot the American captain and fifty-odd passengers who claimed American citizenship in spite of their hirsute and swarthy mien. The American navy, more sail than steam, converged on Key West, ready to do battle to the best of its ability with tragically obsolete equipment. But this crisis was settled amicably on the diplomatic level, and the navy returned to its peaceful, delightful idleness, and the Americans returned to their busy isolation.

In 1889 there was more serious trouble over Samoa, whose excellent harbor, Pago-Pago, was looked upon with envy by the Americans, British and Germans. The Wilkes expedition had surveyed and claimed the island group for the United States in 1839; an American naval officer had seen the possibilities of the port in 1873 and had concluded a treaty with the local king, but the Senate took no action on the treaty. Five years later a commercial treaty was arranged, and then Britain and Germany obtained similar treaties. Civil strife in the islands conspired to make the work of white imperialists easy, and the Germans in particular delighted in complex schemes to bring the whole island group under the German flag. In March 1889, during a climax over the question of who owned the islands, with American, British and German warships anchored in the roadstead of Apia, a hurricane blew in and wrecked the ancient American, as well as the German, vessels. This dispute, too, was at length settled decently when on June 14, 1889 a joint protectorate over the islands was arranged, with the three rivals participating in the prey. But, for the moment, it had turned the attention of the American people seaward.

It was against this backdrop that Congress moved to infuse new life into the merchant marine, to the accompaniment of much lurid oratory. There was considerable confusion about the technique to be used in the resurrection: two cures were the chief ones proposed—mail contract subsidies, and higher port dues and duties for foreign ships and goods. The McKinley tariff act was passed in 1890, but there were objections to carrying this sort of thing too far, for the reciprocity treaties were still in force with a score of foreign nations, and more pertinent, the increased cost of imported goods was sure to make the citizen-consumer unhappy. In the debate those who favored the use of the mail contract subsidy appeared to be the wiser men: by following their method fewer people would object, less enemies be made, more votes anticipated. The custom then was to send the foreign mails abroad as they accumulated in the ports by whatever ship happened to be sailing in the right direction, regardless of flag, and paying for the service at a fixed rate. In 1878 American ships, being comparatively few, had been paid $40,152 for carrying U.S. mails, while foreign-flag ships received $159,827 for the same service. In 1890 the foreigners were still being paid much more than the Americans and this was a situation irksome to all but a few land-bound politicians. Why not spend some of this money to help build up the merchant marine?

As a sop to the shipbuilders iron and steel plate were put on the 1890 tariff's duty-free list, and this was intended to stimulate the shipyards. But, since there was a stipulation that such materials could not be used in ships operated in the coastal trade for more than two months a year, the shipowners and builders did not get the full benefit of the act, and it was clear that more drastic measures were in order.

At length, in 1891, when American ships were carrying only 12.5 per cent of the nation's foreign trade, two subsidy bills drawn up by Maine's sea-wise and sagacious Senator William P. Frye passed the Senate: one, the "Mail Ship Bill," concerned mail-carrying steamships; the other, the "Cargo Ship Bill," related to cargo-carrying ships, both sail and steam. The House rejected the Cargo Ship Bill by a slender margin but passed the Mail Ship Bill, although in a mutilated form, having reduced the subsidy payments by one-third. The bill that won the approval of both houses of Congress came to be known as the "Ocean Mail Act of 1891" and the "Postal Aid Law." It marked the first constructive effort in maritime legislation since 1865.

The Act specified that during the first two years of a contract 25 per cent of the crew of a subsidized ship should be Americans, and this percentage rose to 33 per cent in the next three years, and to 50 per cent during the remainder of the contract. By the nation's general navigation laws all the officers had to be American citizens, so the act did not affect them. But its effect on the composition of the crews was drastic, for it meant that no longer could seamen on any waterfront in the world sign on an American ship. Gradually the foreign seamen working on American ships were replaced by men of Irish, British or Scandinavian blood, but with the all-important American citizenship.

By the Act ships were classified according to their size and speed: in the first class were iron or steel steamships of 8,000 or more gross tons, capable of a sustained speed of twenty knots an hour. This class of ships was the only one deemed eligible to carry the mails between American and British ports, and they were entitled to a subsidy of four dollars for every mile logged on the outward trip, following "the shortest practicable route." In the second class were iron or steel steamers which could make an average speed of sixteen knots an hour, and which were over 5,000 tons in size. Such ships rated a subsidy of two dollars per mile on the outward trips. The third class was for iron or steel steamers of 2,500 tons or over, able to make fourteen knots, and these vessels were entitled to one dollar per mile. In the fourth class were steamers, either of wood, iron or steel, which could make an average speed of twelve knots an hour and which were of 1,500 gross tons or over. Such low-caste vessels received sixty-six and two-thirds cents a mile for the outward voyage.

Congress had been moved to pass the measure in an effort to strengthen the national defense and to expand foreign trade, but when the Post Office asked for bids on fifty-three routes the only proposals which were accepted came from lines which were already in operation. To existing lines the Act was manna from heaven: contracts were signed with the Pacific Mail Company, for the New York–Colón, Panama–San Francisco–Yokohama–Hong Kong runs; with the "Red D" Line for the New York–Venezuela route; with the Ward Line for New York–Havana–Vera Cruz; and with the Oceanic Steamship Company for the San Francisco–Hawaii–Australia route. The ships these lines operated at first were all of the second, third or fourth classes—none of them owned first-class steamers of the type that the men concerned with national defense had envisaged as potential commerce-raiders. But because of the Act, better ships were built than would have existed without it, for the lines operating when the act was pending had ordered new vessels in anticipation of the passage of the bill. When the bill became law more steamships were built which qualified for the mail contracts. Contrary to expectations, only one new company was created and sustained by the new legislation, and that was the American Line.

This came about because the International Navigation Company, an American organization, was in a particularly difficult position when the act was passed. The company had bought the old British Inman Line soon after its founder, William Inman, died in 1886, and two modern steamers of 10,600 gross tons were ordered from British yards to improve the service. These sister-ships were the *City of Paris* and the *City of New York*. The company fully expected that the new ships would qualify for the British mail subsidy, which the Exchequer had been giving to Inman, as well as to Cunard and White Star. But before the two ships were completed on the Clyde, the British mail contracts terminated, and upon examining the situation the British government decided that two mail services from Britain to the United States were all that were necessary. Naturally, these two mail contracts went to the

British-owned companies—Cunard and White Star—and the ships owned by the International Navigation Company were left without subsidy. The company knew better than to try to operate in the North Atlantic without a subsidy against Cunard and White Star. Yet they had the two crack liners almost ready to be launched, and even if orphaned by the British decision, there yet remained a hope of saving them from banishment to some less highly competitive route.

In their distress the Americans turned to Congress and made an offer: if Congress would permit the two British-built liners to be registered as American ships and so to qualify for American mail contracts, the company would be happy to build two similar vessels in American yards. The deal appealed to Congress, and the enabling legislation was passed in the spring of 1892. The company ordered its two American-built liners from the Cramp yard in Philadelphia, and in 1894 and 1895 they were launched—the *St. Louis* and the *St. Paul*—two sisterships of 11,600 gross tons each, 554 feet long, with a 63-foot beam and ample compartmentation as a safety factor. Strength enough to enable them to carry guns was built into them, for a wise provision of the Act was that subsidized ships had to meet minimum structural requirements which would render them useful as naval auxiliaries in time of war. Their speed was more than the average twenty knots required of the first-class ships, and both vessels made the run from New York to Southampton in less than seven days—*St. Louis* making it in six days and thirty-one minutes.

Thus the one new line came into existence, and on that count the backers of the Act could claim to have accomplished some good. There was, too, a general improvement in the quality of the new ships built by the few lines which could afford the high construction costs in the United States. But even so, the total tonnage in foreign trade continued to decline, and ten years after the Act had been passed American ships were carrying only 8.2 per cent of the nation's foreign trade.

Throughout the years following the Civil War, while the merchant marine was losing ground in foreign trade and at the same time gaining it in coastal trade, the navy was drifting into a condition of unrelieved incompetence. Thus had it been after the War for Independence, the War of 1812 and the Mexican War. And at the close of the Civil War the American Navy was the largest, if not the most efficient, in the world. The Nation's attitude toward it was what might have been expected: there was so much navy that it was a drain on the Treasury. The few potential enemies were three thousand miles to the east, across the Atlantic ocean, and it was commonly assumed that the United States had fought the last of her wars and that peace was inevitable and permanent. Therefore the cry went up: get rid of these useless warships, with the emphasis on "useless" for the Americans were above all a utilitarian race.

It had made little difference after the earlier wars that the navy had been allowed to languish, for then a merchantman could be converted to a man-of-war by the simple expedient of throwing guns and men aboard her, and presto! there was your navy conjured up overnight. There was no realization in the United States that a revolution in naval warfare was in progress, and this lack of awareness can be traced to the preoccupation of the lawmakers with inland matters, and to their appreciation of the presence of the sea as protection.

But while the United States germinated, wrapped in the oceans as though a bulb well-insulated, in Europe the great transition was being made in naval policy and construction and ordnance. There was much experience for the Europeans to draw upon: the French ironclads in the Crimean War, and the American Civil War, with such choice engagements as *Monitor* vs. *Merrimac* to ponder, and the use of mines, rams, turret-guns and the blockade. Indeed, the Civil War was a testing-ground for naval warfare, and it was so regarded by British and French naval officers, if not by the Americans who, after all, were so busy fighting that they had little time to examine the meaning of their changing equipment, tactics and strategy. In Europe the lessons were learned, and with knowledge came refinements in the use of steam engines, screw propellers, iron and steel hulls, rifled guns and armor plate. Such developments came quickly in the European cockpit, where a naval officer might enjoy a drink and a friendly chat aboard a warship of a neighboring nation on one day, and be shooting at it the next. Thus, as rivalry made for progress in Europe, in the United States the warships were not only growing old—they were becoming obsolete.

What followed, in the years up to the Spanish-American War, is unparalleled in history: the seas protected the states while the republican form of government, working by instinct rather than reason, sensitive to every pressure or lack of it, like an earthworm contracting here and expanding there in response to touch, made decisions which were against all logic but which, in the test, in retrospect, proved exactly right. Thus might a bemused child play on a surface rock on a beach, not knowing whether the tide was rising or falling, and then—the tide having fallen—totter across the sand all unconscious of the peril in which he had been. The irrationality of American policy was to move that old authoritarian, Otto von Bismarck, to remark enviously that God protects women, fools and the United States. To which the corollary was that God loves American sailors.

The process is clear, for there are many records of the period: Gideon Welles continued as Navy Secretary after Lincoln's assassination and to him fell the task of demobilizing the fleet. First went the river-craft, sold or broken up, for it was a rational assumption that they would be needed no longer: another civil war was inconceivable, and the chances that any invader would ever be in a position to operate armed vessels on American inland waters were fantastically remote. Other warships were decommissioned or sold, their crews discharged, and when Welles left office in 1869 there were only fifty-two warships in commission. They were a sorry collection of antiques, and their officers and men were of appropriate quality. Each vessel was a species of cosmopolitan microcosm, with more foreigners than Americans in the crew, and deck officers found a knowledge of two or three languages, in addition to English, most useful in handling the crews. Otherwise they would need the services of an interpreter to make their orders clear to the Scandinavians, Germans, Spaniards and Irish who, knowing no other craft, signed on American men-of-war. The officers, of whom there were too many, were reluctant to leave the service: most of them had been graduated from the Naval Academy, and they were certain of security in the future if they behaved like gentlemen and eschewed arguments with their superiors. On the whole they were a well-disciplined group, and when one of them did get into trouble, usually over the bottle, he could appeal to his Senator or Representative for "justice" and thus have himself reinstated.

The ships, following the pre-war custom, were sent out to their foreign stations, there to show the flag, protect the national trade and dignity. It was a slow death, for there was seldom any reason to fire a gun save as a salute, and except in China the day of the pirates had passed. There was plenty of inactivity—of time to think and to read, but apparently only one officer, Alfred Thayer Mahan, came to profit from these unmartial activities.

In the navy yards corruption was in flower. The politicians, reluctant to permit the closing of even the most uneconomic yards, proceeded to mine the yards as veins of patronage, wherein the faithful voter could always find work and sometimes a sinecure. Upon closer scrutiny the politicians discovered that there was a use in having a navy which they had overlooked: it could be made a source of personal profit to them. Repairs to the ancient hulks, if awarded to the right people, would bring in campaign contributions and ready cash. Why bother to build new warships when there were so many perfectly good old ones, needing only extensive repairs to fit them for sea duty? Like locusts the contractors descended on the navy yards, breaking up old ships and using the timber to rebuild others, in an orgy of graft.

No one in the Navy Department objected, for a minor guerrilla war was going on there between those who advocated steam and those who held out for sail, and the net result of the graft was to strengthen the hand of the reactionaries who opposed the trend to steam and modernity.

The leader of the anti-steam forces was David Dixon Porter, a veteran of the Mexican War, son of old David Porter of *Essex* vs. *Phoebe,* and a Vice-Admiral in 1869. That year, because he had assiduously cultivated the friendship of President Grant, he was put in effective charge of the Navy Department, with an amenable Philadelphia merchant, A. E. Borie, warming the Navy Secretary's chair. Porter, in his new office, became the prototype of the "bull admiral"—the unbending, rigid-minded, autocratic giver of commands. And he detested steam.

His pet enemy was Benjamin Isherwood, head of the Bureau of Steam Engineering, and one of the most talented engineers the navy ever had. But to Porter an engineer was like a red flag to a bull. He thought they were little better than mechanics, inclined to be greasy, sweaty and smelling of the engine room. Such people should not be permitted to lower the tone of the ward rooms with their presence and their eternal talk of pistons and boiler pressures and shafts and valves. The real naval officers, to Porter's way of thinking, were the men in *command* of ships —they were the elite in the naval hierarchy. Such an attitude stemmed, of course, from a need for compensation: the public considered naval officers worthless in peacetime, and as compensation the officers sought a form of life in their midst upon which they could look askance. The engineers were admirably vulnerable: Porter put Isherwood and his engineers in their places by dropping them a full grade in relation to the line, or command, officers. There was no one to stop him. Farragut, full of piety and pride, died in 1870, and was presumed by his intimates to have gone to heaven, where perhaps he identified beyond doubt the voice he had heard at Mobile Bay. Porter became the ranking Admiral of the Navy. Porter's distaste for steam cannot be attributed to the engineers alone, nor to the fact that he had mastered a forceful style in writing which he retained while turning out novels in the heroic manner; he was confronted with the matter of keeping his ships on their foreign stations, where they were leagues away from American coaling-stations and thus at the mercy of the avaricious local coal merchants of Europe, South America and the Far East. One answer to this lack of American coaling-stations was to equip the warships with full sail power, in addition to steam, and to make any captain who burned coal guilty of extravagance unless proved innocent. Wherefore the American warships continued to carry their voluminous sails, cut down their steam power, and their captains dared to use their engines as auxiliaries only in moments when the safety of their ships was endangered. To Porter this solution was not entirely satisfactory, for there were complaints that American ships were capable of steaming only eight or nine knots, while foreign warships were able to make seventeen or eighteen, and he emitted a few bellows on that score, but they were muted by his allegiance to President Grant.

Secretary Borie endured his humiliation as a figurehead for only three months, and he was followed in office by a more malleable man, George M. Robeson of New Jersey. Porter promptly indoctrinated him into the mysteries of naval policy, and the two men ruled the navy for eight years —to the end of Grant's administrations. Those were the years in which the navy vegetated quietly, its vessels inefficient under either sail or steam or a combination of the two.

Under Robeson and Porter the graft continued, and rapidly the navy became a collection of museum pieces, in which the officers took on the protective coloration of museum attendants. In 1872, when the Europeans were building steel ships, Congress authorized three new wooden vessels, to which were added, slowly and at immense cost, nineteen rebuilt ships, five of them monitors. By 1875 naval policy and ship design had reached a condition of stasis. The senior, policy-making officers, looking back over their years of experience, came to the conclusion that the navy had two distinct functions to perform in the event of war: commerce-raiding and coast defense. The deductions seem to have been based on the operations of the Civil War, when the Southern commerce raiders had proved immensely destructive, and on the War of 1812, when coastal defense was in favor. In combination the two techniques seemed vested with more value than they in reality had: *Alabama's* victims were not convoyed by warships, as the merchantmen of any European power would surely be in time of war; and a navy as vestigial as that of the United States could never protect the whole expanse of even one coast. But no matter how fallacious the reasoning, the conclusions worked because there was no war in which to test them.

By 1880 there were only forty-eight American warships in fighting condition, and there was little hope that more would be built. On the credit side of the ledger there was one constructive development: there had been an investigation of the state of the navy by a House Naval Affairs committee in 1876, and this post-mortem resulted in a mass of information printed at Government expense and readily available to anyone who was interested. Too few were interested, and the navy continued to age in a pleasant stupor until 1879. That year, on February 5th, Chili declared war on a Peruvian-Bolivian alliance and set about fighting to determine who owned certain nitrate deposits on the west coast of South America. The war demonstrated that a nation with a navy powerful enough to win command of the sea (in this instance it was Chili), had an enormous advantage over nations with less powerful navies. The Chileans scattered the opposing fleet, and although outnumbered on land, were able to transport soldiers up and down the coast and so to defeat the enemy land forces in detail. The war was grist for the mill at the Navy Department, but it was also disconcerting to consider that the Chilean warships, most of them British-built, were better than any warships that flew the American flag. The Chilean war was followed by threats of the French to build a canal through Panama, and by British efforts to see if the British interests in the Western Hemisphere were expansible. The best the United States could do was to rattle its ancient cruisers in defense of the Monroe Doctrine.

In this atmosphere President Arthur's Navy Secretary, William Chandler of New Hampshire, began to reconstruct the navy. A board of naval officers had been appointed to draw up recommendations for new construction and they had alienated Congressional opinion by asking for thirty-eight new cruisers, as well as twenty-five of the small torpedo boats so popular in Europe, and five rams. Such a request was beyond all reason, thought the Congressmen, and they authorized in 1882 two new cruisers but neglected to appropriate the money to build them. More important in the Navy Act of 1882 was a rule that repairs to old vessels were not to be made if the repairs could not be made for less than 30 per cent of the cost of replacing the vessel. In the same year another board of naval officers was convened, to make recommendations more in harmony with Congressional sentiment. The second board was not so greedy as the first, recommending only that four steel protected cruisers and a dispatch boat be built. Congress found the proposal sufficiently modest to authorize on March 3rd, 1883, and to appropriate the funds for, the construction of three steel protected cruisers and the dispatch boat. Then the Congress lowered the repair cost percentage to 20 per cent of the cost of replacement, and the navy was on the way to a rejuvenation, in steel.

But who was to build the steel vessels? Secretary Chandler had the answer to that question: he had a close friend, one John Roach of Chester, Pennsylvania, a burly Irish immigrant who had acquired a shipyard on the Delaware River. Chandler, in his capacity as treasurer of the Republican party, had enjoyed the pleasure of accepting campaign contributions from Roach, and here was a chance to return past favors. So Roach was given the contracts for the protected cruisers *Chicago, Boston* and *Atlanta,* and for the dispatch boat *Dolphin.* But there was no steel and no knowledge of design for such vessels, and it took three years to finish the four steel ships on British designs. The ships were not well built, and they were full of engineering faults, but the navy and the public loved them, nicknamed them "The White Squadron" and, lacking anything better, lavished their patriotic affections on them.

In the naval lexicon of the times warships were divided into groups: battleships, with heavy armor and low speeds and big guns; armored cruisers, faster than battleships but more lightly armored and gunned; and protected cruisers, which had no belt armor, and only a thin plate over their engines and magazines. The American cruisers were of the last group, but they were not fast enough to run from enemy cruisers of the same class.

It was with this start that naval reconstruction began: in 1885 two more cruisers and two gunboats were authorized; and then, with President Cleveland and Navy Secretary William C. Whitney in office, there came a flood of authorizations—thirty new ships in four years. Still the Treasury continued to show a yearly surplus, and there seemed to be no end to the expanding prosperity of the nation. Among the new ships were the armored cruisers (sometimes called second-class battleships), *Texas* and *Maine,* and they were good ships of their class, able to do nearly eighteen knots. The new protected cruisers that came into service were received with joy by naval officers: they could make nearly twenty knots.

Thus it was with a growing fleet that the nation was able to back up its policy in Samoa in 1889, and to force a fair division of the spoils. In 1891 a more serious incident aroused the national rage: a liberty party from the USS *Baltimore* went ashore in Valparaiso, Chili, on October 16th, and members of the party were attacked by natives in the town. Two American sailors were killed, and the threat of war was very real until the Chilean government made restitution, paying $75,000 to the families of the dead men, thus setting the value of an American sailor's life at $37,500, gold. Two years later there was a revolt in the Hawaiian Islands.

For generations American ships—whalers, merchantmen and men-of-war—had made a habit of calling at the Hawaiian Islands (which their crews knew as the Sandwich Islands), to take on fresh water, fuel and provisions. American traders had established themselves there, and the missionaries, Protestants for the most part, had explained the benefits of Christian morality to the natives and persuaded them to clothe themselves more conventionally, if less healthfully, than was their primitive custom. This God-given mission they had carried on with a great deal of fervor, for Puritanism had not then arrived at the sterile atheism which was its logical destination, and much progress was made in converting the islanders, and in teaching them to mistrust the hairy seamen who came ashore to find a brief respite from the enforced abstinence and continence of shipboard life.

With the passing of time both traders and missionaries had acquired a great deal of fertile land in the islands, and they had become at once pious and prosperous, as befitted their New England origins. Rarely did anything mar the serenity of their island paradise: in 1843 the British cast envious eyes at the islands, thinking of a protectorate; later on the Russians made a clumsy attempt to gain control by sending an agent disguised as a botanist to subvert the King of Hawaii's authority by encouraging his rivals. But the British were busy elsewhere and they lost interest; the botanist was summarily ejected from the islands; and the influence of the Americans continued to grow.

Meanwhile, since a small and isolated state, like Hawaii, has a tendency to move into the orbit of the nearest great power, the proximity of the United States induced closer cultural and trade relations. In 1875 the United States signed a trade treaty with Hawaii which excluded foreign competition and at the same time protected the islands from conquest by any third power. In 1884 Pearl Harbor was ceded to the United States. The Americans in the islands did not lose their national identity; indeed, distance, rather than diluting, intensified their nationalism, and so greatly did they admire the republican form of government with its attendant democratic principles that they persuaded the King of Hawaii to grant a liberal constitution in 1887.

The leader in this constitutional reform movement was a man with a Mosaical beard, Sanford Ballard Dole, a missionary's son born in the islands in 1844, educated as a lawyer in the United States, and returned to Hawaii to live in the luxury which his father's acumen had assured him. The liberal constitution worked very well until 1891, when

Queen Liliuokalani fell heir to the throne and, woman-like, sought to extend her authority by imposing a more autocratic constitution on the islanders. Against this queen of Junoesque physique the Americans led a revolt in January 1893, timing their rebellion to coincide with the presence in Hawaiian waters of USS *Boston,* whose marines landed and formed a cordon around the American Legation. The insurgents, within a matter of hours, proclaimed a republic, elected Sanford Dole as their President, and obtained recognition of their republic from the American Minister, who was their friend and drinking-companion.

The Queen abdicated her throne, under protest but helpless in the presence of the marines, and the Americans sent a commission to Washington to obtain a treaty of annexation, following the Texas precedent. The commissioners were well-received by President Harrison; a treaty of annexation was drawn up on February 14th, but before it could be ratified by the Senate, President Cleveland was inaugurated.

Cleveland, following a less expansive policy, withdrew the treaty from the Senate and sent to Hawaii a special commissioner, J. H. Blount, to report exactly what had happened there. Blount arrived at Honolulu on April 1st, 1893, and he ordered the naval commander to haul down the American flag and to withdraw the marines at once. Then he began his investigation, the upshot of which was a report that the Queen had been wrongfully treated and that force, in the form of the United States Marines, had prevented her retaining her throne. Cleveland directed Blount to tell the Queen that the United States was willing to restore her throne to her if she would grant a general amnesty to all of her subjects who had been involved in the revolt. But the Queen refused this stipulation, insisting that the leaders be beheaded, or at least banished and their property confiscated. This vengeful, feminine attitude was so un-Christian that Cleveland assumed a hands-off policy. The provisional government thereupon wrote a constitution and formally organized a republic, which was proclaimed on July 4, 1894, with Dole as its President. Cleveland's conscience was thus cleared of doubts, and the "Republic of Hawaii" was recognized, while the Queen, giving up all hope of regaining her throne, resorted to annual and futile petitions to Congress to indemnify her for her loss.

These singular events were observed with much interest in American naval circles: the islands would provide an excellent support for the coaling station at Pearl Harbor, only 2,091 nautical miles from San Francisco, and any territorial change that helped to extend the range of the fleet was an addition welcomed by naval officers.

At the time the Hawaiian Republic achieved recognition by the United States an almost imperceptible change was coming over the attitude and thinking of naval officers. The program of naval rejuvenation initiated in 1882 was in full swing, and as the new ships were put into commission they joined the "squadron of evolution" established in 1889 as the nucleus of a modern fleet of which naval officers could be proud. As the naval establishment expanded, so did the world consciousness of its officers. Two factors contributed toward this broadening of the navy's mental horizon: on March 23, 1882, an Office of Intelligence, with a Chief Intelligence Officer in charge, had been created in the Navy Department's Bureau of Navigation, and naval officers were sent abroad to collect data on the naval habits and strength of potential enemies. Spasmodic efforts to obtain such information had been made before the Office of Intelligence was organized, but there had been no coherent plan, no consistent policy and no selection of qualified officers for such specialized duty. Haphazard collections of fact and fancy by civilians were of little or no value in an age of steel and steam warships and rapidly changing ordnance: the times called for experts who could grasp at sight the implications of a new type of warship or gun. In the tightly knit circles in which naval officers existed, any information from abroad which concerned developments in foreign navies was certain to start arguments, inspire comparisons and stimulate thought.

The second, and more influential factor, in naval thought was the Naval War College at Newport, Rhode Island, which had been started on October 6, 1884, with Admiral Stephen B. Luce as President. To this seat of higher strategic education went the most promising of the navy's senior officers. There they came into contact with, and were exposed to the thinking of, Captain Alfred Thayer Mahan. Mahan had taken the unassimilated mass of historical naval facts and from them deduced that naval power was the sine qua non of a nation's greatness. As Matthew Fontaine Maury had distilled physical principles from the data in old log-books, so Mahan developed, from a study of naval history, principles which appeared to govern the rise and fall of nations. The end-product of Mahan's thinking was imperialism, undiluted, and this fitted the aspirations of the navy very well at that time.

The mood, of course, was not one peculiar to naval officers: they simply reflected in their specialized field the revival of the New Manifest Destiny which was emerging in the nation's consciousness. Foreign trade had grown mightily, with exports rising in value from $750 millions in 1882 to $1,030 millions in 1892. With trade expansion came a need for new markets for manufactured goods, but unhappily there were few unattached markets of any value left for the new imperialists to acquire. And there were rivals in the field of empire-building, for other nations were also discovering that the industrial revolution made better sense if its products were assured of markets. In this impolite search for markets the world's navies played a useful part, especially when the opposing power was equipped with inadequate warships.

In August 1884 the French became involved in a war with China, and on the River Min the virtues of high explosives and torpedo-boats were demonstrated when a French torpedo-boat, the 16-knot "Number 46," exploded the Chinese *Yang Woo* with such force that bodies and portions thereof littered the rooftops of Foochow, a mile away. Among the rapt observers of the engagement were the ships' companies of the American squadron—*Enterprise, Monocacy, Trenton* and *Juniata*.

Then Japan, a late starter in the family of aggressive and expansible nations, was moved to test its new naval power in a war with China. There were 41 million Japanese and 300 million Chinese—a disparity in numbers that led the Americans and British to sympathize with the Japanese David against the Chinese Goliath. In this brief war the interplay of motives was complex: the Japanese had acquired a patina of modernity, of which their navy was a concrete expression, and close at hand lay Korea, whose King rendered annual tribute to China, and whose trade with Japan was restricted. It is probable that the Japanese wanted to deal with the Koreans as Commodore Perry had dealt with Japan: break down the artificial isolation and bring to the hermit kingdom the blessings of world relations. There were, too, reasonable expectations that Korea would fall completely into the control of either China or Russia, thus bringing, in either case, an uncomfortably powerful nation close to Japan. The Korean government was tricky, corrupt and far too pliable for Japan's peace of mind. Thus matters stood when a revolt started in Korea and Chinese troops moved in to support the King's government. Japan, too, moved in troops, and on July 23, 1894, Japanese soldiers attacked the King's palace at Seoul.

The naval war began two days later when a squadron of three large Japanese cruisers routed two smaller Chinese warships—the cruiser *Tsi Yuen* and the gunboat *Kwang Yi*—in a spirited action in Caroline Bay on the west coast of Korea. There was great carnage aboard the *Tsi Yuen,* and the Chinese later protested that the Japanese had fired without warning and before a declaration of war. The Japanese claimed that the Chinese had made the first belligerent motions. Whoever fired the first shot, it was without a doubt fired according to the best oriental traditions: the head of the Chinese Navy was an Admiral Ting, an ex-cavalry officer who was, as were all Chinese military men, a keen student of the writings of Sun Tsu. And Sun Tsu had written, in 500 B.C., that "All warfare is based on deception." But there were also Japanese studies based on the writings of Sun Tsu, and the Mikado's navy was well aware of the ancient master's principles of war. At any rate, when *Tsi Yuen* limped into port at Wei-hai-wei she was a ghastly sight, with blood splashed high on her funnels and numerous seamen crushed under large fragments of heavy armor plate. A British officer who inspected the work of the Japanese guns was fascinated at the effect of one six-inch shell which had glanced from the steel deck and exploded in the conning-tower where it blew a gunnery lieutenant to bits, leaving his head perched on the top of a speaking-tube.

Meanwhile the Japanese flying squadron of cruisers had gone on to attack and sink a British-owned merchantman, the *Kowshing,* which was transporting Chinese troops to Korea. This action the British government allowed to pass unnoticed, without protest, although when the word went out that the Japanese had added an inhuman touch to their work by slaughtering great numbers of Chinese left swimming in the sea after *Kowshing* sank, there was considerable criticism from the British public. By applying Christian standards to the Japanese conduct the British arrived at strange conclusions: on the charge that the Japanese had fired before a declaration of war there was a large amount of precedent that made such action legal—from 1700 to 1870 in only ten cases had a declaration of war come before the shooting started. By the then current niceties of international law it was possible to excuse the Japanese for sinking the *Kowshing,* which after all was transporting enemy troops. But as for shooting the helpless survivors in the water, there was no excuse for that, and it was commonly attributed to the incomplete synthesis of Western civilization and Japanese traditions.

As the war progressed it became clear that the Japanese had learned more than modern gunnery and engineering: they had selected for their own use those principles of war which brought the best results, regardless of ethical origin. The principles of Sun Tsu appeared to have a greater practical value than those of the international law evolved by Europe throughout the centuries.

Two months after *Kowshing* sank, a second naval battle took place at the mouth of the Yalu River; this time twelve Chinese and eleven Japanese men-of-war were involved. The Chinese fleet was larger in tonnage, and theoretically more heavily gunned. But the Japanese ships were swifter, and their ordnance included a larger proportion of the rapid-fire guns then coming into general use. In this engagement four Chinese ships were sunk, one stranded and one was severely damaged, while the Japanese suffered only minor inconveniences. In November Port Arthur fell to a combined land and sea attack in which the Chinese, trapped between fire from land and sea, became panic-stricken. The third and last naval action began in late January, 1895, when the Japanese attacked Wei-hai-wei. The Chinese had by then only a few ironclads left, and thirteen torpedo-boats. Against them the Japanese brought twenty-five warships and sixteen torpedo-boats. The Japanese fleet bombarded the forts from a discreet distance, and in this preliminary action they were aided by their army's artillery. As the naval action developed the Japanese torpedo-boats swirled in and out of the harbor, and in this type of warfare the Japanese proved themselves highly adept in handling the small, fast torpedo-boats with their sixteen-man crews in night attacks on the Chinese warships. Among the torpedo-boats was the *Katoka,* Yarrow-built in England, with one-inch armor: she was the model on which the Japanese had built others of the same class. The last torpedo-boat attack took place at night on February 5th, and the Japanese boats managed to get into close range undetected. Six boats which formed the first division attacked and obtained at least four hits. The Chinese iron-clad, *Lai Yuen,* 2,850 tons and Stettin-built, capsized, her hull protruding above the water. The shrieks of her entombed crew were audible for days; by the time a hole could be cut in her iron bottom they were all dead.

Wei-hai-wei surrendered on February 12th; Admiral Ting killed himself to atone for his defeat; and the few remaining Chinese warships afloat were taken to Japan as spoils of war. On April 17th the Treaty of Shimonoseki was signed, and by its terms the Japanese won the "independence" of Korea, the Liao-tung peninsula, Formosa, the Pescadores, two hundred million taels as indemnity, and the opening of four Chinese ports to foreign trade. The cost to Japan: 1,005 killed, 4,922 wounded, 16,866 died of disease. It was a cheap price to pay for victory and for recognition as a new and powerful nation.

To the strategists and tacticians at the Naval War College this war offered a case history worth serious study. Naval matériel was in a state of continuous flux: ingenious means of killing enemies were being devised and improved upon with great rapidity. Here, then, was a laboratory test, made at the expense of the Chinese, and there were lessons to be learned from it. The use of torpedo-boats was clearly beneficial; the rapid-fire Hotchkiss guns had proved admirable; mines were disappointing; iron-clad battleships essential. There was no doubt that the higher explosives were effective both on armor plate and human flesh.

While the American Navy was mulling over such matters, and debating the possible value of the pneumatic dynamite guns which had been installed on USS *Vesuvius,* the nation was given an opportunity to test the effect of the New Manifest Destiny. The result was almost disastrous, for the test took the form of a dispute with Britain over Venezuela. Rich gold deposits had been discovered in the interior of Venezuela, and both British and Venezuelan interests were anxious to exploit the fields. This sudden discovery of wealth in what had formerly been considered a worthless wilderness led to a border dispute between British Guiana and Venezuela. For a while it looked as though Britain would go to war with Venezuela, and President Cleveland in 1895 in defense of the Monroe Doctrine insisted that the matter be arbitrated.

He intimated that if his proposal were not accepted there would be war between Britain and the United States.

At that time the American Navy was out-classed, out-gunned and out-numbered by the British, in the ratio of fifty to two in capital ships. Then, quite suddenly, while many American naval officers were drawing up their last wills and testaments, the British government agreed to arbitrate, and the American Navy was spared a series of humiliating defeats. Few men, outside informed naval circles, realized how close to the abyss the United States had come. In this instance, it was the sea and the difficulties the British faced in traversing it, rather than God, that protected the United States. There was to be need of that protection, for in Cuba one of the interminable rebellions against the Spanish authorities was becoming insufferable to large numbers of Americans.

Part VI
SELF-INTEREST

[18] "A Splendid Little War"

This latest in a series of struggles for Cuban independence had begun on a large scale in 1895, and when Spanish General Weyler took command of Spain's forces in Cuba in 1896 he began a reign of terror, packing concentration camps with townspeople to prevent their giving aid to the insurgents. In these camps civilians died in droves from malnutrition and disease. President Cleveland, in his annual message on December 7, 1896, objected to such inhumane conditions and warned that the United States could not remain indefinitely disinterested. Because of American disapproval, General "The Butcher" Weyler was recalled in 1897, but the rebels would settle for nothing less than freedom. In this attitude they were supported by the American public, which had become actively and emotionally embroiled in the revolt and was sending quantities of supplies and large sums of money to the concentration camp victims. Still, nonintervention remained the official American policy, and when President McKinley moved into the White House in 1897 he was hopeful that Spain would prove herself civilized enough to avoid serious trouble with the United States.

But there were powerful and peculiar influences and personalities at large in the United States. American citizens had at least $30,000,000 invested in Cuban sugar and tobacco plantations, mines and railroads, and their money had to be protected. Trade with Cuba amounted to nearly $100,000,000 a year, and that was too much to permit the Spaniards to jeopardize. In New York so incidental a matter as the rivalry of newspapers for increased circulation had an effect on the situation: the papers published the most sensational and violent stories they could find, and the mind of the reading public was inflamed. In the Navy Department there was a new and harmless Secretary, John D. Long, but the Assistant Secretary was an over-stimulated Harvard graduate named

Theodore Roosevelt, by glandular compulsion a devotee of the strenuous life, and by hobby a student of naval history, which at that time meant an admirer of Captain Mahan. Roosevelt with Mahan and Senator Henry Cabot Lodge formed a weird trinity in which Mahan supplied the naval brains, Roosevelt the energy and Lodge the political experience.

While the Cuban rebellion was in progress the "new navy" was growing rapidly, and by 1898 included four battleships of the first class—*Oregon, Iowa, Indiana* and *Massachusetts*—all heavily armored and gunned; the armored cruisers *New York, Texas, Maine* and *Brooklyn;* raiding cruisers *Olympia, Columbia* and *Minneapolis;* thirteen protected cruisers, and, among the smaller vessels, seventeen torpedo-boats and fifteen gunboats. This was approximately three times as much power as the Spanish could muster, and moreover the Spanish Navy had no frenetic character with Roosevelt's energy who could whip it into shape for hostilities.

In late 1897 and early 1898 the Navy Department bustled with unaccustomed activity: Commodore Dewey, equipped with all the information available on the Philippines, went off to head the Asiatic Squadron in December, with instructions from Roosevelt to get the ships in a condition of combat-readiness. Throughout January and February of 1898 the belligerent attitude of the public was stimulated by almost daily reports in the press of the progress the navy was making in the interest of "national defense": new guns mounted on old vessels; ammunition supplies increased; and warships called in from distant stations.

Thus matters stood, with the public enjoying shivers of joy at this sudden realization of the nation's strength, when, on February 9, 1898, the junta of Cuban revolutionists released for publication in New York a letter written by the Spanish Minister in Washington, Dupuy de Lôme, to a personal friend, an editor in Cuba. The letter had been purloined from the Havana post-office, and in it de Lôme spoke of President McKinley as a pot-house politician and caterer to the rabble. There was enough truth in the characterization to make it politically awkward; and with the public already greatly agitated, this insult to their Chief Executive from a noisome Spaniard brought their hatred of Spain to a condition bordering on violence.

Then, on the evening of February 15th, the USS *Maine,* at anchor in the harbor at Havana, where it had gone on a friendly visit only to be made the butt of many insults in the local Spanish press, exploded with a terrific blast. The lives of 260 of the ship's company of 350 were lost. Captain Sigsbee, commanding *Maine,* was not sure what had caused the destruction of his vessel: in his opinion the explosion could have been either external or internal, and he advised prudence in judging the cause until an investigating board could report its findings. A Spanish commission of inquiry was rowed around the wreck, whose top-hamper protruded from the water, and through water-glasses they examined the ship as she rested on the bottom. They decided that there had been an explosion inside the vessel. Then an American naval board of inquiry, consisting of three captains, arrived on the scene, sent down divers, and came up with the theory that the loss of the ship was due to the explosion of a submarine mine. The latter explanation fitted the public's conception of the nefarious methods that were to be expected in any dealings with Spain, and in the ensuing feverish excitement the House and Senate passed, by unanimous vote, a fifty million dollar appropriation bill, the money to be used for the "national defense."

Still it was not too late to avoid war: McKinley sent a proposal to Spain, intimating that the matter could be settled if Spain would stop putting Cubans in concentration camps, declare an armistice, and permit the United States to act as mediator between Cuba and Spain. The Spanish government wriggled painfully on the hook, torn between an ancient pride and modern reality, until April 9th, when they agreed to McKinley's proposals.

By that time pressure had been built up to such an extent that Mc-Kinley, who was inclined to see the hand of God in everything he did not understand, became no longer useful as a safety valve: if the people wanted war, then they must be right. To some men the desires of the public seem based on mystical revelations of the divine will, and McKinley was such a man. He sent a message to Congress on April 11th, reviewing the situation and recommending intervention "In the name of humanity, in the name of civilization, in behalf of endangered American interests . . ." And he asked for authority to use the army, navy and militia to end the rebellion and establish a stable government in Cuba. Congress obliged with a joint declaration declaring that the

Cubans were free and independent, that the Spaniards must relinquish all authority in the island, and that the President was empowered to use the armed forces of the United States to make the resolution a reality. Almost unnoticed in the Congressional uproar, Senator Teller inserted an amendment in the resolution which asserted the government's intention to leave control of Cuba to the Cubans, once the island had been pacified. McKinley signed the joint resolution, Teller Amendment and all, on April 20th, and thenceforth, since he had arrived at his decision only after much prayer, he assumed the attitude of implacable righteousness which was to mark his conduct of the war. On the 21st he ordered a blockade, which was proclaimed the next day as applying to the north coast of Cuba and the port of Cienfuegos on the south coast. Admiral Sampson's North Atlantic Squadron, which had been held in readiness at Key West, steamed out at dawn on the 22nd, ready for a fight or a frolic. The first brush with Spaniards indicated that it might be a frolic: USS *Nashville,* in Sampson's squadron, nearing the Cuban coast, put a shot across the bows of a Spanish merchantman, the 1,741-ton *Buena Ventura,* and the merchantman promptly hove to and was boarded by a seven-man prize crew. It was as easy as that.

Congress got around to passing a declaration of war on the 25th, and, with an eye to the conventions, unanimously voted that war between Spain and the United States had existed since April 21st, 1898.

The navy was in excellent condition for hostilities: McKinley had allocated thirty of the fifty million dollars appropriated in March to the Navy Department, and this was more than enough to buy, charter and equip merchantmen of all sizes for use as naval auxiliaries. Provision was also made for the construction of three battleships and numerous torpedo-boats and torpedo-boat destroyers. Warships already in commission had been formed into three major squadrons: Commodore Winfield S. Schley's Flying Squadron, based at Hampton Roads for use in an emergency; Sampson's North Atlantic Squadron, operating out of Key West; Dewey's Asiatic Squadron at Hong Kong.

As soon as war was declared a frenzied search for merchant vessels began: fifty steamers were chartered or purchased for transport duty, about half of them from foreign lines. When word went out that the government was in the market for ships, the shipowners, whether foreign or domestic, were quick to sense the possible profits: almost without exception they asked and obtained exorbitant prices for their vessels. The lines subsidized by the Ocean Mail Act contracts made a modest contribution to the war: the Atlantic Line's four best steamers, *St. Paul*, *St. Louis, New York* and *Paris,* each of over ten thousand gross tons, were chartered and converted to duty as armed scouts. Four steamers of the Morgan Line, the *El Norte, El Sud, El Sol* and *El Rio,* were bought outright by the government and entered the naval service after their abhorrent Spanish names had been painted out and they had been rechristened *Yankee, Yosemite, Prairie* and *Dixie.* They were small ships, of 4,600 gross tons each, 400 feet in length, single-screw, steel-hulled coal-burners, capable of making close to 16 knots an hour. Guns were mounted in their cargo-ports, beams reinforced, magazines and crews' quarters built into them. Their batteries consisted of ten 5-inch quick-firing breechloaders; six 6-pounders; and two Colt automatic guns. So converted and armed the Morgan liners made excellent auxiliary cruisers. A few other, less efficient, steamers were brought from the subsidized lines and turned into men-of-war. From the coastal service came the merchantmen which the navy converted into the hospital ship *Solace* and the repair ship *Vulcan.*

As had been expected, the foreign-born seamen left the American merchantmen as soon as their ships were bought or chartered by the government. They were thoroughly opposed to risking their lives in a war that was not of their making for a nation that seemed unaware of their existence. But this made little difference: the naval militia of the various states, which had been created by Act of Congress in 1891, and to which many amateur yachtsmen had been attracted, supplied all the men needed to man the naval auxiliaries. When the reservists were puzzled or despairful, not comprehending navy ways, there was always a grizzled old boatswain's mate or marine gunner to make everything clear to them—even the necessity for coaling ship until they thought their backs would break. This was war.

It was April 29th when Spanish Admiral Cervera, with four armored cruisers and three torpedo-boat destroyers, left the Cape Verde Islands and vanished from sight in the ocean wastes. Along the Atlantic coast the whereabouts of these ships became an absorbing mystery, with undertones of panic: no one was sure where they had gone, and from ports as insignificant as Narragansett Pier demands came to the Navy Department for protection, backed often by political pressure. McKinley was prevailed upon to promise a warship would be sent to defend Portland, Maine, from Spanish attack, and Assistant Secretary Roosevelt sent a Civil War monitor to the town's defense. The citizens of Portland felt quite secure with this naval antique, manned by twenty-one New Jersey naval militia, in their harbor. While the whole eastern seaboard, from Portland south to Key West, was on tenterhooks, wondering when and where Cervera would strike, and while a patrol force of the rapidly converted merchantmen was cruising up and down the New England coast, and Schley's Flying Squadron was stripped for action, in the far Pacific an empire was being won by the Asiatic Squadron

Dewey had received a confidential and secret dispatch from Roosevelt, sent on February 25th, ordering him in the event of hostilities to carry out offensive operations in the Philippines; with war declared, Secretary Long sent him a coded cable ordering him to proceed to the Philippines and capture or destroy the Spanish fleet. Long's cable supplemented Roosevelt's, giving Dewey a specific objective, and the Commodore set out from Mirs Bay, on the China coast near Hong Kong, on the afternoon of April 27th. In his squadron were four protected cruisers, including the flagship, USS *Olympia,* a revenue cutter and two gunboats. Six hundred miles to the southeast, across the South China Sea, in Manila Bay Admiral Montojo's fleet of two protected cruisers and five obsolete smaller craft lay at anchor. Admiral Montojo strove to forget, in a round of social festivities, the doom he was certain impended.

Soon after dawn on the 30th the American squadron made its landfall on the coast near Manila, and that evening the ships stood in toward Manila Bay. In the darkness they passed the sleeping batteries on Corregidor and El Fraile safely and entered the bay. Next morning, in the first light, lookouts spotted Montojo's squadron near Cavite, and Dewey ordered the range closed.

The Spaniards opened fire first, their shots falling short or ranging over, and it was 5:40 A.M. when Dewey, looking in his baggy tropical whites like a civilian in pajamas, turned to the captain of *Olympia* and said in a quiet voice: "You may fire when ready, Gridley." Following *Olympia's* example, the rest of the ships opened a steady fire on the Spanish ships, which returned the fire with almost total inaccuracy. One Spanish shell hit near the bridge of *Olympia,* where Dewey stood nobly exposed, but it caused no damage; another shell struck USS *Baltimore* and wounded eight men. The Spaniards in the aged hulks were being massacred, even though their guns still flashed bravely through the clouds of black smoke that eddied and swirled across the bay.

Montojo tried in vain to close, for his guns were of shorter range than the Americans', but the fire from Dewey's ships drove him back. Five times the American squadron steamed back and forth, raking the Spanish ships with 5″, 6″ and 8″ shells. Quite suddenly the Americans broke off the engagement to make a count of their ammunition and casualties and to eat breakfast. At 11:16 A.M., the smoke having cleared away, they returned to deliver the coup de grâce, pouring on a merciless fire at close range.

By 12:30 it was all over. At Cavite a white flag was flying. The big Spanish ships were all either sunk or in flames, and Dewey sent in a gunboat to finish off the small craft. Then he attempted to arrange the terms of a surrender: he demanded that the Spanish put the facilities of the port and the cable to Hong Kong at his disposal, and that they promise that the heavy artillery in Manila would not be used against his ships.

The Spaniards were hesitant, reluctant: they promised not to use the Manila batteries on the American ships, for Dewey had warned that if they did he would bombard the city. But they refused his other demands. Dewey at once ordered the cable to Hong Kong cut, to isolate Manila from Madrid, and sent off his reports of the battle to Hong Kong to be cabled to Washington. At the same time he made an urgent request for ammunition. The few mines in the harbor were swept up: they had never been more than a mental hazard, but they were a menace to navigation.

Dewey had established American sovereignty in the Philippines, but only within range of the guns of his ships. Stoically he gathered the squadron at Cavite, declared Manila blockaded, and sat down to await developments.

Seldom have the limitations of warships operating alone been outlined in so stark a light: without troops Dewey's victory was insubstantial, and his position precarious, for he had not enough men to take and hold Manila. For over three months, during which a strong German squadron entered the bay and acted as though no battle had been fought, he was unable to give substance to his victory.

The news of the battle filtered in to the United States on May 1st, by way of Europe, and the fragmentary reports hinted at the immensity of the Spanish defeat. But not until Dewey's official report was cabled to Washington from Hong Kong was the full story told: then the nation, already immersed in waves of patriotism, found the taste of victory good and ravened for more. At a cost of 8 men wounded the nation had won command of the seas around the Philippines; 381 of the misguided seamen on the Spanish ships were dead or wounded; and no one doubted for a moment that the 7,500,000 Filipinos, then in various stages of enlightenment, would soon be freed of the Spanish yoke and allowed to live in the sunshine of republican liberty. This was the organ-music of imperialism, and the public was transported into ecstasies of joy and wonder.

Dewey was the hero of the hour, and McKinley rose to the occasion handsomely, promoting him to Acting Rear Admiral at once. On May 7th Roosevelt resigned as Assistant Secretary, dashed off to his commission as a Lieutenant-Colonel in the Rough Riders, and ultimately to the Presidency: it was physically impossible for him to sit in an office while his country was at war. Two days later Captain Mahan arrived in Washington, called back to duty from Rome, where he had been enjoying the pleasures of retirement. The Roosevelts placed their Washington home at his disposal, and he became a member of the Naval War Board created by Secretary Long. There his logical mind and vast knowledge made his opinions respected, if not always put into practice.

All haste was made to get reinforcements and ammunition and troops off to Dewey from San Francisco; then the main theater of action and focus of public attention shifted to the Caribbean.

The action in the Caribbean was nearly as fast as it had been in the Philippines. The Spanish squadron under Cervera, which had vanished on April 29th, was next reported to have passed Martinique on May 12th. A day later Schley's Flying Squadron left Hampton Roads for Key West. But still no one knew where Cervera was headed: he might try to intercept USS *Oregon,* which was on her way north from Bahia, Brazil, after a run at forced draught from San Francisco by way of Cape Horn. Or he might be looking for a place to refit and refuel.

Sampson thought hard and decided that the Spaniards would head for San Juan, Puerto Rico, where there was a navy yard, and it is likely that Cervera wanted to reach San Juan but was frightened off when he learned that Sampson was hunting for him there. Schley was sent to look in at Cienfuegos, Cuba, to see if Cervera had put in there. Meanwhile, by keeping well to the south, Cervera had avoided the armed merchantmen which were being used as scouts, and the heavy warships, and found refuge at Santiago, Cuba, on May 19th. (One of his torpedo-boat destroyers had fallen by the wayside, unable to stand this pace: she later limped into San Juan.) There the combined squadrons of Sampson and Schley found him and set up a constant patrol off the harbor mouth.

The lack of action goaded the Americans into a novel attempt to seal the channel with a block-ship. A collier, the *Merrimac,* was made ready, and when volunteers for the perilous mission were asked for, nearly every man stepped forward—for not since Lieutenant Richard Somers had taken the ketch *Intrepid* into Tripoli in 1804 and exploded into immortality had there been such a chance for glory. Lieutenant Richmond Pearson Hobson, an assistant naval constructor who had been adapting the collier to her new role, was selected because he knew more about the ship than anyone else. In the early hours of June 3rd, Hobson, with seven other volunteers, steamed into the channel. Shells from the forts disabled *Merrimac's* steering-gear, control was lost, and she sank too far inside the harbor to be of any use in blocking the channel. Hobson and his men were rescued by the Spaniards, and in the afternoon Cervera sent his chief of staff out under flag of truce to inform Sampson, in magniloquent terms, that the brave men were all alive and well.

The public, now that the enemy squadron had been located, could enjoy the war without fear of being shot at: Hobson became the current hero—he was young and dashing, Dewey old and nearly deified. In the army energy replaced reason, and troops and supplies poured into Tampa, Florida, which had been designated as the principal port of embarkation. Liason with the navy was either bad or non-existent, and there were no joint war plans. But it was clear that since Cervera was at Santiago a major effort should be directed against that port, and the army was ordered to get ready to sail on June 7th. A rumor that a Spanish squadron was at large postponed the sailing date until June 14th, by which time the report had been proved unfounded. Convoyed by the navy, thirty-two transports carrying seventeen thousand troops and eighty-nine war correspondents steamed away from Tampa, and arrived off Santiago on June 20th.

Then the question arose: what was the best way to use the troops? Demonstrating the ancient, congenital inability of the sailor to understand the soldier, Admiral Sampson suggested that it would be nice if the soldiers would assault the harbor forts, take them, and thus permit the warships to steam into the port and sink the Spanish squadron. But the army, under General Shafter, was not sure that the forts could be taken, and there was also a matter of prestige to consider: if the army followed Sampson's suggestion, the victory would be a naval one, and the army was becoming conscious of the values of publicity. Shafter refused to sacrifice his troops to make a naval holiday.

At length it was decided to land the army at a point eight miles away from Santiago and to march overland against the port, taking it from the rear. But there were not enough small boats on the transports to unload the troops and supplies, and on the 22nd Sampson came to the rescue, gallantly permitting the navy to help the army disembark. Then the troops began a slow advance on the city.

Cervera was caught between the American Army, most of whom were regulars and tough fighting men, and the American Navy. And the trap was closing slowly but surely. More Spanish troops marched in to reinforce Santiago, and Cervera was able then to withdraw his sailors from the forts they had helped to man, and to return them to duty on their ships. Escape seemed impossible: by night the American warships kept their searchlights on the harbor mouth—not even a fishing-smack

could clear the port undetected. By day the Americans kept up a fault-
less patrol; when one ship left the line to coal at Guantanamo Bay forty
miles away, another closed the gap in the line. In the blockading squadrons were the battleships *Iowa, Indiana, Massachusetts:* the armored
cruisers *New York, Texas, Brooklyn;* protected cruisers *New Orleans*
and *Marblehead,* and soon the battleship *Oregon* came to join the patrol.
With only four armored cruisers and two torpedo-boat destroyers in
Cervera's squadron, the odds were very much against survival, unless
the ships were to languish at anchor until they could be surrendered.
But in supreme command of all Spanish forces in Cuba was General
Blanco, a proud old blade, and the indignity of seeing the Queen's ships
remain at anchor, seemingly afraid to go out and fight, rankled in his
mind. He conferred with a German naval officer in Havana, and quite
suddenly Cervera had orders to make a sortie at once.

July 3rd, at 9:30 A.M., Cervera began to lead his ships out of the harbor. On USS *Brooklyn,* Commodore Schley's flagship, the signal was
instantly wig-wagged: "THE ENEMY FLEET IS COMING OUT OF THE HARBOR."
Sampson had gone off in *New York* to confer with General Shafter,
leaving standing orders which Schley took to mean that he was in command in Sampson's absence. The Spaniards cleared the harbor in forty
minutes. Schley ordered his ships to close and engage the enemy.

At 10:15 Cervera's flagship, *Marie Teresa,* was on fire and headed for
the beach; five minutes later *Oquendo* followed her, after a duel with
Texas. Vizcaya and *Cristóbal Colón* were fast, and they set off at full
speed to flee the holocaust, with *Brooklyn* and *Oregon* and *Iowa* in full
pursuit. Other American ships ran the destroyer *Pluton* on the rocks, and
saw her sister-ship, *Furor,* explode and sink. At 11:15 *Vizcaya* gave up
and was run aground: as the American ships streamed past the flaming
wreck, Captain Philips of *Texas* injected a curious note of humane
sentiment into the battle by shouting: "Don't cheer, boys, the poor devils
are dying!" Other than that cry, no one seemed to notice that a war
being fought out of purely humanitarian motives killed men just as
thoroughly as any other kind of war. The "poor devils" continued to
die: *Colón* turning to beach forty-five miles west of Santiago at 1:30 P.M.,
as *Oregon* came into range and bracketed her with 13-inch shells.

The navy presented the nation with the victory in time to make the morning editions on the Fourth of July, 1898. Casaulties: Spanish, 600 killed or drowned, 1,700 taken prisoner, including Admiral Cervera; American losses: 1 killed, 1 wounded.

The army, having taken San Juan Hill on July 1st, plugged doggedly along and ground to a halt in front of Santiago. The Spaniards were informed that if all the soldiers in the province—some 24,000 of them—would lay down their arms quietly, they would be transported back to Spain at the expense of the American government. It was a primitive but effective form of psychological warfare: the Spaniards were war-weary; many of them had been in Cuba for three years, longing for home, and they agreed to the terms of the surrender on July 17th.

With the release of the fleet from the blockade of Santiago, there was no fighting left for the navy to do: troops were transported to Puerto Rico, the blockade continued, prizes jammed the harbor at Key West—but the nearest enemy ships were thousands of miles away.

Spain was not willing to let her Philippine empire go by default, after one battle, to the Americans, and a squadron of her best remaining ships was hastily assembled under Admiral Camara's command and started off for Manila by way of the Suez Canal. The squadron reached Port Said on June 26th, passed through the canal and steamed into the Red Sea. Meanwhile the Naval War Board (and one can detect the thinking of Mahan in this instance) ordered a squadron made ready to start for the coast of Spain, in an effort to draw Camara back to protect his motherland. With Cervera's fleet demolished or on the rocks, a major part of the American naval force in the Atlantic could be used against Spanish ports, and with this goal in view preparations went ahead. But it never became necessary to carry them out: Camara, as expected, was called home. And on July 26th peace overtures were made by Spain through the good offices of the French Ambassador in Washington.

The Americans by then had taken Ponce, in Puerto Rico, and were marching on San Juan, where hostilities were ended by word that a peace protocol had been signed in Washington on August 12th. The protocol provided that peace commissioners meet in Paris, and by its terms Spain agreed to relinquish all claim to Cuba, to cede Puerto Rico and minor Caribbean islands, as well as Guam, to the United States.

But the protocol did not settle the Philippine matter: indeed, on the day it was signed Manila was still in Spanish hands and Dewey, thanks to the broken Manila–Hong Kong cable, was not aware of the signing. He had been reinforced with ten thousand troops brought across the Pacific in the merchantmen-transports, and in August he was in a position to attack the city.

The Spanish General in Manila was willing to surrender if a way could be found to save his personal dignity and military reputation along with the honor of Castille. In addition, he preferred the Americans to the Filipino insurgents as victors. He would not surrender without a fight, and yet he wished to avoid bloodshed. Negotiations were initiated to meet his requirements: the march on the city was to be a bloodless affair, and the guns of the warships were to fire in the general direction of Manila but they were to be sure not to hit anything. While these war-like gestures were going on his surrender was to be demanded by Dewey, by means of a flag signal. Thus, confronted by such overwhelming force, he would be able to surrender in the best hidalgo manner, without blot on his escutcheon. These arrangements were put into operation at 9:00 A.M. August 13th, Manila time, and they were carried out to the general satisfaction of everyone except the insurgents, who found themselves barred from the city.

News of the capitulation of Manila reached Washington on the 16th, and McKinley was extremely puzzled: should the archipelago be taken under the eagle's wings and thus protected from the voracious power of other, less Christian, nations? Or should they be allowed to remain free and to stew in their own juice? But that would mean civil wars unending, and almost certainly foreign intervention. The problem was a difficult one, but with God's guidance the President decided that benevolent philanthropy demanded that the United States save the Philippines, take up the white man's burden and bring the blessings of civilization to the islanders. He sent word to the Commissioners at Paris that there was only "one plain path of duty—the acceptance of the archipelago." The Spanish commissioners objected when the Americans offered to take the islands off their hands, and at the same time to pay Spain twenty million dollars, which was roughly the amount of the Philippine debt. After much disputation, during which the Americans delivered a virtual ultimatum, the Spanish commissioners yielded, and the treaty was signed on November 10, 1898. By its terms Spain lost not only all her Caribbean possessions, and Guam, but the Philippines too. In return for the archipelago they were to be paid twenty million dollars, and Spanish merchantmen were to have the right to continue trading with the Philippines for ten years on the same terms as American vessels.

The treaty now faced a divided Senate, wherein the debate was carried on with more acrimony than usual: Senator Lodge, working for annexation, led the administration forces. The anti-imperialists fought a strong rear-guard action which they finally lost when the treaty was approved on February 6, 1899, by fifty-seven to twenty-seven votes—or one more than the necessary two-thirds majority.

The navy, at war's end, had become enormously popular, for the battles of Manila Bay and Santiago were recognized as the keystones of victory in the Pacific and Caribbean. By contrast the army had appeared muddle-headed, wasteful of lives and money. Naval personnel had increased from 13,750 to 24,123 officers and men, and 123 merchantmen, yachts and tugs had been converted to naval service. At least thirty worthwhile prizes had been taken into Key West, without the use of privateers which both the Queen Regent of Spain and McKinley had agreed to eschew.

It had been, as John Hay wrote to Roosevelt, "a splendid little war," but on closer examination it was apparent that there were elements of phenomenal luck in the undertaking. The navy was good only when compared with the Spanish Navy, and the Spaniards were terrible. American gunnery at Manila Bay had scored less than 5 per cent hits on the Spanish ships, and the average at Santiago was no better. Fortunately the Spanish were even worse as marksmen. The merchant marine had been proved inadequate: it was unable to provide all the ships needed, making it necessary for the government to buy vessels from foreign nations. Happily, enough vessels were acquired to serve the needs of the army and navy in such a short war. Indeed, it had been "a splendid little war," with the emphasis on "little." A splendid big

Bird's-Eye View of Deck of U.S.S. *Massachusetts,* at
Brooklyn Navy Yard (1905)

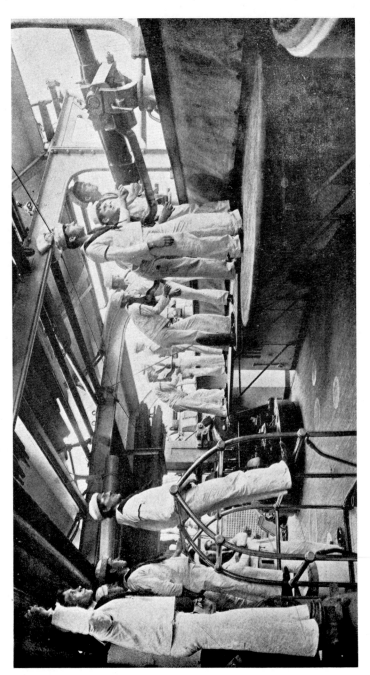

Target Practice on U.S.S. *Massachusetts*

war, against a major power, might well have ended in an American defeat.

But the Americans, despite the defects of their army, navy and merchant marine, had won an overseas empire in little more than three months. The war had been entirely unpremeditated murder, and it had the added virtue of being motivated by the highest Christian principles. The nation was now ready to embark on the business of empire in the ageless European tradition, complete with rebel tribesmen in the form of Filipino insurrectionists. It was unfortunate that such benighted primitives should combat the Star and Stripes, unable to see the advantages of American rule and aspiring to nothing less than independence, but they represented, after all, one of the responsibilities which the nation had so confidently assumed and then left to the armed forces to handle in a savage jungle war which did not end until the rebels were thoroughly enlightened.

Having taken leave of its traditional policy of isolation, the United States hurriedly acquired more possessions in the Pacific. It was clear that naval bases and coaling stations would be useful in protecting our new interests in the Far East. In the summer of 1898, while the fighting was still in progress, the Hawaiian Islands had been annexed in accordance with the islanders' government's wishes. A year later the problem posed by the Samoan Islands, on the route to Australia, was settled by mutual agreement: the United States took possession of Samoa, with its coveted harbor of Pago-Pago, while Germany accepted the rest of the island group and Britain was made happy by German concessions elsewhere. In the same year uninhabited Wake Island was acquired by simple annexation, and so a line of potential bases dotted the route to the Far East: Hawaii, Midway (which USS *Lackawanna* had surveyed and taken possession of in 1867), Wake, Guam and Manila.

The United States was at last a power in the Pacific, and as the twentieth century opened, the nation, like an eaglet newly emerged from its nest and proud of its strength, looked eagerly toward the far and unknown horizons.

[19] *"Sleeping: Do Not Disturb"*

1900 A.D.—the year was greeted by Americans with the respect reserved for momentous milestones: the republic had overrun its boundaries and in an excess of exuberance reached across the seas. There was no time to sum up the years since 1776, and to learn the lessons thereof: the mood was progress and the tense was future. The nation, set in a new framework that extended six thousand miles across the Pacific, entered a period of transition and adjustment. The United States was at last a world power, striding brash and ignorant across the world stage.

No one expected eternal peace: that much was evident to the young nation. But the public was not greatly concerned about adjusting the navy and the merchant marine to the realities of the power politics in which the nation was involved.

The navy sloughed off its excess of converted merchantmen and yachts, keeping only a dozen of the best as permanent auxiliaries. The war had provided a severe trial for the fighting ships: ordnance, gunnery, engine design had been tested in battle and found barely adequate against a third-rate foe. The officers, as a group, had justified their Naval Academy training, proved themselves under fire, displayed high qualities of courage and decorum. At last they had a fleet of which they could be proud, and they developed their own special sense of duty and of selfless service: nothing quite like this had happened since the War of 1812, and it is a remarkable fact that among the men who served in the Spanish War were officers of the same type that Preble would have admired: Joel Pringle, William Leahy, Harry Yarnell, Thomas Hart—then young whippersnappers, but destined to fill positions of authority in the greater wars to come.

The merchant marine reverted to the tendencies it had displayed before the war: in coastal shipping, where profits were secure, there was a steady growth. The tonnage of ships registered in foreign trade fluctuated mildly around the 900,000-ton mark. In 1901 foreign vessels were carrying 91.8 per cent of American foreign trade. The habit of seafaring had been lost.

Captain Mahan saw this happening, and he thought that the lack of interest in the condition of the merchant marine and the navy was a source of potential danger to the nation. Valiantly but in vain he strove in his writing to impress upon the public the importance of sea power. Too many people were beyond his reach: either they could not read or could not afford to buy books and magazines. In his effort he had the active support of Roosevelt, who, having become Vice President in 1901, acceded to the Presidency in September of that year, following the death by assassination of President McKinley. Roosevelt, aged forty-three, was still full of nervous animation, still deeply interested in naval matters. He and Mahan kept up a steady interchange of ideas on the subject, and since both favored a navy large enough to carry out the nation's commitments overseas, the result was a sudden growth of warships.

It was evident, in the early years of the twentieth century, that the United States could no longer depend upon its merchant marine as a source of fighting ships suitable for offensive war: the types were too divergent, the demands of naval warfare too exacting. A few swift auxiliary cruisers were the most that the merchant marine could be expected to provide in time of war. The navy, if it was to win battles, must look to its own efforts and its own ships. Congress was incited to authorize new battleships, armored cruisers, scout cruisers and submarines.

The matter of personnel was a difficult one: there were, in 1901, only 883 officers and 25,050 men in the navy. With Roosevelt in the White House there came a sudden emphasis on efficiency in handling the ships. There were continuous drills for officers and men, less shore leave at the delightful ports of Southern California, Maine and Rhode Island. The only way to learn how to fight a ship was to take her out to sea and put her through her paces under conditions as close as possible to those the ship would meet in battle. This meant months of hard and grueling work, with little praise and less pay, no matter how well the work was done.

As the new ships joined the fleets there were not enough officers and men to man them properly, and that meant more work for all hands. Congress raised the authorized limit of enlistments and increased the number of appointments to the Naval Academy, but in both cases the number of applicants failed to provide men enough to fill the berths in the ships in commission.

This was symptomatic of the nation's conception of a navy: let those who like it join it, we the taxpayers will foot the bill—the navy can fight the wars. There was a kindred attitude toward the merchant marine: let the seamen, those coarse and foul-mouthed beasts who were no good on land, work and sail the ships. What if there weren't enough merchantmen flying the American flag? The British, German, French and Dutch ships were serving very well as carriers of American exports and imports.

In this attitude there was much sound commonsense: the forecastles of the merchantmen were at once verminous and fetid, the food unpalatable, the work dangerous and hard, the wages low. The coal-burners had made mechanical stokers of human beings, and only the toughest men could stand the work. There were still sailing ships, now practically all schooner-rigged, and on them conditions were as bad as on the steamers: in the latter a man baked in the engine-room, in the former he froze in the rigging. In contrast, there were fortunes to be made ashore.

• But if the American people were not concerned with the sea, the President more than compensated for their apathy. His interest found expression in the acquisition, by means more practical than ethical, of what was to become the Panama Canal. For generations the United States had been interested in the Panamanian isthmus, owned by Colombia, seeing therein the site of a potential canal. In 1826 Secretary of State Clay had proposed the matter for discussion at the Panama Congress; twenty years later, by Article 35 of a treaty with Colombia (then known as New Granada), the United States had guaranteed the neutrality of the isthmus so that unhindered transit would be certain. This provision was inspired by the necessity of linking newly-won California with the Eastern states. In 1849, when the gold rush strained trans-isthmian travel facilities to the breaking point, and moving passengers and freight across the isthmus became a source of great profits, an alternate route across Nicaragua was considered, and Nicaragua granted a concession for the construction of a canal across its territory to an American company. For lack of capital the concession was never acted upon, and then, with the completion of the railroad across the isthmus from Colón to Panama, the need was no longer a pressing one. The project of a canal was allowed to drop until 1881, when the Frenchman, Count de Lesseps, with a concession obtained from the Colombian government, undertook to construct a canal by 1892. In 1889 the de Lesseps company, having spent $266,000,000 without completing the project, became bankrupt, and in 1891 the concession was extended for ten years.

When the war with Spain began, the navy's need for a canal became painfully evident: USS *Oregon,* which had been ordered to leave the Bremerton Navy Yard in Washington on March 1st, 1898, did not arrive at Key West until May 26th, having perforce rounded Cape Horn to reach the eastern seaboard. Dramatic as *Oregon's* dash was, with the nation following the news of her progress breathlessly, it was clear to everyone that she could have made the trip in less than half the time had there been a canal. The lack of a canal was felt as acutely when Camara's squadron was poking around in the Red Sea, threatening to steam against Dewey in Manila: the reinforcements nearest to Dewey, aside from two monitors sent from San Francisco, were in the Atlantic ocean.

With the winning of the Philippines, and the bright promise of trade there, the nation had possessions overseas which might some day need protection, and that protection could be furnished much more expeditiously if the warships could be shuttled back and forth through a canal. Otherwise the fleet would have to be divided into two portions, for Europe was always a potential source of wars, and the United States could not leave her eastern seaboard unprotected while there were tensions in Europe. It was hard enough to assign ships to the West Coast in peace: the citizens of the eastern ports had come to think of the visits of the warships, with their by no means inconsiderable pay-rolls, as a source of traditional profits, and furthermore, the mayors of eastern ports could exert influence on the disposition of naval vessels, in the interest of partisan politics. But with a canal it would be possible to please these important people, and then, as danger threatened, concentrate the ships in either the Atlantic or Pacific. The shipping industry was also involved: the route from San Francisco to New York, by way of a canal, would be shortened by some nine thousand miles, and from New York to Manila by nearly six thousand miles—a saving in time and distance which meant that each ship could make more frequent trips and therefore greater profits. The saving to the coastal trade vessels plying between east and west coasts would be enormous.

So matters stood in 1902, and the one chance for the French company to salvage something from the wreckage of their enterprise was to sell the rights to build the canal, and the work done on it, to the United States. After much Yankee and Gallic haggling the price of forty million dollars was found to be mutually acceptable, and in the summer of 1902 Congress authorized the President to buy the French concession for not more than forty million dollars. But, next year Colombia became difficult: her government objected to the transfer of the French franchise to the Americans, refused to ratify the treaty unless a goodly amount of the price should find its way into the pockets of worthy Colombian citizens. The very thought of being refused by Colombia outraged Roosevelt, a man of fantastic patriotic pride, and he voiced his decisions: let the canal be built, regardless of Colombia's sentiments in the matter.

A revolt, instigated by the French, who had the most to lose, and with the connivance of the Americans, who had the most to win, broke out in the isthmus on the evening of November 3rd, 1903, and the Republic of Panama was proclaimed. On that day, in the harbor of Colón, were three American gunboats—USS *Nashville,* USS *Boston* and USS *Dixie.* They had orders to keep Colombian ships fifty miles away from Panama, to prevent Colombian troops from landing on the isthmus, and to keep service uninterrupted on the oceanic railroad. The United States Marines landed to patrol the railroad, as well as to protect American lives and property—always a worthy reason for marines to take a situation in hand. In the excitement there was one casualty—a Chinese was shot by the Colombians.

A few hours after news of the revolt reached Washington on November 6th the State Department recognized the Republic of Panama as a sovereign state, and by a treaty concluded twelve days later the United States obtained from the new republic a concession to build the canal, including a strip of territory five miles wide on either side of it, together with "any other lands that might be necessary to the construction and maintenance of the canal." At the same time the United States guaranteed the independence of the Republic of Panama. The Senate ratified this treaty on February 23, 1904, by a vote of sixty-six to fourteen, and the United States agreed to pay Panama ten million dollars in cash, and an annuity of a quarter of a million dollars, to begin nine years after Panama ratified the treaty. Panama ratified at top speed. Colombia felt unjustly treated: to see all this money going to Panamanians, when it might have gone to Colombians, put a severe strain on Pan-American good-will. But Roosevelt was willing to risk Colombia's displeasure, and the criticism of political opponents at home. By his lights, his cause was "righteous."

Even before the treaty had been ratified by the Senate, Roosevelt began to stress the need for reviving the merchant marine. A utilitarian, first and always, he had the fait accompli of the canal project, and full use must be made of it. When he reported to Congress on December 7, 1903, he recommended that Congress form a commission to investigate and report "what legislation is desirable or necessary for the development of the American merchant marine and American commerce, and incidentally of an ocean mail service, of adequate auxiliary naval cruisers and naval reserves." And he went on to point out that the British and Germans had surpassed the Americans in trans-Atlantic service with better and faster ships, and that cargo ships were even more important than swift mail steamers.

Congress duly created a Merchant Marine Commission a few months later, composed of five Senators and five Representatives, to look into the situation. After holding nation-wide hearings the commission issued its final report in January 1905, at the same time submitting a bill which recommended immediate action before "conditions became still more desperate." The bill was a panacea for all the merchant marine's ills: it was designed to promote the national defense, increase foreign commerce, and revitalize the merchant marine by providing subsidies for foreign-trade ships and deep-sea fishing craft. It recommended that ten new mail services be established and that ships on those routes be subsidized by mail contracts. Such was the majority report, to which seven of the ten commissioners subscribed; the three minority members were in favor of using discriminating duties and port dues instead of direct or mail subsidies to encourage shipping. It was a notable effort to do something constructive about the merchant marine, but it failed, even in modified form, to pass the Senate in 1906, and over nine-tenths of the nation's foreign trade continued to be carried in foreign-flag vessels. The nation was simply too busy with domestic problems to worry about maritime affairs.

While the Americans were internally occupied, the Europeans had been showing an unmannerly appetite in their search for markets in the Far East. Japan had been deprived of most of the fruits of her victory over China. Her special interests in Korea and Formosa were all that remained to her of the spoils. Germany had secured and fortified Kiao-chau, on the China coast opposite Korea; Russia had taken Port Arthur in the north, and Talien-wan, and built Dalny for her trans-Siberian railroad; Britain picked up Wei-hai-wei, and Mirs Bay near Hong Kong; France took Kwang-chau to the south; and Italy seized Sanmen, south of the Yangtze. China had the look of a nation about to be vivisected: each of the five nations involved expected to control the trade of the hinterland their seaport holdings served, and there was an excellent chance that American trade would be frozen out of Chinese markets by special tariffs imposed by the Europeans. This was a cause for grave concern in the American Department of State.

John Hay, Secretary of State under both McKinley and Roosevelt, was a wise and fast-moving man, and he was prompt to oppose this dismemberment of China, with which the United States had enjoyed trade relations ever since 1786, when the first American commercial agent had been sent there. But Hay had no way of enforcing his diplomacy, no warships with which he could overawe either Britain or France or Germany, and so he appealed to St. Petersburg, Berlin and London, sending to each in September 1899 a politely-worded note asking them to respect China's open or "treaty" ports and to maintain identical tariffs in their zones of influence. When each of the three nations expressed approval of the notes, Hay so informed the others and the "Open Door" policy became generally accepted. The principle had been made effective without the use of guns. It was reiterated at the time of the Boxer Rebellion, when American warships, marines and troops helped to put down that revolt, and Hay took advantage of the occasion to send another note to the powers asking them to respect China's territorial integrity. The nations all agreed to this, and the door to American trade in China remained open. Still, the agreement was a fragile one: Hay's policy rested on an appeal to the nations' better nature not to profit from China's inability to protect herself, and not to brand themselves as unenlightened people by making colonies out of the ancient celestial empire. And, of course, this moral suasion, a delicate fabric, was ripped to shreds at the first test of reality, when the Japanese decided to go to war with Russia.

There had been bad blood between the two nations since the 1850s, when the Russians had appropriated northern islands from the Japanese, and in 1875, when Japan was forced to cede half of Sakhalin Island to Russia, matters were made worse. The animosity grew when Russia took Port Arthur away from Japan after Japan had taken it from China. By 1900 the Muscovites had made Manchuria a zone of influence and they were becoming involved in Korea. In addition, there was boundary trouble between Russia and Japan on Sakhalin Island, and negotiations had been carried on for several years in an attempt to find a peaceful solution to the problem. These were matters diplomacy might have solved, had the will for a solution existed on both sides. But on February 5, 1904, the Japanese broke off negotiations. This had happened before and no one in Russia was very much worried about it—the arguments could always be resumed. This time they were resumed in an unexpected manner.

On the night of February 8th, while the Japanese diplomats were being banqueted by the Russians in St. Petersburg, Japanese torpedo-boat destroyers nosed into the roadstead at Port Arthur and without warning loosed their torpedoes at the anchored Russian ships. Three of Russia's best ships were hit and severely damaged. Two days later the formal declarations of war followed. The American naval officers were aghast at such an impolite way of opening a war, and even the British, who had signed an Anglo-Japanese treaty of alliance in 1902, found the method unsporting. That the attack had paid off in results was only too certain: the Russian ships remaining were not at all anxious to come out of the harbor, and the Japanese thoughtfully laid a mine field in the channel one night, and then began to blockade the port. Once the Russians, lured by some Japanese light cruisers, went out to fight the visible enemy, but the decoys fled and when the Russian ships turned back to port they ran into the mine field and lost another ship. That made them even more reluctant to meet the Japanese in battle, and not until August 10th, when the Russian ships were driven out of port by the Japanese army, did they fight again. Then they were defeated and dispersed, although not without having inflicted damage on the Japanese fleet, and the victors returned to their blockade, calmly ferrying troops across from Japan to seize and hold the ground from the Russian soldiers.

All that Russia had left in the way of ocean-going warships was her Baltic fleet, and they were ordered to the Far East, leaving Libau in October, 1904, rounding the Cape of Good Hope and reaching Madagascar in time to learn that Port Arthur had fallen to the Japanese army and navy. Undecided about their next move, the Russians were encouraged by the arrival of reinforcements in March, 1905, from the Baltic by way of Suez, and the combined fleets, with their train of supply ships, steamed across the Indian ocean, up through the Malacca Straits and into the South China Sea. Admiral Togo, already a hero by Japanese standards because of the success of his surprise attack on Port Arthur, decided to wait for the Russian fleet in his home waters, confident that they would take the short and easy route north to Vladivostok. The Russians left Camranh Bay in mid-May, and met Togo in the battle of Tsushima Straits, between Korea and Japan, on May 27th. The result was a Russian disaster.

Nothing further could be gained by Russia in further fighting, and Roosevelt, in the guise of dove of peace, offered the good offices of the United States to bring about peace. The peace conference opened on August 9th, 1905, at the Portsmouth, New Hampshire, Navy Yard, and ended when the treaty of peace was signed two weeks later. It had not been the intention of the Japanese to fight a long war, but rather one marked by a calculated economy of effort and aimed at maximum gains. By the peace treaty the Japanese won the limited victory they had hoped for: Russia gave up her leases of the Kwantung peninsula and pulled out of Port Arthur, and Manchuria, and left Korea as a Japanese zone of influence.

The British could not help being proud of their ally, in whose naval service Royal Naval officers had been advisers. The Japanese, since they could defeat the Russians so easily, were obviously worth cultivating. In the United States, at the Naval War College, the war was food for much thought, and the lessons to be learned from it, aside from the technical ones, were that surprise attacks could be expected from Japan, and that you could not apply Christian ethics in dealing with Asiatics on the war-path—they simply did not follow the tenets of Christianity in matters of life or death. Unfortunately there was no way to disseminate the lessons of the Russo-Japanese War through the fleets. A monthly publication of good technical standards, the "United States Naval Institute," edited and published by naval officers, was not required reading. Even if it had been there was little in it at that time which would have served as a useful warning: the Japanese had performed twice in the same manner—it would take three times for the pattern to be clear to everyone.

The Russians, of course, denounced the Japanese for the sneak attack on Port Arthur, but the Japanese replied that they had suspended diplomatic negotiations and were signatory to no pact which made it necessary for them to declare war overtly. Because of the ensuing debate, in the third Hague Convention in 1907 provision was made to embalm in international law the rule that hostilities should not start without either a prior declaration of war or an ultimatum with a conditional declaration of war attached. For those who put their faith in the pledged word, the move seemed a long step forward on the road from barbarism.

The Russo-Japanese War had provided a stringent test for the Open Door policy, but by reason of John Hay's efforts the policy survived, although in modified form. As soon as the shooting began he had sent notes to the neutral powers asking them to join the United States in requesting Japan and Russia to keep hostilities localized and to recognize the neutrality of China. Since this was to the advantage of the neutrals, they gave Hay the support he needed, and China's dismemberment was kept to a minimum.

Roosevelt and Mahan did not have sufficient faith in the ethics of international relations to expect that Hay could continue to devise his requests for international morality, and to make them even partially effective forever. He had worked wonders with appeals to justice and reason and decency, but his position was like that of a Salvation Army girl collecting donations from the inmates of a waterfront saloon: there would be no trouble until the fighting started. And against that moment it behooved the United States to build as many and as efficient warships as possible. With sufficient sea power the United States would be able to enforce its highly moral diplomacy and to use its influence to spread the beneficent American culture throughout the world. This was surely one of the most naïve forms of imperialism the mind of man had ever devised: it partook of the fervor of crusading for a special form of government, and it included undertones of religious motivation, since one aspect of it was to bring Christianity to the benighted heathens, be they Mohammedan or pagan as in the Philippines, or Buddhist or Confucian, as in China. Such a potentially explosive approach to world affairs made a large navy mandatory: there was no choice about it.

Against this grandiose attitude, shared not by Roosevelt and Mahan alone but by many high ranking naval officers, the nation posed its proverbial inertia in maritime affairs and the wondrous workings of politics in a democracy. Overseas bases were neglected because Congress would not appropriate the money necessary either to build, strengthen or maintain them. And Congress had an excellent reason for not spending funds in distant lands: no votes from job-holders would accrue to the law-maker who spent money beyond the continental limits. Better, far, to allocate the dollars to navy yards like those at Boston, New York, Philadelphia, Norfolk, San Francisco, where employment would be provided for citizens who would show their appreciation at the polls, and where the beneficiaries of contracts could be expected to donate to political campaign funds in time of need. In 1903 there was not a single American naval base in Asiatic waters, and the ships of the Asiatic Squadron were dependent on dockyards at Nagasaki and Hong Kong. And without bases in the Far East, the navy's wings were clipped. On another move the President met rebuff: he tried to bring some efficiency into the maze of the Navy Department's eight bureaus, whose duties frequently overlapped and among which responsibility was fugitive. So it had been since 1842, when the bureau system was created, and so it continued to be in 1904. The proposal was made to create a Naval General Staff, composed of line officers, who would have authority over the bureau chiefs and who would act as advisers to the Navy Secretary. But Congress was not willing to let naval officers assume too strong a position in policy-making matters, and the opposition to the idea was enough to defeat it.

But if the Roosevelt-Mahan policies suffered these major defeats, they won major gains too. A febrile young officer named William Snowden Sims, who had seen much service abroad as a naval attaché and observer, was chagrined to find that dismal gunnery was a hall-mark of the American Navy. What was the use of building all these ships if they couldn't hit their targets? Sims had sent in such detailed reports on European navies that he had won Roosevelt's praise when the latter was Assistant Secretary of the Navy, and by 1902 good gunnery had become a fetish in Sims' mind. But the senior officers were repelled by his incessant and importunate attempts to improve American gunnery, and, risking his future career, Sims appealed directly to Roosevelt for action. As a result Sims was appointed "Inspector of Target Practice," and he applied British gunnery techniques, as well as improvements on them, throughout the navy. Within a few years American warships were shooting more accurately than anyone had dreamed possible.

A second reform was carried out in the same period: Roosevelt created, from the vessels of the five traditional squadrons, two large fleets: the Atlantic Fleet, in which all the battleships were concentrated, and the Pacific Fleet, in which armored cruisers were the largest type of vessel. By this arrangement both coasts were protected, the Atlantic against possible trouble with Germany, which was becoming surly and ambitious, and the Pacific against Japan, which felt that it had a great deal of lost time to make up in order to bring the whole world into the Mikado's household.

The more immediate threat came from Japan, which considered that the peace arranged by Roosevelt at the end of the Russo-Japanese War had not been as profitable to Japan as the military situation then warranted. Further cause for ill-will grew out of discrimination against

Japanese laborers in California by Americans who saw their standard of wages imperiled by cheap Japanese labor, and who vented their prejudices by passing restrictive laws and by segregating Japanese school-children. To the Japanese, who were firmly convinced that they were descended from the Sun Goddess, this attitude was a gratuitous insult from the white barbarians. When the resentment rose to government levels in Japan, Roosevelt decided to apply his policy of "Speak softly and carry a big stick" by sending the battle fleet on a cruise around the world.

On December 16, 1907, the sixteen battleships of the Atlantic Fleet, with two supply ships, a repair ship and a fleet tender, steamed out of Hampton Roads, bound for the Far East by way of Cape Horn. Six destroyers accompanied them, and a newfangled invention, the wireless, kept them in touch with shore. The fleet proceeded leisurely down the east coast of South American, rounded Cape Horn, and steamed up to Magdalena Bay in Lower California, where they had a month's target practice. Then they went on to California, Washington and Oregon, to the tremendous pleasure of the local inhabitants, and finally steamed away for Hawaii, and thence to New Zealand, Australia and the Philippines. Between Manila and Japan the ships weathered a typhoon, in which the battleships lost some men and boats, but all finally arrived in Yokohama in October where they were subjected to a fervent welcome by the Japanese. The threat of war vanished in torrents of rice wine, whiskey and beer, and when, after a week of festivities both hosts and visitors were near exhaustion, the warships started home by way of Suez, reaching Hampton Roads in February, 1909. They had steamed nearly 54,000 miles, without major trouble, and when Roosevelt came down from Washington to review them his heart was nearly bursting with pride and joy. For the fleet was largely his own creation.

While the ships had been away the President had been having more trouble with a Congress which had grown obstinately tired of being told what to do. The pacifists, headed by Andrew Carnegie, had been sniping at his building program even before the fleet left on the world cruise, and this strange congerie of religious and idealistic characters was still hard at work, fighting his every effort to build more battleships. From the navy's point of view the pacifists were both misguided and misinformed: HMS *Dreadnought,* which the British had launched on an unsuspecting world in 1906, after hurriedly and secretly building it, was an 18,000-ton battleship with a speed of 21 knots, and guns that made every other battleship obsolescent: she carried ten 12″ rifles in five twin turrets, and mounted only a few lesser pieces for use against torpedo-boat destroyers. She was the first "all big gun ship," and she could have sunk any other battleship then afloat. But it was difficult to make a pacifist understand such matters, and a spirit of resignation pervaded the upper ranks of the navy. Indeed, the resignation, blended with complacency, became so widespread that a minor guerrilla war, a bloodless one, began between the young and vigorous officers, Sims among them, and the barnacled old sea-dogs. The result was an article inspired by the rebels, written by Henry Reuterdahl, which appeared in *McClure's* magazine for January, 1908. Reuterdahl, with only a few minor errors of fact, laid bare the structural faults of American men-of-war, to wit: their armor plate was so low that when the ships were fully loaded their armor was either close to, or in some cases, below the waterline, where it offered no protection; the ships had so little freeboard that their guns would all be useless in rough weather; turrets and ammunition hoists were poorly designed; there were only 20 destroyers in commission whereas the British had 155; anti-torpedo defense was poor; promotion by seniority instead of selection was creating superannuated captains and admirals. The cause of all this, wrote Reuterdahl, was the bureau system, and thus there began a last spirited attack by Roosevelt on the bureau chiefs. This time, as in 1904, he lost to the politicians who could not bring themselves to create a Naval General Staff, and who by that time, after seven years of Roosevelt's often autocratic demands, were inclined to oppose him on any project, no matter what its merits.

In the navy there was much woeful shaking of heads on March 4, 1909, when William Howard Taft, erstwhile Secretary of War, became President. Roosevelt, as Assistant Secretary and as Chief Executive had done more to rebuild and rejuvenate the naval service than any previous President: there were now 1,096 officers and 44,500 enlisted men, and the United States had a navy second only to Britain in size. In addition to the construction of new ships Roosevelt had accomplished a less tangible but more important thing: he had alerted large numbers of the American people to the existence of their navy, and to the role it could be expected to play in time of war. To an incalculable extent the expansion of the fleets and the world cruise had made the American people less provincial, more conscious of their country's role in world affairs. In contrast to the out-going, Africa-bound President, Taft was as anticlimactic as a glass of milk after a clambake.

In the next four years frustration marked the naval and maritime policies of the administration. A depression hampered the efforts of the "Big Navy" advocates to keep abreast of the Anglo-German naval building race which was then well under way. Political factions made sport of naval appropriations, and the pacifists were active. There were but a few constructive accomplishments: Secretary of the Navy George Meyers rearranged the Navy Department bureaus, making them more efficient by a clearer assignment of responsibility; an army-navy joint board abandoned the idea of building a naval base in the Philippines, settling instead for one in Hawaii, and this project met the approval of Congress in 1909, when funds were voted to begin construction at Pearl Harbor. Another small appropriation in 1911 enabled the navy to do some work on its base at Guantanamo, from which the approaches to the Panama Canal could be guarded. Taft, trying hard to carry out Roosevelt's policies without quite understanding their implications, asked Congress for two battleships each year, and, except in 1912, when only one was voted, he was able to obtain the authorizations and appropriations. The result was a navy in which there were plenty of battleships, but few smaller, supporting craft, and the strategists bewailed the unbalanced offensive and defensive power of such a fleet. But there was one virtue in having the big ships built: they could not be improvised in a few months, in the way destroyers could, and once they were in commission the most complex part of the navy was built.

Having this navy, Taft seems to have been unaware of its limitations. Foreign policy stressed the interest of the United States in the "Open Door" in China, but without Hay's gracious and cogent touch. Demands were made that the American Government, and American bankers, be permitted to invest money in Chinese railroads, as a means of wedging the door to China open. Such efforts, labeled "Dollar Diplomacy," and made without prior consultation with the powers concerned, were destined to fail. For it was evident to all the world that the United States could not back up her demands in the Far East with guns, and that the commitments of her foreign policy were no longer synchronized with her ability to enforce them in Asiatic waters. In the Caribbean and in Latin America, "dollar diplomacy" was more practical, for the small republics in that area were within easy reach of American warships and marines.

In Europe, during Taft's administration, there were internal rumblings as British and German shipyards exuded more and larger warships. The Kaiser, with his realm thoroughly industrialized, wanted colonies and markets. But Britain had most of the world's colonies, and the British Isles lay athwart the routes the German merchantmen and warships must take if they were to reach foreign lands. Britain therefore was the first barrier to Teutonic dreams of conquest overseas. In the Western Hemisphere the Monroe Doctrine limited German penetration to commerce carried on by conventional methods, and furthermore, there were no German bases close enough to the United States to make a war against the Americans practical. The Atlantic Fleet—the "battle fleet"—regardless of its lack of small supporting cruisers and destroyers, was still too large for the Germans to hold in light esteem.

In March 1913 the bumbling Taft became a private citizen and Woodrow Wilson took office as President. He was a minister's son, had started an unsuccessful and short-lived law practice, and then became a college professor, university president, and Governor of New Jersey. In short, he was an intellectual politician whose principles were provincial American and thus it was natural for him to be an advocate of American neutrality in a war between Britain and Germany. The sides were lined up in Europe: Germany, Austria-Hungary and Italy against Britain, France and Russia, in a delicately balanced armed peace. Then, on June 28, 1914, an Austrian archduke was murdered at Serajevo by a Serbian revolutionist. With Germany's backing, Austria-Hungary declared war on Serbia. One by one the European nations were caught up in the maelstrom: Russia mobilized to help Serbia; Germany declared war on Russia, then on France, and drove against France through neutral Belgium. Britain, with her channel ports threatened, her allies attacked and her future threatened, declared war on Germany on August 4, 1914. The formalities had all been observed—except when inconvenient, as in the case of Germany's disregard of Belgium's neutrality.

Wilson promptly extended an offer of the good offices of the United States to effect a peaceful solution to the holocaust. This well-intentioned interjection of morality was refused, and the President proclaimed the neutrality of the United States. The American problem now was the enforcement of this neutrality.

There is, in the human mind and body, a yearning for that dark and comfortable pre-natal period when the womb insulates the unconscious foetus from the realities of life. To this blissful, somnolent condition the United States, under the leadership of Wilson, attempted to return in the first years of the First World War. Such a biological tour de force was found to be impractical.

The state of the American merchant marine was such that only 9.7 per cent of American foreign trade was being carried in American ships. American tonnage in foreign trade had passed the 1,000,000 mark in 1913, for the first time since 1886, and it had reached 1,066,288 tons in 1914. The grand total of American tonnage was 7,928,688—including deep-sea fishing craft, shipping on the Great Lakes, and the coastal trade vessels. Sail had not by any means gone out of style, but it had passed its peak when the *Thomas Lawson,* an enormous seven-masted steel-hulled schooner of 5,200 tons was built at Fore River in 1901–2. Her 7 spars carried 43,000 square feet of canvas, and she could freight 8,000 tons of coal. But she was wrecked and no one cared to duplicate her, although schooners of modest size continued to be built and to be used in carrying lumber on the west coast and bulky freight on the east coast. The American ships in foreign trade were, by 1914, almost exclusively steamers of less efficiency than comparable British and German vessels. American capital could not trust government and would not become embroiled in shipping in an era when the anti-trust laws made each combination of shipping lines and supporting companies an object of suspicion and possible legal action. The great oil companies owned scores of ocean-going tankers, but found it profitable to register many of them under foreign flags. The Dollar Line and the Munson Line were the only two new lines of any great importance that had come into being since the turn of the century. As soon as war was declared the ships of the belligerents were put to work as transports, ammunition ships and naval auxiliaries, and there were not enough American merchantmen to carry the nation's commerce.

To meet this crisis the government was forced to take strong measures. By the Panama Canal Act (1912) foreign-built merchantmen could be registered under the American flag if they were not over five years old, and on August 18, 1914, Wilson signed an emergency bill which removed the age limit. A flight to the protection of the American flag and neutrality began: within three months over eighty merchantmen of good size, averaging 3,500 gross tons each, were registered in the United States for foreign trade. Most of them came from Britain, but there were many neutral vessels among them.

In August 1914 the wheat crop was being harvested on the western plains, and grain cars jammed the terminals in the port cities until the railroads were forced to put an embargo on further shipments: there were not enough ships to carry the grain to Europe. Thus, even more drastic measures were called for, and a bill was proposed which was designed to create a Shipping Board and to put the government into the shipping business by authorizing the board to buy and operate ships. But critical as the times were, government ownership was at that moment too radical a departure from the conventional concept of the functions of government, and the measure was defeated by Congress in the fall of the year.

In the following months a long overdue piece of legislation was passed: the Seaman's Act. Its genesis was a curious one: when the White Star liner *Titanic* ripped her hull open on an iceberg shortly before midnight on April 14, 1912, and dove into the frigid waters of the North Atlantic a few hours later, carrying 1,513 men, women and children out of the 2,201 aboard to their deaths, the civilized world was shocked and bewildered. *Titanic* was the latest thing in ships—the largest— 46,000 tons—in the world, and she was thought to be unsinkable, with her double-bottom and sixteen watertight compartments. But now, quite suddenly, she was gone, and with her men and women whose lives made news. The headline writers had a field day, pulled out all the stops, and whipped up public interest to a frenzy. Dozens of unlamented merchantmen had preceded her to the depths, but this disaster involved not only crew but passengers, and a shipping line had a moral, if not a legal, responsibility to its passengers to carry them safely across the seas. No similar relation existed between shipping line and crew: the seamen were presumed to know the perils of seafaring, and they were paid for the work they did and the risks they took. And as *Titanic* sank some of her fear-crazed crew had tried to force their way into the life-boats, had attempted even to take the life-belts off the backs of other men. Clearly, seamen were of a low and unprincipled nature.

A direct result of the loss of *Titanic* was an increased interest in maritime safety, and this coincided with the efforts of Andrew Furuseth, head of the International Seamen's Union, to improve working conditions afloat. In 1913 a bill which would have bettered working conditions, and with them safety at sea, was passed by Congress but Taft had shelved it with a pocket veto, being perhaps over-sensitive to the influence of shipping lines whose profits would have been less had the bill become law. But in the winter of 1914–15 seafaring was even less attractive than it had been in peace, and it was both humane and practical to improve conditions. In such circumstances the Seamen's Act became law on March 4, 1915. It was the seamen's Magna Carta, giving them certain minimum rights, such as the division of every 24-hours at sea into two or more watches for deckhands and into three watches for the black gang in the engine rooms. In its safety provisions the Act specified that three-quarters of the crew must be able to understand orders; provision was made for better life-saving equipment, for inspections, for regular lifeboat drills so that passengers and crew would know their boat stations in case of emergency.

Meanwhile the idea of government ownership of merchantmen had not been allowed to die: private capital was still unwilling to take the risk, and yet the nation had to have ships. In the summer of 1916 a ship-purchase bill modeled on the one that had been defeated in 1914, and like it providing for the creation of a Shipping Board, was passed by Congress. Wilson's signature made the bill law in September.

Division of public opinion was sharp about the necessity for the "Shipping Act of 1916," as the legislation was called: the farmers of the mid-West, who had never realized how closely their livelihoods depended on the sea until the war-created shortage of shipping raised ocean freight rates and made it difficult for them to move their harvests, were very much in favor of government ownership and operation of ships: such ownership held out the promise of more profitable farming. The shipping interests, fearful of the osmotic pressure of government competition, thought it would be better if the money were used as subsidies for existing lines. In both groups the national interest was subordinated to the interests of those who formed and supported the competing groups. But the first function of a state is to *be,* to maintain its identity and its freedom, and the government, faced with the possibility of becoming embroiled in the war, was conscious that provision had to be made for a merchant marine, for ships that would be useful as naval auxiliaries, and, incidentally, for government regulation of water-borne commerce. The Shipping Board was empowered to build, buy and charter merchantmen, and on that basis the government was able to provide millions of tons of transports and cargo vessels when they were most needed.

The navy, in the years when Europe was at war and the United States remained neutral, suffered silently. So strict an interpretation of neutrality did Wilson make that he forbade army and navy officers to speak publicly or write for publication about the war. Mahan, retired though he was, and close to death, was effectively muzzled, and the nation as a whole was unable to know what the wise old gentleman thought about the war. This censorship of officers was not as undemocratic as it appeared at first glance: in 1910 Sims had blundered when he made an oration in London's Guildhall, where he and some eight hundred sailors from his command, USS *Minnesota,* were luncheon guests of the Lord Mayor. Then Sims had said: "If the time should ever come when the British Empire is menaced by a European coalition, Great Britain can rely upon the last ship, the last dollar, the last man, and the last drop of blood of her kindred beyond the sea." For a few days the remark caused an international hubbub, until it was made clear that Sims was speaking for himself, and not for the United States Government. So, when Wilson silenced the officers, without in any other way infringing upon their rights as citizens, he was simply taking precautions. If he held such an inflexible view of neutrality, it was because idealists are prone to deal in absolutes.

Wilson's Secretary of the Navy was a newspaper editor from North Carolina, by name Josephus Daniels. His character shone forth in that age as that of a God-fearing liberal, sincere, high-principled and good-natured. He was also innocent of any knowledge of the navy, and in the field of foreign affairs his mentality was parochial. In short, he was an amiable, provincial type who would have made an excellent Bible-salesman. His first approach to naval matters was thoroughly democratic, almost Jeffersonian: he thought that the navy might be useful as a means of educating the godless, underprivileged sailors, and there was an antique graciousness in the idea of turning the instruments of death to some human good. He suggested an arms limitation conference, and this was a sweetly reasonable idea: the difficulty was that Britain and Germany were getting ready to go to war. But he was not utterly naive: when his arms conference was turned down, he refused to abandon the American building program. He simply cut it down to a reasonable size.

Soon the new Secretary found that large northern corporations—and such corporations were then to a southern liberal more maddening than picadors to a bull—were making excessive profits on naval supply contracts. Daniels planned to keep these "monied interests" from battening on the navy by creating government-owned companies and plants to supply the navy with guns, ammunition, coal, oil and armor plate. It is quite possible that it never entered his head that such government-owned and operated plants would provide a large number of jobs for the politicians' friends. In Congress his plans were thwarted, but he began to expand navy yards with a Southerner's regional pride, and these yards were a distinct political asset.

At the same time he undertook these reforms he made an admirable attempt to bring a modicum of democracy into the caste-bound navy, seeking to find ways of making it possible for an enlisted man to become an admiral. This enraged the officers, whose attitude toward enlisted men was firm, paternal and benevolent, partaking of the affection a man has for his dog or his horse. Morale of officers in the navy sagged, and consolation was denied them when Daniels, in July 1914, forbade alcoholic liquors for drinking purposes on warships and in naval establishments. All that could be salvaged from his order were the bursts of Homeric laughter in the wardrooms when word went around that he had been banqueted aboard a warship and that each course had included a wine sauce, the meal being topped off by rum mousse. But if morale among the officers reached a new low, among the enlisted men it improved immensely: they could now hope to enter the Naval Academy by competitive examination, and, more important, it became easier to get out of the service with an honorable discharge than it had ever been before.

Wilson's Assistant Secretary of the Navy was a tall and wealthy young man, Franklin Roosevelt, of New York State. He was then an arrogant product of Groton and Harvard who loved the masses of mankind if not the individual specimens. His dealings were chiefly with labor leaders whose followers worked in the navy yards, and with the less important politicians who wanted a few scraps of patronage. He was an expert handler of small sailboats, and the navy had become his hobby, although not to such an extent that he lost his balanced judgment in regard to naval affairs. In the Navy Department he acquired political experience and a smattering of naval strategy.

The navy itself was slightly dazed by the election that had brought it this triumvirate of rulers: the college professor whose specialty was jurisprudence; the North Carolina editor who wanted to turn the navy into an educational institution; the patrician New Yorker with the small, tight mouth and the pince-nez that would mist in the slightest fog. The New Yorker was young and he could learn, but the other two? It was difficult to try to add to Wilson's immense fund of learning, and Daniels was already settled in a mental groove that detoured any form of violence.

But in Europe the violence was limitless, and spreading across the seas it inevitably touched, tested and finally ruptured the web of isolation Wilson tried so hard to weave about the United States.

The navy was not ready for war: Congress would not authorize, in 1914, more than 51,500 enlisted men, and 70,000 were needed; officers were by law to number no more than 1,898, and 2,658 were needed. The navy had thirty of what the public knew as "battleships," but only twenty-one of these were in commission, and of these, only eight were of the dreadnought type. Britain had twenty modern dreadnoughts, and Germany thirteen. There were 51 American destroyers: Britain had 167, and Germany 130. No help could be expected from Wilson: he had a liberal's early distrust of military men; he had never been to sea, and at this time, when his support might have been enough to improve the navy, it was not forthcoming.

For six months after the war in Europe started Wilson resolutely refused to prepare the navy for war. Then, in February 1915, Germany announced the establishment of a war zone around the British Isles and warned neutral vessels to keep out of the zone if they wanted to avoid being sunk by submarines. Wilson protested, in vain, and on May 1st the SS *Gulflight,* an American vessel, was torpedoed and two American lives were lost. Six days later the 30,000-ton Cunard liner *Lusitania,* en route to Liverpool from New York with 1,959 persons aboard, sighted the Old Head of Kinsale, on the southernmost point of Ireland, at about 2 P.M. Without warning, U-boat Number 20, Leutnant-Kapitan Schweiger commanding, loosed a torpedo from a range of 700 meters and scored a hit on the ship's starboard side, just abaft the bridge. Within 22 minutes *Lusitania* dove bow first beneath the waves, and 1,198 of her passengers and crew were lost, among them 124 Americans. This was sheer murder, and Wilson's reaction was to turn the other cheek: in a speech made three days later at Philadelphia he said: "There is such a thing as a man being too proud to fight," an ideal few Americans could comprehend. Diplomatic notes protesting the sinking without warning of passenger vessels were sent to Germany, but still the sinkings continued. Finally it occurred to Wilson that it would be wise to look to the nation's defenses.

In July, 1915, the third note of protest went to Germany, and at the same time Wilson asked the army and navy to draw up plans for increasing their strength. To the navy this was a pleasant surprise. In the Navy Department the General Board, which had been created in 1900 and was an outgrowth of the Naval War Board of the Spanish-American War, was supposed to advise the Secretary of the Navy. They had offered much advice but Daniels was loath to act upon it. To be *asked* for advice was highly flattering, and the General Board, which was composed of the navy's elder statesmen, the officers who by experience and knowledge were best fitted to know what the navy needed, delivered its recommendations. There should be, opined the Board, a five-year building program which would result in the construction of ten battleships, six battle cruisers, ten scout cruisers, fifty destroyers, nine fleet submarines and fifty-eight coast submarines, as well as thirteen auxiliaries and enough personnel to man existing ships properly. Much to the navy's delight the Administration accepted the Board's recommendations in the first four categories, and even backed an increase of fleet submarines from nine to fifteen, and of coast submarines from fifty-eight to eighty-five.

The debate in Congress lasted for eight months, during which Wilson asked publicly for "the greatest navy in the world" in a speech made at St. Louis on February 3, 1916, but at last, in August 1916 the Naval Act was passed. In its final form it approved the General Board's original recommendations, and, perhaps sensitive of the time already lost in oratorical flights, decreed that the ships be built in three instead of in five years.

While the debate raged Wilson had sent a very stern note to Germany on the continued sinkings of neutral ships, and on May 4th, 1916, Germany agreed to respect neutral vessels and to give warning before sinking merchantmen. This arrangement worked very well, and it looked at the moment as though American neutrality had been enforced and virtue had triumphed. In the fall of 1916 Wilson was re-elected on the theory that he had kept the nation out of war. But on January 31st, 1917, Germany announced the beginning of unrestricted submarine warfare, and specified the course a weekly American vessel would be permitted to follow on its way to Falmouth, England. The vessel was to fly a checkered flag and to be painted like a zebra so that it could be identified by the U-boat captains. The Germans had become over-confident, calculating that their submarines could sink enough British merchantmen to starve the British Isles into surrender before the Americans could be of any practical help. The note informing the United States of this new type of warfare was doubly bitter medicine for Wilson to take: it enraged him by its disregard for the laws of nations, and it proved his technique of armed neutrality a dismal failure. The baser elements among mankind were breaking into the cloistered, isolated democracy, and all his attempts to bring about peace by the use of reason had been made in vain.

The chances of a German victory became notably stronger when a revolt in Russia began on March 17th and thousands of German troops were freed from the northern front for use in the lines in France. That same month five American merchantmen were sunk by submarines. Wilson's house of cards collapsed: the cultured, humane man who abhorred war was face to face with reality. On April 2, 1917, he asked Congress to "formally accept the status of belligerent" which Germany had forced upon the United States. Four days later Congress declared war on Germany, and the navy radio station at Arlington snapped out the message to all ships and stations: "The President has signed act of Congress which declares that a state of war exists between United States and Germany."

Part VII
UNFINISHED DRAMA

[20] *First Act*

The British had been fighting submarines for two years and eight months, and they had learned a good deal about the business. All that they knew was laid before their new ally, whose naval representative in London was Rear-Admiral William Snowden Sims, the enfant terrible of the service. Sims was given the unvarnished truth about Britain's desperate situation: the submarines—and there were 120 of them in commission—were sinking so many merchantmen that Britain would be starved into surrender by autumn unless something could be done to cut down the losses. In February 1917 the Germans had sunk 536,334 gross tons of allied and neutral merchant and fishing vessels; in February the total sunk had risen to 603,440 tons, and in April the rate of losses was still rising, with longer days and fairer weather approaching.

Sims, on April 14th, hurriedly dashed off a cable to the Secretary of the Navy, urging that "maximum number of destroyers be sent, accompanied by small anti-submarine craft." The destroyers were to patrol the seas west and south of Ireland, and the small craft were to act as an inshore patrol. Ten days later a squadron of six destroyers, the eighth destroyer division of the Atlantic Fleet, fully equipped for war, left Boston harbor after nightfall, bound for Queenstown, Ireland. On May 4th, in the morning sunshine, the six slender and graceful four-stackers steamed up the channel to Queenstown amidst the applause of the Irish, who had mysteriously learned that the Americans were due. Commander J. K. Taussig, ranking officer of the little flotilla, together with his five fellow destroyer captains, were invited to dine that evening with the man for whom they were to work, Vice-Admiral Sir Lewis Bayly. The Admiral was waiting for them as they trudged up the hill to Admiralty House in Queenstown, and after a brief exchange of amenities he asked Taussig: "When will you be ready to go to sea?" Taussig replied: "We are ready now, sir." He could not have found a better answer, and Bayly was delighted. These were the kind of men he appreciated, and the type of ship he understood best of all.

The shortage of destroyers in the British Navy was at that time acute: there were two hundred of them in commission, but of these nearly a hundred had to be attached to the Grand Fleet at Scapa Flow in case the German High Seas Fleet attempted another sortie like the one that had ended the year before in the battle of Jutland. The German fleet had its complement of destroyers, and the British could not take the risk of throwing their dreadnoughts and battle-cruisers into a fight without being able to match the Germans ship for ship. The hundred-odd other destroyers remaining available for anti-submarine duty were not enough: they were needed in the English Channel as escorts for the troop and supply ships crossing to France, in the seas around the southern and western shores of Ireland, in the Mediterranean, along the Atlantic coast of France, and as protection for the troopships from Canada. Wherever there were submarines there was a need for destroyers, and this was a situation that had not been foreseen by the Admiralty. The idea of unrestricted submarine warfare was one alien to the British mind: it was unsporting, like shooting a sitting bird, and it was indecent to kill non-combatants in war. For war then had its regulations, sanctified by law and custom, based on honor and observed by honest fighting men. The Germans had brought an inhuman Teutonic lack of decency into the game, and it had taken the British some time to get adjusted to this uncivilized form of warfare.

In European waters the U-boats had forced epochal changes in naval tactics, design and strategy. Early in the war, in the North Sea, a German submarine had fired a torpedo at, and missed, a British cruiser. The cruiser steamed full speed at the submarine, which submerged, and in plain sight under water remained as safe from attack as the cruiser roared overhead as though in another world. Admirals Jellicoe and Madden together heard of this encounter, and Madden suggested that a mine be designed that could be dropped on submarines. The Admiralty was asked to design such a weapon, and the result was the "depth charge," a steel cylinder loaded with explosives, and fired by a simple mechanism that was activated by the pressure of the water. Destroyers could carry twenty or more depth charges in racks on their sterns, and because of their speed, handiness and shallow draft they turned out to be the ideal type of ship to use against the submarines. Originally the destroyers had been developed as a reply to the torpedo-boat, and had been named "torpedo-boat *destroyers*." By 1914 they had all but eliminated the torpedo-boats as a naval type, when suddenly the submarine was found to have replaced the torpedo-boat as their natural enemy.

The British officer who knew most about destroyers and submarines was Lewis Bayly, Commander-in-Chief at Queenstown, and so it was that the Americans learned how to use destroyers against U-boats from an expert. Bayly had started his career at sea in 1872, as a navigating cadet in HMS *Ariadne*, a heavily sparred steam frigate, and he had worked his way up to flag rank in years of sea duty in the Far East, off West Africa, in the Caribbean, Mediterranean, and the waters around the British Isles. He had become an expert in torpedoes and in destroyers early in his career, and when, in July 1915, the Admiralty became worried about the losses caused by U-boats he was asked for suggestions to stop the sinkings. Bayly said that he could stop the submarine campaign if he were given authority covering the western approaches to the British Isles, including the entrance to the British Channel, the coast of Ireland, St. George's Channel, Bristol Channel, and the Irish Sea. He also asked for as many small patrol craft as could be spared, and was promised the steam sloops then nearing completion as anti-submarine vessels.

Before the arrival of the American destroyers Bayly had only thirteen coal-burning, 16-knot sloops, and a few trawlers and drifters to protect the merchantmen bound for the English Channel and Liverpool. In desperation the British had devised "Q-ships" to combat the submarines. These were merchantmen heavily armed with guns mounted behind bulwarks and in false deck-houses, manned by volunteers from the British Navy. To the U-boat commander a Q-ship looked exactly like any other innocent freighter, with her crew's wash flying from the rigging, and her people lounging about the deck in the slovenly manner expected of merchant seamen, bearded, unkempt, their clothes in tatters. When a submarine torpedoed such a ship most of the crew of the stricken vessel would tumble in simulated confusion into the ship's boats and pull frantically away from their ship. Then the submarine would surface, to pick up prisoners as proof of the sinking and to finish off the merchantman with gunfire. The moment the submarine broke water the men who had remained behind on the Q-ship would pull, at their captain's signal, the levers that collapsed the bulwarks and cleared the guns, hoist the battle flag, and begin to pour shells into the submarine's fragile hull. At least twenty Q-ships were in commission in 1917, and they accounted for twelve U-boats.

The British had pondered and rejected the use of the convoy system which had proved itself so valuable in earlier wars against the privateers and armed raiders of the enemy. There were objections to the use of the system as late as May 1917: there were not enough British warships to offer the proper attention to the convoys; it was claimed that the merchantmen could not keep station at sea; the convoys would be restricted to the speed of the slowest merchantmen and there were too many 8-knot freighters; the large assemblage of ships was presumed to make a larger target for the U-boats; much time would be lost in gathering the ships of a convoy together in port—in the eighteenth century some ships had swung at anchor for two months waiting for a convoy to form. But as more and more American destroyers arrived at Queenstown these objections were over-ruled by the necessity of trying anything that held out even a faint hope of cutting down losses to submarines. A test of the convoy system was arranged in May, when 8-knot merchantmen in Gibraltar were formed into a convoy and escorted by British destroyers to England without loss. The merchantmen had kept their position in the convoy perfectly, they had zigged and even zagged, and from the date of their arrival—May 20th, 1917—the convoy system was a proved success. Next day the Admiralty adopted the system for all merchant vessels, and the key to the victory at sea had been identified.

Rapidly the American destroyers were fitted out and ordered overseas to the war zone. With them to Queenstown went their repair-ships, USS *Dixie* and USS *Melville*. So urgent was the need for destroyers that the five ancient coal-burners of the first destroyer division, 430-ton ships stationed at Manila, were ordered to proceed to Gibraltar by way of Suez. Much to the surprise of their officers and men they weathered the typhoons of the South China Sea and reached the Rock in safety.

U.S.S. *Kentucky* (1905)

U. S. NAVAL MESSAGE

NAD NR3   M   XRAFT V ANON P GR 16

Cap T

DESPATCH RECEIVED AT NAVY YARD, PORTSMOUTH, N. H., VIA   RADIO 0612 3 SEPT 1939

ACTION   ALNAV
FROM   ACTING SECNAV

3503 ENGLAND AND FRANCE ARE NOW AT WAR WITH GERMANY
YOU WILL GOVERN YOURSELF ACCORDINGLY 0530

COPIES TO

COMDT.	X	MANAGER	X	SUPPLY OFFICER	X	SAGAMORE-R-13 -	WANDANK S-29
CAPT. OF YARD	X	C.O. PRISON		COMM. OFFICER	X	MAR. BKS. NAVHOSP NAVPRIS	

Naval Message Announcing Outbreak of World War II

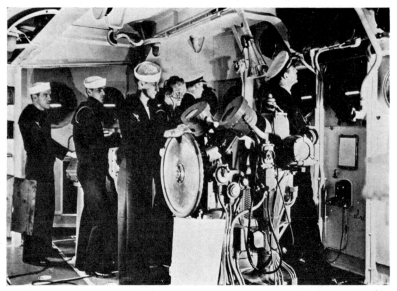

The Bettmann Archive

Navigating Bridge of the U.S.S. *North Carolina* (U.S. Navy Photo)

Their commanding officer was a bright-eyed, if unimaginative, character named Harold Stark. The more modern oil-burning destroyers were sent to Bayly, who worked them relentlessly, fitting them into operations with the British warships and displaying a monolithic impartiality in the assignment of duties.

Bayly made only one distinction between the British and Americans: he did not interfere in the internal discipline of the American ships, leaving Captain Joel Poinsett Pringle, the senior American officer in Queenstown, to worry about that. Bayly made Pringle his U.S. Chief of Staff and in that capacity Pringle's name was entered in the British Navy List, a formality which the British considered a great honor. The destroyers from America were followed by seven L-class submarines, of 450-tons displacement, under the command of Captain Thomas Hart, and they, with their tender, USS *Bushnell,* were stationed at Berehaven, Ireland. Bayly permitted only one American submarine at a time to be at sea, and he made certain that his officers knew the time of the submarine's departure, her general location and the time of her arrival back in port. He had trained his destroyer captains to shoot first and ask questions afterwards and he wanted no victims of mistaken identity on the casualty lists. The American sub-chasers, under Captain A. J. Hepburn, arrived safely, and they were found to be useful when working with the American seaplanes based in Ireland. The sub-chasers had the latest type of listening gear, and the seaplanes could spot the U-boats for the sub-chasers, which would then converge over the indicated position of the submarine, and tracking it by their sound equipment, drop depth charges over the area.

By the fall of 1917 Bayly had over thirty American destroyers under his command, ranging in size from the 750-ton class to the 1,200-ton ships. The latter were 314 feet in length, with a beam of 30 feet, and a speed of 35 knots. They carried depth charges, four 4″ guns, one light antiaircraft gun and four triple torpedo tubes. As a general rule each destroyer was given five days a month to refit in Queenstown; the rest of the time they alternated between six days at sea and two in port. But schedules were highly elastic, and were frequently disrupted by the importance of an incoming convoy or a special alarm. The *Leviathan,* bringing over the first division of American troops, had orders to go to Liverpool, where she could be docked, there being no dock large enough to hold her in the United States, and as she neared the Western Approaches, as Bayly's bailiwick was called, he sent out eight American destroyers under the command of Captain Alfred Johnson to escort the huge ship to port. There were submarines in the area, and if anything happened to *Leviathan,* loaded with soldiers, there would be trouble on the home front in the United States, where mothers were still humming "I didn't raise my boy to be a soldier." *Leviathan* was given three rendezvous points through which she was to pass on her way across the Irish Sea to Liverpool, and the eight destroyers rushed to meet her at the first rendezvous at the appointed time. The destroyers waited two hours for her, in weather of low visibility, and then proceeded to the next rendezvous. Still *Leviathan* did not appear, and the destroyers steamed hard for the third and last appointed area, where they finally sighted the transport and escorted her safely in to Liverpool. An inquiry was made into the cause of the fiasco and it brought to light the reason the destroyers had missed *Leviathan* at two rendezvous: the captain of the transport thought the appointed spots were too dangerous and he had steamed wide of them.

Gradually the losses to submarines were cut down by the use of the convoy system: from 875,023 tons in April, 1917, they dropped to 458,723 in October, and to 277,934 in April of 1918. By that time the American navy had bases scattered from Corfu in the Mediterranean to Scotland, and the importance of Queenstown faded as Brest, France, became the major American base overseas, complete with dirigibles, seaplanes, destroyers, mine-sweepers and repair ships.

The American Navy made one other major contribution to the allied victory: a great mine barrage was laid across the North Sea, between Scotland and Norway, a distance of 250 miles, with the water averaging in depth 100 fathoms. Using the type of mine that exploded on contact, it was estimated that 400,000 mines would be needed to form an effective anti-submarine barrage, and the Americans simplified the problem by inventing a new mine which had a tendril of copper wire. The wire was buoyed close to the surface and any metal object touching it would explode the mine. 100,000 of these new-type mines would be enough to make the barrage and in November, 1917, the idea was given official blessing. Within a year the American minelayers, which were converted coastal steamers from the Eastern seaboard, had put down 56,571 mines, while the British had 13,546 to their credit. How many U-boats were blown up in the North Sea mine barrage no one will ever know: German records show that between forty and fifty U-boats were lost without the cause being certainly known, and of these it is probable that at least six touched the lethal antennae of the North Sea mines. Even more effective was the lowering of the German U-boat crews' morale: not knowing when their ship would set off a mine and they be blown to bits was a mental hazard, and it created such a nervous strain the best work could not be expected of them.

The officer in charge of all the multifarious activities of the American Navy in the war was Admiral William S. Benson, Chief of Naval Operations in the Navy Department. He was a man of considerable tact and tremendous accomplishments in a difficult job. Overseas he had the vain and temperamental Sims to handle, and simply by letting Sims have a long leash he got the best results. At home he had Secretary Daniels to contend with, and he displayed an unswerving loyalty to the North Carolina editor. The naval building program and the expansion of naval personnel were his responsibility, and both were handled with speed and efficiency. 248 destroyers were authorized in 1917 and 1918, and many of them were built at top speed by semi-skilled workmen. Yet there were few that were not well built, and one of the Bath-built ones, the USS *Allen,* fought out of Queenstown in 1918, and twenty-three years later took part in another war. Less than half the destroyers authorized were finished in time to see action in 1918, but 116 sub-chasers, as well as many mine-layers and mine-sweepers were commissioned in time for service overseas. A division of battleships was sent to give the British fleet enough power to make it suicidal for the German fleet to come out of harbor. Three other battleships were based at Bantry, Ireland. American cruisers helped to protect the convoys in the Western Atlantic, escorting them to the point where British and American destroyers based in Europe could relieve them of the duty. Under Benson naval personnel reached a peak of 497,000 officers and men at war's end. Of these some 50,000 were regulars, about 250,000 came from the naval reserves which had been formed in 1916, and the rest were the green hands rushed through the great training stations like those at Great Lakes, Illinois, and Newport, Rhode Island. Daniels' educational program suddenly became a series of courses on how to deal out death to the enemy with guns, mines, depth charges, bombs and torpedoes. Twelve thousand energetic women donned a special type of uniform and went to work in naval establishments: they were called "yeomanettes," and their martial duties were performed with the typewritten forms without which the navy would have been bewildered.

Over 2,000,000 American troops were transported overseas, and among them were 30,000 marines. At first, when the United States entered the war, trained soldiers were scarce, and there were few army divisions fit to move into the front-line trenches. But there were the 5th and 6th Marine regiments and they were formed into the Fourth Marine Brigade. The Brigade—7,500 men—went to France in the summer of 1917 and fought as a part of the 2nd U.S. Army Division. Before the fighting ended the Brigade had need of 14,000 replacements, to whom the veterans imparted the spirit of the corps.

The regular marines in this brigade were unique: they were the nation's best fighting men. Their corps tradition went back to 1775 and included every war and semi-war the United States had ever fought. They were the mercenaries who were likely to know nothing but gunnery and rifles and bayonet-work and two words of Latin: "Semper Fidelis," the motto of their corps. They had served with the navy as gun crews aboard cruisers and battleships, and ashore in China, the Philippines, Cuba and in Latin America wherever there was trouble, for when American lives and property are in danger the marines can be landed without a declaration of war. As fighting men there has never been anything quite in their class, although it is possible that a regiment of youthful West Point graduates, if properly indoctrinated in the amphibious tactics which are marine specialties, could aspire to rival them. Both groups have funds of proud traditions from which their members can draw inspiration.

In France the marines fought magnificently, and with revolver, rifle and machine-gun taught the Germans to have a high regard for the corps. Belleau Wood, Chateau-Thierry, Soissons and Blanc Mont became names to add to the battle honors won at Yorktown, Chapultepec and Antietam. A quarter of a century later an abstracted look came into men's eyes as they talked of the marines before Blanc Mont ridge, in the Champagne country, recalling how the thin line had sloped forward, thinning where the shrapnel and high-explosive and nickel-jacketed bullets hit, but always moving up. A French officer, from the north of France and not given to sudden emotions, saw them advance and said: "But this is inhuman valor—the good God Himself could not stop those men."

The transportation of two million fighting men from the United States to Europe entailed a tremendous effort by the U.S. Shipping Board. The Board, although created in September, 1916, did not settle down to work as an effective agency for months. As though in an ivory tower, the five members of the Board, civilians all, spent the winter of 1916–17 making a survey of shipping line services and ocean freight rates. Then, in the spring of 1917, the wholesale destruction of shipping by submarines forced them to act. The Chairman of the Board, William Denman of California, after consultation with the nation's builders of wooden ships, sent a confidential report to Wilson advising, strangely enough, the construction of wooden ships. From this report grew the Emergency Fleet Corporation, created on April 16th by act of Congress. The fledgling corporation was under the control of the Shipping Board, and Wilson persuaded an army general, George W. Goethals, to head the emergency agency. Goethals, by reason of his work on the Panama Canal, was considered one of the nation's best construction experts, but he could not get along with his fuzzy-minded civilian superior, Chairman Denman, nor did he have any faith in the wooden-ship program. As months went by with much activity but few ship launchings, Goethals remarked that "birds are still nesting in the trees" which were to be used in building wooden ships. Then he resigned. But his criticism was effective, and the shipbuilding program was changed to include the construction of steel vessels. Congress made limitless funds available for the work, which, belatedly begun, was not soon ended.

While contracts were being awarded for the construction of ships and shipyards, the submarines were industriously sinking every ship in sight, and the Shipping Board was hard pressed to find the tonnage needed to transport men and munitions and supplies overseas. Hurriedly the Board purchased 233 vessels from foreign nations, including even some ramshackle Japanese freighters; 87 Dutch merchantmen were taken by right of angary; 97 enemy vessels were seized, including the 54,000-ton, 907 feet long *Leviathan,* which had been built in Germany as the *Vaterland,* and was capable of carrying 12,000 troops at one time. 331 other foreign vessels were chartered, and the Shipping Board requisitioned all the suitable vessels in the American merchant marine, in both foreign and coastal trade, as well as ships under construction, whether for foreign or domestic accounts. So many of the coastal trade's ships were taken that Senator Wesley L. Jones was inspired to proclaim "It is safe to say that the war was really won by our coastwise merchant marine." All these ships, foreign and domestic, with the tonnage made available by Britain (whose ships carried 49 per cent of the American troops overseas), represented the means on hand to project American power into the European battles.

This tonnage was augmented by the efforts of the Emergency Fleet Corporation, which, after a slow start, began to launch in 1918 large numbers of the ships for which it had awarded contracts the year before. This was work in which the whole nation became involved: prefabrication of sections and standardization of design and equipment made it possible for inland plants to supply parts for the ships. Special shipyards were created and at one period 625,000 were employed in the nation's shipyards. As the new ships came into service men were found who could be trained to operate them: close to ten thousand deck and engineering officers were turned out by seventeen navigation and nine engineering training schools operated by the Shipping Board.

A publicity campaign to induce young men to go to sea met with great success when the good wages and comfortable quarters were advertised. The seamen signing on a ship built by the Emergency Fleet Corporation were given steam-heated quarters, with built-in bathtubs and shower baths and good food. The officers were even more regally treated: the captain of a 5,000-ton, war-built freighter had a large cabin with a bathroom attached, in which a porcelain tub and a toilet reposed in gleaming silence. He had, too, an office, with desk, table and armchair, wherein he might transact the ship's business. The chief mate had a cabin and private bath under the bridge; the second and third mates and the engineering officers each had their own cabins, and their duties were lightened by communal lavaboes. Thousands of men from both coastal and inland states harkened to the lures of the publicity campaign and went off to sea, where by comparison with the lot of the foot soldiers in the trenches, dodging shells and bullets and gas attacks, suffering from influenza and trench-feet, they were infinitely better off.

The public was meanwhile being subjected to a barrage of inspirational information about the merchant marine and the shipbuilding program. By posters, motion pictures, news releases and speeches tailored to any length, they were told that "Ships Will Win the War," and that the nation must build a "Bridge of Ships" to Europe. When one yard launched a vessel in thirty-seven days, other yards were spurred to greater efforts to beat the record. The new shipyards, like that at Hog Island on Newark Bay on the Delaware River, were gigantic industrial establishments, designed to make the best use of the new prefabricated techniques then being applied to steel shipbuilding. At Hog Island, once the flow of materials was regulated (after the war was ended), two 7,500-ton ships a week could be completed and delivered. By May, 1919, there were 223 shipyards in the United States, with 1,122 ways—compared with 130 yards with 398 ways in 1917. The very magnitude of the effort heightened the pride of the nation in the merchant marine, and there were few Americans who did not think, in 1919, that the United States had regained its ancient and traditional place as a leading maritime nation. That same year the Shipping Board released its third annual report, and the cost of the "Bridge of Ships" was found to have been, up to June 30th, $3,602,398,733.84.

When the fighting was suspended on November 11, 1918, the yards were filled to capacity with new building, and work on this was not halted. As a result the Shipping Board acquired more and more vessels, reaching a total of 1,792 in 1921. By every possible means—by purchase, charter, requisition, angary and new construction—the Shipping Board had, during the war, increased the amount of shipping available for war use to ten million tons—an increase of nine million tons. When all these ships came home after the war, and after the need for them in world relief and reconstruction had fallen off, they totaled more tonnage than the nation could possibly use. In the fall of 1920 a brief period of depression began which acutely affected the world's merchant marine, and hundreds of American ships went to join those surplus vessels already laid up in quiet backwaters along the coasts of the United States which became known as "ship graveyards." In reality these ships were as useless as spent bullets that had missed their targets, and the billions of dollars they had cost to build were irretrievably lost.

The military victory having been won, Wilson embarked for Europe, pursued by the howls of the opposition, but determined in his strong-minded fashion to write a just and durable peace. The war had been fought "to end wars," and "to make the world safe for democracy": nothing must stand in the way of these noble aims. Unfortunately, in Paris, where the peace conference opened in January, 1919, Wilson had to deal with men who were inured to the inhumanity of man toward his fellowmen. Clemenceau, Lloyd George and Orlando, of France, Britain and Italy, were practical politicians with no trust whatever in paper treaties and little in God. But then Wilson was a product of the most cut-throat school of politics known in the United States—the faculty politics of an American university. The years of dog-eat-dog maneuverings in which he had taken part at Princeton had sharpened his wits, without, however, giving him an appreciation of the abysmal depths to which international power politics can sink. At least, on the campus and in the faculty club, when a professor had an argument which he could sustain on a high moral level he was sure to strike a responsive chord in even the opposition's mind, and he might even, by logic and an appeal to justice, win his point, and with it an increased slice of the college budget for his department or perhaps that coveted chair in ethnic history. But at the conference table in Versailles, Wilson's opponents were not fellow professors, or provincial New Jersey politicians, but men thinking in terms of the life and death of their nations. By contrast the tribal strife on the campus had been unreal: it was as though it had been carried on in a vacuum. Wilson's proposals found no response in their bitter, sceptical minds: Clemenceau, "The Tiger," as he was called, was the product of another, more practical world; specifically, he was a citizen of a nation that had been twice invaded by the Germans. He thought Wilson's faith in mankind was based on a false premise and that it was sheer folly to talk about a "just peace" where Germans were concerned. Idealism of Wilson's sort might be applicable in the United States, with the nearest enemy three thousand miles away across the seas, but in the European cockpit it would be suicidal. Lloyd George and Orlando, like Clemenceau, found the ideas of this latter-day Jeffersonian from the new world a nuisance.

But after more than five months of wrangling the peace treaties were written, and as a part of them there was a pet plan of Wilson's for a League of Nations. The Senate rejected both the treaties and the League; in the presidential campaign of 1920 the issue was taken to the public, and the Republicans won the election by more than six million votes. A joint resolution of Congress ended the war with Germany officially on August 25, 1921, and the nation settled back to enjoy a normal state of isolation, far from the turbulence of Europe.

It is futile to speculate on what would have happened had the United States accepted and become a member of the League of Nations. But the mere proposal of the creation of the League was enough to make men pause and consider, for it was not widely known that the idea of an association of nations banded together to prevent war was as old as recorded history. The world had been changed by the war: there was a republic in Germany; bewhiskered communists were running a new regime in Russia. In Italy a dictatorship was formed; in Britain a labor government came to power. There were newly-created nations in the Balkans and in Central Europe and they rapidly became as nationalistic as any ancient kingdoms. The Austro-Hungarian Empire was at an end. The old order was changing and being constantly challenged: it had brought nothing but tragedy. This inquiry into causes by large numbers of people was then a new spirit, but it was not widespread in the United States, where an expression of it took the curious form of 919,799 votes cast for the Socialist Party's candidate for the Presidency in the elections of 1920.

The Americans were not concerned with the outside world, and this was a normal reaction from war and war-weariness. The United States had less to show for its participation in the war than any other nation, for Wilson had been determined not to profit by the defeat of the Germans. Naval officers had envy of the German islands in the Pacific, but their wishes had no influence and the Marshall, Marianas, Palau and Caroline islands went to Japan, and Nauru, New Guinea and Western Samoa to the British Empire. The United States had nothing to show for its effort, and the Americans, a practical people, were led to believe that they had pulled Europe out of the abyss and had received nothing in return, not even a note of thanks. There was a general belief that America's entry into the war had been a ghastly mistake: all that remained were the 350,000 casualties, the enormous debts and the memory of days when men had been fighting for their country. In a sudden revulsion of sentiment the Americans left Europe to fend for itself, and returned to the business of making a living.

The reaction inevitably affected the navy: there was an almost undignified scramble to get out of uniform, and the process of demobilization went on rapidly, impeded only by the need to transport the soldiers home from Europe and to sweep up the North Sea Mine Barrage. Both tasks were swiftly accomplished, the naval personnel was reduced from a war-time peak of 500,000 to less than 200,000 within a year after the fighting ended. Back to their hearths and homes went nearly 300,000 naval reservists, to enjoy the pleasures of civilian life far from the austerities of naval service. One sailor, in the Queenstown Command, when asked what he planned to do after the war, replied that he was going to take an oar back to the United States and then start marching inland with it until some one asked him "What is that thing you are carrying?" At that point, said the sailor, he would lay down his oar and live for the rest of his life.

[21] *First Intermission*

The new President, Warren G. Harding, took office in March of 1921. He was a newspaper publisher from Ohio who had become a Senator. In the latter capacity he had performed his duties with an undistinguished normalcy which made him the natural choice of a nation surfeited with Wilson's incandescent idealism. Harding was a man of impulsive personal morality, although of staid, almost bishop-like appearance, and it would have been difficult to find anyone who reflected more faithfully the temper of the times. Of himself he wrote: "I am a real idealist and an altruist, handicapped only by an instinct to keep one foot on the ground while I am reaching for the stars." As a native of an inland state, he could not be expected to know anything about the sea and ships, but it was apparent to everyone that there were more warships than the world needed, and that a reduction in taxation would follow naval disarmament. The navy had come out of the war with an enormous amount of new tonnage, and only three vessels of any consequence had been lost—one destroyer and a revenue cutter torpedoed, and an old cruiser sunk by a mine.

Thus, when Senator William Borah of Idaho, a state famed for its potatoes, suggested an arms limitation conference in 1921, Harding took the idea to his heart, for mind he had little, and in November the nine nations with interests in the Pacific sent their delegations to Washington. In the conference hall they were jolted out of their cynicism by the opening speech made by Secretary of State Charles Evans Hughes. Hughes confronted the assembled representatives of the United States, Great Britain, France, Italy, Japan, China, Portugal, Belgium and Holland with a specific plan to limit warships and to prevent further fortifications in the Pacific. To that end, he informed the delegates, the United States was willing to abandon its building program and to scrap 15 ancient battleships, a total reduction of 845,740 tons. The British, who had already junked over half of their fleets, including 38 battleships, were to stop building new battle-cruisers and to scrap 19 additional ships, making the British sacrificial offering at the conference 583,375 tons. Japan was to reduce her actual and projected tonnage by 448,928 tons. At length, among the five leading naval powers, there was agreement on a program which closely followed Hughes' proposals. The ratios of naval tonnages were set at 5–5–3 in capital ships for the United States, Britain and Japan, and at 1.7 for France and Italy. For ten years no capital ships were to be constructed. No accord could be reached on the numbers of submarines, cruisers and destroyers which each navy should have, for every nation, in accordance with its location and wealth and manpower had a different idea of the value of these types of vessels. But it was agreed that new cruisers should not exceed 10,000 tons, and aircraft carriers of over 27,000 tons were not to be built. The ratios were applied to the amount of carrier tonnage a nation could have, the United States and Britain being allowed 135,000 tons each of this type, and Japan 81,000 tons. Hope for a permanent peace was very real in 1921, and on the chance that the disarmament treaty might last it was agreed that the age at which a battleship or aircraft carrier might be replaced by new construction was twenty years. It was agreed among the five powers that no further construction of bases in the Western Pacific would take place. The treaty by which these sensible measures were accomplished was called the Five Power Treaty, and because of it international naval building rivalry was postponed for fifteen years.

Other treaties were produced at the Washington Conference: the Four Power Treaty, by which the United States, Britain, France and Japan agreed to respect each others' possessions in the Pacific ocean and to settle disputes arising from these possessions by joint conference. The Nine Power Treaty was signed, and by its terms all the nations at the conference solemnly swore to protect the national integrity of China. The "Open Door" policy seemed once again to be in effect, and for the moment, provided always that the treaties were honored by the nations that had signed them, the foreign commitments of the United States were in balance with the nation's ability to protect and enforce them.

There were other moments when the Harding administration had a momentary effect on the navy: Edwin Denby, Harding's Navy Secretary, enthusiastically cut naval expenditures and unwisely became involved in a scandal. Soon after becoming Secretary of the Navy Denby transferred the naval oil reserve fields at Elk Hill in California and Teapot Dome in Wyoming to the Department of the Interior, whose Secretary, Albert Fall, promptly leased them to oil companies. Investigation showed that Fall had received bribes totaling $400,000 from the oil companies, and in the ensuing publicity Denby, whose role in the matter had been that of a stupid and innocent bystander, was forced to resign. On August 2, 1923, his spirit broken by the troubles he and his ill-chosen cronies had brought upon him, Harding died, and the Vice-President, Calvin Coolidge, became the nation's Chief Executive.

Coolidge, like Harding, was the product of machine politics, but unlike his predecessor, he was virtuous in the Puritan sense. He had been born in Vermont and had absorbed some of the taciturnity and frugality which are characteristic of the region's inhabitants. He had been graduated from Amherst College, in Massachusetts, where liberalism and hard work and wisps of clerical influence combined to give him a pragmatic, almost stoic, approach to the world's woes. He was not a man to lead a crusade, but rather a routine lawyer become politician, and an honest man. He had had little to do with nautical matters, and the navy expected and received little encouragement from him. Appropriations dwindled in accordance with the regime's policy of economy; more and more warships were decommissioned and laid up in reserve; re-enlistments became increasingly infrequent.

There remained, however, the two great aircraft carriers, the 33,000-ton *Lexington* and *Saratoga,* converted from battle-cruiser hulls. They were all that had been saved of the six 42,500-ton battle-cruisers that had been building when the Washington Conference consigned them to the scrap-heap. Ten light cruisers of 7,500-tons each were completed in 1923–25, and three 2,164-ton submarines joined the fleet in 1926. These, with the five battleships completed from 1920 to 1923, and some of the numerous destroyers that had been completed too late for war service, were the only modern ships in commission. But they formed a tidy little nucleus of some defensive value, and the navy loved them.

Coolidge apparently thought them a necessary evil, and to avoid the need for building more warships in the categories not covered by the

Washington conference, he called a meeting of the naval powers at Geneva, Switzerland, in 1927, to attempt to limit the construction of submarines, cruisers and destroyers. This conference failed dismally. A seamy character, a lobbyist named William B. Shearer, paid by the ship-building interests, ensconced himself in a lush flat in Geneva and began a one-man propaganda campaign against naval limitation. Even had there been no Shearer taking pot-shots at the dove of peace it is likely that the conference would have failed. France and Italy would not send delegates to it, but only unofficial observers. Britain, the United States and Japan bogged down in a dispute over whether cruisers should be built with 6-inch or 8-inch guns. After several months of argument the conference curdled and the delegates returned to their homelands. On this sour note the Coolidge administration's interest in naval matters ended, and there is little reason to doubt that he was happy to be rid of such pesky matters as arms conferences when he retired from public life in March, 1929.

His successor was one Herbert C. Hoover, who had been Secretary of Commerce for eight years, and who during the war had handled relief matters in Europe with great success. He was a mining engineer who had risen to the top in his profession, made a great deal of money and seen much of the world. He was, by religion, a Quaker, and therefore a man of peace. Naval officers detested him, and failed to appreciate the metallic qualities of efficiency and precision that marked his quite mechanical regime.

The failure of the Geneva conference threatened to inaugurate a world-wide naval race, and to avert this useless expenditure of funds Hoover and Ramsay MacDonald, Prime Minister of Britain, called another conference which met at London in early 1930. Meanwhile a peculiar piece of business had been accomplished in the form of a treaty known as the Pact of Paris, or the Kellogg Pact. This pact had been approved by the Senate in January, 1929, and it represented a record of good intentions to which sixty-two nations ultimately subscribed. The nations signing it renounced war "as an instrument of national policy." No one had any great faith in the pact: it was more like a prayer offered by an optimistic agnostic in extremis. It contained no provisions for the punishment of any nation that might suddenly decide to go to war.

But no one thought it strange that an arms conference should be called within a year after a pact that outlawed war had been signed, and the London conference opened with the habitual contentious arguments between France and Italy. The United States and Britain were in substantial agreement before the conference started, due to personal conversations held between Hoover and MacDonald in the fall of 1929. The Japanese ultimately concurred in limiting the size and tonnage of ships in the categories not covered by the Washington conference. The troublesome problem of 6″-gun and 8″-gun cruisers was settled by dividing cruisers into two classes, light and heavy, and total cruiser tonnages were limited. A maximum size was set for submarines and destroyers, and in all three categories ratios were equitably applied. Thus, Japan reached equality in submarines with the United States and Britain; in destroyers the ratios were settled on the basis of 10–10 for the United States and Britain, and 7 for Japan. In battleships the ratio became 15–15–9, with Britain scrapping five capital ships, Japan one, and the United States three. The capital ship building holiday was extended to 1936.

The results of the conference, to which France and Italy did not subscribe, represented solid accomplishments in a time of diminishing national incomes. A sudden deflation in the values of American securities in October and November of 1929 heralded a depression that was to become world-wide. But, in case conditions, whether economic, political or military, changed, the treaty drawn up in London contained an "escape clause" by which a signatory nation might announce that she would no longer be bound by the treaty limitations.

As soon as the London Naval Treaty had been ratified by the Senate the navy had an objective to aim for—a "treaty navy," that is, a navy that would consist of the full numbers of ships in each category that were permitted by the treaty. It was to be years before the ships were built, for as the business depression continued government expenditures, including naval appropriations, were drastically cut. The pay of officers and men was reduced, and the service seemed well on its way to becoming a species of national fire department, with the equipment not to be moved except in emergencies. Under such conditions the efficiency of the fleet deteriorated rapidly: funds were lacking for everything from fleet maneuvers to time-lock safes in which to file the war plans. Only in one way was the depression helpful: the officers and men in the service remained in it, reluctant to leave for civilian life in which millions were unemployed. This cadre of experienced officers and men formed the brains and heart of the service in future expansion.

The navy, in 1932, could look back on twelve years of small appropriations. In but one branch of the art of naval warfare had much progress been made, and that was in aviation. The Navy's General Board, on August 30, 1913, had called attention to the nation's dangerous lack of military and naval aircraft, and had given a résumé of the preparations then being made in Europe for the use of aircraft by armies and navies, as well as recommendations for the establishment of a suitable naval air service for the United States. As a result of the Board's recommendations, a Board of Aeronautics was formed on October 9, 1913, and that Board recommended the establishment of a naval air station and training school at Pensacola, Florida, the purchase of fifty airplanes, one fleet dirigible and two small dirigibles for training purposes. A year later the navy owned only twelve airplanes of various incongruous types, all wholly unfit for serious work by reason of their slow speed and small carrying capacity. In its report to Secretary of the Navy Daniels on November 17, 1914, the General Board urged that Congress be asked to appropriate "at least $5,000,000, to be made available immediately, for the purpose of establishing an efficient air service." The money, of course, was not immediately forthcoming, for Wilson was then passing through his strict neutrality phase, and it was not until 1916 that the funds were appropriated. During the war the naval air patrols gained much practical experience and proved their value as antisubmarine weapons when operated in co-ordination with surface craft.

But with the end of the war a debate on the effectiveness of planes and surface ships took the nation by storm. What was the use of paying for a large battleship if it could be sunk by an inexpensive plane? The public was entranced at the idea of finding an inexpensive way to defend the nation. The verbal strife waxed bitter and confused as tests were made: navy planes dropped bombs on warships anchored off the Atlantic coast, and then army planes repeated the performance on other ships. But the ships proved difficult to hit and to sink, and there was no actual proof that a plane could sink a battleship until the old German *Ostfries-land,* which was used as a guinea-pig, after resisting bombs of 250, 600 and 1,000 pounds, finally succumbed when 1-ton bombs were used. The navy triced up its defenses, pointing out that the German ship was an old, pre-war, obsolete type, and further tests were arranged. Among the target ships in the new tests was a modern battleship, the *Washington,* which had been marked for the junk-yard by the Washington conference. *Washington* proved that battleships of modern design were not easy victims of airplanes, for after taking many hits by bombs and 14″ shells she was still afloat and had to be given the coup de grâce with gunfire from the 14″ rifles of the *Texas.* The tests on *Washington* cast doubt upon the more extreme claims of the air fanatics, who screamed that the experiments had been rigged to favor the battleship, but as far as the navy was concerned valuable lessons were learned, and the effort to create a larger naval aviation service was intensified.

An old collier, the *Langley,* had been converted into an aircraft carrier in 1922 (four years after the British had commissioned HMS *Argus* as a carrier), and *Langley,* with *Lexington* and *Saratoga,* became the ships with which the navy learned the value of aviation. On their flight decks hundreds of officers qualified as carrier pilots. Throughout the 1920s naval aviation profited as plane types increased in efficiency: scout planes were put on cruisers and battleships; torpedo planes made their appearance; the range of patrol planes was extended from year to year. In 1919 a navy plane, the NC-4, had flown across the Atlantic to Portugal by way of the Azores and proved that the ocean was no longer an impassable barrier to aircraft. In 1925 a record of eighteen hundred miles of continuous flying was set in an attempt to fly from the Pacific coast to Hawaii. The technique of aiming a plane as though it were a rifle and releasing the bomb with the target in the sights was invented by marine corps fliers and resulted in dive bombers as a plane type which the armies and navies of the world soon imitated.

The center of research and development of naval aviation in the early years was the Naval Aircraft Factory in the Philadelphia Navy Yard. The Factory had been established in 1917 to manufacture patrol planes and in the spring of 1917 it was turning out two planes a day. At war's end, with a naval aviation force of three thousand pilots and two thousand planes, which soon were obsolete, the Factory turned to the development and testing of the new types of planes, and sought new means of using them. A practical catapult was devised at the Factory, by means of which planes could be launched from cruisers and battleships. Arresting-gear which enabled planes to land safely in the restricted area of a carrier's deck was invented. Experiments made at the Factory in the use of metal alloys in the structure and gondolas of early dirigibles led to the substitution of metal for wood in the construction of planes.

Working with the fleet, lighter-than-air craft were found useful in fleet maneuvers as long-range scouts. The airships *Shenandoah, Los Angeles* (German-built), *Akron* and *Macon* were commissioned, but all of them except *Los Angeles* came to tragic ends, breaking up in storms that placed too great a strain on their huge bulks. *Los Angeles,* small when compared to *Akron's* and *Macon's* 6,500,000 cubic feet of helium gas capacity, continued to operate until 1932, when she was at last decommissioned. She had been superseded in her work as a long-range scout by the new patrol planes that were less expensive to keep up and less of a loss if shot down. The smaller dirigibles continued to be kept in operation, although no one was quite sure how useful they might be in time of war.

Heavier-than-air craft in the naval service were gradually increased in number after 1926, when a naval appropriation bill authorized one thousand planes. By 1930 the thousand planes had been procured. There was never any difficulty in manning these planes: young ensigns just out of the Naval Academy, after a spell of sea duty on surface ships, applied for pilot-training by the hundreds. Only the physically perfect were accepted and put through the training courses at Pensacola. That there were so many officers who aspired to be naval pilots was due to several factors: a pilot received 50 per cent more pay than the surface vessel officer; he cut a dashing figure in the society of the day, when pilots were still rare and daring creatures; and he was, in a very real sense, the captain of his own "ship" when he was piloting a plane. Many of the navy's senior officers applied for flight training and went to Pensacola to win their wings as pilots or aerial observers, for to have wings meant a better chance when the time came for promotion. The young officers called the old ones "Pensacola admirals," and it was not often that an instructor, a junior officer, dared to recommend that one of these high-ranking students be sent home without his wings.

These men and planes, and the high efficiency which they brought to the naval service, to some extent made up for the lack of new shipbuilding which had reduced the American Navy to 101 underage ships totaling 728,050 tons in 1932. That year there were only 9,423 officers and 81,093 men in the navy. Japan admitted having 184 underage ships of 726,000 tons, and so confident was she of her strength and invulnerability that she began a rapid conquest of Manchuria on September 18, 1931, in spite of her obligations under the Nine Power Treaty and the Kellogg Pact. The United States, alone, was in no condition to stop her.

Man's hope that reason will be applied to international affairs is perennial, and even while the Japanese were mopping up and consolidating their conquest in Manchuria, another conference for the limitation and reduction of armaments met at Geneva in February 1932. The head of the American delegation, Hugh Gibson, reminded the delegates that their nations had pledged themselves not to wage aggressive war when they signed the Kellogg Pact, and that therefore weapons which could be used in an aggressive war should be abolished. This was a strange and a confusing approach to the problem, for no one knew exactly which weapons were offensive. But Gibson proposed special restrictions on tanks and heavy mobile guns; a diminution of standing armies; abolition of lethal gases and bacteriological warfare; practical measures to protect civilians from aerial bombs; the abolition of submarines and the extension of the naval treaties made at Washington in 1922 and at London in 1930. At the same time he advocated a reduction in the tonnage each nation had been permitted by the treaties signed at those conferences.

The difficulty in cutting down naval tonnage lay in the fact that the United States Navy was not built up to treaty limits, and therefore any reduction by Britain or Japan would simply be a gift to the Americans, bringing the American Navy closer to combat equality with the others. It was as though an unarmed wayfarer had asked a brigand to throw away his gun and fight on equal terms with bare fists. No sensible robber would for a moment consider such folly. The conference quickly became immersed in whirlpools of arguments: the French valued submarines for their defensive value; the British esteemed them as offensive weapons. For more than two years the conference lingered on before it quietly expired.

In the fourteen years from the Armistice to the fall of 1932 the trials of the navy were miniscule compared to those of the merchant marine. The bright vision of a great merchant marine held out at the end of the war faded swiftly away. It had been expected that the Panama Canal would increase the use of ships in carrying freight from coast to coast, and this increase did develop, but not to the extent predicted. Efforts were made to hold the position won on the seas in the war years: the Merchant Marine Act of 1920 was designed to extend American shipping lines throughout the world by the use of mail subsidies, and by making it easy for American citizens to buy and operate the Shipping Board's surplus vessels. But this act made no provision for the replacement of obsolescent ships, and the merchant marine declined both in quality and quantity. In the post-war depression, when freight rates dropped in 1921 to 30 per cent of the 1919 rates, there were few companies anxious to buy ships of any sort at any price. Later on, when trade revived, much of the cargo-carrying of the world was once again in British hands. There was little attempt at constructive legislation, although the Merchant Marine Act of 1928, besides endorsing the policy of the act of 1920, attempted to protect what shipping remained by making financial help available to shipowners who wanted to modernize their vessels. But in spite of such encouragement the merchant marine continued to decline.

The reasons for this were many and their effect cumulative: it cost more to operate American-flag vessels, whose crews' wages were fixed by law. The higher costs of labor and materials in the United States made ships built in American yards cost approximately 30 per cent more than British-built ships. And when American ships were in service they could find cargo to carry overseas, but seldom could they fill their holds for the return trip, for foreign goods were almost invariably carried in ships of the nation that produced them or in ships of the nation that had traditionally and by custom and usage carried them. Immigration restrictions limited one formerly good source of revenue; high tariff helped to cut down ocean-borne commerce. Private capital was not willing to enter such a precarious business, for not only could more profits be made in other enterprises, but also there remained a wholesome fear of anti-trust legislation, to which the shipping interests were particularly sensitive.

The modern plumbing in American vessels was not enough to attract American citizens to life on the sea, which was still a dog's life, with engine room temperatures running well above a hundred degrees and dehydrating the engine room force, and the members of the deck department often inadequately protected from the weather simply because they could not afford to buy warm clothes. Ashore, a seaman was still a strange and alien being, presumed to have at least one venereal disease, and when drunk given to veering alarmingly in his walk.

From a trifle more than 17,000,000 tons in 1921, the merchant marine dwindled to 13,500,000 tons in 1932, including foreign, coastal and lake shipping. The most obvious reason for the decline, and the reason least possible to evaluate in terms of its effect, was the public's apathy for the sea, and the politicians' faithful reflection of this attitude. The century-old pattern repeated itself: Americans did not take to the sea when there was a chance to make a fortune ashore, and when depression ashore ended that chance, there were few ships sailing. It was common in 1932 to find men with engineers' tickets signing on as oilers and wipers; others, qualified as third mates, were happy to find berths as quartermasters or able-bodied seamen.

The American people in the autumn of 1932 were in no mood to be concerned with the world beyond the seas. There were troubles enough at home: the depression had shown no signs of abating, and nearly twelve million people were unemployed. Against a dolorous background of poverty and bitterness the presidential elections were held. Hoover, a victim of circumstances beyond his control, served as a puppet of forces only dimly understood. He went about the business of campaigning honestly, without making the florid promises expected of politicians, marshaling his facts like so many samples of gold-bearing ore. His opponent, Franklin Roosevelt, was a more complex character. After the First World War, in which he acquired a taste for government service as Wilson's Assistant Secretary of the Navy, Roosevelt had campaigned unsuccessfully for the Vice-Presidency. In August of 1921, while sailing a small boat off the Maine coast near Campobello, New Brunswick, he had seen a forest fire ashore and had beached his craft to help fight the flames. Back on Campobello Island, he had taken a swim, and in the next few days he became increasingly ill. Too late the sickness was diagnosed as infantile paralysis: he was paralyzed from the waist down. He was then thirty-nine years old, and a less courageous man would have been content to congratulate himself on merely being alive. Roosevelt, drawing on his innermost mental and physical resources, set about recovering. During the next seven years, slowly and painfully he regained a partial use of his legs. What happened to his mind during those years of enforced physical idleness is not yet clear and must await a definitive biography by some psychiatrist who is endowed with the quality of mercy. Those who were close to him during this period noted that the ordeal of his illness had humbled his once arrogant spirit, that he read much history and biography, that his thinking on social welfare matters became deeper and broader. In 1928 he had recovered sufficiently to win the election for Governor of New York State, an office which he held until he was nominated by the Democrats in 1932 as their candidate for the Presidency.

During the campaign, as a means of proving his vitality, Roosevelt traveled seventeen thousand miles across the nation, speaking frequently, displaying an infectious enthusiasm and unbounded optimism. Radio broadcasting, which in the elections of 1928 had played a large part, was even more widely used by the politicians of both parties in 1932. And Roosevelt's voice, a flexible, resonant admixture of Groton and Harvard accents, was admirably adapted to the medium. Hoover's flat tones were, by contrast, lacking in color and conviction. In the final count of ballots Hoover had 15,761,841 votes and Roosevelt 22,821,857.

The nation had the impression that the President-elect was a man who would master events, rather than by them be mastered. Hope entered the downcast hearts of naval officers, for Roosevelt was a man who knew and understood their problems. When he took the oath of office in March, 1933, the world was in a bodeful state, and the life-noises of the earth's peoples were full of strident, discordant sounds.

In Russia Joseph Stalin had entrenched himself in power in the Kremlin and was imposing his concept of communism on the peasants; in Italy Benito Mussolini had persuaded the Italians that their mortal enemy was communism and that the blood of the Roman legionnaires still ran in their veins; in Japan a military clique had proved, in Manchuria, that aggression still paid; in Germany a psychotic Austrian named Adolf Hitler had become head of the government. In each of these nations the rulers believed that they were acting in the best interests of their subjects, and in each an indigenous secret police enforced this belief. But no matter how nationalistic their motives, their objectives conflicted. Thus Russia desired to extend the dubious blessings of the communist state to the rest of the world, by invisible maneuvers rather than by armed force; Germany was anxious to demonstrate, by armed force if need be, that the Germans were a master race destined to rule the world; Japan yearned for, and was willing to fight to obtain, a Far Eastern empire, as a prelude to world conquest; Italy aspired to make the Mediterranean an Italian lake and to recreate a modern Roman Empire along its shores. Four worlds would have been necessary for the fulfillment of the ambitions of these powers, and at the time there was available only one, of which large areas were already controlled by Britain, France, China and the United States, all quite satisfied with the existing territorial divisions of the world. The depression and the unrest that accompanied it had become world-wide: nourished by that unrest, the new totalitarian forms of government battened. The nations whose governments were based on the principles of Anglo-Saxon democracy, being pacifist by nature, struggled in a net woven of economic woes and sought to cure their troubles by the use of reason rather than armed might. But, since they had possessions to protect, they assumed postures of passive self-defense; China tried to strengthen her army and air force; France sought safety behind the fixed fortifications of the Maginot Line, a modern version of the Chinese Wall; Britain put her faith in her fleet and in the twenty miles of salt water that separates the British Isles from the continent of Europe. The United States, with three thousand miles of water as a barrier, became involved in a new experiment in government, called the "New Deal," which had a tremendous effect on the American Navy and merchant marine.

An aspect of the "New Deal," which was paternalistic in nature, was the appropriation of huge funds to be spent on public works, on the theory that such spending would revive the national economy. The President was given wide powers in the allocation of these funds, and whenever it was not politically inconvenient Franklin Roosevelt made portions of the moneys available to the navy. Soon after he took office the naval renaissance began: in June 1933, $238,000,000 from the National Recovery Act appropriations were allocated to improve and increase the navy. With these funds construction of thirty-two warships was made possible.

These ships were the first of the "new navy," and they represented, in the efficiency of their propulsion machinery, a clean break with engineering design and shipbuilding tradition. Formerly shipbuilding firms had built both the ships and their machinery to navy specifications and delivered the finished item to the navy. But the Bureau of Engineering, under Admiral S. M. Robinson, had by 1933 made great progress in the development of experimental "high pressure high temperature steam" propulsion equipment. By means of this equipment steam was generated and superheated so that each ton of fuel delivered more energy than could be obtained from the conventional marine engineering plant. This was something new in the naval world of that era, although such installations were common ashore. The new high pressure and high temperature steam was first tried out in destroyers of the *Porter* class, commissioned in 1936, but in these ships the machinery which used the steam was not adequate, for it was patterned after British naval designs best suited for steam of lower pressures. The apparent need was to build new turbines, gears and special machinery for the new steam pressures, but when the navy approached the shipyards to obtain this equipment they encountered much inertia, for the yards were reluctant to modernize their machinery production practices. As a result the navy contracted for machinery capable of handling the high pressure steam with inland corporations which were willing and able to deliver the proper equipment. From then on, as the new machinery began to come to the shipyards, the yards themselves became hull-building and assembly plants for warships whose machinery had been built elsewhere. This revolution in shipbuilding practice was not achieved without much verbal strife within the navy itself, and much controversy between the navy and the shipyards and the navy and ship machinery manufacturers. In May 1935 Rear Admiral Harold G. Bowen became Chief of the Bureau of Engineering and he continued Robinson's struggle in behalf of the new propulsion equipment. As the new machinery gradually proved its value in terms of fuel, weight and space saved, which could be used to obtain greater range and armament, the opposition evaporated, and the navy's warships became, by a conservative estimate, 25 per cent more efficient than those of any other navy.

In 1934 the Vinson-Trammell Act was passed, having for its objective the creation of a treaty-strength navy by 1941 at the latest. This was a well-reasoned piece of legislation: building was planned on an orderly basis, without any sudden spasm of activity, in every class of combat ship. In this building program the President took a keen interest: a less intelligent man might have resorted to an austere isolationism and washed his hands of the bloody involvements of Europe and Asia. But as early as May 31st, 1934 Roosevelt gave evidence that his sympathies were with Britain in the support of world peace. That month Admiral Sir Lewis Bayly made a trip to the United States to dedicate a plaque in the Naval Academy chapel to his war-time Chief of Staff, Joel Pringle. After the rituals were completed Bayly was invited by Roosevelt to see a naval review off New York from the flagship, USS *Indianapolis*. When the fleet had steamed by, on the way back to New York, Roosevelt dictated a message to Bayly to give to King George V, saying: "No matter what people may say, nor what they may do; our two countries must keep together, and work together, for the peace of the world." This message Bayly delivered to the King, and the Admiralty was duly informed of its contents.

Roosevelt was much too agile a politician to have made such a statement publicly, for within the United States a strong spirit of isolationism was abroad in the land. Confirming the then general belief that American participation in the First World War had been a mistake, a Senate investigating committee in 1934 disclosed that munitions firms and bankers had made tremendous profits from the war, and (so reasoned the politicians in search of a scapegoat) if the capitalists made money in war, they must have been in favor of it. The public was easily gulled by such specious reasoning, and the pacifist ranks were enlarged by the addition of numerous isolationists. Their arguments were further strengthened by the failure of foreign nations to pay their war debts to the United States. From this failure, and the determination that it should not happen again, grew the Johnson Act of 1934, which barred nations in default on their war debts from borrowing money in the United States. This Act was followed, on August 31, 1935, by the Neutrality Act, which provided that when war broke out abroad "the President shall proclaim such fact, and it shall thereafter be unlawful to export arms, ammunition, or implements of war" from the United States to the belligerent nations. Furthermore, the Neutrality Act regulated by licenses the export of munitions to any country; forbade the use of American vessels as carriers of armaments to belligerent states, and restricted travel by American citizens on vessels of belligerent nations. The Act, in short, was an abdication of the basic principle of "freedom of the seas" for all American vessels; it was passive defense become slumberous, the sleeping puppy curled up in a ball. In the Navy Department wry comments were made, to the effect that now there would be no use for a navy—the coast artillery could defend the nation, American rights stopped at the three-mile limit. Roosevelt approved the legislation, but not without a few warning words. He said that the arms embargo provisions "might drag us into war instead of keeping us out"; that no one could anticipate the future. He signed the Act because, as he said, "it was intended as an expression of the fixed desire of the Government and the people of the United States to avoid any action which might involve us in war." Thus isolationism came to full flower: the nation had made it clear that the United States would not fight unless attacked, and since it was unthinkable that any nation would be foolhardy enough to want to fight the United States, the country retired behind this mental Maginot Line and the lachrymal events in Europe and Asia seemed more than ever to be routine matters in the alien life of a distant world. In Japan, Germany and Italy it may be presumed that the naval and military strategists breathed sighs of relief when the Neutrality Act became law: now they could lay their plans and count on a long period of American impotence in world power politics.

The London Naval Treaty was due to expire in 1936, and there was not much expectation that an extension of it could be made: Japan had withdrawn from the League of Nations, and become a nation looked at with disgust by honest sailormen, for she was suspected of cheating on the tonnage limitations of her cruisers and destroyers. Nevertheless the second London Naval Conference convened in December 1935. After five weeks of debate the Japanese delegation withdrew. The United States, Britain and France managed to agree on limiting the size and armament of various types of warcraft, if not on the number of each type that could be built. This parley, the last pre-war arms limitation conference attended by American officers, had an air of unreality about it: there were so many escape clauses in the final document that the treaty was nearly meaningless.

Various nations were making their arrangements for war on a purely amoral, realistic basis: Japan had taken the North China provinces of Jehol and Chahar in 1933; the Italians had invaded Ethiopia in 1935 and made use of poison gas against the enemy; Germany had repudiated the restrictions on her armed forces embodied in the Versailles peace treaties in March 1935 and had begun to re-arm openly; a month later Germany announced that she was starting to build submarines once more, and the British, forsaking France, signed a naval treaty with the Germans by which the Germans agreed to limit their surface fleet to 35 per cent of Britain's tonnage in surface vessels provided they could build as many submarines as Britain had. This was pure power politics and it gave added strength to the American isolationists, who were usually men of such high principle that they found reality repugnant. In the spring of 1936 the Germans marched into the Rhineland, which had been demilitarized, and once again German troops faced French troops in an armed truce. In July a civil war began in Spain, with the Russians supporting the legally-elected government, and the Germans and Italians supporting the rebels under a general named Francisco Franco. In this struggle the United States assumed an attitude of rigorous neutrality. An American heavy cruiser, the USS *Quincy,* was ordered to Gibraltar and to Spanish ports to evacuate American citizens, but beyond that no concrete effort was made that interfered with the unbridled ferocity of the war. In November Japan and Germany signed the Anti-Comintern Pact, which led the democracies to believe that Soviet Russia was the chief enemy of Italy, Germany and Japan. At the time, Joachim von Ribbentrop, the German Foreign Minister, said: "Japan will not suffer the expansion of Bolshevism in Eastern Asia; Germany is a bulwark against this pestilence in the heart of Europe. Finally, Italy will carry the anti-Bolshevik banner in the South."

Meanwhile Roosevelt had turned his attention to the condition of the American merchant marine. He had been fully informed of the slovenly state into which the merchant fleet had fallen by reports from the Post Office Department and the Department of Commerce: the war-built freighters had been outmoded by modern foreign vessels; only a few fast passenger ships had been built because of the Merchant Marine Act of 1928. In the spring of 1935 he asked Congress to remedy the situation with new legislation. For the following year there was great activity in the halls of Congress as the merchant marine's future was being determined. Some congressmen wanted government ownership of the merchant fleet; other wanted subsidies with government control; some wanted no subsidies of any sort; a few favored subsidies without government control. In the end a compromise bill was passed. Roosevelt signed it on June 29th, 1936. This bill, which became known as the "Merchant Marine Act of 1936," contained the following statement of policy: "Section 101. It is necessary for the national defense and development of its foreign and domestic commerce that the United States shall have a merchant marine (a) sufficient to carry its domestic water-borne commerce and a substantial portion of the water-borne export and import foreign commerce of the United States and to provide shipping service on all routes essential for maintaining the flow of such domestic and foreign water-borne commerce at all times, (b) capable of serving as a naval and military auxiliary in time of war or national emergency, (c) owned and operated under the United States flag by citizens of the United States in so far as may be practicable, and (d) composed of the best-equipped, safest, and most suitable types of vessels, constructed in the United States and manned with a trained and efficient citizen personnel. It is hereby declared to be the policy of the United States to foster the development and encourage the maintenance of such a merchant marine."

To carry out this policy the bill provided for the creation of a five-man Maritime Commission, which replaced the Shipping Board. The ocean-mail contracts, which in effect were disguised subsidies, were to be replaced by direct subsidies in the form of payments for the difference between the cost of operating American and foreign vessels; the same principle applied to the building of new ships—the Maritime Commission was ready to pay the difference between the cost of building a ship in an American yard and in a foreign yard. These construction subsidies were not to exceed one half of the total cost of the vessel, and the vessel had to be of a type which would be useful in time of war. Since private capital had found no reason to be attracted to the shipping industry in the 1930s, the financial arrangements of the Act were lenient: if a company wanted to obtain a new ship and was willing to pay one-fourth of the construction cost, the Maritime Commission would advance the rest of the funds needed, contract for the building of the ship, taking the company's one-fourth of the cost as a down payment and spreading the rest of the payments over a period of twenty years, with interest at $3\frac{1}{2}$ per cent annually. The Act provided that officers and men on subsidized cargo vessels must be citizens of the United States, and that steps be taken to develop a force of trained officers and seamen for the merchant fleet. In charge of the program Roosevelt placed Joseph Kennedy, a flagrantly Irish Bostonian capitalist.

Kennedy proved to be a competent Chairman, and by the fall of 1937 blueprints had been prepared for standard types of cargo-carriers (the "C-1," the "C-2," and "C-3"), which had the approval of the Navy Department, whose naval architects had had a hand in the designs. Variations on these basic designs were permitted, but each vessel had to meet speed and structural specifications set by the Navy Department.

The Maritime Commission had evolved a long-range program of shipbuilding which called for the construction of five hundred modern ships within ten years. It was hoped that private capital would, because of the generous nature of the financial provisions of the Act, furnish the intiative in ordering these vessels through the Commission. But the depression was still in effect; millions were still not gainfully employed; world trade had not revived to such an extent that capital was willing to risk money in shipping; nor was the political atmosphere of the time conducive to government and capital working together. In 1938 it was apparent that if the merchant fleet was to be revived the government would have to do the job. Otherwise there would not be enough ships for the national defense. Fortunately the Act provided that if shipping companies did not order enough vessels to provide a modern merchant marine, the Maritime Commission might build ships for government ownership.

In February 1938, Rear-Admiral Emory Scott Land became the Maritime Commission's Chairman, Joseph Kennedy having been appointed Ambassador to the Court of St. James. Land was an expert on ship construction, aged fifty-nine, an energetic and profane man. Kennedy had left the Commission after setting two major aims for it: to get new ships and to rationalize the use of ships on American routes. Land placed the emphasis on new construction, for at that time, although the United States had 1,420 ships of 8,200,000 gross tons, about 90 per cent of them had been launched in 1918–21, and only 38 of them were less than 10 years old.

And in the fall of 1938 the Commission obtained permission from Roosevelt to begin building ships for its own account. There were then only 20 C-2s under construction; and the Maritime Commission was authorized to start at once a building program for 150 freighters. They were to be built within three years, and they were all of simplified and standardized designs, C-1s, C-2s, C-3s, and tankers—powered by either diesel or steam, and capable of carrying large amounts of cargo, either for peace or for war. All of them were convertible for use as naval auxiliaries. By the end of 1938 the macabre pattern of the tapestry being woven in the Foreign Offices of Europe and Asia was becoming apparent to everyone.

On July 7th, 1937, Japan had again attacked in China, this time intent on total conquest; on December 12th an American gunboat on the Yangtse, the USS Panay, was attacked and sunk by Japanese planes. The United States demanded and received an apology and full restitution for the damage done. In the same month Nanking fell and the Japanese troops looted and raped and slaughtered in a frenzy of primitive blood-lust that surpassed in cruelty even Franco's Moors' behavior. Germany had meanwhile been re-arming rapidly, and in March 1938

· 438 ·

German troops took over Austria, without having to fight for it; two months later the American Congress enacted the Twenty-Percent Naval Expansion Act, authorizing the construction of 46 warships and raising the authorized naval tonnage to 1,557,000 displacement tons. The Expansion Act provided, too, for twenty-six naval auxiliaries. In previous administrations authorizations of this nature had been taken as evidence of intentions, as policy, and they were frequently left as "paper ships," for money was not appropriated to build such ships as had been authorized. In this instance most of the money was forthcoming: enough of it to fill the slipways of government and private yards with new construction for the navy. In the fall of 1938 the Germans threatened Czechoslovakia with war unless the Czechoslovaks should cede their Sudetenland, inhabited by people of German ancestry but Czechoslovakian citizenship, to Germany. Czechoslovakia had military treaties of alliance with Britain, France and Russia, not one of which was willing to go to war for a treaty. The result was the Munich pact, by which Hitler agreed to refrain from further territorial demands if only he could have the Sudetenland. To this Britain and France agreed, (Russia not being present at Munich), and Czechoslovakia lost her most highly fortified region to the Germans. In the next March the Germans marched into the Czechoslovakian provinces of Bohemia and Moravia. Hitler entered Prague, ancient and lovely capital of Bohemia, as a conqueror in an armored car. That same month Madrid fell to Franco; and when in April Italy invaded Albania it was only a minor incident in the terrestrial tragedy. In May Hitler and Mussolini formed a military alliance, called "The Axis." On August 19th the Russians and the Germans concluded a trade agreement, and four days later they signed a non-aggression pact. By these two treaties, involving the exchange of Russian raw materials for German armaments, and various supplementary provisions of mutual benefit, Hitler secured his eastern boundary from attack and was left free to go to war. For the moment it looked as though evil had everywhere been victorious, for these events were all body blows at human liberty and human happiness. Throughout the summer of 1939 the Germans had been threatening Poland: on September 1st, German troops invaded Poland, and the world was at war again, for this invasion could not be localized: Britain and France had guaranteed the independence of Poland—and they would rather fight than suffer the shame of another Munich. They declared war on Germany.

The President's first move was to proclaim on September 8th that a state of limited emergency existed: the chief effect of this proclamation on the navy was to raise the strength of authorized enlisted personnel from 131,485 to 191,000 men, and to permit the recall to active duty of naval personnel on the reserve and retired lists. Minor blessings incurred by the state of limited emergency included a simplification of legal formalities in the procurement of land, materials and equipment, and, ultimately, the elimination of competitive bidding. And, if the President so desired, he could turn the Coast Guard over to the avuncular jurisdiction of the navy.

In those years from 1933 to the invasion of Poland, the American people played little part in European and Asian affairs. But slowly, against the somber backdrop of war in China, in Ethiopia, in Spain, in Albania, and the bloodless victories of Germany in Austria and Czechoslovakia, the United States moved toward an improved defensive position, not only in merchant marine matters, but in numbers of warships built and building. On February 28, 1933, the United States Navy consisted of 15 first line battleships; 3 aircraft carriers and 1 under construction; 20 cruisers and 5 under construction; 222 destroyers and 8 under construction; 82 submarines and 2 under construction. This was a total of 342 ships, with 16 building; in tonnage—1,000,270 tons built and 78,060 tons building. On July 1st, 1939, there were 15 battleships and 8 building; 5 carriers and 2 building; 37 cruisers and 4 building; 221 destroyers and 43 building (54 had been built in 1934–39, many old ones stricken from the Navy List); 94 submarines and 20 building. The totals: 373 vessels built, 77 building; the tonnages—1,277,290 built, 454,880 building. Thus, at the outbreak of war, the navy had increased by 25 per cent over its 1933 tonnage: qualitatively the improvement was even greater, for the new ships were faster, more heavily gunned, and of greater range than the old vessels. There had also been an attempt to improve the bases from which the warships and naval planes operated.

Congress had ordered the Navy Department to make a report on what action was desirable in regard to building and improving naval bases, and the naval board had turned in its report in January 1939. It recommended 23 new or expanded bases in the Pacific, with the island of Guam as a key base. In this way American naval power would have been extended 3,300 miles westward from Hawaii, and a Japanese naval spokesman quickly pointed out that "It would be placing a gun at a neighbor's door." There was much debate in Congress on this point. A highly fortified Guam would have cost a great deal of money; would have perhaps precipitated a Japanese attack. On January 19, 1939, Roosevelt let it be known by means of his press secretary, Steve Early, that he did not support the idea of fortifying Guam—that he was opposed to the idea—but that he approved deepening the harbor on the island so that seaplanes could land safely and supply ships enter the harbor with less trouble. In due time Chairman Vinson of the House Naval Affairs Committee drafted a bill that started improvements on eleven other naval and air bases in the Atlantic and Pacific which had been given priority in the Naval Board's report.

Meanwhile reports of a curious experiment which had been held for three months beginning in December 1938 on board the USS *New York* were arousing excited interest in the Navy Department. The *New York* had been equipped with a set of radar,* made by the Naval Research Laboratory, and early in 1939 the set was given thorough tests at sea. When it became apparent that the device could locate ships in the night, when they would otherwise have remained invisible, the officer commanding the ships involved, Vice-Admiral Alfred W. Johnson, sent an enthusiastic report to Washington. As a veteran of many stormy nights on convoy duty out of Queenstown in 1917–18 he was quick to see the potential value of the invention, whose origin in the United States may be traced back to 1922.

That year two civilian scientists employed by the navy, a physicist named Dr. Albert Hoyt Taylor, and his associate, Leo Clifford Young, were experimenting with short wave radio in Washington, transmitting radio signals across the Anacostia River. During the experiments they noticed that vessels moving on the river distorted their signals, and as a result they sent a report to the Navy Department on September 27, 1922, suggesting that with radio detection equipment destroyers several

* The word is a Navy abbreviation for "radio detection and ranging" equipment.

miles apart could detect any enemy vessel between them, regardless of smoke screens, fog, or darkness. The navy was not impressed with this discovery in 1922, but providentially, on July 2, 1923, the Naval Research Laboratory, on the Potomac River in Washington, District of Columbia, was formally opened. Funds for the Laboratory had been appropriated in 1916, but war had postponed its establishment. Its mission was: "To increase the safety, reliability, and efficiency of the Fleet by application of scientific research and laboratory experimentation on naval problems." In this laboratory Dr. Taylor was appointed Superintendent of the Radio Division, and was thus in a position to continue his experiments with short wave radio. In 1925 the Laboratory developed radio transmitting equipment which could send out pulses of radio energy: by beaming the pulses against the Kennelly-Heaviside layer that blankets the earth's atmosphere, and by measuring the time the reflected pulse took to return, the height of the layer could be determined. This was the basic principle upon which radar came to be gradually developed.

In June, 1930, while Taylor and Young, assisted by L. A. Hyland, were working on a high-frequency landing system for aircraft, Hyland noticed that planes passing over the area covered by the transmitter and the receiver were reflecting the radio waves. Military aviation developments had by that time made detection of aircraft a major problem, and on November 5, 1930 a report by Dr. Taylor called "Radio Echo Signals from Moving Objects" was submitted to the Navy Bureau of Engineering. Two and a half months later the Bureau ordered the Laboratory: "Investigate use of radio to detect the presence of enemy vessels and aircraft. Special emphasis is placed on the confidential nature of this problem." Throughout 1931 and 1932 the idea was developed, and when radio pulses instead of regular radio waves were used, after Young recollected the Kennelly-Heaviside experiments, modern radar was born. Other scientists at the Naval Research Laboratory were assigned to help Young, among them Dr. Robert M. Page, and Robert C. Guthrie. At this time Captain Harold Gardner Bowen, of the Bureau of Engineering, became convinced of the importance of the work, and he persuaded Congress to back the experiments. In 1935 the Naval Appropriations Committee allotted $100,000 to the Laboratory for the development of radar. In April 1937 the USS *Leary*, a four-stack destroyer, was equipped with a test set with which she was able to detect aircraft some forty miles away. Meanwhile Admiral William D. Leahy, Chief of Naval Operations, with Charles Edison, Assistant Secretary of the Navy, had seen radar demonstrated at the Laboratory, and from then on the invention was given full official support. Work began on a practical shipboard model, which was installed on the USS *New York* in December 1938. When that set had proved its value, and been further improved, a contract was awarded, in October 1939, to a commercial company for six sets of radar. Throughout this period of trial and error the Laboratory kept the U.S. Army Signal Corps fully informed of progress made in developing the new detection equipment.

On the diplomatic front the administration had been preparing the ground in the Western Hemisphere for a united stand against aggression in the new world by any European power. Roosevelt had initiated a "good neighbor" policy in 1933 and that had been the guiding rule of the nation's diplomacy in Central and South America. Successive conferences—at Montevideo in 1933, at Buenos Aires in 1936, and at Lima in 1938 had resulted in the formation of an entente cordiale between the twenty-one republics of the Western Hemisphere. In September 1939, soon after the invasion of Poland, the Foreign Ministers of the twenty-one American republics met in Panama to consider what measures of self-protection they could take to insulate themselves from the impact of war in Europe. From this conference came, on October 2nd, the Declaration of Panama, which ruled that the waters adjacent to the North and South American republics were "of inherent right" free from hostile acts by warring nations.

Germany and Italy were notified of this resolution on October 3rd and informed that by it the twenty-one American republics had decided that "no hostile acts shall be performed by participants in the war" within an area of sea that blanketed the Western Hemisphere as far north as Canada with a three hundred mile wide "neutrality zone." By this same agreement, which the United States proposed and which the other republics accepted, provision was made for a patrol of the forbidden area by warships and planes of the American republics, operating either in concert or separately. To make the patrol effective the navy began to recommission some of its 111 laid-up World War I destroyers.

Still in effect in the United States was the Neutrality Act of 1935. It had been amended in 1936 and 1937, but the arms embargo provision remained in the law and when Germany invaded Poland, France and Britain were no longer able to take delivery of munitions made in the United States. Orders for planes, machine tools, artillery and shells had been placed in American factories when France and Britain were neutral: now that they were suddenly become belligerents the law forbade their obtaining these goods. Not until November 4th, 1939 did Congress repeal the arms embargo provision, and then with the stipulation that belligerent France and Britain must pay cash for the products they had ordered, and must carry them to Europe in their own vessels. New sections to the Neutrality Act were passed which prohibited American merchantmen in foreign trade from being armed and forbade their entry into belligerent ports. The theory was that if a ship was not armed it could not fight, and if it kept away from other people who were fighting, it would necessarily avoid getting mixed up in the dispute. The Department of State thoughtfully issued a map for publication, explaining the areas within which American ships could not proceed and outlining the belligerent coasts with which they could not trade. Submarines of the warring powers were excluded from the territorial waters of the United States, and American citizens were barred from the combat zones.

While these steps were being taken to protect the Western Hemisphere from the war in Europe the German army had knifed through Poland in a new type of warfare called "blitzkrieg," or "lightning war," in which the tactics of planes and tanks and motorized infantry were synchronized. The Poles' conventional type of army was overwhelmed in a few weeks. On September 27th Warsaw surrendered; two days later Russia and Germany partitioned the defeated nation. On November 30th Russia invaded Finland: the Finns held off their giant enemy for months, fighting them to a standstill until the weight of Russian numbers and the Russian artillery made a negotiated peace advisable in March of 1940. In that winter of 1939–40, the war between Germany and the British-French alliance was dormant: it was as though someone had stopped a clock, and so confusing was the effect on Americans that this period of suspended martial animation became known as the "phony (i.e. counterfeit) war."

This phase ended abruptly on April 9, 1940, when the Germans invaded Denmark and Norway. In Denmark there was little opposition; the Norwegians fought gallantly, aided by a British-French expeditionary force which was too small to do more than fight a delaying action. On May 10th the German army invaded the Netherlands, Luxembourg, Belgium and France, using the same tactics that had worked so well in Poland. Prime Minister Chamberlain of Britain, the architect of Munich and of appeasement of the Germans, resigned: Winston Churchill became the King's First Minister. For years Churchill had warned the world of Germany's intentions but he had not been heeded. He symbolized in his personality and even in his appearance the stalwart traits of character that had made England the keystone of a great empire: pugnacious, well-fed, eloquent, familiar with every gambit of diplomatic and political chicanery, he was a Cromwellian figure come to power when the need for such a man was greatest. But he was too late to save Britain from an initial defeat: within three weeks the British expeditionary force on the continent had been defeated and driven to the beaches at Dunkerque, whence close to 300,000 of them were evacuated and brought home by all manner of small craft from the British Isles. On June 10th, when it was evident that the French and British had lost the campaign, Italy declared war on them and attacked in the south of France. On June 17th France asked Germany for an armistice, and the American Congress passed a resolution forbidding the transfer of territory in the Western Hemisphere to the victorious Germans. This was done to prevent the Germans from making use of the French and Dutch possessions in the new world as springboards for attack on any of the American republics. The armistice between France and Germany was signed at Compiègne on June 22nd, and two days later France and Italy concluded an armistice. On June 27th Russia seized Bessarabia and Bukovina from Romania and began to send petroleum from the Romanian oil fields to the Germans.

All these events were duly reported in the press of the United States. They were related by radio commentators to whom millions of Americans listened. The more dramatic aspects of them were seen by addicts of the cinema in newsreels and documentary films. Still the real nature of Hitler and the Germans was not comprehended by the American public: there had been so much anti-German propaganda in the First World War, so much pacificism and isolationism after it, that reports of German atrocities were discounted by large segments of the population. Indeed, the accounts of German cruelty were difficult for complacent Americans to credit: what had happened in Germany to the Germans seemed then incredible. A whole nation had permitted itself to be degraded and tribalized by Adolf Hitler and in the process the ethics of Christianity had been supplanted by the glorification of brutality. The result was pure evil, judged by any civilized standards. In Poland the Germans were eradicating the educated and governing classes, as well as those of Jewish faith, and planning to turn the surviving Poles into a race of serfs. Such a callously devised and executed program had not appeared in the world since the Spanish conquistadors had applied the same technique to the ruling class and the priesthood of the ancient Mayan and Aztec and Inca empires, and enslaved the leaderless remnants of those races. A great majority of the American people found the reports from Europe incredible: it was alien to any experience they had ever known. But it was fact, as they learned later.

Confronted with the disasters that had overtaken the British and French and the Low Countries and Norway and Denmark, the American government obtained from Marshal Pétain, the senescent head of the French government whom the Germans permitted to rule a part of France, a promise that the French fleet would never be surrendered to the Germans. The belligerents were officially informed that the United States would not permit the transfer of any territory from one non-American power to any other American power. This reaffirmation of the Monroe Doctrine was effective because the American Navy was large enough to support it. In July 1940 the Foreign Ministers of the twenty-one American republics met at Havana and declared that an act of aggression against any American republic by a non-American state would be considered an act of aggression against all the signatory republics, and that each of the twenty-one republics would take steps to counter subversive activities aimed at disrupting the welfare of the republics. The great and unsolved problem of American naval strategists at this time was posed by the British Navy: suppose the Germans invaded the British Isles and Britain surrendered? What would happen to the British fleet? Would it be turned over to the Germans, or would it retreat to fight from Canadian bases? The only way to be safe was to build more warships, and on July 19th the Two-Ocean Navy Bill was passed. This Act, following as it did the Eleven Percent Naval Expansion Act of June 14th, 1940, increased the tonnage of combatant ships authorized from 1,724,480 tons to 3,049,480 tons. Funds were promptly voted for the authorized ships, and $150,000,000 went to expand existing shipbuilding facilities and to create new shipyards. But warships take a long time to build, and could Britain hold out for the necessary time? It seemed doubtful, and in August a Joint Canadian–United States Defense Board was organized. From this move the Germans could surmise that the Monroe Doctrine had been extended throughout the whole Western Hemisphere and that the Americans would fight with the Canadians to defend the Doctrine, should the need arise.

In the German High Command plans were being made for an invasion of the British Isles by twenty-five army divisions. But there were two major obstacles to this operation: the Royal Air Force and the Royal Navy. On July 10th the action began, swelling from nocturnal attacks to include mass daylight raids by German bombers and pursuit planes. The Royal Air Force suddenly became Britain's first line of defense. The navy remained away from the British Channel, where his Majesty's ships would have been choice targets for the German dive bombers operating from the coast of France. For months the aerial battles raged with varying intensity: on September 15th the Germans lost fifty-six planes. Two days later the invasion plan was postponed indefinitely: the Royal Air Force had denied the Germans mastery of the air over the invasion area; the Royal Navy had not been called upon to repel an attempt to invade. From July 10th to October 31st, 1,733 German planes had been destroyed and 643 damaged: the Germans could not afford to continue taking such heavy losses. This battle, called "The Battle of Britain," confirmed the American faith in the sea as a means of protection. If the German army divisions could not cross twenty miles of salt water to reach England, how could they be expected to traverse the Atlantic?

Throughout 1940 the Roosevelt Administration had obtained billions for defense. To make the defense program appear to be a coalition effort, above partisan politics, Roosevelt appointed two Republicans to his Cabinet on June 20th. The Navy Secretary so appointed was Franklin Knox, who had been a "Rough Rider" in the Spanish-American War of 1898; the Secretary of War was Henry Stimson, who had served in Hoover's Cabinet as Secretary of State. These appointments confused and enraged the Republicans, and Roosevelt found their reactions highly amusing. On the same day that these appointments were announced, the Burke-Wadsworth bill to draft American men into the army was introduced in Congress. This bill became law on September 16th, and a month later 16,400,000 men between the ages of 21 and 35 registered for the draft. By the bill's provisions 800,000 were to be selected for military training, but they were not to be used outside the Western Hemisphere except on American soil.

On September 3rd Roosevelt informed Congress that he had arranged, by executive agreement, to trade fifty American destroyers of the First World War type to the British for the right to build and operate naval and air bases in eight British possessions in the Western Hemisphere. Leases on these bases were for a 99-year period, and Roosevelt called their acquisition "an epochal and far-reaching act of preparation for continental defense in the face of grave danger." The bases were located on Newfoundland, Bermuda, in the Bahamas, Jamaica, St. Lucia, Trinidad, Antigua and British Guiana. There was much criticism of the method by which the agreement had been made; some thought it unconstitutional. But 1940 was an election year and animosities reached fever heat. On November 5th Roosevelt was elected for a third time (a record) in defiance of the unwritten law that no man should be president for more than two terms. His opponent, Wendell Willkie, received 22,304,755 votes to Roosevelt's 27,243,466.

But with these bases under American control American planes and warships were able to extend the neutrality patrol far out to sea, and to report their findings when they chanced to see a German submarine. If the British escorts of British convoys had their radio tuned to the right frequency they could pick up valuable information.

On December 29th, in a radio speech to the nation, Roosevelt said: "The nub of the whole purpose of your President is to keep you now, and your children later, and your grandchildren much later, out of a last-ditch war for the preservation of American independence and of all the things that American independence means to you and to me and to ours." And he went on to say: "Some of us like to believe that even if Great Britain falls, we are still safe, because of the broad expanse of the Atlantic and of the Pacific. But the width of these oceans is not what it was in the days of clipper ships. At one point between Africa and Brazil the distance is less than from Washington to Denver—five hours for the latest type of bomber. And at the north of the Pacific ocean, America and Asia almost touch each other. Even today we have planes which could fly from the British Isles to New England and back without refueling. And the range of the modern bomber is ever being increased." Even while he spoke, in the mountain passes of Greece the Greeks were driving the Italian invaders back into Albania, hopeful that help from the United States would be forthcoming, for Roosevelt had sent a message to their king, saying, "As your majesty knows, it is the settled policy of the United States government to extend aid to those governments and peoples who defend themselves against aggression."

But aside from facilitating large shipments of relief supplies to Greece there was nothing the United States could do then to help the Greeks. Throughout the closing months of 1940 German mass bombing attacks by night had made life in England a fearful ordeal; on October 8th there was a heavy raid on London; on November 14th Coventry underwent a "blitz" bombing attack; late in December the Germans dropped incendiary bombs on London and there were widespread fires. It was noted that the drops of water from the fire-hoses glistened on the window panes, and that the light they reflected from the fires was as red as blood. So ended 1940, the most momentous year in European history since 451 A.D., when Attila the Hun went down to defeat at Chalons.

On January 6, 1941, the President delivered an eloquent address on the state of the nation to the 77th Congress, in which he said: "In the future days, which we seek to make secure, we look forward to a world founded upon four essential freedoms. The first is freedom of speech and expression—everywhere in the world. The second is freedom of every person to worship God in his own way—everywhere in the world. The third is freedom from want—which, translated into world terms, means economic understandings which will secure to every nation a healthy peacetime life for its inhabitants—everywhere in the world. The fourth is freedom from fear—which, translated into world terms, mean a world-wide reduction of armaments to such a point and in such a thorough fashion that no nation will be in a position to commit an act of physical aggression against any neighbor—anywhere in the world. This is no vision of a distant millennium. It is a definite basis for a kind of world attainable in our own time and generation." But before these worthy, almost Wilsonian aims could even begin to be achieved the Axis powers had to be beaten on the field of battle, and to this end the President, in the same address, called for "ships, planes, tanks, guns," for use by those nations which were fighting for their freedom. At the time, China was resisting Japan, to the best of her ability; in Europe, Britain and Greece were the only nations actively fighting the Axis.

Britain had become an island besieged and blockaded, and she was suffering tremendous shipping losses to Axis submarines, mines and air-craft. Without ships to import food and munitions the British Isles could not long survive, and thus not idealism alone but sound common-sense and self-interest on the part of the United States dictated a policy of giving all possible help to Britain, particularly in the field of shipping.

The British merchant fleet in June 1939 had numbered 6,772 vessels of 17,891,000 gross tons; to this total had been added 8,000,000 tons of allied and neutral shipping and 400,000 tons of captured Axis shipping. Of this total of about 26,000,000 tons, 4,000,000 tons had been allocated to the British army and navy for military purposes, and nearly 5,000,000 tons had been sunk because of the war by January 1941. The shipping that remained had to be used in an uneconomic fashion: the conti-nent of Europe was closed to England as a source of foodstuffs; lumber could no longer be brought from near-by Scandinavia, nor iron ore from the European mines. Imports now had to be brought from great distances—from Canada and the United States, South America and Australia. The route to the Far East by way of the Mediterranean and Suez was no longer safe, and time-consuming voyages had to be made around the Cape of Good Hope. Accumulated shipping losses had, by

November 1940, passed the replacement rate of the oft-bombed British shipyards, and in December the British Ministry of Supply announced that it had contracted for the construction of two shipyards and sixty cargo ships in the United States. Both the yards and the ships were to be built by the Todd-Kaiser interests.

The sixty ships were to be built to a standardized design, devised so that large sections of them could be prefabricated. Steam-reciprocating engines provided the propulsion, and they had a speed of 11 knots. They were unlovely ships, of 10,800 deadweight tons, but 60 of them would be able to carry 300,000 tons of war cargo to the British Isles. Later, after the design had been improved, this type of ship came to be known as the "EC-2" or "Liberty ship." Some called them "Plain Janes" and Roosevelt dubbed them "ugly ducklings." The prototype of all these vessels was a British standard "tramp" freighter that Joseph L. Thompson and Sons, Ltd., had been building for years on the River Wear, on the northeast coast of England, but this fact was lost sight of in the subsequent publicity that attended the launching of American-built "Libertys."

To offset losses while awaiting the delivery of new ships the British had bought, by December 1940, 130 American-owned vessels, of which 86 were of more than 1,000 gross tons. The rest were small craft which were converted into mine-sweepers and mine-layers. At the time, the United States was planning to turn every ship it could spare over to the British, and to take over British shipping routes in the Pacific with American ships so that more British ships would be freed for use in the Atlantic battle zones.

Fortunately the Maritime Commission had been alert to the menace of a new unrestricted submarine war, and soon after the invasion of Poland the Commission's program had been accelerated. The 150 ships which had been planned for completion at the rate of 50 a year in 1938, as a part of the normal, authorized program of 50 ships a year for 10 years, had been ordered completed in 2 years. By October 1940, 47 of these ships had been completed; in December the yards were packed with new construction—176 ships of 1,462,000 gross tons were on the ways. These were ships of the C-1, C-2 and C-3 designs, as well as variations of these types and fast tankers. They were all ships which could be converted readily to war-time use as troop carriers, or supply ships, or naval auxiliaries.

In January 1941 Roosevelt asked for two hundred EC-2s, or "Libertys," and this meant that new shipyards would have to be constructed to handle the order. Many of the old sites of the First World War yards were available, and the process of refurbishing them began at once. Throughout this same period of great urgency and expanding ship-building activity, the government expedited the training of thousands of shipyard workers. The Maritime Commission intensified its program, which had been started in 1938, of training officers and men for the merchant fleet. In January 1941 the Merchant Marine Academy at King's Point, New York, was established to perform the same functions for the merchant marine that the Naval Academy performed for the navy.

In March the Lend-Lease Bill—which had been tagged "HR 1776" in order to make the opposition appear to be voting against a historic date associated in the minds of Americans with the Declaration of Independence—was passed and signed by the President. This Act lifted the "cash and carry" restrictions on purchases in the United States by nations which were fighting aggressors. Toward the end of the month the Coast Guard seized by a right of angary all German and Italian merchantmen in American ports, as well as the ships of the nations they had conquered. In April the State Department announced that an agreement had been reached with the Danish Minister in Washington by which the United States was granted the right to con-struct and operate air bases and facilities in Greenland. Marines were immediately landed on the island, whose coast had been surveyed by the U.S. Coast Guard.

While these various prudent arrangements were being made a verbal tempest arose over the extent and purpose of the Pan-American "neu-trality patrol," which had been functioning for a year and a half in the waters of the Western Hemisphere. It is doleful to relate, but the exist-ence of this patrol greatly incensed the political opponents of the Presi-dent, whom they suspected of playing at being a naval strategist, and whose paternalistic form of democracy they disdained. No President since Lincoln had inspired such mistrust and detestation, and his every effort to help Britain was beclouded and distorted by the venomous hatred of those who opposed his "New Deal."

The matter of patrols was an abstruse one to the general public, and Roosevelt did not take the nation into his confidence. When he used the word "patrol" his opponents suspected that it was a synonym for "convoy." But the President could improvise with mercurial mental agility, and he explained to a press conference late in April that there was a difference between "patrols" and "convoys." A "patrol," he said, meant warships that searched the sea to find out if any potential aggressors lurked in certain areas; "convoys" were warships that escorted merchantmen in order to protect them from aggressors. And he informed his audience of reporters that, using his authority as Commander-in-Chief of the navy, the patrols would be continued.

The patrols by surface ship and planes had been extended, as the need arose, as far as two thousand miles out to sea, well into the North Atlantic war zone from which navigators had been warned by Germany in March. The new bases leased from Britain had been put into immediate construction and operation, and planes and ships fanned out from them looking for German surface raiders or submarines. If an American ship or plane operating out of the American base at Bermuda located a German submarine, the American did not attack, but gave the nearest British warship and base a precise idea of where to find the enemy. In this way, convoys could be routed away from the danger spot, and British ships and planes could converge on it. The work of the American ships and planes proved to be a great help to the hard-pressed British, who were able, because of it, to concentrate more of their escort vessels in areas closer to the British Isles. A secondary advantage was that the patrol induced a state of readiness in the American Navy, giving many officers and men invaluable experience in warlike operations.

Overseas, that spring, military and diplomatic affairs were going badly for the democracies: the Germans had come to the rescue of the Italians in Greece, had driven through Yugoslavia with their armored divisions and bombers. In April Athens fell and the swastika flag flapped idly from the Acropolis. Greece was the fourteenth nation to fall, by force of diplomacy or battle, to the Germans. In North Africa the German Afrika Corps under General Erwin Rommel, aided by the Italians, had re-taken Bengasi and started a counter-offensive which was not to end until they had reached a position that threatened Egypt, the Suez Canal and the Near East. In Moscow, Japan and Russia signed a neutrality pact. German submarines and planes were taking such a toll of British shipping in the Atlantic and Mediterranean that Roosevelt issued an order for 112 more of the EC-2s, the "Libertys," and 100 of the Maritime Commission's standard type ships—the C-1s, C-2s, C-3s, and tankers—for the British. The ships were to be paid for out of Lend-Lease funds, and from that point on the merchant building programs of the Americans and the British became so intermingled that they were indistinguishable.

In May the days began to lengthen over the North Atlantic and fair weather became increasingly prevalent, making the work of the German submarines and bombers much easier to perform. On May 21st a German submarine gave the SS *Robin Moor,* an American vessel en route to South Africa, thirty minutes' warning: in that time the boats were lowered and passengers and crew abandoned ship. Then the Germans sank their vessel, and for from two to three weeks the passengers drifted about in the small boats before they were rescued. This was but an incident in the battle of the Atlantic: as May drew to a close there were reports of growing British shipping losses in the North and South Atlantic and in the Mediterranean.

The Germans were using new and faster types of submarines, and they were attacking at night, often on the surface, specializing in torpedoing tankers with their inflammable loads of aviation gasoline. Long-range planes flew from bases in Norway in a great semi-circle out to the westward of the British Isles and in to bases in France. Such planes spotted and bombed the convoys, and radioed their location to the submarines. Convoys were easily detected from the air: often as many as sixty ships formed one convoy, forced together by the lack of sufficient escort vessels, and moving at a speed of only eight knots an hour. The Germans made use, too, of a handful of fast capital ships as commerce-destroyers, and of heavily-armed merchantmen as raiders, which they used much as *Alabama* had been used in the Civil War. British shipping being repaired in British yards was subjected to frequent bombing attacks; the waters around and the navigable rivers in England were strewn with all manner of ingeniously contrived mines which tied up a thousand mine-sweeping ships and twenty thousand men.

Britain was in desperate straits when Roosevelt proclaimed, on May 27th, an "unlimited state of national emergency." In a radio address that evening he pointed out that the Axis objective of world domination could never be achieved unless they first obtained control of the seas, and that if they failed to obtain control of the seas they would certainly be defeated. And Britain was all that stood between the Axis and the domination of the seas by Germany and Italy. Roosevelt mentioned the fact that the Atlantic Fleet, under Admiral Ernest J. King, had been greatly increased in strength during the past year, and that ships and planes were being added to the neutrality patrol as rapidly as possible. One of the new additions was the 35,000-ton *North Carolina,* commissioned on April 9th—the first new battleship to join the fleet since 1923. In May three old battleships, one aircraft carrier, four cruisers and nine destroyers were detached from the Pacific Fleet and sent to the Atlantic. That month 483 ocean-going warships were either under construction or on order for the two-ocean navy; and private shipyards had contracted for 890 vessels of 5,700,000 tons, both for the merchant marine and for use by the Navy; the United States had turned a total of 260 freighters over to Britain, most of them ancient and rusty relics of the 1917–21 building. But they would have to do until the new Maritime Commission ships and the prefabricated Libertys began to be completed in greater numbers.

On June 22nd, 1941, the Germans quite suddenly invaded Russia. There had long existed in Germany a theory that if the Germans had access to the immense Russian resources of manpower, oil, timber, wheat and minerals, the possibilities of conquest would be limitless. Now the theory awaited the outcome of battle. Soon the Russian and German armies were engaged along an 1,800-mile front stretching from the Black Sea to the Arctic Ocean, and the Russians had reason to be thankful for their own previous aggressions which had won for them territory that acted as a buffer zone to the advancing German armies in Poland, in Romania, in the Baltic States and in Finland. Slowly the Russian armies fell back, their peasant-soldiers fighting magnificently, as they have throughout all history, despite inadequate arms and tactics. This was a struggle of Titans, as Pan-Slavism fought Pan-Germanism with equal savagery. Aid, in the form of military supplies, was quickly dispatched to Russian White Sea and Siberian ports from the United States.

On the 7th of July the President announced that United States Marines had been landed in Iceland, under an agreement reached with the Prime Minister of Iceland. These troops replaced the British and Canadians who had been garrisoning this northern island which had become so valuable as an air and naval base protecting the convoy route to Europe. With the establishment of American bases on the island, the neutrality patrol could function even more effectively than before. The submarines were still as active as ever, but the future that Britain faced seemed less ominous, now that the Germans had to fight a war on two fronts, with Russia on the East and Britain on the West. In the United States there were many who found it difficult to distinguish the communist form of government from that of Nazi Germany, and who said, in effect, "a plague on both your houses." How great the difference actually was, is a matter for the historians of the future to decide.

Roosevelt had his own definite ideas on the subject: any nation that fought Germany was a friend of democracy, and as much aid as possible should be given to the Russians, who, no matter what their government, were traditionally friends of the American people.

These matters began to crystallize in early August. At 7:30 A.M. on Saturday, August 9th, HMS *Prince of Wales,* with Prime Minister Winston Churchill aboard, sighted American destroyers of Placentia Bay, Newfoundland, and shortly thereafter entered the great bay. Roosevelt, on USS *Augusta,* was awaiting the Prime Minister for a series of conferences which began almost immediately. This meeting, which had been kept a secret from the world, was well protected: besides *Augusta,* the cruiser *Tuscaloosa* and the battleship *Arkansas* and a division of American destroyers were in the bay. HMS *Prince of Wales,* after a stormy voyage during which her escorting destroyers had been unable to keep up with her, had been met by three Canadian destroyers. Overhead American seaplanes flew patrol. While the officers and men of the two navies visited each others' ships, exchanging professional talk and gifts, the Prime Minister and the President, each attended by a coterie of military and diplomatic and economic aides, worked in conference. These talks lasted intermittently until *Prince of Wales* left the bay at 5 P.M. on Tuesday, August 12th. During the conferences there had been drawn up in Roosevelt's cabin on USS *Augusta* the "Council of Placentia," which was a joint declaration of certain principles which both nations held in common. On August 14th the official text of this declaration, which came to be known as "The Atlantic Charter," was released. It proved to be a verbal banner to which all men of good will could subscribe, for it displayed an idealism which was applicable on a global scale, in the Wilsonian manner. In part, the text read: "Sixth, after the destruction of the Nazi tyranny, they hope to see established a peace which will afford to all nations the means of dwelling in safety within their own boundaries, and which will afford assurance that all men in the lands may live out their lives in freedom from fear and want;

"Seventh, such a peace should enable all men to traverse the high seas and oceans without hindrance . . ." In the desperate years ahead this Charter was accepted and endorsed by all the democratic nations, including Russia.

This was not the only matter discussed at the momentous meeting of the elected heads of the English-speaking race: the problems of supplying food and munitions through Lend-Lease were reviewed, and on August 15th a joint message from Roosevelt and Churchill, the aristocrats, was given to Joseph Stalin, the Georgian cobbler's son, informing him that Britain and the United States were co-operating to supply Russia with her most urgent needs, and suggesting a meeting in Moscow of their representatives in order to work out joint problems aimed at the defeat of Germany. To this suggestion Stalin acceded, and so facilitated what later became a flood of Lend-Lease goods, borne to embattled Russia over the North Atlantic and North Pacific oceans, for the most part in American ships. At the time, a goal of fourteen hundred ships to be built by the end of 1943 had been set for American shipyards.

In this moment of great events, there was a bill before Congress which was to determine whether the selective service act should be extended for another 18 months. The bill had been approved in the Senate by a vote of 45 to 30, and when it came before the House on August 12th, it was passed by a vote of 203 to 202. By the slender margin of one vote the conscript army of the United States had been saved from dissolution, and complacent isolationism defeated.

On the Atlantic by the autumn of 1941 the navy's "neutrality patrol" had developed into an undeclared war against the German submarines. On September 4th the USS *Greer,* a 1,200-ton, four-stacker destroyer first commissioned in 1918, was steaming along 175 miles southwest of Iceland, headed for Reykjavik with mail and urgent freight. Shortly after breakfast a British patrol plane warned her that a submarine had just been sighted less than a dozen miles ahead. *Greer,* at flank speed now, commenced zigzagging, and soon picked up the submarine on her listening gear. The plane dropped four depth charges in the general neighborhood of the U-boat. At 12:48 P.M. the submarine attacked, firing a torpedo at *Greer,* which took evasive action and eight minutes later tossed a pattern of eight depth charges. The submarine fired another torpedo, which was avoided, and *Greer* scattered eleven more depth charges. Then contact with the submarine was lost: it is doubtful if her commanding officer knew the nationality of the destroyer at which he had aimed his torpedoes, for *Greer's* silhouette was the same as that of the fifty destroyers that had been traded to Britain for bases.

This engagement, the first attack on an American naval vessel since the Japanese had sunk USS *Panay,* brought orders from the President for the navy to "shoot on sight" any vessel attempting to interfere with American shipping, or with any shipping under American escort, as well as any hostile craft encountered in waters upon which the security of the United States depended. While the navy was carrying out these orders, of which public approval was general, the USS *Kearny,* a 1,630-ton destroyer commissioned in 1940, was torpedoed about 350 miles off Iceland, soon after midnight on October 17, 1941. She had been steaming behind a convoy bound from Iceland to the New World and when the convoy had been attacked by submarines, and a tanker hit, she had moved ahead fast and fired a pattern of depth charges. Then she was hit on the starboard side, amidships, by a torpedo, and, although disabled she made port safely. Eleven of her people had been killed and seven wounded in the blast of the exploding torpedo. Roosevelt declared ten days later, in fiercely melodious tones: "We Americans have cleared our decks and taken out battle stations."

On October 30th the USS *Salinas,* a navy oiler launched in 1921, was hit while in waters to the southwest of Iceland by two torpedoes. Strenuous damage-control work saved her from sinking. A day later, in the same vicinity, the USS *Reuben James* was hit amidships by a torpedo and sank immediately. She was an old four-stacker, first commissioned in 1920, and of her crew of 150 officers and men, 100 were lost. She, with other destroyers, had been escorting a convoy to Iceland.

In this twilight stage between peace and declared war, American merchantmen were attacked, and seamen killed. By October 22nd ten American-owned vessels, of which six flew the Panamanian flag, had been lost because of the war. The *City of Rayville,* 5,883 tons, sank when she hit a mine in Australian waters on November 9, 1940; *Charles Pratt,* 8,902-ton tanker, was torpedoed and sunk off the West African coast on December 21st, 1940; *Robin Moor* was torpedoed, shelled and sunk in the South Atlantic on May 21st, 1941; *Sessa,* 1,700 tons, was torpedoed and sunk southwest of Iceland on August 17, 1941; *Steel Seafarer,* 5,714 tons, was bombed and sunk by a German plane in the Gulf of Suez on September 5, 1941; *Montana,* 1,900 tons, was torpedoed and sunk off Iceland on September 19, 1941; *Pink Star,* 6,850 tons, was torpedoed and sunk off Iceland on September 19, 1941; *I. C. White,* 7,052 tons, a tanker, was torpedoed and sunk in the South Atlantic on September 27th, 1941; *Bold Venture,* 3,222 tons, was sunk 500 miles south of Iceland on October 16, 1941; *Lehigh,* 4,983 tons, was torpedoed and sunk off West Africa on October 19, 1941.

Public opinion in the United States was not greatly influenced by the attacks on merchantmen. But the public was proud of its navy in a latent, absent-minded way: before public interest and emotions were aroused a warship had to become involved in some major disaster. Thus, when USS *Kearny* was hit, and when USS *Reuben James* went down, the public's wrath rose.

On the day *Kearny* was torpedoed, the House of Representatives voted almost two to one that American merchantmen should be armed. This was the first weakening in the Neutrality Act of 1939. But not until

—denotes vessels flying Panamanian flags.

November 13th were the sections of the Act that prevented American vessels from being armed and from carrying cargoes to belligerent ports fully and finally repealed. Then at last the 1,375 merchantmen flying the American flag could fight when attacked.

As the American vessels returned to their various ports, those built under Maritime Commission auspices were able to be equipped with guns rapidly because of the naval specifications which had been injected into their design. On ships built without war in mind, the job was more difficult, entailing in many cases the making of structural changes before the guns could be properly mounted. There was no shortage of gun crews: the navy had been quietly training officers and men for this duty ever since the preceding April.

With the lifting of the Neutrality Act restrictions, the flow of Lend-Lease supplies increased tremendously. In October the first British convoys left for Murmansk with munitions for the embattled Muscovites. American ships were shepherded across the North Atlantic to Liverpool with supplies for the British Isles; made the long trip around the Cape of Good Hope and up the Red Sea; voyaged across the Pacific to Vladivostok, Singapore and Rangoon. Seldom was there anything spectacular in this activity. Ships in convoy steamed slowly, sometimes making only five knots an hour. Days and nights of routine quiet were broken briefly by the daylight attacks of bombers and by the night attacks of submarines in the northern seas. Then, after the suddenly erupting flames of a torpedoed tanker and the swift counter-attacks of the escort vessels had subsided, there was again an intense calm, and once more life at sea was hard and dull and fraught with ennui. But this steadily expanding, undramatic effort marked the beginning of American mastery of the seas. Thus does a sea gull break its shell and discover the world. No longer were the oceans protective barriers alone. Suddenly they became for the United States a means of conveying American responsibility in the service of democracy to the far places of the earth.

[22] *Second Act*

For many months now, the Americans had been preoccupied with the news of the fighting in Russia, in North Africa and in the air over Britain. But in the Far East the Japanese had been moving south along the China coast and they had all but encircled the Philippines. Hainan Island had been seized in February 1939; the Spratly Islands (seven hundred miles southwest of Manila) and the Paracels in the next month. In July Secretary of State Hull announced the abrogation of the commercial treaty between Japan and the United States, the abrogation to become effective January 1940, in accordance with the terms of the treaty. Thus was the way cleared for an impeccably legal embargo on the shipment of war materials to Japan. On September 15th a truce between Russia and Japan, whose troops had been fighting a small-scale undeclared war along the borders of Manchuria and Mongolia, was signed in Moscow.

In the next spring Japanese planes resumed large-scale raids on Chungking, then capital of China. During that summer the militarists in Japan rose to power, ousted the assuasive Yonai cabinet and brought in Prince Konoye as Prime Minister. He was a noted hypochondriac over whom they had full control. On August 1st Konoye proclaimed the formation of a totalitarian regime in Japan and gave notice to the world that Japan intended to establish a "Co-Prosperity Sphere," a "New Order," in "Greater East Asia." On September 22nd the Japanese and the French government headed by Marshal Pétain signed the Hanoi agreement which permitted the establishment of Japanese air bases and garrisons in Indo-China. On September 27th, Japan joined the Axis in a military alliance by which Italy, Germany and Japan agreed to assist each other in every way possible if any one of them were attacked by the United States. To avoid the embarrassment of being allied with a non-Aryan race, the Germans decreed that the Japanese were "honorary Aryans."

Nine months later, on July 26, 1941, the President froze Japanese assets by Executive Order: American-Japanese trade soon ended under the impact of this decree. That same day the Japanese government invoked the National Mobilization Law. Three days later Japanese troops took over the Camranh naval base in Indo-China. In October the Japanese cabinet was re-formed, with a dyspeptic General named Hideki Tojo as Prime Minister. He was of the opinion that the United States had acted unfairly in placing an embargo on the export of American oil and supplies to Japan, and he thought that under conditions then existing Japan was like a man with his head in an iron bucket. In short, by some curious discrepancy between reality and the aspiration of Japan, the Japanese militarists considered that they were encircled by alien and unsympathetic powers.

Against this storm on the far horizon the United States had taken several precautionary steps, aside from the general increase in armaments: in July the armed forces of the Philippine Islands had been placed under the command of American army and naval officers. Command of American and Filipino army units in the Far East thus was given to Lieutenant-General Douglas MacArthur, who had served with distinction in the United States Army and then become an employee of the Filipinos. In command of the naval forces was Admiral Thomas C. Hart, Commander-in-Chief, Asiatic Fleet, a veteran of the Queenstown Command, and an expert in submarine warfare. In September Hart urgently recommended that the United States Marines in China, as well as all naval units in Chinese waters, be withdrawn at once. Throughout this same period of mounting tension, American civilians were repeatedly urged to leave the Far East; additional troops and planes were sent to MacArthur, and submarines to Admiral Hart.

In Tokyo that September, at the Imperial Naval War College, Admiral Isoruku Yamamoto assembled his fleet admirals and staff officers to formulate the final plans for a naval campaign in the Pacific. These conferences lasted from September 2nd to 13th, and in that time the basic plans were perfected. They included a plan for an air raid on Pearl Harbor, on the island of Oahu in the Hawaiian Islands. Yamamoto had conceived the idea of this raid nine months earlier, and had detailed

Rear-Admiral Takijiro of the 11th Air Fleet to make a study of the operation.

On November 5th the directives for the general attack in the Pacific were issued to all fleet commanders: the key operation was to be the attack on Pearl Harbor, where numerous units of the American fleet were habitually anchored on week-ends. To the Japanese the American Navy represented the one great obstacle to the success of their over-all plan of naval conquest in the Pacific: if the Pacific fleet at Pearl Harbor could be inactivated for a long period, nothing could stop the offensive.

The task force that was to attack Pearl Harbor consisted of two commands: an advance expeditionary force of three light cruisers, twenty submarines, five midget submarines and six ships of the train, all commanded by Vice-Admiral Mitsumi Shimizu, Commander-in-Chief, 6th Fleet; and a striking force of six carriers, two battleships, three cruisers, sixteen destroyers and eight train vessels, under the command of Vice-Admiral Chuichi Nagumo, Commander-in-Chief, 1st Air Fleet.

On November 14th the striking force calmly began to gather at Hitokappu Bay, in the sere and lonely Kurile Islands to the north of Japan. Three days later a special envoy from Japan, Saburo Kurusu, arrived in Washington to find out if the United States could not be persuaded to accede to Japan's program for a "New Order" in East Asia.

Secretary of State Hull talked with Kurusu and the Japanese Ambassador to the United States, Admiral Kichisaburo Nomura, on the 18th. He mentioned how patient the United States had been with the Japanese, and told the two emissaries that in the present situation the extremists in Japan appeared to be looking for trouble, and that it was up to the Japanese government to make an extra effort "to take the situation by the collar." Hull, a fierce old man from Tennessee, seems to have been unaware that the Tojo cabinet, which had come to power on October 18th, was at once extremist and the only government Japan had: there was no government to take Tojo and his cabinet by the collar—they themselves were the government.

Two days later the Japanese envoys gave Hull their proposal, which would have restored commercial relations between the two nations, given Japan all the oil it needed and stopped Lend-Lease aid to China. Hull, in turning down the offer, told Kurusu and Nomura that the American people were opposed to the concept of a "New Order" in Asia, even as they were opposed to it in Europe. Japan, he made clear, must pull out of China and renounce her expansible habits if she wanted to resolve the dilemma. But Japan was unwilling to surrender the conquests she had made in China: the negotiations were deadlocked.

On November 21st, after this conference, there was little hope left in Japanese naval circles that war could be avoided. On November 25th the striking force was ordered to leave Hitokappu Bay, and soon after dawn on November 26th (Japanese date) Admiral Nagumo's ships steamed out of the bay. December 8th (Japanese date) had been set for the attack on Pearl Harbor, yet Nagumo's orders from Yamamoto were that in case the negotiations in Washington succeeded two days before the attack date, the ships were to return to port.

The striking force took the unfrequented northern route. Blacked out, observing complete radio silence, held to a speed of 13 knots by the vessels of the train, the warships headed for a refueling rendezvous at 41 degree North, 170 degrees East.

On the day after the striking force sortied from Hitokappu Bay, Hull gave Kurusu and Nomura the American counter-proposal: if Japan would withdraw her troops from China and Indo-China, a reciprocal, most-favored-nation trade agreement would follow, and, among other blessings, there would be peace in the Far East.

The Japanese envoys were crestfallen at this invitation to give up their "Co-Prosperity Sphere" in East Asia, and it was with misgivings that they forwarded the proposal to Tokyo. Three days later Hull warned the American government that the problem had become one for the military forces to solve: diplomacy had failed.

The United States government, committed to peace, was unable to declare war. Even had the desire existed on the part of the administration, it is certain that a resolution calling for war would have been defeated in Congress. There was nothing to do but await an overt act on Japan's part, and "war warning" messages were sent to the outpost commanders in the Pacific.

On December 1st (Japanese date) the Japanese cabinet approved the start of hostilities against the United States; next day the formal order for the attack was issued. President Roosevelt arrived in Washington from Warm Springs, Georgia, where he had been resting, called back by the failure of the Hull-Kurusu negotiations. It was clear that the situation was deteriorating rapidly, for throughout this period the army and navy had been intercepting Japanese diplomatic messages and decoding them.

Meanwhile the navy, which had been tracking Japanese fleet units by their radio signals, found that several carriers had simply stopped sending: these carriers were presumed to be in ports in Japan.

On December 4th (Hawaiian date) Nagumo's striking force fueled at sea from the fleet tankers and continued on toward the east, unhampered now by the slow vessels of the train. On the 5th the pilots were briefed for the attack: Japanese espionage reports continued to come in, pin-pointing the position of the major fleet units in Pearl Harbor. On December 6th there were eight battleships, eight cruisers, twenty-nine destroyers and forty-one lesser vessels in port.

Early that day the striking force was eight hundred miles north of Oahu, and the message "Climb Mount Niitaka," which was code for "proceed with attack," was received. Southward the warships drove at twenty-four to twenty-six knots through the daylight hours of December 6th, and on through the night, unseen and unsuspected.

In Washington that evening the President, who had been kept constantly informed of the progress of the negotiations by Hull, sent a final appeal to the Mikado, saying, in part: "I address myself to Your Majesty at this moment in the fervent hope that Your Majesty may, as I am doing, give thought in this definite emergency to ways of dispelling the dark clouds." The message was sent at 9 P.M. that evening, as night cast a protective mantle over the striking force.

At 6 A.M. on Sunday, December 7th, 200 miles north of Oahu, the 6 carriers began launching their planes. By 7:15 A.M. their decks were clear: 360 planes were in the air—81 fighters, 135 dive bombers, 104 horizontal bombers, 40 torpedo bombers. The warships turned and withdrew toward the northwest while the planes sped for Pearl Harbor, flying high in the clear morning sunshine.

At Oahu there had been tenuous indications of impending trouble: the USS *Condor,* a costal minesweeper, while 1¾ miles southwest of

Pearl Harbor, had sighted an unidentified submarine periscope at 3:50 A.M., in an area from which American submarines were barred. The USS *Ward,* an old four-stacker built in 1918, began a search for the submarine, located and sank it soon after 6:45 A.M. At 7:02 A.M. an army mobile radar unit picked up a large number of planes bearing down from 3 degrees East of North, 132 miles away. These were presumed to be either a flight of army bombers or of planes from an American carrier, both of which were expected that morning.

At 7:55 A.M. nine Japanese dive bombers hit Ford Island Naval Air Station. The Commander of Patrol Wing 2, Rear Admiral Patrick Bellinger, broadcast from Ford Island the message: "Air raid, Pearl Harbor. This is *not* drill." A few minutes later the Commander-in-Chief, United States Fleet, Admiral Husband Kimmel, sent out a similar message.

The attack developed in five distinct phases: Phase One, in which torpedo planes struck at the moored battleships and cruisers while dive bombers neutralized the air fields on Oahu, lasted until 8:25 A.M., and turned the port area into an inferno of exploding ships and burning fuel oil. Phase Two was a fifteen minute lull in the attack. Phase Three began at 8:40 A.M. when horizontal, high level bombers, and toward the end, dive bombers, attacked the warships. By this time pools of burning oil were spreading over the surface of the water. Phase Four consisted of dive-bombing attacks against ships in the harbor, and lasted from 9:15 A.M. to 9:45 A.M. Men from the ships swam through the burning oil toward the sea-wall on Ford Island, against which slight waves splashed and smothered the flames, creating a fire-free lane a few feet wide hard by the sea-wall. Along this wall men from the Air Station leaned over and pulled the survivors from the water: one Chief Petty Officer grasped by the wrists a man who had swum through the fire and the burned skin came off the swimmer's arms like gloves. Phase Five began at 9:45 A.M., when the last of the attacking planes had withdrawn. All but 27 of the 360 planes in the raid were recovered by their carriers, between 10:30 A.M. and 1:30 P.M. Then the striking force retired at high speed to the northwest.

At small cost the Japanese had won a great victory. The United States Navy and Marine Corps suffered 2,835 casualties, of whom 2,086 were killed, 749 wounded survived. The army lost 194 killed in action, of 600 casualties. The United States was denied, by severe damage or sinking, the use of 8 battleships, 3 light cruisers, 3 destroyers and 4 miscellaneous vessels. 188 army and navy planes were destroyed. Luckily, no carriers were in port that day, and nine battleships, including the new *North Carolina* and *Washington,* were in the Atlantic where they were serving to help insure the delivery of Lend-Lease goods.

In Washington it was 1:20 P.M. when the Japanese attacked Pearl Harbor. The President was peeling an apple in the White House study, topping off a lunch with his chief adviser, Harry Hopkins, when Secretary Knox telephoned the news from the Navy Department at 1:47 P.M. The President's first reaction was to utter an incredulous cry of "No!" Then rage entered his heart, as it did that of every good citizen of the United States.

Throughout the United States the news of the raid on Pearl Harbor was attended by much consternation. This was especially so on the West Coast, where a Japanese sea-borne attack was expected momentarily. In San Diego, that Sunday afternoon, crowds of people converged, lemming-like, on the waterfront and stood gazing silently out to sea. At no previous time had so many people become suddenly conscious of the immensity of the ocean wastes, out of which an enemy could suddenly strike, protected from discovery by the vastness of the ocean, in which a task force could steam for days without being detected. In San Francisco, on December 8th, the sirens heralded a black-out, and the army's primitive radar equipment reported flights of wild-fowl as "squadrons of carrier-based enemy planes." In New York, too, there was great anxiety, springing from the fear that the Japanese had synchronized their attack on Pearl Harbor with the Germans, and that therefore a German air raid on New York was imminent. This fear was without foundation.

Japanese strategy had been based on the assumption that the United States was, as Admiral Sankichi Takashi said, "a crazy-quilt of heterogeneous population, lacking entirely in national consciousness and the spirit of loyalty." That this was a grave misconception the Americans were quick to prove. In the first days of frenzied excitement naval recruiting stations were packed with vengeful young Americans, anxious to get their hands on a Japanese. The hatred that Roosevelt had attracted, and which had led Sakichi Mitsui to write that "The United States is already divided into two great camps and is on the brink of a revolution," was now directed at the Japanese. For the nonce, partisan political disputes in America were forgotten, and the nation presented a united front to the enemy.

The usual formalities of declaring war were observed: the President appeared before Congress on December 8th at 12:29 P.M. and asked Congress to declare "that since the unprovoked and dastardly attack by Japan on Sunday, December 7, a state of war has existed between the United States and the Japanese Empire." As requested, Congress quickly declared war, with but one non-conforming vote. On the morning of December 11th Germany and Italy declared war on the United States, and the Congress that same day, with a single abstaining vote, declared war on Germany and Italy. With the exception of Argentina, the American republics allied with the United States by the Havana Agreements joined in the war against the Axis, and the conflict soon became, in a literal sense, world-wide. Twenty-six nations opposed "the Axis," which then consisted of Germany, Italy, Japan, Finland, Hungary, Romania, Slovakia and "Manchukuo," as the Japanese called Manchuria.

In this global strife the offensive power of the United States was destined to play a decisive part. Years later, when Churchill was asked what the real turning point of the war had been, he unhesitatingly replied: "Pearl Harbor. Up to that all was doubtful; after that nothing could prevent the victory of the great Allies." Before that victory could be won, many American lives and much of the basic resources of the United States were to be expended: of these the sea was to exact its tribute, as the price of victory.

The idea that the United States might be defeated did not enter the thinking of the vast majority of the American people: defeat was inconceivable, victory inevitable. It was purely a question of time. This attitude sprang from an appreciation of the nation's human and industrial resources. The enemy's conception of Americans as a mongrel people grown soft with wealth and easy living was confuted by the depth of anger and the ferocity of purpose the nation displayed.

The President swiftly began to direct this will to victory, synchronizing it with the material resources of the nation, not neglecting to inject into the broth the idea that the war was being fought "for liberty under God," a concept pleasing to those who identified God with their personal well-being.

Off to Pearl Harbor flew Navy Secretary Knox, to obtain a first-hand estimate of the damage there. Details of the American losses were a tightly guarded secret, but Knox, the very personification of honesty, told reporters: "The air attack simply took us by surprise. We weren't on air alert." The blame for this lack of an air alert fell on the three commanding officers on the island of Oahu: the two generals in command of army ground and air forces there, and Admiral Husband E. Kimmel, whose ships had borne the brunt of the attack.

Kimmel had been picked by the President to be Commander in Chief of the Pacific Fleet, over the objections of Secretary Knox, but with the support of Admiral Harold Stark, Chief of Navy Operations, and he was the unwitting victim of circumstances beyond his control. To maintain a completely effective air patrol of the areas around Oahu, Kimmel would have needed 250 patrol planes. Yet he had only 49 such planes in flying condition at his disposal. Within the following five years eight distinct investigations and inquiries sought to fix the responsibility for American losses at Pearl Harbor, without, however, arriving at any unanimous conclusion save that the Japanese were to blame.

But since, by naval standards, Kimmel had to assume the blame, he was replaced by Admiral Chester Nimitz, a gimlet-eyed native of Texas, aged fifty-six. Disguised as a civilian, after having been chosen by Knox to relieve Kimmel, Nimitz made his way by train and plane to Oahu, to retrieve what he could from the wreckage.

Admiral Ernest Joseph King, egg-bald but amorous, sixty-three years old, was strongly recommended by Knox for the job of Commander in Chief, U.S. Fleet. The President, who had been prejudiced against King in the beginning, was finally persuaded that he had outstanding ability, and following Knox's recommendation, selected him for the over-all command of naval forces at sea. The bumbling Stark, who, as Chief of Naval Operations, was primarily an administrative officer, without much consciousness of the fleets at sea, remained in that duty until March 1942, when his job was given to King, who thus became CINCUS * and CNO.** King's selection was a logical one: he was a qualified naval aviator, a tough and vindictive man with a reputation for being a "sun-downer," that is, an officer who insists on having his men back aboard ship by sun-down. Such men, although of limited intelligence, make useful leaders in war, and of this fact the President was aware. King gradually replaced the Navy Department's bureau chiefs with younger and vigorous officers, among them a then modest and unassuming admiral named Randall Jacobs, who took over from Nimitz the Bureau of Navigation, which in May 1942 became the Bureau of Naval Personnel.

On the first day of 1942 the navy was being run by the following men: Commander in Chief, U.S. Fleet, Admiral King; Chief of Naval Operations, Admiral Stark; Commander in Chief, Pacific Fleet, Admiral Nimitz; Commander in Chief, Atlantic Fleet, Vice-Admiral Royal Ingersoll; Commander in Chief, Asiatic Fleet, Admiral Thomas Hart. Hart had been foresighted and without blame when the Japanese attacked, and he was therefore not affected by this kaleidoscopic shifting of the navy's high command posts. He had disposed his ships of the Asiatic Fleet so that they were ready for just such an attack, and small as were the naval forces at his disposal—a heavy cruiser and two light cruisers, thirteen aged destroyers, twenty-nine submarines, a handful of supply ships and motor torpedo boats, thirty naval patrol planes— they fought with brilliance in the ensuing months.

Fifteen days after Pearl Harbor Prime Minister Churchill arrived in Washington to confer with the President and from their informal conversations came many vital decisions. On January 1, 1942, a declaration pledging that all the nations fighting the Axis would co-operate in the war and would not make a separate peace with any of the Axis nations with whom they were at war was signed by representatives of twenty-six nations in Washington. In this Declaration of Washington the principles of the Atlantic Charter were subscribed to by the signatory nations. From it grew the United Nations as an organization. To

* Commander in Chief, U.S. Fleet.
** Chief of Naval Operations.

· 470 ·

obtain complete strategic collaboration between the British and the Americans a "Combined Chiefs of Staff" was formed, and its existence announced on February 6, 1942. Four American officers, who comprised the American Joint Chiefs of Staff, Generals George Marshall and Henry Arnold, Admirals Ernest King and Harold Stark represented the United States on this board of highest strategy. The British members were Field Marshal Sir John Dill, Admiral Sir Charles Little, Air Marshal A. T. Harris and Lieutenant General Sir Colville Weymss. At a later date Admiral William Leahy, USN, as the President's chief naval adviser, became a member of the group.

An Allied Military Mission began to function in Moscow, where they were the object of much suspicion, and an Allied Military Council began to operate in Chungking.

These were the links that bound together the four major powers; and they served their purpose extremely well, in spite of the awkward fact that Russia was not at war with Japan.

In Washington, during those first momentous weeks of 1942 the decision was made to defeat Germany first. This was not unanimously favored by all the nations involved: the nations of the Pacific naturally wanted the full force of the Allied offensive to be directed against Japan. But Germany had greater resources for making war than did Japan, and Germany was closer at hand, and already engaged on four fronts— in Russia, in Africa, in the air over Europe, and at sea. By contrast, no front against Japan existed except in China, and Japan itself was inaccessible as a target because of the vast distances which protected her from the United States and Britain. With Germany defeated, Japan's fate would be certain.

In this strategy, the United Nations had the advantage of sea power and because of this could reinforce each other as circumstances dictated, applying their strength where and when it was most needed against either enemy. Thus the navy was faced with a two-fold task: to fight a delaying action against the Japanese in the Pacific, and to win control of the sea from the submarines in the Atlantic. For without this control the fighting men and the munitions fabricated in the United States could not be brought to the point of contact with the enemy.

On December 7th, 1941, personnel totaled 325,095 officers and men in the navy, plus 70,425 in the Marine Corps, and 25,002 in the Coast Guard, (which had been transferred to the Navy on November 1, 1941.) By the end of the month, 40,000 additional volunteers had been accepted for naval service, and a great training program had been instituted. Within the next year nearly 900,000 volunteers entered the service, and they were trained in time to man the new ships as they were completed.

To handle this influx of men, the four permanent naval training stations, at Newport, Rhode Island; Norfolk, Virginia; Great Lakes, Illinois and San Diego, California, were expanded, and three new stations were established, at Sampson, New York; Farragut, Idaho and Bainbridge, Maryland.

To obtain officers in the number needed, a series of programs was begun in the colleges, based on the experience gained in the Reserve Officers Training Corps units which had been established in various universities before Pearl Harbor. The aviation cadet program (V-5) produced pilots; the reserve midshipman program (V-7) indoctrinated future officer material; and within 2 years under the V-12 program, there were 66,815 young men studying in 241 colleges at government expense to prepare themselves for a naval career.

In the early stages of the war, the navy, because of the nation's will to fight, was never at a loss for adequate manpower. When, on February 1, 1943, men began to enter the navy through Selective Service, it was chiefly because the army objected that the best of the country's youth were being attracted to naval service by means of the navy's recruiting system, although conscription for naval service would have been inevitable sooner or later.

But if there were plenty of men at the navy's disposal, there were far from enough ships. By the loss of the battleships at Pearl Harbor the aircraft carrier was suddenly placed in the position of being the major unit in naval warfare, and there were only seven first-line and one escort carrier in commission, with several large carriers of the *Essex* class building. The first escort carrier was the USS *Long Island,* and she had been converted in early 1941 from the merchantman *Mormacmail,* a vessel built under the Maritime Commission program. Tests proved the *Long Island* a valuable warship, and more such escort carriers were ordered, converted in the last half of 1941 from Maritime

Commission C-3 hulls and tankers. In 1942 this program was greatly accelerated, as the navy discovered the full power of carrier-borne planes. These small, "baby flat-tops," came to be used as escorts for convoys, as transports for airplanes, and as combatant carriers, working with the fleets. Fifty-four cruisers were being built, but only eighteen heavy cruisers and nineteen light cruisers were in commission at the end of 1941. There were only ninety-nine modern destroyers in commission, although over two hundred were building, and close to a hundred of the over-age four-stackers were at work, from Iceland to the China Sea. The navy was not well equipped with submarines, of which only forty-two had been commissioned since 1932. But there were eighty building, sixty-six ancient vessels useful chiefly as training ships, and a few special type submarines fit for combat duty.

The navy's modern submarines were excellent ships, built at Portsmouth, New Hampshire; Groton, Connecticut; or Mare Island, California. From 1933 on, the design of these ships had been gradually improved with each successive class, so that the more recent of them were powerful vessels of nearly fifteen hundred tons surface displacement, with a length of three hundred feet, beam of twenty-seven feet, draft of thirteen feet, nine inches. They could make twenty knots on the surface, and nine submerged, and their armament consisted of ten to fourteen torpedo tubes, six to ten forward and four aft, and a 3-inch, 50-caliber deck gun. Such ships could carry three dozen torpedoes, and they were manned by a ship's company of fifty-five officers and men. Their surface range was fifteen thousand miles, and they were made to order for the war in the Pacific, where on their first combat patrols they proved their worth. Soon two other yards began to produce submarines: the Cramp Shipbuilding Company, in Philadelphia, and the Manitowoc Shipbuilding Company in Wisconsin. From the latter yard completed ships were tried out on the Great Lakes, and then, by way of the Chicago Drainage Canal, taken down the Mississippi to New Orleans, where their shake-down cruises began.

There were few landing craft in the navy in 1941, and those were of an experimental design. In 1942, as the Japanese demonstrated the value of this type of craft, a billion-dollar program for these craft was started and a top priority given the program. Navy and merchant marine building programs had already filled existing yards to capacity, and to obtain the landing-craft new yards were built, many of them inland, in the Mississippi Valley, and along the banks of the Ohio. In the last six months of 1942 nearly 250,000 tons of landing craft were built, and this tonnage included a host of new types of ships, ranging from tank-landing ships 300 feet long to small boats. As the war progressed and experience in amphibious landings on hostile beaches was gained, the variety of these special types increased, so that it included amphibious tracked craft, and special ships for landing personnel, guns, vehicles, and supplies.

Thus, although the outbreak of war found the two-ocean naval building program represented mostly by partially completed hulls and machinery, the foundation for accelerated construction had been laid, and many months of effort had been put to good effect. The warning of impending trouble had been heeded, if not early enough, then at least in time to permit the United States to take the offensive much sooner than the enemy had believed possible.

The navy had been authorized to have 15,000 planes in 1940, and this complement was raised to 27,500 on January 7, 1942. The new models that were delivered in 1942 included the "Avenger" torpedo planes, and there were improved radio systems, self-sealing gas tanks, heavier guns, de-icing systems, and greater power plants. These improvements reflected the contents of combat reports from the fleet which told of the superior speed, maneuverability and fire-power of Japanese planes. The number of naval pilots rose from 4,525 in June 1941, to 11,240 in June 1942, and nearly $813,000,000 worth of aircraft and facilities were delivered in the same period. Close to $4,000,000,000 worth of aircraft and facilities were on order.

As the navy's shipbuilding and plane procurement programs were being intensified, the President, early in 1942, asked for the construction of eight million deadweight tons of merchant ships in 1942 and sixteen million tons in 1943. At the time of Pearl Harbor the total carrying capacity of the merchant fleet was approximately eleven million tons, and although this was a smaller total than the records showed for 1937, the fleet was of better quality. 185 new and highly efficient vessels, of over 2,000,000 deadweight tons had been built in 1939, 1940 and 1941.

Many of the old ships had been withdrawn from service; others had been sold to the British to replace their war losses. The Maritime Commission's 1937 plan to build fifty vessels a year for ten years had been raised to the scheduling of four hundred ships a year in 1941. In 1937 there had been but ten shipyards in the United States capable of building ocean-going vessels: in December, 1941, there were forty great yards at work, on the Pacific, Gulf and Atlantic coasts, and on the Great Lakes. In the closing weeks of 1941 the first two Liberty ships were completed, having taken nearly nine months to build.

The goal set by the President of 24,000,000 deadweight tons of shipping could never have been reached had it not been for the Liberty ship design: from 2 delivered in 1941 the number of Libertys rose to 542 in 1942 and to 1,232 in 1943. The amount of time required to complete a Liberty fell to 4 months in mid-1942, to 55 days at the end of the year, to 39.2 days at the end of 1943, when 80 yards held contracts for Liberties, and employed, at the peak of the program, 702,000 men and women. This tremendous building activity created new techniques of shipbuilding: welding replaced riveting to an extent no one had believed possible; large ship-sections were prefabricated; a close liaison was maintained between the suppliers of parts and the hull assembly lines in the yards. One energetic man, Henry Kaiser by name, discovered the profitable secret of building ships by working with government money, and the shipyards he operated completed hundreds of merchantmen.

Cost was no consideration in this program: speed of building was of paramount importance. As a result, there were great waste and much extravagance, which the public could charge to the price of winning the war. Throughout the war the Maritime Commission remained under the chairmanship of Admiral Emory S. Land, and he was the driving force behind the building program.

To operate the ships the War Shipping Administration was created on February 7, 1942, and this bureau too was administered by Admiral Land, who thus became the czar of American shipping, in charge of both building and operating the merchantmen. The War Shipping Administration was given the power to purchase, charter, or requisition any of the nation's privately-owned ships for its own use, or for use by the army and navy. Vessels not needed by the army and navy were placed in the United Nations merchant shipping pool, and were operated by the shipping lines, which thus became agents of the government. The Combined Shipping Adjustment Board was created on January 26, 1942 to adjust and concert in one harmonious policy the work of the British Ministry of War Transport and the shipping authorities of the United States government. This Board served as a clearing house for information as to the need for and availability of ships, and was of course subject to the decisions of the Combined Chiefs of Staff.

By all these various organizations—Combined Chiefs of Staff, Joint Chiefs of Staff, Navy Department, Maritime Commission, War Shipping Board, Combined Shipping Adjustment Board—the maritime elements of the war were provided and put to use. When there was conflict between the claims of the army, the navy and the civilian population for portions of the nation's limited production, a "War Production Board" decided which claim would contribute most to victory, and to that claim gave priority. In this way the United States became not only the arsenal but also the shipbuilder of the United Nations.

The first year following the attack on Pearl Harbor was the most difficult of the war. In the Pacific the Japanese, displaying an admirable grasp of amphibious operations, invaded and conquered at will.

In December, Guam, all but defenseless, fell quickly to them, and Wake Island was captured after a stalwart defense. The main force of the Japanese attack was directed to the south, toward the Philippines, Malaya and the Netherlands East Indies. There was little to stop them. The army planes in MacArthur's command were caught on the ground at Iba and Clark fields in the Philippines; ten hours after the attack on Pearl Harbor they were being decimated by Japanese fighter planes and bombers from Formosa. Hong Kong fell on Christmas, and by that day, the invasion of the Philippines was well under way. In Malaya Japanese landing forces were moving down the peninsula toward Singapore.

The Japanese expansion was harried by what slender resources were at the disposal of the Allies in the Far East. Admiral Tom Phillips, of the Royal Navy, set out from Singapore with the new battleship *Prince of Wales* and the old battle-cruiser *Repulse,* accompanied by a few destroyers, in an attempt to halt an invasion convoy nearing the Malayan coast on December 10th. His force was detected through a rift in the clouds, and both capital ships, as well as a destroyer, were sunk by Japanese torpedo and bombing planes in a brief engagement. Admiral Hart had ordered his surface vessels to southern waters in November, and as the Japanese moved against Borneo he sent four ancient destroyers against the invaders. The destroyers came upon the Japanese force shortly after midnight on January 24th, and in a night torpedo attack, called the Battle of Macassar Strait, inflicted severe losses on the enemy. On February 11th, Admiral Hart was directed to turn operational command of the American naval forces in the southern seas over to Vice-Admiral Helfrich of the Netherlands. On February 27th an allied naval force, under Rear Admiral Karel Doorman of the Netherlands, consisting of nine destroyers, two heavy and three light cruisers, engaged superior enemy forces protecting an invasion convoy in the Battle of the Java Sea, and was defeated. Of the cruisers, only USS *Houston* and HMAS *Perth* remained afloat, and they, with the rest of the American-British-Dutch-Australian forces, were bottled up in the Java Sea by the Japanese. The two surviving cruisers were sunk on the night of February 28–March 1, as they attempted to run the Sunda Strait. Of the surface ships from this whole allied "ABDA" force, only four American destroyers reached Australia.

Meanwhile Singapore had fallen, on February 15th, and in the Philippines the American ground forces had been bottled up on Bataan. There was obviously little hope that they would be relieved, and yet morale remained high, especially on Corregidor, "The Rock" in Manila Bay where the Fourth Regiment of the Marine Corps, the "North China Marines," manned the defenses while the soldiers were fighting on Bataan. So good, in fact, was morale, that when MacArthur sent out the following message, there was much argument as to whether it was necessary:

> "FORT MILLS, P.I.
> January 15, 1942

"Subject: Message from General MacArthur
"To: All Unit Commanders

"The following message from General MacArthur will be read and explained to all troops. Every company commander is charged with personal responsibility for the delivery of this message. Each headquarters will follow up to insure reception by every company or similar unit.

'Help is on the way from the United States. Thousands of troops and hundreds of planes are being dispatched. The exact time of arrival of reinforcements is unknown as they will have to fight their way through Japanese attempts against them. It is imperative that our troops hold until these reinforcements arrive.

'No further retreat is possible. We have more troops in Bataan than the Japanese have thrown against us; our supplies are ample; a determined defense will defeat the enemy's attack.

'It is a question now of courage and determination. Men who run will merely be destroyed but men who fight will save themselves and their country.

'I call upon every soldier in Bataan to fight in his assigned position, resisting every attack. This is the only road to salvation. If we fight we will win; if we retreat we will be destroyed.

'MacArthur' "<br>"By command of General MacArthur."

Unkind critics of this excellent officer opined that his years of employment by the Filipinos had put him out of touch with the tenacity in combat of the average American soldier. But on March 11th, on orders from the President, MacArthur departed by motor torpedo boat and plane for Australia, accompanied in his recession by an entourage of staff officers and by his domestic ménage. He was much too valuable a general to permit the Japanese to capture, and General Jonathan Wainwright was left to surrender to the enemy, which he did early in May.

By that time the Japanese had moved into the Solomon Islands, and Port Moresby in Australia was threatened.

The navy had managed to salvage little from the onslaught: of the 200,000 tons of Allied shipping in Manila Bay at the start of the war all but one ship escaped under naval escort to the south. In the process of fighting against the Japanese the value of air power had been demonstrated: much of the dependable information about enemy ship movements in the early days of the war came from the patrol planes of Patrol Wing Ten, whose pilots could be depended on to report a heavy cruiser as a heavy cruiser and not as a battleship. And it was clear

· 478 ·

that whenever the Japanese had controlled the air over a surface engagement the Allies had been defeated. These lessons were taken to heart: the emphasis on new construction was placed on carriers, and the inadequate antiaircraft batteries of American warships were improved by the addition of more and faster-shooting guns. As reports of enemy ships sunk by the fleet submarines came in, surpassing even Admiral Hart's expectations, this class of warship won the full appreciation it had hitherto lacked. The navy, in short, was learning as it fought.

In the first six months of the Pacific war the navy could undertake only a few offensive actions: on January 31st a carrier task force commanded by Admiral William Halsey, Jr., raided the Marshall and Gilbert Islands without losing a ship. This raid served the double purpose of raising civilian morale in the United States and obtaining information about these islands which lay on the flank of the supply lines to Australia and New Zealand. In February Halsey took command of another task force built around the carrier *Enterprise* and this force bombed and shelled the Japanese conquerors on Wake Island and went on to raid Marcus Island; in March Admiral Wilson Brown, with *Lexington* and *Yorktown,* raided Salamaua and Lae on New Guinea, sinking and damaging many enemy vessels at light cost to the Americans. On April 18th Tokyo received its first sample of what the future held in store for it when 16 twin-motored army bombers, having been ferried on the USS *Hornet* to within 850 miles of the city, dropped 16 tons of bombs on the Mikado's home soil. The military value of this raid was slight: the most the army claimed for it was that it resulted in the concentration of Japanese planes in Japan, at a time when they might have been more usefully employed in the South Pacific. But in the United States news of the raid was received with amazement and jubilation. On May 7th the Battle of the Coral Sea began: that morning an American task force commanded by Admiral Frank Fletcher, consisting of the carriers *Yorktown* and *Lexington,* eight cruisers (two of which were Australian), and numerous destroyers, made contact with the new Japanese carrier *Shoho,* which was sunk by American carrier-based planes. Next morning two more Japanese carriers were located and attacked, one of which was heavily damaged by planes from the

American carriers. Planes from the Japanese carriers hit both *Yorktown* and *Lexington,* damaging the latter so severely that she had to be sunk by torpedoes from an American destroyer, in an attempt to conceal her loss from the enemy. American losses in this engagement were, besides the *Lexington,* the tanker *Neosho* and the destroyer *Sims,* 66 planes, and a total of 543 personnel casualties. In this first battle between American and Japanese carriers, fought while the ships were 150 miles apart, the Americans won a tactical draw and a strategic victory. Both forces lost one carrier, but the Japanese move southward had been checked. There were then only four American carriers left in the Pacific: *Yorktown, Hornet, Saratoga* and *Enterprise.* The Japanese had nine such craft in commission.

Soon after the Battle of the Coral Sea, radio messages were intercepted and decoded which revealed that the Japanese were about to launch an attack in strength against Midway Island. Emergency repairs were made on *Yorktown* and all the American forces available in the Central and South Pacific were rushed to the area threatened. These forces consisted of the carriers *Yorktown, Hornet* and *Enterprise,* fourteen destroyers, twenty submarines, seven heavy and one light cruisers. These vessels were formed into two task forces, one under Admiral Frank Fletcher, the other under Admiral Raymond Spruance. On Midway the Marine Corps air group was alerted, and reinforced by army bombers from Hawaii.

On June 3rd the enemy forces were sighted by Ensign Jack Reid, flying a navy patrol bomber several hundred miles to the southwest of Midway. In the afternoon a squadron of army bombers, B-17s, launched a high-level bombing attack on this force and claimed hits on several ships. During the night navy patrol planes attacked the invasion force with torpedoes. Next morning Midway was hit by planes from Japanese carriers, while planes from Midway attacked and severely damaged one enemy carrier. Then came the attacks from the American carrier-based planes: Torpedo Squadron 8, from *Hornet,* attacked a group of four carriers, and scored several hits, although only one man in the squadron survived the attack. Then the torpedo planes from *Enterprise* and *Yorktown* hit the same group of carriers and took severe losses. The Japanese fighter planes were drawn down to engage these low-flying torpedo planes, and before the fighters could recover altitude, dive bombers from *Enterprise* roared over two carriers, turning them into flaming hulks, and these dive bombers were quickly followed by more from *Yorktown,* which damaged another carrier. One Japanese carrier still remained unscathed, and planes from this ship attacked *Yorktown,* damaging her with three bomb and two torpedo hits. Fletcher, who was Senior Officer Present, moved his flag from hard hit *Yorktown* to *Astoria* and signaled to Spruance at 1615 on June 4th that he would follow Spruance's lead.

Meanwhile, planes from *Enterprise* reached the Japanese carrier in a synchronized dive-bombing and torpedo-plane attack and set her ablaze. When *Hornet's* squadrons arrived on the scene this enemy carrier was not worth wasting bombs on, and *Hornet's* planes concentrated their attack on a battleship and a heavy cruiser, inflicting damage on both. Airplanes from Midway came out to polish off the already mortally injured enemy forces, and army B-17s, in a high-level bombing attack, claimed hits on a heavy cruiser. As June 4th ended the Japanese forces were in full retreat. In the next two days planes from *Enterprise* and *Hornet* sought out and attacked several cruisers and destroyers. On the last day of the battle—June 6th—as *Yorktown* was being towed toward Pearl Harbor, and the destroyer *Hammann* was alongside, putting a salvage party aboard the carrier, a Japanese submarine lunched three torpedoes at the slow moving vessels. *Yorktown* was hit by two and *Hammann* by one of the torpedoes. *Hammann* exploded and sank instantly, and *Yorktown* followed her to the bottom the next morning. In this battle the Japanese lost four great carriers: *Akagi, Hiryu, Kaga* and *Soryu;* and one heavy cruiser, the *Mikuma,* as well as hundreds of the Japanese Navy's best pilots. Not since 1592, when Hideyoshi was defeated by a Korean fleet under Admiral Yi-Sun, had the Japanese Navy been so thoroughly routed. For the Americans it was a great victory, and the last of the purely defensive battles the navy had to fight in the Pacific.

Prime Minister Churchill arrived in Washington June 18th, 1942, and despite the brilliant naval victory at Midway, the future looked foreboding to the Allied cause. The Japanese had landed in the Aleutians on June 8th at Attu, Kiska and Agattu, but these landings were in the nature of a feint and were thus estimated by the Combined Chiefs of Staff. Still, the landings caused considerable alarm on the Pacific coast, and the United States did not have the forces available to recapture the islands. On the day of Churchill's arrival in Washington, tanks of General Rommel's Afrika Corps broke through the British lines before Tobruk, and 3 days later Tobruk fell, and 25,000 troops were captured by the Germans. The British Eighth Army prepared to make a final desperate stand inside the Egyptian border, at El Alamein. In Russia although Moscow and Leningrad were still holding out, the Germans had swept through the Ukraine and the Crimea to Sevastopol. In the Atlantic the German submarines were taking a heavy toll of Allied merchantmen.

The Germans, during the first eight months of 1942 kept an average of fifty-seven U-boats constantly at sea. There was little the United States could do to protect its shipping from these lethal craft: there were not sufficient planes and anti-submarine vessels and trained men to protect even the coastal shipping, and it became the practice for coastwise vessels to duck into the nearest port at dusk, and to set forth again at dawn. In June 141 ships were lost, representing 707,000 tons of shipping which were sorely needed. Slowly the submarines were driven from east coast waters, only to appear in the Gulf of Mexico and in the Caribbean. In the struggle against them the Americans profited greatly from the experience gained in the neutrality patrol and from the acquisition of the eight bases which had been traded for the fifty four-stack destroyers in 1940. The British, too, were helpful, making their latest devices and techniques available to the Americans, so that there was a complete interchange of information. By the use of convoys in the Gulf of Mexico and in the Caribbean, by intensified air patrols with planes and small dirigibles, the submarines were gradually forced to concentrate on the convoy lanes in mid-Atlantic, beyond the range of aircraft.

Both radar and sonar were put to use in detecting the submarines; the sonar being sound gear which broadcast underwater sound waves that were reflected by any submarine in their path. To evade the sonar the submarines were equipped with "pillenwerfers," or "pill-ejectors," which released pills that made a screen of bubbles capable of reflecting the sonar waves, and confusing to the attacking vessels. In the continuing search for a way to detect submarines American scientists, working with the navy, managed to keep one step ahead of the enemy's efforts to avoid detection.

Most perilous run of all the convoy routes was that to Russia, by way of the North Cape of Norway and on down to Murmansk or across the White Sea to Arkhangelsk. In the late spring and during the summer, as the ice moved down from the Arctic, the convoys had to make their way between the North Cape and the ice. In this area, which took on the semblance of a bottleneck, the ships were exposed to attack by German submarines, German and Finnish bombers, and the threat of attack by German capital ships such as the *Tirpitz* or the *Hipper,* or the *Scheer,* which could put out from the Norwegian coast, where they lurked in Trondhjem fjord.

One such convoy which set out from Iceland in June 1942 lost nineteen of thirty-five cargo ships to bombs and torpedoes, in spite of a covering force consisting of two American and two British cruisers, one American and one British battleship, a British aircraft carrier and nine destroyers. The convoy's close escort included six destroyers, four corvettes, seven trawlers, two submarines, two anti-aircraft ships and three life-saving ships. Scouting ahead of the convoy were four Russian and nine British submarines. Of this convoy only eleven ships reached Arkhangelsk with their cargoes of tanks and planes and guns. Such losses were not uncommon in the early days of the war, and the hazards of the route brought from Ivan Maisky, Soviet Ambassador in London, the following lyric tribute: "The Russian convoys are a Northern saga of heroism, bravery, and endurance, and the price had to be paid. This saga will live forever not only in the hearts of your people but also in the hearts of the Soviet people, who rightly see in it one of the most striking expressions of collaboration between the allied nations." Despite heavy initial losses, in the three and a half years from October 1941 to March 1945, the Muscovites received 91.6 per cent of the tremendous quantities of war supplies shipped to them over the northern route.

The convoys bound for the British Isles traversed seas almost as perilous as those around the North Cape. Convoys of sixty or more merchant vessels gathered in such ports as Halifax, New York and

Norfolk, to begin their long journey to Iceland and Liverpool. By taking the northern route they were able to remain under the protection of the land-based airplanes which flew from bases in Newfoundland, Greenland and Iceland. Even so, they were frequently attacked by groups of ten or more submarines.

In July, 1942, Congress authorized an additional expansion of naval construction. The Act of July 19, 1940 had provided for an increase of 1,425,000 combatant and auxiliary tons; the Acts of December 17 and 23, 1941, and of May 13, 1942, had provided for 350,000 additional tons of combat ships and 800,000 tons of auxiliaries. To this enormous program Congress added the authorization, on July 9, 1942, for the building of 3,100,000 tons of combat and auxiliary vessels. This meant that a two-ocean navy was no longer considered large enough: the United States was going to build a navy capable of seizing control of any or all of the world's oceans. It was hoped that this navy, with its congeries of fleets, would be completed by 1947, through an acceleration of the ship production program. For the program, as for that of the Maritime Commission, the Congress appropriated the funds with unusual celerity: in the seven months following the attack on Pearl Harbor, Congress appropriated over twelve and a half billion dollars in cash for the navy, along with authority to contract for nearly five billion additional dollars worth of ships, supplies and equipment. Of this total approximately one-third was to be devoted to aviation. The navy had, in fact, become as air-minded as the Air Force, and with the well-founded conviction that air power adds more to sea power than it takes away from it.

In the Atlantic war October 24, 1942, was a memorable day, for then the British Eighth Army, under General Montgomery's command, began its offensive at El Alamein, and a huge troop and supply convoy left American east coast ports. Next day two more convoys cleared British ports, and these three convoys, numbering in all some seven hundred vessels, moved against French North Africa, following a decision which had been made by the Combined Chiefs of Staff four months earlier. The Commander in Chief of the Allied force was General Dwight D. Eisenhower, U.S. Army, and all Allied naval forces in the expedition were commanded by Admiral Sir A. B. Cunningham, R.N.

The troops involved in the expedition were American and British.

The three task forces, covering twenty-five square miles of sea, but lost in the immensity of the ocean wastes, converged west of Gibraltar on November 7th, when five attack groups formed and set off for their designated landing points. Sunday, November 8th, was the day set for the landings, which were to be made at Oran and Algiers in the Mediterranean, and in the vicinity of Casablanca on the Atlantic coast of Africa. The forces assigned to land at Algiers and Oran were supported by British naval units, and these landings were made without great difficulty; although the French fought at Oran for two days, Algiers surrendered after a token resistance.

In the Casablanca area the landings were more complex: the orders called for landings at Fedala, 14 miles north of Casablanca, at Port Lyautey, 51 miles north of Fedala, and at Safi, 125 miles south of Casablanca. Once these landings had been made, Casablanca could be taken by land. The naval force supporting these landings was commanded by Admiral H. K. Hewitt, and included the carriers *Ranger* and *Wasp*, the battleships *Washington* and *Texas,* cruisers *Augusta, Wichita, Tuscaloosa, Philadelphia* and *Brooklyn,* and numerous destroyers, all drawn from the U.S. Atlantic Fleet. Safi and Port Lyautey were taken without trouble, but at Fedala, soon after the first troops had been landed, shore batteries opened fire on the supporting naval forces. These batteries were not silenced until early in the afternoon.

In Casablanca the battleship *Jean Bart* fired her 15-inch guns from her berth in the harbor, and although bombed by nine navy dive bombers and sunk in shallow water, she continued to fire throughout the ninth and tenth. A light French cruiser, accompanied by two destroyer leaders and five destroyers, sortied from Casablanca and after encountering the American covering force, were all either beached or sunk. Of the French warships in Casablanca, only eight submarines managed to escape.

With the French warships disposed of, the landings at Fedala were speedily completed. Army pursuit planes were flown from American carriers to provide the nucleus for an American air force in Africa; the ten tons of initial equipment per man began to be landed. The fighting did not lull until the afternoon of the tenth, when Admiral Jean François

Darlan, commander of all the French armed forces under the control of Pétain's government at Vichy, having been awarded the titular leadership of France by the Americans, agreed to order the French to stop fighting their liberators. Thus the nice French sense of honor was satisfied. On November 11th, the transport *Joseph Hewes,* the destroyer *Hambleton* and the oiler *Winooski* were torpedoed. *Hewes* sank within an hour, and the others were ultimately taken to Casablanca for repairs. On the 12th two more transports were torpedoed, the *Hugh Scott* and the *Edward Rutledge.* It was presumed that these attacks were made by German or Italian, rather than Vichy-French, submarines.

When the French ceased fire on the 11th, the operation, so far as it concerned American naval forces, was at an end. From then on the navy's task was one of insuring the delivery of the 1.5 tons of supplies each soldier in the North African campaign required every month. During the next 3 months 800 ships brought 6,500,000 tons of supplies and equipment to North Africa.

The German reaction to this invasion of North Africa was fast and infuriated: their submarines had been caught out of position, and the surprise had been complete. They were enraged at Darlan's defection from the Vichy-French government they had patronized, and German troops proceeded to over-run the remaining unoccupied portion of France. At Toulon the French scuttled the remnants of their fleet to prevent the Germans from obtaining them.

Meanwhile at sea the submarines intensified their efforts to cut the supply lines to Russia, Britain, and North Africa. The wolf-packs of U-boats increased in size and in the months from October 1942 to June 1943, they sank 603 vessels, totaling 3,546,000 tons.

In the Pacific, following the Battle of Midway, a pause occurred in the fighting, while the opposing fleets refitted and made ready for the next campaign. This was not long delayed.

By early August the Japanese offensive had reached its outermost limits. Their forces were entrenched in the Aleutian Islands of Attu, Agattu, Kiska and Rat. The South China, Celebes, Banda and Java Seas had become Japanese lakes; the Netherlands East Indies, Indo-China, Siam and Malaya were under Japanese control, and their forces had occupied the Nicobar and Andaman islands in the Bay of Bengal. The northern shore of New Guinea and the island of New Britain had been taken by their amphibious forces against slight opposition, as had the Gilbert Islands of Makin and Tarawa. In May the Japanese had taken Tulagi in the Solomons; in July they began to build an airfield on Guadalcanal. These conquests represented a potentially great empire, which the Japanese expected to retain and develop after the Americans became weary of fighting and returned to their habitual life of ease and frivolity.

The Americans had other plans afoot, and as news of Japanese atrocities reached them their determination grew. Radio station JOAK in Tokyo had announced the execution of three of the army pilots who had flown off USS *Hornet* to raid Japan; Japanese brutality in the Philippines, Hong Kong and Singapore had been so sadistic that they were rightly classified as an outlawed nation. The quality of mercy was not in them.

Troops and planes from the United States, as well as Australian veterans withdrawn from the North African campaign, had been sent to Australia to protect the thinly populated sub-continent which the Japanese threatened from the north. To assure this front of adequate supplies and reinforcements the Americans were creating a string of bases in the South Central Pacific, leading from Hawaii to Palmyra to Canton to the Samoan Islands, and thence to the Fiji Islands, New Caledonia and Brisbane, Australia. A second line of supply, further removed from possible Japanese attack, led to the Society Islands, where Bora-Bora became a fueling station, and down to New Zealand. None of these island bases had been developed to their full war potential, but soon they were the scenes of bustling activity. The navy's war-born Construction Battalions, called "Sea-Bees," and formed around a core of experienced construction workers, remade the face of many an islet, built docks, dredged harbors, erected cantonments, hospitals, leveled the ground for airfields, distilled weird and highly potent alcoholic concoctions from sugar and raisins and fruit juices.

In August, when the supply line to Australia was serving to deliver men and planes and supplies to MacArthur's command, reconnaissance flights showed that the Japanese had nearly completed their airfield in

Guadalcanal in the Solomons. If they were permitted to complete the field, from it they would be able to raid the American supply line to Australia. To remove this threat to the supply line the Americans undertook a desperate campaign to capture and hold the airfield on Guadalcanal.

This first major offensive operation was planned and commanded by Vice-Admiral R. L. Ghormley, USN, and the forces involved included the First Marine Division, the Second Marine Regiment, the First Marine Raider Battalion and the Third Defense Battalion, under the command of General A. A. Vandergrift, USMC. The Marine units were concentrated in New Zealand during June and July.

Three naval task forces were to provide cover for the operation. Two of these forces were commanded by Vice-Admiral Frank Fletcher, USN; they were, first, an air support force under Rear Admiral Leigh Noyes, USN, with three carriers, a new battleship, five heavy and one light cruisers, and a few divisions of destroyers; second, an amphibious force commanded by Rear Admiral Richmond K. Turner, USN, consisting of six heavy cruisers, two of which were Australian, one light Australian cruiser, accompanying destroyers and twenty-three transports. The third task force was formed of land-based planes based on Samoa, the Fiji Islands and New Caledonia, all commanded by Rear Admiral John S. McCain, USN. McCain's planes were ordered to co-operate with planes from MacArthur's command in Australia and New Guinea —an achievement easier to order than to effect.

Of these forces, that of Admiral Turner was the one most involved in the following days, and command of his screening cruisers was given to Rear Admiral V. A. C. Crutchley, a British naval officer on loan to the Australian Navy.

On the morning of August 7th the marines landed on Tulagi and Guadalcanal, taking the enemy by surprise. On Tulagi there was bitter fighting, but on Guadalcanal the airfield was immediately taken as the Japanese retired into the jungle. By the afternoon of August 8th the marines had Tulagi under control, and the primary objectives of the operation had been achieved. The cost to the Americans was one transport and one destroyer sunk, another destroyer damaged, all as a result of Japanese air raids, and twenty-one planes lost.

On the evening of the 8th, while unloading of the supply ships was progressing at Tulagi and on Guadalcanal, and while Admiral Noyes' carrier force was withdrawing to refuel away from the submarine infested waters, Admiral Crutchley made his defensive dispositions for the night. *Vincennes, Quincy* and *Astoria* were assigned to cover the channel north of Savo Island, with *Chicago* and HMAS *Canberra* patrolling to the south of them. The American destroyers *Blue* and *Ralph Talbot* patrolled the waters south and north of Savo Island. Crutchley's flagship, HMAS *Australia,* lay off Guadalcanal, hard by USS *McCawley,* Admiral Turner's flagship. On the chart the dispositions looked excellent, and when that evening word came from a scouting plane that a Japanese force which included cruisers and "seaplane tenders" had been sighted three hundred miles northwest of Guadalcanal, no change in the disposition of the cruisers and destroyers was thought necessary. At a late night conference which Turner called aboard USS *McCawley,* both Turner and Crutchley found no reason for disquietude. That evening Crutchley asked Turner what he thought the Japanese force's objective was, and Turner said that he suspected they were headed for Rekata Bay, on Santa Isabel 125 miles away, whence they could launch torpedo planes against the Allied fleet units. To prevent this he had ordered the "seaplane tenders" bombed the next day.

But the Japanese Admiral, Mikawa by name, had more urgent plans: his force of five heavy cruisers and three destroyers headed for Guadalcanal at flank speed, and in the early hours of August 9th sped in south of Savo Island at 1:45 A.M., undetected by USS *Blue* whose radar was of a primitive type. The Japanese fired their torpedoes at unsuspecting, semi-alerted *Chicago* and *Canberra,* then bore to the north and opened fire on *Quincy, Astoria* and *Vincennes.* The supply ships were now but lightly protected, and Mikawa had orders to attack them. But a shell from an American gun had hit his plotting room and ruined his charts, and he turned tail and fled, at 2:15 A.M., leaving the supply ships unharmed. This Battle of Savo Island cost the Allies four heavy cruisers sunk—*Quincy, Astoria, Vincennes* and *Canberra,* and one, the *Chicago,* heavily damaged. The loss of life was enormous: 952 American officers and men, and 84 Australians.

The supply ships, left without the protection of five heavy cruisers, were at once withdrawn, before their unloading had been completed. The marines were thrown on their own resources, which, as it turned out, were adequate to the occasion. For ten days they were all but isolated from reinforcements and supplies, and the Japanese bombed them by day and shelled them at night. The positions held by the marines on Guadalcanal and Tulagi became small oases of American power, surrounded by Japanese-dominated air and water.

The campaign for Guadalcanal settled down to a war of supply, as each side sought to reinforce its positions in the area. Sea battles raged in the surrounding waters, and in the air over Guadalcanal marine fighter pilots shot down scores of the highly-inflammable Japanese planes. The marines fought without giving or asking quarter, and so effectively that the Japanese came to complain that they were fighting unfairly. This was a notable tribute from the Japanese, who were schooled to savagery and deception. Not until December was the First Marine Division replaced by soldiers of the Army's 25th Division, and by that time the American Navy had won control of the waters and air around Guadalcanal.

Great progress toward winning this control had been made in the Battle of Santa Cruz Islands, on October 26th, when four Japanese and two American carriers exchanged blows. The battle cost the Americans the carrier *Hornet* and the destroyer *Porter,* and resulted in damage to the carrier *Enterprise,* the cruiser *San Juan* and the destroyer *Smith.* The battleship *South Dakota* took a bomb hit on her Number Two turret. While the American force was under attack by Japanese planes, planes from *Hornet* and *Enterprise* were working over the Japanese ships. The American air groups reported four hits with 1,000-pound bombs on a carrier, and additional hits on a battleship, three heavy cruisers and a destroyer leader. But the greatest damage suffered by the Japanese force was represented by the estimated 110 carrier-based planes shot down as they attacked the American surface vessels. The loss of these Japanese planes meant that four enemy air groups had been slaughtered, and the Japanese carriers had to retire to replenish their complements of planes and pilots.

Definitive control of the waters and air around Guadalcanal was not won until November, in a great battle which began on the morning of

November 11th. Word came to Admiral Halsey, who had relieved Admiral Ghormley as Commander, South Pacific Forces on October 18th, that the Japanese were mounting an invasion attempt on a large scale.

To oppose this offensive Halsey had two new battleships, four heavy and four light cruisers, twenty-two destroyers, and *Enterprise*. The carriers *Lexington, Yorktown, Wasp* (torpedoed by a submarine), and *Hornet* had been lost, and of the carriers left (*Saratoga, Ranger* and *Enterprise*), only damaged *Enterprise* was available for use in the South Pacific. In contrast, the Japanese force included two carriers, four battleships, five heavy cruisers and some thirty destroyers, as well as transport and supply ships.

On the 11th three American transports arrived off Guadalcanal, and were subjected to an air attack by the Japanese; next day a second group arrived and began unloading. This group too was bombed, ineffectively, for marine fighter planes shot down twenty-four of the twenty-five attacking torpedo and bombing planes. One of the damaged planes made a suicidal dive on the *San Francisco,* killing thirty men.

The main enemy forces were meanwhile coming down from the northwest, and to oppose them Admiral Turner assigned to Rear Admiral Daniel Callaghan two heavy and three light cruisers and eight destroyers. With this force Callaghan was to fight a delaying action until the carrier-battleship force under Admiral Kinkaid, 600 miles to the southward, could reach the Japanese.

On the night of the 12th Callaghan's force had shepherded the supply ships out of the area and returned to patrol the bay. Shortly after midnight the radar screens showed enemy vessels inside the bay, to the northwest. The night was moonless, and the opposing forces were at point-blank range when the darkness was split by searchlights from the Japanese destroyers. Both sides opened fire instantly, and as the battle raged before the fascinated gaze of thousands of marines on Guadalcanal, ships were seen to explode and vanish, the beach shuddered under the impact of the explosions, and waves created by the recoil of the ships' guns slapped against the sand. In the fitful, deceptive light of vari-colored tracers and high-explosive shells exploding against steel, twenty-six Japanese warships were counted, including the battleship *Hiyei,* heavy and light cruisers and destroyers. Early in the battle Admiral Norman Scott, on *Atlanta,* was killed when his crippled ship was taken under fire by a heavy cruiser, and shortly after that a salvo from the *Hiyei* hit the bridge of *San Francisco,* killing Admiral Callaghan and Captain Cassin Young. The American force was now without an officer of flag rank, and command of the ships devolved to a junior officer, Lieutenant-Commander Bruce McCandless, thirty-one years old, who had survived the hits on the bridge of *San Francisco.* McCandless had no way of letting the rest of the ships know that Callaghan was dead, and so he took command of the force, and the battle continued without pause, and with undiminished fury. After the first fifteen minutes of battle, of the American force only three destroyers remained undamaged, and in the next nine minutes only one of these remained unscathed. In all, during those murderous twenty-four minutes, four destroyers and the *Atlanta* were hit so hard that they were lost, and eight of the other nine ships were crippled, *Juneau* so badly that she made an easy target for a Japanese submarine on the 13th, when she too was lost. The Japanese losses included the *Hiyei,* which was finally sunk by planes on the 13th as she lay dead in the water, one cruiser and three destroyers, by a conservative estimate.

On the 14th, before daylight Japanese cruisers and destroyers shelled the airfield on Guadalcanal, and were driven off by motor torpedo boats. After dawn planes from the field scored hits on two heavy and two light cruisers, and the main Japanese invasion force, north of Guadalcanal, was subjected to air attacks. As this force neared Guadalcanal, the two battleships of Halsey's command, the *Washington* and *South Dakota,* under Rear Admiral W. A. Lee, Jr., reached the scene early in the evening of the 14th. He was at once ordered to conduct a search and to intercept enemy forces that might enter the area. The radar screens scanned the sea and air ceaselessly.

Soon after midnight radar contact was made by *Washington* with six or seven enemy ships in the bay, and *Washington,* closely followed by *South Dakota,* opened fire with full radar control. Both of the enemy target vessels vanished after being hit by several broadsides of 16-inch shells from the battleships, which then sought other victims. There was a flurry of action as the American and Japanese light forces engaged, and then, when Admiral Lee could find no more targets in the bay, the two battleships pursued the enemy past Savo, and were rewarded by finding a second enemy group.

Using full radar control again, *Washington* engaged the enemy, singling out the battleship *Kirishima*, and so heavily damaging her that she sank a few hours later. *South Dakota*, her radar temporarily out of order, drew within searchlight range of the Japanese and as a result was considerably damaged. The remaining enemy vessels were dispersed by fire from the battleships and forced to flee to the northward. *Washington* and *South Dakota* retired to the southward.

At dawn on November 15th four Japanese transports which had been beached on Guadalcanal were bombed by planes from the airfield, and their destruction was completed by the destroyer *Meade*. Thus the naval "Battle of Guadalcanal" ended.

The American Navy had won a major victory and from then on the Allied position on Guadalcanal was never seriously threatened. What had begun as a defensive operation ended as the foundation for an offensive that was not to stop until Japan surrendered.

In the United States hundreds of thousands of officers and men were being trained for the war at sea. Specialists' schools, for radar, and radio and aviation, as well as a score of other specialties, were established. As men came from the basic training schools they were assigned to that specialty for which aptitude tests proved them best suited. The help of scientists had been enlisted, and synthetic training devices were being devised that reproduced battle conditions in training centers and sped the task of training large numbers of men in the complicated art of modern sea and air warfare.

In the greatest secrecy, on December 2, 1942, on a squash court beneath the stands of the University of Chicago's stadium, scientists pulled the restraining graphite rods out of the world's first experimental atomic fission pile. Pile #1 was tested successfully on that day, but at the then current rate of production it would have taken 70,000 years to produce enough uranium to make an atomic bomb.

Pile #1 was the result of a letter written to President Roosevelt by Albert Einstein, a mathematician and theoretical physicist of great repute. The letter had been delivered to President Roosevelt on October 11, 1939 by an economist named Alexander Sachs. It depicted the feasibility of making atoms explode in such a manner that they would be useful in defeating an enemy. Roosevelt was intrigued, and being a man of vision, he had given his support to the idea.

Within the five months following the successful testing of Pile #1, further developments aimed at mass producing uranium and making atomic bombs were under way. It was decided to give the army major control of further developments, and plans were made for the construction of the necessary plants at Oak Ridge, Tennessee; Los Alamos, New Mexico; and Hanford, Washington. On May 1st, 1943, army engineers, working in a newly-created, secret "Manhattan Engineer District," were placed in charge of the project. In the ensuing years they drew upon the resources of American, British and Canadian industry and science to a tremendous extent.

While the possibilities of this powerful new explosive were being studied, the navy, trusting neither God, Roosevelt, nor Einstein, continued with its shipbuilding and personnel training work.

Most entrancing of these programs was that by which women became subjected to naval discipline. On July 30, 1942, the "Women's Reserve" was established, and members thereof became known as "WAVES," derived from their official appellation of "Women Accepted for Volunteer Emergency Service." At first it was thought that a thousand officers and ten thousand enlisted women would be enough for the navy to handle, and to this end officers' training schools were organized, one at Smith College in Northampton and another at Mt. Holyoke College nearby. Training centers for enlisted Waves were established in Oklahoma, Indiana and Wisconsin. All of the recruits and officers were volunteers, and all had to meet high educational requirements: officers had to be college graduates, and enlisted Waves had to have at least two years of high school. Natty uniforms were designed for them by Mainbocher, whose name was synonymous with fashionable styles. And, for the first time in the navy's history, women, en masse, were handled with scientific care. In the First World War there had been yeomanettes, but their duties had been restricted to office and clerical work. With the Waves the navy began to plumb the limitless depths of women's abilities.

The navy selected for the head of this organization a woman named Mildred McAfee, after such sagacious ladies as Meta Glass, President of Sweet Briar College, and Dean Gildersleeve, of Barnard College, had refused the job. Miss McAfee was well known in the field of female education, for she was President of Wellesley College. Rapidly she acquired a reputation for light and pleasant speech-making at official functions.

On January 9th, 1943, the Navy Department announced proudly that a training school for Waves was about to open at Hunter College, in the Bronx, New York City, and that this school would be able to train up to 5,000 Waves at one time. The officer in command of this establishment was Captain William Faulkner Amsden, renowned as an excellent ship-handler, who had been taken off convoy duty in the South Pacific to train incipient Waves. Such assignments are proof of the inscrutable workings of the Navy Department. In this case there is corroborative evidence that Amsden's assignment was due in part to the fact that his daughter was famed, in naval circles, for her serene beauty and for the uprightness of her character. For the navy that was proof enough of Amsden's ability to handle the task. Indeed, in this instance, the Bureau of Naval Personnel was right.

At first, at USS *Hunter College,* as the training school came to be called, female Marines and Coast Guardswomen (the latter called "Spars"), as well as Waves, were trained. But since it would never do for women in the Marines and the Coast Guard to be indoctrinated in navy ways, separate schools were later set up for the Spars and female Marines in which they could learn the proper worth of their respective organizations.

From the Bronx training school, under Amsden's command, issued some 80,000 Waves, many of whom went on to further training at specialists' schools to win specialty ratings in such esoteric but essential fields as aircraft plotting, aerial camera repair work, cartography, aviation machinist work and meteorology. At least three-fourths of the Waves who marched forth from Hunter College after six weeks of basic training were destined to take over the duties of men on shore-duty in the navy and thus to free them for combat duty with the fighting fleets. The Waves themselves were not permitted, by law, to be stationed in the combat zones.

The effect of this splendid body of disciplined women on the war was great and inspiring. Commanding officers at air stations and in navy yards who were at first aghast at the thought of women cluttering up their establishments, soon became among the Waves' most enthusiastic supporters. It was discovered that the presence of Waves in a naval establishment served to raise morale and resulted in a marked improvement in the appearance of officers and enlisted men, who were quick to appreciate the value of a woman.

Less well-known to the public, because it was less publicized, was the work of the Navy Nurse Corps, which at one time numbered 10,968 nurses. Many of these nurses, who were all commissioned officers, worked in the combat zones, either ashore or on board hospital ships. They won the undying gratitude of thousands of wounded sailors and marines. It is related (and the tale is difficult to verify) that one sorely wounded marine, upon regaining consciousness in a naval hospital plane flying over the Pacific, looked up into the blue eyes of the navy nurse on flight duty, a petite and cherubic blonde-haired girl, and was convinced that he was at last in heaven.

Women were also found to be useful in the accelerated shipbuilding program of the Maritime Commission. As a shortage of manpower in the shipyards developed in late 1942, due to the workings of Selective Service and the competition from other war industries, women were hired to fill the need. They quickly proved themselves adept at welding, and at related tasks which did not demand great physical strength. By the time the program reached its peak, in 1944, 100,000 women, representing 17 per cent of the total persons employed in shipyards building Maritime Commission vessels, were women. On the Pacific coast in particular the women were employed in the yards: at one time 26 per cent of the workers employed by the Oregon Shipbuilding Company were women, who were quite willing to hide their charms behind a welder's mask and stitch the steel plates together for the same pay that a man earned for the same job.

In the last two weeks of January 1943, President Roosevelt and Churchill met at Casablanca and announced that the objective their nations sought was the unconditional surrender of their enemies.

On February 2nd the valiant Russian defenders of Stalingrad went on the offensive and trapped the German forces besieging the city. This marked the start of a broad Russian offensive along the whole length of their enormous front, and from the ferocity of their attack the Germans recoiled. The British Eighth Army was entering Tunisia. In May the Germans and Italians trapped in Tunisia at Cape Bon surrendered to the Allies, and then, after gathering up renewed strength, the Americans and the British made an amphibious assault on Sicily on July 10th. In this operation the European theater saw the use to which American ingenuity had been put: special landing craft poured tanks and men ashore; floating piers were assembled and they linked the bigger supply vessels to the shore. The Allies showed at Sicily that they had mastered the problem of maintaining a steady flow of supplies to an army, without the use of massive port facilities. The lesson was lost on the German High Command, for when undertaken on a gigantic scale in the next year at Normandy, they still believed it an impossible feat.

In the Atlantic in 1943 the war against the submarines raged with its accustomed fury. Gradually this campaign had settled down to a battle of wits, as both sides built up their forces. In the first six months of 1943 the Germans constantly maintained nearly a hundred submarines at sea. American plane production was rising, more destroyers were being commissioned every week, and the skill of anti-submarine force personnel was increasing with experience.

In the last few months of 1942 the Germans had found a means of evading radar: they had invented a receiver by which they could locate radar waves from planes or surface vessels before the radar could locate them. The American Navy, faced with a decrease in submarines sunk, devised radar equipment that worked on a band the German receivers could not pick up. For over a year the Germans remained mystified by this new type of radar.

During 1942 eleven escort carriers had been commissioned, and in the first half of 1943 this type of ship, with their twenty-odd planes and their crews of over eight hundred officers and men, began to help convoy the merchantmen across the Atlantic. With the help of very-long-range planes, equipped with radar and flying patrols out of bases in the British Isles, Iceland and Newfoundland, the submarines no longer led an easy life. To help locate a submarine which had submerged after being sighted by aircraft, the Americans invented a "sonobuoy," which located the submarine by sound and transmitted the sound to the plane. By dropping a few of these in the area in which the submarine was known to have submerged the plane could maintain contact with it.

Nonetheless, there were heartbreaking reports of sinkings: in January a convoy of nine tankers and four escorting warships cleared Trinidad for Gibraltar. Attacked by submarines, beyond the reach of aircraft in mid-Atlantic, seven of the nine tankers were sunk. In March, in attacks on four convoys, the submarine wolf packs sank thirty-eight ships. In May the battle of the Atlantic reached one of its recurring crises: that month the Germans kept 120 submarines at sea, and of these 44 were sunk. In one forty-eight hour period, when submarines attacked a convoy of 34 merchantmen and 8 escorting warships, 12 merchantmen were sunk and 5 submarines were destroyed. For the Germans this was too great a price to pay, and in June their submarines were less numerous in the North Atlantic. July marked further Allied victories, for that month 46 submarines were destroyed, 32 of them by aircraft. For the first time the monthly total of submarines sunk passed that of merchantmen torpedoed. In July the escort carriers flew their planes 24 hours a day, and the mid-Atlantic area which had been unpatrolled by planes now became subjected to intensive search by the planes from the escort carriers that accompanied the convoys. Admiral Karl Doenitz, director of the German submarine campaign, ordered his craft to stay on the surface and fight the attacking planes, and this was a ghastly mistake: the planes strafed the anti-aircraft crews on the submarines' decks and blasted the ships' hulls with bombs. By the end of July 1943 the submarine menace had been checked, and the convoys could sail with a reasonable expectation of arriving at their destinations, whether in Murmansk, Arkhangelsk, Liverpool, Algiers, Casablanca, or Basra in the Persian Gulf, where port facilities had been installed through which munitions and supplies were sent to Russia.

Thus matters stood in August when Roosevelt journeyed to Quebec, Canada, to confer with Prime Minister Churchill for the fifth time since Pearl Harbor. With them were their military strategists and their foreign ministers. At this meeting it was decided to speed the invasion of Italy, where Mussolini had been denuded of power and office, and to recognize the French Committee of Liberation, whose spiritual leader was the attenuated, intransigeant General Charles de Gaulle. The main purpose of the conference was to concert plans for the defeat of Japan, and among these plans was one to give increased military aid to China.

T. V. Soong, China's Foreign Minister, represented the Chinese ruler, Generalissimo Chiang Kai-shek, at this council of war. In the course of the discussions the decision was reached that more pressure could be brought to bear on Japan, by sea, air and land attacks, without seriously diminishing the force of the offensive in Europe.

In the Pacific three offensives developed: in the South, Central and North Pacific. To the southward, in the area around the Solomons and New Guinea, after the Japanese defeat in the naval Battle of Guadalcanal, American sea, air and land forces were greatly strengthened. In the three months following that batttle the American forces won complete control of Guadalcanal. The calculated risk which had marked the beginning of the campaign in the Solomons had turned out successfully, despite the haste with which the initial forces had been assembled and landed. The line of supply to MacArthur was no longer threatened, and the approaches to the Hawaiian Islands were secure, as were communications between Hawaii and the continental United States. The three strong points on the route to Australia—Samoa, the Fijis and New Caledonia—had become powerful bases. The Japanese had lost in the South Pacific because they had obstinately refused to change their plans to recapture Guadalcanal. Lacking the mental flexibility to shift their power against the American supply line at Samoa or in the Fiji Islands they had continued to expand their strength in futile attacks in the Solomons, in which they had committed their forces piecemeal. In the war of attrition that developed in that region they were doomed to ultimate defeat by the superior resources of the United States. As the men and weapons became available in the south, the Americans advanced westward, up the New Guinea coast and up the Solomons, threatening the Japanese base at Rabaul.

In April 1943, Japanese code messages had been intercepted and decoded which disclosed the itinerary Admiral Isoruku Yamamoto was to follow on an inspection trip in the South Pacific. On the 25th he was ambushed by army pursuit planes, and the bomber he was flying was shot down in flames over Kahili airdrome on the south coast of Bougainville. Thus this brilliant and venomous strategist, who had first seen war at the Battle of Tsushima Straits in 1905, went to join his ancestors. He was succeeded by a defensive-minded admiral named Mineichi Koga. By November 1943 the Americans, Australians and New Zealanders had made landings at Munda, Kolombangara, Vella Lavella, Salamaua, Lae, Finschhafen and Bougainville. The campaign in the central Solomons was won. In these efforts the army and its air forces proved highly useful. The soldiers developed into amphibious troops who, with experience, became nearly as effective as the marines. The air force enjoyed its biggest victory in March, when army bombers located a Japanese convoy and in three days of battle over the Bismarck Sea claimed to have sunk twelve merchantmen and ten destroyers and cruisers. This engagement was hailed as a great victory for air power over sea power by the extremely talented public relations officers who worked for the air force.

In the North Pacific there was some unfinished business to attend to: the Japanese were still entrenched in the outermost islands of the Aleutian chain, and this was disquieting to the people of the west coast states. In May 1943 the navy escorted soldiers to Attu, landed them on the beach, and so delivered them into one of the war's most eerie battles. In snow and fog and gales the soldiers fought an enemy whose fanatical courage they had underestimated. With defeat certain, the Japanese indulged in a suicidal charge that took many American lives. Organized resistance on this island did not end until after eighteen days of battle, when all but a few of the Japanese had been annihilated. In August, Kiska was occupied by American and Canadian soldiers, after a covering naval force had bombarded the island. The soldiers who stormed ashore found that the Japanese had withdrawn from the island several days earlier.

In the Central Pacific the navy was gathering its strength for the opening moves of a campaign which was designed, as was the South Pacific campaign, to protect the flank of MacArthur's forces as they advanced toward the Philippines and Japan. This Central Pacific campaign, more than any other, was the navy's war.

Throughout the summer and fall of 1943 new carriers of the 27,000 ton *Essex* class, and carriers converted from cruiser hulls, and escort carriers, came through the Panama Canal to join the fleet. Admiral

Nimitz had sent them on shake-down raids against Marcus and Wake Islands, and their planes had bombed Tarawa and Makin and Apamama in the Gilbert Islands in the fall. Throughout October and the first half of November they had attacked these formerly British islands intermittently and it was thought that much damage had been done to the Japanese installations at Makin and Tarawa.

On November 19th a great task force, commanded by Admiral Raymond Spruance, USN, master of strategy and tactics and one of the leaders at the Battle of Midway, neared Tarawa and Makin. On the 19th and 20th both islands were subjected to heavy bombardments by carrier-based planes and surface vessels. On the 20th soldiers were landed on Makin and after a brief and violent engagement captured the island at a cost of 66 killed, 187 wounded. The Second Marine Division began to land on Tarawa the same day. These marines had seen 3,000 tons of shells and bombs wreck the surface of Betio Island in the Tarawa atoll, and to most of them it did not seem possible that many Japanese could have survived such a bombardment. But as the first waves of landing craft neared the beach and encountered a hail of fire from Japanese pillboxes, bunkers and dug-outs, the realization came that this landing was not going to be easily made. The Japanese had been preparing Betio for just such an assault for fifteen months and they had made the island into a fortress. Everything they had been able to get had been put to use in building fortifications. Cocoanut logs, sand, concrete, steel rails, as well as guns ranging in size from light machine guns to eight-inch coast-defense rifles were blended into one formidable defensive machine. Fields of cross-fire had been plotted, whereby one position was protected from assault by several others. An estimated four thousand picked Japanese troops who had survived the aerial bombs and surface ship shells without undue inconvenience manned these defenses. They considered their handiwork impregnable.

At first, as the leading three waves of marines landed, it looked as though the Japanese were right. Machine-gun and mortar fire pinned the marines to a narrow beachhead, and as the tide went out, many of the landing craft carrying the fourth and fifth waves grounded on reefs and the men in these waves had to wade ashore, under enemy fire, in water that was up to their necks. That night, when for some inexplicable reason the Japanese did not counter-attack, the beachhead was reinforced by tanks and more marines.

On the 21st the marines began a day such as their corps had not known since Blanc Mont. Dawn exposed their positions clearly and they were caught in an enfilading fire. The American warships moving in and, with dive-bombers from the carriers, began to attack enemy strong-points. But for the marines there was nothing to do, but advance—training had erased the idea of retreat from their consciousness—and they began to reduce the enemy bunkers with flamethrowers, Bangalore torpedoes, grenades, and demolition charges. Each strong-point had to be taken by groups of marines who were under fire from other concealed dug-outs. Like so many surgeons, probing and testing, they worked the island over until it was in their control. That was seventy-six hours after the first wave had been landed. 988 marines died in this assault, and 2,164 were wounded. In the Pacific, which was to be the scene of many other mortal struggles, when men spoke of Betio on Tarawa atoll they came to call it "Bloody Betio."

Much was learned from this battle. The landing-craft were proved inadequate; more and better amphibious tractors were needed; tractors that could walk over coral reefs. 3,000 tons of explosives were not enough for one square mile—armor-piercing shells and rockets were needed to level such fortifications as those on Betio. More thorough reconnaissance of beaches and underwater obstacles, and a greater appreciation of the effect of wind and tide on the low-lying coral atolls were needed. But one basic fact had been proved: the marines were without peers as fighting men.

Soon naval construction battalions were hard at work on Betio, repairing and enlarging the air-strip, building docks and clearing channels. This bit of earth captured from the Japanese in the Central Pacific became a stepping stone on the road to Tokyo. By the end of 1943 planes from Betio were flying against the Marshall Islands to the westward.

In the United States the war effort was reaching a peak as 1943 drew to a close. 568 combatant ships, displacing 1,582,004 tons, were built that year, as well as 1,508,442 tons of auxiliaries and landing craft. Among the new warships were 15 large carriers and 50 escort carriers, with a total displacement of 641,813 tons. 23,144 naval aircraft were produced in 1943, and of these, 16,371 were combat types. To fly these planes the navy had some 24,000 pilots. The total number of officers and men and women in the naval service reached 2,252,606 on December 31, 1943, and there were, in addition, 391,620 in the Marine Corps and 171,519 in the Coast Guard. On September 8, 1939, there had been only 156,198 in all three organizations. Belatedly, the navy became conscious of the offensive power of rockets, whose value had been lost sight of in the years following the War of 1812. In 1943, $11,921,000 worth of rockets were procured by the navy, whereas none had been bought in the year before. From companies making electronic equipment the navy acquired, in 1943, $251,964,000 worth of radar gear and $57,351,000 worth of sonar gear.

In the aggregate, these ships and men and planes and equipment represented the two-ocean navy authorized in 1940. Had "Teddy" Roosevelt and Captain Mahan been alive they would have beamed with pleasure at the sight of so much power being put to such good use.

In the Atlantic, during the early autumn of 1943, the Germans began to equip their submarines with a new type of torpedo—the "acoustic torpedo." These were admirably suited for submarine warfare: since they were drawn to their targets by the noise of ships' propellers it was not necessary for the submarine to come to periscope depth to line up the target. An acoustic torpedo was simply fired toward the noise a ship made and the hydrophone in the torpedo steered it toward the ship's propellers.

In an attack on an Atlantic convoy on September 19, 1943, the Germans used these torpedoes and sank three escort vessels and six merchantmen. At this point the close liaison between the navy and civilian scientists proved its worth: working with information supplied by British and American Intelligence services, the scientists deduced the kind of hydrophone the Germans were using in their torpedoes. Then they invented a device which could be towed behind the escort and merchant vessels. This invention was a "noise-maker" that misled the torpedoes.

When the Germans returned to the fray in October, well-supplied with the new torpedoes, the Allied ships had enough "noise-makers" to nullify the attacks. The acoustic torpedoes were bewildered, and they circled the "noise-makers" behind the ships until their fuel was exhausted and they sank. In this brief offensive German submarines were sunk at the rate of seven for each merchantman lost.

By that time the shipyards of the United States had produced enough shipping to replace the tremendous losses the Allies had suffered in the previous years, and new ships were being built faster than the submarines and bombers could sink them.

When the President early in 1942 directed the Maritime Commission to build 8,000,000 deadweight tons of shipping in 1942 and 16,000,000 tons in 1943, few had believed such an accomplishment possible. But in 1942, 8,091,833 tons had been built, and in 1943, 19,270,746 tons came off the ways. The goal of 24,000,000 tons in 24 months had been exceeded by over 3,000,000 tons. From 2 Liberty ships launched in 1941 the number had risen to 542 in 1942 and 1,232 in 1943. At the same time other types of vessels launched rose from 101 in 1941 to 218 in 1942, to 717 in 1943. Among the latter were 31 escort carriers.

There was so much cargo-carrying tonnage available by the end of 1943 that the Maritime Commission was able to change the emphasis on new ship construction from the Liberty to the Victory type ship, and to harken to the request of the Joint Chiefs of Staff for ships of more specialized types.

The Liberty ships, for which no contracts were awarded after April, 1944, had been built in four types: dry cargo, tanker, tank carrier and collier. Their speed was only 11 knots. The Victory type, with geared-turbines instead of the Liberty's reciprocating steam engines furnishing the propulsion, could make from 15½ to 18½ knots. Production of them began in November 1943, and the first of the new type—the *United Victory*—was completed on February 29, 1944. The Victory ships were built in two distinct types, as dry cargo ships and as troopships. The ones used for general cargo purposes had a deadweight tonnage of 10,600 tons, and they were 455 feet and 3 inches in overall length, with a beam of 62 feet and a draft (loaded) of 28½ feet. Their cruising radius was 20,500 miles, and they were well fitted for the task of carrying men, munitions and supplies over the great distances that separated the United States from the fighting fronts. From New York to Liverpool by convoy took seventeen days, from New York to Basra, by way of the Cape of Good Hope, took seventy days. From San Francisco to Syndey, Australia, was a twenty-eight day voyage, and from Seattle to Kiska took twelve days. But with the backlog of Liberty ships and the certainty of obtaining Victory ships from American shipyards beyond the range of enemy bombers, these lengthy voyages were, as logistic problems, no longer to be feared. The yards could supply all the cargo-carriers and troopships needed, and the specialized military types as well.

Among the military types were the landing ship, tank, or LSTs, of which the Maritime Commission had built fifteen in 1942 and sixty in 1943, and the Attack Transports (the navy's "APA") and the Cargo Attack Ships (the "AKAs"). These were the ships which became the most important in the Maritime Commission's program for 1944, for without them and the host of other specialized types, ranging from crane ships through twenty-six different types of landing craft to rocket ships and water barges, the planned invasion of Europe could not be carried to a successful conclusion.

While this gigantic building program was being carried on in the United States, with the shipyards building both naval and merchant tonnage on an intense twenty-four-hour-a-day schedule, in preparation for the landings on the continent of Europe, in the Pacific the armed forces were making modest advances over the great distances that separated them from their ultimate objectives.

In the first half of 1944, by a series of amphibious, airborne and paratroop landings, MacArthur's forces moved westward along the north coast of New Guinea from the bases at Salamaua, Lae and Finschhafen. Saidor on New Guinea was taken, and Hollandia and Aitape. The Admiralty Islands to the north, with their airfields and the great harbor at Manus, were in Allied hands early in April. Rabaul was isolated. In May the Allied forces moved on to Wakde and Biak. By these well-timed and skillfully-executed advances over 125,000 enemy troops were passed by and left "to rot upon the vine." Australian, American and New Zealand soldiers, aided by the United States Marines, took part in these landings, working together without friction.

Whenever necessary the Navy's Seventh Fleet, commanded by Vice-Admiral Thomas Kinkaid, furnished the fast transports, the preliminary bombardment by surface vessels and the landing craft for MacArthur's forces. With each landing the technique improved, and among the indispensable men were the landing craft crews, Coast Guardsmen for the most part, who had never before left home. When, as at Hollandia, the army fighter planes were unable to provide effective support from their bases four hundred miles away, carrier-based planes were put to use to soften up strongpoints and to protect the landings.

In all these bitterly fought landings the troops faced not only the fanatical Japanese, but also the normal hazards of the region, an alien world of malaria, rain and mud, myriad insects and obscure tropical diseases, heavy undergrowth with tangling vines and thorns, strange beasts and reptiles.

In the Central Pacific the navy was advancing westward along the road to Tokyo. The Gilbert Islands of Tarawa, Makin and Abemama were quickly developed as forward bases, and from them the next step forward led to the Marshall Islands. Of these coral atolls little was known. They had been mandated to Japan after the First World War, and, since the Japanese did not permit visitors, they had become islands of mystery which few Americans had seen. Charts for the waters surrounding them were unreliable, and the extent of their fortifications was unknown.

Aerial reconnaissance reported Wotke and Taroa well-fortified, and it was decided to pass by these islands, as well as Jaluit and Mili, and to concentrate the attack on Kwajalein Atoll, the largest in the Marshalls, sixty-six miles long, with a great lagoon which could hold all the warships in the world. On several of this atoll's coral islets, such as Roi, Namur and Kwajalein, there was room enough to build extensive airfields and shore installations. These three islands therefore became the targets for the largest amphibious operation yet undertaken in the Central Pacific. Admiral Spruance, in whose mind brilliance and realism were neatly balanced, was in command.

On January 20, 1944, the attack began. Carrier planes bombed and strafed the installations on the target islands and made widespread raids on neighboring islands in the Marshall group. On the next day the bombardment was continued, with surface ships joining in the attack. The navy had learned its lesson at Tarawa, and this time the enemy islands were saturated with such a concentration of high explosives that they were swept incessantly by wave after wave of steel and fire.

When the marines of the 4th Division stormed ashore on the northern islands of Roi and Namur on February 2nd, they met a shell-shocked enemy amid scenes of utter devastation. With their customary élan the marines secured both islands in 27 hours of fighting, at a cost of 129 killed, 436 wounded and 65 missing. 3,472 Japanese were killed on these two islands. On Kwajalein, largest of the target islands, soldiers of the 7th Division, veterans of Attu, went about their work doggedly, killing nearly five thousand Japanese in a six-day battle. By February 8th the whole of Kwajalein Atoll was in American hands.

Nine days later a fast carrier task force from Spruance's fleet raided Truk, which had acquired the reputation of being a center of enemy sea and air power. The attack caught the Japanese by surprise, and for two days American planes and ships bombed and cannonaded the island fortress. In this engagement the Japanese lost 201 planes and 19 ships, among them 2 light cruisers and 3 destroyers. American losses amounted to 17 planes lost and minor damage to one warship.

Concurrently an amphibious attack was launched on Eniwetok Atoll, west of Kwajalein, with a landing force composed of marines and soldiers. Following the now formalized bombardment by planes and ships, the marines took Engabi, the northern island of the atoll, in six hours, and then joined the soldiers in the task of exterminating the Japanese on the atoll's southern islands. After two days of fighting, during which the marines lost 196 killed and 550 wounded, Eniwetok was under control. Its capture marked the end of one phase of the Pacific war, for Eniwetok was the last of the coral atolls that had to be taken by savage fighting.

The next operations were to be aimed at islands of volcanic origin, whose mountains were honeycombed with caves from which the Japanese had to be rooted out with flame-throwers and demolition charges. To investigate these future targets, on February 23rd a fast carrier task force commanded by Admiral Marc Mitscher raided the Marianas (Ladrone) Islands of Saipan and Tinian and Japanese-occupied Guam. 135 enemy aircraft were destroyed, as well as 2 cargo ships, at a cost of 6 American planes. These raids were a portent of the future, and the Japanese High Command, 1,500 miles to the north in Tokyo, reacted by sending reinforcements into the islands. The intentions of the Americans were crystal-clear: only one feint had been made to distract the enemy's attention, and that feint consisted of a modest raid on February 4th, when a task force bombarded the naval base at Paramushiru in the northern Kuriles.

Up to that time, except for the raid by the pilots of the twin-motored bombers flown off the *Hornet,* the only American fighting men who had come closer to the home islands of Japan were the submariners.

At the time of Pearl Harbor, Admiral Hart's twenty-nine submarines had constituted the whole of the navy's submarine force in the western reaches of the Pacific. But the Pacific quickly became the hunting ground for nearly all the navy's submarines, as operations in the Atlantic were restricted to testing new ships and training new crews.

Soon after Pearl Harbor the order had gone out to the submarines, with Presidential approval: "Execute unrestricted air and submarine warfare against Japan," and this order showed a realistic comprehension of the nature of the enemy. The United States was bound by the London Naval Treaty of 1930 to such restrictions in submarine warfare that, had the terms been observed, few ships but Japanese men-of-war could have been attacked. Since that treaty had been signed the concept of total war had returned to plague mankind, and in contrast to that concept the terms of the London Naval Treaty appeared unrealistic and embued with wisps of idealism which could cost the lives of many valorous fighting men. It would have been sheer madness to have abided by the terms of that treaty: this was not a war that could well be fought with a Froissart-like romanticism by the United States, while the Japanese abided by none of the rules of civilized warfare. To the submarines the order was tantamount to the words "Shoot on sight!" and in the first year of the war they accounted for 580,390 tons of enemy merchantmen and 140,000 tons of warships.

This merchant tonnage sunk represent approximately 10 per cent of the gross tonnage at Japan's disposal when the war started. In following years the strangulation of Japan's supply lines continued unremittingly as the building of American submarines increased, from eleven in 1941 to thirty-four in 1942, to fifty-six in 1943 and seventy-nine in 1944.

The Americans' affinity for submarines came as a great surprise to the

Japanese, who had not credited them with any great skill as submariners because the United States had always advocated the abolition of submarines as instruments of warfare. The miscalculation was a mortal one, for the Japanese hope of victory was founded on the theory that after a swift conquest of the South Pacific area they would be able to develop the resources of that region, and with a abundance of oil and rubber and minerals and foodstuffs, carry on a war in defense of their conquests indefinitely. They estimated that the amount of shipping they would lose could be replaced by new construction and ship seizures, but in the first two years of the war the submarines proved the theory fallacious. Japanese merchantmen, in spite of being herded into convoys, were constantly in danger of submarine attack. The Empire's resources, great though they were, could not be fed into Japan's war industries without ships to transport them to the home islands. In those first two critical, formative years of war the submarines prevented the flow of raw materials from reaching such a volume that the Japanese could build a self-perpetuating war machine that would make their position impregnable.

Tankers, next to warships, were the submarines' favorite targets, and so many of these had been lost by the spring of 1944 that the operations of the Japanese fleet were drastically handicapped. Later on, the work of the submarines was made easier by the use of electric, trackless, target-seeking torpedoes. Submarines carried out reconnaissance duties, reaching to the Inland Sea, the innermost recesses of Japanese naval power, and they carried weapons, radio equipment and medical supplies to the hard-pressed guerrillas fighting in the Philippines. All their work was carried on without publicity, and the submarines became so fabulous a branch of the service that there were more volunteers for submarine duty than there were submarines to man. It is doubtful that the 50 per cent additional pay the submariners received had a great deal to do with the popularity of the service. In these narrow, tubular ships so packed with machinery that they themselves seemed like huge torpedoes, Americans with an aptitude for gears and levers and complex engines found full expression of their talents. They thought their work fascinating, for it took on the added excitement of a big-game hunt, with the sea as substitute for the African veldt. Men who served in these big, black-painted undersea raiders became so attached to their ships that they were unhappy and ill-at-ease on surface ships. Submariners considered themselves the elite of the navy, and not without good reason, for they sank 1,750 of Japan's steel merchant vessels and they broke the back of the Japanese merchant marine.

In contrast to the increasing effectiveness of the American submarines, the German undersea craft continued to be kept on the defensive in the first half of 1944. In that period each merchantman sunk cost the Germans two submarines, and this ratio was achieved chiefly because the Allied detection equipment became so efficient that German submarines were unable to send even brief radio messages without disclosing their position. Once a submarine's approximate position was known, an arsenal of anti-submarine weapons could be brought against it. Allied surface vessels—destroyers, destroyer-escorts, frigates and corvettes—equipped with radar and sonar gear, and aircraft, both land-based and escort-carrier based, worked together with the harmony gained by experience. The German submarines were depth-bombed with such gratifying efficacy that morale among the U-boat crews plumbed the depths of fatalism.

In June, Admiral Ingersoll reported: "Recently on a brilliant moonlight night one of our destroyer escorts sighted a submarine, fully surfaced, silhouetted against the moon. The destroyer escort immediately rang up full speed and headed for the submarine, opening fire with all her guns. The submarine elected to fight it out and opened fire with her deck guns and machine guns, tracers passing high over the bridge of the destroyer escort. The submarine maneuvered at high speed and fired a torpedo. The destroyer escort closed the range rapidly, following the sub's evasive maneuvers and burying the sub under a withering fire at point blank range, with machine guns and 3-inch forecastle guns. The range finally closed until the submarine was only 20 yards away. All fire on the submarine having ceased at this point the destroyer escort rode up on the forecastle of the submarine where she stuck. Men began swarming out of the submarine and up onto the destroyer escort's forecastle. The destroyer escort opened up on them with machine guns, tommy guns and rifle fire. Ammunition expended at this time included several general mess coffee cups which happened to be at the gun stations. Two of the enemy were hit on the head with these. Empty cartridge cases also proved effective for repelling the boarders. During this heated encounter the destroyer escort suffered her only casualty of the engagement, when a husky seaman bruised his fist knocking one of the enemy over the side. At this stage of the battle the boatswain's mate in charge forward with a 45 Colt revolver and a Chief Firecontrol-man with a tommy gun accounted for a number of those attempting to board. The destroyer escort then decided to back off to stop any more enemy trying to board her. Again the running battle was resumed, hits falling like rain on the sub's topside. Even shallow depth charges were used against the submarine. The destroyer escort rammed a second time and then the submarine rolled slowly over. Personnel on the escort's deck had a clear view into the conning tower which was ablaze. A torpedoman threw a hand grenade which dropped through the sub's conning tower before exploding. The submarine finally sank with her Diesel engines still running, and the conning tower hatch open, fire blazing from it. The commanding officer of the destroyer escort was a young Lieutenant Commander in the Naval Reserve, who came on active duty in 1941." The incident was unusual only because the combatants came to such close grips: in most cases the submarines were sunk with impersonal efficiency by Allied planes and warships.

Having won control of the sea routes that led to the Mediterranean and to the British Isles, the Allies were able to carry out their plans for the invasion of Germany by way of France. At a conference held in Washington in May 1943, and attended by the President, Prime Minister Churchill and the Combined Chiefs of Staff, formal commitments were made by the British and the Americans to insure that the invasion would be a success. The date of the invasion was set, for planning purposes, as the spring of 1944. Further details were worked out at the Quebec Conference in August. Three months later, at Teheran, Iran, the Heads of State and the Combined Chiefs of Staff met with Generalissimo Stalin and his advisers, and the invasion date was set so that it would coincide with the Russian spring offensive.

The situation in Europe, as 1944 began, was not one that encouraged optimism. In Italy the Allies were blocked at Cassino, after having fought their way up from the Straits of Messina and from amphibious landings made in the Gulf of Salerno. The Italians, having ousted Mussolini, had signed an armistice in September 1943, by the terms of which they surrendered most of their naval vessels to the Allies. The surrender of these vessels, among which were six battleships, eight cruisers, twenty-seven destroyers and nineteen submarines, permitted the release of numerous Allied warships from duty in the Mediterranean. In January, 1944, in order to flank Cassino, the Allies landed at Anzio, where their beachhead was sealed off and contained by the Germans. On the Russian front the energetic and courageous Muscovites, their equipment supplemented with weapons and vehicles from British and American factories, had crossed the Dnieper River, lifted the siege of Leningrad, isolated the Crimea, and were nearing the Polish border. But Berlin was still over six hundred miles away. In the air over German-occupied Europe Allied planes flying from Italian and British bases were cascading tons of bombs on factories and railroad centers, weather permitting. The Germans were moving their aircraft and munitions plants underground, into mines and caves, building jet-propelled fighter planes which were superior to anything the Allies had, and devising rocket-propelled weapons that could reach the British Isles from launching sites along the coast of France and the Low Countries. There were intelligence reports that the Germans, too, were developing an atomic bomb. Along the Atlantic coast of the continent the Germans had thousands of conquered men at work on fortifications that were designed to make costly and difficult the invasion they knew was sure to come. Minefields were laid in coastal waters; pill-boxes, barbed wire, anti-tank ditches, stakes to impale Allied parachutists were installed. Batteries of guns and mortars were sited to cover potential landing areas on the beaches. Month by month these defenses grew stronger.

It was, therefore, with a sense of great urgency that the Allies formulated their plans for the invasion. The Combined Chiefs of Staff were confronted with a shortage of landing craft, without which the invasion could not even be attempted. The shipyards in the United States were urged to increase their production of landing craft such as the DUKWs, a 2½-ton tracked and armored amphibious truck which had been found invaluable in the invasion of Sicily, the LCVP (Landing Craft,

Vehicle and Personnel), the LCM (Landing Craft Mechanized), the LST (Landing Ship, Tank), the LCI (L), LCR (S), which were large and small rubber landing craft. In the first six months of 1944 nearly twenty thousand of these and other specialized types of landing craft were completed.

The amount of shipping needed to support such an undertaking as the cross-Channel invasion was enormous. At Salerno, where in the first 18 days 189,000 troops, 30,000 vehicles and 108,000 tons of supplies had been landed, each army division required the use of 30 LSTs, 39 LCIs, 24 LCTs, 9 transports, 4 cargo ships, and scores of small landing craft to reach shore and to have a chance to remain alive there. And Salerno, compared to the projected invasion at Normandy, was a minor operation.

Shipping which had been assigned to the support of the Italian front was diverted, in the closing months of 1943, to the task of transporting American troops and supplies to the British Isles. Huge troop convoys steamed across the Atlantic, pouring men into Britain, springboard of the coming invasion, at the rate of 150,000 men each month. Cargo ships brought their food and weapons and the infinite variety of supplies upon which the troops depended. By June 6, 1944, 1,533,000 completely-equipped American soldiers were in the British Isles. At the same time these men and their supplies were being ferried across the ocean, planes were being flown by way of Newfoundland, Iceland and Scotland to insure continued Allied air supremacy in the European area. Under naval protection, tankers carried the gasoline and cargo ships the bombs without which the aerial armadas would have been helpless.

All Allied naval forces assigned to take part in the invasion were placed under the command of Admiral Sir Bertram Ramsay, RN, who in turn was responsible to General Dwight Eisenhower, Supreme Commander, Allied Expeditionary Force. Nearly 102,000 American naval officers and men, serving in 2,479 warships and landing craft, were directly involved in the invasion. Of these, 87,000 men manned the landing craft and the smaller escort vessels; 15,000 others manned the combatant ships. In the battleships and cruisers marine sharpshooters were assigned to pick off floating mines.

On June 6th, 1944, at 2 A.M., following several days of heavy aerial

· 513 ·

attack on German installations along the coast of France, three Allied airborne divisions were dropped behind the coastal fortifications of the Normandy beaches. They proceeded to disrupt German communications, while, at 3:14 A.M., the heavy bombers began to saturate the beaches with high explosives. Soon after dawn, at 5:50 A.M., the naval phase of the assault began, as warships moved in behind the minesweepers to cannonade the coast. Forty minutes later the landing craft, manned by Coast Guardsmen, protected by a canopy of fighter planes and the shell-and-rocket fire of the warships, hit the beaches, let down their ramps, and the first waves of infantry stormed ashore.

The small landing craft continued to shuttle between the beaches and the transports lying off-shore, while the larger landing ships disgorged their tanks and men and vehicles on the beach and then returned to English ports to reload and repeat the performance endlessly. As the first waves of troops poured ashore they were pinned down by accurate machine-gun and mortar fire, and in this crisis a group of destroyers moved in close to the beach and gave the infantrymen fire support.

There was little doubt that the Allies could seize a beachhead: Guadalcanal, Tarawa, Kwajalein, Eniwetok, North Africa, Sicily, Salerno and Anzio were proof that this could be done. The doubtful element in the invasion was whether the Allies could build up and expand the Normandy beachhead before the Germans could bring overwhelming forces to bear against it. In the effort to get men and supplies ashore that followed the initial hard-fought landings, the naval forces played a major part.

Having brought the troops to the British Isles, and then across the Channel, landed them, and given them fire support, the navy had to make sure that the troops continued to get all the weapons and supplies that they could use. There were no large ports in the invasion area, so the Allies created artificial ports. Of these there were two kinds, the two British-designed and built "Mulberries," and five "Gooseberries," or small-boat shelters. The "Gooseberries" were formed by sinking old and damaged warships and merchantmen close to the beaches, where they acted as a breakwater for small craft. The "Mulberries" consisted of specially-built concrete caissons which were towed across the Channel and sunk off the beaches; between the sunken caissons and the shore, floating pierheads were constructed, and these piers were connected with the land by causeways supported by pontoons and barges. In these large artificial harbors ocean-going ships could tie up alongside the floating piers and discharge their cargoes in quiet water. By June 8th the first pontoon causeway was in operation; by the 10th all the "Mulberries" and "Gooseberries" were in position. For a week men and vehicles and supplies poured into the beachhead, and then, on the 18th, a northeast gale hit the area. For three days the gale lasted, building up heavy seas that wrecked the "Mulberry" off the American beachhead.

Only the British "Mulberry" and the five small "Gooseberries" now remained as harbors. There was still no major port in Allied hands, and an operation to take Cherbourg was begun. While the soldiers approached Cherbourg from the rear, on June 25th an Allied naval fire support group, commanded by Rear Admiral Morton Deyo, USN, and composed of the battleships *Arkansas, Texas* and *Nevada,* two American and two British cruisers and eleven destroyers, began to bombard the shore batteries around Cherbourg. Spotting planes and Shore Fire Control Parties directed the fire of the warships so accurately that nineteen of twenty-one designated inland targets were destroyed. The cost to the naval force was fourteen killed and twenty-eight wounded. Two days later the soldiers captured Cherbourg.

The port of Cherbourg and its cargo-handling facilities had been wrecked by the Germans, who had also put down layers of mines in the harbor. British and American salvage units quickly began clearing away the wreckage, and early in July the port was in limited operation. The beaches still carried the bulk of the invasion traffic, and in such volume as the Germans had not believed possible. This miscalculation— the belief that the Americans could not supply themselves over the beaches—was one of the most fatal of the many mistakes the German General Staff made. They clung to the belief that the Allies could not expand their beachhead without a major port in spite of the evidence given them at Sicily, when the DUKWs and landing craft and floating piers had carried eighty thousand men, seven thousand vehicles and three hundred tanks ashore in two days. The lesson was lost on the Germans, who were confident that their counterattacks could be mounted before the Allies in Normandy had the strength to withstand them.

Contributing to their miscalculation was the work of the Allied air forces, which bombed bridges and airfields and strafed with machine-gun, cannon and rocket fire the German divisions that attempted to move toward the Normandy beachhead.

By July 25th enough men and weapons and supplies had been landed over the beaches to permit the army to attack successfully in the St. Lô and Avranches area. From that day on, the Germans fought a losing war. Dieppe was taken by the Canadians on the 31st of August, and a week later was being used as a port; Le Havre fell in September and in October its harbor facilities were in operation; unloading began at Rouen in mid-October; Antwerp, liberated from the Germans by the British and Canadians became an important unloading point late in November. The Allies faced the winter with their lines of supply secure: the battle for the ports had been won, as had the battle of transportation across the seas. With their reinforcements and cargoes of food and munitions under the good guardianship of the Allied navies, the armies and air forces were free to seek out and destroy the German enemy.

While the Allies were engaged in this admirable endeavor, on the other side of the world the Japanese were being brought closer to defeat. The basic strategy to be followed in the Pacific war had been approved at Washington, in May, 1943, and it had been elaborated at Quebec in August and at Cairo in November of the same year. At Cairo an agreement was reached by the President, Prime Minister Churchill and Generalissimo Chiang Kai-shek, that their nations would fight Japan until that country surrendered unconditionally. Then, all the lands Japan had conquered would be returned to their rightful owners, all territory taken from the Chinese since the Sino-Japanese War of 1894 would be returned to China. Japan was to be stripped of all the islands she had seized or occupied in the Pacific since 1914. In brief, it was planned to turn Japan into a fifth-rate power, incapable of waging war. Korea was, "in due course," to become free and independent.

These were specific political objectives which, it was hoped, would be attained by following the military strategy that had been evolved at Quebec in August, 1943. This strategy was based on the conviction that the best place to fight the main Japanese armies was on the Tokyo plain, where defeat of the enemy would be conclusive. There would have been little profit in fighting the Japanese in China, in the region of Hangchow, and then having to repeat the blood-letting in Japan itself. Therefore, so that the Japanese might be brought to battle in Japan, the approved route was the one that led directly to Tokyo. This entailed the advance of MacArthur's forces to the Philippines and the simultaneous campaign in the Central Pacific to protect his flank. It was clear that the war effort in China would, because of the Japanese blockade of the supply routes to that nation, necessarily be restricted to a defensive, holding campaign.

At the Quebec conference in 1943 the specific routes which were to be followed on the road to Tokyo were charted by the Joint Chiefs of Staff. At that conference General H. H. Arnold, eupeptic chief of the army's air force, suggested a plan for the bombing of Japan by B-29 planes flying from the Mariana Islands. The plan was later approved, for these islands had to be taken anyhow, for the use of the ground forces on the way to Japan.

It was June, 1944, before the Marianas were within reach of American amphibious attack. By that time the Americans had created new techniques and new weapons, and had become skilled in their use. Among these new weapons, which fitted the American temperament as easily as an oar the hand, was the fast carrier task force. A task force of this nature was organized around a nucleus of from eight to ten big carriers of the *Essex* class, with six to eight light fast carriers of the *Independence* class, six to eight fast battleships, eight to twelve cruisers, and perhaps seventy-five destroyers. Such a force represented nearly a million tons of combatant ships manned by about one hundred thousand men and capable of putting over a thousand planes in the air. Its tactical speed was nearly thirty knots an hour and it could cruise at twenty-five knots without difficulty.

When a ship suffered battle-damage, or when its engines broke down, huge floating dry-docks at the advance bases could repair minor and major injuries. From these advance bases hundreds of unheroic fleet oilers, supply ships, ammunition ships and escort carriers acting as plane transports, could steam to a rendezvous with the task force and replenish its needs. With their help the force was able to stay at sea for as long as two months at a time. This solution of the problem of supply was a secret the Japanese never fathomed. The fast carrier task force could bring its tremendous offensive power to bear against one objective, vanish, protected by the immensity of the sea, and then appear a few days later, hundreds of miles away, equally powerful and destructive.

It was such a force as this that attacked the Marianas in a three-day foray that started on June 11, 1944, as a preliminary to the invasion of Saipan, Guam and Tinian. In this invasion of the Marianas over 600 warships, 2,000 planes and 300,000 naval, marine, coast guard and army personnel were to be involved. The chain of command in the operation led from Nimitz at Pearl Harbor to Spruance, commander of the Fifth Fleet, and of all air and land forces in the operation, to Mitscher, commander of the fast carrier task force, and R. K. Turner, who had charge of the amphibious landing force.

Following the established formula the carrier planes of the fast task force first destroyed enemy aircraft in the Marianas and then began bombing the airfields and defenses on Saipan and Guam and Tinian. On the 13th the fast battleships moved in to cannonade Saipan and Tinian, while minesweepers and underwater demolition teams composed of expert swimmers cleared the waters off Saipan.

Then, on the 14th, the fire support groups, formed of old battleships and cruisers and destroyers, began their bombardment of Saipan. In the offing, Spruance's fleet and the fast carrier task force cruised protectively, alert to intercept any incursion the Japanese might attempt.

Next day the amphibious force, supported by planes from the escort-carriers, approached the island of Saipan. At 5:45 A.M. the old battleships, cruisers and destroyers began the last bombardment of the beach defenses on the island's west coast. The marines climbed into their landing craft from the transports, and at the reef which protects Saipan were transferred to armored and tracked amphibious vehicles, called "Buffaloes," or "amphtracs," which carried them over the reef and up on the beach. The first marines reached shore at 8:40 A.M. and were met by heavy machine-gun and mortar fire. That day, as the marines of the 2nd and 4th Divisions were landed, they suffered severe casualties from Japanese artillery and mortars sited in the mountain caves overlooking the beaches. On the 16th the soldiers of the 27th Army Division were brought ashore as reinforcements and they, with the marines, began a slow advance across the island under harassing fire. This was a new type of warfare: the enemy had made the best possible use of Saipan's seventy-two square miles of rough and mountainous terrain, and there were nearly thirty thousand Japanese defenders, all determined to kill as many Americans as possible before they themselves were killed.

By the 23rd the swing to the north end of the island was under way, with the 27th Army Division in the center, flanked by the 4th Marine Division on the east coast and the 2nd Marine Division on the west. The soldiers, fighting as a division for the first time, were not trained to marine standards, and their progress was slow compared to that of the marines. Lieutenant-General Holland Smith, USMC (in command of all troops once they were landed), told the army division's commander to attack, and when the army general sent out an order merely to hold, General Smith promptly relieved him of his command. This was no reflection on the troops of the 27th Division: they were National Guardsmen, and no one expected them to be as good as marines, who had been trained from the bear-pits at Quantico and Parris Island to the point of contact with the enemy to believe that marines are the best fighting men on earth and that it would be better for them to die than to disprove that reputation.

In the meantime the warships of Spruance's 5th Fleet (which included Mitscher's Task Force 58), had won a major victory over units of the Japanese fleet. On the first day of the landings on Saipan word had come to Spruance that a large enemy task force was moving toward the Marianas, obviously intent on destroying his fleet and then proceeding to break up the landings being made on Saipan. To accomplish this aim the Japanese carriers were to launch their planes far from the American fleet, to attack that fleet, and then to land on the airfields at Guam and Rota to refuel and rearm and return to battle. Once the American fleet had been sunk, the landing force on Saipan, cut off from supplies and reinforcements, could be eradicated in a leisurely manner.

Spruance's primary mission was to protect the Saipan landings, and yet here was a tasty target—a large enemy fleet, in which there were reported to be five carriers. If Spruance were to send his warships off to the westward to fight the Japanese carriers, there was a chance that the Japanese might send other forces from the north or the south to wipe out the landing force. Mindful of his primary mission, Spruance sent his carriers and fast battleships to the westward to meet the Japanese, but not so far away that they could not return to meet any surprise attack the Japanese might have planned. In the north Spruance had another carrier task force which had been ordered to bomb Iwo Jima and Chichi Jima in the Volcano and Bonin Islands, and thereby discourage the Japanese from flying planes down from Japan to Tinian, whence they could harry the landing force. This northern force performed its task on the 15th and 16th, and then was in a position to protect Spruance's right flank.

The battle began on the 19th, when American carrier-based planes intercepted the Japanese planes as they attacked the American fleet prior to attempting landings on Guam and Rota. To the Japanese the results were astonishing. American planes had thoroughly bombed the airfields on which the Japanese expected to land, and the runways were pitted with holes. Hundreds of American planes were in the air over the carriers and over the airfields and their pilots shot the Japanese out of the air and burned them up on the ground with such joyful enthusiasm that the fight became known as "The Marianas Turkey-Shoot." On this same day, in the waters off Yap, south of Guam, American submarines sank two Japanese carriers, the *Shokaku* and the *Taiho*. American planes and antiaircraft batteries, in the day's work, destroyed 402 enemy planes, at a cost to the Americans of 27 planes lost and slight damage inflicted by Japanese planes on 4 warships.

Spruance, having won air control over the Marianas, and having depleted the Japanese carrier plane strength, was now free to pursue the retreating Japanese. Search planes swept the sea to the westward of Guam on the 20th, and in the late afternoon reported the location of the Japanese fleet: it was barely within range of the American carrier-based planes. Shortly before sunset planes from Admiral Mitscher's fast carriers thundered off the flight decks and headed to the west. They attacked the Japanese fleet as darkness mantled the area, sank one carrier, the *Hitaka*, damaged three others as well as one battleship and three cruisers, at a cost of sixteen planes shot down. Nightfall ended the engagement, and the planes turned to find their carriers in the night. Night landings on carriers are at best precarious affairs, and on this night the planes were coming in with their gasoline tanks nearly empty, and often unable to identify the particular carrier from which they had flown. Many pilots made water landings near the American vessels and were fished out of the sea by cruisers and destroyers; others landed on the first carrier they could find.

While this scene of wild confusion was going on, with planes crash-landing in the sea as their gasoline ran out, and others stacked up over the carriers in landing circles waiting their turn to land, Mitscher made one of the most drastic decisions an admiral ever made: he ordered the ships of the task force to use their searchlights as beacons to guide the planes home and to speed the rescue of pilots who had made water-landings. In an instant the area was a blaze of light—an illuminated target visible for scores of miles. But there were no Japanese planes left to take advantage of this gallant gesture.

The Japanese fleet fled on to the westward during the night and on the 21st had passed the point beyond which Spruance could not let his carriers go without leaving the Saipan landing force unprotected. In this battle, called "The First Battle of the Philippine Sea," the Americans lost a total of 106 planes—33 shot down in action, and 73 lost in the landing melee on the night of the 20th. But the Japanese naval air force was never to recover from the effects of the battle.

On Saipan the marines and soldiers continued their advance, threw back a suicidal attack launched by the frenzied Japanese before dawn on July 7th, and kept at the work of fighting an enemy who had to be either dug out of, or sealed into, their mountain caves. In this work they were constantly supported by the guns of the warships and the planes from the escort-carriers. On the 9th organized resistance was declared at an end on Saipan, although there were still numerous unorganized Japanese who were willing to die for the Mikado. But some 26,000 of them had been killed by the marines and the soldiers, at a cost to the Americans of 3,441 dead or missing and 11,465 wounded, out of a total force of 48,000 marines and 20,000 soldiers committed to the battle.

Saipan was a milestone in the Pacific war. Its capture brought Japan, 1,285 miles to the north, within range of B-29 bombers. The Japanese began to plan the evacuation of school-children from Tokyo: on the 18th Prime Minister Tojo resigned, unable to withstand the shame of having lost Saipan. The Americans had an opening wedge in the Marianas, and Guam and Tinian were doomed.

The most striking feature of the attack on Saipan was that it was carried on at the same time that the Allies were engaged in a tremendous effort to strengthen the bridgehead on the Normandy beaches, 12,500 miles away. This was war on a truly global scale, yet it was being waged by a United States only partially mobilized. Unlike the British and the Russians, the Americans were not subjected to stringent measures by which every Russian and British man and woman was assigned to a specific job in the war effort, at the cost of their personal freedom. The war was not close enough to the United States to make such drastic measures necessary. Yet the Americans, by adapting their industrial equipment to the needs of war, had produced the weapons which were essential to victory. On June 30, 1944, there were 1,107 combatant ships in the navy, among them 23 battleships, 13 big carriers, 9 light carriers, 63 escort-carriers (scores more of these had been loaned to the British), 52 cruisers, 370 destroyers, 368 destroyer-escorts, 208 submarines. There were also 39,858 landing craft, 907 auxiliaries, and 34,071 planes on hand. The Maritime Commission had launched 920 vessels in the first 6 months of 1944, and in the same period, for shells, rockets and guns, radar and loran, torpedoes and depth charges, the navy spent $1,304,-352,000. Because of such astronomical figures it became customary in the United States to say that machines would win the war.

This, of course, was nonsense. The fighting men, given the weapons they needed, were taking and holding the ground. Up to June 30, 1944, 31,880 naval, marine and coast guard personnel had died, 19,483 of them in battle. 25,974 others had been wounded; 9,313 were listed as "missing." 4,762 were prisoners of war. The Navy's Bureau of Personnel (formerly the Bureau of Navigation), listed 3,623,205 men and women in the navy, marine corps and coast guard. 59,036 of them were pilots. All of them had been trained according to their aptitudes in a program which made full use of synthetic training devices. Experts from the fringes of the motion picture business, the documentaries and the commercial films, donned naval uniforms and worked amicably with sundry Hollywood patriots to produce hundreds of specialized training films that undoubtedly accelerated the training programs. The navy's consciousness of the value of films in the training and indoctrination of recruits rose gradually to the upper ranks of the naval hierarchy, and naval camera crews began to cover every naval operation. Thousands of feet of this film were made available to the newsreels and documentary film producing units. In this way the public was exposed to some excellent war films which gave them a partial realization of the scope and violence of the war. It was believed that such films inspired civilians working in shipyards and war plants to greater efforts, and whether this was so or not, at least the films, with their animated maps and their scenes of actual battle, enlarged the mental horizons of those who saw them. Millions of Americans had never heard of Saipan before the marines landed there; other once esoteric place-names were soon to become familiar.

In the South Pacific MacArthur and his forces were being wafted along under the protection of the 7th Fleet and the Army's 5th Air Force to Noemfoor, where resistance was feeble, and to Sansapor, where the landings were unopposed. Thus the thirteen hundred mile progression up the coast of New Guinea was completed, and MacArthur with his troops and impedimenta were in a position to be moved on to Morotai and from there to the Philippines. Although sixty-four years old in 1944, he had displayed a creditable ability to learn the new ways of amphibious warfare, to appreciate the value and limitations of aircraft and to outwit the Japanese. The Philippines, which were to him akin to the Holy Grail the crusaders sought, were almost within reach, separated from Sansapor by less than a thousand miles of blue water, across which the navy could be depended upon to transport him.

For the moment the navy was otherwise occupied: after Saipan, Guam was assaulted on July 21st by forty thousand marines and twenty thousand soldiers, and Tinian, separated from Saipan by a narrow channel, was stormed by forty thousand marines on July 24th. On August 1st Tinian was proclaimed secure, and nine days later organized resistance on Guam ended. As soon as these three islands were in American hands their development as staging areas for further moves to the west and as bases for the B-29 bombers began. The Navy's Construction Battalions, aided by army engineers, rapidly altered the landscape of each island. Using great earth-moving equipment they cut down hills and leveled areas for landing fields. Hard-surfaced roads were built and harbors cleared; hospitals, barracks, recreation fields and port facilities were installed. The Construction Battalions turned Tinian into one of the world's largest airfields, with six runways, each two miles long, and lined with revetments for the B-29s.

When the Marianas had been secured, Spruance went ashore to plan future operations, and Admiral Halsey, after two years shore duty, returned to command the fleet on August 26. The 5th Fleet, although the ships comprising it were the same, now became known as the 3rd Fleet. By this change of names it was hoped that the Japanese would be led to believe that the Americans had two great fleets, each with its Fast Carrier Task Force, whereas in reality there was only one fleet.

On September 12th, Halsey's planes raided the Central Philippines and encountered only slight aerial opposition. Next day he recommended to Nimitz that the landings planned for several islands in the Western Carolinas be canceled, and that landings on Leyte in the Philippines be made as quickly as possible. Nimitz forwarded Halsey's recommendation to the Joint Chiefs of Staff, then meeting with the British members of the Combined Chiefs of Staff at the Second Quebec Conference. The American strategists asked MacArthur what he thought about advancing the scheduled landings on Leyte, and after two days of silence word came from MacArthur's headquarters that he was ready to change his plans so that the landings on Leyte could be advanced from December 20th to October 20th. Ninety minutes later Nimitz and MacArthur had their orders to carry out the Leyte landings on October 20th.

Because of this change of plans, landing operations projected for the Palaus, Yap and Mindanao were abandoned. Only Peleliu, Anguar and Ulithi in the Palaus remained to be taken by the Central Pacific forces. Morotai, only 626 miles from Leyte, was in MacArthur's operational area and it was his responsibility to take that island.

The landings on these last of the intermediate bases on the way to the Philippines began on September 15th at Peleliu, in the Palau Islands, after the usual pre-invasion air raids by carrier-based and land-based planes, and bombardments by surface vessels. Widespread task force strikes on Japanese airfields from Celebes to Mindanao assured the landing forces of air supremacy in the area. Peleliu was a costly and a bloody fight: of the 25,000 marines who went ashore there, 1,241 were listed as killed or missing, 4,883 wounded. On this island, whose area was only six and a quarter square miles, a ridge runs down the center, and this ridge, with numerous inter-connecting caves, was a natural fortress. The airfield on Peleliu, the main objective of the landing force, was captured by sunset on the 16th, but the rest of the island was not conquered until mid-October.

Six miles to the south of Peleliu troops of the 81st Infantry Division stormed Anguar Island on September 17th, and within a few days had the island under control. Work on a field for heavy bombers was promptly started there. After Anguar, a combat team from the 81st Infantry moved on to take Ulithi Atoll, 400 miles southwest of Guam. There the troops landed on the 23rd of September and found that the Japanese had evacuated the atoll. The anchorage at Ulithi has an area of about 112 square miles, and it rapidly became the fleet's westernmost anchorage and supply base—4,000 miles from Pearl Harbor. Concrete barges loaded with supplies for the fleet were brought to Ulithi and there used as floating warehouses. As the supply ships arrived their cargoes were transferred to the concrete barges, known as the "crockery fleet," and these barges in turn refueled and provisioned and rearmed the combatant ships at Ulithi. An airfield was built at Ulithi, and one of the atoll's islands, Mogmog by name, became a recreation center for fleet personnel. The Japanese never appreciated the amount of naval strength that was being readied there, and the importance of the atoll was lost on their High Command. It was, indeed, beyond their ability to imagine the transformance of this quiet lagoon into a modern floating naval base.

On Morotai, MacArthur's forces were put ashore by the navy on September 15th, and, since there was only unsubstantial resistance, casualties were light and the island was taken without difficulty. The stage was now set for the return to the Philippines.

The Fast Carrier Task Force, after protecting the amphibious landings in the Palaus, resumed the attack on the Philippines. Manila Bay and neighboring targets were raided by carrier planes on September 21st and 22nd, photographic reconnaissance of the Leyte area was completed by September 24th. There was slight opposition to these attacks, Japanese air strength in the Philippines having been all but destroyed in the raids made during the period from September 9th to 15th.

After a fortnight's rest the task force was back at work again, sweeping in a great arc from Okinawa to Luzon to Formosa, and on to the Central Philippines, which was raided on October 19th. In this operation some 55 enemy vessels were sunk and over 480 planes destroyed.

Next morning the navy began to land the American Expeditionary Force on the beaches of Leyte Gulf, and the great General MacArthur himself waded ashore from a landing craft, through the surf, in water up to his knees. He was happy to be back on the soil of the country which had once hired him to look to its defenses.

Engaged in landing the troops were over 650 ships of Kinkaid's 7th Fleet, an armada of battleships, cruisers, and destroyers, 18 escort carriers, 53 assault transports, 54 assault cargo ships, 151 landing ships (tank), 16 rocket ships, 72 landing craft (infantry). On the first day four army divisions were landed and the beachhead was made secure against slight opposition.

Halsey's 3rd Fleet, with the Fast Carrier Task Force led by Marc Mitscher, stood off to the north, busily giving support to the landings by raiding the airfields on Formosa and in the Philippines. On the day of the landings a Japanese search plane found the carrier task force and reported its location to Admiral Takeo Kurita in Singapore, whose command included nearly two-thirds of the major units in the Japanese Navy.

Japan could not permit the landings on Leyte to continue uncontested: if the Americans were permitted to establish themselves in the Philippines, then they could sever communications between the home islands of Japan and the conquered lands south of the Philippines. Japan itself would be sealed off, blockaded and besieged. Forced to a decision, the Japanese committed their remaining ships to a final battle. The plan to wipe out the Leyte beachhead was cunningly devised. The operations of three separate forces were synchronized: two of them moved up from the south, the third, down from the north, converging on Leyte from three directions.

The southernmost of the three forces was to approach Leyte through the Surigao Strait, to debouch from that strait in the night, and to wreak havoc with the landing armada.

The central force, coming up from Lingga, close to Singapore, included Japan's two super-battleships, the *Yamato* and the *Musashi,* each of which displaced 72,809 tons and carried a main battery of nine 18.1-inch guns. This force was to navigate the torturous San Bernardino Strait north of Samar and to steam down against the Leyte landing vessels.

The northern force, which included four carriers, and two battleships with flight decks on their sterns, was to engage Halsey's fleet.

Before dawn on October 23rd the submarines *Darter* and *Dace,* patrolling the channel between the Dangerous Ground and Palawan, encountered the central force, reported it, and then sank two heavy cruisers. Carrier-based planes located both the central and the southern forces on the 24th and the planes of the Fast Carrier Task Force attacked them. The northern force was found on the 24th, too late for attack that day. Carrier planes attacked it on the morning of the 25th.

Meanwhile the southern force, on the night of October 24–25, had entered Surigao Strait and was proceeding toward Leyte. Vice-Admiral J. B. Oldendorf, commanding the American naval forces at the northern end of the Strait, had disposed his light warships along the sides of the Strait, where they lay waiting for the Japanese. His battleships and heavy cruisers sealed the exit from the Strait to Leyte Gulf. Into this trap the Japanese force (two battleships, a heavy cruiser and four destroyers), steamed unwittingly. Shortly before midnight sections of American motor torpedo boats attacked with torpedoes. A few hours later the destroyers, led by USS *Remey,* joined the party. Then, as the Japanese ships came within range of the heavy guns of the American battleships and cruisers, they were all but annihilated. One Japanese destroyer and the heavy cruiser escaped sudden obliteration by a quick reversal of course, but the cruiser was sunk by aircraft on the 26th. In this engagement, the "Battle of Surigao Strait," no American ships were sunk, although the destroyer *Albert W. Grant* was heavily damaged by shell-fire, and only stalwart work by her damage-control organization saved her from sinking.

The central force, aiming for San Bernardino Strait, was subjected to heavy aerial attacks by planes from the Fast Carrier Task Force during the 24th. *Musashi* was hit repeatedly by bombs and torpedoes in a series of synchronized attacks by dive bombers and torpedo planes in the Sibuyan Sea. After the fifth attack, having been hit by ten torpedoes, the gigantic vessel capsized and sank. *Yamato* was hit by several bombs which caused only minor damage to her 9-inch armored deck. Admiral Takeo Kurita, on *Yamato,* sent part of his force westward, including damaged vessels, to escape the narrow confines of the Sibuyan Sea, and soon thereafter Halsey had word of the Japanese northern force bearing down against him. Halsey, apparently convinced that Kurita with his full force was in retreat, turned his attention to the northern force, which was the only one of the three Japanese forces that included carriers. But that night Kurita led the unharmed part of his fleet through San Bernardino Strait and continued undetected along the coast of Samar toward Leyte. Soon after sunrise on the 25th, *Yamato* and her accompanying battleships, cruisers and destroyers came upon Rear Admiral C. A. F. Sprague's six escort carriers, three destroyers and four destroyer escorts which were silhouetted against the rising sun. At 6:58 A.M. *Yamato* opened fire on the escort carriers nearly twenty-two miles away with her 18.1-inch rifles. So began the "Battle off Samar." The escort carriers launched their planes, and the destroyers and destroyer escorts laid smoke screens, but at about 9:00 A.M. the escort carriers began to be hit. *Gambier Bay* was sunk, and four others damaged by surface fire. Then, in a valiant effort that would have warmed the hearts of Preble, Farragut, Dewey and Pringle, with guns blazing, three American destroyers and four destroyer escorts charged the Japanese battleships and fired their spreads of torpedoes. Three of the American vessels were sunk by the enemy's heavy guns, and Kurita led his force on, until they were within twelve thousand yards of the escort carriers. Quite abruptly, then, as many Americans on the escort carriers were fumbling for the words of dimly-remembered prayers, Kurita reversed his course and broke off the engagement. The Americans had lost heavily: 2 escort carriers sunk (the second was the *Saint Lô*, one of a group to the southward which had been attacked by suicide planes), 2 destroyers, 1 destroyer escort and 105 planes.

Why, with a complete victory within his grasp, did Kurita suddenly stop his attack? The answer is locked in the labyrinth of his mind. Post-war interrogations showed that he was not sure himself of the course of his thinking. Apparently he had been informed that the southern Japanese force had been destroyed, and that the northern force, with its carriers, was being routed. He could have moved on, completed the destruction of the escort carriers and destroyed the Leyte landing armada. But he knew that Oldendorf's battleships were in the Leyte area. (He did not know that they were almost out of ammunition.) He feared the planes of Halsey's fleet, as well as the American land-based planes, which might be expected to attack him at any moment. He had been under air attack for two days, had had his cruiser-flagship sunk under him by submarines, had seen in how workmanlike a fashion the planes had sunk *Musashi*, *Yamato's* sister-ship. He was tired, an old man slightly punch-drunk. His own force was damaged and his communications were poor. All these factors had to be considered. For two hours Kurita mulled the situation over, while his ships re-formed and made repairs, circling in a singular manner north of Leyte. Then the admiral decided not to carry out the attack but to withdraw through San Bernardino Strait. This decision made, Kurita, throwing away the chance for a major victory in Leyte Gulf, left the scene of his minor victory, and with all the speed his ships could make he fled over the horizon.

The northern force, of which the Japanese carriers were a part, had meanwhile come to a grievous pass. Halsey's planes had located this force late in the afternoon of the 24th, and during the night the American carrier task force steamed northward at flank speed, and launched its planes before dawn. The Japanese force was attacked by these planes well to the north of Cape Engaña (northeasternmost point of land on Luzon Island), at 8:40 A.M.—just at the time when Kurita was closing with the escort carriers off Samar. At about this time, word was sent to Halsey that the escort carriers needed help, and he dispatched some carriers and fast battleships to assist them. By the time these 3rd Fleet units reached the waters off Samar, Kurita had entered San Bernardino Strait, and was within range of attack only by aircraft. That afternoon the carrier planes attacked the retreating enemy, causing considerable damage to three cruisers and four battleships.

That part of Halsey's fleet which had remained in the north spent a busy day finishing off the Japanese in what came to be known as the "Battle off Cape Engaño." The enemy had one big carrier, three smaller ones, the two hybrid battleships with flight decks aft, five cruisers and six destroyers. By 6:00 P.M. all four carriers had been sunk, as well as a light cruiser and a destroyer, and much damage had been done to the battleships. The cost to the Americans was forty planes lost in combat, and the light carrier *Princeton,* which had been so severely damaged by enemy dive bombers on the 24th that she had to be sunk by torpedoes from her escorting destroyers.

The Japanese, after the battles of Surigao Strait, Samar and Cape Engaño, which collectively are known as "The Battle for Leyte Gulf," were never again able to put a fleet of any great power to sea. Japan's navy had been eliminated as a threat to future operations, and Leyte was saved, thanks to Halsey and to the men of the 3rd Fleet, and Kinkaid and the men of the 7th Fleet. MacArthur, who had commanded his troops to make the beach area at Leyte secure and to wait for the final decision being made at sea, could now carry on with his program for the liberation of the Philippines.

After a brief rest the Fast Carrier Task Force was back at work, ravaging Luzon in six raids from November 5th to the 25th, and again on December 14, 15 and 16th. On December 15th the navy put more troops ashore on Mindoro in the Philippines; on January 9th, 1945, landings were made in the Lingayan Gulf. In this latter amphibious operation, 1,033 naval vessels of all types, and over 273,000 officers and men, were involved. Within five days following the unopposed landings the navy put nearly 185,000 troops ashore.

The Pacific, whose distances had helped to protect Japan's conquests, was no longer an insurmountable barrier: with warships and planes and merchantmen the Americans had won naval and aerial supremacy on the vast ocean, and had turned it into an open road. Over a hundred years earlier a Russian, Alexander Herzen, had remarked: "The Pacific is the Mediterranean of the future." By 1945 his prediction was well on the way to realization: hundreds of naval transport planes linked the United States with Hawaii, Australia, Kwajalein, Ulithi, Guam and intermediate bases. The B-29s were flying from Guam, Saipan and Tinian to Japan in seven hours and twenty minutes. This projection of American power across seven thousand miles of salt water was made possible only because the United States had won control of the seas.

The first large-scale raid on Tokyo by B-29s based on the Marianas took place on November 24th, 1944. Other B-29s had been operating on a modest scale from Chengtu in China, and they had bombed Tokyo in July. But their work was restricted by the fact that all their gasoline and oil and ammunition had to be flown in over the Himalaya Mountains, since China's ports were tightly blockaded by the Japanese. The raids by large numbers of B-29s had to await the completion of airfields on Saipan and Guam and Tinian: then, with their supplies assured by the navy, the big bombers were able to function with moderate efficiency.

During the winter of 1944–45, the morale of the men who flew the B-29s from the Marianas sank to a low point. More courageous men than these never flew planes. Yet they doubted the efficiency of their work. They were flying over Japan at altitudes of 30,000 to 35,000 feet, and at that height the winds often attained a velocity of 200 miles an hour. Bombing under such conditions was at best haphazard and inaccurate, and many of the pioneers were lost to antiaircraft fire and enemy fighter planes. The crews of planes damaged over Tokyo and forced to land at sea on their way back to the Marianas had little chance of being rescued unless they came down within six hundred miles of Saipan, where they would be within reach of the navy's rescue planes.

To heighten the efficiency of the B-29s the Joint Chiefs of Staff asked the marines to take Iwo Jima. Spruance, in command of the fleet since January 27, with Mitscher commanding the Fast Carrier Task Force, and Turner commanding the amphibious forces, planned the landings on Iwo Jima for February 19, 1945. The island, lying 625 miles north of Saipan and 775 miles from Honshu, largest of Japan's home islands, had been bombed methodically ever since June 15, 1944, by carrier-based planes and by army and marine planes flying from the Marianas. Three days before the landings at Iwo hundreds of planes from the Fast Carrier Task Force attacked Tokyo and Yokohama and for two days bombed and strafed airfields and specific targets in the area. This low-level, precision bombing raid resulted in heavy damage to such targets as aircraft shops, factories and engine works which the high-flying B-29s had been unable to put out of business. A Japanese escort carrier was sunk at Yokohama, and 499 enemy planes were destroyed, 177 of them on the ground, at a cost of 49 American planes. Following this raid the carrier task force moved down to Iwo Jima to join the warships giving that island its final pre-invasion bombardment.

For three days Iwo Jima was bombed by the fleet's carrier-based planes and by army planes flying from the Marianas. Surface ships moved in to add their shells and rockets to the bombardment. While destroyers provided close fire support, beach reconnaissance parties, underwater demolition teams and minesweepers carried on their work. In all, nearly 800 warships with more than 220,000 men were engaged in the invasion of the 8 square mile island.

On the 19th, in the clear dawn with the waters around Iwo flat as a mill-pond, the invasion fleet arrived off the island. The LSTs let down their ramps and disgorged their amphtracs, which began to get into line. LCIs, armed with rockets that could pierce three feet of concrete, moved in close to the beach and blasted at pill-boxes. A great force of B-29s from the Marianas soared over Iwo and loosed tons of bombs on the island; dive bombers and fighter planes from the carriers launched their bombs and rockets at strong-points. Over all this island the surface ships, battleships, cruisers and destroyers, poured their fire. It was difficult to see how anything could remain alive on Iwo.

The first assault waves landed at 9:00 A.M., and they encountered only moderate resistance. In the first hour two battalions of tanks were put ashore.

Then suddenly, when it was clear that this landing was the main effort, and not a feint to draw the Japanese from the west side of the island, Lieutenant General Tadamichi Kuribayashi concentrated his weapons against the landing area. Fire from machine guns, and from mortars, 20 mm. guns, rocket-launchers and artillery sited in Mt. Surabachi to the south and in the hills to the north raked the marines on the beaches. The Japanese had dug themselves in, gone underground into caves and pill-boxes built beneath the surface of Iwo's volcanic soil. There were 22,000 Japanese manning these interlocking defenses and they had to be killed, a few at a time, with flame-throwers and phosphorus shells and hand grenades.

During the 20th one of the island's three airfields was captured, and on the next day the marines of the 4th and 5th Divisions were reinforced by the 3rd Division, which had been held in reserve. There were now sixty thousand marines on Iwo, and the fighting grew in intensity. Star-shells from the warships lit the scene at night and by their light the marines threw back numerous counter-attacks. On the fifth day the American flag was raised on the top of Mt. Suribachi, and part of the second airfield was taken. By the 25th the marines had captured nearly half the island, including the two best airfields.

From then on the battle was a series of costly attacks on the hundreds of interlocking subterranean caves and tunnels from which the Japanese fought fanatically. On March 3rd the first damaged B-29 made an emergency landing on Iwo, after a raid on Japan. On the 16th organized resistance ended, but the cave-fighting continued sporadically. By the time this type of fighting—which may have been a foretaste of the kind of wars that will be fought in the future—ended, over 5,500 marines had been killed and nearly 13,700 wounded. The Japanese defenders, with the exception of a few prisoners, were dead.

On April 7th, when the B-29s from the Marianas raided Tokyo they had an escort of long-range fighter planes which flew from Iwo Jima to help protect the big bombers from Japanese intercepters. Quickly the airfields at Iwo were enlarged so that they could land B-29s safely, and in the following months the B-29s made more than two thousand landings on Iwo. Rescue planes based on Iwo could fly close to the coast of Japan to pick up the crews of B-29s that had crash-landed at sea. Iwo was taken just in time, for on March 9th, Major General Curtis LeMay, commander of the B-29s in the Marianas, ordered his planes to begin a series of low-level raids with fire bombs on Japan. As soon as these raids started the B-29s proved their value: acres of Japanese cities went up in flames.

Having made it possible for the B-29s to operate from the Marianas, and having contributed immeasurably to their safety by taking Iwo

Jima, the navy went about the gratifying business of attacking Japan proper. The Fast Carrier Task Force had returned to strike Tokyo late in February, and on March 19–20 the Inland Sea was raided. At the same time, preparations were being made to land on Okinawa, largest of the Ryukyu Islands, only 350 miles from Japan itself.

Okinawa, with an area of 450 square miles, well-watered, with several good anchorages and sites for many airfields, could be made into a powerful base for an offensive against Japan. From it planes could disrupt communications between Japan and the Chinese mainland, and it could be used as a staging area for the planned invasion of Japan.

The island was not entirely strange to the American Navy. Commore Matthew Calbraith Perry had used the port of Napa on Okinawa as a base for his squadron in 1853, when he was trying to win a treaty of commerce and amity from the Japanese. That year extensive surveys had been made, including even the dimensions of the fortress of Shuri, with notes on the thickness of the castle's concave walls. When all Perry's ancient but valuable information was brought up to date by air reconnaissance in 1945, the Americans had a good fund of information about the target island.

The capture of Okinawa was entrusted to Admiral Spruance, aided by Admirals Turner and Mitscher. General S. B. Buckner, USA, was to command the ground forces once they had been landed.

The usual heavy naval and aerial bombardment commenced on March 25th, one day after a fleet of seventy-five minesweepers began clearing the waters around the island. A large-scale feint was made by part of the landing force toward the southern end of the island, where the Joint Expeditionary Force had no intention of landing. The landings were to be made on the southwest coast, where there were six miles of beaches, and where two airfield were not far inland. While the warships and planes pounded Okinawa with high explosives for seven consecutive days, the invasion fleet steamed toward the island. In that fleet were over 1,200 ships of all kinds, including 318 combatant ships. 548,000 American naval, marine, coast guard and army personnel were involved in the operation, as well as a British Carrier Force.

On the first of April, which was Easter Sunday, the marines and soldiers began to land at 8:30 A.M. There was no strong resistance, and within four hours both airfields had been captured. Before sunset 50,000 troops had been put ashore, and with them many of the T-6 tanks made buoyant by pontoons that could be discarded in shallow water. The marines and soldiers rapidly crossed the island, and then the 1st and 6th Marine Divisions bore off to the northward, while the soldiers of the 7th and 96th Infantry Divisions turned to the south, where most of the 110,000 Japanese troops had been concentrated in expectation of a landing there. In the south there was to be desperate fighting, but it was in the waters off Okinawa that the Japanese struck the heaviest blows.

The navy had been aware that the nearness of Okinawa to Japan was a double-edged weapon: that from Japan planes could fly down to raid the invasion forces. The Japanese had previously shown an aptitude for sacrificial suicidal attacks by flying planes loaded with explosives into the American ships. This type of pilot was a member of the "kamikaze," or "Divine Wind" corps, members of which were quite willing to kill themselves for the Mikado. In the last part of 1944 the suicide planes had damaged several of the big carriers, and there appeared to be only one way to stop them from doing more damage: that was to shoot down the suicide planes before they got within striking distance of the fleet. The Fast Carrier Task Force had raided the airfields on Kyushu and Formosa time after time, and still there were always planes left for the suicidal work. Fortunately the navy was well supplied with shells fitted with proximity fuses—that is, shells which did not need to make a direct hit on an enemy plane before exploding, but were expoded electronically when they came within a few yards of the enemy. And, since the best protection against these attacks was warning that the suiciders were on their way, a picket line of destroyers and smaller ships was formed off Okinawa to protect the landing vessels. These vessels, operating under Rear Admiral Morton L. Deyo, were a part of the Fire Support Task Force, and as the suiciders came down from Kyushu the ships on the picket line were the first targets they saw. Fifty miles further down the coast the landing force vessels were anchored.

During the first four days close to 240,000 tons of supplies had been landed on the beaches at Okinawa, and there were five divisions of American troops on Okinawa. The cargo ships and transports were nearly empty. Then, late on the afternoon of the 6th, the suicide planes made their biggest attack: hundreds of enemy planes were picked up on the radar screens of the ships on the picket line; carrier planes shot down 248 of them; antiaircraft guns knocked down 39 more. But 22 others crashed into American ships.

The Japanese penchant for self-destruction was not restricted to the "kamikaze." On the day of the great air attack the 72,809-ton battleship *Yamato* sortied from the Inland Sea, with an escort of one cruiser and nine destroyers. *Yamato* was to be beached on the south coast of Okinawa and there to be used as a fortress to help stem the American advance. But as she cleared the Inland Sea she was sighted by an American submarine which reported her to the 5th Fleet. The planes of the Fast Carrier Task Force, under Admiral Mitscher, located the Japanese force on April 7th shortly after mid-day, and within an hour she had been hit by five bombs and nine torpedoes, all on her port side. At 2:20 P.M. this gigantic vessel capsized and exploded. The cruiser and four of the destroyers were also sunk by air groups from the carriers.

The suicide planes continued to raid the fleet off Okinawa, and they soon developed a co-ordinated technique, whereby six of them aimed at one ship.

Three, four or five of the six planes would inevitably be shot down, but there was a good chance that at least one plane would get through the curtains of antiaircraft fire to complete its mission by crashing against the target ship. The ships on radar picket duty suffered most heavily, an estimated thirty-four of them being sunk between March 26th and June 21st, when Okinawa was declared secure. Close to 250 vessels of all classes were damaged during those months of furious battle, most of them by suicide planes. Valor was routine on the picket line. Thus, USS *Bryant,* a destroyer of high repute, was going to the aid of stricken *Laffey* when she herself was hit on the port bridge by a suicide plane and lost 27 men. Undaunted, *Bryant* recovered and continued on her errand of mercy.

One particularly deadly type of plane was the "baka" or "idiot" plane, which was small enough to be carried under a twin-motored bomber until within range of the ships. In each "baka" plane a suicide pilot was ensconced, and when the "baka" was cast off by its mother plane, rockets drove it toward its target under the guidance of the pilot. In its warhead was at least a ton of high explosives, and its speed was so great that it was difficult to hit. But the twin-motored planes that carried the "bakas" made good targets.

With such weapons the Japanese expected to do so much damage to the fleet that the Americans would abandon the Okinawa operation. This was an utterly unrealistic hope, for the idea of calling off the conquest of Okinawa was not even considered by the Americans.

While the battle for Okinawa raged, at sea and on land, and while in Germany the inner defenses were crumbling, President Franklin Roosevelt died of a cerebral hemorrhage, on the afternoon of April 12, 1945, at Warm Springs, Georgia. The shock to the American people was great: in New York an American naval officer's young wife, who throughout her youth had known no other President but Roosevelt, was so stricken by the news of his death that birth pains were induced, and she immediately gave premature birth to a daughter. In Washington the citizens loitered outside the White House gates, much as others before them had done when Lincoln died. At the news of his death, there was rejoicing in Germany and Japan, and among the more virulent of his domestic political enemies. There is no doubt that Roosevelt took arbitrary, unneutral steps that were leading the United States toward war with Germany in 1941; there is also no doubt that he was greatly surprised when the Japanese attacked Pearl Harbor. But this man, complex and devious in character, was against the positive evil that Hitler and Mussolini and Tojo represented. Of that fact there can be no doubt.

Roosevelt was succeeded by Harry S. Truman, erstwhile Vice-President, a God-fearing and rational politician from Missouri. Truman had crossed the ocean in the First World War and had served in France as an artillery officer. In the army he had acquired an abiding respect for generals, and his sense of humility had become highly developed. As President of the United States he considered himself the servant of the people, rather than their leader.

In Germany, at the time of Roosevelt's death, the American Ninth Army was crossing the Elbe, only fifty miles from Berlin. The Russian Army was on the outskirts of that city, and everywhere the Allies were advancing. Within a few weeks this vise tightened and eliminated the German armies. On May 3rd Berlin fell to the Russians, and it was reported that Hitler had committed suicide in the ruins of the city. There was scant reason to doubt the veracity of the report, for Hitler was in a sorry state by the time the Russians began besieging Berlin: he was then taking vitamin, glucose and caffein injections to stimulate his energy, and he was suffering from coronary sclerosis, colitis and bodily tremors. The idea of capture by the Russians was surely enough to frighten him into killing himself.

On May 7th, 1945, at Rheims, France, at 2:41 A.M., General Alfred Jodl, on behalf of the German High Command, signed an "Act of Military Surrender" whose first clause read:

"We the undersigned, acting by authority of the German High Command, hereby surrender unconditionally to the Supreme Commander, Allied Expeditionary Force and simultaneously to the Soviet High Command all forces on land, sea, and in the air who are at this date under German control."

Next day, in the one hundred and sixty-ninth year of the independence of the United States, President Truman proclaimed the victory over Germany, and predicted that "The power of our peoples to defend themselves against all enemies will be proved in the Pacific war as it has been proved in Europe."

Off Okinawa the sea and air battle was being carried on with undiminished ferocity. Repeated strikes by carrier-based fighter planes were made on the airfields of Kyushu, and still the suicide planes attacked. On May 11th they came down in force: seventy-two were destroyed in the air, but two crashed into the USS *Bunker Hill*, a 27,000-ton carrier, and killed 392 of her people.

The carriers replied by steaming north against Kyushu and trying to wipe out the Japanese planes on the ground. In the next ten days 101 Japanese planes were destroyed, but additional damage was done to the carrier force, when *Enterprise* was hit by a suicide plane.

On May 28th, with Okinawa secure, Halsey relieved Spruance. Admiral John S. McCain became the commander of the Fast Carrier Task Force, relieving Admiral Mitscher, and the sweeps against Kyushu continued from June 2nd to June 9th, interrupted only by a typhoon that moved through the area. By June 10th there were not enough enemy planes left on the Kyushu airfields to justify using the Fast Carrier Task Force against them, and the carriers retired to Leyte Gulf for rest and repairs and supplies. In three months, at the cost of 557 American planes, the fast carriers had destroyed 2,336 Japanese aircraft. Their next mission was to consist of pre-invasion raids on the Japanese home islands.

The Joint Chiefs of Staff had ordered Nimitz and MacArthur in April to prepare for the invasion of Japan, which was scheduled to begin on November 1st, with the invasion of Kyushu. Honshu was to be invaded in the spring of 1946. In these two operations nearly five million American soldiers, sailors, marines and coast guardsmen were slated to be involved.

It was estimated that there were five million Japanese still in arms, nearly two million of them in the home islands. Japan's volcanic terrain, with its countless terraces, ravines, and small streams, was admirably suited for defense. The ground was inconvenient, save on the Tokyo plain, for tank warfare, and the defenders could quickly burrow underground. The Japanese had a belief that their islands were formed from the excretions of ancient gods, and that their soil was sacred. Thus, to man's natural determination to defend his home, would be added a spiritual frenzy. The invasion of Japan would be a repetition of Tarawa, Saipan, Iwo Jima and Okinawa on an enormously enlarged scale.

The United States forces in the Pacific had suffered 300,000 battle casualties up to July 1st: the assault on Japan would cost in the neighborhood of one million more Americans killed and wounded. It would be a ghastly invasion, on a scale much larger and tougher than the landings on the Normandy coast had been. Convoys carrying the troops and supplies to the landings in Japan would have to cross hundreds of miles of ocean on their way from the Marianas, the Philippines and Okinawa. Japan had 9,000 aircraft left which were operational and 5,000 of them had been prepared for suicide attack on the invasion fleet.

In preparation for the invasion of Kyushu, Okinawa became a great airbase, packed with bombers and fighters. The B-29s continued their fire-bomb raids from the Marianas. On July 1st, McCain's Fast Carrier Task Force, as part of Halsey's Third Fleet, steamed north from Leyte to carry out the first pre-invasion raid on Japan. Nine days later the force launched its planes 170 miles southeast of Tokyo, and the airfields and industrial plants in the area underwent a thorough bombing and strafing. There was little opposition, for the Japanese had moved most of their planes to the north in order to preserve them from attack. The 3rd Fleet moved up the coast of Japan, to strike northern Honshu on July 14–15, and Hokkaido, shelling mills and factories and oil refineries along the coast.

While these men and planes and ships were carrying out their missions, a curious experiment was taking place on a desert in New Mexico.

The scientists had produced their first atomic bomb and they were ready to prove that it worked. On July 14th the bomb was placed on a one hundred foot high skeletal steel tower in the most desolate part of the 2,000 square mile Alamogordo Reservation, thirty miles from the nearest village. Shortly after midnight on July 16th, in great secrecy, over 300 of the scientists who had been working on the development of the bomb, and some 250 army officers and men, were assembled at the site of the test. It was raining heavily, and there were uneasy moments while a thunderstorm played around the horizon. But by 4 o'clock the rain had ended, although there were still flashes of distant lightning. The spectators were instructed to lie flat on the ground, with their heels toward the bomb and their eyes shaded. At 5:30 A.M. (Mountain War Time), Monday, July 16th, 1945, the bomb was exploded. It was as though a miniature sun had been born on earth: a huge globe of fire shot into the sky, twisting, convoluting, multi-hued, rising to an altitude of 41,000 feet. At the same time there came a deep and guttural roar from the mass of exploding atoms.

The scientists broke into a grotesque little dance of joy, and their leaping shadows were similar to those of the ancient Mayas who had worshiped the Sun.

Word of the successful test was rushed to the Secretary of War, Henry Stimson, and on to Potsdam, where Truman, Stalin and Prime Minister Clement R. Atlee of Great Britain were in conference. President Truman, following the recommendations of his military and diplomatic advisers, decided that Japan should be warned to surrender, and a joint ultimatum from the United States and Great Britain was sent to Prime

Minister Suzuki of Japan on July 26th, threatening the "full application of our military power." Two days later Suzuki scornfully rejected the ultimatum. Then the orders were given to use the atomic bomb on Japan.

By that time the 3rd Fleet had attacked the coast north of Tokyo, and carrier planes had bombed Yokosuka Naval Base in Tokyo Bay, wrecking *Nagato,* the next to the last Japanese battleship still afloat. The planes had been turned loose to find targets on the Inland Sea, and there they had raided Kure naval base on July 28th. Merchant ships and railroads were attacked, and two days later the planes were back over Tokyo, and the fast battleships were shelling the coast of Honshu. The navy was carrying out its assigned mission. Those few naval officers who knew of the atomic bomb were none too sure that it would mean the end of the war.

As soon as reports of the first explosion of an atomic bomb had reached Potsdam, steps had been taken to ready a bomb for explosion on Japan. The materials were flown to San Francisco and loaded on the cruiser USS *Indianapolis,* which left at once for the Marianas. More of the explosive element was flown by three B-29s from California to Tinian in the Marianas in the first days of August. General Carl Spaatz, in tactical command of army air forces in the Pacific, had orders to have the first bomb dropped on one of four target cities in Japan at any time after August 3rd. These target cities were all of military importance.

On August 4th (United States date), the crew members of six B-29s at Tinian were briefed: three of the planes were to take off at 1:45 A.M. the next morning to report on weather over three of the target cities; two planes were to accompany the B-29 *Enola Gay,* which was to carry the atomic bomb. Captain William S. Parsons, USN, was to make the final adjustments in the assembly of the bomb after *Enola Gay* was airborne. In that way, if the B-29 crashed on the take-off, no great damage would be done to Tinian.

At 2:45 A.M., an hour after the weather planes had taken off, the *Enola Gay,* piloted by Colonel Paul W. Tibbets, Jr., roared off toward Japan. En route Captain Parsons completed the assembly of the bomb, and the reports from the weather planes came in: there was good visibility only over Hiroshima, a city of 400,000 souls.

It was 9:15 A.M., by the navigator's watch, Monday, August 6th, 1945 (Japanese date), when the dark, slender, gracefully curved bomb fell from the *Enola Gay*. At that moment, on the Eastern seaboard of the United States, it was Sunday evening, August 5th, and many Americans were just beginning to eat their Sunday dinners.

The bomb exploded in the air over Hiroshima at a time when thousands of the inhabitants were going to work. Eyewitnesses reported its burst was a blue-white flash, of intense heat, followed by a blast of air and the thunderous rumble of the explosion. The man-made tower of smoke and dust and death reached an altitude of nearly 50,000 feet.

By this primitive type of atomic bomb, whose explosive force was equal to only 20,000 tons of TNT, between 60,000 and 70,000 people were killed, many of them vaporized, and 50,000 more were injured. 60 per cent of Hiroshima's buildings were destroyed. *Enola Gay,* unscathed, flew back to Tinian.

Next day the news of the explosion of the atomic bomb was released to the world. The civilian public's first reaction was one of stunned surprise, for the secret of the development of the bomb had been well kept. Its use induced a ferment of thinking. Expressions of terror and horror were widespread. From the Vatican came word: "The use of atomic bombs in Japan has created an unfavorable impression on the Vatican." But the announcement of the bomb's power gave men and women in the armed forces reason to hope that the war might soon be ended.

In Moscow, at 8:30 P.M. (Moscow time), August 8th, Foreign Commissar Molotov announced to a press conference that Russia declared war on Japan, effective August 9th. While he was reading the formal declaration of war to the assembled reporters, another B-29, *The Great Artiste,* was en route to Japan with an atomic bomb of improved type, whose explosive force was equal to perhaps 40,000 tons of TNT.

As *The Great Artiste,* piloted by Major Charles Sweeney, neared the coast of Japan the reports from the weather planes narrowed the choice of target cities to Nagasaki, population 230,000, site of the Mitsubishi steel works and armaments plant. A few minutes after mid-day on August 9th (Japanese date), the bomb was released over the city. In the subsequent explosion 40,000 men, women and children were killed or dissolved, and 40,000 were injured. The column of smoke, composed of dust that had once been flesh and blood, wood, stone and steel, mushroomed to a height of 60,000 feet. *The Great Artiste* flew on to Okinawa.

A day later the Japanese government sued for peace, making use of the good offices of the neutral Swiss government. There followed several days of haggling over the terms of the capitulation which, as proposed at Potsdam, were not entirely acceptable to Japan. The Japanese had no wish to surrender unconditionally: they were anxious to keep their Emperor. Their army was still nearly intact, and they had a large air force. But their navy and merchant marine had been destroyed and without these their homeland was doomed to invasion, and the people to terrible and unknown privations. The Japanese were not sure how many more atomic bombs the United States had; they suspected that only a few had been made, but they had no way of knowing that the bomb exploded over Nagasaki was the last one then in existence. Surrender was certainly advisable, and the atomic bomb offered the Japanese government a chance to surrender without loss of face: the bombs were quite evidently miniature, man-made suns, and for a nation whose people believed themselves to be descendants of the Sun Goddess, the bombs offered proof that the Sun Goddess had a worthy rival in the creators of the atomic bombs. There was little shame connected with surrender to the masters of such a planetary, mystical force.

During the last few days of the war, while negotiations were still being debated, the 3rd Fleet bombed and shelled the coast of Honshu while its planes raided the airfields and factories. Throughout this period there were also raids by masses of B-29s and smaller bombers flying from the airfields of Okinawa and the Marianas. On August 13th Tokyo was again attacked by carrier-based aircraft, as though to emphasize to the Japanese the futility of further resistance.

In Washington, at 6:10 P.M. on the afternoon of August 14th, the Chargé d'Affaires of the Swiss Legation, Mr. Max Grässli, trotted up the steps at the State Department and delivered a note to Secretary of State James Byrnes which contained the text of Japan's formal capitulation. Fifty minutes later at a White House press conference, President Truman released the news that the war had been won. Nothing then remained to be done but to arrange for the formal signing of the "Instrument of Surrender" in an appropriate atmosphere.

On board the battleship USS *Missouri,* anchored in Tokyo Bay, on September 2nd, at 9:04 A.M., the emissaries of the Emperor of Japan and of the Japanese government signed the document, the second paragraph of which stated: "We hereby proclaim the unconditional surrender to the Allied Powers of the Japanese Imperial General Headquarters and of all Japanese armed forces and all armed forces under Japanese control wherever situated." Admiral Chester Nimitz represented the United States of America at the surrender ceremonies.

The Japanese were permitted to retain their Emperor, but he was to be subject to the orders of "The Supreme Commander for the Allied Forces," General Douglas MacArthur, who thus reached the apogee of a varied and colorful career. Japan's conquests were shorn from her; all that remained of the ill-got empire were the home islands of the Mikado. The vanquished nation reverted territorially to the status which she had enjoyed in 1868.

Thus ended the war with Japan.

[23] *Second Intermission*

In the achievement of victory the American merchant marine played a part which, being taken for granted, was largely unappreciated. Military secrecy cloaked the sailings and routes of the great convoys, one of which in the days before the Normandy landings included 167 vessels. During the war 733 American merchantmen were lost—77 of them on the Murmansk run alone—and nearly all of these ships went to their doom anonymously, without benefit of the chastely-phrased communiqués which recorded episodes in the progress of the army and navy and air forces.

5,638 American seamen were listed as killed or missing during the war, and these men, being volunteers, were among the bravest in their country's service. So many of them were lost in the spring of 1942, when

German submarines were cruising in the coastal waters of the Atlantic seaboard, and when anti-submarine defenses were rudimentary, that the life expectancy of an American seaman became very brief. As a result many seamen cautiously refrained from going to sea, and ship delays reached an average of forty-five a month. The War Shipping Administration saw the writing on the wall: what good would the new ships be if there were not enough men to sail them?

This possibility called for immediate preventive measures, and the War Shipping Administration created a "Recruitment and Manning Organization" which sought seamen for the merchant fleet. Industry was combed for men with previous seafaring experience and almost a hundred thousand such men, who had drifted into jobs on shore, were persuaded to return to the sea. Congress in 1943 passed a law guaranteeing such men re-employment and seniority rights when they returned from the wars. With the 55,000 professional seamen and officers who had been following the sea in December 1941, these additional hands were enough to man the ships until the training program began to produce seamen in large numbers. As the newly trained seamen came from the training schools they formed a pool of manpower on which the merchant fleet could draw as the need arose. Approximately 75 per cent of the merchant seamen employed were supplied by the shipping line operators and the maritime unions. Only when the operators and the unions could not supply the men needed did the Recruitment and Manning Office draw on the pool of training school graduates.

Soon after the United States entered the war the seafaring unions agreed to a "no-strike" pledge for the duration of the war. Their employer throughout the war was the United States Government, which, through the War Shipping Administration, had requisitioned in April, 1942, the use of nine hundred sea-going cargo and passenger vessels, many of which had been in the coastal trade. There was no need for the unions to strike for more pay: wages were high, and there were large bonuses for the crews of ships which entered the combat zones. Seamen were exempted from the draft, and many a man who preferred to take his chances at sea at high pay in a merchantman, rather than fight as a soldier or sailor, joined the merchant service. A vociferous minority among the seamen were firm admirers of Russian communism, but since

Russia was an Ally in the war against Germany, these indigenous American communists sailed as bravely and worked as hard as though the safety of their own country were at stake.

This ideological aspect of the manpower problem was not without its lighter moments: on the West Coast a labor leader named Harry Bridges, head of the International Longshoremen's and Warehousemen's Union, controlled the loading and unloading of ships at West Coast ports. Many of his followers were Scandinavians, not mentally agile, and up to the time of the invasion of Russia by Germany they had been told, time after time, until they had it firmly fixed in their minds, that the war was "imperialistic and capitalistic," and that they should not hurry to load and unload ships engaged in shoring up the tottering edifice of rival capitalistic states.

Then, overnight, with the invasion of Russia, the war stopped being "capitalist-imperialist" and became democratic, and the longshoremen were told that they should bend every effort to get the ships loaded. This sudden change of directions was at first puzzling to them, but they finally understood the need for speed, and then they worked as busily as beavers for the duration of the war, and many ships loaded with munitions and supplies for the Russian armies sailed from West Coast ports after remarkably fast cargo-handling had filled them to capacity. The longshoremen, too, throughout the war, honored the "no-strike" pledge.

From Pearl Harbor to the signing of Japan's surrender the American merchant marine moved 268,252,000 long tons of cargo. In the course of delivering and picking up this cargo, the ships steamed into remote South Sea harbors unvisited by American vessels for over a hundred years, as well as into the great ports of Europe. Because of them the seas became a means of linking the Allies, and of shifting and applying offensive power to any given point at a predetermined time. Raw materials—such as bauxite, manganese, copper, chrome, uranium-bearing ore, nitrates, sisal, henequen, cocoa beans, wool, hides and skins, burlap, sugar and coffee—which were needed to support the war effort of the United States, were imported from South America, Africa, the Middle East, India, Australia and New Zealand.

To handle this vast cargo "lift" new methods of stowage and loading were applied: deck cargoes took on a new importance when they consisted of planes, amphibious craft, vehicles, mobile generators, as well as the usual lumber and drums of lubricating oil. Tankers were fitted with platforms on which planes could be carried; whole trains of freight cars were lightered out to ships anchored in American ports and the ships were loaded directly from the lighters or "carfloats." Terminals, at which freight might pile up, were kept reasonably clear by co-ordinating shipments by rail, truck and barge with the cargo capacity of ships in port and the port's facilities for handling cargo. All this was in the domain of the War Shipping Administration, which also attended to such matters as 42,076 repair jobs for vessels in the Allied Shipping Pool, the transfer of 509 vessels to foreign registry under Lend-Lease, and the allocation of ships to the army and navy, which at one time used three-fourths of the tonnage at the War Shipping Administration's disposal.

The period immediately following the end of the war was one of intensified activity for the merchant marine. A great hue and cry went up in the United States for the prompt return of the millions of fighting men still far from the comforts of home and such amenities of life as the corner drug store and the neighborhood theater. The task of transporting these men fell to the merchant marine.

The War Shipping Administration had begun to operate a "troop return fleet" soon after the surrender of the German armies and this fleet was enlarged as soon as Japan capitulated. 97 Victory ships, converted into transports capable of carrying 1,500 men, and over 300 Liberty ships, converted so that they could transport 550 men each, were assigned to the troop return fleet. In time this fleet came to number 546 vessels, with a carrying capacity of 580,000 men. Warships as well as merchantmen were pressed into service in the scramble to bring the men home, and by December 1st, 1945, nearly 3,500,000 men had been returned to the United States.

The demand for shipping was enormous, for with the coming of peace, greatness had been thrust upon the United States, and the world looked to the United States for shipments of food, clothing, machinery, medicine, tools, seed and livestock. This was a responsibility the nation was able to discharge, for there were 5,529 merchant-type vessels flying the American flag, and their total tonnage was 56,797,700 deadweight tons. Of these ships, 4,221 were being operated by the War Shipping

Administration at war's end. Their capacious holds could carry the cargoes of peace as easily as the weapons of war. In the month of December, 1945, the War Shipping Administration listed twelve hundred sailings—four hundred more than in the busiest month of the war.

Of course, it could not last forever: there were more American merchant vessels than anyone could possibly use in time of peace. The merchant fleet, which had consisted of 1,310 vessels of 11,544,000 deadweight tons on September 1st, 1939, and which at that time had represented 14 per cent of the world's tonnage, had suddenly become so large that it represented 51 per cent of the world's tonnage. 1,396,400 men and women had been involved in building these ships, 800,000 of them in the ship yards, and the rest in plants that kept a steady stream of supplies flowing to the yards. A merchant shipbuilding capacity of 25,000,000 tons a year had been created. The cost of building and operating the merchant fleet was at least $22,500,000,000; the ships themselves represented an investment of some $15,000,000,000. On March 2, 1946, the Allied Shipping Pool was dissolved and most of the American-built ships returned to the jurisdiction of the Maritime Commission.

To conserve the best of these vessels as a national asset, Congress passed a law called the "Merchant Ship Sales Act of 1946," which was approved on March 6, 1946. This Act began with the brave and oft-used words: "It is necessary for the national security and development and maintenance of the domestic and the export and import foreign commerce of the United States that the United States have an efficient and adequate American-owned merchant marine (1) sufficient to carry its domestic water-borne commerce and a substantial portion of its water-borne export and import foreign commerce and to provide shipping service on all routes essential for maintaining the flow of such domestic and foreign water-borne commerce at all times; (2) capable of serving as a naval and military auxiliary in time of war or national emergency; (3) owned and operated under the United States flag by citizens of the United States; (4) composed of the best-equipped, safest, and most suitable types of vessels, constructed in the United States and manned with a trained and efficient citizen personnel; and (5) supplemented by efficient American-owned facilities for shipbuilding and ship repair, marine insurance, and other auxiliary services."

By the terms of the Act prices were set at a low level: the minimum price for Liberty ships was set at 31½ per cent of the war-time cost of construction; the minimum price for other types of dry-cargo vessels was set at 35 per cent of cost; for tankers, it was 50 per cent of cost. First choice of ships at this great bargain sale was given to American citizens, who could buy ships with a down payment of 25 per cent of the purchase price, the balance to be paid over a period of twenty years, with depreciation figured at 5 per cent per year and the interest rate on the unpaid balance set at 3½ per cent per year. In practice, this meant that an American could buy a Liberty ship which had cost about $1,750,-000 to build for $584,000; and a Victory ship for $1,065,000. There were 44,000,000 tons of shipping from which to choose, and the man in charge of disposing of them was Vice-Admiral William Ward Smith USN (Ret.), who replaced Admiral Land as Chairman of the Maritime Commission on June 3rd, 1946.

The liberal terms of the Act made it possible for American shipping lines to buy the best of these vessels—the Maritime Commission C-type vessels and the tankers. By the beginning of 1947 the Maritime Commission (which took over the functions and duties of the War Shipping Administration when that bureau was abolished on September 1, 1946), had sold 818 vessels, for a total of $732,000,000. Of these ships 296 were sold to American operators, who bought 179 C-type ships, 53 Libertys, 48 tankers, 3 Victorys and 13 coastal vessels. Foreign governments or nationals bought the rest of the 818 ships sold; among their purchases were 311 Libertys, and only 46 C-type vessels.

There was an inevitable surplus of Libertys, of which there were 2,500 at the end of the war—nearly half the total ships the Maritime Commission could either sell or lay up in the reserve fleet. Because they had been designed after the model of a time-tested British tramp ship, the Libertys were eminently suitable for tramping. But in this field of seafaring the Americans had long been out-classed by the British, for tramping involves many associated elements: it presupposes an alert consular service whose employees are on the lookout for cargoes; it depends to a great extent on custom and usage; and it entails long voyages, lasting sometimes for more than two years, which American seamen have been loath to undertake.

The position of the United States as a maritime power was adversely affected in the crucial, formative years after the defeat of the Axis by the high cost of operating American ships. As Norway, Denmark, France, the Netherlands and Britain made progress in peace they quickly placed ships on the world trade routes. Their vessels could be operated at much less cost than American ships, because of the higher American wages and living standards. A British merchantman could be operated for 41 per cent of the cost of operation of an American vessel of the same type. Government subsidies and operating differentials offered some help to the Americans, but such subsidies were at best subject to the whims of the political party in power, and on such a basis it was hazardous for shipping operators to formulate long range plans. Increasing costs drove many operators to register their ships under the Panamanian or Honduran flags, where they could escape the expense of American wages and regulations. It was estimated, in early 1947, that 101 American ships were flying the flags of Panama and Honduras.

American ships plying the coastal and intercoastal routes, although free from foreign competition, were affected by rising costs to such an extent that the railroads were able to threaten their profits. In this situation the national security was involved, for vessels in the domestic trade habitually form 70 per cent of the American merchant marine. In time of war they are the nation's one sure source of shipping, for they are readily available, being constantly operated on routes close to the United States. Yet, on September 1, 1946, there were only 101 dry-cargo vessels, of 917,270 tons, in the coastwise and intercoastal trade, compared to 312 such vessels on September 1, 1939. So uninspiring were the prospects for profits in this once lucrative business that operators were reluctant to enter it with vessels bought from the great war-created merchant fleet.

In 1947 the government was committed to a policy of relinquishing the operation of ships to private operators: 750 of the 900 large vessels which had been requisitioned during the war had been returned to private operation by July, 1946, and only 27 were still in government service on January 1, 1947.

As the pattern of maritime decline which had followed the First World War was repeated after the Second World War, it was accompanied by the customary public somnolence: the American people were simply not aware of what was happening to their merchant marine, and there was no one in the Maritime Commission or in the shipping lines capable of arousing the public's interest. Faithfully, undramatically, the process of decay took its established course.

The surplus war-built ships were assigned to permanent anchorages on the Gulf, Pacific and Atlantic coasts, in ice-free waters. There were nine of these "Reserve Fleet Anchorages" in all, on the James River in Virginia, at Suisun Bay, California, Mobile, Alabama, Astoria, Oregon, Olympia, Washington, Beaumont, Texas, Wilmington, North Carolina, Brunswick, Georgia, and on the Hudson River, north of New York City.

Early in 1947 there were 1,681 idle ships, most of which were Libertys, moored at these anchorages. Choice targets though they were, they represented a means of defense which was worthy of constant care. For the United States had reached a condition in world affairs similar to that of Britain in the nineteenth century, when it was said that, "The frontiers of England at war are the shores of the enemy." But that these ships in the inactive fleet would be kept in good condition was likely to be an empty hope: the cost of keeping a Liberty ship for twenty years was estimated at about fifty thousand dollars, and this amount of money, when multiplied by the number of ships in the reserve fleets, seemed large to the economy-minded Congress that assembled in Washington in January 1947. At that time shipbuilding had all but ceased in the United States, and there were prospects that the active American merchant marine would dwindle to a fleet of about 11,000,000 deadweight tons, compared to 9,300,000 tons in the pre-war active fleet. America's inactive fleet might reach 25,000,000 deadweight tons, compared to 2,400,000 tons in 1939. In any event, the ships and men had done their job: whether it would all have to be done over again was a matter for the statesmen to decide.

The navy's adjustment to peace, although so painfully abrupt that it left the statesmen little with which to implement their policies, was in the time-honored, democratic tradition. The fighting men wanted, quite simply, to go home. Thousands of their fellow servicemen were dead: the navy, marine corps and coast guard listed total casualties at 146,950 officers and men, as of October 18, 1945: 55,633 killed, 80,238 wounded, 9,573 missing (nearly all of whom were dead), and 1,506 prisoners. The dead had not all met an instant and a painless death: many of them had been trapped in stricken submarines or in flaming planes or surface ships; among the wounded were many who were maimed for life, and there were those who, their minds unable to bear the insanity of war, had themselves become insane. With Japan defeated, the normal reaction of naval personnel, 84.5 per cent of whom were reservists, was to return to the pursuits of peace. They had known the reality of war—not simply the words describing it. They had had more than enough of the slaughter, and in the expression of their desire for a peaceful life lay conclusive proof of the congenital distaste Americans have for war. So irresistible among army personnel was this urge to return to civilian life that soldiers in Paris and Manila staged highly unmilitary demonstrations whose theme was "I want to go home!" "Home," for most American fighting men, whether sailors or soldiers, meant not only the apple pie in the oven, the use of the family automobile and the dulcet, pliant charms of feminine companionship, but also freedom from the restrictions on personal liberty that military discipline entailed, a chance to begin or resume careers, and an end to the dull-eyed battle weariness.

Demobilization in the navy was not as impassioned and undignified as in the army, but it was nonetheless so swift that the navy seemed to melt away. On September 2, 1945, there were 3,408,347 officers and men and women in the navy; fifteen months later there were only 491,663. The navy's losses in the war amounted to 157 combatant ships: the 2 battleships lost at Pearl Harbor—*Arizona* and *Oklahoma;* 5 carriers, 6 escort carriers, 7 heavy and 3 light cruisers, 71 destroyers, 11 destroyer escorts and 52 submarines. In addition, 544 auxiliary ships and landing ships had been destroyed. But at war's end, when Japan had nothing but 51 submarines and 36 destroyers left in operational condition, the American Navy consisted of 40 carriers, 79 escort carriers, 24 battleships, 3 battle cruisers, 33 heavy and 57 light cruisers, 450 destroyers, 359 destroyer escorts, and 263 submarines. This tremendous armada, whose smallest turret gun would be considered heavy artillery on land, was quickly reduced so that it conformed to the needs of peace. In 1947 there were 25 carriers (10 of which were escort carriers), 2 battleships,

12 heavy and 25 light cruisers, 143 destroyers, 30 destroyer escorts, and 80 submarines in the active fleets. Aircraft on hand had dwindled to 15,983, from a peak of 41,272.

The surplus ships were laid up in inactive fleets, their guns and machinery protected by grease and plastic cocoons that were devised to prevent rust. Their hulls were coated with a plastic paint that would protect them for five years in salt water. Then they would have to be drydocked for repainting. More than two thousand vessels in all were scheduled to be given this preservative treatment, and they could be made mechanically ready for use on ten days' notice.

Constricted though the active post-war navy was, it still remained the greatest and most mobile striking force in the world. The kind of warfare that had to be carried on in order to defeat the German submarines and to drive the Japanese back to their home islands had forced innumerable technical improvements on the navy.

In the anti-submarine warfare, besides the use of radar and sonar and loran, a new type of depth-charge had been devised. This was the "hedgehog," a British invention which the Americans were quick to adopt. The "hedgehog" was an anti-submarine weapon in which twenty-four projectiles were mounted in a projector on surface ships. All twenty-four projectiles could be fired in 1.8 seconds, and they would explode only on contact with the submarine. In this way, the crew of a submarine under attack could never be sure how close to destruction they were until a roaring explosion resolved their doubts.

In the war against Japan, aircraft armed with rockets, bombs and guided missiles became the fleets' long-range guns. The carriers, as the source of the planes, were the ships that could deliver the most powerful and destructive attacks on the enemy. The planes themselves, toward the end of the war, became the source of increasingly lethal weapons: target-seeking, self-guiding glide-bombs were loosed from naval planes against Japanese shipping, and plane-borne rockets reached a diameter of 11¾ths inches and a length of ten feet, three inches. To protect the carriers from enemy attack, the carrier task forces were ringed with a circle of ships that included battleships, cruisers and destroyers, their decks all crammed with antiaircraft weapons, such as 20 mm., 40 mm. guns in multiple mounts, and the 5-inch guns whose shells were equipped with proximity fuses. Against "kamikaze" attacks on the carriers the escorting vessels could throw up a curtain of fire.

The navy the United States had when the war ended represented what the navy had learned while fighting. When the war began the Germans were far ahead of the Allies in research and new inventions, and the Japanese had grasped the fact that air power adds more to sea power than it takes away. Hampered by small appropriations, the democratically-governed nations could not compete in laboratory work with their militaristic enemies, but when the fighting ended the democracies were surpassed in only a few fields by German inventions.

Most dangerous of the Germans' naval inventions were submarines fitted with the "schnorchel," a device that drew air from the surface and so enabled submarines to cruise submerged for weeks at a time. The Dutch had invented this submarine breathing-tube in 1940, but the Germans had neglected to develop it until it was too late to change the course of the war.

The prototype of the submarine of the future was the German Type 26, which was designed too late for construction during the war. The plans for the Type 26 called for a hull streamlined for submerged operations, capable of an underwater top speed of twenty-four knots, and powered by a hydrogen-peroxide engine. Equipped with a "schnorchel," such a vessel could cruise submerged across the Atlantic, and its detection would have been almost impossible by either surface ship or aircraft with the detection gear in use in 1945. By this type of U-boat, every submarine in the American Navy was out-moded.

The Germans had used missiles launched and guided from planes in attacks on Allied ships in the Bay of Biscay in the fall of 1943, but, lacking a navy, their guided missiles were of limited use, being restricted to the range of the planes that carried them. They had made great progress in the field of rockets, such as the V-1s and V-2s with which they had bombarded London from launching sites on the coast of France and the Low Countries. But when the war ended there was no fuel known to science by which a rocket could be driven for more than five hundred miles.

These technical achievements by the Germans were over-shadowed by the development of atomic power, which was a joint product of American, British and Canadian inventiveness. When the actual effectiveness of the atomic bomb had been proved at Hiroshima and at Nagasaki, there was an immediate out-pouring of warning words from the scientists who had devised the bomb. They were among the gentlest of men, and their knowledge of humanity reflected an educational background in which laboratory work had all but excluded history. The wisest of them, Doctors A. H. Compton, Enrico Fermi, E. O. Lawrence and J. R. Oppenheimer, reported on June 16, 1945, just after the Alamogordo test had been successfully carried out, that "We have, however, no claim to special competence in solving the political, social and military problems which are presented by the advent of atomic power." They were, in fact, like obstetricians who balk at the practice of pediatrics. Other scientists who had worked on the bomb were suddenly beset with guilt complexes as a result. Happily, they could seek absolution for their sense of guilt in religion, and thus free their minds of a heavy responsibility. Others, politically virginal, banded together into organizations whose aim was to arouse the public's concern over the advent of atomic power.

The American Navy's approach to the problem of atomic power was purely practical. A series of tests was arranged in the summer of 1946, and these tests took place in a remote lagoon in the South Pacific, at Bikini atoll. A Joint Army-Navy Task Force, commanded by Admiral William H. P. Blandy, carried out the tests with a force of 42,000 men, 150 planes and 230 ships. Two of the improved Nagasaki-type bombs, which made use of plutonium instead of the uranium used in the Hiroshima-type bomb, were exploded—one in the air several hundred feet over the carefully dispersed target fleet, and another on the surface of the lagoon. The results of these tests made it possible for the navy to form an estimate of the best type of ship design for atomic warfare, the tactical distances by which ships should be separated while at sea, their anchoring distances in port, the strategic disposition of types of ships, the number and location of repair yards and bases, and the kind of equipment needed in them. Of all the test ships at Bikini, the submarines were the least affected by the explosions.

The emphasis on future warships turned immediately to submersible types of craft, for they were the ships capable of best sustaining the flash heat, radio-active rays and blast effect of atomic bombs. Other types might be able to survive in a future war, but they would have to be built to withstand enormous pressures, like the whalebacks of the Great Lakes, and they would need special equipment to neutralize radio-active rays.

Fortunately the navy was aware of the implications the future held for sea power. Construction of the battleship *Kentucky* and the battle cruiser *Hawaii,* which were in process of completion when the war ended, was halted in 1946, and it was planned to turn them into missile-launching ships, and to embody in them as many of the lessons learned at Bikini as possible. Selected officers and men were trained in atomic defense. The navy instituted a basic research program, for which 90 universities, with contracts in 1947 of about $22,000,000, carried on over two-thirds of the work.

Under this program technical progress would move forward in many fields, and the navy could expect to learn much which could be applied to the development of jet and rocket powered planes moving at transonic and supersonic speeds, anti-submarine weapons, methods of communication between submerged submarines, methods of launching guided-missiles from underwater vessels, improved electronic gunsights, computers, fuses, bomb-sights, nuclear power and nuclear explosives, atomic power by fusion or fission, the prevention of imperfections in metals, and dozens of unmentionable projects. The war had made the Navy, for the first time, extremely conscious of the value of scientific research, and there was a fair chance that, given the funds for research and for applying the results of research in new construction of ships and planes, the navy would not have to fight the next war with the weapons of 1945.

There was great interest in naval circles in the Arctic regions, over which the air route to the United States from Europe is relatively short. At the end of 1946 the navy was maintaining only twelve active bases outside the continental United States, and of these four were in northern waters, at Kodiak, Adak and Attu in Alaska, and in Greenland. The others were in Pearl Harbor, Guam, Subic (in the Philippines), Argentia, Newfoundland, San Juan, Puerto Rico, Trinidad in the West Indies,

Guantanamo, Cuba, and Balboa, Canal Zone. Emphasizing the navy's interest in getting cold weather operating experience were the expeditions to the Arctic and Antarctic made by naval task forces in 1946 and 1947. In the Antarctic, where Captain Nathaniel Palmer had sought seals in 1820, and where, in 1839, ships of the expedition led by Captain Charles Wilkes, USN, had been driven along the ice barrier by gales, Rear Admiral Richard E. Byrd, USN, in 1947, commanded an expedition of twelve ships and four thousand officers and men. This expedition tested all sorts of naval equipment in sub-zero temperatures, and proved that icebergs, fog, snow and high winds are not sufficient obstacles to prevent naval operations and the support by surface vessels of land and air warfare in polar regions. To many of the officers and men of Byrd's command, veterans of the Pacific war, the establishment of a base on the Antarctic continent was a novel and exacting beachhead landing, in which the human body proved more adaptable than any mechanical equipment.

After the war, adjustments were made in the education of officer and enlisted personnel in the navy. With the full approval of the Secretary of the Navy, James V. Forrestal (who had succeeded to the job when Franklin Knox died in April, 1944), a plan was put into effect by which it was hoped that about half of the future officers in the navy would be graduated, after being educated at the navy's expense, from civilian universities. In this way, the rigid thinking of the Naval Academy graduates might be leavened by association with officers whose viewpoint, being partially civilian, would be larger in scope. The synthetic training devices which had served their purpose so well in war were an established and accepted means of indoctrination and training at war's end. There was much emphasis placed on electronics in the training schools. Only in the navy's system of selecting officers for promotion had there been no great change. The selection boards, composed of as many as eleven officers, none of whom was by training or inclination a personnel expert, continued to be convened at irregular intervals. Membership on such boards depended to a great extent on the availability of ranking officers: many of the best officers were too occupied with urgent duties to serve on selection boards. After taking an oath of secrecy, board members proceeded to a discussion of the current situation, and then to a round-table discussion of individual cases, based on the evidence supplied by an antiquated form of "fitness" report and on the service reputation of the officers concerned. From the decisions of the selection boards, arrived at by secret ballot and majority vote, there was traditionally no appeal, and not infrequently justice was ill-served by the well-meaning board members. Yet the navy countered any criticism of the board's selections with haughty references to the integrity of the board members, rather than by an admission of their human fallibility.

Relations between the navy and the army and the air forces became very bitter when the defeat of Japan released them from the necessity of full co-operation. President Truman, with simple logic, proposed that there be a merger of all the armed forces, and this suggestion simply exasperated the navy, which feared that in the merger it would be relegated to the position of the Coast Guard, a lowly estate, in naval opinion. Sentiment in the navy was most aroused against the pretensions of the Army Air Forces, whose grandiose operations during the war had been publicized by public relations officers and by correspondents who enjoyed special favors in return for their support of Air Forces' plans and policies. This feeling was particularly bitter after the Battle of Midway, when the Air Forces claimed to have done much damage with high level bombers. The navy then had no way of knowing just how much damage the high-flying bombers had done, and the tendency in naval circles was to ask for pictures of the sinking ships, and if no pictures were forthcoming, to write the Air Forces' claims off as laudable expressions of suppressed desires.

Not until the war was over did the navy find a star witness, one Captain T. Aoki, who had commanded the Japanese carrier *Akagi* at the Battle of Midway. When interviewed, Aoki opined that at Midway it was the carrier-based dive bombers that had turned back the Japanese fleet, and that the Japanese had lost four carriers to carrier-based dive bomber attack. He was of the opinion that the high-level bombing to which the army was addicted was not effective against surface ships, and he could not recall one hit being scored by high-level bombers during the battle. Still, it was within the realm of possibility that if the Air Forces had interviewed Aoki first, he might have given them the pleasure of an answer that would have proved their value to their own satisfaction.

Early in 1947 the President was still struggling to merge the armed forces, and it was proclaimed that the army, navy and air forces had arrived at a plan by which they would all be united under a Secretary of National Defense, although retaining their own Secretaries in the Cabinet. This merger had the appearance of a "mariage de convenance," without any mutual affection in the hearts of the participants. Not until midsummer was the union legalized, with James V. Forrestal as head man.

Even while these nuptials were being avoided by the surly parties, an organization of limitless importance to the future welfare of the United States was hard at work in Washington. This was the National War College, located at Fort Humphreys, in the buildings that had formerly housed the Army War College. In the summer of 1946 a first class of a hundred students had inaugurated the college. These hundred men were all carefully picked: thirty each came from the army, navy and air forces, ten from the State Department, and their average age was about forty-two years. The object of the ten-month course they entered was to study the integration of the nation's defense and its foreign policy. In two world wars the commitments of the United States had been greater than the power at hand to enforce them. The National War College offered hope that in the future the foreign policy of the United States would be such that the armed forces would be able to support it instantly.

The first Commandant of this new school was Vice-Admiral Harry W. Hill, one of the navy's most intelligent admirals, and his deputies were Major General A. M. Gruenther, USA, Brigadier General T. H. Landon, AAF, and George F. Kennan, of the State Department, perhaps the best informed man in the government on the motives and character of the Russians. Experts in education, history, foreign affairs, industry, labor and finance were drawn from civil life to lecture to the students. In theory the foreign policy of the United States would no longer be a mystery to the men who would, when words failed, have to enforce it with men and guns, ships and planes.

War did not seem unavoidable late in 1947. It seldom does. On behalf of peace an organization called the United Nations had been established, and its Charter had been ratified by fifty-one nations during September and October of 1945.

The United Nations, as an organization, was functioning in a realistic fashion in 1947, with member nations attempting to wring concessions and compromises from each other, and sometimes succeeding. There remained considerable unrest and mistrust abroad in the world, and the United States Navy continued to try to maintain the vestiges of its power in a condition of continuing offensive readiness. It became apparent to all Americans that the war had not ended, like a baseball game, with the teams departing peacefully for home. In its wake the war had left many problems, and the struggle to create a more rational world faced many obstacles. Europe's machine shop had always been Germany, and now Germany lay in ruins, pounded by bombers and artillery; the German people remained unrepentant, shrewd, ingratiating in the presence of British, French, Russian and American armies of occupation. In Italy the people had abandoned the idea of acting like Roman Legionaries; the Japanese seemed docile and resigned, although they continued to think in terms of centuries. The victors were not much better off: Britain, that small, invincible nation of islanders, suffered appallingly from war-weariness, yet so great-hearted were her people that they continued to ration their own food so that Germans might be kept from starving. A Labour Government, headed by Clement Attlee, began to experiment politely with socialism at home. Abroad, the British Empire was in process of diminution, as the British disburdened themselves of commitments they no longer had the power to support. France's economic life was disorganized by the years of war and occupation, and her people bore the mental injuries of wounded pride and the physical injuries of malnutrition. China continued to engage in civil war, in which non-communists fought communists. Poland, on whose behalf France and Britain had gone to war, had been partitioned again, for the fifth time, when Russia absorbed over half of her territory. Russia emerged from the war greatly expanded in area and population: in addition to half of Poland, she had claimed and taken for her very own the

Baltic States of Latvia, Esthonia and Lithuania, parts of Finland, the once Romanian province of Bessarabia, portions of Slovakia, the Kurile Islands north of Japan, and the southern half of Sakhalin Island. The Russians began a five-year plan to revive the nation, at the same time being careful to keep their munitions factories and armies in readiness to defend themselves against the perfidy which they seemed unable to avoid associating with the Anglo-Saxon democracies. Throughout great areas of Asia and Europe hunger and cold and suffering were widespread.

Only in the United States was there an appearance of peace and well-being, with ample food, clothing, and shelter for everyone. Millions of Americans who had been uprooted and sent overseas to fight in strange lands were home again. There were 8,300,000 men and women in the army when Germany admitted defeat, and they, with the 4,063,458 men and women who were in the navy, marine corps and coast guard at the time of Japan's surrender, formed a segment of the population whose awareness of the world did not stop at the borders of the United States. In one way or another they had been exposed to war, and their knowledge of the world enlarged. Many of them had found God in strange places. At least half of them had served in foreign lands or on the high seas, and they had seen how warships and merchantmen had changed the Pacific ocean from a tremendous ocean moat upon which the Japanese counted for protection into a broad highway over which troops could be carried, bases seized and aircraft supplied. In the Atlantic they had seen planes and warships and merchantmen used to bring Germany and Italy to defeat. The course of the war was not a matter of academic interest to them: their futures depended on the tides of battles fought thousands of miles from home. Including the people in the armed forces, more than 75 million Americans were engaged directly in the war effort. It is, of course, impossible to assess the effect of the war on the thinking of Americans, but there were straws in the wind that showed the way Americans felt about the world in 1947.

Isolationism was dormant, for there was full support by the United States for the United Nations. There was a tendency to minimize the value of the sea as a protection against attack from the air, and this was a result of an overly-publicized concept of air power. There was a general belief that the next war would be fought with labor-saving devices: it was termed "push-button warfare," and the people were not fully aware that they had just won a war of that sort. Of approximately 14,000,000 men and women mobilized for the Second World War, only 1,500,000 were infantrymen or marines who had to carry their weapons to the point of contact with the enemy: the rest of the fighting men were fighting with machines of one sort or another—planes, tanks, ships, artillery and trucks. From this hope of applying labor-saving devices in any future war sprang the public's apathy to continuing conscription of soldiers in time of peace: to a nation fond of mechanical gadgets, the idea of shooting rockets and guided missiles with atomic warheads at any enemy mad enough to declare war on the United States seemed a reasonable way to carry on war. The fallacy of this type of thinking was bewailed by such experts as Secretary of State George Marshall and Dr. Vannevar Bush, chairman of the Joint Research and Development Board which had been created in 1946 to co-ordinate army and navy research activities.

It was impossible in 1947 to forecast what weapons would prove decisive in the next war. Only one thing could be predicted without reasonable doubt, and that was that soldiers would have to be transported, landed and kept supplied until they had won and could hold the enemy's land. To that end, the nation that could win control of the seas would be the victor.

There was but one weapon against which the sea was no protection at all. Throughout the war the belligerent powers had carried on laboratory experiments aimed at making use of biological agents as weapons. In the United States the government perforce looked to its defenses against the use of bacteria by the enemy, and great progress was made in the culture and care of bacteria, viruses, fungi, rickettsies and toxic agents developed from living organisms. These invisible weapons could cause disease or death to plants, animals or human beings, and, although their use might be outlawed by international agreement, the sanctity of the pledged word had fallen into such disrepute that the United States had to be prepared for any eventuality. Germs borne by the winds cannot distinguish one nation from another, and the only defenses against such weapons are anti-toxins, retaliatory counterattacks with similar agents, and the maintenance of an indomitable civilian morale.

In 1947 most Americans could discern but one potential trouble-maker on the international scene: this was Russia, and Russia was a wracked and ruined nation, very slowly regaining her strength. Her leader, the venerable Georgian brigand Stalin, had forged a totalitarian police state that would be a handy weapon for the next Generalissimo who appeared on the steppes as ruler of all the Muscovites. Unhappily, the warm-hearted Russian people were governed by six million communists, and the minds of these communists were enslaved by an ideology evolved from the Marxist theory of socialism. This ideology could not be dis-carded: without it the crimes of Russia's communist rulers against the Russian people would have no justification in the eyes of those who had committed them. There were no psychiatrists in Russia who could free them from this psychosis. Caught in their ideological bear-trap, there was no way for the communists to stop being communist, short of fleeing Russia, renouncing their whole creed and embracing religion. Even then their motives were suspect in the democratic world: having become renegades from one set of beliefs, there was no certainty that they might not disavow whatever their current ideological alliances might be.

The Americans, who since Hitler's armies had marched into Poland had been accustomed to having an international villain at large in the world, were quick to cast Russia as the villain in the post-war world. In this attitude they were aided by the recalcitrant attitude of Russian statesmen and by the fanatical hatred communism inspires in devout Christians. There was no immediate danger, in 1947, that the two opposing creeds might cause a polarization of opinion that would result in Christians equipped with atomic weapons setting out on a twentieth-century crusade against communists, also equipped with atomic weapons. In such a war Christianity would be useful as a means of maintaining the morale of civilian populations and of strengthening their will to resist, but it would be a difficult war to fight without killing most of the participants by one means or another.

In that event, civilization would not be entirely destroyed, and the words of Theodoridas, a Greek who lived twenty-one centuries ago, would be worth recalling—

"A shipwrecked sailor, buried on this coast,
    Bids thee take sail;
Full many a gallant ship, when we were lost,
    Weathered the gale."

BIBLIOGRAPHY

Albion, R. G.: *Forest and Sea Power, The Timber Problem of the Royal Navy, 1652–1862* (1926).

Allen, G. W.: *Naval History of the American Revolution* (1913).

American Neptune, The, a quarterly published by The American Neptune, Inc., Salem, Massachusetts.

Bayly, Admiral Sir Lewis, RN: *Pull Together!* (1939).

Bennett, F. M.: *Steam Navy of the United States* (1896).

Bigelow, John: *France and the Confederate Navy, 1862–1868* (1888).

Boynton, C. B.: *The History of the Navy During the Rebellion* (1867).

Brooks, N. C.: *A Complete History of the Mexican War* (1849).

Bulloch, James D.: *Secret Service of the Confederate States in Europe, or How the Confederate Cruisers Were Equipped* (1884).

Cave, C. J. P.: *Clouds and Weather Phenomena* (1943).

Chadwick, Admiral F. E.: *The Relations of the United States and Spain* (1909–1911).

Chapelle, H. I.: *History of American Sailing Ships* (1935).

Clark, Arthur H.: *The Clipper Ship Era* (1910).

Cole, Charles W.: *French Mercantilist Doctrines Before Colbert* (1931).

—— *Colbert and a Century of French Mercantilism* (1939).

—— *French Mercantilism, 1683–1700* (1943).

de Koven, Mrs. Reginald: *The Life and Letters of John Paul Jones* (1913).

Esquemeling, John: *Bucaniers of America* (1684).

Essex Institute, Salem, Massachusetts: publications of.

Force, Peter: *American Archives* (1837–1853).

Hakluyt Society, The: publications of (1846–1946). The Centenary Volume issued for 1946 contains a list of the works published by the society.

Harvard University, Graduate School of Business Administration: *The Use and Disposition of Ships and Shipyards at the End of World War II* (1945).

Hawks, Francis L.: *Narrative of the Expedition of an American Squadron to the China Seas and Japan . . . under the Command of Commodore M. C. Perry, United States Navy* (1856).

James, William: *Naval History of Great Britain from the Declaration of War by France in 1793 to the Accession of George IV,* London (1824).

Livezel, William E.: *Mahan on Sea Power* (1947), contains an excellent bibliography.

Maclay, Edgar S.: *A History of American Privateers* (1899).

—— *A History of the United States Navy* (1901).

Mahan, Alfred Thayer, Captain, USN: works of.

Marine Research Society, The, Salem, Massachusetts: publications of.

Marvin, W. L.: *The American Merchant Marine: Its History and Romance from 1620 to 1902* (1902).

Metcalf, Clyde H.: *A History of the United States Marine Corps* (1939).

Morison, Samuel Eliot: *Maritime History of Massachusetts* (1921).

———— *Admiral of the Ocean Sea* (1942).

———— *Operations in North African Waters, October 1942–June 1943* (1947).

Morris, E. P.: *The Fore-and-Aft Rig in America* (1927).

Niles, H.: *The Weekly Register* (1811–1826).

Paullin, C. O.: *Navy of the American Revolution* (1906).

———— *Diplomatic Negotiations of American Naval Officers, 1778–1883* (1912).

Peabody Museum, The, Salem, Massachusetts: publications of.

Porter, David D., Admiral, U.S.N.: *The Naval History of the Civil War* (1886).

Robinson, W. M.: *The Confederate Privateers* (1928).

Scharf, J. T.: *History of the Confederate States Navy* (1887).

Semmes, Raphael, Admiral, C.S.N.: *Service Afloat and Ashore* (1851).

———— *Service Afloat, or the Remarkable Career of the* Sumter *and* Alabama (1887).

Sims, W. S., Admiral, U.S.N., and Hendrick, B. J.: *The Victory at Sea* (1920).

Smith, Edgar C.: *A Short History of Naval and Marine Engineering* (1938).

Smyth, H. D.: *A General Account of the Methods of Using Atomic Energy for Military Purposes under the Auspices of the United States Government, 1940–1945* (1945).

Spears, John R.: *The History of Our Navy, 1775–1897* (1897).

———— *The American Slave Trade* (1901).

———— *The Story of the New England Whalers* (1908).

———— *The Story of the American Merchant Marine* (1910).

Sprout, Harold and Margaret: *The Rise of American Naval Power, 1776–1918* (1939).

———— *Toward a New Order of Sea Power; American Naval Policy and the World Scene, 1918–1922* (1940).

Tourtellot, Arthur B.: *The Charles* (1941).

Toynbee, Arnold J.: *A Study of History* (1933–1939).

Trevelyan, George Otto, Sir: *The American Revolution* (1905).

United Nations: *Official Records of the Atomic Energy Commission, including the First Report of the Commission to the Security Council* (June 14–December 31, 1946).

U.S. Government, Department of State: *Peace and War—United States Foreign Policy, 1931–1941* (1942).

————, ———— *A Report on the International Control of Atomic Energy* (1946).

———— Joint Congressional Committee on the Pearl Harbor Attack: *Investigation of the Pearl Harbor Attack* (Majority and Minority Views) (1946).

———— Manhattan Engineer District, The: *The Atomic Bombings of Hiroshima and Nagasaki* (1946).

———— Reports of the Secretaries of Navy and of War and of Generals Marshall and Arnold and of Admiral King (1941–1946).

———— Report to the Secretary of War on Biological Warfare by George W. Merck (1946).

———— United States Maritime Commission: Annual Reports to Congress.

———— *United States Strategic Bombing Survey (Pacific War)* (July 16, 1946).

———— *Wartime Production Achievements, or Report of the Chairman, War Production Board* (October 9, 1945).

U.S. Naval Institute Proceedings, published monthly at Annapolis, Md.

The full text of the letter written after the battle of Trafalgar (page 145) may be found in *Naval Yarns,* compiled and edited by W. H. Long (London, 1899). President Harding's description of himself (page 419), is from a letter he wrote to John Kendrick Bangs during the presidential campaign of 1920. An article and editorial bearing on Admiral Sir Lewis Bayly's visit to the United States (page 433) appeared in *The Times* (London) on July 30, 1934. A copy of the letter dictated to Bayly by President F. D. Roosevelt is in the Admiralty files. The original of the Theodoridas quotation (page 564) is in *The Greek Anthology.*

STATISTICAL APPENDIX

A NOTE ON TONNAGES

"Displacement tonnage" is the term used to denote the tonnage of warships. It is the calculated weight of water displaced by them.

Merchant vessels are measured in three ways: *

(*a*) "Gross" tonnage is the capacity of the space inside the hull, plus the space inside the above-deck structure, available for crew, passengers, cargo, and stores, with a few minor exceptions.

(*b*) "Net" or "registered" tonnage means the space available for passengers and cargo. It is the tonnage remaining after the space taken up by the crew's quarters, officers' cabins, bridge, fuel, and propulsion machinery have been deducted from the gross tonnage.

(*c*) "Dead-weight" tonnage represents the weight in long tons required to depress a vessel from the light water line (i.e., with only equipment and machinery aboard) to load line. Thus, it is the weight of personnel, stores, fuel, and cargo which a vessel is designed to carry safely.

"Cargo" tonnage refers to the weight of cargo in long, short, or metric tons and it is not a measure of a vessel's size.

TABLE I

RECAPITULATION OF U.S. NAVY LOSSES IN THE SECOND WORLD WAR

Battleships, 2	Motor torpedo boats, 69
Aircraft carriers, 11	Tank landing ships, 40
Heavy cruisers, 7	Medium landing ships, 9
Light cruisers, 3	Tank landing craft, 67
Destroyers, 71	Infantry landing craft, 22
Destroyer escorts, 11	Support landing craft, 6
Submarines, 52	Tugs, 10
Minelayers, 3	Tankers, 6
Minesweepers, 24	Troop transports, 21
Submarine chasers, 18	District patrol craft, 36
Gunboats, 12	Misc. district craft, 152
Coast Guard vessels, 15	Cargo vessels, 4
Seaplane tenders, 3	Misc. auxiliaries, 22

Source: Navy Department, October 5, 1945

* The terms "gross" and "net" tonnage refer to space measurement, 100 cubic feet being called 1 ton.

TABLE 2

ANALYSIS OF EMPIRE, ALLIED, AND NEUTRAL MERCHANT SHIPPING LOST BY ENEMY ACTION FROM THE OUTBREAK OF WAR, SEPTEMBER 3, 1939, TO VE DAY, MAY 8, 1945

CAUSE	BRITISH EMPIRE		U.S.		ALL OTHER ALLIES		NEUTRAL		TOTAL	
	No.	Gr. Tons	No.	Gr. Tons	No.	Gr. Tons	No.	Gr. Tons	No.	Gr. Tons
					Gross Tons in Thousands					
U-Boat	1,360	7,620	440	2,740	670	3,260	300	930	2,770	14,550
Mine	340	830	15	90	75	210	90	270	520	1,400
Surface craft .	210	970	13	90	87	460	20	50	330	1,570
Aircraft	440	1,590	58	360	202	770	50	110	750	2,830
Other or unknown causes	220	370	12	30	138	330	30	60	400	790
TOTAL	2,570	11,380	538	3,310	1,172	5,030	490	1,420	4,770	21,140

In addition the following tonnages were lost owing to marine risks: British Empire, 610 ships of 1,120,000 gross tons; Allies other than United States of America, 261 ships of 710,000 gross tons; and Neutrals, 490 ships of 680,000 gross tons.

Notes

(a) The enemy-action losses include ships of all tonnages. Marine losses include ships of 100 gross tons and over.
(b) Ships under enemy control or working for the enemy are not included.
(c) Finnish, Hungarian, Italian, and Japanese ships are included prior to the dates on which these countries became enemies. Losses of Italian ships after Italy became a cobelligerent are included.
(d) French ships are included up to the date of the collapse of France. After that date Free French ships are included, but not Vichy-controlled vessels.
(e) Five U.S. ships lost by enemy action prior to December 7, 1941, are included in neutral losses.

Source: Admiralty, June 13, 1945

TABLE 3

ANALYSIS OF GERMAN U-BOATS SUNK IN SECOND WORLD WAR

Cause	U.S. and Other Allied (Except British Empire) Forces Under U.S. Control	British Empire and Other Allied (Except U.S.) Forces Under British Control	Total Assessments
Ships	30½	205½	236
Shore-based aircraft	45	179½	224½
Carrier-borne aircraft	32	18½	50½
Joint ship/shore–based aircraft	7½	21½	29
Joint ship/carrier–borne aircraft	6	4	10
Submarines	1	25	26
Bombing raids on U-boats afloat in enemy ports	29	8	37
Subtotal	151	462	613
Other losses including those owing to mining by Bomber Command, etc., precise details of which are not yet available		100	
Final Total			713

Source: Admiralty, June 10, 1945

Table 4

MERCHANT FLEETS OF THE WORLD—PREWAR AND POSTWAR

SEAGOING IRON AND STEEL STEAM AND MOTOR MERCHANT-TYPE VESSELS OF
1,000 GROSS TONS AND OVER

(Excludes vessels on the Great Lakes and inland waterways and special types
such as channel vessels, icebreakers, cable ships, etc., and vessels owned
by the U.S. Army and Navy)

FLAG	MERCHANT FLEET AS OF SEPTEMBER 1, 1939			MERCHANT FLEET AS OF JUNE 30, 1946		
	No.	Gross Tons	Dwt. Tons	No.	Gross Tons	Dwt. Tons
TOTAL, ALL FLAGS	12,798	58,270,374	80,600,600	12,445	71,000,408	99,219,900
United States ..	1,379	8,125,756	11,681,700	4,861	35,363,598	50,389,300
British Empire	3,319	17,770,919	24,053,700	3,159	18,064,293	24,009,600
Argentina	45	196,627	267,700	64	310,623	430,000
Belgium	72	356,862	494,000	46	242,670	341,600
Brazil	122	413,646	541,600	136	490,423	669,700
Bulgaria	8	22,306	29,700	—	—	—
Chile	50	153,959	180,900	46	151,227	196,800
China	100	204,062	276,000	73	246,479	344,300
Colombia	—	—	—	2	7,354	11,100
Costa Rica	—	—	—	1	1,068	1,500
Cuba	12	17,504	21,700	8	11,738	14,400
Denmark	379	1,041,756	1,575,800	208	640,864	952,600
Danzig	4	5,162	7,400	—	—	—
Dominican Republic	1	1,973	2,200	—	—	—
Ecuador	—	—	—	1	1,120	1,300
Egypt	23	98,177	128,000	7	19,119	29,100
Eire	—	—	—	13	33,109	52,300
Estonia	94	176,376	274,400	13	21,209	30,900
Finland	232	530,285	826,000	125	252,761	372,000
France	555	2,678,435	2,998,800	262	1,370,836	1,612,800
Germany	854	3,915,978	5,177,100	242	800,590	1,160,100
Greece	436	1,697,986	2,791,000	146	619,320	1,006,200
Greenland	—	—	—	1	1,151	900
Honduras	27	82,068	90,500	34	140,553	167,900
Hungary	6	22,748	39,900	1	1,022	1,500
Iceland	—	—	—	5	7,245	7,900
Italy	667	3,178,120	3,910,800	123	576,199	691,700
Japan	1,180	5,102,346	7,145,400	327	1,085,969	1,432,100
Latvia	73	199,058	325,600	18	46,013	73,400
Lithuania	3	4,330	6,800	—	—	—
Mexico	10	23,815	31,600	17	79,336	118,800
Netherlands ..	537	2,670,149	3,424,600	291	1,591,103	2,035,800

Table 4—*Continued*

MERCHANT FLEETS OF THE WORLD—PREWAR AND POSTWAR

FLAG	MERCHANT FLEET AS OF SEPTEMBER 1, 1939			MERCHANT FLEET AS OF JUNE 30, 1946		
	No.	Gross Tons	Dwt. Tons	No.	Gross Tons	Dwt. Tons
Nicaragua	2	3,023	4,200	1	1,109	1,600
Norway	1,072	4,499,086	6,931,200	607	2,933,972	4,477,000
Palestine	2	4,147	7,000	5	9,809	14,300
Panama	130	719,041	1,105,600	164	868,855	1,329,000
Peru	7	25,834	31,100	10	37,648	46,200
Philippines ...	33	82,695	105,200	17	46,780	65,000
Poland	31	113,644	101,200	28	93,746	128,200
Portugal	54	197,307	263,200	66	262,329	364,000
Rumania	25	101,807	129,000	6	26,995	18,400
Spain	217	749,681	1,051,700	257	879,286	1,253,100
Sweden	484	1,311,763	2,033,100	443	1,437,535	2,204,000
Switzerland ..	—	—	—	7	32,690	50,900
Thailand	2	2,622	2,000	1	1,311	1,000
Turkey	67	173,847	223,800	58	151,148	192,000
Uruguay	5	13,791	14,300	3	11,989	18,900
U.S.S.R.	354	1,135,783	1,597,900	488	1,851,675	2,626,700
Venezuela	27	70,089	93,200	28	71,613	97,500
Yugoslavia ...	98	375,811	604,000	26	104,926	176,500

Note: Included in the above figures but excluded from the United Stated are U.S.-owned merchant vessels operating under the following foreign flags.

FLAG				No.	Gross Tons	Dwt. Tons
TOTAL				526	3,223,571	4,681,500
British Empire				341	2,008,885	2,842,200
Belgium				7	50,327	74,900
Brazil				1	6,937	4,400
Chile				4	21,257	32,600
China				11	79,071	118,000
France				13	93,445	139,400
Greece				14	100,771	150,500
Honduras				2	6,536	10,200
Japan				1	3,252	5,400
Netherlands ..				6	28,202	42,300
Norway				23	181,923	280,400
Panama				3	14,373	23,700
Poland				5	14,633	21,500
U.S.S.R.				95	613,959	936,000

Source: U.S. Maritime Commission, October 11, 1946

TABLE 5

CHARACTERISTICS OF VESSELS BUILT UNDER U.S. MARITIME COMMISSION CONTACTS

Type	Dwt. Tons	Machinery	Sea Speed
Liberty Types			*Knots*
EC2-S-C1 (dry cargo)	10,500	Recip. steam	11
Z-EC2-S-C2 (tank carrier)	9,475	do	11
Z-EC2-S-AW1 (collier)	11,000	do	11
Z-ET1-S-C3 (tanker)	10,665	do	11½
Victory Types			
VC2-S-AP2 (dry cargo)	10,730	Turbine	15½
VC2-S-AP3 (dry cargo)	10,600	do	17
VC2-S-AP5 (troopship)	5,914	do	17
Dry Cargo and Combination Types			
C1-A (cargo)	7,240	do	14
C1-A (cargo)	7,416	Diesel	14
C1-B (cargo)	9,050	Turbine	14
C1-B (cargo)	9,005	Diesel	14
C1-S-D1 (concrete cargo)	5,200	Recip. steam	10
C1-S-AY1 (troopship)	2,587	Turbine	15
C1-M-AV1 (cargo)	3,840	Diesel	11
C2 (cargo)	9,722	Turbine	15½
C2 (cargo)	8,656	Diesel	15½
C2-F (cargo)	9,133	Turbine	15½
C2-G (cargo)	9,036	do	15½
C2-S (cargo)	10,048	do	15½
C2-T (cargo)	9,274	Diesel	15½
C2-SU (cargo)	9,613	do	16
C2-S-A1 (cargo)	8,160	Turbine	16½
C2-S1-A1 (cargo-pass.)	6,945	do	17
C2-S-B1 (cargo)	7,400	do	15½
C2-S-E1 (cargo)	9,581	do	15½
C2-S-AJ1 (cargo)	10,360	do	15½
C2-S-AJ2 (cargo)	10,231	do	15½
C2-S-AJ3 (combat cargo)	7,750	do	15½
C3 (cargo)	12,562	do	16½
C3 (cargo)	11,976	Diesel	16½
Cargo Pass.	9,021	Turbine	16½
C3 (cargo-pass.)	9,937	do	16½
C3 (cargo-pass.)	9,000	Diesel	16½
C3-M (cargo)	12,120	Turbine	16½

TABLE 5—*Continued*

CHARACTERISTICS OF VESSELS BUILT UNDER U.S. MARITIME COMMISSION CONTRACTS

Type	Dwt. Tons	Machinery	Sea Speed
Dry Cargo and Combination Types			*Knots*
C3-S-A1 (cargo)	12,525	do	16½
C3-S-A2 (cargo)	12,515	do	16½
C3-S-A3 (C3-E) (cargo)	9,902	do	16½
C3-S1-A3 (troopship)	7,529	do	16½
C3-S1-B1 (aircraft tender)	7,272	do	16½
C3-S1-N2 (destroyer tender)	6,659	do	16½
C3-S-BH1 (cargo)	12,630	do	16½
C3-IN (cargo-passenger)	9,000	do	16½
C3-P (cargo-passenger)	9,916	do	16½
C4-S-A1 (troopship)	14,600	do	17
C4-S-B1 (tank carrier)	8,369	do	17
C4-S-B2 (troopship)	5,379	do	17
N3-S-A1 (coastal cargo)	2,847	Recip. steam	10
N3-S-A2 (coastal cargo)	2,842	do	10
L6-S-A1 (lake ore carrier)	15,580	do	10½
L6-S-A2 (lake ore carrier)	15,690	do	10½
Passenger Types			
America (passenger)	14,331	Turbine	22
P1-S2-L2 (troopship)	1,848	do	19
P2-S2-R2 (troopship)	10,530	do	19
P2-SE2-R1 (troopship)	12,200	Turbo-elec	19
Refrigerated Cargo Types			
R1-M-AV3 (refrig. cargo)	3,450	Diesel	11
R2-ST-AU1 (refrig. cargo)	6,500	Turbine	18½
Tanker Types			
T1-M-A1 (coastal tanker)	1,600	Diesel	10
T1-M-A2 (fleet oiler)	1,448	do	10
T2-SE-A1 (tanker)	16,655	Turbo-elec	14½
T2-SE-A2 (tanker)	16,433	do	15½
T3-S-A1 (tanker)	16,400	Turbine	15½
T3-S-BF1 (tanker)	18,500	do	16
T3-S2-A1 (tanker)	18,276	do	18
T3-M-AZ1 (tanker)	17,910	Diesel	15

Note: Design characteristics are for identification purposes and are not warranted to be those of any particular vessel.

Source: U.S. Maritime Commission, 1946

TABLE 6

THE POSTWAR UNITED STATES MERCHANT MARINE OF 1,000 GROSS TONS AND OVER, ESTIMATED TO BE AVAILABLE AS OF DECEMBER 31, 1946

STEAM AND MOTOR DRY-CARGO VESSELS

(Excluding vessels in inland-waterway service, vessels on the Great Lakes, certain special types, military types, vessels acquired by capture and foreign-owned vessels requisitioned by the United States)

TYPE	NUMBER	DWT. TONS
American-built Liberty	2,418	25,768,900
Canadian-built Liberty	65	676,000
Victory (VC2-S-AP2, VC2-S-AP3, VC2-S-AP4)	410	4,457,900
Victory (VC2-S-AP5)	117	678,300
Coastal Cargo (N3-S-A1, N3-S-A2, N3-M-A1)	96	275,100
C1-ME-AV6 (coastal cargo)	1	5,000
C1-M-AV1 (coastal cargo)	216	1,080,000
C1-M-AV8 (coastal cargo)	1	5,000
C1-MT-BU1 (coastal cargo)	4	15,200
R1-M-AV3 (coastal cargo refrig.)	17	78,300
R1-S-DH1 (coastal cargo refrig.)	7	32,200
C1-S-D1 (concrete cargo)	22	120,800
C1-A	64	469,800
C1-B	83	749,300
C1-S-AY1 (troop transport)	11	27,900
C2 cargo	301	2,808,400
C3 cargo	163	1,868,600
C4 cargo	75	632,700
C5-S-AX1	4	96,000
R2-ST-AU1	9	58,500
R2-S-BU1	6	48,600
S4-SE2-BD1	32	86,400
S4-SE2-BE1	32	89,600
Passenger combination	1	14,400
Mississippi Shipping Co. (combination)	6	54,000
C2 combination	12	106,300
P2 (P2-S2-R2, P2-S2-R4; P2-SE2-R1, P2-SE2-R3)	21	193,900
C3 combination	18	172,500
P1-S2-L2 (transports)	2	4,200
VC2-S1-AP7 (passenger and cargo)	3	27,000
United States private construction	199	1,304,700

TABLE 6—*Continued*

THE POSTWAR UNITED STATES MERCHANT MARINE OF 1,000 GROSS TONS AND OVER, ESTIMATED TO BE AVAILABLE AS OF DECEMBER 31, 1946

TYPE	NUMBER	DWT. TONS
Emergency Fleet Corp. construction	301	2,256,200
Foreign construction	50	295,400
Dry-cargo total	4,767	44,557,100
Tanker total	1,065	14,518,600
GRAND TOTAL	5,832	59,075,700

STEAM AND MOTOR TANKERS

(Excluding vessels in inland-waterway service, vessels on the Great Lakes, vessels acquired by capture and foreign-owned vessels requisitioned by the United States)

TYPE	NUMBER	DWT. TONS
Z-ET1-SC3 (converted Liberty)	61	646,700
Coastal tankers (T1-M-A1, T1-M-A2, T1-M-BT1, T1-M-BT2)	87	216,600
T2-SE-A1, T2-SE-A2, T2-SE-A3, and T2	527	8,761,100
T3-S-A1	19	310,900
T3-S-BF1	4	74,000
T3-S2-A1 and T3-S2-A3	33	605,600
T3-M-AZ1	1	17,600
T3-S-BZ1	3	69,000
United States private construction	219	2,641,800
Emergency Fleet Corp. construction	99	1,034,500
Foreign construction	12	140,800
Tanker total	1,065	14,518,600
Dry cargo total	4,767	44,557,100
GRAND TOTAL	5,832	59,075,700

Note: The foregoing figures will be reduced to the extent that American-flag vessels are transferred to foreign flags as a result of purchases made under the Ship Sales Act.

Source: U.S. Maritime Commission, 1947

TABLE 7

UNITED STATES MERCHANT FLEET IN SECOND WORLD WAR

	NUMBER	DWT. TONS
Ships built by U.S. Maritime Commission, 1939–June 1, 1946	5,828	56,762,948
Delivered in May, 1946	8	80,941
Merchant fleet owned by U.S. government and U.S. citizens, May 1, 1946 (includes dry-cargo of 1,000 gross tons and over and tankers of 1,600 gross tons and over)	5,849	58,106,700
U.S.-owned ships under WSA control (389 allocated to carry UNRRA cargo, 768 to carry International Programs cargo, 161 troop ships)	3,286	34,134,600
Lend-Lease	425	3,806,000
Army	255	1,999,000
Navy	700	5,846,200
Reserve fleet (includes 3 dry-cargo and 24 tankers incomplete) ....?	685	6,631,100
Vessels returned, sold, or interim chartered to U.S. private citizens	498	5,689,800
Number of men in U.S. Merchant Marine Labor Force, May, 1946 (includes shore reserve)		225,000

Source: U.S. Maritime Commission and War Shipping Administration, June 1, 1946

Index

[NOTE: An italic figure in a group of page references indicates the point of main discussion. No italics are used when all page references are of equal importance.]

Acadie, 29
Achilles, the, 99, 100
acoustic torpedo, 503
Adam, Po, 232
Adams, John, 79, 80, 105, *122-133,* 250
Adams, John Quincy, 191, 197, 198, 204-205, 240, 250
Adams, Sam, 68
Adams, 171
Admiralty Islands, 505
Adriatic, 286
Adventure, 116
Adventure-Galley, 34-35
Aeronautics, Board of, 424
airplane carriers, 425, *479-481*
airplanes, 474
Aix-la-Chapelle, Treaty of, 56, 57, 62
Akagi, 481
Akbar, 237
Akron, 426
Alabama, 295, 314, 315, *316-320,* 454
Alabama claims, 319
Alaska, 106; acquisition of, 331-332
Albania, 439
Albany, 16
Albert W. Grant, 528
Alcide, 62, 63
Aleutians, 106, *481-482,* 486, 500
Alfred, 78, 79, 81, 82
Algiers, 122, 136
Allen, 411
Alliance, 97, 105
Allied Military Council, China, 471
Allied Military Mission, Moscow, 471
Allied Shipping Pool, 547, 548
Amelia, 298
Amelia Island, 155, 213
America, 189
American-Canadian border, 205
American East India Company, 115
American Line, 344
American republics: enter World War II, 468; meetings of, 443, 446
American Steamship Company, 333

American Turtle, 89
Amiel, Montagu, 299
Amity, 217
Amsden, William Faulkner, 495
Anderson, Major, 291
Andrea Doria, 79, 82
Andros, Sir Edmund, 29-30
Anglo-American treaty, 120-122
Anglo-French treaty, 1778, 90
Anglo-German naval building race, 392, 393
Anguar Island, 525
Ann Alexander, 229
Annapolis Royal, 39
Anne, Queen, 37, 40
Ann McKim, 236-237, 267
Anson, George, 54
Antarctic, 245
Antelope, 236
Anti-Comintern Pact, 436
anti-slavery bills, 212-214
anti-submarine warfare, 553
Aoki, T., 558
Architect, 267, 268
Arctic regions, 284, 556-557
Arctic whaling, 337-338
Arethusa, 90
Argall, Samuel, 14
Argo, 93, 94
Argus, 137, 138, 425
Ariadne, 407
Ariel, 236, 316
aristocrats, English, 66-67
Arizona, 552
Arkansas, 456, 515
Arkansas River, 7
Armada, Spanish, *11-12*
Arms Limitation Conference, 419-420
Army Air Forces, 558
Arnold, Henry, 471, 517
arresting-gear, 426
artificial ports, 514-515
Ashburton Treaty, 214
Aspinwall, C. S., 266, 267

Astoria, 489
Atlanta, 351, 492
Atlantic, 284
Atlantic Charter, 457, 470-471
Atlantic Fleet, 389, 393, 405-406, 455; on
    world cruise, 390
Atlee, Clement R., 540, 560
atomic bomb, 493-494, *541-543,* 555
Attack Transports, 505
Augusta, 456, 457, 485
Aulick, J. H., 277
Austerlitz, 145
Australia, 487, 505
Australia, 489
Austria: conquest of, 439; French alliance
    with, 63
Avenger torpedo planes, 474
aviation, 424-427
Axis, The, 439; composition of, 1941, 468;
    nations opposing, 468
Ayllon, Lucas Vasquez de, *5-6*
Aztecs, 11

baby flat-tops, 473
bacteria, as weapon, 562-563
Bainbridge, William, 126, 168, 170
baka plane, 536-537
Baker, T. H., 299
Baltic, 284
Baltic trade, 111
Baltimore, 165, 170, 298; Battle of, 181-
    182; blocade of, 1812, 171
Baltimore, 126, 352, 369
Baltimore clipper schooners, *184-185,* 212
Bancroft, George, 251
bankers, 335
Barbary States, 109, *136-143*
Barclay, Robert Heriot, 172
Barnes, Reuben, 128
Barney, Joshua, 93, 165-166, 180-181, 189,
    192
Barracouta, 319
Barron, James, 142-143, 149
Barry, John, 82, 93, 126, 231-232
bases, 440-441; destroyers traded to Britain
    for, 448; island, 487; neglect of, 388; in
    World War I, 410; after World War II,
    556-557
Battle of Britain, 447
battleships, 352
Bay Colony, 18
Bayly, Sir Lewis, 405-406, 407, 409, 433
Bay of Biscay, 99
Bayonne Decree, 155
Beauregard, Pierre G., 292
Bedford, 108
Belle Poule, 90
Bellinger, Patrick, 466

Bellomont, Lord, 34, 35
Belvidera, HMS, 160, 161
Benson, William S., 411
Bering, Vitus, 106
Bering Strait, 106
Berkeley, Vice-Admiral, 149
Betio, 502
Betsy, 112
Bible, King James version, 12
Biddle, James, 276
Bikini Atoll, tests at, 555, 556
Biloxi, 106
Bismarck, Otto von, 347
Black Ball Line, 217
Blackbeard, 32-33
Blanco, Don Pedro, 214, 215, 373
Blenheim, Battle of, 37
Blessing of the Bay, 19
blitzkrieg, 444
blockade: Civil War, 296, 302*ff.,* 321*ff.,*
    346; of Cuba, 366; War of 1812, 168-
    169, 173, 178, 179
Blockade, Proclamation of, 320
blockade-runners, 322-325
Blockading Squadrons, North and South
    Atlantic, 302-303
Blockading Squadron, Western Gulf, 303
Blonde, 95
Bloody Forties, 285
Blount, J. H., 354
Blue, 489
Board of Aeronautics, 424
Bohemia, 439
Bold Venture, 459
Bolton, 81
Bon Homme Richard, 97
Bonita, 256, 261
Bonnet, Steed, 43
Borah, William, 419
Borie, A. E., 348, 349
Boscawen, Vice-Admiral, 62, 64
Boston, 18, 19, 57, 61, 67, 70, 208
Boston, 351, 354, 382
Boston Massacre, 67-68
Boston Packet, 217
Boston Tea Party, 70
bounties of 1813, 206
Bowditch, Nathaniel, 144-145
Bowen, Harold G., 433, 442
Boxer Rebellion, 385
Boyle, Thomas, 189, *190-191*
Brandywine, 88
Brandywine, 264
Brazil, trade with, 332
Bridges, Harry, 546
Briggs, James, 112
Britannia, 271
British: attitude, toward American trade,

1805, 146; evacuation of Boston, 81; impression of American seamen, 109; treatment of prisoners, 185-190
British merchant fleet, 450
British Navigation Laws, repeal of, 265
British Navy: after Civil War, 330-331; in 1812, 167
British seamen, desertion of, *150*
British ships, in Civil War, 319-323
Broke, Philip, 169-170
Brooke, John M., 296, 303, 305
Brooklyn, 326, 364, 373, 485
Broughton, Nicholson, 76, 77
Brown, Charles, 200
Brown, John, 293
Brown, Wilson, 479
Bruat, Admiral, 282
Brunel, Isambard K., 331
Bryant, 536
B-29s, 531, 533, 539, 542, 543
buccaneers, 32
Buchanan, Franklin, 251, 296, 304-307, 308, 326
Bucklin, Joseph, 69
Buckner, S. B., 534
Budd, Captain, 276
Buena Ventura, 366
buffer states, European, 455
Bulloch, James D., 295, 315, 320
Bunker Hill, 70
Bunker Hill, 538
Bureau of Naval Personnel, 470
Bureau of Navigation, 470
Burgoyne, General John, 89
Burke, Edmund, 66
Burke-Wadsworth Bill, 448
Bush, Vannevar, 562
Bushnell, David, 89
Bushnell, 409
Butler, B. F., 313
Byrd, Richard E., 557
Byrnes, James, 543
Byron, Vice-Admiral, 91, 92

Cabot, John, 48
Cabot, 79, 81
Cabrillo, Juan Rodriguez, *7-8*
Cairo Conference, 516
Calais, 11
Calhoun, 301
California, 7, 106, 250, 252-256; Japanese in, 390
California, 266
California gold rush, 265-267
Callaghan, Daniel, 491, 492
Camara, Admiral, 374
Canada: French in, 63; in War of 1812, 171-172

Canadian-American border, 205
Canadian fisheries, 336
Canadian privateers, 31, 36
Canary Islands, 14, 109
Canberra, 489
Canceaux, 77
Canning, George, 150, 197, 198
Canton, 109, 110, 235
Cape Breton Island, 39, 55
Cape Engaño, Battle off, 530
Cape Fear River, 5, 43
Cape Horn, 113
Cape Mendocino, 10
Cape Town, 109, 110, 111
Cape Verde Islands, 113
Capitol, burning of, 181
Cargo Attack Ships, 505
cargo-carriers, 437
Cargo Ship Bill, 343
Caribbean area, 4, 100-101; minor islands, to U.S., 374, 376; after Seven Years' War, 66; Spanish American War in, 371-376
Carnegie, Andrew, 390
Carnes, Jonathan, 127
Car of Neptune, 202
Carolina, 9
Caroline, 128
carpetbaggers, 330
Carr, Sir Robert, 26
carrier-borne planes, 473
carriers, airplane, 425, 479-481
Cartagena, 54
Casablanca Conference, 485, 496
Cassino, 511-512
Catalina Island, 8
catapult, 426
Cathay, 4
Catherine of France, 9-10
Catholics: and Protestants, 56; in China, 239
Cavendish, 11
Central Pacific, 500, 506
Centurion, the, 54
Cervera, Admiral, 367-368, 371-374
Chahar, 435
Challenge, 268, 272
Chamberlain, Neville, 445
Chandler, William, 351
Charles II, 25, 26, 27, 29, 36, 50
Charles V, 4, 5
Charles VI, 55
Charles Daggett, 234
Charles Pratt, 459
Charles River, 18
Charleston, 37, 57, 98, 325, *327-328*
Charlestown, 18
charts, wind and current, 264-265
Chasseur, 190, 191

Cherbourg, 515
Cherub, 175, 176, 312
Chesapeake, 112, 148, 149, 156, 160, 163, 169, 170
Chesapeake Bay, 10, 14, 103
Chiang Kai-shek, 516
Chicago, 351, 489
Chichi Jima, 520
Chicorana, Francisco, 5
Chili, 350-352
China, 7, 420, 431; commercial treaty with, 240; commission houses in, 235-236; fur sales to, 106-107; Japanese invasion, 435, 438; in Russo-Japanese War, 387; threatened dismemberment of, 384; war with France, 356; war with Japan, 356-359
China trade, 231, 234-235
Chinese-Japanese War, 461
Choiseul, 91
Christianity, 563; Hitler and, 446; in Japan, 275
Chrysolite, 268
Churchill, Winston, 445, 468, 498, 511, 516; first conference with Roosevelt, 456-457; at Washington Conference, 470-471
City of New York, 344
City of Paris, 344
City of Rayville, 459
Civil War, 291-329; blockade-runners, 322-325; European trade and, 320-321; loss of life in, 329; privateering in, 297-302
Clay, Henry, 380
Clemenceau, 416, 417
Clermont, 201-202
Cleveland, Grover, 354, 359, 363
Cleveland, Richard, 128-129
Clinton, Sir Henry, 94, 98
clipper ships, 212, 236-238, 267-274, 335-337; builders of, 270; for California trade, 268-274; crews of, 272-274; opium, 236; speed of, 270-271
Coast Guard, 472
Cochrane, Vice-Admiral Sir Alexander, 176-181
Cockburn, George, 170, 179-181
codfish, 17, 19
Colbert, 35
Collier, Sir George, 95
Collins, E. K., 283-284
Collins, Gamaliel, 222
Colombia, 380, 382, 383
colonies, after Revolution, 106
colonists: expedition against Port Royal, 31; expedition against Quebec, 31-32; independence of character, 28; lack of unity between, 67; seizure of British store ships, 76-77; self-reliance of, 26; in 1750, 57

colonization, end of, 198
Columbia, 364
Columbus, Christopher, 3, 4
Columbus, 78, 79, 82, 112-116
Combined Chiefs of Staff, 471, 476
Combined Shipping Adjustment Board, 476
Comet, 189, 190
Committee of Safety, 74
communism, 431, 563
Compton, A. H., 555
Concord, 70
Condor, 465
Confederate money, 324
Confederate Navy, 293-297
Confederate States of America, 291
Confidance, 183
Congress, 163, 169, 254, 255, 305-308
Congréve, 281
Connecticut River, 16, 18
Conner, David, 256-259, 316
conquistadors, 4
Constellation, 122, 124-126, 130, 131, 163
Constitution, Federal, 114
Constitution, 122, 124, 125, 131, 137, 140, 141, *161-165,* 169, 173, 192
Construction Battalions, 487
Continental Congress, 70, 76, 89
Convention of 1818, 205
convoy system, 408, 410, 453, 483-484, 497-498, 513, 544
C-1s, C-2s, C-3s, 454
Cook, Captain James, 107, 112
Coolidge, Calvin, 421-422
Co-Prosperity Sphere, 461, 464
Coquette, 237
Coral Sea, Battle of the, 479-480
Cornwallis, Lord, 104
Corregidor, 477
corsairs, of Barbary States, 136
Cortez, Hernando, 5
Corwin, 338, 339
cotton, 23, 26
Council of Placentia, 457
Courier, 217
Couronne, 318
Coxetter, L. M., 299
Creighton, William, 90
crews for American ships, 333-334
Crimea, 482
Crimean War, 280-282
Cristobal Colon, 373
Cromwell, Oliver, 18, 24, 25
Cromwell, Samuel, 247
cruisers, 352
Crutchley, V. A. C., 488, 489
C-type ships, 549
Cuba, 5, 360, *363-376*

Cumberland, 305-307
Cunard, Samuel, 284
Cunard Line, 344, 345
Cunningham, Sir A. B., 484
Cushing, Caleb, 239-240
Cyane, 252, 253, 255
Czechoslovakia, 439

Dace, 527
Dacres, James Richard, 161-163
Dahlgren, John Adolf, 327
Dahlgrens, 295
Dale, Richard, 125, 132, 137
Dale, 252, 253, 255
Daniels, Josephus, 398-399, 400, 411, 412, 424
Darlan, Jean François, 485-486
Darter, 527
Dartmoor Massacre, 191
Dartmoor prison, 186, 188-189
Da Souza of Whydah, 214, 215
Davis, C. H., 314
Davis, Jefferson, 291, 292, 294, 298, 319
Deane, Silas, 96-97
Deane, Stewart, 112
de Barras, 103, 104
Decatur, Stephen, 125, 126, 138, 141, 156, 157
Decatur, 258
Deception Island, 227
Declaration of Independence, 212
Defense, 83, 84
de Gaulle, Charles, 498
de Grasse, 102-103, 104
de Guichen, Compte, 101
De la Motte, Admiral, 62
Delaware, 125
Delaware River, 16; Swedes along, 21, 27
De La Warr, Lord, 14
de Lesseps, Count, 381
de Lesseps Company, 381-382
democratic government, 117
Demologos, 248
de Moscoso, Luis, 5, 7
Denby, Edwin, 420-421
Denman, William, 413
Denmark: German invasion of, 445
Depression, Great, 423, 429, 437
depth charge, 406-407
Derby, Elias Hasket, 98, 111, 129-130
De Ruyter, Admiral, 27, 50
Desire, 19
de Sota, Hernando, 5, 6-7
d'Estaing, Count, 91-92, 95, 98, 101
Dévastation, 281, 282
Dewey, Admiral, 364, 366, *368-370,* 372, 375
Deyo, Morton L., 515, 535

Dill, Sir John, 471
dirigibles, 426
dive bombers, 425
Dixie, 367, 382, 408
Doenitz, Karl, 498
Dole, Sanford Ballard, 353, **354**
Dollar Diplomacy, 392-393
Dollar Line, 394
Dolphin, 351
Dominican friars, **7**
Donnegal, 140
Doorman, Karel, 447
Downes, John, 175, 233
Downie, Captain, 182-183
Dragon, 93
Drake, Sir Francis, 10-12
Dreadnaught, 284, 391
Dromo, USS, 153-155
Dublin, 252
Duc de Durac, 97
Dudingston, William, 69-70
Duff, 139
Dunkerque, 11, 445
Dunkirk, 62, 63
Dunmore, Lord, 80
DuPont, Samuel F., 294, 302-303
D'Urville, Dumont, 246
Dutch, 8, *15-17,* 21, 23; war with, 24-25; war with English, 24-28
Dutch East India Company, 16
duties, discriminating, 209-210

Eagle, 89, 99, 100
Early, Steve, 441
East, Far (*see* Far East)
East India Company, 70, 109; American, proposed, 115
East Indies, 27
Echo, 299
EC-2 (*see* Liberty ships)
Edgar, the, 39
Edison, Charles, 443
Edward, 82
Edward Rutledge, 486
Eighth Army, British, 484-486
Einstein, Albert, 493
Eisenhower, Dwight, 484, 513
El Alamein, 482, 484
Eleven Percent Naval Expansion Act, 447
Eliza, 275
Elizabeth, Queen, 11-12
Elk Hill oil reserves, 421
embargo acts, 119, 121, 152-153, 156, 157, 158, 177
Emergency Fleet Corporation, 413, 414
Empress of China, 110, 111
Endicott, Charles M., 231-233
Endymion, 190

England, 3-12 (*see also* Great Britain): alliance with Prussia, 63; and slave trade, 52; at end of 17th century, 35; bombing of, 447, 449; impressment of U.S. seamen, 126, *149-150,* 166; maritime supremacy of, 25; results of Seven Years' War, 66; rise of nationalism in, 25; rivalry with France, *31-40;* trading acts, 23-24; wars with Dutch, 24-28

English Channel, invasion across, 513
English immigrants, 219
Eniwetok Atoll, 507
Enola Gay, 541, 542
Enterprise, 131, 132, 133, 137, 138, 356, 479, 480, 481, 490, 491, 538
Ericsson, John, 249, 308, 310
escort carriers, 472
Essex, 137, 147, 173-174, 176, 229, 312, 472
Essex Junior, 175, 176
Ethiopia, Italian invasion of, 435
Etna, 261
Europe: and Civil War, 320-321; armed peace in, 393; German-occupied, bombing of, 512
Europeans in Far East, 384
Expansion Act, 439
Experiment, 112, 131
explosives, high, 356-359
exports, 23, 25-26; in 1715, 44-45; taxation of, 28

Fall, Albert, 421
Falmouth, Maine, burning of, 77-78
Falmouth, 264
Fame, 60, 211
Far East, 384; trade with, *109-112,* 333
Farragut, David Glasgow, 212, 281, 294, 303, *311-312,* 314, 318, 325, 326, 349
Fast Carrier Task Force, 524-535
Federalists: an Embargo Act, 156-157; New England, 159
Ferdinand Maximilian, Prince, 325
Fermi, Enrico, 555
Ferrelo, 8
Fiji Islands, 234
Finland, Russian invasion of, 444
Fire, Great, 27
Fire Fly, 202
Fire Support Task Force, 535
Fishing industry, 19, 22, 23, 26, 43, 44, *48-49;* after War of 1812, 203-209; deepsea, in 1831, 209
Fitch, John, 199
Five Brothers, 301
Five Power Treaty, 420
Flambeau, 133

flat-tops, baby, 473
Fletcher, Benjamin, 33
Fletcher, Frank, 480, 488
Florida, 4, 6, *8-10, 66,* 95, *105,* 135, 210
Florida, 295, 314, 315
Flying Cloud, 269
Flying Fish, 244, 245, 246
Folger, Barzillai T., 227
Forbes, John M., 237
foreigners as crews, 333-334
forests of New England, 22
Formosa, 359, 384
Forrest, Captain, 257, 258
Forrestal, James V., 557, 559
Fort Caroline, 9
Fort Moultrie, 292
Fort Nassau, 16
Fort Orange, 16
Fort Sumter, 291, 292
Forty-Niners, 271
Forward, 256
Foudroyante, 281
four freedoms, 449-450
Four Power Treaty, 420
Fox, Gustavus V., 311
France, 8-10, 431; aid to colonies, *89-92;* alliance with Austria, 63; alliance with U.S., 118, 121, 122, 124; and Japan, 276, 277, 279; and Panama Canal, 381-382; and U.S., 1794-99, 121-127; at end of 17th century, 35; gains after American Revolution, 105; invasion of, 445, 511-516; losses in Seven Years' War, 65; revolution in, 117-118; rivalry with England, 31-40; surrender of, 445; undeclared war with, 121-133; war with China, 356
Franciscan friars, 6, 10
Franco, Francisco, 435
Franklin, Benjamin, 90, 105
Franklin, 275
Frederick the Great, 63
freebooters, 32
Freely, 301
Frémont, John C., 254
French, 20; east of Alleghenies, 62-63; smuggling by, 28
French and Indian Wars, 30, 55, *62-66,*
French Committee of Liberation, 498
French Navy, 91, 107; decline in power of, 38; defeat of, 121; scuttling of, 486; in World War II, 446
French pirates in Revolution, 86
French privateers, 29, 38
French trading posts, 29-30, 62
Friendly Cove, 113, 114
Friendship, 231-233
frigates, 163-165, 241-243

Frobisher, Martin, 11
frontier: end of, 341; settlements, 37
Frye, William P., 343
Fulton, Robert, 199-202
Fulton II, 248
Fulton's Folly, 201
Furor, 373
furs, 44; smuggling of, 28
fur trade, 17, 19; on West Coast, 106-107
Furuseth, Andrew, 396

Gage, General, 70
Galatea, 95
Gallatin, Albert, 134, 156
Gallup, John, 20
Galveston Island, 213
Gambier Bay, 528
Ganges, 125, 227
Gardener, George W., 226
Gaspé, 68-70
Gates, General Horatio, 89
General Armstrong, 190
General Pickering, the, 99, 100
Geneva Naval Conference, 422, 427
George, 128-129
George I, 40, 52
George II, 52-53, 65
George III, 65
George V, 433
George and Susan, 339
George's Bank, 207-208
Georgia, 267
German immigrants, 218
Germans: advance eastward, 482; weapons of, 554-555
Germantown, 258
Germany, 431; announces unrestricted submarine warfare, 401; in Far East, 384; invasion of, via France, 511-516; in 1935, 435; shipbuilding in, 392, 393; sinks neutral vessels, 400-401; in Spanish War, 435; trade agreement with Russia, 439
germ warfare, 562-563
Gerry, Elbridge, 123
Ghormley, R. L., 488, 491
Gibraltar, 37, *105*, 129
Gibson, Hugh, 427
Gifford, Acting Master, 328
Gilbert Islands, 479, 501, 506
Gillespie, Captain, 254
ginseng root, 110, 111
Glasgow, the, 81, 82
Glide, 234
Gloucester, 208
Goethals, George W., 413
Golden Eagle, 99-100
gold in Venezuela, 359-360

gold rush, 265-267, 380
good neighbor policy, 443
"Gooseberries," 514-515
Gordillo, Francisco, 5
Gosnold, Bartholemew, 13
Gourgues, Domonique de, 10
Governor Tompkins, 189
grain-ships, 340-341
Grand Alliance, 36, 37
Grand Banks, 208, 335
Grand Turk, 111
Grant, Ulysses S., 348
Grässli, Max, 543
Graves, Thomas, 73-74, 77, 78, 103
Gray, Robert, 112-116
Great Artiste, 542, 543
Great Britain, 431; American troops in, 513; and Venezuela, 359-360; bombing of, 454-455; in Far East, 384; ships from U.S. in, 450-451
Great Britain, 331
Great Fire, 27
Great Lakes, 29
Great Plague, 27
Great Republic, 270, 282-283
Great St. Julian, 38
Great Western, 283, 331
Greece, 449; Germans in, 453
Greene, Lieutenant, 309-310
Greenland, 452
Greer, 458
Grenville, 66
Greyhound, 319
Gridley, Captain, 369
Griffiths, John Willis, 238, 267, 269
Gruenther, A. M., 559
Guadalcanal, Battle of, 487-493
Guam, 374, 376, 377, 441, 476, 507, 518, 520, 523
Guerrière, 161-165, 168
Guinea coast, 50, 51, 58
Gulflight, 400
Gulf of Mexico, 106
gunboats, 180; "Jeffs," 151-152, 171
Guthrie, Robert, 442

Hague, 105
Haiti, 4, 5; French in, 135-136
Half Moon, 16
Halifax, 64, 155
Halifax, 77, 148, 149
Hall, Samuel, 237, 270
Hallet, Captain, 110
"Halls of Montezuma," 262
Halsey, William, Jr., 479, 491, 524, 526-530
Hambleton, 486
Hammann, 481

Hancock, John, 67, 68, 217
Hanford, 494
Hannah, 69, 76, 93
Hanoi Agreement, 461
Haraden, Jonathon, 99-100
Harding, Captain, 83
Harding, Warren G., 419-421
Harriet, the, 110
Harris, A. T., 471
Harrison, W. H., 172
Hart, Thomas, 378, 409, 462, *470*, 477, 508
Hartford, 311, 326
Hatteras, 316, 318
Havana, 7
Havana Agreements, 468
Hawaiian Islands, *352-355*, 377, 556
Hawk, 81
Hawke, Admiral, 73
Hawkins, Sir John, 11, 12, 15, 50
Hay, John, 376, 384-385, 387, 388, 392
Hazard, Captain, 82, 93
Heard, 235
heavier-than-air craft, 426
hedgehog, 553
Helena, 237
Helfrich, Vice-Admiral, 477
Henry, 144
Hepburn, A. J., 409
Herald, New York, 301-302
Herbert, Admiral, 30
Hero, 222
Herzen, Alexander, 530-531
Hessions, 89
Hewes, Joseph, 79, 96
Hewitt, H. K., 485
Heywood, Lieutenant, 255
Hill, Harry W., 559
Hillyar, Captain James, 175, 176
Hiroshima, 541-542, 555
Hiryu, 481
Hitaka, 520
Hitler, Adolf, 431, 439, 446, 538
Hiyei, 491, 492
Hobson, Richmond Pearson, 371-372
Hog Island Shipyard, 415
Holbourn, Admiral, 63
Holland, 8, 101-102 (*see also* Dutch); at
    end of 17th century, 35; Pilgrims in, 17;
    truce with Spain, 16
Hollandia, 506
Holmes, Sir Robert, 33
Hong Kong, 276, 277, 476
Honshu, 539, 540, 541, 543
Hood, Sir Samuel, 103, 104
Hoover, Herbert C., 422, 423, 429, 430
Hopkins, Ezek, 79, 80, 81, 82
Hopkins, Harry, 467
Hopkins, John B., 79

Hopkins, Stephen, 79
Hornet, 192, 479, 480, 481, 490, 491
hospital ships, 88
Hotchikiss guns, 359
Houqua, 237
Houston, 477
Howard, Lord, of Effingham, 11, 12
Howe, General, 70, 121
Howe, Richard, 62, 91, 92
Howe, Sir William, 88, 89
Howe, Tyringham, 81
HR 1776 (*see* Lend-Lease)
Hudson, Henry, 16
Hudson Bay, 40
Hudson River Valley, 16-17
Hughes, Charles Evans, 419
Hughes, Sir Edward, 104-105
Hugh Scott, 486
Huguenots, 9, 30
Hull, Cordell, 461
Hull, Isaac, 161-163; talks with Kurusu
    and Nomura, 463-464
Humphreys, Joshua, 163-164, 282
Hunter, Charles G., 260
Hunter, Robert, 45-46
Hussey, Christopher, 46-47
Hyland, L. A., 442

Iceland, U.S. Marines in, 456
I. C. White, 459
Idzu, Prince, 278
Illinois, 267
immigrants, 218-219, 221
imports, 23, 26
impressment of seamen, 126, *149-150*, 166
Incas, 11
Indentured servants, 15
Independence, 218, 255
India, 56, 68, 109
Indiana, 364, 373
Indianapolis, 433, 541
Indian Ocean, 33
Indians, 4, 7, 10, 20
Indigo, 45
Indo-China, Japanese in, 461-462
Industry, 108
Ingersoll, Jonathan, 111
Ingersoll, Royal, 470, 510
Inman, William, 344
International Navigation Company, 344,
    345
Intrepid, 141-142, 371
Invasion, European, via France, 511-516
Iowa, 364, 373
Ireland, 12
Irish immigrants, 218
iron, 26

iron-clads, 303-304; in Civil War, 294-295;
French, 281
iron works, 295
Isabel, Doña, 6
Isherwood, Benjamin Franklin, 294, 348,
349
island bases, 487
isolationism, 377, 417-418, 433-434, 435,
458, 561-562
Italy, 511-513; enters Albania, 439; in Far
East, 384; invades Greece, 449; seizes
Ethiopia, 435; in Spanish War, 435
Iwami, Prince, 278
Iwo Jima, 520, *531-533*

Jackson, Andrew, 191, 213, 241
Jack the Painter, 97
Jacob Bell, 315
Jacobs, Randall, 470
Jamaica, 5, 25; prisons in, 186
James, Duke of York, 25, 26
Jamesina, 236
James Monroe, 217
James River, 13
James II, 29, 37
James III, 37
Jamestown, *13-15*
James, William, 164
Jane, 301
Japan, 384, 431; advances, 1939, 1940, 461-
462; commercial treaty between U.S.
and, abrogated, 461; dissatisfaction with
American-made peace, 389; joins Axis,
461; neutrality pact with Russia, 454;
opening of, 274-280; outermost en-
trenchments of, 486-487; Russia declares
war on, 542; surprise attacks by, 385-
387, 463-467; surrender of, 543-544;
treatment of whalers, 227; truce between
Russia and, 461; warned to surrender,
540-541; war with China, 356-359, 435,
438; war with Russia, 385-387; weapons
used against, 553-554
Japanese, atrocities of, 487
Japanese Navy, first route of, 481
Java, 109
Java, 168, 173
Java Sea, Battle of, 477
Jay's treaty, 119-122
Jean Bart, 485
Jefferson, Thomas, 123, 134-135, 141, 151-
153, 156, 198, 250
Jefferson Davis, 299
"Jeffs," 151, 180
Jehol, 435
Jellicoe, Admiral, 406
Jenkins, Robert, 53
Jersey, 87-88, 139

Jesuits, 10
jet-propelled fighter planes, 512
Jews in Europe, 446
Jodl, Alfred, 538
Johnson, Alfred, 410, 441
Johnson Act of 1934, 434
Joint Canadian–United States Defense
Board, 447
Joint Chiefs of Staff, 476
Joint Research and Development Board,
562
Jones, Catesby Ap. R., 296, 307, 308, 309
Jones, Ichabod, 74
Jones, Paul, 79, 82, 89, *96-98*, 99, 105, 192
Jones, Thomas, 252
Jones, Wesley L., 414
Joseph Hewes, 486
Judith, 301
Juneau, 492
Juniata, 356
Jutland, Battle of, 406

Kaga, 481
Kaiser, Henry, 475
Kaiser Wilhelm, 393
Kanagawa, Treaty of, 279
Katoka, 358
Kearney, Lawrence, 238-239
Kearny, 458, 459
Kearsage, 317-319
Kellogg Pact, 422-423, 427
Kendrick, John, 112-114, 116
Kennan, George F., 559
Kennebec, Maine, 13, 17, 18
Kennedy, Joseph, 437, 438
Kentucky, 556
Keppel, Admiral, 90
ketches, 49
Key, Francis Scott, 182
Kidd, William, 34-35
Kimmel, Husband E., 466, 469
King, Ernest J., 455, 469-471
King George, 93
King George's War, 55-57
King William's War, 31
Kinkaid, Thomas, 491, 505-506, 526
Kirishima, 493
Kirwan, Richard, 144
Knox, Franklin, 448, 469, 557
Koga, Mineichi, 500
Konoye, Prince, 461
Korea, *356-359*, 384, 387, 516
Kowshing, 357-358
Kuribayashi, Tadamichi, 532
Kuriles, 276
Kurita, Takeo, 526, 528, 529, 530
Kurusu, Saburo, 463-464
Kwajalein Atoll, 506-507

Kwang Yi, 357
Kwantung Peninsula, 387
Kyushu, 538-539

labor, during World War II, 545-546
La Citoyenne, 133
La Concorde, the, 102
La Couche, 38
Lady Washington, 112-116
Lae, 479
Lafayette, Marquis de, 103, 104
Laffley, 536
Lafitte, Jean, 213
La Guadaloupéenne, 133
L'Aigle, 133
Lai Yuen, 359
Lake Erie, Battle of, 172
Land, Emory Scott, 438, 475, 549
landing craft, 473-474, 505-506, 512-513, 515-516
Landon, T. H., 559
Langley, 425
La Pauline, 133
La Seine, 133
Laudonniere, Rene de, 9
Lave, 281, 282
Law, George, 266, 267
Lawrence, E. O., 555
Lawrence, James, 151, 169, 170, 171, 192, 193
Lawrence, the, 172
League of Nations, 417, 435
Leahy, William D., 378, 443, 471
Leander, HMS, 147, 148
Lear, Colonel Tobias, 142-143
Leary, 443
Le Croyable, 125
Ledyard, John, 107, 112
Lee, Ezra, 89
Lee, W. A., Jr., 492
Lee, 78, 83
Legazpi, 8
Lehigh, 459
Leipsic, 172
LeMay, Curtis, 533
Lend-Lease, 452, 457, 460, 512, 547
Leningrad, 512
Leopard, 149, 150, 160
Lesseps, Count de, 381
letters-of-marque, 56, 125
Levant, 254
Leviathan, 409-410, 414
Lexington, 70
Lexington, 77, 82, 277, 279, 421, 425, 479, 480, 491
Leyte, 524-530
Liberty, 67

Liberty ships, 451-452, 454, 475, 547, 549, 551; types of, 504
licensing of American vessels, 166-167, 177, 179
lighter-than-air craft, 426
Light Horse, 111
Lightning, 270
Liliuokalani, Queen, 354
Lincoln, Abraham, 291ff., 311, 320
Lindsay, Captain Benjamin, 69
L'Insurgente, 126
Little, Captain, 139
Little, George, 184
Little, Sir Charles, 471
Little Belt, the, 157
Little Juliana, 303
Livingston, Harriet, 201
Livingston, Robert, 134, 135-136, 200
Lloyd George, David, 416, 417
Lodge, Henry Cabot, 364, 376
Lôme, Dupuy de, 364
London, burning of, 27
London Company, 13, 14
London Naval Conferences, 422-423, 435
London Naval Treaty, 435
Long, John D., 363, 368, 370
Long Island, 18; smuggling on, 28; whaling on, 45-46
Long Island, 472
loran, 553
Los Alamos, 494
Los Angeles, 106
Los Angeles, 426
Louis XIV, 33, 35, 37, 40
Louis XV, 40, 62
Louis XVI, 89-90, 91, 117
Louisbourg, 55-56, 63-64
Louisiana, 135, 136
L'Ouverture, Toussaint, 135
Low, Ned, 33
Lower California, 7
Loyalists, 81
LSTs, 505-506
Luce, Stephen B., 355
Lundy's Lane, Battle of, 182
Lusitania, 400
Luxembourg, invasion of, 445
Luzon, 530

Mabel, 339
McAfee, Mildred, 494-495
MacArthur, Douglas, 462, 476, 477-478, 487, 488, 505, 517, 523-526, 539, 544
McCain, John S., 488, 538
McCandless, Bruce, 492
McCawley, 489
McClure's Magazine, 391
MacDonald, Ramsay, 422, 423

Macdonough, Thomas, 182-184, 193
Macedonian, 167, 168, 279
McGrath, George, 189
Machias, Maine, 74
McKay, Donald, 269, 270
McKay, Lauchlan, 269
Mackenzie, Alexander Slidell, 247
McKim, Isaac, 236-237
McKinley, William, 363, 364, 365, 366, 368, 370, 379
McKinley tariff act, 342
Mackinnon, Bryce, 300-301
McLane, 256
McLean, General, 94
Macon, 426
Madagascar, 33, 34
Madden, Admiral, 406
Madison, James, 108, 157
Madras, India, 56
Maginot Line, 431
Mahan, Alfred Thayer, 348, 355-356, 364, 370, 379, 388, 389
Maidstone, 140
mail contract acts, 332-333
Mail Ship Bill, 343
Maine, 13, 17
Maine, 352, 364-365
Maisky, Ivan, 483
Makassar Strait, Battle of, 477
Makin, 501
Malaya, 476
Maley, Lieutenant-Commander, 131
Mallory, Stephen Russell, 294-295, 303, 305
Malplaquet, Battle of, 37
Malta, 136
Manchukuo, 468
Manchuria, 387, 427, 468
Manhattan, 276
Manhattan Engineer District, 494
Manhattan Island, 16, 33-34
manifest destiny, 252, 253, 277, 280, 356, 359
Manila, 8, 10, 375, 377
Manila Bay, 368-370
Manly, John, 78
Marblehead, 19, 208
Marblehead, 373
Marcus Island, 479
Marcy, Samuel, 251
Marcy, W. L., 251
Margaret, 275
Margaretta, 74-75
Mariana Islands, 507, 517-518
Maria Theresa, 55
Marie Teresa, 373
Marine Corps, 124, 472; creation of, 78-80
Marines: and Hawaii, 354; in China, 462;

in Greenland, 452; in Iceland, 456; in Panama, 382; in World War I, 412-413
Maritime Commission, 437-438
Marlborough, 37, 39
Marshall, George, 471, 562
Marshall, James Wilson, 123, 265
Marshall Islands, 497, 502, 506-507
Martinez, Don Estevan, 114
Mary, William and, 30
Mary, 33
Massachusetts, 13, 17-19, 28, 29
Massachusetts, 115, 258, 259, 275, 364, 373
Matagorda, 29
Maury, Matthew Fontaine, 263-265, 296
May Flower, the, 17
Meade, 493
Meares, John, 113
Medina Sidonia, Duke of, 11
Mediterranean, 136-137
Melville, Herman, 226
Melville, 408
Memnon, 267
Mendoza, 7
Menendez, Pedro, 9, 10
mercenaries, 89
merchant marine: in 1914, 394; in 1932, 429; packet lines, 216-221; Roosevelt, T. R., and, 383-384; ships sold to private operators, 550; ships under foreign flags, 550; after War of 1812, 209-212; after World War II, 547-551; in World War I, 474-475, 544-547
Merchant Marine Academy, 452
Merchant Marine Acts, 428, 436
Merchant Marine Commission, 383
Merchantmen: American, in 1805, 146; government ownship of, 396-397
Merchant Ship Sales Act of 1946, 548-549
Mermaid, 91
Merrimac, 303-310, 371; and *Monitor,* 308-311
Mexican War, territory ceded by, 263
Mexico, 5, 8, 9, 10, 252; Ferdinand Maximilian, Emperor of, 325; war with, 254-263
Meyers, George, 392
Middle Passage, the, 51, 59-61
Midway, Battle of, 558-559
Midway Island, 377, 480-481
Mikado, 278, 279, 280
Mikawa, Admiral, 489
Mikuma, 481
Milan Decree, 151
Mindanoa, 530
mine barrage, across North Sea, 410-411
minelayers, 410-411
mines, 359, 406
Minneapolis, 364

Minnesota, 305, 309
Minute Men, 70
Mississippi, 250, 256, 257, 277, 279
Mississippi River: in Civil War, 311-313; French on, 29; Spanish losses east of, 66
Missouri, 250, 544
Mitscher, Mark, 507, 518, 520, 521, 526, 531, 534, 536, 538
Mitsui, Sakichi, 468
Mobile, 106, 325-326, 327
Moby Dick, 226
Molasses, rum, and slaves, 51
Monhegan Island, 17
Monitor, 304; and *Merrimac*, 308-311
Monk, Admiral, 24
Monocacy, 356
Monroe, James, 122, 136, 150, 197, 198
Monroe Doctrine, 198, 248, 359, 393, 446, 447
Montagu, John, 73
Montana, 459
Montauk, 237
Montcalm, 64
Montezuma, 132
Montgomery, Captain, 254
Montgomery, Sir Bernard Law, 484
Montojo, Admiral, 268-269
Montreal, fall of, 65
Moody, Parson, 56
Moore, Midshipman, 74-75
Moore, William, 35
Moors, 3
Moravia, 439
Morgan Line, 367
Mormacmail, 472
Morocco, 136
Morotoi, 525
Morris, George, 305, 306
Morris, Richard, 137
Morse, John Hamilton, 145
motion pictures, World War II, 522-523
Mount Vernon, 129, 130
Mowat, Henry, 77, 78
"Mulberries," 514-515
Mulford, Samuel, 45-46
Munich Pact, 439
Munson Line, 394
Murray, Alexander, 93
Musashi, 527, 528, 529
Muscovites, 106
Music, 301
Mussolini, Benito, 431, 512
Mystic River, 19

Nagasaki, 542-543, 555
Nagato, 541
Nagumo, Chuichi, 463-465
Nancy, 78

Nanking: fall of, 438; treaty of, 239
Nantucket, 46-48, 68, 228
Napier, Henry, 178
Napoleon, 107, 135, 145, 148, 157, 173
Napoleon, 215
Napoleon III, 281
Narraganset Bay, 68-69
Narvaez, Panfilo de, 5, 6
Nashville, 366, 382
National Recovery Act, 432
National War College, 559
Nautilus, 138
Naval Academy, 240
Naval Aircraft Factory, 425-426
naval air patrols, 424
Naval Articles, 80
Naval Committee, 79
naval training stations, 472
Naval War College, 355, 359, 387
Navigation Acts, 23-24, 25, 210, 334
Navy Bill, 1827, 240-241
Navy department, creation of, 123
Navy Nurse Corps, 496
NC-4, 425
Negroes, 4, 50-52; in Dartmore prison, 188
Nelson, Lord, 145
Neosho, 480
Netherlands, invasion of, 445
neutrality, becomes American policy, 118
Neutrality acts, 434, 444, 459-460
neutrality pact between Japan and Russia, 454
neutrality patrol, 458
Nevada, 515
New Amsterdam, 18, 24, 26-27
New Bedford, 228
New Breton, 29
Newburyport, 208
New Deal, 431-432, 453
New England, 178; and slave trade, 51-52; fishing industry, 203, 335-337; French and Indian War, 31; seamindedness of, 21; shipbuilding in, 27-28, 43-44
Newfoundland, 28, 38, 40
Newfoundland Banks, 19, 31, 40, 48-50, 105, 191, 204, 208
Newfoundland Conference, 456
New Guinea, 505
New Hampshire, 30
New Mexico, 540
New Netherlands, 16, 27
New Orleans, 106, 311, 313, 321; Battle of, 191
New Orleans, 373
Newport, 51, 57, 61, 92, 101
New Providence Island, 80-81
New York, 16, 27, 30
New York, 364, 367, 373, 441, 443

New Zealanders, 505
Ney, Marshal, 173
Niagara, 172, 234
Nicaragua, 381
Nicholas I, 280
Nicholas, Samuel, 80
Nicholson, Colonel, 38, 126
Nicholson's Non-Importation Bill, 148, 152
Nicolls, Richard, 27
Nieu Nederlandt, the, 16
Niles Register, 297
Nimitz, Chester, 469, 470, 501, 518, 524, 539
Nine Power Treaty, 420, 427
Nocton, 173
noise-makers, 503-504
Nomura, Kichisaburo, 463-464
Nonata, 256
Non-Intercourse Act, 157
Normandy, 48, 497, *513-516*
Norsemen, 3
North, James H., 295
North, Lord, 70, 104
North Africa, 482, *484-486;* Allied victory in, 497; in World War II, 453-454
North America, 12
North Carolina, 455, 467
Northerner, 272
North Pacific, 500
North Sea, 11; Battle of, 24; mine barrage across, 410-411
Northwest, 109-116
Northwest America, 113
Northwest Passage, 4, 7, 16
Norway, German invasion of, 445
Nova Scotia, 20, 29, 40, 204
Noyes, Leigh, 488
Nymphe, HMS, 178

Oak Ridge, 494
O'Brien, Jeremiah, 74-75
Oceanic Steamship Company, 344
Ocean Mail Act, 343-344, 367
Office of Intelligence, 355
officers of frigates, 242-243
Offshore Grounds, 227
Ohio, 249, 258, 267
Okinawa, 280, *534-537,* 539
Oklahoma, 552
Oldendorf, J. B., 527, 529
Oldham, Mr., 20
Old Mill prison, 88
Olympia, 364, 368-369
Olyphant, 235
Open Door policy, 384-385, 387, 392, 420
open ports, China, 384
opium trade, 236, 238-240
Oppenheimer, J. R., 555

Oquendo, 373
Ordronaux, Jean, 190
Oregon, 8, 205, 250, 252
Oregon, 246, 267, 364, 371, 373, 381
Oregon Shipbuilding Company, 496
Oreno, 234
Oriental, 267-268
Orlando, V. E., 416, 417
Ostfriesland, 425

Pacific: English in, 10-11; English trade in, 114; Japanese losses in, 499; war in, 499-500
Pacific, 217, 218, 284
Pacific Fleet, 389; ships transferred from, 455
Pacific Mail Line, 267, 333, 344
pacifists, 390, 392; in World War II, 434
packet rats, 220-221, 272
packets, 216-221, 283-287
Pact of Paris, 422-423
Paddock, Ichabod, 46
Page, Robert M., 442
Paixhan guns, 248, 259-260
Pallas, 97
Palmer, N. B., 222-223
Palo Alto, Battle of, 253
Panama, 52, 382-383; Declaration of, 443
Panama, 237, 267
Panama Canal, 380-383, 392, 413, 428, 500
Panama Canal Act, 395
Pan-American conferences, 443
Pan-American neutrality patrol, 452-453
Panay, 438, 458
Panuco River, 7
Paragon, 202
Paris, 367
Paris, Peace of, 65, 105
Parson's Sailors Physician, 273
Parsons, William S., 541
Pasha, Hobart, 323
patrols, World War II, 443-444, 452-453
Patrol Wing Ten, 478
Paul Jones, 237
Peace of Paris, 65, 66, 105
Peacock, 192, 244, 245, 246
Pearl Harbor, 353, 355, 392; attack on, 462-467; blame for, 469
Pearson, 97
Pease, Samuel, 33
Pedee River, 5-6
Peele, Jonathan, 127
Peleliu, 524-525
Pendleton, Isaac, 222
Penn, Admiral, 25
Pensacola, 106
Pensacola admirals, 426-427
Pensacola Bay, 9

pepper, 127
Pepperell, William, 55
Perch, 89
Perry, Matthew Calbraith, 212, 248-250, 256-261, 534; opens Japan, 274-280
Perry, Oliver Hazard, 172, 192, 193, 211
Perry, 299
Perth, 477
Peru, 9
Peru, 234
Pescadores, 359
Pétain, Marshal, 446, 461, 486
Peters, Hugh, 19
Petrel, 301
Petrita, 256
petroleum, 338
Philadelphia, 57; blockade of, 1812, 171; Continental Congress in, 70; Howe in, 88; school for midshipmen, 251
Philadelphia, 137, 140, 141, 485
Philip II, 8-9
Philip V, 36-37
Philippines, 7, 8, 11, 461, 462, 476, 524, 525; American sovereignty in, 369-370; Spanish American War in, 363-369
Philippine Sea, First Battle of, 521
Philips, Captain, 373
Phillips, Captain, 126, 127
Phillips, Tom, 476
Phips, Sir William, 31-32
Phoebe, 175, 176, 312
Phoenix, 202
"phony" war, 444-445
picaroons, 130-131
Pickering, 99, 100, 138
Pico, Don Andres, 255
Pierce, John, 147
Pilgrims, *17-18*
Pinckney, Charles, 122
Pink Star, 459
Piracy, *32-35*, 43; off Quallah Battoo, 231-234
pirates, 109-110, 210, 211-212; and slave trade, 213; French, 86
Pitt, William, 63-64, 66
Pizarro, 5, 6
Plague, Great, 27
Plattsburg, 182-183
Pluton, 373
Plymouth, 13, 17-18, 30
Plymouth, 277
Pocahontas, 13-14
Pocahontas, 229
Point Loma, 8
Poland: German invasion of, 439-440; partition of, 444
politicians, 348

Polk, James, 251
Polly, 210, 211
Ponce de Leon, Juan, 4
Porpoise, 244, 245, 246
Port Arthur, 358, 384, 385, 386, 387
Porter, Captain David, 173, 174, 175, 212
Porter, David Dixon, 327, 348-350
Porter, John L., 303
Porter, 432, 490
Portland, 340
Portland, 38
Porto Bello, 52
Port Royal, 9, *38-39;* colonial expedition against, 31
ports, artificial, 514-515
Portsmouth, 57, 208
Portsmouth, 254, 255
Portugal, 8
Postal Aid Law, 343
Potomac, 233-234
Potsdam Conference, 540
Pounds, Thomas, 33
Powhatan, 277, 279
"Practical Navigator, The," 145
Prairie, 367
Prebel, 255
Preble, Edward, 126, *137-143*, 193
prefabricated ships, 451-452, 455
prejudice, race, 390
preservative treatment of ships, 553
President, 137, 157, 160, 169
Prevost, Sir George, 182-184
Prince de Neuchatel, 190
Prince of Wales, 456, 457, 476
Princessa, the, 114
Princeton, 249, 250, 529
Pringle, Joel, 378, 409, 433
prisoners, War of 1812, 185-190
prison ships, 87-88
privateering: background of, 297-298; during Civil War, 297-302; growth of, 98-99
privateers, 82-86, 93-95, 104-106; American, 90-91; in 1814, 189-192; French, in American waters, 121-127; John Adams and, 125-126; Tory, 93-94; in War of 1812, 179, 184-185
Protector, 139
Protestant and Catholic, 56
Providence, 61
Providence, 82
Province, 54
Provincetown, 208
Prussia, English alliance with, 63
Puerto Rico, 4, 5, 374
Puritans, 12, *18-20*
Putiatin, Efimii Vasilievitch, 278

Q-ships, 407-408
Quakers, 52, 212, 228
Qualla Battoo, 231-234
Quebec, 39, 155; capture of, 64-65; colonial
  expedition against, 31-32
Quebec Conferences, 498-499, 511, 516-517
Quedagh Merchant, 35
Queen Anne's War, *37-40*
Quexos, 5
Quincy, 435, 489
Quitman, John A., 260, 261, 262

Rabaul, 505
Raccoon, 175
race prejudice, 390
radar, *441-443*, 482-483, 493, 553; new
  type of, 497
railroads, formation of steamship com-
  panies by, 333
Rainbow, 238, 267, 269
Raisonnable, 95
Rajah, 127
Ralph Talbot, 489
Rambouillet Decree, 157
Ramillies, Battle of, 37
Ramsay, Sir Bertram, 513
Randolph, Edward, 28-30
Randolph, 93
Ranger, 89, 96, 485, 491
Rappahannock, 315
Raritan, 258
Raritan and Delaware Canal, 249
Rebecca, 53
reciprocal trade treaties, 209-210, 336
reconstruction, 329; naval, 1883, 352
Recruitment and Manning Organization,
  545
Red D Line, 344
Red Sea men, 33-34
Red Star Line, 217
Reefer, 256
re-exportation, 120, 121
Reid, Jack, 480
Relief, 244
Remey, 527
Reprisal, 77, 105
Repulse, 476
Resaca de la Palma, Battle of, 253
Reserve Fleet Anchorages, 551
Retaliation, 125
Reuben James, 459
Reuterdahl, Henry, 391
Revolutionary War, 73-106
revolution in France, 117-118
Rhett, William, 37-38, 43
Rhode Island, 30; slave trade in, 51, 52,
  68

Ribault, Jean, 9
Ribbentrop, Joachim von, 436
Ricci, Matteo, 239
Rice, 45
Richard, 147; vs. *Serapis*, 97-98
Riley, Mrs., 285
river steamers, 198-203
Roach, John, 351
Roanoke, 305
Roanoke Island, 11
Robert E. Stockton, 249
Roberts, Captain, 323
Robeson, George M., 349-350
Robin Moor, 454
Robinson, S. M., 432, 433
Rochambeau, 101, 104
Rochester, 38
rocket-propelled weapons, 512, 554
Rodgers, John, 143, 157, 160, 161, 241
Rodney, Admiral, 101-102, 103
Rogers, Moses, 201, 202-203
Rogue River, 8
Rolfe, John, 15
Rolla, 298
Romania, Russian invasion of, 445
Rommel, Erwin, 454, 482
Roosevelt, Franklin D., 388-392, 429-430,
  432, 456-457, 465, 493-494, 498, 511;
  and merchant marine, 436; Assistant
  Secretary of Navy, 399; death of, 537;
  elected for third term, 448; four free-
  doms, 449-450; message to George V,
  433; message to Mikado, 465; proclaims
  "unlimited state of national emergency,"
  455; speech of Dec., 1940, 448-449
Roosevelt, Nicholas, 200
Roosevelt, Theodore, 364, 368, 370, 376;
  and Panama Canal, 380-383; and Russo-
  Japanese War, 386
Roscius, 219
Ross, Major-General, 179-180
Rossbach, Battle of, 63
Rossie, 165-166, 190, 298
R.O.T.C., 472
"Rouges' Harbor," 37
Rough Riders, 370
Rousseau, 90
Royal African Company, 50-51
Royal Air Force, 447
Royal Navy, 25, 27, 34; after Seven Years'
  War, 66; impression of seamen into, 68;
  in 1775, 73; in 1780-81, 101; in World
  War II, 447
Royce, Captain, 227
Rule of 1756, 119
Rum, molasses, and slaves, 51
Rumsey, James, 199

Rush, Richard, 197
Russell and Company, 235
Russia, 222-223, 353; aid from U.S., 456; and Japan, 275, 276, 278-282; and Korea, 356; declares war on Japan, 542; in Far East, 384; invaded by Germans, 455-456; neutrality of, in Civil War, 332; neutrality pact with Japan, 454; sale of Alaska, 331-332; in Spanish War, 435; trade agreement with Germany, 439; truce between Japan and, 461; after World War II, 563
Russian-American Company, 331
Russian Revolution, 402
Russians: in California, 173; claim of, to Oregon, 205; drive westward, 512; on West Coast, 106-107
Russian ships, 280, 281
Russo-Japanese War, 385-387
Ryswick, Treaty of, 35

Sachs, Alexander, 493
safety, maritime, 396
sailships, last flourish of, 340-341
St. Antonia, 186
St. Augustine, 9, 10, 11
St. Eustatius, 102
St. John, Newfoundland, 19
St. John's River, 4, 9
St. Lawrence, Gulf of, 39, 62, 84-85, 105
St. Lawrence, 191, 305
Saint Lô, 529
St. Louis, 345, 367
St. Martin, 102
St. Paul, 345, 367
Saipan, 507, 518-521
Sakhalin Island, 385
Salamaua, 479
Salem, 18
Salem Atheneum's library, 144
Salerno, 512
Salinas, 459
Sallie, 301
Sally, 95
Saltonstall, Dudley, 79, 94, 95, 139
Samar, Battle off, 528
Samoa, *341-342,* 352, 377
Sampson, Admiral, 366, 371, 373
Sampson, 132
Samuel Russell, 267
Samuels, Samuel, 284-286
San Clemente Island, 8
San Diego, 106, 467
San Diego Bay, 8
Sandwich, Earl of, 73
Sandwich Islands (*see* Hawaiian Islands)
San Francisco, 106, 268, 271, 340, 467
San Francisco, 491, 492

San Juan, 490
San Juan Hill, 374
San Mateo, 10
San Quentin Bay, 7
Santa Barbara, 106
Santa Cruz Islands, Battle of, 490
Santa Monica Bay, 8
Santiago, 54, 372
Santo Domingo, 5, 6, 11
Sarajevo, 393
Saratoga, 183, 258, 277, 279, 421, 425, 480, 491
Saucy Jack, 215
Savannah, 325, 327
Savannah, 95, 203, 253, 255, 298, 299
Savo Island, Battle of, 489
Sawyer, Herbert, 160, 161
Saxony, 63
Scapa Flow, 406
Schimmelpfennig, Alexander, 328
Schley, Winfield S., 366, 368, 373
Schley's Flying Squadron, 366, 368, 371
schnorchel, 554
school for midshipmen, 251
schooner, 44, 49-50
Scorpion, 261
Scott, Norman, 492
Scott, Winfield, 258, 259, 262
Scourge, 260
screw propeller, 249
Sea-Bees, 487
Sea Gull, 244, 245
Sealing, 222-223
Seaman's Act, 395-396
Sea Witch, 267, 269, 271
Secession, 291
Segura, Fray, 10
selective service act, 448, 457-458
Selman, Captain John, 77
Semmes, Raphael, 294, 296, *316-319*
Serapis, 97
Sessa, 459
Sevastopol, 482
Seven Years' War, *62-66,* 119
Severn, 38
Seward, William H., 332
Shafter, General, 372
shallops, 22, 49
Shannon, 169
Shark, 252, 253
Sharon, 229
Shaw, Lieutenant-Commander, 132-133
Shaw, Major, 111
Shearer, William B., 422
shed plan, 135
Shelvack's Island, 154
Shenandoah, 314, 315, 319-320, 426
Sherman, W. T., 302, 327, 328

Shimizu, Mitsumi, 463
Shimonoseki, Treaty of, 359
shipbuilding, 18-20, 27-28, *43-45*
Ship Island, 312
Shipping Act of 1916, 396-397
Shipping Board, 395, 396, 397, 413, 437;
    purchases from foreign nations, 414, 415
ships, early, types of, 22
Shirley, William, 55
Shoho, 479
Shokaku, 520
Shortland, Thomas George, 189, 191
Shrewsbury, Duke of, 34
Shubrick, William Branford, 255
Siberia, 106
Sicily, 497
Sigsbee, Captain, 365
Sims, William Snowden, 389, 396, 405,
    411
Sims, 480
Singapore, 477
Sino-Japanese War, 516
Siren, 137, 138, 141
Sirius, 283
Sitka, 106
S. J. Waring, 299-300
slave-breeding farms, 214
slave factories, Africa, 58
slave-running, clipper ships, 212
slavery, and Civil War, 291
slaves, 14; in colonies in 1715, 52; profit
    on, 61; smuggling of, 28
slave ships, 43, 60-61, 212
slave trade, 40, 50-52, *57-61, 212-216*
Sloat, John Drake, 253
sloops, 22, 49
Small, Elisha, 247
Smith, David, 222
Smith, Francis P., 249
Smith, Holland, 519
Smith, John, 13-14
Smith, Robert, 134, 138
Smith, William Ward, 549
Smith, 490
smuggling, 23, 26, 28, *32-35,* 210-211; re-
    vival of, 68; of slaves, 213
Social Contract, The (Rousseau), 90
Solace, 367
Solomon Islands, 478
Somers, Lord Chancellor, 34
Somers, Richard, 138, 142, 371
Somers, 247
sonar, 482-483, 553
sonobuoy, 497-498
Soong, T. V., 499
Soryu, 481
South, after Civil War, 329
South America, 54, 332

Southampton, 277, 279
South Carolina: in Queen Anne's War, 37-
    38; secession of, 291
South Dakota, 490, 492, 493
southern colonies, 23
Southerners, westward movement of, 330
South Pacific, Japanese losses in, 499
Sovereign of the Seas, 269, 270
Spaatz, Carl, 541
Spain: in American Revolution, 95-96, 98,
    101; gains of, after Revolutionary War,
    105; losses in Spanish American War,
    374, 376; in Seven Years' War,.65, 66;
    truce with Holland, 16
Spaniards, 3-13
Spanish: claim of, to Oregon, 205; smug-
    gling by, 28
Spanish American War, 363-376; in Carib-
    bean area, 371-376; in Philippines, 363-
    369
Spanish armada, *11-12*
Spanish Empire, 36
Spanish War, 435, 439
Spars, 495-496
Spencer, Philip, 247
Spice Islands, 7
Spitfire, 77, 261
Sprague, C. A. F., 528
Spruance, Raymond, 480, 481, 518-521,
    524, 534, 538
Staghound, 269
Stalin, Joseph, 431, 457; at Potsdam, 540;
    at Teheran Conference, 511
Stalingrad, 496
Stamp Act, 66
Stanton, Secretary, 308
Stapleton prison, 186-187
Stark, Harold, 409, 469-471
Star of the West, The, 291
Stars and Stripes, 89
steam, high pressure, high temperature, 432
steamboats, 198-202
steam engine, 198
steam packets, *283-287*
steamships, 202-203
Steel Seafarer, 459
Stevens, John, 111, 200, 202, 303
Stevens, Robert L., 202, 303-304
Stewart, Charles, 138
Stimson, Henry, 448, 540
Stockton, Robert Field, 249, 254, 255
Stoddert, Benjamin, 124, 133-134
Stoeckel, Baron, 332
Stornoway, 268
Subercase, Governor, 38-39
submarine: clam-shaped, 89; U.S., 473
submarine warfare, 405-407, 413, 482, 486,
    497-498; German, 401, 510-511; of fu-

Submarine warfare (*Continued*)
  ture, 554-556; U.S., in Pacific, 508-510;
  in World War II, 450-451, 454, 456, 458
Sudetenland, 439
Suez Canal, 333
Suffren, 102, 104-105
suicide attack, Japanese, 535, 536-537
Sulu Sea, 246
Sumatra, 109, 127
Sun Tsu, 357, 358
Superior, 227
Supply, 277
Surigao Strait, Battle of, 527-528
Surinam, 27
surveying the Southern Ocean, 244-247
Susquehanna, 277, 278, 279
Sutter, John A., 264
Suzuki, Minister, 541
Swallow Tail Line, 218
Swedes along Delaware, 21, 27
Sweeney, Charles, 542

Taft, William Howard, 391-393
Taiho, 520
Takashi, Sankichi, 467
Takijiro, Rear-Admiral, 463
Talbot, Silas, 93
Tallyrand, 123, 130
Tampa Bay, 6, 7
Tarawa, 501-502
target practice, 389
Tattnell, Commander, 258
Taussig, J. K., 405-406
taxation of colonial exports, 28
Taylor, Albert Hoyt, 441-442
Taylor, Zachary, 254
Tea, monopoly on, 70
Teapot Dome oil reserves, 421
Tecumseh, 326
Teheran Conference, 511
Teller Amendment, 366
Tenedos, 169
Tennessee, 325-326
Terrible, 104
territories, in World War II, 445, 446
Texas, 250, 252
Texas, 352, 364, 373, 425, 485, 515
Thomas Lawson, 394
Thompson, Joseph L., and Sons, Ltd., 451
Tibbets, Paul W., Jr., 541
Tillman, William, 299-300
timber, 44
Ting, Admiral, 357, 359
Tinian, 507, 518, 520, 523-524
Titanic, 395-396
tobacco, 15, 23, 26, 44; smuggling of, 28
Tobruk, 482
Todd-Kaiser interests, 451

Togo, Admiral, 386
Tojo, Hideki, 462, 463, 522
Tokyo: bombing of, 479, 543; first large-
  scale raid on, 531
Tom Bowline, 192
Tonnante, 281, 282
Tories, native, 93
Tornado, 341
torpedo-boats, 356-359, 407
torpedoes, 326; acoustic, 503
Toulon, 486
Toulon fleet, 91
Townshend, Charles, 67
Townshend Acts, 67, 68
trade: early, 23; in 1847, 265; licensed,
  166-167; after Revolution, 106
Trafalgar, 145
training program, naval, 472
transportation, World War I, 412, 413-414
treaty navy, 423
Treaty of 1783, 105
treaty ports, 239, 384
Tredegar Iron Works, 304
Trenton, 356
Tripoli, 136-143
True Blooded Yankee, 189
Truk, 507
Truman, Harry S., 537, 540, 543, 558, 559
Truxton, Captain, 126, 127, 130
Truxton, 257
Tsi Yuen, 357
Tucker, John, 117
Tulagi, 488
Tume, Lieutenant, 54
Tunis, 136
Turner, Richmond K., 488, 489, 518, 531,
  534
Turtle, American, 89
Tuscaloosa, 456, 485
Twenty Percent Naval Expansion Act, 439
Twiggs, Levi, 262-263
Two-Ocean Navy Bill, 447
Tyler, John, 239
Tyng, Captain Edward, 55

U-boats, 405-407, 413, 427-428, 435
U-boat warfare (*see* submarine warfare)
Ukraine, 482
Ulithi Atoll, 525
Union, navy yards owned by, 293
United Nations, 470, *560-561*
United States: aid to British shipping, 450;
  commercial treaty with Japan, abrogated,
  461; enters World War II, 468; inde-
  pendence of, acknowledged, 105; Japa-
  nese dissatisfaction with, 389-390; losses
  to Japan, 476-477; neutrality of, 118,

394; overseas empire, 377; undeclared war with France, 121-133

United States, 122, 124, 125, 163, 164, 167, 252, 253

U.S. air forces, merged with army and navy, 559

U.S. army, merged with navy and air forces, 559

United States Navy: in 1812, 160; in 1845, 250; 1900–1914, 378-402; in 1914, 399-400; 1933-1937, 440; in 1941, 471-472; in 1942, 470, 484; in 1944, 502-503; after Civil War, 347-348; demobilization, World War II, 552-553; losses, World War II, 552-553; merged with army and air forces, 559; under New Deal, 431-432; relations with army and air force, 558; research into atomic power, 556; tests of atomic power, 555; world cruise of, 390

Urdaneta, Fray Andres de, 8

Utrecht, Treaty of, 40; Article 16 of, 50, 52

Valley Forge, 89

Vancouvor, Commodore, 116

Vandalia, 277, 279

Vandergrift, A. A., 488

Vaterland, 414

Vengeance, 97, 130, 132

Vera Cruz, 9, 256-260

Vernon, Admiral, 53-54, 57

Versailles, 416-417

Vesuvius, 359

Vichy, 486

Victory ships, 504-505, 547, 549

Villaret, 121

Vincennes, 244, 245, 246, 264, 489

Vinson, Frederick M., 441

Vinson-Trammell Act, 433

Virginia, 80

Virginia, 95, 305

Virginia Capes, 103

Virginia Company, 14

Virginius, 341

Vixen, 137, 138, 256, 257, 259

Vizcaino, 12

Vizcaya, 373

Vladivostok, 386

Voltaire, 90

V-1s and V-2s, 554

Von Tromp, Admiral, 24

Vulcan, 367

Wachusett, 315

Waddell, James I., 319

Wainwright, Jonathan, 478

Wake Island, 377, 476, 479

Walker, Sir Hoveden, 39-40

Walloons, 16

Walpole, Sir Robert, 40, 53

Wampanoag, 331

Ward, 465

Ward Line, 344

War Hawks, 159, 171

Waring, S. J., 299-300

War of 1812, 158-159, *160-193;* American collusion with British, 170-171; end of, 191; unpopularity of, 158-159, 170-171, 177-178, 181

War of Jenkins' Ear, 53-55

War of Spanish Succession, *37-40*

War of the Austrian Succession, 55-57

War Production Board, 476

Warren, Commodore, 56

Warren, Joseph, 68

Warren, Sir John, 166-168, 170, 176

Warren, 95, 254, 255

War Shipping Administration, 475-476, 545, 547-548

warships, types of, 241-243

Washington, 425, 467, 485, 492, 493

Washington Conferences, 470, 481-482, 511

Washington, D.C., in War of 1812, 181

Washington, George, 70, 76, 78, 114, 118, 122

Washington Naval Conference, 419-420

Wasp, 192, 485, 491

Waterman, Robert, 271-273

Watson, S. E., 262

Waves, 494-496

weapons of World War II, 553-555

Webb, William H., 237, 270

Webster, Daniel, 239

Welles, Gideon, 293-294, 302, 314, 347

West, Ebenezer, 111

West Coast, Spanish on, 106

western territory, 105

Westervelt, Jacob, 270

West Indies, 4, 5, 10, 23, 25, 27, 57, 85-86, 102, 103, 111, 120, 209-212; and slave trade, 213; British, 18, 155; French, 118-119; starvation in, 108

Wetmore, 235

Weyler, General, 363

Weymouth, 13

Weymss, Sir Colville, 471

whaleboat navy, 151

whaleboats, 337-340; in 1901, 340; in Revolution, 74

whales: attacks by, 226, 229-230; types of, 226

whaling grounds, 226-227

Whaling industry, 43, *45-48,* 57, 108, 173-174, 223-231

Whigs, 74

Whipple, Abraham, 69, 79, 82

Whitby, Captain, 148
White House, burning of, 181
White Squadron, 352
White Star Line, 344, 345
Whitney, William C., 352
Wichita, 485
Wilkes, Charles, 244-247
Wilkes expedition, 341
Wilkes' Land, 246-247
William, King, 34, 35
William of Orange, 30, 37
Williams, Captain, 139
Williamson, William P., 303
Willkie, Wendell, 448
Wilmington, 325, 327-328
Wilson, Woodrow, 393, 394, 395, 396,
   397, 399; in Europe, 416-417
Winslow, John A., 317-318
wireless telegraphy, first use of, 390
Wolfe, James, 64
women: in gold rush, 273-274; in World
   War II, 494-496
Women's Reserve, 494-496
Woodbridge, Admiral, 90
wooden ships, 413
Worden, John L., 308-310
World War I, 393-416; American troops in,
   412; beginning of, 393; peace treaties,
   417; results of, 417-418; U.S. enters, 402
World War II: conditions after, 560-561;
   dead and missing, 522; events leading to,

438-440; German surrender, 538; Japan
surrender, 543-544; labor during, 545-
546; organizations, 476; Pacific area, 499-
500; U.S. enters, 468

Xavier, St. Francis, 275
XYZ affair, 123, 130

Yamamoto, Isoruku, 462, 499-500
Yamato, 527, 528, 536
Yang Woo, 356
Yankee, 367
Yankees, 178-179
Yarmouth, 93
Yarnell, Harry, 378
Yeo, Rear-Admiral Sir James, 176
Yeomanettes, 412
York, 301
Yorktown, 103, 104
Yorktown, 479, 480, 481, 491
Yosemite, 367
Young, Cassin, 492
Young, Leo Clifford, 441-442
Young Eagle, 54-55
Yucatán, 256, 261
Yugoslavia, 453

zee rovers, 32
Zephyr, 236
Zouave, 306